Lifespan Development Across Cultures
Second Custom Edition

Compiled by Cathleen Erin McGreal, Ph.D., for Michigan State University

Taken from:
Human Development: A Cultural Approach
by Jeffrey Jensen Arnett

Cultural Anthropology, Third Edition
by Nancy Bonvillain

Language, Culture, and Communication: The Meaning of Messages,
Seventh Edition by Nancy Bonvillain

Infants and Children, Seventh Edition
by Laura E. Berk

Life Span Development: A Topical Approach
by Robert S. Feldman, Ph.D.

Lives Across Cultures: Cross-Cultural Development, Fifth Edition
by Harry W. Gardiner and Corinne Kosmitzki

Cross-Cultural Explorations: Activities in Culture and Psychology, Second Edition
by Susan Goldstein

Health: Making Choices for Life
by April Lynch, Berry Elmore, and Jerome Kotecki

Human Sexuality in a World of Diversity, Ninth Edition
by Spencer A. Rathus, Jeffrey S. Nevid, and Lois Fichner-Rathus

Cover Art: Images courtesy of Cathleen Erin McGreal, Ph.D.

Taken from:

Human Development: A Cultural Approach
by Jeffrey Jensen Arnett
Copyright © 2012 by Pearson Education, Inc.
Upper Saddle River, NJ 07458

Cultural Anthropology, Third Edition
by Nancy Bonvillain
Copyright © 2013, 2010, 2006 by Pearson Education, Inc.
Upper Saddle River, NJ 07458

Language, Culture, and Communication: The Meaning of Messages, Seventh Edition
by Nancy Bonvillain
Copyright © 2014, 2011, 2008 by Pearson Education, Inc.
Upper Saddle River, NJ 07458

Infants and Children, Seventh Edition
by Laura E. Berk
Copyright © 2012, 2008, 2005, 2002, 1999, 1996, 1993 by Pearson Education, Inc.
Published by Allyn & Bacon
Boston, MA 02116

Life Span Development: A Topical Approach
by Robert S. Feldman, Ph.D.
Copyright © 2014, 2011, 2008 by Pearson Education Inc.
Upper Saddle River, NJ 07458

Lives Across Cultures: Cross-Cultural Development, Fifth Edition
by Harry W. Gardiner and Corinne Kosmitzki
Copyright © 2011, 2008, 2005 by Pearson Education, Inc.
Published by Allyn & Bacon
Boston, MA 02116

Cross-Cultural Explorations: Activities in Culture and Psychology, Second Edition
by Susan Goldstein
Copyright © 2008 by Pearson Education, Inc.
Published by Allyn & Bacon
Boston, MA 02116

Health: Making Choices for Life
by April Lynch, Berry Elmore, and Jerome Kotecki
Copyright © 2014 by Pearson Education, Inc.
Glenview, IL 60025

Human Sexuality in a World of Diversity, Ninth Edition
by Spencer A. Rathus, Jeffrey S. Nevid, and Lois Fichner-Rathus
Copyright © 2014, 2011, 2008 by Pearson Education, Inc.
Upper Saddle River, NJ 07458

This special edition published in cooperation with Pearson Learning Solutions.

All trademarks, service marks, registered trademarks, and registered service marks are the property of their respective owners and are used herein for identification purposes only.

Pearson Learning Solutions, 501 Boylston Street, Suite 900, Boston, MA 02116
A Pearson Education Company
www.pearsoned.com

Printed in the United States of America

3 4 5 6 7 8 9 10 V0ZN 17 16 15 14

000200010271725405

EEB

ISBN 10: 1-269-14163-5
ISBN 13: 978-1-269-14163-5

CONTENTS

SECTION 1

INTRODUCTION:
CULTURE AND DEVELOPMENT

MODULE 1-A

THE NATURE OF CULTURE

Tibetan monks at the Dilgo Kyentse Gompa, after the death of Tibetan lama Urgen Tulku.
(Corbis/Alison Wright/Corbis)

Preview

- What is culture? What features are usually included in definitions of culture?

- What elements of culture are regarded as universal, and why?

- How can members of a society both share and not share culture?

- How is culture learned and transmitted?

- How can culture be both adaptive and maladaptive?

- What are some forces of cultural integration?

- How is culture based on symbols?

- How do cultures change from within and through contact?

- What are the dynamics of global culture change today?

Taken from *Cultural Anthropology*, Third Edition, by Nancy Bonvillain.

3

At the beginning there was on the earth only a single man; he had neither house nor tent, for at that time the winter was not cold, and the summer was not hot; the wind did not blow so violently, and there fell neither snow nor rain; the tea grew of itself on the mountains, and the flocks had nothing to fear from beasts of prey. This man had three children, who lived a long time with him, nourishing themselves on milk and fruits. After having attained to a great age, this man died. The three children deliberated what they should do with the body of their father, and they could not agree about it; one wished to put him in a coffin, the other wanted to burn him, the third thought it would be best to expose the body on the summit of a mountain. They resolved then to divide it into three parts. The eldest had the body and arms; he was the ancestor of the great Chinese family, and that is why his descendants have become celebrated in arts and industry, and are remarkable for their tricks and stratagems. The second son had the breast; he was the father of the Tibetan family, and they are full of heart and courage, and do not fear death. From the third, who had inferior parts of the body, are descended the Tartars, who are simple and timid, without head or heart, and who know nothing but how to keep themselves firm in their saddles.

From David L. Snellgrove and Hugh Richardson, *A Cultural History of Tibet.* © 2003 Orchid Press, reprinted by permission of the publisher.

This Tibetan narrative, describing the origin of the Tibetan people and two ethnic groups who live near them, tells us much about Tibetan attitudes toward themselves and other peoples. These attitudes are part of the core of Tibetan culture, that is, Tibetans' understanding of the world, its origins, and the people who inhabit it. In the beginning, the story depicts the world as an idyllic, peaceful place, without harsh weather and hardship. The Tibetans and their neighbors descend from the same founder. But the story also tells us what qualities the Tibetans believe differentiate them from others. They praise the Chinese for their arts and accomplishments but disapprove of their trickery. They are disparaging and condescending toward the Tartars. And they think of themselves as people of courage and kindness.

The narrative also gives us information about burial practices. Each brother advocated a method of burial that is practiced in different societies around the world: interment in the ground, cremation, and exposure to the elements. These practices are aspects of culture, how people organize their lives. The story thus provides insight into features of Tibetan culture. We learn about how Tibetans view themselves and their neighbors, how they think about their relationships with other groups, and some practices they engage in. In this module, we will explore what culture is and how cultural practices and attitudes change.

◇ WHAT IS CULTURE?

The basic definition of culture: the behaviors, values, and attitudes shared by a group of people. This module expands on this definition. Although defining what culture is may sound like a simple task, anthropologists have struggled to define and specify culture since the late nineteenth century, when anthropology was established as a discipline. The British social anthropologist Edward Tylor was the first to attempt a formal definition. Writing in *Primitive Culture* in 1871, he stated, "Culture is that complex whole which includes knowledge, belief, art, morals, law, custom, and any other capabilities and habits acquired by man as a member of society."

To what extent is culture shared? For example, what could you say about "American" attitudes toward self and others and "American" ways of organizing life?

Tylor's definition captures several significant features that most definitions of culture include today. It focuses on the holistic quality of culture ("that complex whole") and embraces all the activities, attitudes, and beliefs of human beings. Significantly, these are traits people "acquire." That is, people's attitudes, beliefs, and ways of acting are learned rather than inherited, instinctual, or automatic. Finally, Tylor stressed that people acquire culture "as a member of society." People live and interact with other people, learning skills and attitudes from them, and in turn transmitting their knowledge and beliefs to others.

Since Tylor, anthropologists have expanded on and refined the definition of culture innumerable times. By the 1950s, Alfred Kroeber and Clyde Kluckhohn had collected more than one hundred definitions, and all differ according to their focus and the theoretical orientation that underlies them (Kroeber and Kluckhohn 1952). Nevertheless, all the definitions include statements about human behavior and activities in families, groups, and communities, and about people's selectively shared knowledge, attitudes, values, and beliefs.

As we shall see, anthropologists use the term "culture" in two distinct senses (Sewall 2008, 42). In one meaning, "culture" refers to a set of beliefs and practices that are analyzed and abstracted from people's actual lived experiences. The second meaning of "culture" refers to a particular identifiable group of people (a "society") who, to varying degrees, share or participate in social life.

Cultural knowledge refers to the information people have that enables them to function in their social and physical environments. Some of this information is practical—how to make a living, what kinds of clothes to wear and shelters to build, and so on. Other cultural knowledge is less obvious—for example, people share knowledge about the world, why people do the things they do, what a person can expect from others, and so on. This kind of cultural knowledge is expressed in people's attitudes, values, and beliefs, including ethical values about what is right and wrong and what is proper and improper behavior. Cultural knowledge thus includes religious beliefs and scientific theories about the past, the world, people and their origins, and people's relationships to plants, animals, and the natural world.

In addition to cultural knowledge, social and cultural skills are included in the definition of culture, such as the activities and practices that people engage in to obtain their food, clothe and shelter themselves, and make or procure goods needed for their households. Cultural behaviors include the ways that people organize themselves to provide leadership, make decisions, and carry out communal activities. In all societies, people need to develop modes of subsistence and economic exchange, methods of social control and conflict resolution, and principles of leadership and governance. They need to organize families and provide for child care and socialization. Other aspects of culture, such as religion and artistic expression, are also part of the human experience. People share similar basic societal needs with members of other societies, but the strategies and institutions they develop to satisfy or cope with those needs vary.

Thus, people in all societies have their own specific thoughts (cultural knowledge) and behaviors (cultural skills) that vary from group to group. Although each society is unique, they all share similarities with others. In today's world, cultural influences are spreading in the context of global processes that include ways of organizing economies, purchasing goods and services, and communicating through the arts, travel, and the Internet. Elements of this global culture emanate from many parts of the world. Although Europe and the United States provide powerful centers for this global culture, economic, political, and artistic influences also come from Asia, Africa, and Latin America as well.

The cultural knowledge of these Sami includes everything there is to know about reindeer, living in the Arctic, and coping with citizenship in the modern state society of Norway.
(The Image Works/Topham/The Image Works)

cultural knowledge
Information that enables people to function in their society and contributes to the survival of the society as a whole.

What is global culture? This question is widely debated among social scientists. What thoughts, behaviors, tools, and skills do you identify as making up today's global culture?

REVIEW

Culture includes cultural knowledge (people's ideas, attitudes, beliefs, and values) and cultural skills (people's activities and behaviors for living and organizing their lives). People's thoughts and behaviors are mutually reinforcing. Some aspects of culture deal with concrete knowledge, such as what food to eat, how to build a shelter, and what clothes to wear. Other aspects of culture deal with abstract ideas, such as how people are expected to behave, what attitudes are appropriate in given situations, and value systems. Concrete and abstract components of culture and their behavioral analogs are present in all human societies. At the same time that each culture is unique, a developing and expanding global culture also spreads economic, political, and aesthetic influences throughout the world.

cultural models
Shared assumptions that people have about the world and about the ideal culture.

norms
Sets of expectations and attitudes that people have about appropriate behavior.

◇ CHARACTERISTICS OF CULTURE

Although each society is unique, a number of characteristics in their organization and functioning are universal. To begin, any culture is a product of a group of people who share and transmit some basic attitudes and assumptions about the world. In addition, aspects of culture tend to interrelate and function together with some consistency to form a coherent system of behaviors and beliefs. Through their cultures, people adapt to their life situations and to changes in their social and physical environments. Anthropologists often state that culture is shared, learned, adaptive, and integrated. And although these general principles make sense, as we shall see, they are not entirely unproblematic. Perhaps we can also state that cultures consist of a constellation of shared meanings and that these meanings are reflected in and reinforced by the behaviors in which people engage. Furthermore, meaning is both produced and interpreted by members in their interactions with one another. That is, culture is both meaning and practice.

Culture Is Shared

Humans are by nature social creatures; that is, we do not live as individuals alone. Rather, we live with other people in families, households, and communities of various sizes and relationships. The way we behave, our attitudes about right and wrong, our ideas about the world we live in are all formed through our interactions with others. We do not act alone, and we do not have ideas all to ourselves. Together with these other people, we are societies. As defined, a society is a group of people who live within an acknowledged territory, who could potentially interact with one another, and who share certain practices and values. Societies are held together by social structures that organize family life, means of making a living, and ways of arriving at decisions and establishing methods of leadership.

However, to say that culture is shared is not to say that all members of a particular society have exactly the same attitudes and do exactly the same things in the same way. Rather, the general principles of culture may be shared but there may be many differences in how people experience and think about their lives. For example, not all Americans vote or believe that voting is efficacious, but most would staunchly defend everyone's right to vote. Thus, voting is included in the broad cultural conception of legitimate governance in the United States.

Societies can function as groups to minimize conflicts because their members agree about the basic parameters of living. If this were not so, people would not be able to coordinate their activities or agree on what to do next. And even though they might speak the same language, they would not be able to accurately interpret each other's meanings and intentions if they did not share basic cultural assumptions about the world. These shared assumptions, or **cultural models,** form a background ideology in terms of which behavior becomes relatively coherent and consistent.

Despite cultural models, there are disagreements and conflicts within any community. In all communities, some people are more fully committed to general societal norms than others. Societal **norms** are sets of commonly held expectations and attitudes that people have about appropriate behavior. Although these norms are generally held to be valid within each culture, not everyone acts in accordance with them.

Deviance from expected and appropriate behavior occurs in every community. Some types of deviance are tolerated whereas others are not. In fact, behavior that may be considered deviant within a community as a whole may be a marker of identity for a particular group. For example, body piercings or tattooing might violate adult conceptions of beauty, but teenagers may engage in these physical alterations to conform to youthful standards.

This young woman was photographed in traditional Burkina Faso garb with her aunt.
(The Image Works/Imapress/Charreire/The Image Works)

Violent behavior such as assault and murder are deviant acts that are not tolerated in most societies. Other kinds of violence that occur within the family, though, such as spousal abuse, may be tolerated, even if not condoned.

People occupying different social roles and statuses may hold opposing views about the existing social order and prevailing cultural norms. For example, age may be a factor in the way people organize their lives and in the kinds of attitudes that they hold. Younger and older people have different experiences and different frames of reference. Opposing activities and norms for older and younger people may be relatively stable, though; that is, as younger people age, they adopt the lifestyles and norms of their elders. Differences between the young and the old may also signal ongoing social and culture change, if young people introduce new ways of living as they replace their elders through the normal aging process.

Gender differences are another common source of distinctions in people's activities and attitudes. Issues of gender will be explored in depth, but here we can note that gender is a complex cultural concept through which people assign particular roles and convey particular attitudes. Gender as a social construct differs from sex, which is a biological attribute. In most societies, women and men usually have certain specific tasks that they fulfill in their homes and communities. The relationships between men and women in the family and in the public sphere influence the ways they experience their lives. For example, men and women are likely to have different ideas about their rights and responsibilities, depending on which gender is the dominant decision maker and authority in the household. Women who have the major share of the household and child-rearing responsibilities may feel burdened and restricted, or they may feel challenged and fulfilled. In societies that sanction violence against women and permit men to abuse their wives, women's experience of household life certainly contrasts sharply with men's.

Like differences in age and gender, other status differences in society result in incomplete sharing of culture. Such differences also may be a source of social tension and cultural disagreement. For example, members of elite groups may reap greater economic and social benefits from the way in which society is structured than do members of marginalized or oppressed groups. Although differences of experiences, attitudes, and opinions vary within all societies, such differences are likely to be sharper in complex, heterogeneous societies than in small, relatively homogeneous ones where people interact more personally with one another. Class, race, or ethnicity may segment large societies, creating group cultural distinctions in how people organize their lives. In addition, people who belong to different religions may apply different philosophical orientations and moral principles to their daily lives.

Thus, members of different groups in stratified societies may have different attitudes and values. For example, when economists and politicians in the United States tell us that the economy is booming, this does not mean that everyone is doing well. The wealthy and those who own shares on the stock market experience an economic boom very differently from workers whose factories have been relocated abroad, or from people on welfare. Thus, a culture is not fully shared in a diverse society.

Differences in social groups and in the ways that members of distinct groups live may remain relatively stable for long periods of time. However, tensions and struggles over cultural norms and values may lead to significant societal changes.

In the diverse society of Bolivia, this peasant woman of the Andes does not fully share the same culture as her counterpart in La Paz, the capital.
(The Image Works/Kike Calvo/V&W/The Image Works)

subculture
A group whose members and others think of their way of life as different in some significant way from that of other people in the larger society.

Hasidic families are an American urban subculture among many in New York City. Their subculture is distinguished through ethnic background and religious beliefs and practices.
(Corbis/Alain Keler/Sygma/Corbis)

People can acquire any culture if they are raised in it, just as people can learn any language.
(Dreamstime LLC/Lyoung403b/Dreamstime)

In addition to differences derived from distinct social roles and statuses, some societies contain groups that participate in identifiable subcultures. A **subculture** is a group of people who think of themselves, and are thought of by others, as different in a significant way from the majority of people living in the society. Members of subcultures interact more frequently among themselves than with "outsiders," and share attitudes and practices that distinguish them from other groups.

In complex, multiethnic societies, including American society, ethnic groups may comprise subcultures, especially if members retain allegiance to their native country, use their native language, and observe ethnic food, preferences, and family relations. Some occupational groups may also function as subcultures. For example, police officers may work and socialize together, have shared vocabulary, and share expectations of life patterns, cooperation, and mutual aid.

All of these sources of difference modify our understanding of culture as a constellation of shared behaviors and beliefs. Still, when people interact within the same society, they must share some basic premises about social order and social values. If they did not, community cohesion would disintegrate, and the groups within the society would separate.

Culture Is Learned

Culture is transmitted from generation to generation and is learned mainly in childhood and during maturation. We learn not only our behavior but also our attitudes and values. The ability to acquire culture in this way makes humans highly adaptable to different cultural environments. Humans are born with a potential to learn whatever knowledge and skills are practiced in their communities. They do this through the process of **enculturation**—learning one's culture through informal observation and formal instruction, beginning in earliest childhood. Children learn the culture that they are exposed to, as the Case Study "Daughter from Danang" illustrates. We all can acquire any culture if we are raised in it, just as most people can learn any language. Through these processes of exposure and learning, people acquire their culture and transmit it to others.

Although most human cultural behavior is the result of learning, this behavior is also influenced by inherited drives as well as acquired needs. People must fulfill important physical and survival needs, just like all living creatures. People need to eat, drink, sleep, eliminate body wastes, and engage in sexual activity. And, like other primates, people also need to interact with one another to obtain food and protection. Culture intervenes and influences the ways in which people satisfy these needs.

For example, each culture has attitudes about what kinds of foods are edible and suitable for human consumption. People do not eat everything that is edible in their environment; they select some foods and reject others, expressing these choices as preferences and prohibitions, or **taboos.** In the United States and Canada, most people consider eating insects distasteful, but many peoples of Australia, Asia, Mexico, and Africa consider insects a delicacy. The Maasai of Kenya and northern Tanzania drink the blood of their cattle. Koreans farm puppies for meat. Religion-based taboos forbidding Hindus to eat beef and forbidding Muslims and Jews to eat pork further illustrate the mediation of survival needs through culture. Further, people also have norms about how many meals to have, when to eat them, and which kinds of foods to eat at each meal.

Although all people need to sleep, they normally do so at a culturally prescribed time and place. No matter how tired you are at work, it would probably be inappropriate to lie down on the floor or your desk to sleep. People follow culturally prescribed rules about where and when to eliminate body wastes. Most people are taught not to urinate or defecate in public under any circumstances, for example. In fact, doing so may be a criminal offense. All cultures also have norms about when and how to satisfy sexual urges appropriately. These norms include strong taboos that prohibit sexual relations between parents and their children and between siblings.

enculturation
Process of learning one's culture through informal observation and formal instruction.

Watch the Video
Anthropology of Childhood on www.pearsoncustom.com/mi/msu_mylabs

taboos
Norms specifying behaviors that are prohibited in a culture.

How many meals do you eat in a day, and at what times? What kinds of foods do you eat at each meal? If you ate eggs at different mealtimes, how might you prepare them differently for each meal, and why? What do your answers to these questions reveal about your cultural norms and values?

CASE STUDY

DAUGHTER FROM DANANG

Mai Thi Hiep was born in Danang, Vietnam, in 1968. She was the daughter of a Vietnamese mother and an American soldier who had abandoned Hiep's mother when she became pregnant. In 1975, her Vietnamese mother, troubled by the chaos of war, participated in "Operation Babylift," an American government program that placed racially mixed children from Vietnam for adoption in the United States, wanting to protect her child and expecting her to be returned later. Hiep's mother also feared reprisals from Vietnamese angered by the U.S. intervention in Vietnam.

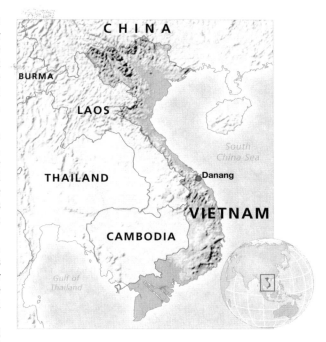

At age seven, Hiep was sent to the United States, where a single woman adopted her. Hiep became Heidi and grew up in the small town of Pulaski, Tennessee. Heidi recalls that her adoptive mother advised her not to tell people that she was Vietnamese because of the racial climate in Pulaski. Heidi learned to think of herself as American. She forgot her native language quickly because she had no other Vietnamese people to speak with, and acquired all of the tastes and attitudes of American teenagers. By 1997, Heidi had married an American serviceman and became the mother of two young daughters.

Heidi longed to reconnect to her birth mother and to her Vietnamese family. By an odd coincidence, Heidi and her mother were contacting various agencies at about the same time, trying to find one another. Heidi located her mother and arranged for Heidi to visit her family in Danang. Before the trip, Heidi spoke of "going home." It was ". . . going to be so healing for us. It would make all those bad memories [of war and separation] go away."

Reuniting with her Vietnamese family was deeply moving, but Heidi found the sights and sounds of Vietnam strange. She was shocked by the poverty of people on the streets and of her own family. At the first dinner, she did not know the etiquette of how to eat (dipping food from common plates into sauces rather than the American custom of placing a quantity of food on one's own plate), and was not used to the spiciness of the cooking. Within a few days, more problems surfaced. Heidi's mother never left her alone, holding her hand as they walked through the streets, touching and hugging her whenever she could. Although Heidi began to ". . . feel a little smothered," she was also a little "jealous" of the "love and unity" characteristic of Vietnamese kinship ties.

Her mother asked Heidi to help a sister who was extremely poor. Heidi gave her money, but when her sister asked for more, Heidi felt "insulted . . . I didn't come here to be anybody's salvation, I came here to be reunited." This was not what she had imagined. She wanted to "escape back to the world I feel comfortable in." For Heidi, love and asking for financial support were incompatible needs, but to her Vietnamese kin, asking for money didn't lessen the integrity of their love.

Before Heidi's departure, their final meeting revealed the stark contrasts between Heidi's expectations and those of her family. Her brother began to talk about their mother's advancing age and her need for material and emotional support. He said that, for twenty-two years, ". . . we, your siblings, have been taking care of our mother. We hope that now you will assume your filial responsibility toward her," meaning to send money monthly. Again, Heidi was shocked, but her mother understood her negative reaction to this direct request for financial help: "What does she know about the Vietnamese notion of love and emotion? She's used to living in a different way." Heidi's brother added, "We are trying to understand your situation and we hope you'll try to understand ours. . . . As a Vietnamese, I thought what I said was normal." Although saddened by her family's situation, Heidi could not respond the way they expected. "It's not how I wanted it to be."

From a cultural perspective, the complex, conflicting expectations of both Heidi and her Vietnamese relatives were understandable and appropriate, given the cultural contexts in which each lived and the attitudes and values that they had learned. Although Heidi was born Vietnamese, she had become an American. Because her family remembered her as the child known as Hiep, they expected her to conform to their own system of values. Heidi interpreted her family's expectations through the lens of American culture because most of her socialization had been in the United States.

This story demonstrates how cultural learning molds people to regard their society's practices and values as normal and natural. Understanding other people's reactions from their own perspective requires insight and empathy.

From *Daughter from Danang*, PBS American Experience. Directed by Gail Dolgin and Vicente Franco. © 2003 PBS.

Societies enculturate children in culturally specific ways. In many societies, children are expected to learn skills informally by observation and imitation. That is, they watch and observe their parents or other elders and learn by trying to do the same thing. Adults may offer guidance, but, for the most part, the child learns by doing and is an active participant in the process. This type of learning takes place in all communities in some contexts, but training and education also take place in formal settings such as schools in some societies.

Casual observation of others as they interact informally also plays a role in enculturation. Through observation, children learn attitudes: They hear what people have to say about themselves and others, and what they think of other people's behavior. They listen to people express their beliefs about the world. Through these conversations and interactions, children learn what is valued and what is criticized by members of the community. In these contexts, they thus gain a sense of personal identity as well as a sense of the world and their place in it.

Culture Is Adaptive

When anthropologists say that culture is adaptive, they are usually referring to behaviors and beliefs that respond to environmental constraints and opportunities that ensure a community's survival. People must adapt to their environment, and culture is their chief mechanism of adaptation. Because of their capacity for adaptation, humans can survive in nearly any environment. Further, people can modify their environments and create artificial ones to enhance survival. Cultural adaptations often involve technological innovation and the elaboration of material culture. For example, people living on islands or along coasts construct rafts, canoes, and boats to cross rivers, bays, and oceans, and people everywhere make a vast array of tools and equipment to help them obtain food and perform other kinds of subsistence tasks. The tools and practices that enable people to satisfy their survival and adaptation needs make up what is called a **cultural core**.

cultural core
Practices by which people organize their work and produce food and other goods necessary for their survival.

Although adaptation through culture is a fundamental and universal process, not all cultural practices are adaptive. Some practices may be maladaptive or have unintended negative consequences as circumstances change. Sometimes solving one problem may lead to new, unforeseen problems.

The archaeological record gives us some clues about how agricultural techniques that turned out to have unforeseen negative consequences contributed to the decline of several large and prosperous ancient cultures in both the Eastern and Western Hemispheres. For example, Sumer in ancient Mesopotamia (what is now southern Iraq) had developed large city-states by 3000 B.C. The Sumerian economy was based on intensive farming, made possible by extensive irrigation systems that channeled water from the Tigris and Euphrates rivers to fields. Sumerian farmers produced a greater yield of crops than farmers in the region produce today (Sasson 1995).

Over time, crop yields declined. One reason for the eventual fall of Sumerian civilization was that intensive irrigation increased salinization, or salt content, in the soil. As the land deteriorated, Sumer was no longer able to support large populations without a decline in living standards (Peregrine 2003).

The Industrial Revolution provides a more recent example of unintended negative consequences. Industry's ability to supply millions of people with an ever-increasing amount and variety of products has led to pollution, contamination, and overexploitation of natural resources and nonrenewable energy resources. Many practices, like the heavy reliance on chemical fertilizers and pesticides commonly used in industrial agriculture, are maladaptive in the long run, although they may increase productivity in the short term.

Thus, the idea that culture is adaptive needs to be considered in context. That is, a particular practice may be adaptive in one situation but not in another. For instance, farming techniques used in temperate climates to increase crop yields may be counterproductive in the Amazon rain forest because the topsoil there is too thin and relatively infertile to sustain them. This is exactly what is happening in parts of the Amazon today, where environmentally inappropriate farming techniques are harming the long-term viability of the soil (Schmink and Wood 1992).

This cropduster's payload is carefully regulated because chemical fertilizers may contaminate food and deplete land productivity in the long term. (The Image Works/Jack K. Clark/The Image Works)

■■■■ CASE STUDY

MALADAPTIVE ADAPTATIONS: KURU AND MAD COW

In 1910, a new disease appeared among the South Fore (pronounced For'ray), a farming people of New Guinea. This progressive disease, called *kuru* (meaning "trembling" or "fear" in the Fore language), affects the central nervous system and slowly leads to complete physical incapacitation and death. Victims gradually become unable to sit or walk unaided, focus their eyes, speak clearly, or even swallow. Death usually occurs six to twelve months after the onset of symptoms, although some people may survive as long as two years.

☐ South Fore People

Investigation of the spread of kuru during the 1950s led to suspicion that it correlated with ritual cannibalism by women. In Fore society, as elsewhere in New Guinea, women are the primary farmers, growing sweet potatoes, yams, and other vegetables. They also care for the domesticated pigs each household keeps. Men clear the fields and hunt, but do little farm labor. Women live in small huts with their children and pigs, and men reside communally in a "men's house," eating and sleeping away from their families. Fore culture emphasizes concepts of pollution and danger, against which rituals serve as antidotes. This includes the belief that women pose a threat to male strength and vitality. Men and women also participate in different social and ceremonial activities.

In the early 1900s, South Fore women began practicing cannibalism as part of their mourning ceremonies when a female relative died. This ritual involved eating the brains and body parts of the deceased kin. According to anthropologist Shirley Lindenbaum (1979), this practice had some adaptive value because it provided needed protein, particularly for women. As the population increased and more land came under cultivation, sources of animal protein had declined. In addition, men had access to more high-quality protein than women because they claimed greater rights to the pigs. They believed that other sources of protein, such as insects, frogs, and small mammals, were not only unfit for men but might threaten their health and vigor. Thus, women may have turned to cannibalism to secure more protein.

When a South Fore woman died, her female relatives dismembered her body and ate it. Some of the meat was given to children of either sex, but adult men rarely ate it because of the belief that contact with women (and, logically, eating their flesh) was dangerous and polluting. The Fore did not associate cannibalism with kuru, but they were alarmed by the high incidence of the disease, particularly among women. They attributed kuru to sorcery, a common cause of illness and death in their belief system. When someone died of kuru, kinspeople tried to identify the evildoer, usually accusing someone who might have had reason to wish the victim harm.

Between 1957 and 1968, when the disease was at its height, about 1,000 people died in the South Fore population of 8,000. The fact that nearly all the deaths were of adult women added to the social and economic burden, because women produced the crops, tended the pigs, and gave birth. In some villages, nearly half of the adult female deaths and nearly all of the deaths of children between ages 5 and 16 were due to kuru (Foster and Anderson 1978).

The riddle of kuru was not solved until the late 1960s, when the anthropologist-virologist Carlton Gajdusek discovered that the disease was transmitted by a prion, the same kind of agent responsible for mad cow disease. Prions, slow-acting proteins that attack and destroy brain tissue, remain dormant for years after they are ingested but eventually cause progressive damage to the brain. Thus, when South Fore women and children ate the brains of their female relatives, they unknowingly ingested the cause of their own deaths. The incidence of kuru began to decline after the Australian colonial administration in New Guinea persuaded the Fore to give up ritual cannibalism.

████ **CASE STUDY** CONTINUED ─────────────────

The Fore had adopted a maladaptive practice. Similarly, the spread of mad cow disease in Britain in the 1980s and 1990s resulted from a procedure that seemed financially beneficial in the short term but ultimately proved disastrous. Companies began to use bonemeal derived from sheep brains as cheap protein filler for cattle feed. However, some of the bonemeal was infected with a disease called scrapie, caused by agents of the family of prions similar to those that caused kuru. When cattle ate the infected bonemeal, they developed symptoms similar to those manifested by the Fore.

Once mad cow disease became known and its source identified, more than 140,000 cows in Britain had to be slaughtered to prevent the disease from spreading. In 1996, some people in Britain who died of a prion-caused disease now identified as Creutzfeldt-Jakob disease were thought to have become sick after eating beef infected with mad cow disease. As a consequence, more British cattle were slaughtered to stem a potential epidemic. The European Union banned the export of British beef from 1996 to 1999, and nearly half of the country's 11 million cattle were destroyed. Some British cattle imported into Canada and the United States also were destroyed.

The U.S. Department of Agriculture now bars importation of cattle and many cattle by-products from Britain and most other European nations. The Food and Drug Administration has also banned the use of beef proteins or hormonal extracts from cattle organs in medicines, dietary supplements, and cosmetics. The economic loss to the European and Canadian cattle industry has been disastrous. Using cheap sheep brains to fatten cattle ended up costing millions of dollars and many lives.

Mad cow disease, like kuru among the Fore, demonstrates that people sometimes engage in practices that seem to make sense when first introduced but have consequences in the long term that are maladaptive and even life-threatening. These two syndromes are vastly different in their cultural causes, one stemming from religious beliefs and the other driven by the economic motive to cut costs. However, they share a similar process, namely, that seemingly sensible behavior often has unforeseen and dangerous consequences.

> What are some other examples of "maladaptive" adaptations in today's world?

── ■

Culture Is Integrated

cultural integration
Tendency for people's practices and beliefs to form a relatively coherent and consistent system.

Cultural integration refers to the observation that people's practices and beliefs form a relatively coherent and consistent system. Cultures are not simply random collections of activities but, instead, are patterned and interrelated in systematic ways. For example, behaviors that take place in one domain, such as political organization, tend to be compatible with and support behaviors taking place in other domains, such as family organization. Anthropologists recognize that terms such as *economy, social organization, family organization,* and *government* are not discrete, separable units of activity but are closely intertwined. For example, economic activities are usually integrated with, affect, and are affected by other kinds of activities. The work of obtaining food and other goods and services is often performed by people who occupy particular social roles and statuses. Gender roles may assign men and women different kinds of work in contributing to their household economies. Also, social norms or, in complex societies, laws enacted by legislators and policies formulated by political agencies tend to be consistent with particular economic consequences and to reinforce particular economic goals.

The shared ways that people organize their lives are major integrating factors. In some societies, religious beliefs permeate and guide all aspects of daily life. Religion then becomes an overarching, integrative system of beliefs and practices. People in societies integrated by religion might perform daily rituals to bless and safeguard themselves and their families; they may recite prayers when hunting or planting crops to ensure success; and they may ask for spirit protection when engaging in any dangerous activity. People in these societies believe that the human and spiritual realms are not separable but that spiritual forces are omnipresent and continually affect their lives.

Naturally, not all aspects of cultural behavior and belief are internally consistent or integrated with all others. Thus, the concept of cultural integration needs to be understood loosely, as a process of adjustment and change, not as static and rigid. Humans and their experiences are not so neat and tidy. Nevertheless, cultural systems as wholes tend toward consistency. A consequence of this consistency and integration is that change in one societal domain causes change in others (see the Case Study "Women and Work in the United States," for example). Societies are not bounded units (either of people or ideas); rather, external influences from other peoples or internal tensions and innovations lead to changes in practices and attitudes.

▮ CASE STUDY

CONSEQUENCES OF CULTURAL INTEGRATION: WOMEN AND WORK IN THE UNITED STATES

In the United States, changes in women's participation in paid employment have affected both their roles in other spheres of life and the prevailing attitudes about men and women (Fox and Hesse-Biber 1984). Women's rates of employment began to rise significantly during World War II, as a consequence of the nation's military and economic policies. As millions of men entered the armed forces, millions of jobs necessary to support the economy and the war effort were left vacant. Public policy encouraged women to do their patriotic duty by working in factories and offices, where they had previously met resistance and discrimination. The banner of women's rights, which had won American women the right to vote in 1920, was raised again.

After the war, many women returned to exclusively domestic roles, but others remained in the work force, partly for personal reasons and partly to improve their family's standard of living. Also, work outside the home gave women a degree of financial equality with their husbands. Women's economic gains contributed to rising rates of divorce because wives could sometimes afford to leave unhappy marriages, and husbands could leave if they felt that their ex-wives could be at least partially self-supporting (Costello et al. 1998). In intact families, greater financial equality as well as the greater amount of time that women spent outside the home contributed to shifting the roles of husbands toward some household and child-care responsibilities.

By the late twentieth century, the percentage of marriages that ended in divorce had risen, and the social stigma formerly associated with divorce had all but disappeared. Also, women's paid employment and opportunities to make prominent contributions in public arenas had expanded. Today, more legislators, governors, and heads of government agencies are women. Women's leadership roles in religion have also broadened; many Protestant and Jewish denominations ordain women ministers and rabbis. More women have advanced educational degrees and are more accepted in formerly male-dominated occupations and professions, such as law and law enforcement, the military, and the building trades.

Changes in women's roles have also affected how men think about themselves and their work. Husbands now expect their wives to contribute to household incomes. And work roles for men have become more flexible. A father could be a stay-at-home Dad if his wife's work brought in more money than his or if he simply preferred that role. And society has become more accepting of men working in certain jobs traditionally associated with women, such as nursing and elementary school teaching.

Thus, within a mere fifty years, changes in one societal sphere in the United States led to changes both in other spheres and in people's thoughts and behaviors. These multiple and interrelating effects illustrate how cultural integration can lead to cultural transformation.

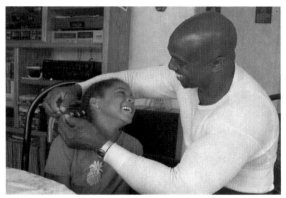

Changes in the roles and status of women in American society have affected men's lives as well as the society as a whole.
(The Image Works/Geri Engberg/The Image Works)

Culture Is Based on Symbols

People's behaviors and understanding of the world are based on meanings expressed through symbols. A **symbol** is a word or object that represents or stands for an idea, event, meaning, or sentiment. Language is a pervasive and powerful symbol system. Words in any language are just sequences of sounds, but each sequence is a symbol of or represents something other than the sounds themselves. The collection of sounds in each word in this sentence, for instance, stands for some arbitrarily assigned meaning.

Symbols permeate human culture in ways other than language. Objects, art, and artistic performances may represent powerful cultural ideas and attitudes. The colors and designs of national flags, for instance, come to be associated with complex levels of meaning. People can understand those meanings by examining the contexts of flag use, the way people talk about their national colors, and the way people react to them. Flags are used to symbolically represent a country, a territorial and cultural unit differentiated from all other similarly organized territorial and cultural units. Flags take on additional associations, demonstrated by the emotional reactions they can trigger in observers. People may use

symbol
A word, image, or object that stands for cultural ideas or sentiments.

What emotional reactions can images of national flags stir? How has the American flag been used to display both positive and negative feelings about the U.S. government or its policies?

their country's flag in ways that show their attitudes and political beliefs. For example, in the United States, after the al Qaeda attack on 9/11, flag pins became necessities for many political figures and represented a show of support for the "war on terror" that the United States undertook.

Religion, too, is a domain filled with symbolic meanings. Believers invest tremendous importance in objects considered to have religious significance. Ordinary objects and substances used in rituals take on sacred properties. Books, cups, images, pieces of cloth or wood, or foodstuffs can be symbols of beliefs and can evoke powerful emotions and dramatize sacred actions. Symbolic culture thus includes both sacred and secular meanings and all the ways in which those meanings are communicated.

Culture often is expressed in symbolic interaction between individuals using verbal and nonverbal language. Thus, language can also be used to challenge basic assumptions encoded in ordinary speech. For example, a dialect of Caribbean immigrants and their descendants in Great Britain, called Afro-Lingua, focuses on the ways that standard English transmits common cultural assumptions about race in the uses and meanings that associate *white* with "good" and *black* with "bad." For example, in common English expressions, "a black day" means a day when things go drastically wrong, and "a black sheep" means an outcast family member (Bones 1986, 46). Afro-Lingua speakers might refer to "a white day" and "a white sheep" in equivalent contexts. In addition, Afro-Lingua also changes syllables in some English words to highlight cultural and political meanings: The word *politics* is transformed into *politricks,* and *oppression* becomes *downpression* (Wong 1986, 119).

Humor is another form of symbolic cultural communication. For example, Western Apache communities in New Mexico have a repertoire of joke routines that ridicule Anglos by imitating and exaggerating their intrusive, domineering communicative styles (Basso 1979). Apaches find these Anglo communication styles insensitive at best or even offensive. Scorned behaviors include making direct eye contact with or staring at interlocutors, touching another person while talking to him or her, calling casual acquaintances "friend," and asking intrusive, personal questions. Through their informal comic routines, Apaches share the opposite norms and values.

Both the changes in English expressions used by speakers of Afro-Lingua and the joking routines of Western Apaches demonstrate the ways that symbolic behavior can be used to challenge dominant values. Through symbolic practices, people can forge their unity with others and can simultaneously develop and transmit messages of resistance. Afro-Lingua speakers defy commonplace notions of race and power; Western Apaches resist communicative norms imposed on them by dominant Anglo society.

Culture Organizes the Way People Think About the World

Through exposure to cultural symbols, enculturation, and the acquisition of shared cultural concepts, people develop ways of thinking about themselves, their lives, other people, and the world. Culture, therefore, consists of systems of meaning produced and interpreted by members. Underlying shared concepts and meanings become so ingrained that they are taken for granted, assumed to be true. People understand them as natural and commonsense. These are **naturalized concepts,** ideas thought to be essential and to exist in nature. Since people understand these naturalized concepts to be part of the "natural" world, they are unaware of their cultural origins and do not question their legitimacy. Indeed, they don't think about them at all. And these taken-for-granted suppositions have all the more influence on people because they are not consciously thought about.

All societies have a core of naturalized ideas, based on societal norms. For example, in most capitalist societies, it is taken for granted that people want to own property and obtain wealth. It is assumed that people are naturally competitive and want to continually acquire more property, own larger and more expensive houses, and have unlimited access to possessions. Yet people in these societies generally may not understand that their attitudes and values about property and wealth stem from the kind of economic system they live in. Models of gender are also deeply naturalized in people's behaviors and attitudes. We come to believe that men's and women's roles and value are derived from qualities, feelings, and needs inherent in women and men rather than understanding that these gender models are largely derived from culture. In other words, people who lack an anthropological perspective think that their attitudes and values are natural and universal rather than products of their culture. Thus, naturalized concepts orient people's thinking about themselves and the world, forming a background ideology that gives meaning to people's behaviors and attitudes. To the extent that they shape the way we view other cultures, they are also a source of ethnocentrism.

Although all cultures have fundamental organizing concepts, these principles may be challenged from within the society. In all societies, members of different subcultures or subgroups hold alternative and

GLOBALIZATION

Afro-Lingua is a language that was created to symbolically challenge the basic assumptions encoded in the ordinary speech of European colonizers of the Caribbean.

What would you learn about cultural communication from studying in your workplace or dorm?

naturalized concepts
Ideas and behaviors so deeply embedded in a culture that they are regarded as universally normal or natural.

What are some examples of culture wars in U.S. society today? What are some examples of countercultures in U.S. history?

These Chinese and American children are forming group identities based on symbiotic culture.
(Getty Images/Hulton Archive/Getty Images; PhotoEdit/Michael Ventura/PhotoEdit, Inc.)

conflicting values. Alternative views may be discussed and debated in the context of mutual respect or they may erupt in more contentious challenges, in what some observers refer to as **culture wars.** Expressions of antipathy between conservatives and liberals over many social policy issues in the United States, such as gun control, abortion rights, gay rights, and immigration policy, are examples of so-called culture wars.

On the other hand, individuals and groups engaging in practices with underlying meanings that conflict with prevailing assumptions and norms may be participants in a **counterculture**—an alternative culture model. Members of a counterculture view themselves as being in active opposition to dominant cultural themes and values. For example, the hippies of the 1960s openly rejected prevailing puritanical attitudes toward sex, the materialism of contemporary society, and the militaristic policies of the government as it escalated the war in Vietnam.

Challenges to widely recognized assumptions often come from members of groups that are marginalized or oppressed, or who hold different **worldviews** than those of the dominant groups or elites. For example, apartheid, South Africa's dominant racist cultural ideology until the 1990s, was imposed by a powerful white minority that had inherited power through colonial rule. That rule was challenged by the majority of black South Africans, who eventually overturned that ideology and rebelled against the government that oppressed them. Black South Africans asserted not only their political rights but also their right to replace the cultural model of white supremacy with one of racial equality. Thus, many political movements seek more than a reordering of social and political forces. They also seek the institutionalization of new cultural models as organizing principles in their society.

Similarly, through symbolic culture, some segments of a society might resist the official culture or offer an alternative cultural model. In the Middle East and North Africa, women's challenges to the ideology of male dominance often take the form of poetry and song, a low-risk context for expressing discontent. Bedouin women, for example, recite poetry and compose songs expressing their longings for love and respect. Song lyrics express passion and joy in attentions they receive from clandestine lovers (Abu-Lughod 1986; 1990). Artistic genres thus permit women to verbalize private feelings that run contrary to accepted norms of female deference and modesty.

Table 1 summarizes the characteristics of culture as it is defined in this module. This section then closes with a story in the In Their Own Voices section (pages 18–19) about an anthropologist's field experience that highlights the challenges of understanding cultures as unique collections of symbols and meanings.

culture wars
Internal disagreements in a society about cultural models or about how society or the world should be organized.

counterculture
An alternative cultural model within a society that expresses different views about the way that society should be organized.

worldview
A culture-based, often ethnocentric way that people see the world and other peoples.

⊙—| Watch the **Animation**
Characteristics of Culture on www.pearsoncustom.com/mi/msu_mylabs

REVIEW

Characteristics of culture include the fact that it is shared. Individuals who belong to a culture share assumptions about the world and develop cultural models and societal norms and taboos that define how one should and should not behave. Members of different subcultures in a society share culture differently. Culture is also learned through enculturation. We are enculturated both formally and informally through social interactions with other members of society. Culture is adaptive in that people change their culture when needed or when influenced to change. The knowledge, skills, and tools people use to survive and adapt are referred to as the cultural core. Culture is integrated—that is, aspects of culture are interconnected and mutually reinforcing. Thus, cultural integration means that change in one aspect of culture leads to changes in other aspects. The existence of culture wars and countercultures within a society illustrates, however, that cultures are not fully shared or rigidly integrated, that alternative cultural models coexist. Culture is based on symbols, and language is the most important symbol system people use. Symbolic objects and symbolic communication are used in diverse contexts, such as religion and humor. Culture influences the way people organize their experience and their worldview. They use naturalized concepts to apply their cultural assumptions to their own and other people's ways of life.

TABLE 1 Characteristics of Culture

Culture Is Shared	Behavior, attitudes, and ideas are formed through interaction with others. **Norms:** Sets of expectations and attitudes that people have about appropriate behavior. **Subculture:** A group whose members interact more frequently among themselves and share attitudes and practices that are distinct from others.
Culture Is Learned	Culture is acquired rather than inherited. **Enculturation:** The learning of one's cultural behaviors, attitudes, and values.
Culture Is Adaptive	Aspects of behavior and belief are responses to environmental constraints and the need to ensure a community's survival. **Cultural core:** Basic practices that function to satisfy people's adaptive needs.
Culture Is Integrated	Practices and beliefs that form a relatively coherent and consistent system. **Cultural model:** Comprehensive shared ideas about the ideal culture.
Culture Is Based on Symbols	People's behavior and understanding of the world are based on meanings expressed through language, art, and symbolic objects. **Symbols:** Words, images, or objects that stand for cultural ideas or sentiments.
Culture Organizes the Way People Think about the World	**Naturalized concepts:** Ideas and behaviors so deeply embedded in a culture that they are regarded as universally normal or natural. **Worldview:** The culture-based way that people see the world and other peoples. **Counterculture:** Alternative cultural model within a society that expresses opposition to dominant social and political views.

GLOBALIZATION

Culture contact, a major force in the process of globalization, leads to several strategies and consequences of culture change, including acculturation, assimilation, and reactive adaptation.

culture contact
Direct interaction between peoples of different cultures through migration, trade, invasion, or conquest.

syncretism
Process by which a cultural product is created when people adapt a cultural item selectively borrowed from another culture to fit their existing culture.

assimilation
Process by which a less numerous and less powerful cultural group changes its ways and cultural identity to blend in with the dominant culture.

acculturation
Process by which a group adjusts to living within a dominant culture while at the same time maintaining its original cultural identity.

◇ CULTURE CHANGE

Cultures are dynamic systems that respond to societal and historical changes from numerous sources. The view of "traditional" or indigenous societies as static and timeless is untenable. All societies experience innovation from within and influences from outside origins. Some sources of culture change are internal, emerging from new practices and attitudes, technological innovations, or adaptations to the consequences of earlier practices. Other sources of culture change emerge as people borrow ideas or artifacts from their neighbors or from people with whom they interact through migration, trade, or other contacts. Some borrowings take place in friendly interactions during **culture contact,** but others are forced on people, as in conquest or foreign intervention.

Although it may be possible to identify original sources of change as internal or external, in practice these are interconnected processes. For instance, cultural changes stimulated by external sources then typically undergo further change through internal processes. People usually adapt outside cultural borrowings to their own cultures. They may borrow only parts of a cultural item, whether a story or a way of organizing economic activity, and combine those parts with items that already exist in their cultural repertoire. For example, in the realm of religion, people often combine elements of their traditional beliefs with those that they learn from external sources as a consequence of culture contact. This process, called **syncretism,** is seen in religions such as Santería, which combines traditional Afro-Caribbean beliefs in magic and witchcraft with Roman Catholicism. Spanish colonizers in the Caribbean derisively called this religion of the Yoruba—and other Bantu slaves from Nigeria, Senegal, and the Guinea Coast—Santería, "Way of the Saints."

Anthropologists have other terms to describe the kinds of internal change that take place following culture contact, depending on the power relations between peoples and the extent of change. **Assimilation** occurs when a less numerous and less powerful group changes its ways to blend in with the dominant culture. In assimilating, people abandon or modify their prior beliefs and practices and adopt the cultural repertoire of the dominant population. For example, immigrants may voluntarily change their national and cultural identities by assimilating the language and culture of their new country. Assimilation is also sometimes forced on people by a dominant culture, especially in the context of conquest and colonization.

A group's adjustment to living within another, more dominant, culture while at the same time maintaining its original cultural identity is called **acculturation.** For example, many Native Americans in the United States and Canada adopt many features of dominant American culture such as the economic and political systems, but maintain their own languages, family systems, and religious beliefs. The term **cultural pluralism** describes a stratified society that contains many diverse cultural groups who ideally live together equally and harmoniously. Other complex changes that occur through combinations of external and internal processes include economic transformations, such as **modernization,** based on industrialism and a market economy.

Internal Culture Change

Early anthropologists, such as Edward B. Tylor, believed that cultures evolve through various stages, from a simpler and more primitive state to a complex and more culturally advanced state. To Tylor and his nineteenth-century contemporaries, middle-class Euro-American culture represented the pinnacle of this **cultural evolution,** which other cultures could naturally and eventually achieve. Others treated the concept of cultural evolution as analogous to biological evolution, claiming that some cultures were naturally superior to others, modeled on the concepts of competition and the survival of the fittest. This faulty reasoning, known as **social Darwinism,** claimed that the wealth and power of Western societies were due to their natural and cultural superiority rather than to the consequences of historical processes. Social Darwinists saw competition between societies as based on similar processes as biological evolution. However, they failed to recognize that particular events and developments in fact contributed to the ability of some societies to dominate others. They also used models of efficiency and progress, analogous to biological processes, in their analyses of cultural development and change.

Today, however, evolutionary biologists study the adaptive value of social behavior, cognitive skills, and the capacity for both material and symbolic culture, all of which have contributed to the evolutionary success of the primates, and which all living human groups possess equally. Thus, **culture history** may be a more apt term than cultural evolution for ongoing culture change in which people respond and adapt to their environment and experiences. In adapting, people make themselves. That is, people develop, define, and direct their own cultural and ethnic identities, a process called **ethnogenesis** (Hill 1992). This concept of culture change views human beings as agents in their own history, continually creating and re-creating the conditions of their lives.

Some changes in societies are not intentional, like ethnogenesis, but result from gradual shifting of public norms and private sentiments. For example, in art and public performance, certain behaviors and language use that were unacceptable in the past have become standard, although not without arousing conflict among some sectors of the population.

Since the 1960s, the content of American films has changed considerably. In previous periods, violence generally was shown only from a distance, and its effects on the human body were not made explicit. Today, the depiction of explicit violence and its effects is commonplace. Nudity and sexual activity also have become routine in American films and videos, and language is not censored as it was in the past. These changes reflect changes in attitudes and values rather than in technology. And these changes are embedded in the wider social and political contexts of the times. The Motion Picture Production Code of the 1930s, which imposed strict limits on language, subject matter, and sexual representation, has been replaced by a rating system identifying film content. Publicized ratings warn potential viewers who do not want themselves or their children exposed to particular content.

Another source of internal culture change is the adaptations that people make by inventing new technologies and skills to better adjust to existing conditions or to deal with new problems. **Inventions** usually are based on previous tools, knowledge, and skills in a process called **innovation.** New environmental challenges and opportunities stimulate innovation and the invention of new adaptive strategies. Some technology-based cultural transformations are so sweeping that they are referred to as revolutions, such as the economic and technological changes termed the "Industrial Revolution." Political forms of **revolution,** in which people try to overturn the social and political order and replace it with new forms of society and culture, are another widespread form of internal culture change that has been a part of the history of many state societies.

cultural pluralism
Condition in a stratified society in which many diverse cultural groups ideally live together equally and harmoniously without losing their cultural identities and diversity.

modernization
Complex culture change, both internal and external, based on industrialism and a transnational market economy.

cultural evolution
Belief of early anthropologists that cultures evolve through various stages from a simpler and more primitive state to a complex and more culturally advanced state.

social Darwinism
Early belief that cultures compete for survival of the fittest, as in the process of natural selection in biological evolution.

culture history
Ongoing culture change in which people respond and adapt to their environment.

Aboriginal star singer Archie Roach, shown here with Ruby Hunter, was a member of Australia's "Stolen Generation." Roach was put into a Salvation Army home at age three and then fostered out to three different white families. (Corbis/John Van Hasselt/Sygma/Corbis)

What are some problems with applying principles of biological evolution to explanations of culture change?

IN THEIR OWN VOICES

HAMLET AND THE TIV

An anthropologist's effort to explain Shakespeare's Hamlet *to Tiv villagers in central Nigeria illustrates how far both the anthropologist and the Tiv culture shape the way they think about the world. When Laura Bohannan lived among the Tiv, they were a farming people living in small villages. Village life centered on groups of families related through men, with fathers, sons, and brothers forming the core of households. After marriage, women moved from their families to live with their husband's relatives. Men prepared fields for planting, but women planted seeds, weeded the plants, and harvested crops. In addition to their families, men depended on their age-mates—other men of the same age group—for help in times of trouble.*

Bohannan was prompted to tell the story of Hamlet because she thought it had a universal meaning that people everywhere would understand in the same way. The Tiv elders also thought the story had universal meaning—but a different one. To both Bohannan and the elders, their particular understanding seemed obvious, showing how powerful cultural assumptions can be. If you need to refresh your memory on what Hamlet is about, read the summary at http://shakespeare.palomar.edu/lambtales/LTHAMLET.HTM. To read the rest of Bohannan's amusing and insightful article, search the Internet for "Shakespeare in the Bush."

The following excerpt expresses the views of both Bohannan and Tiv villagers on the meaning of the play.

I began in the proper style, "Not yesterday, not yesterday, but long ago, a thing occurred. One night three men were keeping watch outside the homestead of the great chief, when suddenly they saw the former chief approach them."

"Why was he no longer their chief?"

"He was dead," I explained. "That is why they were troubled and afraid when they saw him."

"Impossible," began one of the elders. "Of course it wasn't the dead chief. It was an omen sent by a witch. . . ."

Slightly shaken, I continued. "One of these three was a man who knew things"—the closest translation for *scholar*, but unfortunately it also meant *witch*. "So he spoke to the dead chief saying, "Tell us what we must do so you may rest in your grave," but the dead chief did not answer. . . .

There was a general shaking of heads round the circle. "Had the dead chief no living brothers? Or was this son the chief?" . . .

"He had one living brother who became the chief when the elder brother died. In our country the son is next to the father. The dead chief's younger brother had become the great chief. He had also married his elder brother's widow only about a month after the funeral." . . .

"He did well," the old man beamed and announced to the others. "I told you that if we knew more about Europeans, we could find they really were very like us. In our country also," he added to me, "the younger brother marries the elder brother's widow and becomes the father of his children. Now, if your uncle, who married your widowed mother, is your father's full brother, then he will be a real father to you. Did Hamlet's father and uncle have one mother?"

His question barely penetrated my mind; I was too upset and thrown too far off balance by having one of the most important elements of Hamlet knocked straight out of the picture. Rather uncertainly I said that I thought they had the same mother, but I wasn't sure—the story didn't say. The old man told me severely that these genealogical details made all the difference and that when I got home I must ask the elders about it. . . .

Determined to save what I could of the mother motif, I took a deep breath and began again. "The son Hamlet was very sad because his mother had married again so quickly. There was no need for her to do so, and it is our custom for a widow not to go to her next husband until she has mourned for two years."

"Two years is too long," objected the elder's wife. "Who will hoe your farms for you while you have no husband?"

I gave up. . . .

"That night . . . the dead chief again appeared, and . . . Hamlet followed his dead father off to one side. When they were alone, Hamlet's dead father spoke."

"Omens can't talk!" The old man was emphatic. . . .

"It was Hamlet's dead father. It was a thing we call a *ghost*." I had to use the English word, for unlike many of the neighboring tribes, these people didn't believe in the survival after death of any individuating part of the personality. . . .

"Dead men can't walk," protested my audience as one man.

I was quite willing to compromise. "A ghost is the dead man's shadow."

But again they objected. "Dead men cast no shadows."

"They do in my country," I snapped. . . .

IN THEIR OWN VOICES CONTINUED

"Anyhow," I resumed, "Hamlet's dead father said that his own brother, the one who became chief, had poisoned him. He wanted Hamlet to avenge him. Hamlet believed this in his heart, for he did not like his father's brother." . . .

"Now Hamlet's age-mates," I continued, "had brought with them a famous storyteller. Hamlet decided to have this man tell the chief and all his homestead a story about a man who had poisoned his brother because he desired his brother's wife and wished to be chief himself. Hamlet was sure the great chief could not hear the story without making a sign if he was indeed guilty, and then he would discover whether his dead father had told him the truth. . . . It was true, for when the storyteller was telling his tale before all the homestead, the great chief rose in fear. Afraid that Hamlet knew his secret he planned to have him killed." . . .

This time I had shocked my audience seriously. "For a man to raise his hand against his father's brother and the one who has become his father—that is a terrible thing. The elders ought to let such a man be bewitched." . . .

I then pointed out that after all the man had killed Hamlet's father.

"No," pronounced the old man, speaking less to me than to the young men sitting behind the elders. "If your father's brother has killed your father, you must appeal to your father's age-mates; they may avenge him. No man may use violence against his senior relatives. . . . But if his father's brother had indeed been wicked enough to bewitch Hamlet and make him mad that would be a good story indeed, for it would be his fault that Hamlet, being mad, no longer had any sense and thus was ready to kill his father's brother."

There was a murmur of applause. Hamlet was again a good story to them, but it no longer seemed quite the same story to me. . . .

The old man made soothing noises. "You tell the story well, and we are listening. But it is clear that the elders of your country have never told you what the story really means. No, don't interrupt! We believe you when you say your marriage customs are different, or your clothes and weapons. But people are the same everywhere; therefore, there are always witches and it is we, the elders, who know how witches work. We told you it was the great chief who wished to kill Hamlet, and now your own words have proved us right. . . .

"Sometime," concluded the old man, "you must tell us some more stories of your country. We, who are elders, will instruct you in their true meaning, so that when you return to your own land your elders will see that you have not been sitting in the bush, but among those who know things and who have taught you wisdom."

From Laura Bohannan, "Shakespeare in the Bush," *Natural History* (August/September 1966).

CRITICAL THINKING QUESTION

What Tiv cultural assumptions and values caused them to interpret the story of *Hamlet* differently?

External Culture Change

Culture change also occurs through contact with other peoples as individuals migrate, trade, invade, intermarry, or interact in other ways. People learn ideas and skills and borrow tools, foods, clothing, and luxury items from other people with whom they have direct or indirect contact. This process, called **diffusion,** is responsible for the spread of material objects and cultural practices from one place to another.

Diffusion may be local, such as the spread of the invention of blow darts and the use of poisons among some native peoples of South America. Diffusion also can be widespread, even global within geographic constraints, such as the invention of agriculture, which spread east and west along certain latitudes over thousands of years, based on the cultivation of diverse kinds of grain. In addition to diffusion, independent invention may account for the appearance of similar cultural traits in different parts of the world. An example is the invention of writing systems, which likely occurred more than once in prehistory among different peoples in the ancient Middle East, Mexico, and China.

Invasion and conquest also are common causes of external culture change. Most early state societies probably developed partly through the process of expanding into neighboring territories and incorporating the peoples living there (Carniero 1970). Colonization or conquest not only forced indigenous peoples to accept foreign goods and practices but also compelled them to alter many of their cultural practices to conform to their conquerors' ways. The attitudes and values of subject peoples eventually transformed as well to be more consistent with the changes in their behavior. However, subjects of colonial or conquered states are not passive pawns in national and global policies and processes. Rather, indigenous peoples make choices and engage in actions that, in their views, best achieve their goals of maintaining their communities while adapting to their

ethnogenesis
Ongoing process in which people develop, define, and direct their own cultural and ethnic identities.

inventions
New technologies and systems of knowledge.

innovation
Process by which new technologies and systems of knowledge are based on or built from previous tools, knowledge, and skills.

revolution
Process by which people try to change their culture or overturn the social order and replace it with a new, ideal society and culture.

diffusion
Spread of ideas, material objects, and cultural practices from one society to another through direct and indirect culture contact.

GLOBALIZATION

Today, as in the past, diffusion is a major force in the process of globalization, as concepts, technologies, languages, and symbols spread from one culture to another, aided in part by past conquests and the history of colonization.

reactive adaptation
Coping response to loss and deprivation of captive, conquered, or oppressed peoples.

changing conditions. Some of these strategies accommodate to dominant norms, but other processes may overtly or covertly express subversion and resistance.

The imposition of British colonial rule on the Luo of Kenya in the nineteenth century, for example, led to many interrelated changes in the economic, social, and political systems of that tribal society. The Luo (speakers of the Luo language, today known mainly as the Karivongo) settled in Kenya and Tanzania in the fifteenth or sixteenth century, migrating south from the Sudan. In the Sudan, their economy had been centered on cattle herding but shifted gradually to farming after they arrived in Kenya. This change affected gender relations because men had been primarily responsible for herding the cattle and women were the farmers. Following Luo custom, land was owned communally by groups of relatives headed by men, but women actually controlled the production and distribution of crops resulting from their labor. In the colonial and postcolonial periods, however, women's rights to the land and their economic independence were undermined by British land reforms.

In 1899, the British colonial government imposed policies aimed at consolidating individual holdings that were intentionally scattered in different locations. Traditional Luo patterns of landholding gave individuals use rights in scattered parcels so that they could obtain food resources in different ecological zones. People thus could plant a variety of crops suited to each zone. British authorities did not understand this custom, however; in their view, the traditional system was inefficient. In keeping with European ideals, the British combined landholdings into single parcels, which were registered in the names of male heads of households.

In addition, British colonial authorities imposed hut taxes that had to be paid in cash. To obtain cash for taxes, Luo men as heads of households often had to find wage work away from their local communities. At the same time that taxation was a financial burden, men benefited from colonial policies. Participating in the cash economy gave them access to valuable manufactured goods, and their official status as individual landowners gave them greater power and authority. To raise more cash, Luo men turned land production over from home use to cash crops for export, making families more dependent on more expensive imported food to sustain themselves. The Kenyan government continued these land policies after independence in 1960.

Colonized or conquered peoples have responded to external sources of culture change in diverse ways, including assimilation and acculturation, discussed earlier in the module. Another kind of outcome is **reactive adaptation,** in which people react against loss, deprivation, and oppression through passive resistance or violence. Traditional religious leaders and beliefs may play a role in social movements aimed at restoring or revitalizing the traditional culture. A classic example of a

What do these television and movie scenes suggest about changes in American social and cultural norms over the past 60 years?
(Photofest/Photofest; Alamy Limited/AF archive/Alamy)

REVIEW

Culture change can result from either internal or external forces, which usually are mutually reinforcing. Internal culture changes can come about from technological inventions or innovations within a society or can be introduced through culture contact and spread through borrowing, or diffusion. In syncretism, people modify and adapt borrowed items of religious belief and practice to fit their own culture. Culture history and ethnogenesis describe change processes within a society that are self-defining as well as adaptive to both internal and external stimuli. Although the capacity for culture is an important adaptation in human evolution, culture change does not involve cultural evolution, an outdated idea based on beliefs in human progress, racial superiority, and social Darwinism. Outcomes of culture contact include, among others, assimilation and acculturation. Cultural pluralism describes culturally diverse societies in which groups have equal status under the law. Reactive adaptation is an outcome based on unrelieved stresses, often expressed through either violence or spiritual revitalization movements. Sweeping social and culture changes involving both internal and external factors stem from economic and political changes, such as the processes of modernization and revolution.

revitalization movement is the Ghost Dance movement of the North American Plains Indians (Wallace 1956; Mooney 1965). This arose in 1889, at a time when native peoples had been forcibly confined to reservations after brutal military campaigns. Most of their land had been taken from them, and measles and smallpox had decimated their communities. Reduced to poverty and dependence on rations meagerly handed out by the U.S. government, a spiritual reawakening took place.

Begun by a northern Paiute prophet named Wovoka, the Ghost Dance movement predicted an imminent end to the world during a cataclysmic earthquake, to be followed by the reappearance of Native Americans who had died and the disappearance of white people. Although Wovoka taught the necessity of establishing peace, harmony, and good moral principles, his message was distorted by frightened settlers and government officials who feared an armed uprising of impoverished and beleaguered native people. Performances of the Ghost Dance were banned, and participants were threatened with imprisonment.

Finally, after outlawing the dances and harassing participants, government officials in charge of the Lakota reservations in South Dakota sent Army units to arrest Ghost Dance adherents. The units entrapped more than 300 Lakotas and massacred them at Wounded Knee Creek on December 29, 1890. This final tragedy put an end to Ghost Dance performances. Since then, the message of the Ghost Dance has changed from foretelling the end of American control to focusing on personal improvement and spirituality (Kehoe 1989). Nevertheless, Wounded Knee continues as a potent symbol of U.S. government policies that crushed native peoples and their indigenous cultures.

revitalization movement
Type of nonviolent reactive adaptation in which people try to resurrect their culture heroes and restore their traditional way of life.

Watch the Video
Ghost Dance Movement on www.pearsoncustom.com/mi/msu_mylabs

◇ GLOBAL CULTURE

It is commonplace to hear people say that cultures throughout the world are becoming more similar, that a kind of **global culture** is spreading to all corners of the earth. Global culture "clubs" are springing up on the Internet for people who want to participate actively in this ongoing trend. The term *globalization* can apply to many historical periods when developing states expanded their boundaries, incorporating and transforming neighboring societies. In addition, the spread of proselytizing religions (Christianity, Buddhism, Islam) contributed to fundamental changes in the societies they affected, beyond the domain of religion itself but including social relations, economic and political systems, and aesthetic and ethical values. Today's globalization stems from economic and political processes that have expanded from their original centers in Europe and the United States, as the major capitalist industrialized regions, to many other countries. These processes have affected national governments, urban centers, and the cultures of traditional and indigenous peoples everywhere.

Globalization has multiple and complex cultural consequences, summed up by three concepts: homogenization, polarization, and hybridization (Holton 2000). Proponents of the homogenization theory claim that contemporary globalization is creating a homogenized world culture dominated by similar values and practices. They stress the influence of Euro-American economic and political forces, associated with cultural values and norms. Multinational companies stimulate consumer buying throughout the world, and Hollywood images create and transmit an idealized version of

global culture
A constellation of technologies, practices, attitudes, values, and symbols that spread internationally and enmesh nations and communities throughout the world in networks of power and influence.

GLOBALIZATION

Today's globalization stems from economic and political processes that spread their influence through consumerism, the mass media, and information technologies. How should we evaluate the consequences of this globalization?

American society. Homogenization also stems from the internationalization of elite classes and interests. In this view, elites from disparate countries identify more with each other than they do with their own compatriots, participating in and promulgating similar values. However, although Western influence is of course significant, homogenization theorists may overstate the global role of Euro-American culture and may understate processes of resistance.

The concept of polarization emerges in part as a reaction to homogenization. That is, the pressure toward homogenization creates antagonisms because members of other societies with different values and practices react against the influence of Euro-American culture and assert their own national and cultural identities. Discussions of polarization tend to focus on a dichotomy of West and non-West, especially centered in the Islamic, Afrocentric, and Confucian worlds (Holton 2000, 147). Resistance to homogenization may be motivated by authentic antiglobalization forces, particularly among indigenous communities, or by the desire to assert alternative globalizing influences.

Finally, the third concept, hybridization, stresses the development of ever-greater variety and vitality through new cross-cultural combinations of cultural elements that result from the worldwide exchange of products, technologies, information, and artistic expression. Hybridization can be fostered by travel, migration, and intermarriage. It also results from exposure to media, especially music and film that promote familiarity with aesthetic forms from other societies. In addition, many migrants are in fact transnational people, going back and forth between their country of origin and their country of settlement for visits to family and friends. These migrants are often active carriers of new forms of cultural expressions from their multiple life contexts. Hybridization is not uniform and allows for local differences in the mixture of cultural forms.

Although culture change is a continual and universal feature of societies, it occurs both locally and globally in the context of "friction" (Tsing 2005, 1) between various societies. And although global interactions have the potential to develop similarities throughout the world, globalizing processes have specific effects on the local level, leading to distinctions in access to products, services, and technologies, and resulting in inequalities in consumption.

Globalizing tendencies are as old as contacts among societies, but the scale and tempo of change has increased dramatically in the last century. The historical origin of contemporary globalization can be traced to European mercantile and colonial expansion of the fifteenth and sixteenth centuries. For hundreds of years, globalization was centered in Europe, especially in Great Britain, France, Portugal, and Spain. In the late nineteenth century, the United States began to influence other regions, particularly Latin America and the Pacific, competing with the European powers. In the mid-twentieth century, after World War II, the centers of world power were concentrated in the United States and the Soviet Union, seen as representing opposing views of economic, political, and cultural orders. After the early 1990s and the dismantling of the Soviet Union, world power centered in the United States, although several countries in Asia, especially China, Japan, South Korea, and India, as well as the European Union, now exert substantial economic and diplomatic influence. Due in part to the speed of transportation, communication, and information technologies, the influence of capitalist economics and political interests intensified and accelerated throughout the world. However, the cultural and political domination of the West is not uncontested and is countered by Asian economic giants. In addition, cultural influences flow from non-Western countries as Asian and African music, comics, video games, and other items of popular culture are adopted worldwide.

Principal agents of globalization are multinational corporations, which control much of the world's industry and commerce, and the mass media. A global network of finance, manufacture, export, and import has developed, incorporating every nation and many local communities. The prices that farmers receive for their crops are affected by worldwide economic forces through linkages from local to regional, and from national to international networks. Wages received in the manufacturing sector are also connected to worldwide patterns of labor and job availability. National and multinational consumer outlets sell their products in nearly every country. Companies such as McDonald's, Coca-Cola, Sony, and Nintendo are icons of global consumerism. Companies and their advertisers create demand for con-

As governments, corporations, and the media spread their political, economic, and cultural influences, the traditional ways of life of indigenous peoples like this Tarahumara woman are increasingly threatened.
(The Image Works/Zuidema Bzdak/The Image Works)

sumer goods through mass communication systems, such as radio, television, the cinema, and the Internet. Although the spread of products, technologies, and information systems seems relentless, these processes are not inevitable but rather are themselves affected by both global and local patterns of consumption and resistance.

The long-term effects of colonialism and the efforts of indigenous and local societies to participate in a globalized, modern economy without sacrificing their cultural traditions, natural resources, economic interests, and social welfare (see also the Anthropology Applied feature) have been studied extensively. Participation remains a challenge, however. Powerful state societies tend to sanction world domination through globalization on the assumptions that technological advances, industrialism, capitalism, environmental exploitation, and democracy are naturally necessary and superior, and that global progress toward those goals is good. Worldwide climate change can be seen as a maladaptive consequence of some of these attitudes. The loss or destruction of other ways of life is seen as sometimes unfortunate but nevertheless inevitable and unavoidable. However, the destruction of indigenous cultures may only be inevitable because the majority of people in the world accept it as such. This too may be a concept that has become naturalized, consistent with profit-oriented notions of progress and development.

taboos
Norms specifying behaviors that are prohibited in a culture.

Do you think the assumptions used to justify globalization are warranted? Why or why not?

REVIEW

Globalization is a process that historically has had many centers of power as states and empires have expanded their borders and have widened their economic and political influence. However, what is usually referred to today as globalization started in the fifteenth and sixteenth centuries with the development of European mercantile capitalism and state expansion affecting African, North and South American, and Asian peoples and nations. Now there are many centers of globalization, carried by a global economy instituted by multinational corporations. Economic and political forces as well as a global culture disseminated by the mass media and information technologies help create similarities in practices and attitudes, but also threaten the loss of traditional ways of life of indigenous societies and cultural diversity among the world's peoples.

ANTHROPOLOGY APPLIED

DEVELOPMENT ANTHROPOLOGY

Development anthropology is a comparatively new branch of cultural anthropology in which anthropologists use their knowledge and skills to help developing countries maneuver through the processes of culture change. Many developing countries want and need help, for example, to balance their economic growth and industrialization with the maintenance of a sustainable environment. Countries also may need help in dealing with the impacts of economic growth and industrialization on their traditional social institutions and systems of social relationships.

The mission statement of the Institute for Development Anthropology (IDA) reflects the goals of developmental anthropologists. The IDA is "an independent, nonpartisan, non-profit, nongovernmental organization with a mission to promote environmentally sustainable development through poverty elimination, equitable economic growth, respect for human rights, gender equity, and cultural pluralism." This is done by applying the comparative and holistic theories and methods of anthropology to "empowering low-income majorities in developing countries." The IDA seeks to enhance the rights of low-income populations to land, natural resources, food, shelter, health, education, income, employment, and participation in democratic and transparent polities. Its activities relate directly to policies involving management and access to productive resources (land, water, forests), credit, employment and enterprise generation, marketing, rural cooperatives, extension programs, resettlement, river-basin development, social forestry, health delivery systems, and education (http://www.developmentanthropology.org/).

As an example of the work that organizations like the IDA do, consider Senegal's decision to permit flooding of the Senegal River valley to sustain traditional riverine economies rather than rely exclusively on damming and irrigation, which would have prevented water from reaching crops and pastures in small landholdings in valleys. The researchers showed that traditional flooding actually made the land more productive than did irrigation. The floodplain could support five to ten times more livestock than irrigated rangeland, and also would sustain the Senegal valley's yield of fish, an important subsistence resource for the people living there.

In 2002, the IDA was awarded a five-year Women in Development research contract, which encompasses projects in women's legal rights; antitrafficking of women and children and antidomestic violence activities; studies on the gender dimensions of population, health, and nutrition; and studies on the gender dimensions of democracy, governance, and the environment. Included under this grant are studies of rural women in central Bolivia; the interplay of ethnicity, gender, class, and caste in Pakistan; the gender dimensions of desertification (the spread of deserts) among pastoralists; and the gender dimensions of water use and water management in central Tunisia.

ANTHROPOLOGY APPLIED CONTINUED

(Getty Images/DESMOND KWANDE/ AFP/Getty Images)

(Corbis/Yann Arthus-Bertrand/Corbis)

(Friedrich Stark/Friedrich Stark)

CRITICAL THINKING QUESTION

Based on these examples, how might you define the role of development anthropologists in relation to the forces of globalization at work in the world today?

◇ MODULE SUMMARY

What Is Culture?

- Anthropologists use the term *culture* to refer to all of the customs, attitudes, values, and beliefs of members of a society. People acquire these elements of culture in the context of their interactions with others. As members of families, social groups, and communities, people learn what kinds of behaviors are considered appropriate and inappropriate.

Characteristics of Culture

- Several characteristics of culture are fundamental to the way all societies function. Culture consists of behaviors and beliefs that are "shared" by members of the group. If this were not the case, people could not achieve common goals. However, social status, age, gender, race, and ethnicity may create differences in how people's lives are organized and in the attitudes and values they hold.

- Culture is learned. That is, people's behavior is the result of learning, and not instinct. Even when human beings must fulfill critical physical and survival needs, their cultures influence how they satisfy those needs. Many of our attitudes and actions seem natural because our enculturation is so strong.

- Culture is adaptive. That is, people adapt to their environments through cultural means. Human beings can survive in nearly any climate and environment because of the inventions and cultural practices that they develop. However, some practices may become maladaptive over time or not be adaptive in a different context.

- Culture is integrated, forming a relatively coherent and consistent system. Change in one aspect of culture usually leads to changes in other aspects. When cultural traits are borrowed from other peoples, they usually are altered and adapted to fit more closely with the borrower's norms and expectations.

- Culture is symbolic. People's behavior and understandings of the world are based on meanings expressed through symbols. Language is the most obvious and powerful symbolic system, but human beings also use objects and rituals to represent deeply held cultural ideas and attitudes.

- Culture organizes how people think about the world. Through learning and interacting with others, members of a society absorb an array of underlying, taken-for-granted assumptions that help to integrate their activities and beliefs. These concepts become naturalized, so they feel innate and commonsensical rather than acquired. Because not all people accept the dominant cultural models of their society, these underlying assumptions can be the source of contention, which may, in turn, lead to change.

Culture Change

- Cultures are dynamic systems that change because of internal and external forces. Internal change may take place over time through invention and innovation, leading to new adaptive strategies, customs, technologies, and ideas. Culture history describes the selective record of change in a society, but cultures do not evolve in the same way as species. People define themselves through a process of ethnogenesis. Broad culture changes, such as modernization or revolution, are internal changes that usually are strongly influenced by external forces.

- Culture change also occurs through culture contact. People may borrow traits from other groups. In the process of syncretism, items borrowed through diffusion are modified to fit the existing culture. Culture changes also may be imposed on a society by another society through invasion and conquest. Colonized people are forced to adopt practices and beliefs consistent with those of their rulers.

- When a cultural group is in close contact with a dominant culture, the people may become assimilated or acculturated. Cultural pluralism describes a society with diverse cultural groups who retain their distinctiveness but live side by side on more or less equal terms. In contrast, conquered and oppressed peoples may undergo reactive adaptation to cope with deprivation and loss.

Global Culture

- A global culture, characterized by consumer spending and fueled by advertising by multinational corporations, is spreading to all parts of the world. Although globalization has helped to unify different peoples in a global economy, it may also lead to a loss of cultural and linguistic diversity.

◇ REVIEW QUESTIONS

1. How is culture shared? How is it not shared?

2. How does the story of Mai Thi Hiep/Heidi Neville illustrate the point that culture is learned?

3. What differences with Western culture did the Tiv's reaction to Shakespeare's *Hamlet* illustrate? Why were the Tiv not surprised that Hamlet's mother married his uncle?

4. Why is culture a functionally integrated system? How does the history of women's entry into the labor force in the United States illustrate cultural integration?

5. What are internal and external culture changes?

6. Why do you think anthropologists are concerned by the loss of a language? In what other ways is culture symbolic?

7. How can culture be both adaptive and maladaptive?

8. What are the characteristics and implications of a global culture?

◇ REFERENCES

Abu-Lughod, Lila. 1986. *Veiled Sentiments*. Berkeley: University of California Press.

Abu-Lughod, Lila. 1990. "The Romance of Resistance: Tracing Transformations of Power through Bedouin Women." *American Ethnologist* 17:41–55.

Basso, Keith. 1979. *Portraits of "The Whiteman."* New York: Cambridge University Press.

Bohannan, Laura. 1966. "Shakespeare in the Bush." *Natural History* 75:28–33.

Bones, Jah. 1986. "Language of the Rastafaris." In *Language & the Black Experience*, ed. D. Sutcliffe and A. Wong. London: Blackwell.

Carneiro, Robert. 1970. "A Theory of the Origin of the State." *Science*, August, 733–738.

Costello, Cynthia, Shari Miles, and Anne Stone. 1998. *The American Woman 1999–2000: A Century of Change—What's Next?* New York: Norton.

Foster, George, and Barbara Anderson. 1978. *Medical Anthropology*. New York: Wiley.

Fox, Mary, and Sharlene Hesse-Biber. 1984. *Women at Work*. Mountain View, CA: Mayfield.

Hill, A. 2002. Tryptamine Based Entheogens of South America. http://students.whitman.edu/~hillap/tryptamine%20based%20Entheogens.htm.

Holton, Robert. 2000. "Globalization's Cultural Consequences." Annals of the American Academy of Political and Social Science. Volume 570:140–152.

Kehoe, Alice. 1989. *The Ghost Dance: Ethnohistory and Revitalization*. New York: Holt, Rinehart & Winston.

Kroeber, Alfred, and Clyde Kluckhohn. 1952. *Culture: A Critical Review of Concepts and Definitions*. New York: Random House.

Lindenbaum, Shirley. 1979. *Kuru Sorcery: Disease and Danger in the New Guinea Highlands*. Palo Alto, CA: Mayfield.

Mooney, James. 1965. *The Ghost Dance Religion and the Sioux Outbreak of 1890*. Chicago: University of Chicago Press.

Peregrine, Peter. 2003. *World Prehistory: Two Million Years of Human Life*. Upper Saddle River, NJ: Prentice Hall.

Sasson, Jack. 1995. *Civilizations of the Ancient Near East, I-IV*. New York: Scribner's.

Schmink, Marianne, and Charles Wood. 1992. *Contested Frontiers in Amazonia*. New York: Columbia University Press.

Sewell, William, Jr. 2008. "The Concept(s) of Culture." In *The Cultural Geography Reader*, eds. Timothy Oakes and Patricia Price, pp. 40–49. London: Routledge.

Snellgrove, David L, and Richardson, H. 2003. *A Cultural History of Tibet*. Orchid Press.

Tsing, Anna. 2005. *Friction: An Ethnography of Global Connection*. Princeton: Princeton University Press.

Wallace, Anthony F. C. 1956. "Revitalization Movements." *American Anthropologist* 58:264–81.

Wong, Aline. 1986. "Planned Development, Social Stratification, and the Sexual Division of Labor in Singapore." In *Women's Work: Development and the Division of Labor by Gender*, ed. E. Leacock and H. Safa, 207–23. Cambridge, MA: Bergen & Garvey.

MODULE 1-B

INTRODUCTION

Many books begin by introducing their readers to the history of the field. This is certainly essential (though sometimes boring), but will come later in this book (you can always skip it if you don't find it very interesting, but we would highly recommend you look at it). As one of the authors, I (Gardiner) would like to begin this book as I begin most of my classes—by relating a few of my own cross-cultural experiences.

In About the Authors, I mentioned that my wife, Ormsin, is from Thailand and we have raised our four children in an Asian American family, where my wife is the Asian, I am the American, and our children are the Asian Americans and I am the minority—the one with the blond hair and blue eyes. I don't like to admit it, but I'm also the shortest, making me a double minority! As you might imagine, raising children in a cross-cultural and bilingual home has resulted in many interesting developmental experiences, some of which may help you better understand the processes involved in cross-cultural human development.

One experience concerns our eldest daughter, Alisa, and the way in which she became bilingual. Our cross-cultural family setting provided a unique opportunity for this to take place. We had been advised that the best approach to helping her become bilingual was to let her hear and speak both languages without emphasizing that they *were* two languages. So, when she was an infant and young child, her mother spent much of the day speaking to her in Thai, while I spoke to her in English. Then, one evening, when she was about three years old, one of my Chinese students came to baby-sit. Alisa opened the door, saw an Asian face, and began speaking Thai. The young lady patiently listened to her and then said, "I'm Chinese and I understand English, but I'll bet you were speaking to me in Thai, weren't you?" I watched as she thought about this and then turned to me and said, "I speak two languages, don't I? Daddy, I speak two languages!" I told her that indeed she did and asked, "What did you think was happening all this time?" Her reply, based on the experience of her unique developmental niche in a bilingual home, was, "I thought it was all one big language and Mommy understood some words and you understood others and I understood them all!"

Throughout the modules that follow, we make reference to how important it is to understand another culture and realize that not everyone has the same understanding of topics and events. Sometimes, when traveling, studying, or working in another culture, our experiences are frustrating, scary, or humorous. I had an opportunity to live in England for three years while completing my doctoral studies at the University of Manchester. During that time, there was one food craving I found nearly impossible to fulfill—*popcorn!* My roommate and I searched everywhere for it. The only place anything resembling it was available was at the cinema. The only problem: It was sticky, caramel-covered "goop," not the white, fluffy kernels sprinkled with salt and hot butter with which we were familiar. Eventually, using the skills of Sherlock Holmes and Doctor Watson, we discovered small (tiny, actually) thirty-kernel bags of popping corn at the airport and bought the entire stock! A few days later, we visited a British family that had befriended these two "Yanks from across the pond" and took some with us. When we asked the husband whether we could make some popcorn, he replied (much to our surprise), "No, that's impossible." When we asked why, he said, "Popcorn grows on bushes. You pick it and put caramel on it." We told him he might be confusing this with cotton, which grows on

Taken from *Lives Across Cultures: Cross-Cultural Development*, Fifth Edition, by Harry W. Gardiner and Corinne Kosmitzki.

Harry Gardiner and his British friends making popcorn 30 years later.
(Courtesy of authors)

bushes but is not eaten. Nevertheless, he supplied us with a pot, and we put in some oil and threw in some kernels. When it began to make noise, we tried to explain that this was the corn popping. When it was done, we showed him. He took one look and disappeared out the back door! A few minutes later, he returned with his neighbors, looked at us, and said, "Do it again!" One day, I think I'll open a popcorn stand at a street corner in London and surprise and amaze the British public with the wonders of popcorn! Now, if I could only get it to grow on bushes! The moral of this story: We all grow up in cultures where we understand what happens around us because the experiences are a familiar part of our environment and our daily lives. These experiences are not always easily understood by those living in different ecological settings.

More than two decades ago, the anthropologist Theodore Schwartz, writing about the acquisition of culture, declared that "anthropologists had ignored children in culture while developmental psychologists had ignored culture in children" (1981, p. 4). Just two years later, John Berry, a Canadian psychologist and pioneering researcher in cross-cultural psychology, noted that the discipline was "so culture-bound and culture-blind . . . [that] . . . it should not be employed as it is" (1983, p. 449). Shortly thereafter, Gustav Jahoda, a well-known European psychologist and early contributor to the developing discipline, was able to express a more optimistic view and point out that cross-cultural studies of human development had been steadily increasing (1986). Yet, at the same time, he also criticized the field for being "too parochial in its orientation" (p. 418).

These were once serious criticisms of the newly emerging field. Fortunately, in recent years, great strides have been made in our approaches to, and understanding of, cross-cultural human development. Throughout this book, we show the progress, excitement, and promise of this increasingly important area of study.

In this module, we set the stage for the rest of the book by introducing some historical perspectives and expanding on some of the major concepts, themes, and issues briefly presented in the Preface. Let us begin by exploring the origins of cross-cultural human development.

◇ WHAT IS CROSS-CULTURAL HUMAN DEVELOPMENT?

The field of cross-cultural psychology is remarkably diverse, and those who contribute to it bring with them a variety of viewpoints, including different definitions of the field itself. In Volume 1 of the revised *Handbook of Cross-Cultural Psychology*, Berry, Poortinga, and Pandey (1997) define **cross-cultural psychology** as *"the systematic study of relationships between the cultural context of human development and the behaviors that become established in the repertoire of individuals growing up in a particular culture"* (p. x). This definition clearly states that this is a *scientific* endeavor that shares with more familiar disciplines the use of theories, scientific methodologies, statistical procedures, and data analysis.

The term human development has also been defined in a variety of ways. For the purpose of this book, we view **human development** as *changes in physical, psychological, and social behavior as experienced by individuals across the lifespan from conception to death.* While this definition encompasses a wide range of experiences, the intention of this book is not to provide exhaustive and comprehensive coverage of all aspects of human development (Aren't you glad to hear that?). Instead, our goal is more limited, focusing on a number of selected topics that provide insight and understanding into how individuals develop and live their lives in different cultural settings. In doing this, we provide examples from literally scores of societies throughout the world. Considering the important dimensions just discussed, and not finding the term **cross-cultural human development** defined elsewhere, we have chosen to view it as *cultural similarities and differences in developmental processes and their outcomes as expressed by behavior in individuals and groups.*

Since we just mentioned the term culture, it should be pointed out that most researchers agree that this is one of the most difficult terms in the social sciences to define. Almost everyone who studies culture has a different way of looking at it, reflecting in part, different theories for understanding the concept as well as for describing various forms of human behavior. E. B. Tylor was the first anthropologist to use the term in his two-volume work titled *Primitive Culture* (1871). He defined culture as *"that complex whole which includes knowledge, belief, art, morals, laws, customs and any other capabilities and habits acquired by man as a member of society"* (p. 1). More than fifty years ago, two other anthropologists, Kroeber and Kluckhohn (1952) compiled a list of 164 definitions of the term.

In 2002, UNESCO, an agency of the United Nations, stated that culture is the *"set of distinctive spiritual, material, intellectual and emotional features of society or a social group, and that it encompasses, in addition to art and literature, lifestyles, ways of living together, value systems, traditions and beliefs"* (UNESCO, 2002, p. 1).

Azuma (2005) has even proposed a new conceptualization of culture "beyond nationality, geography, class, and even ethnicity," which he tentatively calls "functional culture" (p. xii). It is his contention that "traditional culture" of past generations, uncontaminated, and with distinct and static systems "envisioned by cultural anthropologists in the early 1900s no longer exists" (p. xii). Rather, in the contemporary world, individuals come into contact with a variety of cultures as a result of the media, travel, reading, migration, and other activities, including, we might add, such currently popular Internet social networks as Facebook, MySpace, and YouTube. As a result, "cultures interact with and influence each other"; and traditions, which are part of functional culture, are "more fluid or fragmented" than they once were. In fact, cultures today import many of their features from other cultures and societies—features, which Azuma points out, "were quite foreign to people even a half century ago, and change and substitution of elements are constant" (p. xii). However, he goes on to emphasize that global culture does not become homogeneous, because the way in which these features are distributed within cultures will differ as a result of "traditional emphasis, condition of industry and labor, natural resources, climate, or just by chance" (p. xii); and this will determine cultural specificity. He stresses that "such culture forms a developmental niche not as a loose collection of fragments but as a configuration that is structured yet inevitably fluid . . . [and] . . . Human development must be studied as embedded in a dynamically functioning group culture . . . [in which] . . . More lively understanding results from carefully analyzing how specific behaviors interact with cultural conditions that are always bound by time and place" (p. xii). As you will see, later in this module and throughout the rest of this book, Azuma's contemporary view of culture fits very well with our definition and theoretical approach to understanding cross-cultural human development.

In the absence of an as yet commonly agreed-upon definition of **culture,** when we use the term in this book we will be referring to *the cluster of learned and shared beliefs, values (achievement, individualism, collectivism, etc.), practices (rituals and ceremonies), behaviors (roles, customs, traditions, etc.), symbols (institutions, language, ideas, objects, and artifacts, etc.), and attitudes (moral, political, religious, etc.) that are characteristic of a particular group of people and that are communicated from one generation to another.*

A caveat regarding this definition may be in order before we proceed. Since there is no consensus regarding "the" definition of culture (and it is unlikely there ever will be), our definition is a compilation of several previously published definitions combined with some thoughts of our own as to what constitutes this concept. As Shwalb has accurately pointed out, in most comparative studies, culture is "unfortunately equated with nationality, which is convenient for readers to understand . . . but not satisfying. . . ." (personal communication, 2005). He goes on to say that he would like to see culture "better distinguished conceptually from nationality, ethnicity, race, and religion" (personal communication, 2005). We, and many other social scientists, would surely agree, but, as the reader might imagine, this effort, like defining culture, is a most difficult task and better left for another time.

As the field of cross-cultural psychology has evolved, concerns in the area of development have undergone a number of significant shifts. Parke, Ornstein, Rieser, and Zahn-Waxler (1994) succinctly summarized and discussed the changes in developmental focus over the past hundred years by looking at three periods. One hundred years ago, five major areas were of interest: emotional development, the biological basis of behavior, cognitive development, conscious and unconscious processes, and the role of self in development. During the 1950s and 1960s, the focus shifted to learning theory, the rise of experimental child psychology, interest in operant analysis of children's behavior, investigations of infant sensory and perceptual development, and the objective measurement of cognitive understanding among preverbal infants. Today, there is a revitalized interest in emotional development and cognitive abilities of children, the biological bases of behavior, and social relationships. According to the authors, the "most unanticipated theme is the continuing discovery of the precocity of infants and young children—not only cognitively but also socially and emotionally" (p. 8). More recently, Lickliter and Honeycutt (2003) have shown that advances in genetics, embryology, and developmental biology are transforming contemporary developmental and evolutionary theories that challenge once popular gene-centered explanations of human behavior. We will see these points illustrated numerous times throughout this book.

◇ CROSS-CULTURAL HUMAN DEVELOPMENT AND THE OTHER SOCIAL SCIENCES

In commenting on the central role that culture plays in our efforts to better understand behavior, Segall, Lonner, and Berry posed an interesting and critical question: "Can it still be necessary, as we approach the millennium (as measured on the Western, Christian calendar), to advocate that all social scientists, psychologists especially, take culture seriously into account when attempting to understand human behavior?" (1998, p. 1101). At that time, the answer was (a qualified)—yes! Fortunately, as we enter the second decade of the twenty-first century, the situation has dramatically improved and only continues to get better.

When discussing cross-cultural psychology and its subdiscipline of cross-cultural human development, it is obvious they share a long historical connection with general psychology. Although, as the well-known psychologist–anthropologist Otto Klineberg has pointed out, "There is no specific date that can be identified with the onset of interest in cross-cultural comparisons" (1980, p. 34). Jahoda and Krewer have suggested that it might be as early as the seventeenth century since the "dominant perspective of enlightenment philosophy was highly compatible with cross-cultural psychology's model of man" (1997, p. 11). Since the 1960s, much of our psychological research- particularly that, which has emphasized the cross-cultural approach- has focused on the areas of abnormal, cognitive, social, and developmental psychology (Jahoda, 2009).

In terms of the other social sciences, the closest links are to anthropology and sociology with shared interests in specific approaches, methodological procedures, and research interests, including the socialization process and family influences on development. At the same time, this relationship has not always been a smooth one. Some of the difficulties, especially those centering on comparative studies of infant development, were pointed out by Super nearly thirty years ago when he stated that, for several decades, psychology and anthropology "seem to have withdrawn from the interface . . . to tend to their own theories. Very few studies . . . achieve, or even attempt, an integration of infant care and development, on the one hand, with functional and value characteristics of the larger culture, on the other" (1981, pp.-246–247). At the same time, he noted that success in these areas would require researchers to improve their ethnographic knowledge of cultures as well as to develop quantitative baselines of information for use in future studies. As you will discover in reading this book, this is precisely the path that much of present-day, cross-cultural human development research has taken (Gardiner, 2001b).

In a lively and entertaining book titled *Psychology and Anthropology: A Psychological Perspective*, Gustav Jahoda, a psychologist with a true appreciation and understanding of both psychology and anthropology, noted, "Anthropologists have always been concerned with psychology, even if unwittingly. . . . However, this interest has, in many respects, remained narrowly culture-bound, largely ignoring the wider perspectives provided by anthropology" (1982, back cover).

It is our sincere hope that in the future cross-cultural psychologists, in particular those interested in human development, will be able to forge a bond with other social scientists, notably anthropologists, and work together as partners in laying a firm foundation for an empirically based understanding of human behavior that places a greater focus on developmental processes within cultural contexts. A welcome step in this direction has been made with several volumes that focus on emerging concepts and methods for measuring environment (or context) across the lifespan (Friedman & Wachs, 1999; Sternberg & Grigorenko, 2004) and childhood and family life (Weisner, 2002). Another important contribution is the book, *Developmental Psychology and Social Change,* by Pillemer and White (2005) discussing the historical evolution of developmental psychology, its goals, and its current challenges. The chapter by Charles Super on the globalization of developmental psychology is of particular interest. Efforts such as these and others will greatly enrich our understanding of development and the vital role that culture plays in it.

◇ SOME IMPORTANT THEMES

This book differs in significant ways from most other volumes that focus on cross-cultural aspects of human behavior, most notably in its efforts to integrate a variety of important themes. Let us look at these in some detail and discover how they will weave their way through subsequent modules.

A Cross-Cultural Perspective

Over the past two decades, social scientists have become increasingly aware of the contributions that cross-cultural research findings can make to our understanding of human development. Any attempt to include all or even most of these findings in a book of this length would be impossible. Therefore, we have decided to be selective and discuss representative areas of interest using a chronological-within-topics approach. For readers desiring a more comprehensive view of cross-cultural human development, or for those wishing to explore particular topics in greater depth, we refer you to the Further Readings section at the close of each module as well as the references listed at the end of this book. If you are eager to get started, you might consider looking at such classics as *Two Worlds of Childhood: U.S. and U.S.S.R.* by Urie Bronfenbrenner (1970) and a series of volumes on *Six Cultures* by Whiting (1963), Whiting and Whiting (1975), and Whiting and Edwards (1988). Edwards, Weisner, and others discuss the importance of these studies and the contributions of John and Beatrice Whiting in a special 2010 edition of the *Journal of Cross-Cultural Psychology*. There is the revised three-volume *Handbook of Cross-Cultural Psychology* (1997), edited by John Berry and others, which contains several modules relevant to the study of cross-cultural development as well as the role of cross-cultural theory and methodology. In addition, there is the *Encyclopedia of Psychology*, eight volumes providing a definitive guide to the major areas of psychological theory, research, and practice (Kazdin, 2000). Finally, there is the *Handbook of Culture and Psychology* presenting the state of the art of major areas and issues in cross-cultural psychology, including development (Matsumoto, 2001).

Goals for the Field

As to the nature and purpose of the cross-cultural method, Berry, Poortinga, Segall, and Dasen (2002), in a comprehensive overview of cross-cultural psychology, set forth three goals for the field. The first goal involves *testing or extending the generalizability of existing theories and findings*. In earlier writings, Berry and Dasen (1974) referred to this as the "transport and test goal" in which hypotheses and findings from one culture are transported to another so that their validity can be tested in other cultural settings. For example, are parental speech patterns in English-speaking families similar or dissimilar to those in Spanish-speaking families? Are the stages of cognitive development proposed by Jean Piaget specific to certain types of cultures, or are they universal?

The second goal focuses on *exploring other cultures in order to discover variations in behavior that may not be part of one's own cultural experience*. In other words, if findings cannot be generalized, what are the reasons for this, and are these behaviors unique to these other cultures? A good example is a study, by Jablensky and colleagues (1992), that successfully demonstrates that a number of symptoms characteristic of schizophrenia (a serious psychological disorder) exist in ten very different cultures, but that there is no single factor to explain differences in the formation or outcome of the disorder. At the same time, other psychological conditions appear to be "culture-bound" and occur only among certain groups of people. One example is *pibloktoq*, found only among specific groups of Eskimos, in which individuals, with little or no warning, perform irrational acts lasting a few minutes or as long as an hour, for example, ripping off clothes, shouting obscenities, throwing objects, and running wildly into snowdrifts (Kirmayer & Minas, 2000).

The third goal, which follows from the first two, is aimed at *integrating findings in such a way as to generate a more universal psychology applicable to a wider range of cultural settings and societies*. Examples of this include efforts by many cross-cultural researchers to refine and expand the usefulness of several theories, including the various ecological approaches cited in this book.

We would add to this list a fourth goal—*applying research findings across professional disciplines*. For example, preparing students to study, work, and travel abroad; improving minority children's academic and social success in school; assisting counselors, psychotherapists, social workers, and other professionals in better understanding and helping immigrants with the psychological and social adaptation to a new culture; helping managers and employees in public, private, and government organizations meet the challenges of cultural diversity in the workplace at home and abroad and contributing to greater success in business practices and negotiations; and drawing attention to the basic human rights of children, families, women, and others in cultures across the globe.

At this point, you might be wondering, "How can a cross-cultural perspective contribute to our understanding of human development?" In answer to this question, Gardiner (2001b) has pointed to a number of important benefits. First, looking at behavior from this perspective compels researchers to reflect seriously on the ways in which their cultural beliefs and values affect the development of their theories and research designs. Increased awareness of cross-cultural findings provides an opportunity to extend or restrict the implications of research conducted in a single cultural group, most notably the United States and similar Western societies. Nothing helps to reduce ethnocentrism as quickly as looking at behavior as it occurs in other cultures. **Ethnocentrism** is defined as *the tendency to judge other people and cultures by the standards of one's own culture and to believe that the behavior, customs, norms, values, and other characteristics of one's own group are natural, valid, and correct while those of others are unnatural, invalid, and incorrect.* If you have traveled to another culture, it is likely you have experienced ethnocentrism first hand. Can you think of some examples? What were your reactions to these differences?

Second, the number of independent and dependent variables to be investigated can be greatly increased in a cross-cultural design. Examples of studies in which this has been done include investigations of gender differences (Morinaga, Frieze, & Ferligoj, 1993), effects of parent–child relationships in diverse cultures (Gielen & Roopnarine, 2004), and individualism-collectivism and the attitudes toward school bullying of Japanese and Australian students (Nesdale & Naito, 2005). We generally think of an **independent variable (IV)** as *the condition introduced into or systematically manipulated in an experiment by the researcher,* and a **dependent variable (DV)** as *the subject's response or the behavior being measured in an experiment.* For example, you believe that watching violence in television cartoons makes young children more aggressive (your hypothesis). You show one group of children (matched for age, gender, socioeconomic background, etc.) violent cartoons and a similar group cartoons with no violence. You then measure the level of aggression shown by these children when in play situations. Your IV is the amount of cartoon violence to which children are exposed, and your DV is a child's resulting level of aggression when playing with others. Try to think of a hypothesis of your own and identify the IV and the DV.

Third, cross-cultural studies help us to separate **emics,** or *culture-specific concepts,* from **etics,** or *universal or culture-general concepts.* McDonald's is a good example of an emic approach to cultural consumer behavior. The fast food restaurant successfully sells market-specific items in very different cultures such as a Maharaja Mac (chicken burger) in India, McPalta (burger with avocado sauce) in Chile, and McBingsoo (shaved ice) in Korea. The etic approach is well illustrated by the coffee chain Starbucks, which provides a similar store structure in widely different cultures—strong coffee, soft lighting, and comfortable couches and beanbag seating. Can you think of some other examples?

The **emic** (insider) **approach** focuses on a single culture, using criteria that are thought to be relative to it, and studies behavior from *within* the system itself, making no cross-cultural inferences with regard to the universality of any observations. An example is an anthropological field study in which a researcher lives with a group of people and tries to understand the culture through their eyes and experiences, avoiding the ethnocentrism of his or her own cultural background. The **etic** (outsider) **approach,** on the other hand, looks at several cultures, comparing and contrasting them using criteria thought to be absolute or universal, and studies behavior from *outside* the system. An example, which (happily) we don't see as often as we once did in cross-cultural psychology, involves an investigator conducting what has been called "safari research." An illustration is a professor (not very familiar with the field) who goes on vacation to several countries, taking along a favorite questionnaire concerning _____ (you fill in the blank). He or she visits several universities, collects data from available students (who may or may not understand many of the colloquial English language terms), returns home, and publishes the findings as "universal" attitudes of those living in cultures X, Y, and Z.

Separating emics from etics is better accomplished by testing theories or principles developed in one cultural context in another. The work of Freud, Piaget, and Kohlberg are examples. In some cases, findings lend support to the universality of behaviors in vastly different cultural settings (e.g., stages in language development and the sequence and timing of such behaviors as smiling, walking, stranger and separation anxiety, and pubertal development). On the other hand, results have some-times suggested a need for modification of certain culture-bound concepts (e.g., intelligence, medical diagnosis, and, sometimes, gender behavior). For a comprehensive review of some of the significant findings of indigenous (or native) psychologists, see Kim and Yang (2005).

One of the most frequently used approaches to describing, explaining, and understanding similarities and differences in a variety of cultural contexts was presented by Triandis (1989). This is the dimension of **individualism-collectivism** (IND-COL). A culture characterized as **individualist** is made up of *people who are responsible to themselves and their family and whose individual achievement is paramount.* Frequently mentioned examples of such cultures are the United States and most European societies. A **collectivist** culture, on the other hand, is thought to consist of *people who consider the group to be most important with an emphasis on traditions, cooperation, and a sharing of common goals and values.* Cultures so characterized include most of Asia, Africa, and South America. However, in recent years, use of these characteristics has often been too limiting and it has been recognized that components of each are found in most cultures and even within specific individuals (Green, Deschamps, & Paez, 2005; Triandis, 1995). Fischer and his colleagues (2009) have recently reported promising results on the development and validation of a research instrument for measuring the descriptive norms related to individualism-collectivism.

By focusing throughout this book on cross-cultural material, we hope to provide readers with opportunities to expand their awareness and sensitivity to global similarities and differences in human development and to reduce ethnocentric thinking. The cross-cultural perspective complements and extends the work of earlier researchers who successfully presented the more traditional, but often culture-specific, approach to understanding lifespan development by offering a broader world view. By allowing readers to experience variations in behavior not normally found in their own societies (e.g., accelerated formal operational thought among some Asian populations, decreased susceptibility to visual illusions among certain African groups, and highly developed mathematical skills among Dutch children), this perspective contributes to our understanding of human adaptation. Perhaps most important, it encourages a closer look at the interconnections among culture, development, and behavior—a major theme in contemporary developmental psychology.

While we certainly are not the first to stress the importance of looking at cross-cultural data, we believe we give it greater emphasis because, as Segall so aptly stated three decades ago, "It is to . . . theories of ecological, cultural, and socialization forces that we must turn for the most promising insights into why different peoples develop different . . . skills or develop the same skills at different rates" (1979, p. 129).

The mention of socialization practices, and the variety of ways in which we are influenced by ecological factors, leads us to another of our major themes.

An Ecological Model

The importance of viewing behavior within its social setting was first recognized not by psychologists but by sociologists, who stressed the importance of the individual's subjective view. Among the early proponents of this view were C. H. Cooley (1902), W. I. Thomas and F. Znaniecki (1927), and G. H. Mead (1934). When psychologists became interested in the topic, they tended to ignore the social context in favor of the cognitive processes. Such analysis was extended beyond the individual to the study of the environment with the introduction of the concepts of "psychological field" and "life space" by Kurt Lewin (1935). Explicit recognition of the need to study an individual's subjective view of social reality came with the pioneering work of MacLeod (1947) and has been extended by many others, including Triandis (2008).

One of the most important contributions to these evolving ideas, and one on which much of our presentation is based, is the ecological model presented in the work of Urie Bronfenbrenner (1975, 1977, 1979, 1986, 1989, 1993, and 2005). In its original form, this model divided a child's environment into four nested and interrelated systems or contexts (one more was added later) and allowed us to see and understand (within a broad framework) how patterns of interaction

Can you find the Western anthropologist in this picture?
(© Marcin Jamkowski/Adventure Pictures/Alamy)

Noted anthropologist, Dr. Dawn Chatty, discussing local problems with Harsous tribal member in Sahmah, Oman, in the Arabian Peninsula. (© James L. Stanfield/National Geographic Society)

within the family and the wider society are influenced by and in turn influence the connection between development and culture. Each of these systems involves relationships defined by expected behaviors and roles. For example, a child behaves very differently at home, in school, or with playmates. Take a moment and reflect on your own behavior as a child in these settings. Can you remember how your behavior differed in each setting?

When relationships between systems are in harmony, development proceeds smoothly. Consider the relationship between home and school as an example. If expectations are much the same in both settings (e.g., try to do your best work, be careful and neat), individuals are more likely to succeed and do well than if expectations differ significantly from one setting or environment to another. Bronfenbrenner's family-centered approach has allowed others to adapt and apply his model to a variety of contemporary issues and to develop applied programs involving parent education, counseling, disabilities, day care, and early childhood programs. This approach is presented and discussed in detail in Module 2-A.

The Developmental Niche

If Bronfenbrenner is correct in his view that culture and environment make significant contributions to one's development (and we believe that they do), one might ask, "How does this happen and how can we better understand the processes taking place?"

One possible answer is provided by the cross-cultural developmental work of Harkness (2005), Parmar, Harkness, and Super (2004), and Super and Harkness (1986, 1994, 1999, 2002). Based on an extensive series of studies among Kipsigis-speaking communities in Western Kenya, Super and Harkness, a psychologist–anthropologist research team, have presented a way of bringing together and integrating findings from the two disciplines. Called the **developmental niche,** it provides *a framework for understanding how various aspects of a culture guide the developmental process by focusing on the child as the unit of analysis within his or her sociocultural setting or context.* It is compatible, in many respects, with the ideas put forth by Bronfenbrenner and, in combination with it, comprises another major theme of this book. It, too, is presented and discussed in detail in Module 2-A.

A Developmental Orientation

It is well-recognized that most of our behavior does not take place at isolated periods in our lives but rather evolves and continually develops throughout the lifespan. Although the body of cross-cultural research literature is significant, it frequently resembles "a confused mosaic of contradictory findings" (Gardiner, 1994). This may explain, in part, why none of the books that currently examine cross-cultural topics systematically presents a developmental perspective as we do here. Not all of the behaviors covered in this book will always fit neatly into this orientation or be easily explained by some of the other themes or approaches. However, many do and, where appropriate, we demonstrate how these behaviors evolve and change as individuals develop across the lifespan and across cultures.

To illustrate the importance of looking at behavior from a developmental orientation, let us briefly consider the development of memory and attention, or the increased ability to organize information. As children, we begin to think, attend, and store away memories. As adolescents and adults we develop the ability to make inferences, understand reversibility, and make use of abstract thought. Information that may have been remembered in childhood as a list can now be recalled in adulthood as a total pattern. What is your earliest memory? How old do you think you were? Why do you think this memory is so important?

This brings us to another theme that will occur throughout this book—the chronological-within-topics approach.

A Chronological-Within-Topics Approach

In a book of this size, it is impossible to do all things—that is, provide a comprehensive view of development in all the necessary detail and also focus on all the important cross-cultural findings. Recognizing this, we have decided to look at selected topics for which a large literature of cross-cultural research exists and discuss these topics chronologically—from the early beginnings of development through the last years of life.

Using this chronological-within-topics approach, we hope to effectively demonstrate how behavioral processes evolve and change as individuals pass from infancy and childhood through adolescence and into adulthood. As a result, it should become clear that our behavior is dynamic and involves change, which is at times orderly and predictable and at other times chaotic and unreliable, that both individual and cultural similarities and differences exist, and that specific cultural influences become important at different times and in different cultures. This approach includes basic concepts, principles, and theories that describe physical, psychological, cognitive, social, and personality changes that occur across the lifespan in a variety of cultural contexts.

Another Piece of the Developmental Puzzle: The Human Genome

In recent years, findings from the neurosciences have begun to significantly influence the study of human development. It is becoming increasingly necessary to take into account the role of genes and biological principles and their interaction with one's environment and psychological experiences. As Segalowitz and Schmidt (2003) point out, "While we see both cognitive and affective development—the mainstay of developmental psychology—as having interesting parameters being set by neurological factors, new discoveries in developmental neuroscience also highlight the plasticity and adaptability of the system. Patterns of development are both biologically rooted in our brains and heavily influenced by experience. And the biological influences are manifested through experience" (p. 65).

In addition, with the completion of the thirteen-year Human Genome Project (1990–2003), we have seen an explosion in the study of genetics and the discovery of specific genes that may be responsible for a variety of physical illnesses and psychological conditions, including cancer, diabetes, heart disease, multiple sclerosis, asthma, depression, and many others. There are even those who believe this knowledge could lead to the ability to double the lifespan through a variety of new treatments and therapies. For example, a group of Danish researchers have recently predicted that more than half of all babies born since the year 2000 in France, Italy, Germany, the United Kingdom, the United States, Japan, Canada, and other countries with long life expectancies will celebrate their hundredth birthdays (Christensen, Doblhammer, Rau, & Vaupel, 2009).

The Genome Project's goals of identifying all the approximately 20,000 to 25,000 genes in human DNA, determining the sequences of the 3 billion chemical base pairs that make up human DNA, storing this information in databases, improving tools for data analysis, and transferring related technologies to the private sector have largely been accomplished. However, analysis of the data, its application to specific situations, and implications for the legal, ethical, and social issues arising from this project will last long in the future. Nevertheless, its findings are exciting and, in many ways, will change the way individuals and their descendents across cultures will live their lives in the generations yet to come.

Advances in genetic engineering and biotechnology raise serious questions in terms of culture and human development. For example, what if you had a child who was born with a growth hormone deficiency? Would you (if you could afford it) pay large sums of money, perhaps as much as $1,500 to $2,500 or more, for a series of injections to increase the height of your child at critical stages of his or her development? Would you allow genetic engineering to increase the number of neurons in the brain during fetal development in order to have a potentially "smarter" baby?

Carey (2003) points out that in the past, the greatest effect of culture on humans has been to alter the frequency of alleles (paired genes, alike or different, that affect a trait) and/or genotypes (the genetic makeup of an individual, containing both expressed and unexpressed characteristics). Further advances in genetic engineering could allow scientists to create *new* alleles "… thus, changing mutations from a random phenomenon into a deliberate, scientifically guided enterprise" (Carey, p. 216). The result would be individuals with entirely new and unique genotypes that are not now a part of the human genome. We can only imagine (and even that is difficult) what the effect might be on human development and culture.

Physical and cultural changes in human development have always been intertwined. For example, we can observe the many ways in which a culture's attitudes and beliefs about birth control, abortion, and related topics influence its members' social and religious attitudes, as well as its concern with the physical factors of reproductive fitness. A culture's attitudes towards marriage—who and who will not make appropriate partners—affect the ways in which dating and mating are structured. Advances in international travel (and Internet communication) have increased contact among different cultures, sometimes resulting in an increased number of cross-cultural relationships, intermarriages, and bicultural children, with a subsequent reduction in "the reproductive isolation of human populations" (Carey, 2003, p. 215).

Only the future will determine how far the genetic revolution will take us. While genes and their influences will not be one of the major topics upon which we will have much to say, we recognize the importance of this newly expanding research and urge the reader to learn more about it, as will we, when stories related to it appear in various media.

◇ PRACTICAL APPLICATIONS

We believe that a book emphasizing process, content, and skill (at understanding and interpreting cross-cultural behavior), but avoiding unnecessary jargon and seeking a broad perspective, provides a number of benefits to readers. Therefore, part of our focus is on the *everyday experiences* encountered by individuals of differing ethnic backgrounds within their own society as well as between individuals of different cultural settings. We further believe that if readers come to understand the processes involved, they can begin to understand how to apply these principles for a deeper insight into the events and issues that touch their lives beyond the boundaries of their home, neighborhood, classroom, community, and nation. Throughout this book, the material is continually related to issues and concerns that are important and relevant to all of us. Efforts are made to encourage critical thinking that allows one to examine, question, explore, analyze, and evaluate a variety of everyday situations within diverse cultural contexts.

There is an adage that states, "Tell me and I'll forget . . . show me and I'll probably remember . . . involve me and I'll never forget." Simply stated, this is another of our important themes—practical application. Many of today's texts are written for social science majors planning graduate study and frequently emphasize laboratory research—a shortcoming already recognized in our earlier comments on the need for an ecological point of view. While we feel a developmental text should be grounded in carefully researched theory, we also believe that if it is to be maximally useful, it should avoid jargon and focus on readers' "real-life" experiences, and ultimately assist them to relate more effectively with other individuals and in diverse environments. This is especially true today as our world, even at the local neighborhood level, becomes increasingly multicultural.

These goals are accomplished in several ways. In writing this book, we have selected topics that have meaning for one's daily living: socialization (Module 3-A), personality (Module 8-A).

We don't expect you to accept what we say without question. We believe in the adage mentioned earlier, and we try to practice what we preach by providing opportunities for you to question, explore, and analyze the topics presented. In doing this, we hope you will arrive at a better understanding of your own behavior, modifying it where necessary and desirable and developing and improving your cross-cultural interactions with others, now and in the future.

◇ OVERVIEW OF THE BOOK

Since the transition from theory to practice cannot be accomplished simply by reading about applications, we make an effort to present the material in each module in such a way that it explicitly encourages your active involvement.

First, as you notice, each module opens with vignettes focusing on issues and behaviors to be addressed in a particular module. This gives you an idea of what is covered in each module, and it allows you to formulate your own ideas as you read the material. For example, "What are the benefits of studying development cross-culturally?" "What are the effects of culture on socialization?" "How does children's play differ from one culture to another?" "In what ways are adolescents similar or different throughout the world?" "How do cultures treat their elders or older adults?"

Second, within the narrative, each new idea is defined, highlighted, and illustrated with cultural examples (many from the authors' own experiences) that, hopefully, you would find both relevant and entertaining.

Third, real-life examples of cultural variations in childbirth, effects of culture on learning styles, growing old in different cultures, cultural variations in adolescent identity, and other important topics are presented and discussed.

Fourth, throughout the module you are frequently asked to stop and consider what you have read and try to apply ideas and concepts to your own life experiences. When you can do this, you will have a better understanding and are more likely to remember information that is relevant to your life.

Finally, each module closes with a section on "Further Readings." Included are materials from a variety of sources that we think are interesting, informative, entertaining, and easy for you to locate. You will also find several "Study Questions" to help you focus on important points in each module.

◇ SOME CROSS-CULTURAL TEASERS

As we bring this module to a close, we would like to leave you with a few "cross-cultural teasers," or questions for which we provide partial answers. Each of these receives further attention in future modules.

- Are there any universals in human development? If so, what are they? One example of a universal is gender-role assignment. All societies appear to socialize boys and girls into gender roles (e.g., generally allowing more aggressive behavior among boys and encouraging more caring behavior among girls).

- How can we explain cross-cultural differences in such behaviors as dependence and independence? Part of the answer depends on where infants sleep after they are born. The United States is known as a culture that emphasizes individual achievement; parents generally place babies in their own cribs in their own rooms. Japan, a collectivist culture, encourages dependence or interdependence; children are allowed to sleep with parents, often for many years. How does this affect development?

- Adolescents in many of the world's cultures confront the problem of identity, or try to answer the question "Who am I?" For some, living in Nigeria, it is a relatively easy task. For others, growing up bicultural in New York City, it is more difficult.

- Eating disorders, such as anorexia and bulimia, are common in many Western societies. Do young people throughout the world all strive to attain the ideal body image? You may be surprised by some of the answers found in Japan, Australia, and other countries.

- How do different cultures view their elderly? Is grandparenting the same everywhere? We'll give you some answers to these questions from China, Japan, the United States, and other countries.

- How does family life differ from one culture to another? In some societies, the roles of mothers and fathers may surprise you. Did you know children in some cultures become more closely attached to their fathers than to their mothers? Why would this be the case? We'll find out later in this book.

- An increasingly common disorder among older adults today is Alzheimer's disease. Did you know that people suffering from this disease are treated differently by their caregivers if the patient and caregiver are Hispanic, Native American, or Anglo?

- What's important in selecting a marriage partner—money, good looks, security, health? You'll be surprised at some of the views expressed by men and women from cultures around the world. How many chickens or cows do you think you're worth on the marriage market?

Have we gotten your attention? Do you want to know the answers to these and other interesting cross-cultural questions? Would you like to know about some of the similarities and differences in human behavior and how people live their "lives across cultures?" Then turn the page and read on.

◇ SUMMARY

This module introduces the topic of cross-cultural human development and provides definitions of important terms and concepts. Discussion centers on several themes to be used in organizing developmental topics in a variety of cultural settings. These themes include a cross-cultural perspective, an ecological model, the developmental niche, a developmental orientation, a chronological-within-topics approach, and an emphasis on practical applications. Suggestions are given for using the material in ways to help readers develop a greater understanding of, and sensitivity to, those of a different cultural background than their own and develop and improve any cross-cultural interactions they might experience.

◇ STUDY QUESTIONS

Explain what is meant by the term *cross-cultural human development.*

Demonstrate a familiarity with the important themes presented in this module, including the cross-cultural perspective, ecological model, developmental niche, developmental orientation, and chronological-within-topics approach.

Comment on the goals set forth for the field of cross-cultural psychology.

◇ FURTHER READINGS

Dave Barry. (1992). *Dave Barry Does Japan.* New York: Fawcett Columbine. An irreverent view of Japanese culture by one of America's premiere humorists. Witty and sometimes insightful. Contains discussion of such topics as "Failing to Learn Japanese in Only Five Minutes (Very much good morning, Sir)," "Lost in Tokyo (Looking for plastic squid)," and "Humor in Japan (Take my tofu! Please!)."

Michael Brannigan. (Ed.). (2004). *Cross-Cultural Biotechnology.* Rowman & Littlefield. Fifteen essays from international academics and practitioners address a broad range of legal, ethical, and social issues in biotechnology, underscoring the relevance of cultural values. Topics include the International Human Genome Project and research ethics in East Asia.

Hubert J. M. Hermans & Harry J. G. Kempen. (1999). Moving Cultures: The Perilous Problems of Cultural Dichotomies in a Globalizing Society." *American Psychologist, 54,* 1111–1120. The authors discuss the impact of globalization and compare Western cultural tradition with the rest of the world. They comment on the potential influence of cultural connections and some of the complexities associated with cultural change.

Terri Morrison & Wayne A. Conaway. (2006*). Kiss, Bow, or Shake Hands* (2nd ed.). Avon, MA: Adams Media. Updated and expanded guide to international behaviors. Most useful for business travelers but also of value for tourists and travelers or anyone living or interacting with a culture other than their own. Very informative.

James Shreeve. (2006). *The Greatest Journey.* National Georgraphic, *209* (3), 60–73. A very readable account of genes, DNA, migration, and the origins of modern human life and culture.

The Human Genome Project. For information about this project—its history, research, publications, educational resources, and new programs based on data and resources from The Human Genome Project, The Microbial Project, and systems biology—go to this Web site http://www.ornl.gov/sci/te chresources/Human_Genome/home.shtml.

Name: _____ Date: _____

MODULE 1-C

 ACTIVITY

◇ **WHAT IS CULTURE?**

The concept of culture is not an easy one to define. Even among those who study culture and human behavior there are a large number of definitions in use. Perhaps the most straightforward definition is that of Melville Herskovits (1948) who proposed that culture is the human-made part of the environment. Harry Triandis and colleagues (1972) further suggest that culture has both physical components (such as tools, buildings, and works of art) and subjective components (such as roles, values, and attitudes). Recently, the term *culture* has been used more broadly to refer to the common values, beliefs, and behaviors within groups who share a nationality, ethnic heritage, disability, sexual orientation, or socioeconomic class, as well as to those who share a corporate identity, occupation, sport, or college campus. This activity encourages you to explore the meaning of culture by applying several commonly cited criteria (see for example, Baldwin, Faulkner, Hecht, & Lindsley, 2005; Brislin, 2000) to determine whether a specific group is, in fact, a culture.

Directions: Identify a group that you think of as having its own culture. First describe this group, then by answering the questions below, decide whether this group has the characteristics of a culture.

Group Name and Description:

1. Does the group hold shared perspectives, norms, values, or assumptions that direct the behavior of its members? Please give an example.

Taken from *Cross-Cultural Explorations: Activities in Culture and Psychology*, Second Edition, by Susan Goldstein.

2. Is information important to this group handed down through generations (or cohorts) of its members? Please give an example.

3. Does this group have a common language, dialect, or set of terms? Please give an example.

4. Are the perspectives and practices of this group widely shared among its members? Please give an example.

5. Do group members react emotionally when the perspectives or practices of this group are not upheld? Please give an example.

Conclusions: Discuss your conclusions about whether the group you chose to examine is a culture.

◇ REFERENCES

Baldwin, J. R., Faulkner, S. L., Hecht, M. L., & Lindsley, S .L. (Eds.). (2005). *Redefining culture: Perspectives across the disciplines*. Hillsdale, NJ: Lawrence Erlbaum Associates.

Brislin, R. (2000). *Understanding culture's influence on behavior* (2nd. ed.). Orlando, FL: Harcourt Brace Jovanovich.

Herskovits, M. J. (1948). *Man and his works: The science of cultural anthropology*. New York: Knopf.

Triandis, H. C., Vassiliou, V., Vassiliou, G., Tanaka, Y., & Shanmugam, A. V. (1972*). The analysis of subjective culture*. New York: Wiley.

SECTION 2
THEORY AND RESEARCH

MODULE 2-A

THEORIES AND METHODOLOGY

Justin Tyme, an undergraduate major in psychology, has returned from a month in Thailand, where he attempted to collect data for his senior thesis. This was his first visit to a foreign country, and it was a memorable, but unsatisfying, experience. Why? Because Justin was not well-prepared and made several serious (and avoidable) mistakes. First, he traveled to a culture he knew little about (because it sounded exotic). People spoke a language (Thai) he did not understand and which he found difficult to read, write, or speak in the brief time he was there because of its complexity (44 consonants, 28 vowel forms, 5 tones, and written script). He found the weather too hot and humid, the food too spicy, and life in the village where he was doing his research "too slow." He had difficulty finding people to help translate his English-language, Western-designed, marital-role preference scale so that it would have comparable meaning in Thai. He was upset because the few subjects he was able to get often didn't arrive exactly on time (Asians, in general, are not as time conscious as Westerners, especially Americans), and when they did, they usually told him "Mai pen rai" (Don't worry). Finally, representative samples were difficult to obtain in a rural area that would match his samples back in Chicago, Illinois.

Dr. Kitty Litter, an anthropologist from Cornell University, recently spent six months doing an ethnographic field study among a group of Indians in the highlands of Peru. Not only was she fluent in Spanish, the most widely spoken language in the country, but she also had a working knowledge of two native languages— Quechua and Aymara—from two previous trips to the country. She had read extensively about the customs of the tribal groups in this area and was very fond of the food. She especially enjoyed the tropical climate along the coast and the cooler temperatures in the mountains. She had spent considerable time designing the questions she was going to ask and had even prepared a Quechuan-language version of a psychological instrument she hoped to validate while there.

Theories and methodology—sound exciting, don't they? Perhaps not, but these two topics are central to understanding what happens both in cross-cultural human development and in the modules that follow. In this regard, we have two goals for this discussion of theories: first, to provide a foundation for those who do not have a background in human development (or could benefit from a review of major concepts) to appreciate their contributions to our efforts to better understand behavior; second, to provide a framework for identifying complex human behavior and experience as it occurs within different cultural contexts and to explore possible reasons for the similarities and differences that are found in societies around the world. If research (cross-cultural or otherwise) is not carefully designed, conducted, analyzed, and understood, any findings that result are of little value. So, we'll try to make the discussion of these topics as simple, relevant, and interesting as possible.

Taken from *Lives Across Cultures: Cross-Cultural Development*, Fifth Edition, by Harry W. Gardiner and Corinne Kosmitzki.

◇ THEORIES OF DEVELOPMENT

Why do we study human development? There are many reasons, but basically we do it to *understand, explain, predict,* and (in some instances) *control behavior.* To achieve these goals, we need to be familiar and comfortable with theories and their important concepts. As a graduate student in England, I (Gardiner), while trying to select a topic for my doctoral dissertation, was asked by my major adviser whether there were an area of psychology with which I felt particularly uncomfortable. Without hesitation, I immediately replied, "Theories." (I shouldn't say this but, as an undergraduate student, I frequently skipped over theories because I found them boring, confusing, and too abstract.) When it was suggested that I devote the next three years to the development of my own theory in order to decrease this discomfort (a form of theoretical desensitization, I guess), I thought this was a "daft idea." Of course, I didn't tell this to my adviser! However, develop my own theory I did (Gardiner, 1966). Not only did I really enjoy doing my original doctoral research (on "newspapers as personalities"), but, when it was over, I felt much less threatened by theoretical concepts and gained a greater appreciation for the central role theories play in the social sciences. We hope you feel the same way when you reach the conclusion of this module (don't skip over them; they *are* important!).

What Is a Theory?

Simply stated, a **theory** is *a set of hypotheses or assumptions about behavior.* A theory consists of guesses or speculations that allow us to answer such questions as "Why does a particular behavior occur?" For example, why are Chinese children generally calmer, less active, and easier to soothe when distressed than Western children? Why are ethnic customs and values of greater importance to some minority youths than others? What factors most influence the ways in which contemporary cultures treat their elderly?

When we study human development, we can't look at all aspects of an individual's, group's, or culture's behavior. Theories help us organize our ideas and limit what we look at, and serve as a guide (or blueprint) in the collection of data. Sometimes, it seems as if there are as many theories as there are people. In a sense, there are, because each of us has our own informal, unscientific, unverified, and highly idiosyncratic theories. Built up over years of personal observation and experience, these informal theories help us understand the behavior of those with whom we come into contact. For example, when we meet someone for the first time, our informal theory of personality helps us decide whether we like or dislike this person, whether we want to interact with this person again, and so on. However, we must go beyond these informal theories to truly understand and explain the complexity of human development. We need theories that are more formalized and rooted in scientific principles if we are to be able to compare and contrast behavior within and across cultures and draw conclusions about similarities and differences. In the pages that follow, we discuss six theories. While you may (or may not) be familiar with some or all of them, it might be helpful, in terms of our discussion, to think of the theories of Piaget, Kohlberg, and Erikson as traditional or mainstream psychological theories that focus on the individual, with primary attention to internal cognitive processes (e.g., knowing and thinking, moral reasoning, and psychosocial development). On the other hand, the theories of Bronfenbrenner, Super and Harkness, and Vygotsky can be viewed as interactionist theories, because they focus on the interactions between the individual and his or her environment in specific psychological domains (e.g., ecology and the interrelationship of the developing individual and his or her changing physical and social environment, links between children's behavior and the developmental niche in which they are raised, and cultural influences on development of language, thinking, and guided participation).

Before looking at each of these theories, consider a comment made by Judith Rich Harris in her book *No Two Alike*, in which she proposes a new theory of personality but observes, "Someone who thinks up a new theory is the last person who should be trusted with the job of testing it. A new theory should be tested by independent researchers who aren't cronies of the theorist . . . proposing theories and doing research to test them are jobs that should be carried out by different entities" (2006, p. 265). In the case of the theories discussed here, this sometimes happens and sometimes not.

Bronfenbrenner's Ecological Model

In the previous module, we briefly noted that one of the most important contributions to the study of human development within cultural contexts, and one on which much of our presentation is based, is the ecological model presented in the pioneering work of Urie Bronfenbrenner (1975, 1977, 1979, 1986, 1989, 1993, 2005). At the center of Bronfenbrenner's thinking is his contention that human development is a dynamic, interactive process in which human beings create the environments in which they live and that these, in turn, help shape their own development.

Simply stated, this model views behavior and development as a shared function of the characteristics of the individual (biological or genetic factors and personality) and the environment (social, physical, and cultural aspects of one's present surroundings, such as family, school, and neighborhood), along with the larger contemporary and historical contexts of which these are an integral part, such as society and period in which one is born and lives his or her life.

Bronfenbrenner's original model has been "undergoing successively more complex reformulations to attain its present, still-evolving form" (Bron-fenbrenner, 1999, p. 4). Recent versions of this approach (Bronfenbrenner, 2005; Bronfenbrenner & Morris, 1998) have been renamed the *bioecological model*. By doing so, it identifies a child's own biology as a critical environmental factor affecting development, while incorporating earlier concepts, along with new ideas, into a series of propositions that focus more directly on the role of environment and the concept of time. Those readers who want to know more about this evolving model, which remains more theoretical than practical at the moment, are directed to the references mentioned earlier.

In this book, we have chosen to focus primary attention on Bronfenbrenner's earlier model (without the recent propositions), which we believe continues to offer significant advantages for viewing and understanding the connection between culture and human development. Where appropriate, we refer to some of his more recent ideas and formulations.

The **ecology of human development,** as defined by Bronfenbrenner, involves *"the scientific study of the progressive, mutual accommodation throughout the life course, between an active, growing human being and the changing properties of the immediate settings in which the developing person lives, as this process is affected by relations between these settings, and by the larger contexts in which the settings are embedded"* (2005, p. 107). In short, an individual is seen not as a passive, static, and isolated entity on which the environment exerts great influence (much like a *tabula rasa,* or blank slate), but as a dynamic and evolving being that interacts with, and thereby restructures, the many environments with which it comes into contact. These interactions between individual and environment are viewed as two-directional and characterized by reciprocity. For example, while a child's development is being influenced and molded by parents, family, school, and peers, she is, at the same time, influencing and molding the behavior of others. Take a moment and try to think of examples from your own life where situations like this occurred in your family, at school, or among friends. Why were they important?

Bronfenbrenner has suggested that an individual's perception of the environment is often more important than "objective reality," and that this perception influences one's expectations and activities. A recognition and acceptance of the critical role played by the cultural or environmental context seem particularly suited to the study of human behavior and development.

In his critique of traditional research carried out on children, Bronfenbrenner has stated, "Much of contemporary developmental psychology is the science of the strange behaviors of children in strange situations with strange adults for the briefest possible periods of time" (1977, p. 513). In other words, while striving to achieve experimental rigor and control, we have often lost sight of the scientific and practical relevance of our findings by ignoring how the same phenomena might occur outside such artificial environments. One of the other major goals of this book is to stress the relevance and practicality of such findings. For example, while social workers have employed Bronfenbrenner's model since the 1970s, recent studies demonstrate a deeper understanding and wider application of ecological principles in actual practice (Ungar, 2002).

The ecological model allows us to go beyond the setting being immediately experienced—whether in a laboratory, a classroom, or a backyard—and permits the incorporation of indirect, but nevertheless very real, effects from other settings, as well as from the culture as a whole. Bronfenbrenner originally divided the ecological environment into four **nested systems:** *microsystem, mesosystem, exosystem, and macrosystem* (see Figure 1 on page 46). This conceptualization of the ecological environment has been retained in his more recent bioecological model and is given attention

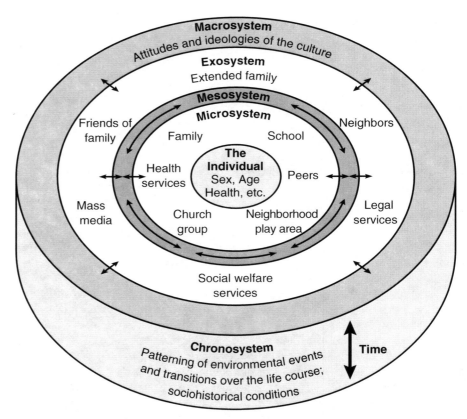

FIGURE 1 Bronfenbrenner's Ecological Model of Human Development

Source: From Kopp, C.B. and Kaslow, J.B., *The Child: Development in a Social Context,* 1st, © 1982. Based on data from *The Ecology of Human Development* by Urie Bronfenbrenner. Electronically reproduced by permission of Pearson Education, Inc. Upper Saddle River, NJ.

in our discussions throughout this book. A fifth system, the *chronosystem*, with its focus on time and sociohistorical conditions, has been mentioned only occasionally in the literature, and seldom by Bronfenbrenner himself. However, as we shall soon see, the concept and importance of time has become a more significant part of the newly reformulated bioecological model and was so recognized in the last integrative book he wrote on his model before he died in 2005 (Bronfenbrenner, 2005).

The Microsystem.   In Figure 1, the first level, the microsystem, is the layer closest to the child and contains those structures with which the child has direct contact, for example, family or preschool and resulting behaviors, such as dependence, independence, cooperation, or competition. This is the most basic level, the one at which individuals engage in face-to-face interactions, and their behaviors frequently reflect social position. Bronfenbrenner (1994) expanded his original definition to include home, church, school, hospital, or day care center. Other factors include the effects of the physical environment on behavior, including background noise, crowding, and the number and types of toys available to a child. For a real-life example of the microsystem, consider Charlie, the youngest child in his family. He attends preschool while his mother and father are at work. It is here that he learns to play "nicely" with other children, share toys, obey the teacher, and develop basic social skills.

The Mesosystem.   The second level, the mesosystem, recognizes that the individual microsystems in which a child functions are not independent but are closely interrelated or connected and influence each other. This layer provides the connection between these structures. According to Bronfenbrenner's newly revised definition, the mesosystem is made up of two or more microsystems (e.g., home and day care, day care and school, or family and peer group). It is the mesosystem that links or ties together information, knowledge, and attitudes from one setting that help to shape behavior or development in another setting. For example, while parents emphasize the importance of learning at home, preschool teachers provide stimulating activities at school that motivate a child to learn more. In this regard, Steinberg, Darling, and Fletcher (1995) looked at authoritative parenting and adolescent adjustment within the ecological setting and reported a number of benefits, including lower levels of delinquency and substance abuse among both male and female adolescents. Charlie's older sister, Sirina, is in second grade and is functioning in the mesosystem. For example, Siri's mother frequently meets with her daughter's teacher, Miss Santiago, to discuss her progress in school and seek advice on improving her study habits at home.

The Exosystem.   Beyond the child's immediate environment are social settings of which he may not be a part but which, nevertheless, interact with one or more structures in his microsystem and influence his development in significant ways. These settings or institutions make up the third level—the exosystem. As defined by Bronfenbrenner, the exosystem includes formal settings, such as parents' place of work or community health and welfare institutions (e.g., hospitals). Bronfenbrenner (2005) provides an example of the link between the home and a parent's workplace for the developing child and of the link between the home and her children's peer group for the developing adult. Other less formal settings might include the extended family (aunts, uncles, cousins, friends, and neighbors). Malinee, Charlie and Siri's older sister, is experiencing daily activities within the exosystem; for example, although she doesn't know much about her father's work, she plays on a mixed-sex soccer team sponsored by his athletic apparel company after school and is learning the importance of team work and discipline.

The Macrosystem.   This is the most complex system and is found in the outermost circle and consists of the customs, values, and laws considered important in the child's culture. The focus is on the consistencies among a wide variety of settings within a given society or culture. For example, in many countries there are striking similarities in the form and function of such familiar settings as school playgrounds, post offices, shopping malls, and even fast food restaurants. This system or level does not pertain to a specific context or environmental setting but is important because it has an effect on all the previous systems. It includes the customs, values, and laws of a child's culture and determines what are acceptable and unacceptable behaviors. For example, Macinnes, the oldest child in the family we have been looking at, is in high school, and, as a result of his accumulated experiences in these previous systems, is considered to be a smart, well-behaved, conscientious, helpful, and law-abiding member of his community and an example for his younger siblings, as well as friends and peers.

The Chronosystem.   In Bronfenbrenner's ecological model, the exact role of the chronosystem is somewhat difficult to describe because it has not received the same attention as have the other four systems. In fact, the term does not always appear in the reformulated bioecological model although the elements that characterize it—time and sociohistorical conditions—constitute a major part of the new model (Bronfenbrenner, 2005). In his final writing, Bronfenbrenner makes the point that "the chronosystem is a methodological construct; the remaining four are theoretical but can also become substantive when put to empirical use" (p. 165). In general, this layer focuses on time as it relates to a child's various environments. For example, it includes the physiological changes that occur as the child matures and his or her reactions to these changes as well as the changed environment in which he or she now functions. Another example is the timing of the death of an important person in the child's life, such as a parent, sibling, or grandparent. Each of the children mentioned above was all exposed to the severe economic difficulties of the year 2009 and beyond. However, due to their age differences, they experienced events in unique ways, and the impact on their development varied. For example, Macinnes became much more aware of economic issues and moral behavior as they affected the country and his family, Malinee had to cut back on some of her activities due a reduction in family income, and Siri and Charlie, because they were so young, didn't always understand what was happening but often heard their parents discussing concerns about money issues.

When studying individual behavior, a great deal of past and present developmental research has tended to view it either at a fixed point in time or, if over a long period of time (and if conducted longitudinally), has assumed little or no change in an individual's personal characteristics or in his or her environmental or ecological setting. As Muuss (1996) has pointed out, "time used to be perceived as synonymous with changes in chronological age. In the ecological model, the constancy or change over time (of both E and P) is essential to assessing the nature of the changes during the life course" (p. 320). Bronfenbrenner has used this chronosystem model to help explain how time simultaneously affects the environment (E) and the person (P). According to Muuss, Bronfenbrenner "emphasizes the interacting nature of these changes, and it is the interacting nature of (E) and (P) that Lewin, and more explicitly, Bronfenbrenner, have brought to our attention" (p. 320).

In his later writings, Bronfenbrenner (2000), while not employing chronosystem terminology, placed increasing emphasis on "time and timing as they relate to features of the environment, as opposed to characteristics of the person" (p. 20)—what he has called "space through time: environment in the third dimension" (p. 20). Much of the progress in this area has emerged from researchers, primarily sociologists, using what Elder has called the "life course perspective." For a discussion of the basic principles of this perspective and recent research, see Elder and Giele (2009).

Muuss provides an example of chronosystem research that might be conducted to investigate behavior among family members and the role time or timing might play in it. He points to the effect the arrival of a new baby might have on parents' interactions with each other and with other children. "By assessing the mother's interaction (with the older siblings) before, during, and after pregnancy, research suggests that the mother's interaction patterns change rather noticeably as a function of these pregnancy/child-bearing conditions" (Muuss, 1996, p. 320). Steinberg and his colleagues in several studies (1987, 1988, 1995) examined the relationship between the timing of puberty and its effects on family relationships and parent–adolescent distance.

The ecological model, with its emphasis on the analysis of specific behaviors in increasingly complex settings, nicely complements our other themes and provides one of the central focal points around which these themes cluster. In fact, such a multilevel approach significantly expands the possibilities for explaining a variety of behaviors, as does our next approach.

Super and Harkness's Developmental Niche

The concept of the developmental niche (at least the "niche" part) was originally borrowed from the field of biological ecology, where *niche* describes the combined features of a particular animal's environment or habitat. Super and Harkness (1994a) use the example of a robin and a pigeon, both of which might live in the same section of a city park but differ in where they build their nests, the kinds of materials they use, and the kind of food they eat from the surrounding environment. The birds create a distinct niche for themselves based on each of these behaviors. The fact that this concept of a niche can be employed in biology and in psychology demonstrates, as we indicated earlier, that there is some unity to scientific efforts. In fact, much of the usefulness of the developmental niche concept lies in its ability to serve as an integrative framework providing connections among culture, socialization, and ecology. In fact, the framework has been used by the authors and others in conducting research in a wide variety of areas, including cognitive, motor, and language development; temperament; sleep and arousal; emotional expression; literacy; and health. It has been used extensively in the study of **ethnotheories,** or *parents' cultural belief systems about the nature of children, the processes of development, and the meaning of behavior* (Harkness & Super, 1996), as well as in intervention programs for inner-city children (Harkness et al., 2005).

As Sara Harkness and her colleagues (2005) have pointed out, the developmental niche concept owes much to the theoretical thinking and research of several earlier pioneers. For example, there are the "culture and personality" studies of the anthropologists Ruth Benedict and Margaret Mead, as well as Beatrice Whiting's idea of parents as "providers of settings" in which children were able to explore a variety of social behaviors. The authors refer specifically to the approach ". . . interwoven in early anthropological accounts of parenting in other cultures, . . . [which] . . . has emerged more recently as a distinctive focus in the developmental, as well as anthropological, literature, drawing from psychological research on parents' ideas as a force in children's development and on the anthropological construct of 'cultural model'" (p. 338). While each of these perspectives resulted in critical contributions, Harkness et al. (2005) state that ". . . none of them accommodate sufficiently two core issues . . . the integration of various elements in the child's culturally structured environment and the endogenous aspects of individual development that alter the specifics of individual-environment interactions. The developmental niche is a theoretical framework that attempts to acknowledge and integrate this set of considerations" (p. 338).

In applying the term to psychology, Super and Harkness (1994a) state that "at the center of the developmental niche, therefore, is a particular child, of a certain age and sex, with certain temperamental and psychological dispositions. By virtue of these and other characteristics, this child will inhabit a different cultural 'world' than the worlds inhabited by other members of his family—and further, the child's world will also change as the child grows and changes" (pp. 96–97). In recent writing, Harkness and her colleagues (2005) state that "the primary view is to take the place of the child and look outward to the everyday world" (p. 338). Harkness (1999) has also pointed out that, while the approach has been used to analyze the niche of single individuals, it has more often been used to compare and contrast cultures or societies "widely separated in geographic place and historical background. However, flexibility in the degree of generalization is a useful feature of the framework, as it has proved useful in examining variation within a single physical community and in documenting changes in child care that are due to migration or seasonal change" (pp. 284–285). See, for example, Eldering (1995).

Every child's developmental niche consists of three interrelated components (see Table 1). First, there are the physical and social settings of daily life in which a child lives (e.g., nuclear family living typically found in many Western cultures versus extended family arrangements found in many Asian or African countries). Aspects of this component include (1) the kind of company a child keeps (e.g., in rural Kenya, families frequently consist of eight or more children, who serve as ready-made playmates and caretakers), (2) the size and shape of one's living space (e.g., in a large North American home, children have their own rooms compared with families living in overcrowded apartments in Tokyo, where small rooms sometimes serve as living, dining, and sleeping areas), and (3) presence or absence of multiple generations living together (e.g., children, parents, grandparents, and other relatives). The differences in these components are clearly observable in the

TABLE 1 Components of the Developmental Niche

1. PHYSICAL AND SOCIAL SETTINGS OF DAILY LIFE

Size, shape, and location of living space

Objects, toys, reading materials

Ecological setting and climate

Nutritional status of children

Family structure (e.g., nuclear, extended, single parent, blended)

Presence of multiple generations (e.g., parents, grandparents, other relatives)

Presence or absence of mother or father

Presence of multiple caretakers

Role of siblings as caretakers

Presence and influence of peer group members

2. CUSTOMS OF CHILD CARE AND CHILD REARING

Sleeping patterns (e.g., co-sleeping vs. sleeping alone)

Dependence vs. independence training

Feeding and eating schedules

Handling and carrying practices

Play and work patterns

Initiation rites

Formal vs. informal learning

3. PSYCHOLOGY OF THE CARETAKERS

Parenting styles (e.g., authoritarian, authoritative, laissez-faire)

Value systems (e.g., dependence, independence, interdependence)

Parental cultural belief systems or ethnotheories

Developmental expectations

case of Kamuzu (living with his mother, aged grandmother, and three siblings in a shack in Soweto) and Jeremy (living with his parents and sister in a wealthy neighborhood of Johannesberg, South Africa) described in the opening vignette of Module 3-A.

The second component of the developmental niche focuses on culturally regulated customs of child care and childrearing practices. These include (1) informal versus formal learning (e.g., family teaching of important skills within most rural African tribal groups versus formal in-school learning characteristic of most Western societies), (2) independence versus dependence training (e.g., independence practiced by most Western parents versus dependence or even interdependence found among the majority of Asian parents), and (3) eating and sleeping schedules (e.g., in many North American and European homes, there are three meals a day at specified times, versus the five to six small meals at unscheduled times customary in many Asian cultures). Again, consider and contrast the educational experiences of Jeremy (who attends an exclusive private school) and Kamuzu (who attends a poorly funded segregated school). Other examples include the customary use of playpens in Holland to keep infants happy and safe and the care of younger siblings by older ones in Kenya (Super & Harkness, 1994a).

Finally, the third component relates to the psychology of the caretakers or the psychological characteristics of a child's parents (e.g., developmental expectations, parental cultural belief systems, and types of parenting styles). According to Super and Harkness (1994a), this component "is an important channel for communicating general cultural belief systems to children, through very specific context-based customs and settings" (p. 98). These authors, like us, see a connection between the developmental niche and Bronfenbrenner's approach when they comment: "Drawing from ecological and systems theory, we suggest that the three components interact with each other as a system . . . to maintain consonance among them. The niche is an 'open system,' however, in that each component interacts independently with elements in the larger culture" (Harkness & Super, 1995, p. 227).

Considering each of these components, think about your family as you were growing up—what were the physical and social settings of your daily life; what kind of childrearing practices or child care did your parents employ; and how would you describe their expectations, belief systems, and parenting styles? By applying this to your own life, you will gain a greater understanding of this approach as well as some of the influences that made you the person you are today. Do you notice differences between you and your siblings?

Super and Harkness propose that these components interact and function as a dynamic but not always completely coordinated system in which the individual and the developmental niche adapt and are mutually influential (see Figure 2). For example, although there is a conformity among certain elements of the niche (ecological settings consistent with parental beliefs), inconsistency can result from many factors, including external influences, limited resources, or historical change. Consistent with their earlier ideas, Super and Harkness (1999) stress that these three subsystems of the niche "constitute elements of the environment as they are culturally structured in the child's experience" (p. 286). They point out that this framework can be equally well applied to adult development by expanding the third component—the psychology of the caretakers—to include the psychology of others (e.g., mates, coworkers) who might affect the adult. For an interesting example of the developmental niche in Somalia, see Box 1.

In an important extension of their pioneering approach to development, Super and Harkness (1999) look more closely at "the environment as culture in developmental research." They discuss, in depth, two anthropological concepts of culture they believe are of critical importance to understanding behavior within context—the immediacy of culture and its integrating nature.

For example, as to the immediacy of culture, it is their position (similar to our comments in Module 1-B) that psychologists (primarily in the past, but many even today) have either ignored culture when considering development or tended to "keep it at great distance from the individual." In this regard, they are critical of Bronfenbrenner's original model, which represents culture as the macrosystem. It is their view that "the macrosystem's placement at the top of a nested hierarchy leaves it with no direct

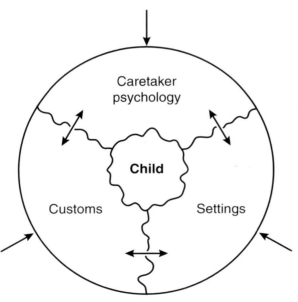

FIGURE 2 A Schematic Representation of the Developmental Niche

Source: From John W. Berry et. al., *Handbook of Cross-Cultural Psychology,* Volume 2, 2nd edition. Published by Allyn and Bacon, Boston, MA. Copyright © 1997 by Pearson Education. Reprinted by permission of the publisher.

BOX 1

CHILDHOOD IN SOMALIA: AN EXAMPLE
OF THE DEVELOPMENTAL NICHE

In an extremely informative and detailed study, Norwegian psychologist Ragnhild Dybdahl explored childhood within the Somali sociocultural context, using the concept of the developmental niche. As part of her study, she conducted open-ended interviews in Mogadishu, Somalia, with twenty mothers, ranging in age from twenty-two to forty (mean age equals thirty), and twenty-three children (mean age equals ten). Most of the women lived with their husbands, and about one-fourth of them had been raised as nomads. The average number of family members was 7.5 and included various combinations of parents, children, grandparents, parents' siblings, and distant relatives staying as long-term guests. Topics of interest included reasons for having children, normative child care, and the roles played by parents and children in the Somali culture.

According to Dybdahl, the first component of the Somali developmental niche is characterized by the culture's economic and health problems; the nomadic way of life, with its emphasis on the extended family and clan; and the child's social and physical settings organized around school and Quaranic school (based on the Koran or sacred teachings of Islam), play, work, and household chores, especially care of younger siblings. The second component is characterized by socialization practices in which the infant, initially spending all its time with its mother, is gradually "distanced from the mother's back, breast and bed to be cared for by someone else." Although formal schooling plays a role, informal education is far more important and is the means by which children are taught such activities as household chores. Quaranic school serves as a mode of traditional education. The third component, based on interview comments from mothers, is characterized by mothers' focus on "physical health, obedience, resourcefulness, helpfulness and hard work," with expectations differing according to a child's age.

Dybdahl reported on the emergence of several themes associated with Somali childhood: (1) a clear responsibility for family and relatives; (2) the importance of such values as pride, hard work, loyalty, and obedience; (3) a constant struggle for survival and good physical health; and (4) the emotional importance attached to children as sources of short- and long-term security.

As a result of her interviews and observations, Dybdahl argues that Somali society represents a mix of "traditionalism and modernism, and collectivism and individualism." According to Dybdahl, her interviews with children provided a look at "the niche from the inside." She points out that "in spite of the difficult living conditions at the time . . . [just before "Operation Restore Hope" in 1989] . . . with war breaking out and relatively poor health conditions, beliefs in the future and in the possibility to change and improve one's life were recurring themes." She suggests that this may be due to a combination of factors, including the nomadic tradition of "moving on to another place," stoicism, and the belief that family and relatives will provide help if needed.

Dybdahl concludes that children must be studied in the "context and culture in which they live, and of which they are a part." Since developmental outcomes in Western societies have often come to be the norm for many of the world's children, "to avoid ethnocentrism and develop a global psychology, it is necessary to do cross-cultural research." Dybdahl is further convinced that, in order to make what she calls the "person-setting interaction" the focus of investigation, anthropologists and psychologists need to combine their efforts and that the developmental niche "might be a fruitful concept for this purpose." For a more recent report on this research, see Dybdahl and Hundeide, 1998.

In follow-up studies, the author used some of her experiences from this study in the design of a successful psychological intervention program with young children and their mothers in the ecological context of war-torn Bosnia and Herzegovina. Findings revealed severe trauma with wide variations in displays of distress that were greatly helped and reduced by means of a simple and inexpensive intervention program adapted to their needs and to an understanding of the developmental niche in which they lived (Dybdahl, 2001, 2002, 2005).

Source: Adapted from "The Child in Context: Exploring Childhood in Somalia," paper presented by Ragnhild Dybdahl at the Twenty-Sixth International Congress of Psychology, Montreal, August 1996. Reprinted by permission.

connection to the individual . . . culture exists as the outermost of several circles, while the developing child stands at the center, insulated from the cultural macrosystem by family, neighborhood, school, and other settings and institutions in the microsystem, mesosystem, and exosystem" (p. 281). Super and Harkness go on to suggest, "The anthropological insistence on the immediacy of culture not only better reflects the phenomenological experience of daily life but also brings the cultural environment into reach for the empirical scientist" (p. 282). We tend to agree with much of this and suggest modifications as you will see in the many examples presented throughout this book.

The integrating nature of culture is seen in the pioneering work of many anthropologists, including Margaret Mead, Ruth Benedict, and John and Beatrice Whiting, and in much of the research being done today. As Super and Harkness (1999) point out, these efforts suggest "a relatively new and promising agenda for interdisciplinary psychologists as they seek a more sophisticated understanding of behavior and development: Look for structures that integrate experience, and look for their immediacy in everyday life" (p. 283). For more on the ways in which culture serves as an integrating force in development and why the authors' expanded cultural perspective on the environment is becoming increasingly important, see Super and Harkness (1999, 2002a, 2002b); Harkness and Super (2003); and Harkness, Hughes, Muller, and Super (2004). Some of their suggested research methods and approaches are discussed later in this module.

Piaget's Theory of Cognitive Development

Jean Piaget (1896–1980), the Swiss-born psychologist, first developed an interest in cognitive development while working with Alfred Binet on intelligence testing in Paris. Piaget became curious about children's thinking and problem solving and why children of the same age made similar mistakes when trying to solve problems. For years, he carefully recorded the cognitive changes he observed in his three children in their home in Geneva. From these and other observations, he theorized that individuals learn by actively constructing their own cognitive world. To Piaget, development is a dynamic process that results from an individual's ability to adapt thinking to meet the demands of an ever-changing environment and, as a result, to formulate new ideas.

According to Piaget's view, normal cognitive growth passes through four distinct periods: infancy, early childhood, middle childhood, and adolescence (see Table 2). Each period is highlighted by the development of age-typical cognitive skills. Although Piaget provided age ranges for these various developmental periods, he recognized that the exact age at which a particular individual enters a specified period could be significantly affected by that person's physical, cognitive, or cultural experience—what Bronfenbrenner has referred to as the *ecological setting.*

It was Piaget's belief that cognitive development occurs as a result of children's attempts to adapt to their environments and to make sense of the many experiences taking place around them. The ability to do this requires the systematic development of progressively more complex mechanisms or structures. At the center of this activity lies the scheme. A **scheme** is *an organized pattern of thought or action applied to persons, objects, or events in an effort to make sense of them.* In short, it is a mental picture of the world and the things in it. For example, infants develop a wide variety of schemes during the first few months, including schemes for mother, breast, bottle, and father's voice. Over the years, increased interactions with the environment result in these schemes becoming more sophisticated and better coordinated, so that by the time an individual reaches formal operations, they are capable of thinking about behaviors and imagining their consequences.

According to Piaget, cognitive development and the ability to adapt to the environment depend on the processes of assimilation and accommodation. **Assimilation** is *the process by which*

TABLE 2 Piaget's Periods of Cognitive Development

PERIOD	APPROXIMATE AGE	DESCRIPTION	COGNITIVE MILESTONES
Infancy	Birth to 2 years	Sensorimotor	Object permanence
Early childhood	2 to 6 years	Preoperational	Egocentric thinking, use of symbols
Middle childhood	6 to 12 years	Concrete operations	Conservation
Adolescence	12 years and older	Formal operations	Abstract thinking

new information and ideas are incorporated or fitted into existing knowledge or schemes. **Accommodation** is *the process of adjusting or modifying existing schemes to account for new ideas and information.* Anyone who has traveled abroad and attempted to make sense of new surroundings or tried to explain new objects or words to a foreign visitor has engaged in assimilation and accommodation—sometimes with success, sometimes with failure, and sometimes with humor! For example, what happens when Hakon from Norway tries to explain the making of a snowman to Yang, who lives in Malaysia and has never seen or touched snow? In this situation, Yang must make use of accommodation and adjust an existing scheme with which Yang is familiar (perhaps shaved ice) or create a new scheme (snow) to explain this new idea of a snowman. Can you recall a situation in which you have had to use assimilation and accommodation to explain an idea to someone else? Did you find it easy or difficult?

It is through active and open interaction with one's environment or surroundings that individuals learn to balance these twin processes of assimilation and accommodation. In terms of Bronfenbrenner's ecological systems approach, these cognitive processes can be said to begin in the family (microsystem); gradually extend to increasingly complex situations that arise in the neighborhood, at day care, or at school (mesosystem); and eventually, as the individual moves into adolescence and adulthood, operate in the workplace (exosystem) and the culture at large (macrosystem).

While there is no doubt that Piaget's theory has had a significant impact on the study and understanding of cognitive development in mainstream Western psychology, his ideas have been challenged on several points. First, some have criticized his emphasis on individual activity occurring apart from social interaction. Such a focus reflects a more individualistic cultural perspective, such as that found in North America and Western Europe, and thereby fails to consider similarities or differences in cognitive development in traditional collectivistic cultures (e.g., China, Japan, and the islands of the South Pacific). Second, some have suggested that Piaget may have overestimated the contribution of motor activity and underestimated the ages at which children are capable of learning and performing a variety of behaviors by themselves. Third, Piaget's claim that once a person moves to a new period of cognitive development, the competencies mastered at that level will be exhibited in other phases of that individual's thinking, does not appear to be fully supported by cross-cultural research findings. While advances may be apparent in some domains of a person's thinking processes, this may not always be true in other domains.

In the beginning, when Piaget was developing his theory and conducting his early studies, he paid little attention to cultural factors and the effects differences might have on cognitive development. However, as Thomas (1999) has noted, "In later years, Piaget did admit some influence of variations in environments, but still considered genetically controlled maturation to be the primary force behind mental development" (p. 65). Whatever one's position is regarding Piaget's theory, it was the first to introduce cognition into developmental psychology and continues to have considerable influence on contemporary research and practice, most notably on social cognition, self-recognition, has been applied to the study of cognitive development in many cultures throughout the world—with varying success. For recent reviews and critiques of Piaget's theory, as well as others presented in this module, see Bergen (2008) and Green and Piel (2010).

Vygotsky's Sociocultural Theory of Development

As we have just noted, Piaget's position was that cognitive development is largely an individual accomplishment, directed and shaped, in part, by the environment (and, in part, by genetics). However, he said little about the importance of the social context in learning. This view was challenged by the Soviet psychologist Lev Semyonovich Vygotsky.

Lev Vygotsky (1896–1934) was one of several children raised in an orthodox Jewish family in Russia. As a young man, he frequently wrote critically about Soviet government policies with which he did not agree. As a result, his scientific writings were banned although his highly acclaimed and influential book *Thought and Language* was finally published in 1934, the year he died of tuberculosis. (For an interesting, and generally ignored, view of how Vygotsky's Marxist orientation influenced the development of his psychological principles and also affected his life, see Gielen and Jeshmaridian, 1999.)

Vygotsky suggested that development is the result of interaction between cultural and historical factors. He believed that the key feature of development lies in matching a child's demands with the requirements of her culture. Vygotsky suggested that there were three major components in this process: the role played by culture, the use of language, and the child's zone of proximal development. Briefly, the **zone of proximal** (nearby) **development (ZPD)** refers to the distance between a child's actual developmental level and the higher-level potential (Vygotsky, 1978). It is *the difference between what children can achieve independently and what their potential level of development might be if given help or guidance.* This concept of the ZPD emphasizes Vygotsky's view that social influences contribute significantly to children's development of cognitive abilities and that mentoring or guidance strengthens their growth.

To tie this into several of the major themes already discussed, let us consider the case of twelve-year-old Dabir, a young Saudi adolescent. We might say that the process of learning, which takes place through mentoring in a number of Dabir's diverse ecological settings (home, mosque, school), defines his developmental niche at a particular time in his life. As Vygotsky would view it, Dabir does not have his own ZPD but participates in a shared ZPD with those around him (e.g., siblings, parents, teachers, and peers). This is also true with regard to Deratu, who does not go to school but learns the important cultural and practical lessons necessary for living in rural Ethiopia from the daily guidance provided by her mother.

While much of Vygotsky's work has been praised for its originality and usefulness, like the pioneering ideas of Piaget, it, too, has its critics. For example, some argue that the zone of proximal development is vague and cannot be adequately measured. Others believe that parts of Vygotsky's theory have been lost or misunderstood in translation and therefore are confusing and incomplete. Nevertheless, the theory still represents an increasingly important contribution to cross-cultural human development, with Vygotsky's zone of proximal development appearing more frequently in educators' teaching methods (Thomas, 1999). As an example, Thomas points out, "Rather than waiting for children to display a particular form of reasoning before attempting to teach skills and knowledge that depend on that form, teachers who follow Vygotsky's lead will attempt to teach the new learnings somewhat before the time children might exhibit their readiness spontaneously" (p. 48).

Interestingly, Bronfenbrenner (2005) points out that Vygotsky, along with others, ". . . served to redefine our conceptions of what a child is, what an environment is, what the nature of interaction is, and what development is—except that we have resisted any effort to think through and be explicit about exactly what these new conceptions are" (p. 63). He even goes as far as to point out that aspects of his model were foreshadowed by Vygotsky's theory and "With respect to the macrosystem, once again it was a Vygotskian concept that paved the way" (p. 100). Vygotsky's theory continues to offer opportunities for finding links between cognitive development within cultural and social contexts, particularly in multiethnic societies such as the United States, Malaysia, India, Canada, Australia, and Continental Europe, where children of different backgrounds approach school and cognitive tasks in a variety of ways.

Erikson's Psychosocial Theory

Erik Erikson, a German-born psychoanalyst and student of Sigmund Freud's daughter, Anna, was the first person to propose a developmental theory encompassing the entire lifespan. Beginning with Freud's stages of psychosexual development, Erikson, a student of anthropology, modified and expanded them to focus greater attention on the social context of development (psychosocial) and less attention on biological and sexual development (psychosexual). Unlike Freud, his emphasis was on the growth of normal or healthy (rather than abnormal or neurotic) personality development, and he was particularly interested in cultural similarities and differences in the socialization of children and the development of identity during adolescence.

Erikson's theory provides a useful framework for attempting to define and unravel some of the major changes in social behavior that take place at various points in the lifespan. As shown in Table 3, he proposed a sequence of eight stages ranging from infancy to later adulthood, each accompanied by a psychosocial crisis requiring resolution if one is to move successfully from one stage to the next. These crises or periods of increased vulnerability and heightened potential involve conflicts between newly developing competencies and a desire to maintain the status quo.

When applying Erikson's theory, as we do at different points throughout the book, there are several points to keep in mind. First, although he assigns an age range to each of his eight stages, these should be considered only as a guide because of differences among individuals. Second, successful resolution of a crisis will depend on how a particular culture views the crisis, the sequence in which a particular stage occurs, and the solution evolving from it. Third, while many of Erikson's

TABLE 3 Erikson's Stages of Psychosocial Development

STAGE	CRISIS	PSYCHOSOCIAL TASK
Infancy	Trust vs. mistrust	Develop first social relationship with primary caretaker(s); develop a fundamental trust in life and the world
Toddlerhood	Autonomy vs. shame and doubt	Explore the social environment outside the primary relationship; recognize self as an individual being
Early childhood	Initiative vs. guilt	Negotiate one's place within social relationships; learn about the impact of one's social behavior on others; develop a sense of power
Middle childhood	Industry vs. inferiority	Learn the importance of social norms and the personal consequences of conformity and nonconformity; develop a sense of competence
Adolescence	Identity vs. role confusion	Find social roles and social environments that correspond to one's identity and principles; form one's own identity
Young adulthood	Intimacy vs. isolation	Negotiate one's own identity within the context of intimate relationships
Middle adulthood	Generativity vs. stagnation	Make a contribution to the larger society; acquire a sense of accomplishment and a place in the world
Late adulthood	Integrity vs. despair	Become an integral and active part of one's family and community; come to terms with one's life and choices

original ideas were based on development in Western societies, we attempt to modify some of these to show their potential usefulness and increased applicability in other cultural and ecological settings.

Kohlberg's Theory of Moral Development

The study of moral development is closely identified with the work of Lawrence Kohlberg, who completed his first research as part of his doctoral dissertation. Responses to a series of **moral dilemmas** (*hypothetical incidents involving a conflict between an individual's desires or needs and the rules of society*) by seventy-two boys, ages ten, thirteen, and sixteen years, were analyzed to determine how moral reasoning developed. For each dilemma, subjects were asked to evaluate the morality of a specific act mentioned in the dilemma. On the basis of these findings, Kohlberg (1981) identified three levels of moral development with two stages in each level, representing a more sophisticated and complex orientation toward justice and normative moral principles (see Table 4).

Most children nine years of age or younger are in the preconventional level, but so are many adolescent offenders and adult criminals. Most adolescents and adults are in the conventional level. The postconventional level is not generally reached before the age of twenty, and then generally only by a minority of individuals.

One of the main assumptions underlying Kohlberg's theory is that these six stages are universal and are present in cultures throughout the world. However, Kohlberg concedes that the stage at which individuals complete their development and the time it takes to be completed may vary from one culture to another.

There have been several criticisms of Kohlberg's theory. First, it is sex-biased because it was originally based on studies of male subjects (without the inclusion of any women) in one American city—Chicago. Second, his stages are culturally biased because they are largely dependent upon Western philosophy, and efforts have been made to apply them to non-Western cultures, which may have very different moral viewpoints. Nevertheless, his contribution to the understanding of the development of moral reasoning is important, and we will attempt to modify some of his ideas to show how they might be made more relevant and applicable to other cultural and ecological settings.

As we move through the rest of the modules in this book, we refer back to each of these theories and show how they help to explain various aspects of human development within a wide range of cultural settings and niches. From time to time, we also indicate how these theories might be expanded and modified to better understand and explain cross-cultural similarities and differences in behavior. We now look at some of the methodological issues and approaches related to the study of cross-cultural human development.

TABLE 4 Kohlberg's Stages of Moral Development

LEVEL	STAGE	BEHAVIOR
I. Preconventional	1. Punishment and obedience orientation	Obeys rules to avoid punishment
	2. Instrumental orientation	Obeys rules to receive rewards
II. Conventional	3. Good-child orientation	Conforms to rules to avoid disapproval by others
	4. Law and order orientation	Conforms to rules to maintain social order
III. Postconventional	5. Morality of contract, individual rights, and democratically accepted law	Accepts and follows laws for the welfare of the larger community
	6. Morality of individual principles and conscience	Believes in and follows self-chosen universal ethical principles

◇ METHODOLOGY IN CROSS-CULTURAL HUMAN DEVELOPMENT

As we noted in Module 1-B, there are many different definitions of culture; therefore, it should not be surprising that there are an almost infinite number of ways to approach and measure cultural differences and similarities. For example, psychologists generally tend to focus on individual behaviors, while anthropologists typically tend to look at the behavior of groups. Those doing cross-cultural research in human development frequently make an effort to look at both individual and group behaviors. This is not always easy because each culture and those who live within it, including parents, peers, teachers, and others, have their own ideas and beliefs about children and the ways in which they should develop.

Imagine you are a social scientist (e.g., psychologist, anthropologist, or sociologist) interested in studying the effects of childrearing practices on children's personality development. Looking at your own culture, you find the range of behaviors limited. So, it seems like a good idea to seek out other cultures, which may have different practices, such as swaddling (found among the Hopi Indians in the American Midwest and many Russian and Chinese families), severe independence training (characteristic of certain African tribal groups), or strict dependence or interdependence training (often noted in Japanese families). Taking this approach offers several benefits. First, you are able to increase both the range of independent variables (childrearing practices) and their effects on the dependent variable (children's personality development). Second, this approach allows (perhaps) for a clearer distinction between biological and environmental influences. For example, if developmental sequences or processes are found to be similar across a variety of diverse cultures, it might suggest that genetic or biological factors are a significant contributor. If, on the other hand, there are wide differences among the cultures, it is more likely that environmental factors play a larger role. Finally, by conducting cross-cultural research in another culture, one becomes aware of his or her own ethnocentric biases that could influence the design, conduct, and interpretation of the results.

Carrying out a cross-cultural study may sound easy. However, here is the heart of the problem: jumping on and off planes in far away and often exotic locations can be exciting, rewarding, and great fun, but it's not all beer and curry! Think about the young undergraduate student, Justin Tyme, in our opening vignette, and consider some other possible difficulties—getting required visas to visit certain countries is often difficult, time consuming, and expensive; you may not be allowed to conduct your research once you get there; you and the local food don't always agree; and you can become frustrated and lonely. In short, you have a great many challenges to meet and resolve. But as Dr. Kitty Litter, the anthropologist in our other vignette, demonstrates, with careful preparation and training, an individual can survive the culture experience and return with important research data. As we see in the next section, although there may be problems in doing cross-cultural research, there are also solutions.

Studying Development Cross-Culturally: Some Methods, Problems, and Solutions

Our intent is not to cover all possible methods, problems, and solutions in this section—besides being impossible, much of this work has been done very well by others. Our aim is twofold: (1) to familiarize you with some of the important information in this area, so that you gain an appreciation for what cross-cultural researchers have to deal with and (2) to prepare you to understand methods and findings you will encounter as you journey through the remainder of this book.

When conducting research in cross-cultural human development, researchers are interested in discovering principles that are universal to all (or most) cultures (etics), as well as principles that are unique or specific to certain cultures (emics)—a distinction we made in Module 1-B. At the same time, they are concerned that the methods they employ are (1) **objective** (*unbiased and not influenced by a researcher's preconceived notions*), (2) **reliable** (*findings are observed consistently and accepted by independent observers*), (3) **valid** (*behaviors and findings are what the researcher claims them to be*), and (4) **replicable** (*other researchers using the same methods report the same or very similar results*).

In this regard, cross-cultural methods are firmly rooted in basic psychological methodology involving the use of experiments (experimental and control groups to test hypotheses), cross-sectional designs (one-time testing of separate age groups), longitudinal designs (repeated testing of same individuals over time), sequential designs (combination of longitudinal and cross-sectional designs), and correlational studies (measurement of relationships between and among variables).

While cross-cultural psychology shares with its sister social sciences a number of similar needs in designing research (e.g., selecting subjects, defining variables, and choosing appropriate measures and methods), it has to deal with unique issues, for example, the complexity of culture, interdependence of culture and self, indigenous (or native) psychology versus universal psychology, communication across cultures, and interpretation of cultural findings. For detailed discussions of some of these issues and approaches to their resolution, see Berry, Poortinga, and Pandey (1997); Cole (1998); Lonner (2005); Matsumoto and Juang (2004); Smith (2004); and van de Vijver and Leung (2000). For more specific discussions of issues related to measurement in cross-cultural human development, see Friedman and Wachs (1999), Keller and Greenfield (2000), and Super and Harkness (2000). For information on conducting fieldwork studies, see the book by Hobbs and Wright (2006).

Matsumoto (2000) discussed some of the critical questions and issues in this area (pp. 130–134); and because many of these also apply to the conduct of cross-cultural human development research, they are summarized here: (1) *theories and hypotheses*—can the theories under investigation be appropriately applied to all cultures in the study, and do the hypotheses have the same meaning for all subjects independent of their cultural backgrounds? (2) *methods*—are the subjects representative of their culture and are they equivalent for comparative purposes, and are all measures (e.g., scales, items) reliable and valid in all cultures under investigation and do they have linguistic equivalence (determined through the method of back translation from original language to target language and back to original language until all meanings are equivalent)? (3) *data and analyses*—are there any unique cultural responses operating and have they been controlled? and (4) *interpretations and conclusions*—are findings and interpretations free of cultural bias and value judgments based on the researcher's own cultural background? These serious and complex questions must be carefully considered and adequately answered if research across cultures is to make significant contributions to our knowledge about similarities and differences in human development.

Because of the seriousness of one of the issues mentioned above—linguistic equivalence—additional comments regarding the translation and adaptation of instruments and materials from one culture to another deserve special attention. The International Test Commission, consisting of members from a number of international psychological organizations, has prepared a set of twenty-two specific guidelines for conducting multicultural studies that anyone interested in conducting cross-cultural research should take into account before designing and carrying out a particular study (see van de Vijver, 2001, for a complete listing of these guidelines). These are divided into four categories: (1) context guidelines focusing on general principles for test translations, (2) development guidelines for enhancing equivalence, (3) administrative guidelines for attaining comparability of administration in the use of different language versions, and (4) guidelines for documentation or score interpretations.

One technique widely used to achieve linguistic equivalence when a researcher is unfamiliar with or not fluent in one or more of the languages to be used in a project is **back translation.** This procedure involves *translating material (instruments, surveys, etc.) from a "source" language, (for example, English), into a "target" language, (for example, Arabic) by a bilingual translator fluent in both languages.* The target translation (Arabic) is then translated by another bilingual translator back into the source (English) language. This continues until there is agreement that the translations are linguistically equivalent. Because this technique often relies on literal translation of the material, ignoring such issues as comprehension and readability, a second procedure involving a group or committee with expertise in a variety of areas (language, culture, psychology, anthropology) carries out the translation process until there is agreement that all language versions are equivalent.

As for the use of specific methods, there are numerous ways in which these can be categorized. One approach is to consider four possible types of cross-cultural studies: (1) investigation of theories and concepts originally developed in Western countries as they may (or may not) apply in non-Western settings (e.g., Piaget's stages of cognitive development and Kohlberg's levels of moral development), (2) replication in one culture of studies previously conducted in another culture (e.g., children's acquisition of language skills, peer pressure during adolescence, and expression of emotion in toddlers), (3) collaborative research in which researchers from two or more cultures participate equally in the design and conduct of a study (e.g., assessment of personality in five cultures, a cross-national study of children's behavior with their friends, and exploration of ethnic identity in Russia, Finland, and South Africa), and (4) administration of test materials designed and standardized in one culture but used in other cultures (e.g., tests of intelligence, personality, and socialization).

A popular approach among psychologists, as well as some sociologists, is **cross-cultural comparisons** in which *individuals from at least two different cultural groups are measured and compared on some aspect of behavior* (e.g., European and Asian attitudes toward the criminal justice system). As for individual methods, a technique widely used by anthropologists in their cultural studies is **ethnography.** Typically, a researcher lives for a time in a culture observing, interviewing, and sometimes testing its members, and produces *a detailed description of a society's way of life, including its attitudes, customs, and behaviors.* The early work of Margaret Mead, Ruth Benedict, and others are examples. More recently, some interesting work has been done in "the ethnography of speaking,"

American anthropologist Margaret Mead, who frequently used ethnographic methods, smiles at a Balinese infant. (© Ken Heyman/Woodfin Camp & Associates)

in which sociolinguists studied variations in conversational language in different social contexts (Hymes, 1996, 1999; Nelson, 1992). Information contained in hundreds of these reports has been classified and indexed in the **Human Relations Area Files (HRAF)** and is frequently used in **hologeistic research,** *projects in which hypotheses about such topics as gender differences in aggression or preference for breast versus bottle feeding can be tested on a worldwide sample of more than 340 societies.*

Another approach that has been around for quite awhile but is receiving increased attention from researchers today is the **narrative method,** which, depending on the researcher, looks at a variety of narrative materials, including stories (oral or written), diaries, letters, and their analyses. For a description and discussion of this approach, see the book *Narrative methods* by Atkinson and Delamont (2006).

Matsumoto points out that "in recent years, there has been an interesting merging of research approaches across disciplines, with an increasing number of scientists adopting comparative techniques for use in single-culture immersion research, and comparative researchers adopting qualitative ethnographic methods to bolster their traditional quantitative approach" (p. 39). We see this as a positive sign that these social science disciplines, often at odds, may be showing signs of understanding and learning from each other.

More recently, Matsumoto and Juang (2008) have cited ecological-level studies in which data are obtained from individuals in several different cultures, summarized or averaged, and used as descriptors for those cultures. Two of the most prominent ecological-level studies of culture are the work of Hofstede (2001, 2004) on work-related values in multinational business organizations and Schwartz's value orientations (1995, 2004), both of which are discussed later in this book.

Keller and Greenfield (2000) look more specifically at some of the contributions developmentalists' research make to cross-cultural psychology—methodologically, theoretically, and empirically. For example, in terms of methodology, they point to the use of "contextualized procedures, such as naturalistic observation, suitable for studying behavior in its cultural context" (p. 52). Theoretically, "developmentalists point to the fact that the culturally constructed behavior of adults can be viewed as an endpoint along a developmental pathway, and that adults provide cultural socialization to the next generation" (p. 52). Finally, empirically, they point out that "a developmental approach leads researchers to investigate the culture-specific shape of developmental stages" (p. 52).

For those who want to know more about cross-cultural research methodology, from a primarily psychological viewpoint, including additional problems and solutions, we recommend the volumes by Segall, Dasen, Berry, and Poortinga (1999) and Berry, Poortinga, and Pandy (1997). Cross-cultural research methodology, as practiced by anthropologists, is discussed in a volume by Ember and Ember (2000).

Let us now take a closer look at some of these issues and several of the research methodologies used in the cross-cultural study of human development, particularly those associated with our two major theoretical viewpoints—the ecological model and the developmental niche.

Methods for Assessing Components of the Developmental Niche

Super and Harkness (1999) have presented, in extensive detail, their suggestions for successfully measuring and assessing the components of the developmental niche. In this section, we provide an overview of their methodology, which, as can be seen in Table 5, involves a combination of psychological and anthropological research techniques. Anyone with a serious interest in the developmental niche approach is advised to consult this important work that blends theory and methodology in a way seldom done in the study of cross-cultural human development. It stands as a model for others in the field and as an example of the effort to bring closer together anthropology and psychology that we hope to see more of in the future.

Looking at Table 5, we find several ethnographic, observational, and formal methods (column one), the component to which a particular method contributes qualitative understanding (column two), and, finally, the component for which a method can furnish quantitative information (column three).

TABLE 5 Methods for Studying the Developmental Niche

METHOD	COMPONENT	
	Identified	*Measured*
Participant observation and ethnographic interviewing	Settings, customs, and caretaker psychology	—
Spot observations and diaries	Settings, customs, and caretaker psychology	Settings (and customs)
Behavior observations	Customs and caretaker psychology	Customs
Semistructured interviews and focus groups	Customs and caretaker psychology	Customs and caretaker psychology
Structured questioning	—	Caretaker psychology and customs
Passive enumeration	Caretaker psychology and customs	Caretaker psychology and customs
Formal methods: free listings, clustering, multidimensional scaling, and consensus analysis	Customs and caretaker psychology	Caretaker psychology and customs

Source: From "The Environment as Culture in Developmental Research" by C. M. Super and S. Harkness, 1999, in S. L. Friedman & T. D. Wachs (Eds.), *Measuring Environment Across the Life Span.* Washington, D.C.: American Psychological Association. Reprinted with permission.

According to Super and Harkness, the first group of methods (participant observation and ethnographic interviewing) is indispensable for selecting and understanding important components or units of the developmental environment, and for providing the foundation for determining what should be measured and how to create hypotheses that will demonstrate how various components of the developmental niche are related to each other. They point out that **participant observation** (*a technique in which an investigator lives for a time with or near a group of people and observes its daily life, activities, and rituals*) and **ethnographic interviews** (*asking group members to describe their culture's typical behaviors, attitudes, beliefs, and values*), if carefully carried out, can help identify elements within each of the three developmental niche components (see Table 1). An example of their use in actual research is in a study by Levy (1996), in which he reports that differences in parental beliefs and practices about learners and teaching in Tahiti and Nepal may be a result of differences in the level of societal complexity in these two cultures.

Other techniques useful in identifying important aspects of all three components, but settings in particular, include spot observations and diaries. Results from **spot observations** (*a series of random unannounced observations of a group, sufficient in number to allow for statistical analysis*) and **diaries** (*written accounts of changes in daily activities kept by participants over varying periods of time, such as a full 24-hour day*) are useful for "describing the physical and social settings of daily life not only in terms of their particular qualities but also in terms of their empirical distributions . . . [and] . . . provide a basis for identifying regularities in settings and activities that may differ between groups, or that one wants to relate thematically to other elements in the niche, or to developmental trends" (Super & Harkness, 1999, p. 304).

Measuring customs (the second component of the developmental niche), according to Super and Harkness, requires (1) a qualitative approach, in which behavioral consistencies are identified either through **direct observation** of a cultural group or by means of **ethnographic descriptions** of its everyday attitudes, beliefs, and behaviors and (2) a quantitative approach producing "measures of individuals' views on the nature and importance of the custom or measures of the frequency of occurrence of the identified practice, or both" (p. 308). They assert that the ideal approach to assessing and measuring the customs component "demonstrates their existence, documents their occurrence, and explains their relationship to the settings of daily life and to the psychological theories that guide them" (1999, p. 308).

Measuring caretaker psychology or parental beliefs and values (the third component of the niche) also requires a combination of qualitative and quantitative approaches. These may include **structured questioning** (frequently based on findings obtained from the methods previously discussed) and **formal methods** originally employed in the cognitive sciences (see Borgatti, 1992, for additional information).

Truly understanding culture and the critical role it plays in human development requires an appreciation of qualitative, as well as quantitative, findings. In the words of Super and Harkness (1999), "Findings in one domain suggest further exploration or reexamination in another, and replication of patterns suggests salient cultural themes" (p. 312). Their unique organizational scheme provides answers to many questions about culture and development while setting forth even more challenges for the future.

Studying Ecological Systems

Unlike Super and Harkness, who constructed their approach to human development and conducted much of their own research in support of it, Bronfenbrenner has primarily been the developer of ideas and hypotheses, while others have carried out research to show the validity of his approach. To illustrate this, let us briefly look at some examples of representative research carried out on each of the four ecological systems.

First, Brown, Lohr, and Trujillo (1990), in an effort to show how the peer microsystem of adolescents becomes increasingly differentiated and influential in one's behavior, reported on the ways in which both positive (acceptance, friendship, status, and popularity) and negative (drinking, smoking, stealing, cheating) behaviors are associated with different adolescent lifestyle decisions.

Second, Muuss (1996) has stated, "A mesosystem analysis examines the quality, the frequency, and the influence of such interactions as family experiences on school adjustment" (p. 325). An interesting example of this is Epstein's study (1983) of the longitudinal effects of family-school-person interactions on student outcomes, which, unexpectedly, reported that the interaction of family and school was of far greater importance and influence than the variables of race and socioeconomic status. Noted among the findings was a continuing influence of the family and school environments far beyond the early childhood years, lending support to the interaction effects among systems proposed by Bronfenbrenner. As an example, the author pointed out that students experiencing the greatest change in independence were those initially scoring low on this behavior (and whose families failed to emphasize decision making), but who attended schools that placed a strong emphasis on student participation.

Third, as you may remember from our original comments, Bronfenbrenner has asserted that decisions made in the exosystem (e.g., in parents' workplaces) can have an extremely important influence on the life of a child or adolescent (even though they are not a part of that setting). Flanagan and Eccles (1993) effectively demonstrated this point in their two-year longitudinal study of changes in parents' work status and their effects on the adjustment of children before and after their transition to junior high school. Results indicated that of four family types identified (based on patterns of change or stability in parental work status), children in deprived and declining families were less competent than their peers in stable or recovery families. Although most of the subjects experienced some difficulty in school adjustment, the transition was shown to be especially difficult for those whose parents were simultaneously dealing with changes in their work status.

Fourth, although the macrosystem, in many ways, is removed from the daily life of an individual, it does consist of extremely important societal influences (political, religious, economic, and other values) that clearly affect human development. Bronfenbrenner (1967) demonstrated the influence of macrosystem values in an early comparison of peer group and adult pressures on children in the United States and the former Soviet Union. At that time, in the Soviet Union, a cohesive core of socially accepted and politically endorsed values left little room for differences in expectations between the adults or peers in one's environment. In the United States, on the other hand, there were frequently unmistakable differences between these significant people, with the result that children and adolescents often found themselves being pulled in different directions. With the breakup of the former Soviet Union, the situation that once existed in the United States (and to a large extent, still appears to) now is much more characteristic of the former Soviet Union as well.

As we close this discussion, it seems only fair to give Bronfenbrenner the last word on the challenge of operationally defining elements of his evolving bioecological model as well as efforts to scientifically measure them. As he states, "Thus far, I have accorded more attention to the conceptual rather than to the operational aspects of this challenge. I did so for a reason; namely, most of the research designs and methods of measurement currently in use in developmental science are not well-suited for what I have referred to elsewhere as 'science in the discovery mode' (Bronfenbrenner & Morris, 1998). To be more specific, these designs and methods are more appropriate for verifying already formulated hypotheses than for the far more critical and more difficult task of developing hypotheses of sufficient explanatory power and precision to warrant being subjected to empirical test. . . . In summary, most of the scientific journey still lies ahead" (Bronfenbrenner, 1999, p. 24). For those interested in reading more about these issues, see any of the several references mentioned in this discussion.

◇ SUMMARY

This module focuses on theories and methodologies used in the conduct of cross-cultural research in general and developmental research in particular. We begin with reasons for studying human development—to *understand, explain, predict, and* (in some instances) *control behavior.* To successfully achieve these goals, we need to use theories or *sets of hypotheses or assumptions about behavior.* We discuss, in detail, six approaches that will receive significant attention throughout this book—Bronfenbrenner's ecological model, Super and Harkness's developmental niche concept, Piaget's theory of cognitive development, Vygotsky's sociocultural theory of development, Erikson's psychosocial theory, and Kohlberg's theory of moral development. We discuss some of the ways in which cross-cultural methods might be classified; distinguish between different types of cross-cultural researchers (natives and sojourners); and comment on specific techniques, including ethnographies, cross-cultural comparisons, and hologeistic studies. We conclude with a discussion of methods for assessing components of the developmental niche as well as ecological systems.

◇ STUDY QUESTIONS

Explain the purpose of theories in the study of human development.

Describe and discuss Bronfenbrenner's ecological model of human development.

Describe Harkness and Super's developmental niche model.

Compare and contrast the human development theories of Piaget and Vygotsky.

◇ FURTHER READINGS

Urie Bronfenbrenner. (2005). *Making Human Beings Human: Bioecological Perspectives on Human Development*. Thousand Oaks, CA: Sage Publications.

> The culminating work by the author, consisting of twenty-three articles written over six decades that describe the historical development of his groundbreaking model. Contains recommendations for future research and applications for the design of social programs and policies for promoting positive development of children and families throughout the world.

Douglas Raybeck. (1996). *Mad Dogs, Englishmen, and the Errant Anthropologist: Fieldwork in Malaysia.* Prospect Heights, IL: Waveland Press.

> A lively account of the author's adventures and misadventures while doing fieldwork, with vivid descriptions of Kelantanese society and culture, kinship, linguistics, and gender relations. Provides a real sense of how an anthropologist conducts and gathers reliable information in cultural settings where often "things go awry."

Susan Goldstein. (2000). *Cross-Cultural Explorations: Activities in Culture and Psychology.* Boston: Allyn and Bacon.

> This book contains nine chapters with ten activities each revolving around case studies, self-administered scales, mini-experiments, and a collection of content-analytic, observational, and interview data allowing "hands-on" experience. Of particular interest is a chapter on "Culture and Psychological Research" that explores major issues and techniques in the conduct of cross-cultural research.

Walter J. Lonner & Roy Malpass. (1994). *Psychology and Culture.* Boston: Allyn & Bacon.

> Each of the forty-three short (five- to six-page) easy-to-read chapters on various aspects of cross-cultural psychology provides personal insights into the ways in which the authors carried out their research, often with revealing comments on the mistakes they made.

F. J. R. van de Vijver. (2000). Types of cross-cultural studies in cross-cultural psychology. In W. J. Lonner, D. L. Dinnel, S. A. Hayes, & D. N. Sattler (Eds.), *Online Readings in Psychology and Culture* (Unit 2, Chapter 6), (http://www.wwu.edu/~culture), Center for Cross-Cultural Research, Western Washington University, Bellingham, Washington.

> This easily accessible online article classifies cross-cultural studies along three dimensions and provides examples and illustrations of cross-cultural methodology.

◇ DEVELOPMENTAL ANALYSIS

INTRODUCTION

Throughout the remainder of this book, you will have the opportunity to explore your own development. By finding ways to apply important concepts to your own life, you will not only better understand them but will also become more aware of whom you are and the various influences (cultural, familial, biological, and social) that have contributed to your unique development.

One difficulty with organizing the large amount of material in a book like this is that most research is not collected in a longitudinal manner. As you read through Modules 3-A, 8-A, you will become familiar with these seven areas of focus: socialization, family, language and cognition, self and personality, social behavior, issues of gender and sexuality and health. As you explore each of these, we recommend you take time to examine how each area has contributed to your development and, in many cases, continues to play a role. Try to relate the many concepts to your own life by jotting down brief examples from your experiences.

◆ DEVELOPMENTAL ANALYSIS   CONTINUED

To help you in this self-exploratory effort, you will find in each module a developmental box presenting the fictionalized life of "Maddi" Skelton, who will be followed throughout the book as she describes her life in terms of the material presented in each module. Her life will be described in the first person from infancy through the later adult years. This will help to provide continuity among the various topics presented throughout the book.

These developmental boxes, beginning with socialization in Module 3-A, will serve as examples of how you might reflect on your own life. Begin by first describing your culture and the ecological system and developmental niche in which you grew up. Subdivide your notes into sections labeled Infancy, Childhood, Adolescence, and Adulthood. Within each section, describe your development in terms of culturally influenced behaviors, such as sleep, feeding patterns, food preferences, attitudes toward caretakers (parents, teachers, siblings), early learning (formal and informal), rites of passage characteristic of your culture, family relations, and any other important aspects of the socialization process that had an effect on the person you are today. Be sure to use concrete examples from your own life. Will you understand these concepts better, you will also have authored your own autobiography—something you will likely treasure and add on to as you make your way through additional life stages.

Enjoy!

Name: _____ Date: _____

MODULE 2-B

 ACTIVITY

◇ **PAGTATANONG-TANONG:**
   AN INDIGENOUS RESEARCH METHOD

This activity evaluates the cross-cultural applicability of the research methods typically used in "Western psychology" and explores an indigenous research method from the Philippines called *Pagtatanong-tanong*.

Directions: Read the scenario and answer the questions that follow.

Scenario: Suppose that you have been trained at your university to uphold the following principles of research:

- The researcher must remain objective. It is important not to become too emotionally attached, or disclose personal information, to research participants.
- Procedures should be standardized. The questions asked of participants and the conditions under which they are asked should be as uniform as possible.
- Participants should not be subject to the influence of others during the testing or interview process (unless it is a condition of the experiment). Thus, participants should be tested or interviewed on an individual basis.

Imagine that you are preparing to conduct a series of interviews in a rural community in the Philippines. Through reading and speaking with experts and members of this community you learn the following about the culture in which you are planning to conduct your research.

- People are unaccustomed to being asked a series of questions in sequence and responding in a regimented manner.
- People are uncomfortable discussing personal opinions or behaviors with a stranger with whom there will be no future relationship.
- People are more comfortable speaking in a conversational manner in which each person discloses information and contributes to managing the process and content of the conversation.
- People may be uncomfortable alone with a stranger, particularly if the stranger is of a different gender or social status.

Taken from *Cross-Cultural Explorations: Activities in Culture and Psychology*, Second Edition, by Susan Goldstein.

1. Describe how you might modify your research methods in order to effectively conduct your interviews. Which research principles would you be willing to reconsider and which principles would you continue to uphold?

Pe-Pua (1989; 2006) and others have described a social science research method indigenous to the Philippines called *Pagtatanong-tanong*. According to Pe-Pua, Pagtatanong-tanong has some of the following characteristics:

- The researcher uses a tentative outline of questions that are revised based on input from the participants.
- The researcher and the participants share equally in determining the content and structure of the interview.
- A relationship is established between the researcher and the participants such that the participants feel comfortable asking the researcher questions and expect that they may have contact with the researcher in the future.
- The researcher starts interviewing with a group of participants. Interruptions in the interview process are not seen as distractions, but as an opportunity to check on the reliability of information obtained.

2. What do you expect about the validity of the information you would collect in the rural community in the Philippines using the Pagtatanong-tanong method?

3. If you are not from the rural Philippines yourself, do you think that Pagtatanong-tanong would yield useful information in your culture? Please explain.

◆ REFERENCES

Pe-Pua, R. (1989). Pagtatanong-tanong: A cross-cultural research method. *International Journal of Intercultural Relations, 13*, 147-163.

Pe-Pua, R. (2006). From decolonizing psychology to the development of a cross-indigenous perspective in methodology: The Philippine experience. In U. Kim, K.-S. Yand, & K.-K. Hwang (Eds.). *Indigenous and cultural psychology: Understanding people in context (*pp. 109-137). New York: Springer.

SECTION 3
SOCIALIZATION

MODULE 3-A

CULTURE AND SOCIALIZATION

Kamuzu Mathebula is fourteen years old and lives in Diepkloof, a section of Soweto, an all-black township outside Johannesburg, South Africa. He lives with his mother, aged grandmother, two brothers, and a sister in a shack made of discarded plastic sheeting and wood with a corrugated iron roof. There is no electricity or running water. Diarrhea and tuberculosis are common here. His mother, a widow, works as a maid for the Martins, an Afrikaner (white South African) family, five miles away. Kamuzu has attended poorly funded segregated schools most of his life. With the end of apartheid (the white-government-enforced system of "separateness") in 1990, his future has been looking better. Rather than working long hours for meager wages in one of the local textile factories, Kamuzu hopes to attend the University of Witwatsrand in Johannesburg and become a doctor and help his people.

Hendrik and Patricia Martin, the Dutch-descended Afrikaner family that Kamuzu's mother works for, have a son named Jeremy who is also fourteen years old. He and his younger sister, Yvonne, live in a wealthy neighborhood of large, well-kept homes. Jeremy's father is president of an import–export company, started by his grandfather, and his mother teaches science at the exclusive private school he and his sister attend. His goal, like Kamuzu's, is to attend the university in Johannesburg and study medicine.

Two young South African boys—the same age, residing just a few miles apart near the tip of the African continent—supposedly live in the same society but have been raised in clearly different environments (developmental niches) by very different families; yet they share a common desire of becoming doctors.

How can we account for the similarities and differences in the development of these two young adolescents? While it is true that Kamuzu and Jeremy share a number of characteristics, in large measure they are a reflection of two distinct cultures—different social contexts, parental belief systems, societal values, and cultural perspectives. Every one of us, like each of them, is influenced by a unique combination of factors, including the genetic material inherited from our ancestors, the family in which we are raised and the style of parenting to which we are exposed, the friends we make and the schools we attend, the historical period in which we are born, and (of pivotal importance) the culture and ecological contexts in which we live out our lives. As Sigel and colleagues (1992) have noted, "Since it is a culture which serves to define values, beliefs, and actions of families, it is imperative and in fact a virtual necessity for the applied developmental psychologist to develop a knowledge base of cultures" (Roopnarine and Carter, 1992b, p. ix.).

Taken from *Lives Across Cultures: Cross-Cultural Development*, Fifth Edition, by Harry W. Gardiner and Corinne Kosmitzki.

Indeed, while this is essential, knowledge of cultures is not enough. To genuinely understand and explain cultural differences in development, we first need to look at the way in which a culture defines these values, beliefs, and actions, and this requires an understanding of the crucial process of socialization.

◇ ECOLOGICAL CONTEXT

As pointed out earlier, our ecological approach looks at human development in terms of the individual within a number of changing environments where growth and development occur as a result of relationships between and among the individual and others surrounding him or her. A child is first studied in the context of the family followed by the community and then the expanded culture. We begin by considering the concept of socialization and its influence on various behaviors across the lifespan and across cultures.

What Is Socialization?

Like many concepts in developmental psychology, socialization can be variously defined. For our purposes, we will view **socialization** as *the process by which an individual becomes a member of a particular culture and takes on its values, beliefs, and other behaviors in order to function within it.* It is through the process of socialization that society teaches desirable behavior while inhibiting undesirable behavior, prepares individuals to become successfully functioning members in its principal institutional settings (family, school, community, and workplace), and guarantees that important traditions (although sometimes modified) will be passed to future members of the culture.

It is far from easy to describe or explain cultural socialization. Contemporary theories focus on the thousands of interactive exchanges between a child and family members over a long period of time during which each is influencing the behavior of the other, making it difficult to assess cause and effect. In addition, explanations have become more complex and multidimensional than those offered by earlier approaches (Grusec & Hastings, 2008).

Edwards (1996) has noted that socialization theories have also undergone substantial revision. For far too long, theories and their proponents were ethnocentric (e.g., proposing that explanations of behavior in one society applied equally well in others). As we frequently note throughout this book, such theories relied heavily on research and assumptions based in Western societies, with the result that theories were either nongeneralizable to other cultures or failed to take into account the richness of human diversity. In a sense, theorists were victims of their own socialization and were promoting a Westernized view of the world that they frequently imposed on the cultures they were studying, rather than letting indigenous behaviors emerge and be recognized. As evidence, Edwards (1989) cites some of her own earlier work in which Mayan children in Zinacantan, Mexico, learned toilet training and other self-care skills by means of imitation and thereby made a relatively easy transition from infancy to early childhood, compared with other cultures in which these activities are characterized by resistance and great difficulty. There would appear to be an entirely different cultural context operating in this Mayan culture than what we tend to see in North America and some cultures of Western Europe. Values important to the successful functioning of these Mayan children are being transmitted in a way that provides a foundation for the development of infants and toddlers, who closely observe and carefully imitate and respond to their elders and others, rather than expecting others to respond to them. A researcher who has made significant contributions to our understanding of socialization, particularly in the area of cognition, is Barbara Rogoff (2003). Her book *Apprenticeship in Thinking* (1990) is recommended for additional reading in this area. Rogoff's approach to this topic has been greatly influenced by the work of the Soviet psychologist Lev Vygotsky, whose work on culture and cognitive development is discussed in detail in the same module. Rogoff developed the concept of *guided participation* to expand on Vygotsky's concept of the *zone of proximal development* "in order to draw attention to the opportunity to learn through participation in nonverbal and tacit forms of interaction as well as through societal arrangements, not just from instruction or scaffolding" (personal communication, 2004). Guided participation emphasizes the bidirectional, or two-way, nature of socialization and the fact that children are active participants in their own socialization. In describing this concept, Brislin

(1993) provides an example familiar to those who have lived in or conducted research in many of the countries in South and Southeast Asia—namely, the cultural requirement that children learn that the right (clean) hand is for eating and the left (unclean) hand is to be used for personal hygiene. If children do not learn this behavior through participation in daily home activities, parents, other adults, or even older siblings will guide the children in the appropriate way. For example, while eating, one of these "teachers" might be seen inhibiting use of the left hand while gently guiding the right toward the food. The point, Brislin says, is "that the children's behavior directs the teacher's behavior. If children learn through simple observation, there is no need for the more active intervention of holding down and guiding hands" (p. 130). Contrast this more directive approach with the observational approach of Mayan child training cited above.

Let us now consider how the socialization process relates to two of our major themes: the ecological model and the developmental niche.

Ecological Model and the Developmental Niche

As we have already noted, socialization is a lifelong process, occurring within a variety of environments or social contexts in which we live, influencing the activities in which we participate, and significantly contributing to our development across the lifespan.

In Module 2-A, we introduced two important themes that are interwoven throughout this book: Bronfenbrenner's **ecological model** and the concept of the **developmental niche.** The ecological model allows us to look at human development as it occurs in its real-world settings or ecological context and is composed of five categories of interrelated systems. It is within these interconnected contexts that socialization takes place and in which we begin to see the development of "lives across cultures."

The socialization process and the interaction between an individual and her or his environment in its various contexts (microsystem, mesosystem, exosystem, macrosystem, and chronosystem) are at the center of the ecological model. For example, if one were interested in comparing and contrasting the self-concepts of adolescents in Israel and Palestine, it would be critical to consider their socialization experiences within their culture, home, school, and among peers as well as their exposure to the media, childrearing practices, parental attitudes and values, and other important influences. In this regard, take a moment and think of your own self-concept. What were some of the socialization experiences that influenced you? Was one more important than another? In what ways?

Likewise, socialization plays a major role in the three interrelated components of Super and Harkness' developmental niche. An interesting example is a study by McDade and Worthman (2004) focusing on "socialization ambiguity." The authors noted that nontraditional lifestyles, such as globalization, were presenting young people in the islands of Samoa with new socialization opportunities along with possibilities of "stress-inducing dissonance" (conflicts resulting from incompatible beliefs and attitudes held simultaneously). Their findings revealed socialization ambiguity to be a significant source of stress on two different islands although the direction varied, possibly an indication of dissimilar socialization objectives on each island. Can you think of any event or situation in your life when you experienced "socialization ambiguity"? Do you recall how it was resolved?

The various aspects of the ecological model and the developmental niche are illustrated in Box 1, which describes some of the ways in which Japanese children become socialized into their culture. To further illustrate this point, we provide three brief examples that will receive detailed attention later. First, if a child is doing poorly in school, this can have an impact on behavior within the family and affect the parent–child relationship in a variety of ways (e.g., neglect or abuse). A home situation involving neglect or abuse can have effects on a child's relationships with parents, peers, teachers, and other family members. In addition, a child's temperament within a particular cultural context (e.g., Brazil or Japan) may affect the way parents interact with that child and, in turn, influence the development of personality and self-concept. Finally, a sick, fussy, or light-sleeping child may keep parents awake at night, making them less effective at work or in their relationship with each other. (Variations in sleep patterns and their relationship to the approaches mentioned above are discussed in the next section.)

With (hopefully) a clear understanding of the ecological model, the developmental niche, and the cross-cultural theme, we are now prepared to look at some cultural variations in socialized behavior.

BOX 1

BECOMING JAPANESE: AN ECOLOGICAL
VIEW OF SOCIALIZATION

In her insightful book on Japanese culture, Joy Hendry (1986) provides a delightful picture of the organization and function of three of the most important microsystems of early childhood development: family, neighborhood, and preschool. Using everyday examples, she shows how these contexts are connected with some of the most important cultural values found in the mesosystem, which, in turn, have significant effects on the surrounding exosystem. In addition, Hendry discusses the strong emphasis the culture places on cooperative behavior; academic achievement; indulgent attitudes toward infants; and the hierarchical nature of parent–child, sibling, and neighbor–child relationships. These fall within the setting of the macrosystem and deepen our understanding of how, accompanied by a traditional respect for age and seniority, these behaviors effectively combine to produce characteristics that are uniquely Japanese.

Hendry describes the family microsystem and the influence of those within it in this way: "The child . . . is in close contact with one set of grandparents and possibly one or two sets of great-grandparents, as well as its parents. . . . Other close relatives are likely to be frequent visitors . . . [and] may well play quite an important part in their early rearing" (p. 36). However, unlike recent developments in Western societies, Japanese fathers tend to play a relatively minor role in early childrearing because "many men [return] . . . home each evening after the children are asleep, and [leave] . . . in the morning before they get up" (p. 38).

According to Hendry, relationships within the neighborhood microsystem are much more institutionalized than in many other countries. For example, "Informal aid is usually given between houses popularly delineated as 'the three opposite and one on either side' (*mukosangen ryodonari*). . . . In this context, mothers of young children meet at the local swings, discuss problems with each other, and occasionally look after each other's children" (pp. 40–41). These neighbors are frequently the first people outside the family with whom the children interact and from which they acquire their first friends. When they enter school, children are organized into a children's group (*kodomogumi*) based on neighborhoods, which arrange "sporting activities, outings and school disciplinary groups [and] . . . gather at a meeting point every morning in order to walk to school together. Thus, the relations established informally at an early age are likely to continue, and even for children whose families move, there are similar groups for them to join in other areas" (p. 42).

The third microsystem, that of the kindergarten or day nursery, is also a highly structured setting in which children are separated according to age "so that most of their contact with other children will be with peers, great emphasis being placed on the ideal that all children should be friends (*tomodachi*) and get on well with one another. . . . Conflict and competition is discouraged [and] . . . every child has a turn eventually to serve and to discipline the others" (p. 43). Later, "after-school classes in English and music provide excellent opportunities for kindergarten classmates to maintain their friendships throughout their school lives" (p. 45).

This short excerpt provides only a glimpse into the complex but interrelated ecological world of Japanese children and their families; we highly recommend that the reader look at Hendry's book for a fuller picture.

Source: Adapted from "Becoming Japanese: The Arenas and Agents of Socialization" by J. Hendry (1993) in R. W. Wozniak (Ed.), *Worlds of Childhood Reader* (pp. 34–47), New York: HarperCollins.

Some Cultural Variations in the Socialization of Behavior

As pointed out in Module 1-B, in a book of this type, with its major focus on cultural similarities and differences, it is impossible to provide as comprehensive a view of human development as do more traditional developmental books. For a general overview of human development principles, we direct the reader to one of these books. Our goal is to consider selected topics for which a large or growing body of cross-cultural research evidence exists and discuss these topics chronologically—from the early beginnings of infancy through the later years of adulthood. Another aspect, unique to this discussion, is the incorporation (and suggested modification) of Erik Erikson's psychosocial theory of development in an effort to place these behaviors within a cross-cultural perspective. (See Module 2-A for a review of the major aspects of this theory.)

We begin our discussion of selected topics, which are followed in a similar fashion in subsequent modules, with a consideration of some of the principal behaviors socialized by most parents across cultures. We turn first to socialization during pregnancy, prenatal development, and birth.

Pregnancy, Prenatal Development, and Birth

Joining a birth preparation class or exercise class during the early stages of pregnancy provides women with opportunities to interact with other mothers or soon-to-be mothers and become socialized into one of the most important experiences of their lives. They must be objective and extremely careful in assessing the information they receive because no two mothers have the same experience and theirs may be quite different from other mothers. However, especially for young first-time mothers, the experience may prove to be very beneficial.

In a recent article, Karen Smith (2005), a language education professor, explored her use of "prebirth gender talk" for the initiation of gender socialization of her baby in the womb following a sex-identifying ultrasound. Findings showed that, in this particular case, gender socialization began in utero, and the labeling of the fetus predetermined the personality for her and also, knowing it was a male, allowed her tone of voice to become "sharper" and "stronger." Presented as a "case study in narrative," Smith documented the words spoken and feelings expressed to her second child beginning in the second trimester, in utero, in an effort to document engendered language and socialization. She concluded that knowledge of the baby's sex imposed social mores upon her "interaction" with it, and she began nurturing specific male traits and stereotypes. To learn more and read a transcript of this mother's "prebirth talk," go to http://www.redorbit.com/news/display?id=158908&source=r_health.

In terms of actual childbirth, women are likely to experience differences in length and difficulty of labor. Yet in the United States there is often a socialization of birth procedures applied to large numbers of mothers-to-be during delivery: placed on their backs, attached to a fetal monitor and IV for delivery of medicine, injection of pain relieving drugs, and administration of an episiotomy to widen the birth area. In some cultures, women hold on to a rope, lie in a hammock, relax in a pool or Jacuzzi, or even squat or kneel on the floor. Doctors and nurses are frequently replaced by midwives, female relatives, family, and friends.

✧ INFANCY

When a newborn arrives in the world, independent of its particular culture, it has many basic needs that require immediate attention. How these needs are met and the manner in which infants are socialized varies considerably across cultures and often among ethnic groups *within* a single society. In fact, as we will see frequently throughout this book, there is often more variability in certain behaviors within cultures than between or among cultures.

It is clear that culture influences patterns of parenting from the first hours of infancy (e.g., when and how parents care for infants, the extent to which they allow them to explore their surroundings, how nurturant or restrictive they might be, and which behaviors they value and socialize). Bornstein expressed it succinctly when he says, "With the birth of a baby, a parent's life is forever altered. Those changes, in turn, shape the experiences of the infant and, with time, the person he or she becomes. Linked, parent and child chart that course together. Infancy is a starting point of life for both infant *and* parent"(2002, p. 33).

There is a wide variety of skills and abilities that are influenced by socialization in this early period—physical (sitting, crawling, walking, grasping), cognitive (language), social (emotional expression, attachment, temperament), and more. Many of these will be discussed later in this book. At this point, let us look at three of the most basic behaviors parents need to socialize.

Sleep

While all babies require sleep, psychological, anthropological, and even pediatric literature reveals considerable variation in cultural sleeping arrangements (McKenna, 2002). According to Harkness and Super (1995), the way sleep is organized, including where and with whom, is an intriguing aspect of culture because, although it is a private rather than public behavior, it is highly structured by different societies and tends to be relatively resistant to change. As these researchers point out, "Parents play a primary role in the assignment of settings and routines for sleep, thus perpetuating a cycle of culture transmission within the privileged context of the family" (p. 227). For example, in a study of Kipsigis farming families in the highlands of rural Kenya in East Africa, Harkness and Super noted that although the next-to-youngest child continues to sleep with its mother and other siblings after the birth of a younger child, it no longer sleeps at the mother's front but rather at her back. This change, along with the termination of breast-feeding and back-carrying, results in a "fundamental shift in the child's physical and social settings of life" (1995, p. 227).

Sleep management is one of the earliest culturally determined parent–child interactions and may provide a useful framework for interpreting cross-cultural differences in the varying emphases placed on such behaviors as autonomy and dependence. Others have made a similar argument with regard to the development of interdependence and sensitivity to the needs of other people.

In a somewhat related effort, aimed at studying development as adaptation, Chisholm (1983) conducted an extensive investigation among Navajo Indians in North America of their use of the cradleboard (a small wooden frame to which an infant is strapped) to determine whether it might cause disruption in mother–infant interaction. (See photo of a Hopi Indian cradleboard at left.) The Navajo cradleboard, or literally "baby diaper," has several purposes, such as infant transport, baby-sitting device, and regulator of infant states including level of physiological responsiveness or arousal and sleep. According to Chisholm, a child is asleep most (as much as 85%) of the time he or she is on the cradleboard, but the numbers of hours on the board may vary from only a few to as many as twenty-three, with fifteen to eighteen being normal. Chisholm concludes that cradleboard use seems to have no lasting effect on a child's behavioral development, and any observed group differences between Navajo and Anglo children are likely a result of sociocultural differences within the infant's environment—what we would attribute to the child's ecological settings and the developmental niche.

Native American children strapped to cradleboards during their first year walk at about the same time as other children.

(© Lionel Delevingne/Stock Boston)

While it is a common practice among middle-class families in the United States and Canada to put young infants in their own room to sleep (in part, to give them an early start down the road to independence), many Mayan mothers (American Indian peoples of Mexico and Central America) view this custom as equivalent to child neglect. On the other hand, interdependence—a prominent personality and cultural characteristic among Japanese—can be attributable, at least in some measure, to the fact that Japanese children (sometimes due to an overcrowded microsystem) frequently sleep with their parents until the age of six or even, in some cases, to the beginning of puberty, when independent sleeping marks a culturally recognized change in one's developmental niche. Similar findings have been found in China, where "all-night co-sleeping" during infancy and early childhood is the norm, decreasing in prevalence with increasing age, and unusual after puberty (Liu et al., 2005). In urban China, the prevalence of regular bed sharing has been found to be 18.2 percent and as high as 55.8 percent in seven-year-olds (Liu et al., 2003), and in Korea 73.5 percent of mothers approve of bed sharing between three and six years of age (Yang & Hahn, 2002).

The parent–child relationship and its effect on the development of dependence, independence, or interdependence can also be viewed within the framework of Erikson's psychosocial theory. According to Erikson's model, which, as we have cautioned, tends to present a predominantly Westernized perspective, social maturation during the first year of infancy is reflected in the development of a feeling of *trust versus mistrust* (e.g., the world is good and comfortable—trust—or threatening and uncomfortable—mistrust). Whichever view develops will depend largely on the parent–infant relationship. For example, many infants learn to trust that if they cry because they are hungry, someone will pick them up and feed them. Parents, on the other hand, learn to trust that their infants will be quieted and comforted when they are fed because the pattern of interaction is consistent.

Similar patterns develop near the end of infancy (during the second and third year) with regard to the second crisis of *autonomy versus shame and doubt*. For example, either children will begin to explore their surroundings on their own (sometimes getting into trouble) and decide for themselves what they want to wear, eat, or do, or they will obediently fol- low the demands of parents and develop doubts about their abilities and feel incapable of making decisions and governing their own behavior.

If we look at trust and independence, as illustrated in the Kipsigis and Japanese examples mentioned earlier, the Western bias inherent in Erikson's theory becomes obvious. In these cultural contexts, social mat- uration is not associated with increased independence but rather with increased interdependence within the family. In both cultures, infants first develop trust and attachment as a result of sleeping with parents. Some degree of autonomy in Kipsigi infants is achieved when breastfeeding ends, and the older child is moved from the mother's front to her back to accommodate the arrival of a new baby. In the Japanese culture, in which a mother sleeps with the child for an even longer period, interdependence would appear to be even stronger than in Kipsigi society. Consideration of these examples strongly suggests that we may need to make adaptations in Erikson's theory when attempting to apply it in another cultural context.

Japanese children often sleep with their parents for the first several years.
(© Inmagine/Alamy)

The practice of **co-sleeping** (*a child sleeping with the parent*) is, in fact, routine in most of the world's cultures, and was the practice in the United States until shortly after the beginning of the twentieth cen- tury. Studies have suggested that the United States and other parts of North America are nearly alone in their expectation that children sleep in their own beds, in their own rooms, apart from their parents (McKenna, 2002). The well-known pedi- atrician Benjamin Spock, to whom generations of American parents have turned for advice on raising their children, stated that "it's a sensible rule not to take a child into the parents' bed for any reason" (Spock & Rothenberg, 1992, p. 213). Super and Harkness (1982), on the other hand, have suggested that the expectation that infants will be able to sleep through the night without some contact or involvement with parents may be "pushing the limits of infants' adaptability" (p. 52). In a study of children in India, aged three to ten years, it was reported that 93 percent of them were co-sleeping (Bharti, Malhi, & Kashyap, 2006). Again, we see the importance of cultural as well as individual and familial differences in the determina- tion of a particular behavior such as sleep patterns. Where did you sleep when you were an infant—in your parents' bed, in a nearby crib, or in a separate room? If you are married and have children of your own, where do they sleep?

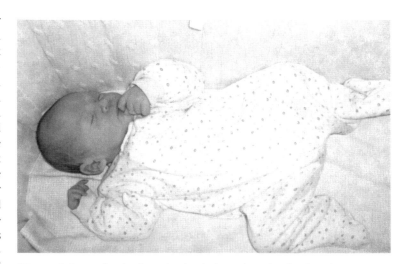

Western infants often begin to develop independence by sleeping alone in their cribs.
(Courtesy of authors)

When considering sleep practices among parents in different cultures, it may not be the specific practice itself but rather the cultural context and values that are the most important consideration. This view supports the ecological and developmental niche themes expressed throughout this book and leads us to another basic infant need requiring socialization—feeding.

Feeding

When infants are not sleeping, much of their time is spent eating. Just ask any new parent! How, what, and when to feed a child is another socialized behavior heavily influenced by the develop- mental niche, social context, parental beliefs, and values of one's culture.

Children need adequate nutrition, before birth as well as during infancy, if they are to grow properly and develop into healthy children and adults. The first two to three years are critical for physical development of the brain. The effects of nutritional deficiencies in infancy can be carried into adulthood and even affect another generation in terms of a mother's poor diet, inability to carry a baby to full term, or delivery of a low-birth-weight infant. According to figures gathered by the United Nations International Children's Emergency Fund (UNICEF) and released in *The State of the World's Children 2009* report, more than 150 million children in developing countries under the age of five are malnourished. This malnutrition contributes to more than half of the nearly 12 million under-five deaths occurring in developing countries each year. This number reflects both good and bad news in the fight against malnutrition. On the positive side, there are fewer malnourished children than a decade ago. However, progress varies significantly among cultural regions. For example, in Latin America and the Caribbean, percentages have declined and are under 10 percent while numbers have actually increased in Africa.

Malnutrition can have an impact on an individual's resistance to disease, as well as normal development of intellectual or cognitive abilities. In fact, Pollitt, Gorman, Engle, Martorell, and Rivera (1993), in a study conducted in Guatemala, report finding a link between inadequate nutrition in infancy and cognitive functioning in adolescence, notably among those living in poor socioeconomic circumstances. In a study among low-income Nicaraguan mothers, findings revealed a clear relationship between maternal beliefs about infant feeding and a child's nutritional level during the first year (Engle, Zeitlin, Medrano, & Garcia, 1996). The authors conclude their study by stating that "behavioral encouragement to eat as observed here did not reflect the sense of responsibility of the mother about feeding [and that] . . . further work is needed to determine the ways in which mothers translate their belief in helping children to eat into feeding behaviors" (p. 443). On the positive side, UNICEF reported that more than 300,000 children were saved from malnutrition in Niger in 2005, but that long-term programs were needed to address the issue.

For a long time, mothers around the world have been told that breastfeeding is the ideal method for providing nourishment to babies. The reasons most frequently mentioned include the fact that breast milk is more easily digested than other types of milk (e.g., milk from goats or cows), it protects against disease by providing natural immunization, and it is (obviously) immediately available. In most non-Western cultures, it is the method most preferred by mothers and strongly encouraged by WABA (World Alliance for Breastfeeding Action), a global network that sponsors World Breastfeeding Week each year and has a Web site containing a large number of resources (http://www.waba.org.my).

It should be noted that recent findings suggest that long-term breastfeeding may have additional benefits for the mother as well (e.g., significantly reducing the risk of developing type 2 diabetes). Using data from two Nurses' Health Studies of more than 150,000 women who had given birth, Steube and her colleagues (2005) found a 15 percent decrease in risk for each year of breastfeeding in the first study and 14 percent decrease in the second. Although not able to explain precisely how breastfeeding may help to protect mothers against diabetes, they suggest it improves insulin sensitivity and glucose tolerance and may help maintain blood sugar balance.

As you might expect, cultural attitudes play a significant role in whether babies are breastfed or bottlefed (Baumslag & Michaels, 2008). Some cultures, many of them in the West, tend to make a woman feel embarrassed about engaging in this natural function in public. When mothers return to work shortly after their child's birth, as many tend to do in North American and European countries, they may be unable to continue breastfeeding. On the other hand, if bottlefeeding is the method of choice, more fathers are able to participate in feeding and bonding with their infants. The United Nations estimates that improved breastfeeding practices could save the lives of almost 1.5 million children a year. Unfortunately, few of the 129 million infants born each year receive optimal breastfeeding (e.g., breast milk with no other foods or liquids for the first six months of life, followed by breast milk and solid or semisolid foods from about six months of age on, and continued breastfeeding for up to at least two years of age along with complementary foods), and some babies are not breastfed at all (UNICEF, 2001). In fact, in 2005, UNICEF stressed that the world had a major opportunity to reduce the toll of HIV/AIDS on infants by supporting exclusive breastfeeding.

At this point, we would like to emphasize that research findings have not yet clearly demonstrated that one method has long-term benefits over the other. If both options are equally available, we would support the opinion of most experts and recommend breastfeeding for the reasons mentioned above. However, we stress that the method is not as important as what happens during the feeding process. The feeding situation provides an excellent opportunity, through socialization, for parents to establish an emotional connection with their infant (attachment or bonding) that has been shown to have important implications for interpersonal relationships throughout the remainder of the lifespan. (For an excellent overview of this topic, see Virginia Colin's 1996 book.)

As one moves through the lifespan, these early cultural experiences with food strongly influence what, when, and how much an individual will eat. For example, which would you rather eat right now—a hamburger with French fries, a bowl of rice with spicy flavored beef, snake on crackers, octopus, grasshoppers, or (perhaps)—after hearing these choices—nothing? Depending on your cultural training, the mention of any one of these meals might make you hungry or completely suppress your desire to eat. While hunger and the feeding process begin biologically, they are individually socialized by cognition, learning, and experiential factors deeply rooted in the culture and often within the immediate family. As with other behaviors, eating preferences may show greater variability within families or within cultural subgroups than they do across cultures. For an interesting ethnographic perspective on cultural food practices in an increasingly globalized world, see Watson and Caldwell (2005).

Crying

All babies cry. But what does their crying mean, and is it responded to in the same or similar way in all cultures? Crying is the newborn's earliest form of communication with those in its immediate surroundings—the world of the micro- and mesosystems. Through crying, a baby lets others know that it is hungry, is not feeling well, has a wet diaper, wants attention, would like its older brother to stop annoying it, or conveys other information about its condition. In a sense, when newborns and infants cry, they are bringing their parents and others into their world and socializing them into understanding what their feelings are when they have no other way of expressing them. Although most parents in diverse cultures around the world can clearly differentiate these cries and distinguish one from another, it is almost impossible to teach this skill to others; experience seems to be the best teacher.

In addition, studies have shown that infants with various disorders (cystic fibrosis, Down syndrome, and others) cry differently than normal babies, and that individuals across cultures can recognize and differentiate among these various cries (Barr, Hopkins, & Green, 2000). Studies have also shown that mothers can discriminate different types of crying in low-birth-weight premature and full-term infants (Worchel & Allen, 1997), that cry analysis can successfully detect effects of prenatal alcohol exposure in newborn infants who do not show clinical signs of abnormality (Zeskind, Platzman, Coles, & Schuetze, 1996), and that crying among hearing-impaired infants differs from those with normal hearing abilities due to the lack of auditory feedback (Moeller & Schoenweiler, 1999). In an important development, Green, Irwin, and Gustafson (2000) have started to synthesize findings from several approaches into a framework that one day could be used to relate crying to early health and development. We know that fathers and other males respond in as nurturing a way to an infant's crying as do mothers and other women.

When and how often should a caregiver respond to a child's crying? If it is responded to frequently, will the child be spoiled? If crying is ignored, will insecurity be the result? These are difficult questions, and not all experts agree on the answers. In general, crying should be responded to frequently, especially during the first year and will not result in spoiling but rather will greatly assist in promoting secure attachment. In terms of Erikson's theory, frequent responding to crying appears to promote attachment as well as assist in resolving the crisis of trust versus mistrust mentioned earlier.

◇ CHILDHOOD

When we use the term **childhood,** we are referring to *the period extending from the end of infancy, about one and a half to two years of age, to just before the beginning of adolescence, typically about the age of eleven or twelve,* depending on the particular culture.

Edwards (1996), in a discussion of the parenting of toddlers, has outlined the developmental tasks she believes children are confronted with during their second and third years. We view each of these as an area of behavior in need of socialization. These include, but are not limited to, learning to function independently or interdependently to become a functioning member of a society, developing the beginnings of a self-concept, understanding sex roles and establishing gender identity, developing a moral conscience and the handling of aggressive behavior, and taking a place in the larger family grouping.

Some children experience difficulties and get "hung up" in the transition between childhood and adolescence.
(© Joe Oppedisano)

When older children enter elementary school, they come under the influence of two very different socialization agents—teachers and peers. In the school setting, the socialization process teaches children more about themselves (their personalities, abilities, and roles) and how to develop social relationships with adults who are not their relatives (teachers) and peers (other students), as well as ways to master some of the challenges of everyday life.

For the remainder of this section, let us consider the effects of socialization on formal and informal learning, as well as academic achievement in classroom settings.

Formal Versus Informal Learning

Most of the socialization experiences of children in nonindustrialized countries take place in informal settings (e.g., within the family or among peers and siblings) and are a fundamental part of one's daily activities. **Informal learning** is not characterized by a defined curriculum and is *generally picked up by means of observation and imitation*. According to Cushner (1990), "The responsibility for learning falls mainly on the learner, making it rather personal, with extended family members often playing a critical role in the act of instruction. . . . Change, discontinuity, and innovation are highly valued" (p. 100). For example, in certain African and South American tribal groups, young boys learn hunting and fishing skills as well as methods for navigating their way through jungles and rivers by observing and imitating adult males in their culture. Girls learn cooking and child care techniques, not in school, but by helping their mothers, aunts, and other women in the daily activities of family and village life. Traditions change very little in some cultures; this is the way it has been for centuries and the way it is almost certain to be long into the future. Some of these skills are also informally taught to American children—how many of you have gone hunting or fishing with one of your parents or have helped prepare meals at home? (For a taxonomy of three types of informal learning—self-directed, incidental, and socialization—see Schugurensky, 2000.)

In other countries, as well as the United States, the majority of children learn important cultural skills as part of their society's formal education system. As Cushner (1990) points out, **formal learning** is *"set apart from the context of everyday life and is typically carried out in the institution we know as school [and is characterized by] . . . an explicit and highly structured curriculum [in which] . . . material is learned from a book that may or may not be useful at a later time"* (p. 100). For a particularly insightful discussion of the failures of formal schooling in African societies, see Serpell's (1993) work on Zambia.

The issue of formal versus informal schooling gives us another opportunity to look at the two crises Erikson says are characteristic of the stage of childhood. As shown in Table 3 on page 55, these are *initiative versus guilt* and *industry versus inferiority*. To put these crises into perspective, let us consider the case of Tamiko and Alexina. Tamiko, aged ten, lives and goes to school in Akita, Japan. Like most children in her country, her success or failure depends more on her effort and character than on her innate ability. She is learning and working productively and harmoniously in mixed-ability groups similar to what she will encounter when she is an adult. Cooperation is seen as essential to the success of the group as well as the individual, and formal instruction occurs with this in mind. In this case, the developmental niche in which early learning takes place will share certain characteristics with the adult niche in which Tamiko will later live and work. The Japanese believe that parents and teachers must coordinate their efforts so that there is a high level of contact between the school and the home throughout a child's formal schooling. For Tamiko and her parents, academic work comes before everything else and involves long hours of study. There is a Japanese expression—"Pass with four, fail with five"—referring to how many hours of sleep are needed in order to succeed.

Tamiko's education actually began prior to entering formal preschool when her mother taught her to read, write, and perform simple mathematics. She spends more hours in school each year than almost any other children anywhere else in the world. This includes her regular classes, followed by several hours in a "juku" (cram school), and finally studying and doing homework at home until the early morning hours. While the latter is not formal in the strict sense of the word, it is nevertheless very serious and regimented. Alexina, also ten years old, lives in Minnesota in the Midwestern part of the United States and is equally serious about her education. However, in her case the focus is more on independence and self-expression. She has learned that autonomy and individual achievement are valued over group collaboration. Getting ahead is a personal goal, as characterized by Alexina's ability to take the initiative to complete assignments on her own.

As with Tamiko, there will be a certain consistency between the values and behaviors present in the developmental niches of childhood and adulthood. Unlike the Japanese, Americans believe that education is to be provided in the school, not in the home. This again points out the distinction between formal and informal schooling mentioned earlier. If you think about the opening module vignettes, Kamuzu's educational experience, while not as rich in opportunities, would be similar in many ways to that of Tamiko (e.g., more cooperative or group learning and more informal home schooling). Jeremy, like Alexina, would be expected to show greater independence, autonomy, and self-expression. Again, in the case of Jeremy and Kamuzu, we observe more variability in their individual educational experiences within the South African culture than we do between the experiences of Jeremy in his culture and Alexina in the United States.

How might we apply Erikson's model and resolution of crises to these four children? In Tamiko's case, *initiative* and *industry* are achieved only after successfully recognizing the need for others to assist in the learning process. The same is somewhat less true in Kamuzu's situation, because his school is underfunded and he had to learn more in the informal settings of his home and community. In Alexina's case, industry is achieved when she is able to take initiative independently and become a "self-starter." Her success in this area is reflected in her school report card, which has a category for "industriousness." In this respect, Jeremy behaves similarly to Alexina. In short, Alexina's culture and Jeremy's subculture view initiative and industry in independent terms, whereas Tamiko's culture and Kamuzu's subculture, to a lesser extent, look at these qualities in interdependent terms. Again, when applying Erikson's theory to non-Western cultures, it is of crucial importance to consider the relevance and cultural definitions of his concepts (e.g., independence and autonomy, initiative and industry). If this is not done, a researcher is liable to make serious misinterpretations of cultural behavior.

Let us close this discussion with an interesting example of informal math learning among some of Brazil's more than two-hundred thousand "Mennios de Rua" and Columbia's "Gamines" or "Chupagruesos"—street children. Many of these children survive by selling fruits and vegetables on street corners. Most of them dropped out of school by the time they were ten, before learning good math skills. Although they conduct scores of informal financial transactions each day without making a mistake, the majority of them are unable to complete a formal, written math problem requiring them to calculate change (not unlike what they do every day) without making numerous errors. Their school (ecological setting) is the street, and it is here that they have been socialized and have learned functional math skills that allow them to survive in the street culture of large Latin American cities where they live. For an interesting discussion of these different cultural practices and the advantages and disadvantages of each, see the book *Street Mathematics and School Mathematics* by Nunes, Schliemann, and Carraher (1993).

◇ ADOLESCENCE

We know that adolescence begins in biology, when hormones that bring about physical changes and prepare the body for sexual reproduction are released into the bloodstream. But adolescent development ends in culture, where one's status is defined by the new role played in society and the transition to adulthood begins. From an ecological or cultural contextual perspective, adolescence is seen as a developmental stage in some, but not all, cultures. According to Cole and Cole (1996), its distinctiveness as a stage depends in large measure on whether "young people reach biological maturity before they have acquired the knowledge and skills needed to ensure cultural reproduction" (p. 629). For example, in the United States and Canada, there sometimes are young adolescents (ages twelve and above) with children of their own who, without a job or educational training, are totally incapable of providing for the welfare of their children or of themselves. Contrast this with the !Kung San living in the Kalahari Desert in Botswana and parts of Namibia and South Africa. Even before reaching the years of adolescence, older children have learned through socialization to hunt animals and gather wild plants as part of their nomadic life. They, like their North American counterparts, are biologically capable of reproduction but already know their developmental niche and have the skills to economically support themselves and a family if necessary.

Adolescence provides another opportunity to dramatically illustrate how the major themes of this book can be used to describe and explain how cultures structure and teach the kinds of activities that Cole and Cole (1996) say need to be mastered in order to "carry out the full process of human reproduction [and how these] . . . shape the psychological characteristics that one develops at the end of childhood" (p. 629). It is at this point in the lifespan that we can again clearly observe the development of "lives across cultures." For example, compare two fourteen-year-old girls growing up in cultures separated by both time and space. Mankushai is a member of the Masai tribe and lives on a flat grassy plain in southern Kenya. Her days are spent in her husband's village working side by side with her mother-in-law cooking and taking care of her young daughter, Consolata. Far away, in the United States, in California, Alisa spends her days in school studying chemistry, calculus, and world history so that she will be able to attend college and prepare for a career as an economist. Each lives in a developmental niche within an ecological system, surrounded by family, peers, and teachers, learning her culture's values, and being socialized into an adult role. But how different their lives are and how different they will continue to be as they move through the lifespan.

Before leaving this topic, let us consider the socialization process from the perspective of immigrants and how they sometimes give up many of the values and customs of their native culture and take on those of their adopted culture, and the effects this might have on their behavior. This can be seen in studies involving first- and second-generation American Chinese adolescents who were compared with Chinese adolescents from Hong Kong, others whose parents had immigrated to Australia, and to European and Anglo Australian adolescents. For example, Chiu, Feldman, and Rosenthal (1992) found that first- and second-generation Chinese American adolescents, in terms of their adolescent problems and the severity of them, were similar to nonimmigrant adolescents. On the other hand, immigration appeared to result in reduced perceptions of parental control, which was unrelated to adolescents' views of their parents' warmth toward them. However, across generations, Chinese American adolescents were found to place less value on the family as a "residential unit," consistent with the values expressed by European and Anglo-Australian adolescents, yet the authors indicated that they still differed from the other groups on this particular value.

Much of an adolescent's time is again spent in the school setting where he or she come under the influence of even more socialization agents, such as involvement in various school organizations, music activities, or sports endeavors. During this period, at least part of their development will be influenced by the presence or absence of rites of passage.

Rites of Passage

In many cultures, the transition from childhood to adolescence is marked by some sort of public recognition. Called **rites of passage,** these are *ceremonies or rituals that recognize or symbolize an individual's movement from one status to another.* These "coming-of-age" experiences vary significantly from one culture to another but, according to a study by Schlegal and Barry (1991), are found in most nonindustrialized societies where nearly 80 percent of girls and close to 70 percent of boys go through some form of initiation.

In eastern Africa, ten- to twelve-year-old boys in the Kaguru tribe are led into the bush, stripped of all clothing, and ritually circumcised while being taught the sexual practices of adulthood by male members of the community. Later, they return to their village, are celebrated at a large feast, receive new names, and are expected to become responsible adult members of their society (Beidelman, 1997). Passage for a Kaguru girl is not as complex as for boys and occurs when she experiences first menstruation and is taught the ways of womanhood by her grandmother or older women in the tribe. She is fortunate in escaping the very painful and widespread practice of female genital surgery (called "circumcision" by some and "female genital mutilation" by others) already experienced by an estimated 100 to 140 million girls and women in twenty-eight countries in Africa, India, the Middle East, and Southeast Asia, a procedure that has no health benefits and is internationally recognized as a violation of human rights (WHO, 2008). The practice is legally outlawed in only three countries—Belgium, Sweden, and the United Kingdom. For more on the prevalence and effects of these practices, see Okedu, Rembe, and Anwo (2009).

The transition from adolescence to adulthood in North America and many other Western countries is not marked by such clearly defined rituals. In fact, many would say there are no true rites of passage experienced by all members of these societies at this particular stage in the lifespan, and if there ever were, they have disappeared. Among certain ethnic groups within the larger society, there may be some commonly experienced ceremonies, such as the Bar or Bat Mitzvah for Jewish boys and girls, that may come close to being a rite of passage. On the other hand, while not experienced by all adolescents at the same time, or by many at all, the following are frequently mentioned as *possible* rites of passage in North American society: graduation from high school or college, successfully passing a driver's test, marriage, or the first job. The lack of commonly accepted rites of passage in these societies may be attributed, in part, to a lack of conformity in developmental niches; for example, two families living next to each other may have significantly different backgrounds, cultural origins, ethnicity, values, and traditions than those found in more homogeneous societies.

Age certainly is not a very helpful marker in cultures like the United States since there are several criteria by which individuals are considered adults (e.g., age sixteen for driving, eighteen for voting, and twenty-one for drinking). American adolescents, and their counterparts in many other countries, often linger in a "cultural limbo" between the ages of twelve to the early twenties when they may (or may not) one day be considered adults.

An exception to the comments made above is the **Vision Quest,** an experience common to many of the more than 500 culturally diverse Native American tribes in North America. Performed primarily as a rite of passage for adolescent males, it begins with the taking of a boy, aged fourteen or fifteen, into a "sweat lodge," where his body and spirit are purified by the heat given off by burning cedar. Sitting with the boy is a medicine man who advises him and assists him with ritual prayers. Later, he is taken to an isolated location and left alone to fast for four days. He prays, contemplates the words of the medicine man, and waits for a vision that will reveal to him his path in life as a member of his tribal culture (Delaney, 1995). As another example, Navajo girls at the time of menarche take part in a rite of passage that involves morning running and the baking of a ceremonial cake.

It is clear from this discussion that different cultures treat their young people very differently. Some provide a clearly defined niche within the microsystem of the family where the parents, elders, and others initiate and prepare their young people to move into the wider realms of the mesosystem, exosystem, and macrosystem and to deal with the challenges and opportunities available to them as recognized adults. Other cultures, such as many Western societies, could do more to prepare their young people for the often difficult transition to adulthood.

In discussing rites of passage, it is important to keep in mind that each culture uses these as a way of helping its adolescents arrive at an understanding of their **identity,** or s*elf-definition as a separate individual in terms of roles, attitudes, beliefs, and values.* In the case of the Kaguru mentioned earlier, adult male identity is achieved when young boys undergo circumcision, and adult female identity is attained when young girls experience their first menstruation. Identity and adulthood are defined and achieved in terms of tribal customs and beliefs. In North American societies, identity is achieved when adolescents demonstrate some measure of independence, initiative, and industriousness although these qualities are not always clearly defined.

The differences between these cultures can be considered in terms of Erikson's fifth crisis—*identity versus role confusion.* Failure to achieve identity in these cultures results in what Erikson refers to as role confusion. The difficulty in terms of this crisis lies in how each culture defines identity and marks the onset of adulthood. In many respects, achievement of identity is less ambiguous in traditional, nonindustrialized societies because rites of passage are clearly defined and adolescents know what is expected of them in order to become an adult. Conversely, in many industrialized societies, true rites of passage (which apply to all members of a given society) do not exist; consequently, there is ambiguity in how identity is defined and achieved. The result is that many adolescents do not know who they are or how they are supposed to behave as adults.

Some theorists and researchers imply that Erikson's theory also applies to preindustrial societies. However, when used to explain such behaviors as identity versus role confusion, the theory contains Western biases (e.g., viewing successful identity achievement as rooted in autonomous judgments). For an extended discussion of identity formation, see Module 8-A.

◇ ADULTHOOD

Developmentalists have historically devoted most of their attention to the earlier part of the lifespan, particularly the years from birth through adolescence. As a result, there is a great deal of research; many findings; and a host of theories describing, explaining, and predicting the events during the first two decades of life. A similar situation applies to cross-cultural human development: only recently have the last three quarters of the lifespan received serious attention. Even so, treatment of topics has been sparse and inconsistent (Zarit & Eggebeen, 2002). Cole and Cole (1993) explain it well: "Since psychologists are sharply divided over the relative roles of biology and culture in the process of development, it is only natural that they should be sharply divided on the question of whether development continues into adulthood and old age" (p. 656).

We know from casual observation that the experience of adulthood varies dramatically across and even within cultures and depends on a variety of factors, including age, gender, socioeconomic status, occupation, family structure, and timing of life events (e.g., marriage, parenthood, grandparenthood, and retirement).

Many psychologists (whose research you will become familiar with in subsequent modules) have paid little attention to developmental changes, including socialization, after adolescence. For example, G. Stanley Hall, who wrote the first book on adolescence in 1904, believed that senescence (old age) began shortly after adolescence ended, generally when one reached the late thirties or early forties (Hall, 1904, 1922). Of course, he based this assumption partly on the fact that life expectancy was much shorter at that time. Jean Piaget, in his theory of cognitive development, proposed that individuals reached the final stage of formal operations during their late adolescence or early adulthood years. Only recently have attempts been made to explain cognitive changes in later adulthood, through the establishment of a stage of post-formal operations.

Two psychologists who did attribute significant developmental changes to the years of adulthood, and some of whose ideas have been subjected to cross-cultural examination, are Lev Vygotsky and Erik Erikson. Vygotsky, a Russian psychologist and one of the founders of the cultural-historical viewpoint, made some of the earliest contributions to our understanding of cognitive development within social settings, or cultures. (His ideas, many of which are similar to those expressed in our major themes, were introduced in Module 2-A.) Erikson, as we have previously noted, is one of a small number of theorists who emphasize cultural and social development across the entire lifespan, separating the years following adolescence into early, middle, and later adulthood. It is in this area that his views coincide most closely with those of the ecological, or cultural context, approach. Limited findings from anthropological, sociological, and cross-cultural studies, particularly those looking at adolescence, tend to support his theoretical assumptions but, as we have previously emphasized, may have to be modified to explain cross-cultural differences.

During early adulthood (early twenties to mid-thirties), in cultures throughout the world, a majority of adults are dealing with the crisis of *intimacy versus isolation* (see Table 3 on page 55). Decisions are made about establishing a close, intimate relationship with another person, or individuals go their way alone and fail to achieve an intimate relationship.

Lefrancois's comment (1996) that age ranges be used only as descriptive guidelines is relevant here in terms of the cultural example we provided in the section on adolescence. Confronting the crisis of intimacy versus isolation usually requires that the individual has achieved a sense of identity, probably is self-supporting, and is involved in a long-term and interdependent relationship. With this in mind, consider fourteen-year-old Mankushai of the Masai tribe in Kenya, East Africa, mentioned earlier. Mankushai lives in her husband's village, cooks his meals, and takes care of her daughter, Consolata. Except for her age, she would appear to be in the stage of early adulthood. What about other cultures, like those parts of India where child marriages are common? In which stage do we put these individuals? Compared with earlier stages of development, there is less cross-cultural research on this stage and the crisis contained within it. This raises additional questions and problems about applying this theory beyond Western societies. We clearly need more critical analysis of ideas and concepts, as well as additional research to extend the cross-cultural usefulness of theories such as these.

When one reaches middle adulthood (mid-thirties to mid-sixties), a new crisis appears that involves *generativity versus stagnation* (see Table 3 on page 55). Middle-aged adults make work and career decisions, raise children, and show concern by guiding the next generation, or they become stagnant, self-absorbed, and self-centered. Some of our earlier comments regarding the role parents play in socialization would appear to be relevant here. It is through socialization within their ecological settings that individuals have the kinds of experiences that help them as adults find a balance between their self-interests and the interests of others. Unfortunately, as with some other areas, there is a lack of cross-cultural findings related to this stage crisis; the need for additional theorizing and research is clear. For the latest in contemporary thinking and research on the psychological, social, and cultural aspects of generativity in the lives of adults, see de St. Aubin, McAdams, and Kim (2003).

Finally, looking once again at socialization, it is in this period of adulthood, as individuals move into the working world, that "globalization" and a clear understanding of cross-cultural differences in business practices become increasingly important. In certain occupations and careers, employees must be socialized to operate within a global organizational culture, or they will not be successful. In addition, some people form relationships with, and often marry, mates from different cultures. In such situations, they encounter differences in the assumptions and values in their own socialization and confront decisions about how they will socialize and raise their own children in multicultural and multiethnic contexts. For insight into the challenges and rewards of a multicultural childhood and its effects on personal identity, see the book *Third Culture Kids* by Pollock and Van Rekn (2001).

◇ LATE ADULTHOOD

During the last period in the lifespan (mid-sixties and after), older adults find themselves dealing with the crisis of *integrity versus despair* (see Table 3 on page 55). According to Erikson, when individuals reach this stage they tend to reflect on their lives. Either they find that they are generally happy and satisfied with their choices, having fulfilled many of their goals and having made their best efforts (integrity), or they find themselves filled with despair over missed opportunities or mistakes made, which leaves them unhappy and dissatisfied. Think about your aging relatives—parents, grandparents, great grandparents (if you are fortunate to have them), aunts, uncles, and others, and even talk with them. How do they view these years of late adulthood? Are they happy or unhappy? What concerns do they have?

Cultural Views of Aging

What role does culture play in shaping the ecological setting in which we age and how we are socialized as older members of the society? We hypothesize that the outcome of the integrity vs. despair crisis of late adulthood might often be negative in some Western societies, which place great emphasis on economic and career success and in which nuclear families are the norm. In these cultures, parents or other relatives in their later years are sometimes seen as burdens to be moved from the microsystem of the family to rest homes in the mesosystem or exosystem. In societies in which young people enjoy the greatest status, the elderly are more often rejected. Contemporary North American society is currently such a society, but given rapid increases in its older population, the ecological setting will soon undergo dramatic changes. An ecological setting that focuses on youth rather than age places an older person in a developmental niche, where either they have few contributions to make or their contributions are not highly valued. In these circumstances, individuals might well feel despair and regret about the past and a real fear of aging.

Contrast this with an Asian, South American, or African culture, in which intergenerational families are the norm and older relatives are looked after by their family or by the village community. Family members look to them as wise and knowledgeable members of the society with much to offer. Rather than attempting to push back the aging process and appear young, many look forward to aging.

People are living longer than ever before, many over the age of one hundred. In fact, several remote areas of the world have become known for having large numbers of people who live unusually long lives. In parts of China, senescence is postponed well into late adulthood, and a disciplined, highly active lifestyle is routine. Some commonly cited reasons for longevity include diet (lots of fresh vegetables, little meat and fat), mutual interdependence, family and neighborhood cohesiveness, and regular exercise. The ecological system is set up to socialize aging individuals as functional members of society well into old age. Contemporary North America, in contrast, is currently not such a society, but given rapid increases in its older population, the ecological setting might soon undergo dramatic changes. What is important to remember is that each culture has its own beliefs about growing old and what roles older people play in society.

It is interesting to note that when Erikson reached the eighth decade of his life, he reviewed his theory and suggested that increases in life expectancy might require a rethinking of his ideas, especially those related to development during adulthood (Erikson, Erikson, & Kivnik, 1986). We encourage others to begin this careful rethinking and, in the process, attempt to apply these new ideas to cross-cultural human development.

◇ SUMMARY

It should be clear after reading this module that universally accepted generalizations about the complex relationships among family, culture, and socialization are sometimes difficult. Numerous variables contribute to cultural differences, including cultural contexts, societal beliefs and values, individual views of children and their place in society, rural versus urban living, family structure, and parenting styles, to mention only a few. However, cross-cultural research on human development also shows that we are gaining a much better understanding of the significant role culture plays in socialization at all levels, from birth through the last years of the lifespan. Traditional, primarily Western, theoretical explanations of human development are, in large part, obsolete and were never very accurate when transported to other cultures in an effort to describe, explain, and predict behavior for which they were never intended.

You are reading this at a time when many societies are undergoing dramatic change in the way they and their family structures operate. In China, the "one-child policy" is having striking effects on traditional family practices; in the former Soviet Union, political and social changes are affecting parental goals and behavior; in Sweden, children's rights have taken center stage; in the United States, high divorce and remarriage rates and large numbers of working mothers are reshaping family relationships. In countries throughout the world, we have seen major changes in the roles played by children and their parents, and yet, as Roopnarine and Carter (1992a) have pointed out, "Perceptions of children and how a culture manages to mesh those perceptions with children's own birthright and value to members of a society, its rituals, functions, and expectations, are not well understood" (p. 251). We have only started the journey toward understanding; much lies ahead of us.

◇ STUDY QUESTIONS

Define the term *socialization*, and explain its importance to understanding cross-cultural human development.

Discuss the components of the developmental niche, and give examples from your own experience.

Explain what is meant by *rites of passage* and the role they play in adolescent identity.

◇ FURTHER READINGS

Naomi Baumslag & Dia L. Michels. (2008). *Milk, Money, and Madness: The Culture and Politics of Breastfeeding.* Santa Barbara, CA: Praeger.
>   The authors convincingly present the medical, cultural, psychological, and economic benefits of breastfeeding to mothers, infants, and the general population. A fascinating, informative, and highly readable book.

Jude Cassidy & Philip R. Shaver (Eds.). (2008). *Handbook of Attachment* (2nd ed.). New York: Guilford Press.
>   Cutting-edge theory and research findings on attachment across a wide range of ages and contexts. An indispensable guide for understanding this crucial developmental process.

Joan E. Grusec & Paul D. Hastings (Eds.). (2006). *Handbook of Socialization.* New York: Guilford Press.
>   Almost all you want to know about socialization, including historical and methodological perspectives; its effects across the lifespan (within and outside the family); and relationship to gender, cognition, emotional competence, and prosocial development.

John Loughery. (1995). *Into the Widening World: International Coming-of-Age Stories.* New York: Persea Books.
>   An edited anthology of twenty-six short stories from twenty-two countries focusing on the adolescent experience and emergence of adulthood. Visit the sun-baked alleys of Cairo, the terrifying forests of war-time Nigeria, a hidden grove in Jamaica, a turkey farm in Canada, a young woman facing an arranged marriage in Malaysia. Fascinating, insightful, and informative reading.

Dennis O'Neil. (2005). *Cultural Anthropology Tutorials.* http://anthro.palomar.edu/tutorials/cultural.htm.
>   This online Web site offers tutorials on a variety of topics related to socialization, including culture, language, social control, culture change, social and political organization, and processes of socialization.

◆ DEVELOPMENTAL ANALYSIS

SOCIALIZATION

My name is Matilda Skelton, but everyone—thankfully—calls me "Maddi." I was named for my great grandmother, who immigrated to the United States from England in 1847. I was born on September 17, 1938, in Elfville, Pennsylvania, a small farming community settled by Irish immigrants (population 1734). The town consisted of a feed and grain store, post office, small grocery store, Catholic Church, school, railroad depot, barber shop, gas station—and not much else! The person I am today was very much influenced by my early socialization experiences in Elfville and with my family. Let me explain.

In terms of my developmental niche, I lived in a rural setting, in a nuclear family, consisting of my two parents, a younger sister, and a younger brother. I spent my early years establishing relationships with members of my family and playmates. I learned to deal with feelings of dependence, independence, cooperation, and competition. My early caretakers were my parents, relatives, or other mothers in town. We didn't have a day care center or preschool when I was young—it was typical of the era for mothers to stay at home while raising their children.

As an infant, I slept in a crib in my parents' room for a couple of months and was then moved to my own room. I was breastfed for nine months. When I cried, my parents picked me up and comforted me. Like most American children, I was part of a formal school system. My siblings, friends, and I walked to a small school consisting of kindergarten through eighth grade, with most classes held together in the same room and taught by the same teacher. My parents and teachers worked together to ensure that I had a good education. I did chores on the farm and enjoyed learning about the animals. When I was fourteen, I began traveling eight miles by bus to attend high school; my ecological system was expanding. In terms of informal learning, my mother taught me to cook and take care of my siblings; my father taught me to drive a tractor and play a guitar. My parents were Catholic, although my mother took religion more seriously than my dad.

As I was entering adolescence during the 1950s, America was characterized by malt shops, Rock 'n' Roll Music, the hula hoop, and "hot" cars. Television was just arriving. At the same time, the nation was plagued by racial injustice, anti-Communist paranoia, and the fear of nuclear war. The closest event to a rite of passage for me was getting my driver's license at the age of sixteen. Like most of my friends, I struggled to establish an identity and often felt confused. After high school graduation in 1956, most of my girlfriends decided to be secretaries, teachers, or nurses.

I decided to go to college and chose an unusual major for girls at the time—business. My first contact with another culture was during my junior year, when I spent a semester in Italy. I was the first in my family to travel abroad or even outside Pennsylvania. It was a wonderful experience and really opened my eyes to the world. In 1962, I traveled to England for graduate work in economics. It was there that I met my future husband—Giorgio Carlo Conte—a student from Italy. He asked me to go out with him seven times before I finally accepted! Socialization can work in surprising (and wonderful) ways.

Giorgio and I were married on March 9, 1968, at my grandparents' home in Coudersport, Pennsylvania. We combined American and Italian traditions. We moved to Minnesota, where I was an economics professor at a wonderful liberal arts college. Giorgio worked at an international bank. Our daughter, Elizabeth Lucia, was born in 1969, and our son, Alexander Donato, was born in 1970. When they were young, we frequently traveled to Italy, so they could spend time with their grandparents and relatives.

I have many fond memories from my childhood, adolescence, and adulthood. I can recall our 1940 Chevrolet sedan; my dad serving in World War II; riding my bicycle to the grocery store; our icebox; a large Philco radio around which we would gather to listen to radio programs; visiting grandparents; and going to the movie theatre on Saturdays to see two films, two cartoons, news, and previews of coming attractions. For 25 cents you got all of this, a candy bar, and a bag of popcorn! Each of these experiences had a socializing effect on me in one way or another. I am now seventy-one years old and continue to go through socialization changes. I'll tell you more about this and other events in my life in the next module. Ciao for now!

Name: _____ Date: _____

MODULE 3-B

ACTIVITY

◇ CLEANLINESS BELIEFS

One of the complaints sojourners often have when they visit another culture is that cleanliness practices are not adequate. This activity will help you to explore your own cleanliness beliefs and put them in cross-cultural perspective.

Directions: For each of the items below, circle the number to indicate your cleanliness beliefs. Where space is provided, respond to the follow-up question.

1. People in my culture value cleanliness.

STRONGLY   STRONGLY
DISAGREE   AGREE

| 1 | 2 | 3 | 4 | 5 | 6 | 7 | 8 | 9 |

Please explain:

2. One should wash one's body before entering a bathtub full of clean water.

STRONGLY   STRONGLY
DISAGREE   AGREE

| 1 | 2 | 3 | 4 | 5 | 6 | 7 | 8 | 9 |

3. Blankets and rugs should be hung out daily to air.

STRONGLY   STRONGLY
DISAGREE   AGREE

| 1 | 2 | 3 | 4 | 5 | 6 | 7 | 8 | 9 |

Taken from *Cross-Cultural Explorations: Activities in Culture and Psychology,* Second Edition, by Susan Goldstein.

4. Shoes should be removed before entering a home.

STRONGLY
DISAGREE

STRONGLY
AGREE

| 1 | 2 | 3 | 4 | 5 | 6 | 7 | 8 | 9 |

5. The left hand should not be used for eating or taking food from communal dishes.

STRONGLY
DISAGREE

STRONGLY
AGREE

| 1 | 2 | 3 | 4 | 5 | 6 | 7 | 8 | 9 |

6. One should use a different washcloth and bar of soap to wash oneself above the waist and below the waist.

STRONGLY
DISAGREE

STRONGLY
AGREE

| 1 | 2 | 3 | 4 | 5 | 6 | 7 | 8 | 9 |

7. One should shower or bathe daily.

STRONGLY
DISAGREE

STRONGLY
AGREE

| 1 | 2 | 3 | 4 | 5 | 6 | 7 | 8 | 9 |

8. Cleaning products should be used in the home to kill germs.

STRONGLY
DISAGREE

STRONGLY
AGREE

| 1 | 2 | 3 | 4 | 5 | 6 | 7 | 8 | 9 |

9. Hands should be washed upon returning home.

STRONGLY
DISAGREE

STRONGLY
AGREE

| 1 | 2 | 3 | 4 | 5 | 6 | 7 | 8 | 9 |

10. One should not eat with one's hands.

STRONGLY
DISAGREE

STRONGLY
AGREE

| 1 | 2 | 3 | 4 | 5 | 6 | 7 | 8 | 9 |

11. One should blow one's nose into the gutter rather than carry the mucus in a cloth or tissue.

STRONGLY
DISAGREE

STRONGLY
AGREE

| 1 | 2 | 3 | 4 | 5 | 6 | 7 | 8 | 9 |

12. The toilet should not be located under the same roof as the place where people eat and prepare food or sleep.

STRONGLY
DISAGREE

STRONGLY
AGREE

| 1 | 2 | 3 | 4 | 5 | 6 | 7 | 8 | 9 |

Reactions:

1. Look over your answers to the questions above. With which cleanliness practices did you AGREE most strongly? What cultural messages were you taught that support these practices?

2. With which practices did you DISAGREE most strongly? What cultural messages were you taught that conflict with these practices?

3. What other cleanliness practices not listed above are important to you?

4. How might someone from another culture view your beliefs if they endorsed the practices with which you disagreed?

5. Look back at your response to item 1. Is there anything you would like to add or change in your answer?

◆ **REFERENCES**

Based on Fernea, E., & Fernea, R. A. (1994). Cleanliness and culture. In W. J. Lonner & R. S. Malpass (Eds.), *Psychology and culture* (pp. 65–70). Boston: Allyn & Bacon, and Waxler-Morrison, N., Anderson, J., & Richardson, E. (1990). *Cross-cultural caring: A handbook for health professionals in Western Canada*. Vancouver, BC: University of British Columbia Press.

SECTION 4

GENETIC FOUNDATIONS AND ENVIRONMENTAL CONTEXTS

MODULE 4-A

GENETIC AND ENVIRONMENTAL FOUNDATIONS

Reprinted with permission from the International Museum of Children's Art, Oslo, Norway

Untitled
Mohamed Salahedeen Abd Hamid
11 years, Egypt

A river flows past a city on one shore and a grassy bank on the other. Animals, birds, vehicles, and people are all part of the complexity of our world. Module 4-A addresses a similarly complex blend of forces—genetic, family, neighborhood, school, and culture—that influence child development.

Taken from *Infants and Children*, Seventh Edition, by Laura E. Berk.

"It's a girl!" announces the doctor, holding up the squalling newborn baby as her parents gaze with amazement at their miraculous creation.

"A girl! We've named her Sarah!" exclaims the proud father to eager relatives waiting for news of their new family member.

As we join these parents in thinking about how this wondrous being came into existence and imagining her future, we are struck by many questions. How could this baby, equipped with everything necessary for life outside the womb, have developed from the union of two tiny cells? What ensures that Sarah will, in due time, roll over, reach for objects, walk, talk, make friends, learn, imagine, and create—just like other typical children born before her? Why is she a girl and not a boy, dark-haired rather than blond, calm and cuddly instead of wiry and energetic? What difference will it make that Sarah is given a name and place in one family, community, nation, and culture rather than another?

To answer these questions, this module takes a close look at the foundations of development: heredity and environment. Because nature has prepared us for survival, all humans have features in common. Yet each of us is also unique. TAKE A MOMENT... Think about several children you know well, and jot down the most obvious physical and behavioral similarities between them and their parents. Did you find that one child shows combined features of both parents, another resembles just one parent, whereas a third is not like either parent? These directly observable characteristics are called **phenotypes**. They depend in part on the individual's **genotype**—the complex blend of genetic information that determines our species and influences all our unique characteristics. Yet phenotypes are also affected by each person's lifelong history of experiences.

We begin our discussion at the moment of conception, an event that establishes the hereditary makeup of the new individual. First we review basic genetic principles that help explain similarities and differences among children in appearance and behavior. Then we turn to aspects of the environment that play powerful roles in children's lives. As our discussion proceeds, some findings about the influence of nature and nurture may surprise you. For example, many people believe that when children inherit unfavorable characteristics, not much can be done to help them. Others are convinced that the damage done to a child by a harmful environment can easily be corrected. As we will see, neither of these assumptions is true. In the final section of this module, we consider how nature and nurture work together to shape the course of development.

❖ ❖ ❖

❖ GENETIC FOUNDATIONS

Each of us is made up of trillions of units called *cells*. Within every cell (except red blood cells) is a control center, or *nucleus*, that contains rodlike structures called **chromosomes**, which store and transmit genetic information. Human chromosomes come in 23 matching pairs (an exception is the XY pair in males, which we will discuss shortly). Each member of a pair corresponds to the other in size, shape, and genetic functions. One is inherited from the mother and one from the father (see Figure 1).

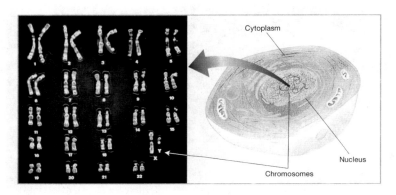

FIGURE 1 A Karyotype, or Photograph, of Human Chromosomes

The 46 chromosomes shown on the left were isolated from a human cell, stained, greatly magnified, and arranged in pairs according to decreasing size of the upper "arm" of each chromosome. The twenty-third pair, XY, reveals that the cell donor is a male. In a female, this pair would be XX.
(© CNRI/Science Photo Library/Photo Researchers, Inc.)

The Genetic Code

Chromosomes are made up of a chemical substance called **deoxyribonucleic acid** or **DNA**. As Figure 2 shows, DNA is a long, double-stranded molecule that looks like a twisted ladder. Each rung of the ladder consists of a pair of chemical substances called *bases*. Although the bases always pair up in the same way across the ladder rungs—A with T and C with G—they can occur in any order along its sides. It is this sequence of base pairs that provides genetic instructions. A **gene** is a segment of DNA along the length of the chromosome. Genes can be of different lengths—perhaps 100 to several thousand ladder rungs long. An estimated 20,000 to 25,000 genes lie along the human chromosomes (Human Genome Program, 2008).

We share some of our genetic makeup with even the simplest organisms, such as bacteria and molds, and most of it with other mammals, especially primates. Between 98 and 99 percent of chimpanzee and human DNA is identical. This means that only a small portion of our heredity is responsible for the traits that make us human, from our upright gait to our extraordinary language and cognitive capacities. And the genetic variation from one human to the next is even less! Individuals around the world are about 99.1 percent genetically identical (Gibbons, 1998; Gibbons et al., 2004). But it takes a change in only a single base pair to influence human traits. And such tiny changes can combine in unique ways across multiple genes, thereby amplifying variability within the human species.

A unique feature of DNA is that it can duplicate itself through a process called **mitosis**. This special ability permits the one-celled fertilized ovum to develop into a complex human being composed of a great many cells. Refer again to Figure 2, and you will see that during mitosis, the chromosomes copy themselves. As a result, each new body cell contains the same number of chromosomes and the identical genetic information.

Genes accomplish their task by sending instructions for making a rich assortment of proteins to the *cytoplasm,* the area surrounding the cell nucleus. Proteins, which trigger chemical reactions throughout the body, are the biological foundation on which our characteristics are built. How do humans, with far fewer genes than scientists once thought (only twice as many as the worm or fly), manage to develop into such complex beings? The answer lies in the proteins our genes make, which break up and reassemble in staggering variety—about 10 to 20 million altogether. Simpler species have far fewer proteins. Furthermore, the communication system between the cell nucleus and cytoplasm, which fine-tunes gene activity, is more intricate in humans than in simpler organisms. Within the cell, a wide range of environmental factors modify gene expression (Lashley, 2007). So even at this microscopic level, biological events are the result of *both* genetic and nongenetic forces.

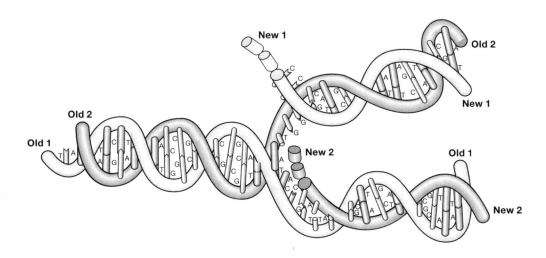

FIGURE 2 DNA's Ladderlike Structure

This figure shows that the pairings of bases across the rungs of the ladder are very specific: Adenine (A) always appears with thymine (T), and cytosine (C) always appears with guanine (G). Here, the DNA ladder duplicates by splitting down the middle of its ladder rungs. Each free base picks up a new complementary partner from the area surrounding the cell nucleus.

The Sex Cells

New individuals are created when two special cells called **gametes,** or sex cells—the sperm and ovum—combine. A gamete contains only 23 chromosomes, half as many as a regular body cell. Gametes are formed through a cell division process called **meiosis,** which halves the number of chromosomes normally present in body cells. When sperm and ovum unite at conception, the resulting cell, called a **zygote,** will again have 46 chromosomes. Meiosis ensures that a constant quantity of genetic material is transmitted from one generation to the next.

The steps involved in meiosis are shown in Figure 3. First, the chromosomes pair up, and each one copies itself. Then a special event called **crossing over** occurs, in which chromosomes next to each other break at one or more points along their length and exchange segments, so that genes from one are replaced by genes from another. This shuffling of genes creates new hereditary combinations. Next, the chromosome pairs separate into different cells, but chance determines which member of each pair will gather with others and end up in the same gamete. Finally, each chromosome leaves its partner and becomes part of a gamete containing only 23 chromosomes instead of the usual 46.

These events make the likelihood extremely low—about 1 in 700 trillion—that nontwin siblings will be genetically identical (Gould & Keeton, 1996). The genetic variability produced by meiosis is adaptive: Because it generates offspring that vary in phenotype, it increases the chances that at least some members of a species will cope successfully with ever-changing environments and will survive.

In the male, four sperm are produced when meiosis is complete. Also, the cells from which sperm arise are produced continuously throughout life. For this reason, a healthy man can father a

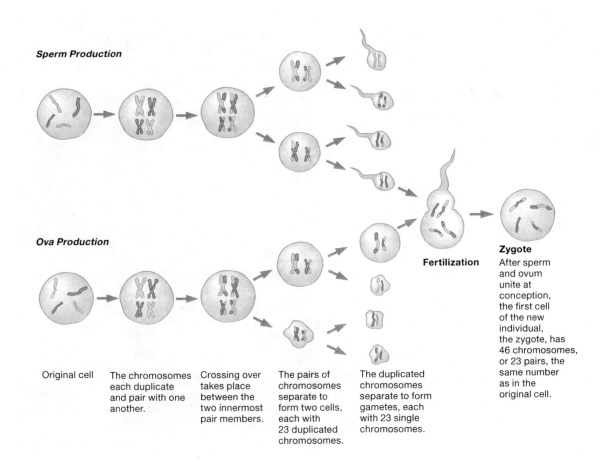

Sperm Production

Ova Production

Fertilization

Zygote
After sperm and ovum unite at conception, the first cell of the new individual, the zygote, has 46 chromosomes, or 23 pairs, the same number as in the original cell.

Original cell

The chromosomes each duplicate and pair with one another.

Crossing over takes place between the two innermost pair members.

The pairs of chromosomes separate to form two cells, each with 23 duplicated chromosomes.

The duplicated chromosomes separate to form gametes, each with 23 single chromosomes.

FIGURE 3 The Cell Division Process of Meiosis, Leading to Gamete Formation

(Here, original cells are depicted with two rather than the full complement of 23 pairs.) Meiosis creates gametes with only half the usual number of chromosomes. When sperm and ovum unite at conception, the first cell of the new individual (the zygote) has the correct, full number of chromosomes.

child at any age after sexual maturity. In the female, meiosis results in just one ovum; the remaining genetic material degenerates. In addition, the female is born with all her ova already present in her ovaries, and she can bear children for only three to four decades. Still, there are plenty of female sex cells. About 1 to 2 million are present at birth, 40,000 remain at adolescence, and approximately 350 to 450 will mature during a woman's childbearing years (Moore & Persaud, 2008).

Boy or Girl?

Return to Figure 1 on page 94, and note the 22 matching pairs of chromosomes, which geneticists number from longest (1) to shortest (22). These are called **autosomes** (meaning *not* sex chromosomes). The twenty-third pair consists of **sex chromosomes**. In females, this pair is called XX; in males, it is called XY. The X is a relatively large chromosome, whereas the Y is short and carries little genetic material. When gametes form in males, the X and Y chromosomes separate into different sperm cells. The gametes that form in females all carry an X chromosome. Therefore, the sex of the new organism is determined by whether an X-bearing or a Y-bearing sperm fertilizes the ovum. In fact, scientists have isolated a gene on the Y chromosome that initiates the formation of male sex organs during the prenatal period. But they also know that other genes, some yet to be discovered, are involved in the development of sexual characteristics (Bhagavath & Layman, 2007; Sekido & Lovell-Badge, 2009).

Multiple Births

Ruth and Peter, a couple I know well, tried for several years to have a child, without success. When Ruth reached age 33, her doctor prescribed a fertility drug, and Ruth gave birth to twins—Jeannie and Jason. Jeannie and Jason are **fraternal, or dizygotic, twins,** the most common type of multiple birth, resulting from the release and fertilization of two ova. Genetically, they are no more alike than ordinary siblings. Table 1 summarizes genetic and environmental factors that increase the chances of giving birth to fraternal twins. Older maternal age, fertility drugs, and in vitro fertilization (to be discussed shortly) are major causes of the dramatic rise in fraternal twinning and other multiple births in industrialized nations over the past several decades (Machin, 2005; Russell et al., 2003). Currently, fraternal twins account for 1 in about every 60 births in the United States (U.S. Department of Health and Human Services, 2010c).

Twins can be created in another way. Sometimes a zygote that has started to duplicate separates into two clusters of cells that develop into two individuals. These are called **identical, or monozygotic, twins** because they have the same genetic makeup. The frequency of identical twins is the same around the world—about 1 in every 330 births (Hall, 2003). Animal research has uncovered a variety of environmental influences that prompt this type of twinning, including temperature changes, variation in oxygen levels, and late fertilization of the ovum. In a minority of cases, the identical twinning runs in families, suggesting a genetic influence (Lashley, 2007).

During their early years, children of single births often are healthier and develop more rapidly than twins. Jeannie and Jason, like most twins, were born early—three weeks before Ruth's due date. And, like other premature infants, they required special care after birth. When the twins came home from the hospital, Ruth and Peter had to divide time between them. Perhaps because neither baby got quite as much attention as the average single infant, Jeannie and Jason walked and talked several months later than most other children their age, although both caught up in development by middle childhood (Lytton & Gallagher, 2002). Parental energies are further strained after

These identical, or monozygotic, twins were created when a duplicating zygote separated into two clusters of cells and developed into two individuals with the same genetic makeup. Identical twins look alike, and as we will see later in this module, tend to resemble each other in a variety of psychological characteristics.
(© Rachel Epstein/Photoedit)

TABLE 1 Maternal Factors Linked to Fraternal Twinning

FACTOR	DESCRIPTION
Ethnicity	Occurs in 4 per 1,000 births among Asians, 8 per 1,000 births among whites, 12 to 16 per 1,000 births among blacks[a]
Family history of twinning	Occurs more often among women whose mothers and sisters gave birth to fraternal twins
Age	Rises with maternal age, peaking between 35 and 39 years, and then rapidly falls
Nutrition	Occurs less often among women with poor diets; occurs more often among women who are tall and overweight or of normal weight as opposed to slight body build
Number of births	Is more likely with each additional birth
Fertility drugs and in vitro fertilization	Is more likely with fertility hormones and in vitro fertilization (see pages 108–109), which also increase the chances of bearing triplets, quadruplets, or quintuplets

[a] Worldwide rates, not including multiple births resulting from use of fertility drugs.

Sources: Hall, 2003; Hoekstra et al., 2008; Lashley, 2007.

the birth of triplets, whose early development is slower than that of twins (Feldman, Eidelman, & Rotenberg, 2004).

Patterns of Genetic Inheritance

Jeannie has her parents' dark, straight hair, whereas Jason is curly-haired and blond. Patterns of genetic inheritance—the way genes from each parent interact—explain these outcomes. Recall that except for the XY pair in males, all chromosomes come in corresponding pairs. Two forms of each gene occur at the same place on the chromosomes, one inherited from the mother and one from the father. Each form of a gene is called an **allele**. If the alleles from both parents are alike, the child is **homozygous** and will display the inherited trait. If the alleles are different, the child is **heterozygous**, and relationships between the alleles determine the phenotype.

Dominant–Recessive Inheritance

In many heterozygous pairings, **dominant–recessive inheritance** occurs: Only one allele affects the child's characteristics. It is called *dominant;* the second allele, which has no effect, is called *recessive*. Hair color is an example. The allele for dark hair is dominant (we can represent it with a capital *D*), whereas the one for blond hair is recessive (symbolized by a lowercase *b*). A child who inherits a homozygous pair of dominant alleles *(DD)* and a child who inherits a heterozygous pair *(Db)* will both be dark-haired, even though their genotypes differ. Blond hair (like Jason's) can result only from having two recessive alleles *(bb)*. Still, heterozygous individuals with just one recessive allele *(Db)* can pass that trait to their children. Therefore, they are called **carriers** of the trait.

Some human characteristics that follow the rules of dominant–recessive inheritance are listed in Table 2 and Table 3 on page 99–100. As you can see, many disabilities and diseases are the product of recessive alleles. One of the most frequently occurring recessive disorders is *phenylketonuria,* or *PKU*. It affects the way the body breaks down proteins contained in many foods. Infants born with two recessive alleles lack an enzyme that converts one of the basic amino acids that make up proteins (phenylalanine) into a byproduct essential for body functioning (tyrosine). Without this enzyme, phenylalanine quickly builds to toxic levels that damage the central nervous system. By 1 year, infants with PKU are permanently retarded.

Despite its potentially damaging effects, PKU provides an excellent illustration of the fact that inheriting unfavorable genes does not always lead to an untreatable condition. All U.S. states require that each newborn be given a blood test for PKU. If the disease is found, doctors place the baby on a diet low in phenylalanine. Children who receive this treatment nevertheless show mild deficits in certain cognitive skills, such as memory, planning, decision making, and problem solving, because even small amounts of phenylalanine interfere with brain functioning (Anderson et al., 2007; Christ et al., 2006; DeRoche & Welsh, 2008). But as long as dietary treatment begins early and continues, children with PKU usually attain an average level of intelligence and have a normal lifespan.

In dominant–recessive inheritance, if we know the genetic makeup of the parents, we can predict the percentage of children in a family who are likely to display or carry a trait. Figure 4 illustrates this for PKU. For a child to inherit the condition, each parent must have a recessive allele *(p)*. As the figure also illustrates, a single gene can affect more than one trait. Because of their inability to convert phenylalanine into tyrosine (which is responsible for pigmentation), children with PKU usually have light hair and blue eyes. Furthermore, children vary in the degree to which phenylalanine accumulates in their tissues and in the extent to which they respond to treatment. This is due to the action of **modifier genes,** which enhance or dilute the effects of other genes.

Only rarely are serious diseases due to dominant alleles. Think about why this is so. Children who inherit the dominant allele always develop the disorder. They seldom live long enough to reproduce, so the harmful dominant allele is eliminated from the family's heredity in a single generation. Some dominant disorders, however, do persist. One is *Huntington disease,* a condition in which the central nervous system degenerates. Why has this disorder endured? Its symptoms usually do not appear until age 35 or later, after the person has passed the dominant allele to his or her children.

Incomplete Dominance

In some heterozygous circumstances, the dominant–recessive relationship does not hold completely. Instead, we see **incomplete dominance,** a pattern of inheritance in which both alleles are expressed in the phenotype, resulting in a combined trait, or one that is intermediate between the two.

The *sickle cell trait,* a heterozygous condition present in many black Africans, provides an example. *Sickle cell anemia* (see Table 3) occurs in full form when a child inherits two recessive alleles. They cause the usually round red blood cells to become sickle (crescent-moon) shaped, especially under low-oxygen conditions. The sickled cells clog the blood vessels and block the flow of blood, causing intense pain, swelling, and tissue damage. Despite medical advances that today allow 85 percent of affected children to survive to adulthood, North Americans with sickle cell anemia have a life expectancy of only 55 years (Driscoll, 2007). Heterozygous individuals are protected from the disease under most circumstances. However, when they experience oxygen deprivation—for example, at high altitudes or after intense physical exercise—the single recessive allele asserts itself, and a temporary, mild form of the illness occurs.

The sickle cell allele is common among black Africans for a special reason. Carriers of it are more resistant to malaria than are individuals with two alleles for normal red blood cells. In Africa, where malaria is common, these carriers have survived and reproduced

TABLE 2   Examples of Dominant and Recessive Characteristics

DOMINANT	RECESSIVE
Dark hair	Blond hair
Normal hair	Pattern baldness
Curly hair	Straight hair
Nonred hair	Red hair
Facial dimples	No dimples
Normal hearing	Some forms of deafness
Normal vision	Nearsightedness
Farsightedness	Normal vision
Normal vision	Congenital eye cataracts
Normally pigmented skin	Albinism
Double-jointedness	Normal joints
Type A blood	Type O blood
Type B blood	Type O blood
Rh-positive blood	Rh-negative blood

Note: Many normal characteristics that were previously thought to be due to dominant–recessive inheritance, such as eye color, are now regarded as due to multiple genes. For the characteristics listed here, there still seems to be general agreement that the simple dominant–recessive relationship holds.

Sources: McKusick, 2007.

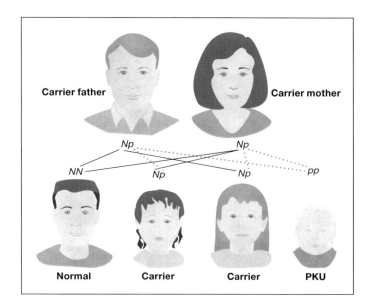

FIGURE 4   Dominant–Recessive Mode of Inheritance, as Illustrated by PKU

When both parents are heterozygous carriers of the recessive gene *(p)*, we can predict that 25 percent of their offspring are likely to be normal *(NN)*, 50 percent are likely to be carriers *(Np)*, and 25 percent are likely to inherit the disorder *(pp)*. Notice that the PKU-affected child, in contrast to his siblings, has light hair. The recessive gene for PKU affects more than one trait. It also leads to fair coloring.

TABLE 3 Examples of Dominant and Recessive Diseases

DISEASE	DESCRIPTION	MODE OF INHERITANCE	INCIDENCE	TREATMENT
AUTOSOMTAL DISEASES				
Cooley's anemia	Pale appearance, retarded physical growth, and lethargic behavior begin in infancy.	Recessive	1 in 500 births to parents of Mediterranean descen[t]	Frequent blood transfusions. Death from complications usually occurs by adolescence.
Cystic fibrosis	Lungs, liver, and pancreas secrete large amounts of thick mucus, leading to breathing and digestive difficulties.	Recessive	1 in 2,000 to 2,500 Caucasian births; 1 in 16,000 births to North Americans of African descent	Bronchial drainage, prompt treatment of respiratory infection, dietary management. Advances in medical care allow survival with good life quality into adulthood.
Phenylke-tonuria (PKU)	Inability to metabolize the amino acid phenylalanine, contained in many proteins, causes severe central nervous system damage in the first year of life.	Recessive	1 in 8,000 births	Placing the child on a special diet results in average intelligence and normal lifespan. Subtle difficulties in memory, planning, decision making, and problem solving are often present.
Sickle cell anemia	Abnormal sickling of red blood cells causes oxygen deprivation, pain, swelling, and tissue damage. Anemia and susceptibility to infections, especially pneumonia, occur.	Recessive	1 in 400 to 600 births to North Americans of African descent	Blood transfusions, painkillers, prompt treatment of infection. No known cure; 50 percent die by age 55.
Tay-Sachs disease	Central nervous system degeneration, with onset at about 6 months, leads to poor muscle tone, blindness, deafness, and convulsions.	Recessive	1 in 3,600 births to Jews of European descent and to French Canadians	None. Death occurs by 3 to 4 years of age.
Huntington disease	Central nervous system degeneration leads to muscular coordination difficulties, mental deterioration, and personality changes. Symptoms usually do not appear until age 35 or later.	Dominant	1 in 18,000 to 25,000 births to North Americans	None. Death occurs 10 to 20 years after symptom onset.
Marfan syndrome	Tall, slender build; thin, elongated arms and legs; and heart defects and eye abnormalities, especially of the lens. Excessive lengthening of the body results in a variety of skeletal defects.	Dominant	1 in 5,000 to 10,000 births	Correction of heart and eye defects sometimes possible. Death from heart failure in early adulthood is common.
X-LINKED DISEASES				
Duchenne muscular dystrophy	Degenerative muscle disease. Abnormal gait, loss of ability to walk between ages 7 and 13 years.	Recessive	1 in 3,000 to 5,000 male births	None. Death from respiratory infection or weakening of the heart muscle usually occurs in adolescence.
Hemophilia	Blood fails to clot normally; can lead to severe internal bleeding and tissue damage.	Recessive	1 in 4,000 to 7,000 male births	Blood transfusions. Safety precautions to prevent injury.
Diabetes insipidus	Insufficient production of the hormone vasopressin results in excessive thirst and urination. Dehydration can cause central nervous system damage.	Recessive	1 in 2,500 male births	Hormone replacement.

Note: For recessive disorders, carrier status can be detected in prospective parents through a blood test or genetic analyses. For all disorders listed, prenatal diagnosis is available (see page 105).

Sources: Kliegman et al., 2008; Lashley, 2007; McKusick, 2007.

more frequently than others, leading the gene to be maintained in the black population. But in regions of the world where the risk of malaria is low, the frequency of the gene is declining. For example, only 8 percent of African Americans are carriers, compared with 20 percent of black Africans (National Center for Biotechnology Information, 2007).

X-Linked Inheritance

Males and females have an equal chance of inheriting recessive disorders carried on the autosomes, such as PKU and sickle cell anemia. But when a harmful allele is carried on the X chromosome, **X-linked inheritance** applies. Males are more likely to be affected because their sex chromosomes do not match. In females, any recessive allele on one X chromosome has a good chance of being suppressed by a dominant allele on the other X. But the Y chromosome is only about one-third as long and therefore lacks many corresponding alleles to override those on the X. A well-known example is *hemophilia,* a disorder in which the blood fails to clot normally. Figure 5 shows its greater likelihood of inheritance by male children whose mothers carry the abnormal allele.

Besides X-linked disorders, many sex differences reveal the male to be at a disadvantage. Rates of miscarriage, infant and childhood deaths, birth defects, learning disabilities, behavior disorders, and mental retardation all are higher for boys (Butler & Meaney, 2005). It is possible that these sex differences can be traced to the genetic code. The female, with two X chromosomes, benefits from a greater variety of genes. Nature, however, seems to have adjusted for the male's disadvantage. Worldwide, about 106 boys are born for every 100 girls, and judging from miscarriage and abortion statistics, an even greater number of boys are conceived (United Nations, 2006).

Nevertheless, in recent decades the proportion of male births has declined in many industrialized countries, including the United States, Canada, and European nations (Jongbloet et al., 2001). Some researchers attribute the trend to a rise in stressful living conditions, which heighten spontaneous abortions, especially of male fetuses. In a test of this hypothesis, male-to-female birth ratios in East Germany were examined between 1946 and 1999. The ratio was lowest in 1991, the year that the country's economy collapsed (Catalano, 2003). Similarly, in a California study spanning the decade of the 1990s, the percentage of male fetal deaths increased in months in which unemployment (a major stressor) also rose above its typical level (Catalano et al., 2005, 2009).

Genomic Imprinting

More than 1,000 human characteristics follow the rules of dominant–recessive and incomplete-dominance inheritance (McKusick, 2007). In these cases, whichever parent contributes a gene to the new individual, the gene responds in the same way. Geneticists, however, have identified some exceptions. In **genomic imprinting**, alleles are *imprinted,* or chemically marked, in such a way that one pair member (either the mother's or the father's) is activated, regardless of its makeup. The imprint is often temporary; it may be erased in the next generation, and it may not occur in all individuals (Everman & Cassidy, 2000).

Imprinting helps us understand certain puzzling genetic patterns. For example, children are more likely to develop diabetes if their father, rather than their mother, suffers from it. And people with asthma or hay fever tend to have mothers, not fathers, with the illness. Imprinting is involved in several childhood cancers and in *Prader-Willi syndrome,* a disorder with symptoms of mental retardation and severe obesity (Benarroch et al., 2007). It may also explain why Huntington disease, when inherited from the father, tends to emerge at an earlier age and to progress more rapidly (Navarrete, Martinez, & Salamanca, 1994).

Genomic imprinting can also operate on the sex chromosomes, as *fragile X syndrome*—the most common inherited cause of mental retardation—reveals. In this disorder, which affects about 1 in

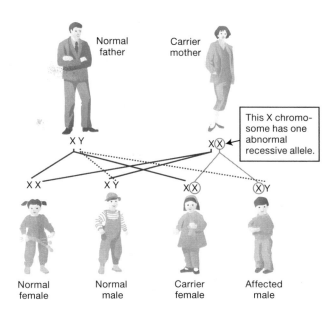

FIGURE 5   X-Linked Inheritance

In the example shown here, the allele on the father's X chromosome is normal. The mother has one normal and one abnormal recessive allele on her X chromosomes. By looking at the possible combinations of the parents' alleles, we can predict that 50 percent of these parents' male children are likely to have the disorder, and 50 percent of their female children are likely to be carriers of it.

4,000 males and 1 in 6,000 females, an abnormal repetition of a sequence of DNA bases occurs in a special spot on the X chromosome, damaging a particular gene. The defective gene at the fragile site is expressed only when it is passed from mother to child. Because the disorder is X-linked, males are more severely affected (Hagerman et al., 2009). Females usually have a normally functioning gene on their other X chromosome (inherited from the father) that partially compensates for the abnormal gene. About 25 to 30 percent of individuals with fragile X syndrome also have symptoms of *autism*, a serious disorder usually diagnosed in early childhood that involves impaired social interaction, delayed or absent language and communication, and repetitive motor behavior (Schwarte, 2008).

Mutation

Although less than 3 percent of pregnancies result in the birth of a baby with a hereditary abnormality, these children account for about 20 percent of infant deaths and contribute substantially to lifelong impaired physical and mental functioning (U.S. Department of Health and Human Services, 2010c). How are harmful genes created in the first place? The answer is **mutation**, a sudden but permanent change in a segment of DNA. A mutation may affect only one or two genes, or it may involve many genes, as in the chromosomal disorders we will discuss shortly. Some mutations occur spontaneously, simply by chance. Others are caused by hazardous environmental agents.

Although nonionizing forms of radiation—electromagnetic waves and microwaves—have no demonstrated impact on DNA, ionizing (high-energy) radiation is an established cause of mutation. Women who receive repeated doses before conception are more likely to miscarry or give birth to children with hereditary defects. The incidence of genetic abnormalities, such as physical malformations and childhood cancer, is also higher in children whose fathers are exposed to radiation in their occupations. However, infrequent and mild exposure to radiation does not cause genetic damage (Jacquet, 2004). Rather, high doses over a long period impair DNA.

The examples just given illustrate *germline mutation*, which takes place in the cells that give rise to gametes. When the affected individual mates, the defective DNA is passed on to the next generation. In a second type, called *somatic mutation*, normal body cells mutate, an event that can occur at any time of life. The DNA defect appears in every cell derived from the affected body cell, eventually becoming widespread enough to cause disease (such as cancer) or disability.

It is easy to see how disorders that run in families can result from germline mutation. But somatic mutation may be involved in these disorders as well. Some people harbor a genetic susceptibility that causes certain body cells to mutate easily in the presence of triggering events (Weiss, 2005). This helps explain why some individuals develop serious illnesses (such as cancer) as a result of smoking, exposure to pollutants, or psychological stress, while others do not.

Although virtually all mutations that have been studied are harmful, some spontaneous ones (such as the sickle cell allele in malaria-ridden regions of the world) are necessary and desirable. By increasing genetic variation, they help individuals adapt to unexpected environmental challenges. Scientists, however, seldom go looking for mutations that underlie favorable traits, such as an exceptional talent or an especially sturdy immune system. They are far more concerned with identifying and eliminating unfavorable genes that threaten health and survival.

Polygenic Inheritance

So far, we have discussed patterns of inheritance in which people either display a particular trait or do not. These cut-and-dried individual differences are much easier to trace to their genetic origins than are characteristics that vary on a continuum among people, such as height, weight, intelligence, and personality. These traits are due to **polygenic inheritance**, in which many genes affect the characteristic in question. Polygenic inheritance is complex, and much about it is still unknown. In the final section of this module, we discuss how researchers infer the influence of heredity on human attributes when they do not know the precise patterns of inheritance.

Chromosomal Abnormalities

Besides harmful recessive alleles, abnormalities of the chromosomes are a major cause of serious developmental problems. Most chromosomal defects result from mistakes during meiosis, when the ovum and sperm are formed. A chromosome pair does not separate properly, or part of a chromosome breaks off. Because these errors involve far more DNA than problems due to single genes, they usually produce many physical and mental symptoms.

Down Syndrome

The most common chromosomal disorder, occurring in 1 out of every 770 live births, is *Down syndrome*. In 95 percent of cases, it results from a failure of the twenty-first pair of chromosomes to separate during meiosis, so the new individual receives three of these chromosomes rather than the normal two. For this reason, Down syndrome is sometimes called *trisomy 21*. In other, less frequent forms, an extra broken piece of a twenty-first chromosome is attached to another chromosome (called *translocation* pattern). Or an error occurs during the early stages of mitosis, causing some but not all body cells to have the defective chromosomal makeup (called *mosaic* pattern) (U.S. Department of Health and Human Services, 2009d). Because the mosaic type involves less genetic material, symptoms may be less extreme.

The consequences of Down syndrome include mental retardation, memory and speech problems, limited vocabulary, and slow motor development. Affected individuals also have distinct physical features—a short, stocky build; a flattened face; a protruding tongue; almond-shaped eyes; and (in 50 percent of cases) an unusual crease running across the palm of the hand. In addition, infants with Down syndrome are often born with eye cataracts, hearing loss, and heart and intestinal defects (Sherman et al., 2007). Because of medical advances, fewer individuals with Down syndrome die early than was the case in the past. Many survive into their fifties and a few into their sixties to eighties. However, more than half of affected individuals who live past age 40 show symptoms of *Alzheimer's disease,* the most common form of dementia (Wiseman et al., 2009). Genes on chromosome 21 are linked to this disorder.

Infants with Down syndrome smile less readily, show poor eye-to-eye contact, have weak muscle tone, and explore objects less persistently (Slonims & McConachie, 2006). But when parents encourage them to engage with their surroundings, children with Down syndrome develop more favorably. They also benefit from infant and preschool intervention programs, although emotional, social, and motor skills improve more than intellectual performance (Carr, 2002). Clearly, environmental factors affect how well children with Down syndrome fare.

As Figure 6 shows, the risk of bearing a Down syndrome baby rises dramatically with maternal age (Schonberg & Tifft, 2007). But exactly why older mothers are more likely to release ova with meiotic errors is not yet known (Martin, 2008). In about 5 to 10 percent of cases, the extra genetic material originates with the father. Some studies suggest a role for advanced paternal age, while others show no age effects (De Souza, Alberman, & Morris, 2009; Dzurova & Pikhart, 2005; Sherman et al., 2005).

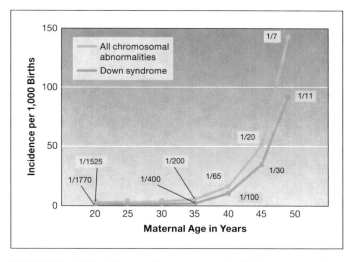

A 6-year-old boy with Down syndrome, at right, plays with a typically developing classmate. Despite impaired intellectual development, this boy benefits from exposure to stimulating environments and from opportunities to interact with peers.
(© Lauren Shear/Photo Researchers, Inc.)

FIGURE 6   Risk of Down Syndrome and all Chromosomal Abnormalities by Maternal Age

Risk rises sharply after age 35. (Adapted from R. L. Schonberg & C. J. Tifft, 2007, "Birth Defects and Prenatal Diagnosis," from *Children with Disabilities*, 6/e, M. L. Matshaw, L. Pellegrino, & N. J. Roizen, eds., p. 85. Baltimore: Paul H. Brookes Publishing Co., Inc. Reprinted by permission.)

Abnormalities of the Sex Chromosomes

Disorders of the autosomes other than Down syndrome usually disrupt development so severely that miscarriage occurs. When such babies are born, they rarely survive beyond early childhood. In contrast, abnormalities of the sex chromosomes usually lead to fewer problems. In fact, sex

TABLE 4 Sex Chromosomal Disorders

DISORDER	DESCRIPTION	INCIDENCE	TREATMENT
XYY syndrome	Extra Y chromosome. Above-average height, large teeth, and sometimes severe acne. Intelligence, male sexual development, and fertility are normal.	1 in 1,000 male births	No special treatment necessary.
Triple X syndrome (XXX)	Extra X chromosome. Tallness and impaired verbal intelligence. Female sexual development and fertility are normal.	1 in 500 to 1,250 female births	Special education to treat verbal ability problems.
Klinefelter syndrome (XXY)	Extra X chromosome. Tallness, body fat distribution resembling females, incomplete development of sex characteristics at puberty, sterility, and impaired verbal intelligence.	1 in 900 male births	Hormone therapy at puberty to stimulate development of sex characteristics; special education to treat verbal ability problems.
Turner syndrome (XO)	Missing X chromosome. Short stature, webbed neck, incomplete development of sex characteristics at puberty, sterility, and impaired spatial intelligence.	1 in 2,500 to 8,000 female births	Hormone therapy in childhood to stimulate physical growth and at puberty to promote development of sex characteristics; special education to treat spatial ability problems.

Sources: Geerts, Steyaert, & Fryns, 2003; Kesler, 2007; Saitta & Zackai, 2005; Simpson et al., 2003.

chromosome disorders often are not recognized until adolescence when, in some deviations, puberty is delayed. The most common problems involve the presence of an extra chromosome (either X or Y) or the absence of one X in females.

Research has discredited a variety of myths about individuals with sex chromosome disorders. For example, as Table 4 reveals, males with *XYY syndrome* are not necessarily more aggressive and antisocial than XY males. And most children with sex chromosome disorders do not suffer from mental retardation. Rather, their intellectual problems are usually very specific. Verbal difficulties—for example, with reading and vocabulary—are common among girls with *triple X syndrome* and boys with *Klinefelter syndrome,* both of whom inherit an extra X chromosome. In contrast, girls with *Turner syndrome,* who are missing an X, have trouble with spatial relationships—for example, drawing pictures, telling right from left, following travel directions, and noticing changes in facial expressions (Kesler, 2007; Lawrence et al., 2003; Simpson et al., 2003). Brain-imaging evidence confirms that adding to or subtracting from the usual number of X chromosomes alters the development of certain brain structures, yielding particular intellectual deficits (Cutter et al., 2006; Itti et al., 2006).

ASK YOURSELF

◆ REVIEW Cite evidence indicating that both heredity and environment contribute to the development of children with PKU and Down syndrome.

◆ REVIEW Using your knowledge of X-linked inheritance, explain why males are more vulnerable than females to miscarriage, infant death, genetic disorders, and other problems.

◆ APPLY Gilbert's genetic makeup is homozygous for dark hair. Jan's is homozygous for blond hair. What color is Gilbert's hair? How about Jan's? What proportion of their children are likely to be dark-haired? Explain.

◆ CONNECT Referring to ecological systems theory, explain why parents of children with genetic disorders often experience increased stress. What factors, within and beyond the family, can help these parents support their children's development?

◇ REPRODUCTIVE CHOICES

Two years after they married, Ted and Marianne gave birth to their first child. Kendra appeared to be a healthy infant, but by 4 months her growth had slowed, and she was diagnosed as having Tay-Sachs disease (see Table 3). When Kendra died at 2 years of age, Ted and Marianne were devastated. Although they did not want to bring another infant into the world who would endure such suffering, they badly wanted to have a child. They began to avoid family get-togethers, where little nieces and nephews were constant reminders of the void in their lives.

In the past, many couples with genetic disorders in their families chose not to bear a child at all rather than risk the birth of a baby with abnormalities. Today, genetic counseling and prenatal diagnosis help people make informed decisions about conceiving, carrying a pregnancy to term, or adopting a child.

Genetic Counseling

Genetic counseling is a communication process designed to help couples assess their chances of giving birth to a baby with a hereditary disorder and choose the best course of action in view of risks and family goals (Resta et al., 2006). Individuals likely to seek counseling are those who have had difficulties bearing children—for example, repeated miscarriages—or who know that genetic problems exist in their families. In addition, women who delay childbearing past age 35 are often candidates for genetic counseling. After this time, the overall rate of chromosomal abnormalities rises sharply (refer again to Figure 6) (Schonberg & Tifft, 2007). But because younger mothers give birth in far higher numbers than older mothers, they still bear the majority of babies with genetic defects. Therefore, some experts argue that mater nal needs, not age, should determine referral for genetic counseling (Berkowitz, Roberts, & Minkoff, 2006).

If a family history of mental retardation, psychological disorders, physical defects, or inherited diseases exists, the genetic counselor interviews the couple and prepares a *pedigree,* a picture of the family tree in which affected relatives are identified. The pedigree is used to estimate the likelihood that parents will have an abnormal child, using the genetic principles discussed earlier in this module. For many disorders, blood tests or genetic analyses can reveal whether the parent is a carrier of the harmful gene. Carrier detection is possible for all the recessive diseases listed in Table 3, as well as others, and for fragile X syndrome.

When all the relevant information is in, the genetic counselor helps people consider appropriate options. These include taking a chance and conceiving, choosing from among a variety of reproductive technologies (see the Social Issues: Health box on pages 108–109), or adopting a child.

Prenatal Diagnosis and Fetal Medicine

If couples who might bear a child with abnormalities decide to conceive, several **prenatal diagnostic methods**—medical procedures that permit detection of developmental problems before birth—are available (see Table 5 on page 106). Women of advanced maternal age are prime candidates for *amniocentesis* or *chorionic villus sampling* (see Figure 7 on page 107). Except for *maternal blood analysis,* prenatal diagnosis should not be used routinely, since other methods have some chance of injuring the developing organism.

Prenatal diagnosis has led to advances in fetal medicine. For example, by inserting a needle into the uterus, doctors can administer drugs to the fetus. Surgery has been performed to repair such problems as heart, lung, and diaphragm malformations; urinary tract obstructions; and neural defects (Kunisaki & Jennings, 2008). Fetuses with blood disorders have been given blood transfusions. And those with immune deficiencies have received bone marrow transplants that succeeded in creating a normally functioning immune system (Williams, 2006).

These techniques frequently result in complications, the most common being premature labor and miscarriage (Schonberg & Tifft, 2007). Yet parents may be willing to try almost any option, even one with only a slim chance of success. Currently, the medical profession is struggling with how to help parents make informed decisions about fetal surgery.

Advances in *genetic engineering* also offer new hope for correcting hereditary defects. As part of the Human Genome Project—an ambitious international research program aimed at

TABLE 5 Prenatal Diagnostic Methods

METHOD	DESCRIPTION
Amniocentesis	The most widely used technique. A hollow needle is inserted through the abdominal wall to obtain a sample of fluid in the uterus. Cells are examined for genetic defects. Can be performed by the 14th week after conception; 1 to 2 more weeks are required for test results. Small risk of miscarriage.
Chorionic villus sampling	A procedure that can be used if results are desired or needed very early in pregnancy. A thin tube is inserted into the uterus through the vagina, or a hollow needle is inserted through the abdominal wall. A small plug of tissue is removed from the end of one or more chorionic villi, the hairlike projections on the membrane surrounding the developing organism. Cells are examined for genetic defects. Can be performed at 9 weeks after conception; results are available within 24 hours. Entails a slightly greater risk of miscarriage than does amniocentesis. Also associated with a small risk of limb deformities, which increases the earlier the procedure is performed.
Fetoscopy	A small tube with a light source at one end is inserted into the uterus to inspect the fetus for defects of the limbs and face. Also allows a sample of fetal blood to be obtained, permitting diagnosis of such disorders as hemophilia and sickle cell anemia as well as neural defects (see below). Usually performed between 15 and 18 weeks after conception but can be done as early as 5 weeks. Entails some risk of miscarriage.
Ultrasound	High-frequency sound waves are beamed at the uterus; their reflection is translated into a picture on a video screen that reveals the size, shape, and placement of the fetus. By itself, permits assessment of fetal age, detection of multiple pregnancies, and identification of gross physical defects. Also used to guide amniocentesis, chorionic villus sampling, and fetoscopy. When used five or more times, may increase the chances of low birth weight.
Maternal blood analysis	By the second month of pregnancy, some of the developing organism's cells enter the maternal bloodstream. An elevated level of alpha-fetoprotein may indicate kidney disease, abnormal closure of the esophagus, or neural tube defects, such as anencephaly (absence of most of the brain) and spina bifida (bulging of the spinal cord from the spinal column). Isolated cells can be examined for genetic defects.
Preimplantation genetic diagnosis	After in vitro fertilization and duplication of the zygote into a cluster of about 8 to 10 cells, 1 or 2 cells are removed and examined for hereditary defects. Only if that sample is free of detectable genetic disorders is the fertilized ovum implanted in the woman's uterus.

Sources: Hahn & Chitty, 2008; Kumar & O'Brien, 2004; Moore & Persaud, 2008; Sermon, Van Steirteghem, & Liebaers, 2004.

deciphering the chemical makeup of human genetic material (genome)—researchers have mapped the sequence of all human DNA base pairs. Using this information, they are "annotating" the genome—identifying all its genes and their functions, including their protein products and what these products do. A major goal is to understand the estimated 4,000 human disorders, those due to single genes and those resulting from a complex interplay of multiple genes and environmental factors.

Already, thousands of genes have been identified, including those involved in hundreds of diseases, such as cystic fibrosis; Duchenne muscular dystrophy; Huntington disease; Marfan syndrome; heart, digestive, blood, eye, and nervous system abnormalities; and many forms of cancer (National Institutes of Health, 2008). As a result, new treatments are being explored, such as *gene therapy*—correcting genetic abnormalities by delivering DNA carrying a functional gene to the cells. In recent experiments, gene therapy relieved symptoms in hemophilia patients and in patients with severe immune system dysfunction. A few, however, experienced serious side effects (Gillet et al., 2009). In another approach, called *proteomics,* scientists modify gene-specified proteins involved in disease (Van Eyk & Dunn, 2008).

Genetic treatments seem some distance in the future for most single-gene defects, however, and farther off for diseases involving multiple genes that combine in complex ways with each other and the environment. Applying What We Know on page 110 summarizes steps that prospective parents can take before conception to protect the genetic health of their child.

This mother sings while delivering medication through a nebulizer to her 2-year-old daughter, who has cystic fibrosis. The child also wears a vest for a twice-daily treatment that pounds her chest to clear her lungs of thick mucus. In the future, such children may benefit from gene-based treatments for hereditary disorders. (© Joey McLeister/MCT/Landov)

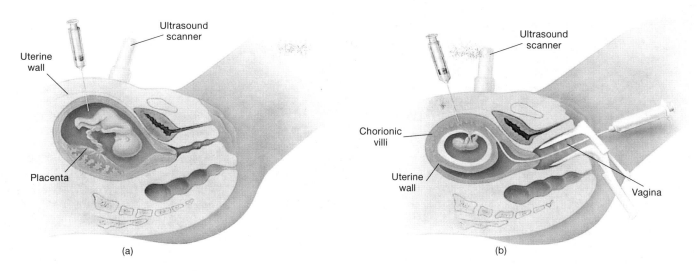

FIGURE 7 Amniocentesis and Chorionic Villus Sampling

Today, hundreds of defects and diseases can be detected before birth using these two procedures. (a) In amniocentesis, a hollow needle is inserted through the abdominal wall into the uterus during the fourteenth week after conception or later. Fluid is withdrawn, and fetal cells are cultured, a process that takes one to two weeks. (b) Chorionic villus sampling can be performed much earlier in pregnancy, at nine weeks after conception, and results are available within 24 hours. Two approaches to obtaining a sample of chorionic villus are shown: inserting a thin tube through the vagina into the uterus and inserting a needle through the abdominal wall. In both amniocentesis and chorionic villus sampling, an ultrasound scanner is used for guidance.

Source: Adapted from Before We Are Born, 7th ed. By K. L. Moore & T. V. N. Persaud, p. 69. Copyright © 2008, reprinted with permission from Elsevier, Inc.

The Alternative of Adoption

Adults who are infertile, who are likely to pass along a genetic disorder, or who are older and single but want a family are turning to adoption in increasing numbers. Those who have children by birth, too, sometimes choose to expand their families through adoption. Adoption agencies try to ensure a good fit by seeking parents of the same ethnic and religious background as the child and, where possible, trying to choose parents who are the same age as typical biological parents. Because the availability of healthy babies has declined (fewer young unwed mothers give up their babies than in the past), more people in North America and Western Europe are adopting from other countries or accepting children who are past infancy or who have known developmental problems (Schweiger & O'Brien, 2005).

Adopted children and adolescents—whether or not they are born in their adoptive parents' country—tend to have more learning and emotional difficulties than other children, a difference that increases with the child's age at time of adoption (Nickman et al., 2005; van IJzendoorn, Juffer, & Poelhuis, 2005; Verhulst, 2008). There are many possible reasons for adoptees' more problematic childhoods. The biological mother may have been unable to care for the child because of problems believed to be partly genetic, such as alcoholism or severe depression, and may have passed this tendency to her offspring. Or perhaps she experienced stress, poor diet, or inadequate medical care during pregnancy—factors that can affect the child. Furthermore, children adopted after infancy often have a preadoptive history of conflict-ridden family relationships, lack of parental affection, neglect and abuse, or deprived institutional rearing. Finally, adoptive parents and children, who are genetically unrelated, are less alike in intelligence and personality than are biological relatives—differences that may threaten family harmony.

Despite these risks, most adopted children fare well, and those with preexisting problems usually make rapid progress (Arcus & Chambers, 2008; Bimmel et al., 2003). In a study of internationally adopted children in the Netherlands, sensitive maternal care and secure attachment in infancy predicted cognitive and social competence at age 7 (Stams, Juffer, & van IJzendoorn, 2002).

SOCIAL ISSUES: HEALTH

THE PROS AND CONS OF REPRODUCTIVE TECHNOLOGIES

Some couples decide not to risk pregnancy because of a history of genetic disease. Many others—in fact, one-sixth of all couples who try to conceive—discover that they are infertile. And some never-married adults and gay and lesbian partners want to bear children. Today, increasing numbers of individuals are turning to alternative methods of conception—technologies that, although they fulfill the wish for parenthood, have become the subject of heated debate.

DONOR INSEMINATION AND IN VITRO FERTILIZATION

For several decades, *donor insemination*—injection of sperm from an anonymous man into a woman—has been used to overcome male reproductive difficulties. In recent years, it has also permitted women without a male partner to become pregnant. Donor insemination is 70 to 80 percent successful, resulting in about 40,000 deliveries and 52,000 newborn babies in the United States each year (Wright et al., 2008).

In *vitro fertilization* is another reproductive technology that has become increasingly common. Since the first "test tube" baby was born in England in 1978, 1 percent of all children in developed countries—about 40,000 babies in the United

Fertility drugs and in vitro fertilization often lead to multiple fetuses. Although these sextuplets are healthy, reproductive technologies can pose grave ethical dilemmas. When three or more fetuses fill the womb, pregnancy complications may be so severe that doctors recommend aborting one or more to save the others.
(AP Images/The Holland Sentinel, Dennis P. J. Geppert)

States—have been conceived through this technique annually (Jackson, Gibson, & Wu, 2004). With in vitro fertilization, a woman is given hormones that stimulate the ripening of several ova. These are removed surgically and placed in a dish of nutrients, to which sperm are added. Once an ovum is fertilized and begins to duplicate into several cells, it is injected into the mother's uterus.

By mixing and matching gametes, pregnancies can be brought about when either or both partners have a reproductive problem. Usually, in vitro fertilization is used to treat women whose fallopian tubes are permanently damaged. But a recently developed technique permits a single sperm to be injected directly into an ovum, thereby overcoming most male fertility problems. And a "sex sorter" method helps ensure that couples who carry X-linked diseases (which usually affect males) have a daughter. Fertilized ova and sperm can even be frozen and stored in embryo banks for use at some future time, thereby guaranteeing healthy zygotes should age or illness lead to fertility problems.

The overall success rate of assisted reproductive techniques is about 35 percent. However, success declines steadily with age, from 40 percent in women younger than age 35 to 8 percent in women age 43 and older (Pauli et al., 2009).

Children conceived through these methods may be genetically unrelated to one or both of their parents. In addition, most parents who have used in vitro fertilization do not tell their children about their origins. Does lack of genetic ties or secrecy surrounding these techniques interfere with parent–child relationships? Perhaps because of a strong desire for parenthood, caregiving is actually somewhat warmer for young children conceived through donor insemination or in vitro fertilization. Also, in vitro infants are as securely attached to their parents, and in vitro children and adolescents as well-adjusted, as their counterparts who were naturally conceived (Golombok et al., 2004; Punamaki, 2006; Wagenaar et al., 2008).

Although reproductive technologies have many benefits, serious questions have arisen about their use. In many countries, including the United States, doctors are not required to keep records of donor characteristics, though information about the child's genetic background might be critical in the case of serious disease (Adamson, 2005). Another concern is that the in vitro "sex sorter" method will lead to parental sex selection, thereby eroding the moral value that boys and girls are equally precious.

Furthermore, about 50 percent of in vitro procedures result in multiple births. Most are twins, but 9 percent are triplets and higher-order multiples. Consequently, among in vitro babies, the rate of low birth weight is nearly three times as high as in the general population (Wright et al., 2008). Risk of major birth defects also doubles because of many factors, including drugs used to induce ripening of ova and delays in fertilizing the ova outside the womb (Machin, 2005; Neri, Takeuchi, & Palermo, 2008). In sum, in vitro fertilization poses greater risks than natural conception to infant survival and healthy development.

SOCIAL ISSUES: HEALTH CONTINUED

SURROGATE MOTHERHOOD

An even more controversial form of medically assisted conception is *surrogate motherhood*. In this procedure, in vitro fertilization may be used to impregnate a woman (called a surrogate) with a couple's fertilized ovum. Alternatively, sperm from a man whose partner is infertile may be used to inseminate the surrogate, who agrees to turn the baby over to the natural father. The child is then adopted by his partner. In both cases, the surrogate is paid a fee for her childbearing services.

Although most of these arrangements proceed smoothly, those that end up in court highlight serious risks for all concerned. In one case, both parties rejected the infant with severe disabilities who resulted from the pregnancy. In several others, the surrogate mother wanted to keep the baby, or the couple changed their mind during the pregnancy. These children came into the world in the midst of conflict that threatened to last for years.

Because surrogacy usually involves the wealthy as contractors for infants and the less economically advantaged as surrogates, it may promote exploitation of financially needy women. In addition, most surrogates already have children of their own, who may be deeply affected by the pregnancy. Knowledge that their mother would give away a baby for profit may cause these children to worry about the security of their own family circumstances.

NEW REPRODUCTIVE FRONTIERS

Reproductive technologies are evolving faster than societies can weigh the ethics of these procedures. Doctors have used donor ova from younger women in combination with in vitro fertilization to help postmenopausal women become pregnant. Most recipients are in their forties, but several women in their fifties and sixties have given birth. These cases raise questions about bringing children into the world whose parents may not live to see them reach adulthood. Based on U.S. life expectancy data, 1 in 3 mothers and 1 in 2 fathers having a baby at age 55 will die before their child enters college (U.S. Census Bureau, 2010b).

Currently, experts are debating other reproductive options. At donor banks, customers can select ova or sperm on the basis of physical characteristics and even IQ. And scientists are devising ways to alter the DNA of human ova, sperm, and embryos to protect against hereditary disorders—techniques that could be used to engineer other desired characteristics. Many worry that these practices are dangerous steps toward selective breeding through "designer babies"—controlling offspring traits by manipulating genetic makeup.

Although new reproductive technologies permit many barren couples to rear healthy newborn babies, laws are needed to regulate such practices. In Australia, New Zealand, Sweden, and Switzerland, individuals conceived with donated gametes have a right to information about their genetic origins (Frith, 2001). Pressure from those working in the field of assisted reproduction may soon lead to a similar policy in the United States. Australia, Canada, and the Netherlands prohibit any genetic alteration of human gametes, with other nations following suit (Isasi, Nguyen, & Knoppers, 2006). But some scientists argue that this total ban is too restrictive because it interferes with serving therapeutic needs.

In the case of surrogate motherhood, the ethical problems are so complex that 18 U.S. states have sharply restricted the practice. Australia, Canada, and many European nations have banned it, arguing that the status of a baby should not be a matter of commercial arrangement and that a part of the body should not be rented or sold (Chen, 2003; McGee, 1997). Denmark, France, and Great Britain have prohibited in vitro fertilization for women past menopause (Bioethics Consultative Committee, 2003). At present, nothing is known about the psychological consequences of being a product of these procedures. Research on how such children grow up, including later-appearing medical conditions and knowledge and feelings about their origins, is important for weighing the pros and cons of these techniques.

Overall, international adoptees fare much better in development than birth siblings or institutionalized agemates who stay behind. By middle childhood, those who were adopted in infancy have mental test scores resembling those of their nonbiological siblings and school classmates, although they tend to achieve less well in school, to have more learning problems that require special treatment, and to be slightly delayed in language skills (van IJzendoorn, Juffer, & Poelhuis, 2005). Children adopted at older ages develop feelings of trust and affection for their adoptive parents as they come to feel loved and supported in their new families (Verissimo & Salvaterra, 2006). However, later-adopted children—especially those with multiple early-life adversities—are more likely than their agemates to have persistent cognitive, emotional, and social problems.

By adolescence, adoptees' lives are often complicated by unresolved curiosity about their roots. Some have difficulty accepting the possibility that they may never know their birth parents.

APPLYING WHAT WE KNOW

Steps Prospective Parents Can Take Before Conception to Increase the Chances of a Healthy Baby

RECOMMENDATION	EXPLANATION
Arrange for a physical exam.	A physical exam before conception permits detection of diseases and other medical problems that might reduce fertility, be difficult to treat during pregnancy, or affect the developing organism.
Consider your genetic makeup.	Find out if anyone in your family has had a child with a genetic disease or disability. If so, seek genetic counseling before conception.
Reduce or eliminate toxins under your control.	Because the developing organism is highly sensitive to damaging environmental agents during the early weeks of pregnancy, couples trying to conceive should avoid drugs, alcohol, cigarette smoke, radiation, pollution, chemical substances in the home and workplace, and infectious diseases. Furthermore, stay away from ionizing radiation and some industrial chemicals that are known to cause mutations.
Ensure proper nutrition.	A doctor-recommended vitamin–mineral supplement, begun before conception, helps prevent many prenatal problems. It should include folic acid, which reduces the chances of neural tube defects, prematurity, and low birth weight.
Consult a physician after 12 months of unsuccessful efforts at conception.	Long periods of infertility may be due to undiagnosed spontaneous abortions, which can be caused by genetic defects in either partner. If a physical exam reveals a healthy reproductive system, seek genetic counseling.

Adoption is one option for adults who are infertile or have a family history of genetic disorders. This couple, who adopted their daughter from China, can promote her successful adjustment by helping her learn about her birth heritage.
(© Golden Pixels LLC/Alamy)

Others worry about what they would do if their birth parents suddenly reappeared. Nevertheless, the decision to search for birth parents is usually postponed until early adulthood, when marriage and childbirth may trigger it. Despite concerns about their origins, most adoptees appear well-adjusted as adults. And as long as their parents took steps to help them learn about their heritage in childhood, young people adopted into a different ethnic group or culture generally develop identities that are healthy blends of their birth and rearing backgrounds (Nickman et al., 2005; Thomas & Tessler, 2007).

As we conclude our discussion of reproductive choices, perhaps you are wondering how things turned out for Ted and Marianne. Through genetic counseling, Marianne discovered a history of Tay-Sachs disease on her mother's side of the family. Ted had a distant cousin who died of the disorder. The genetic counselor explained that the chances of giving birth to another affected baby were 1 in 4. Ted and Marianne took the risk. Their son Douglas is now 12 years old. Although Douglas is a carrier of the recessive allele, he is a normal, healthy boy. In a few years, Ted and Marianne will

ASK YOURSELF

◆ **REVIEW** Why is genetic counseling called a communication process? Who should seek it?

◆ **APPLY** Imagine that you must counsel a couple considering in vitro fertilization using the wife's ova and sperm from an anonymous man to overcome the husband's infertility. What medical and ethical risks would you raise?

◆ **CONNECT** How does research on adoption reveal resilience? Which factor related to resilience is central in positive outcomes for adoptees?

◆ **REFLECT** Imagine that you are a woman who is a carrier of fragile X syndrome but who wants to have children. Would you become pregnant, adopt, use a surrogate mother, or give up your desire for parenthood? If you became pregnant, would you opt for prenatal diagnosis? Explain your decisions.

tell Douglas about his genetic history and explain the importance of genetic counseling and testing before he has children of his own.

⬦ ENVIRONMENTAL CONTEXTS FOR DEVELOPMENT

Just as complex as the genetic inheritance is the surrounding environment—a many-layered set of influences that combine to help or hinder physical and psychological well-being. **TAKE A MOMENT...** Think back to your own childhood, and jot down a brief description of people and events that had a significant impact on your development. Do the items on your list resemble those of my students, who mostly mention experiences that involve their families? This emphasis is not surprising, since the family is the first and longest-lasting context for development. Other influences that make most students' top ten are friends, neighbors, school, and community and religious organizations.

Return to Bronfenbrenner's ecological systems theory. It emphasizes that environments extending beyond the *microsystem*—the immediate settings just mentioned—powerfully affect development. Indeed, my students rarely mention one important context. Its impact is so pervasive that we seldom stop to think about it in our daily lives. This is the *macrosystem*, or broad social climate of society—its values and programs that support and protect children's development. All families need help in rearing their children—through affordable housing and health care, safe neighborhoods, good schools, well-equipped recreational facilities, and high-quality child care and other services that permit parents to meet both work and family responsibilities. And some families, because of poverty or special tragedies, need considerably more help than others.

In the following sections, we take up these contexts for development. Because they affect every age and aspect of change, we will return to them in later modules. For now, our discussion emphasizes that environments, as well as heredity, can enhance or create risks for development.

The Family

In power and breadth of influence, no other microsystem context equals the family. The family introduces children to the physical world by providing opportunities for play and exploration of objects. It also creates unique bonds among people. Attachments to parents and siblings are usually lifelong and serve as models for

The family is a network of interdependent relationships, in which each person's behavior influences that of others. The positive mealtime atmosphere as these teenagers and their parents gather for breakfast is the result of many forces, including parents who respond to children with warmth and patience and children who, in turn, have developed cooperative dispositions.

(Janine Wiedel Photolibrary/Alamy)

relationships in the wider world. Within the family, children learn the language, skills, and social and moral values of their culture. And people of all ages turn to family members for information, assistance, and pleasurable interaction. Warm, gratifying family ties predict physical and psychological health throughout development. In contrast, isolation or alienation from the family is often associated with developmental problems (Deković & Buist, 2005; Parke & Buriel, 2006).

Contemporary researchers view the family as a network of interdependent relationships (Bronfenbrenner & Morris, 2006; Lerner et al., 2002). Recall from ecological systems theory that *bidirectional influences* exist in which the behaviors of each family member affect those of others. Indeed, the very term *system* implies that the responses of all family members are related. These system influences operate both directly and indirectly.

Direct Influences

Recently, as I passed through the checkout counter at the supermarket, I witnessed two episodes, each an example of how parents and children directly influence each other:

◆ Four-year-old Danny looked longingly at the tempting rows of candy as his mother lifted groceries from her cart onto the counter. "Pleeeeease, can I have it, Mom?" Danny begged, holding up a large package of bubble gum. "Do you have a dollar? Just one?"

"No, not today," his mother answered. "Remember, we picked out your special cereal. That's what I need the dollar for." Gently taking the bubble gum from his hand, Danny's mother handed him the box of cereal. "Here, let's pay," she said, lifting Danny so he could see the cash register.

◆ Three-year-old Meg was sitting in the shopping cart while her mother transferred groceries to the counter. Suddenly Meg turned around, grabbed a bunch of bananas, and started pulling them apart.

"Stop it, Meg!" shouted her mother, snatching the bananas from Meg's hand. But as she turned her attention to swiping her debit card, Meg reached for a chocolate bar from a nearby shelf. "Meg, how many times have I told you, don't touch!" Loosening the candy from Meg's tight little fist, Meg's mother slapped her hand. Meg's face turned red with anger as she began to wail.

These observations fit with a wealth of research on the family system. Studies of families of diverse ethnicities show that when parents are firm but warm, children tend to comply with their requests. And when children willingly cooperate, their parents are likely to be warm and gentle in the future. In contrast, children whose parents discipline harshly and impatiently are more likely to refuse and rebel. And because children's misbehavior is stressful, parents may increase their use of punishment, leading to more unruliness by the child (Stormshak et al., 2000; Whiteside-Mansell et al., 2003). In each case, the behavior of one family member helps sustain a form of interaction in the other that either promotes or undermines children's well-being.

Indirect Influences

The impact of family relationships on child development becomes even more complicated when we consider that interaction between any two members is affected by others present in the setting. Bronfenbrenner calls these indirect influences the effect of *third parties*.

Third parties can serve as supports for or barriers to development. For example, when a marital relationship is warm and considerate, mothers and fathers are more likely to engage in effective **coparenting**, mutually supporting each other's parenting behaviors. Such parents are warmer, praise and stimulate children more, and nag and scold them less. In contrast, parents whose marriage is tense and hostile often interfere with one another's child-rearing efforts, are less responsive to children's needs, and are more likely to criticize, express anger, and punish (Caldera & Lindsey, 2006; McHale et al., 2002). Children who are chronically exposed to angry, unresolved parental conflict have serious emotional problems resulting from disrupted emotional security (Cummings & Merrilees, 2010; Schacht, Cummings, & Davies, 2009). These include both *internalizing difficulties* (especially among girls), such as feeling worried and fearful and trying to repair their parents'

Look and Listen:
Observe several parent–young child pairs in a supermarket or department store, where parents are likely to place limits on children's behavior. How does the quality of parent communication seem to influence the child's response? How does the child's response affect the parent's subsequent interaction?

relationship, and *externalizing difficulties* (especially among boys), including anger and aggression (Cummings, Goeke-Morey, & Papp, 2004). These child problems can further disrupt parents' marital relationship.

Yet even when parental conflict strains children's adjustment, other family members may help restore effective interaction. Grandparents, for example, can promote children's development both directly, by responding warmly to the child, and indirectly, by providing parents with child-rearing advice, models of child-rearing skill, and even financial assistance. Of course, as with any indirect influence, grandparents can sometimes be harmful. When quarrelsome relations exist between parents and grandparents, parent–child communication may suffer.

Adapting to Change

Think back to the *chronosystem* in Bronfenbrenner's theory. The interplay of forces within the family is dynamic and ever-changing, as each member adapts to the development of other members.

For example, as children acquire new skills, parents adjust the way they treat their more competent youngsters. **TAKE A MOMENT...** The next time you have a chance, notice the way a parent relates to a tiny baby as compared with a walking, talking toddler. During the first few months, parents spend much time feeding, changing, bathing, and cuddling the infant. Within a year, things change dramatically. The 1-year-old points, shows, names objects, and makes his way through the household cupboards. In response, parents devote less time to physical care and more to talking, playing games, and disciplining. These new ways of interacting, in turn, encourage the child's expanding motor, cognitive, and social skills.

Parents' development affects children as well. We will see that the rise in parent–child conflict that often occurs in early adolescence is not solely due to teenagers' striving for independence. This is a time when most parents of adolescents have reached middle age and—conscious that their children will soon leave home and establish their own lives—are reconsidering their own commitments (Steinberg & Silk, 2002). Consequently, while the adolescent presses for greater autonomy, the parent presses for more togetherness. This imbalance promotes friction, which parent and teenager gradually resolve by accommodating to changes in each other. Indeed, no social unit other than the family is required to adjust to such vast changes in its members.

Historical time period also contributes to a dynamic family system. In recent decades, a declining birth rate, a high divorce rate, expansion of women's roles, increased acceptance of homosexuality, and postponement of parenthood have led to a smaller family size and a greater number of single parents, remarried parents, gay and lesbian parents, employed mothers, and dual-earner families. Clearly, families in industrialized nations have become more diverse than ever before. In later modules we will take up these family forms, examining how each affects family relationships and, ultimately, children's development.

Nevertheless, some general patterns in family functioning do exist. In the United States and other industrialized nations, one important source of these consistencies is socioeconomic status.

Socioeconomic Status and Family Functioning

People in industrialized nations are stratified on the basis of what they do at work and how much they earn for doing it—factors that determine their social position and economic well-being. Researchers assess a family's standing on this continuum through an index called **socioeconomic status (SES)**, which combines three related, but not completely overlapping, variables: (1) years of education and (2) the prestige of one's job and the skill it requires, both of which measure social status, and (3) income, which measures economic status. As SES rises and falls, parents and children face changing circumstances that profoundly affect family functioning.

SES is linked to timing of parenthood and to family size. People who work in skilled and semi-skilled manual occupations (for example, construction workers, truck drivers, and custodians) tend to marry and have children earlier as well as give birth to more children than people in professional and technical occupations. The two groups also differ in child-rearing values and expectations. For example, when asked about personal qualities they desire for their children, lower-SES parents tend to emphasize external characteristics, such as obedience, politeness, neatness, and cleanliness.

In contrast, higher-SES parents emphasize psychological traits, such as curiosity, happiness, self-direction, and cognitive and social maturity (Duncan & Magnuson, 2003; Hoff, Laursen, & Tardif, 2002; Tudge et al., 2000).

These differences are reflected in family interaction. Parents higher in SES talk to, read to, and otherwise stimulate their infants and preschoolers more and grant them greater freedom to explore. With older children and adolescents, higher-SES parents use more warmth, explanations, and verbal praise; set higher academic and other developmental goals; and allow their children to make more decisions. Com mands ("You do that because I told you to"), criticism, and physical punishment all occur more often in low-SES households (Bush & Peterson, 2008; Mandara et al., 2009).

Education contributes substantially to these variations in child rearing. Higher-SES parents' interest in providing verbal stimulation, nurturing inner traits, and promoting academic achievement is supported by years of schooling, during which they learned to think about abstract, subjective ideas (Mistry et al., 2008; Vernon-Feagans et al., 2008). In diverse cultures around the world, as the Social Issues: Education box on the following page makes clear, education of women in particular fosters patterns of thinking and behaving that greatly improve quality of life, for both parents and children.

Because of limited education and low social status, many lower-SES parents feel a sense of powerlessness and lack of influence in their relationships beyond the home. At work, for example, they must obey rules made by others in positions of power and authority. When they get home, their parent–child interaction seems to duplicate these experiences—but now they are in authority. Higher levels of stress, along with a stronger belief in the value of physical punishment, contribute to low-SES parents' greater use of coercive discipline (Conger & Donnellan, 2007; Pinderhughes et al., 2000). Higher-SES parents, in contrast, typically have more control over their own lives. At work, they are used to making independent decisions and convincing others of their point of view. At home, they teach these skills to their children (Greenberger, O'Neil, & Nagel, 1994).

As early as the second year of life, higher SES is associated with enhanced cognitive and language development and with reduced incidence of emotional and behavior problems. And throughout childhood and adolescence, higher-SES children do better in school (Bradley & Corwyn, 2003; Melby et al., 2008). As a result, they attain higher levels of education, which greatly enhances their opportunities for a prosperous adult life. Researchers believe that differences in family functioning have much to do with these outcomes.

Advanced education and material wealth do not guarantee a healthy family life. When children in affluent families lack parental supervision and emotional closeness, they are at risk for academic and emotional difficulties, including poor grades, alcohol and drug use, and anxiety and depression.

(© Inti St Clair/Getty Images/Photodisc)

Affluence

Despite their advanced education and great material wealth, affluent parents—those in prestigious and high-paying occupations—too often fail to engage in family interaction and parenting that promote favorable development. In several studies, researchers tracked the adjustment of youths growing up in wealthy suburbs (Luthar & Latendresse, 2005a). By seventh grade, many showed serious problems that worsened in high school. Their school grades were poor, and they were more likely than low-SES youths to engage in alcohol and drug use and to report high levels of anxiety and depression (Luthar & Becker, 2002; Luthar & Goldstein, 2008). Furthermore, among affluent (but not low-SES) teenagers, substance use was correlated with anxiety and depression, suggesting that wealthy youths took drugs to self-medicate—a practice that predicts persistent abuse (Luthar & Sexton, 2004).

Why are so many affluent youths troubled? Compared to their better-adjusted counterparts, poorly adjusted affluent young people report less emotional closeness and supervision from their parents, who lead professionally and socially demanding lives. As a group, wealthy parents are nearly as physically and emotionally unavailable to their youngsters as parents coping with serious financial strain. At the same time, these parents often make excessive demands for achievement (Luthar & Becker, 2002). Adolescents whose parents value their accomplishments more than their character are more likely to have academic and emotional problems.

SOCIAL ISSUES: EDUCATION

WORLDWIDE EDUCATION OF GIRLS: TRANSFORMING CURRENT AND FUTURE GENERATIONS

When a new school opened in the Egyptian village of Beni Shara'an, Ahmen, an illiterate shopkeeper, immediately enrolled his 8-year-old daughter Rawia (Bellamy, 2004, p. 19). Until that day, Rawia had divided her days between back-breaking farming and confinement to her home.

Before long, Rawia's advancing language, literacy, and reasoning skills transformed her family's quality of life. "My store accounts were in a mess, but soon Rawia started straightening out the books," Ahmen recalled. She also began helping her older sister learn to read and write and explaining to her family the instructions on prescription medicines and the news on television. In addition, Rawia began to envision a better life for herself. "When I grow up," she told her father, "I want to be a doctor. Or maybe a teacher."

Over the past century, the percentage of children in the developing world who go to school has increased from a small minority of boys to a majority of all children in most regions. Still, some 73 million children, most of them poverty-stricken girls, do not start elementary school, and more than 200 million, again mostly girls, do not go to secondary school (UNICEF, 2009a).

Although schooling is vital for all children, educating girls has an especially powerful impact on the welfare

For these girls huddling in an open-air class in a village in Pakistan, attending school will dramatically improve their life opportunities and their nation's welfare. In both developed and developing nations, educating girls leads to gains in family income and relationships that carry over to improved health, education, and economic well-being in the next generation.
(© AP Images/John McConnico)

of families, societies, and future generations. The diverse benefits of girls' schooling largely accrue in two ways: (1) through enhanced verbal skills—reading, writing, and oral communication; and (2) through empowerment—a growing desire to improve their life conditions (LeVine, LeVine, & Schnell, 2001).

FAMILY HEALTH

Education gives people the communicative skills and confidence to seek health services and to benefit from public health information. As a result, years of schooling strongly predicts women's preventive health behavior: prenatal visits, child immunizations, healthy diet, and sanitary practices (LeVine et al., 2004; Peña, Wall, & Person, 2000). In addition, because educated women have more life opportunities, they are more likely to take advantage of family planning services, delay marriage and childbearing, and have more widely spaced and fewer children (Stromquist, 2007). All these practices are linked to increased maternal and child survival and family health.

FAMILY RELATIONSHIPS AND PARENTING

In developed and developing nations alike, the empowerment that springs from education is associated with more equitable husband–wife relationships and a reduction in harsh disciplining of children (LeVine et al., 1991; LeVine, LeVine, & Schnell, 2001). Also, educated mothers engage in more verbal stimulation and teaching of literacy skills to their children, which fosters success in school, higher educational attainment, and economic gains in the next generation. Regions of the world that have invested more in girls' education, such as Southeast Asia and Latin America, tend to have higher levels of economic development (King & Mason, 2001).

According to a United Nations report, educating girls is the most effective means of combating the most profound, global threats to human development: poverty, maternal and child mortality, and disease (UNICEF, 2010). Rawia got the chance to go to school because of an Egyptian national initiative, which led to the establishment of several thousand one-classroom schools in rural areas with the poorest record in educating girls. Because of cultural beliefs about gender roles or reluctance to give up a daughter's work at home, parents sometimes resist. But the largest barrier is that many countries continue to charge parents a fee for each child enrolled in school, often amounting to nearly one-third of the income of poverty-stricken families. Under these conditions, parents—if they send any children—tend to send only sons.

In 2003, Kenya eliminated fees for primary school. Immediately, enrollments of both boys and girls surged—by more than 30 percent. Uganda followed suit, increasing its primary school enrollment by 70 percent (Alter, 2008; RESULTS, 2006). When governments abolish enrollment fees, provide information about the benefits of education for girls, and create employment possibilities for women, the overwhelming majority of parents—including the very poor—choose to send their daughters to school, and some make great sacrifices to do so.

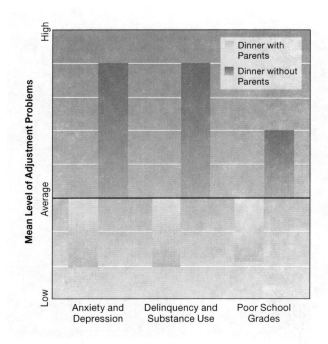

FIGURE 8 Relationship of Regularly Eating Dinner with Parents to Affluent Youths' Adjustment Problems

Compared with sixth graders who often ate dinner with their parents, those who rarely did so were far more likely to display anxiety and depression, delinquency and substance use, and poor school grades, even after many other aspects of parenting were controlled. In this study, frequent family mealtimes also protected low-SES youths from delinquency and substance use and from classroom learning problems.

Source: Adapted from Luthar & Latendresse, 2005b.

For both affluent and low-SES youths, a simple routine—eating dinner with parents—is associated with a reduction in adjustment difficulties, even after many other aspects of parenting are controlled (see Figure 8) (Luthar & Latendresse, 2005b). Interventions that make wealthy parents aware of the high costs of a competitive lifestyle and minimal family time are badly needed.

Poverty

When families slip into poverty, development is seriously threatened. Consider Zinnia Mae, who grew up in a close-knit black neighborhood located in a small southeastern American city (Heath, 1990). As unemployment struck the community and citizens moved away, 16-year-old Zinnia Mae caught a ride to Atlanta. Two years later, she was the mother of a daughter and twin boys, and she had moved into high-rise public housing.

Zinnia Mae worried constantly about scraping together enough money to put food on the table, finding babysitters so she could go to the laundry or grocery, freeing herself from a cycle of rising debt, and finding the twins' father, who had stopped sending money. Her most frequent words were, "I'm so tired." The children had only one set meal—breakfast; otherwise, they ate whenever they were hungry or bored. Their play space was limited to the living room sofa and a mattress on the floor. Toys consisted of scraps of a blanket, spoons and food cartons, a small rubber ball, a few plastic cars, and a roller skate abandoned in the building. At a researcher's request, Zinnia Mae agreed to tape record her interactions with her children. Cut off from family and community ties and overwhelmed by financial strains and feelings of helplessness, she found herself unable to join in activities with her children. In 500 hours of tape, she started a conversation with them only 18 times.

Although poverty rates in the United States declined slightly in the 1990s, in recent years they have risen. Today, about 13 percent—nearly 40 million Americans—are affected. Those hit hardest are parents under age 25 with young children and elderly people who live alone. Poverty is also magnified among ethnic minorities and women. For example, 19 percent of U.S. children are poor, rates that climb to 30 percent for Hispanic children, 32 percent for Native-American children, and 34 percent for African-American children. For single mothers with preschool children, the poverty rate is close to 50 percent (DeNavas-Walt, Proctor, & Smith, 2009).

Joblessness, a high divorce rate, a high rate of adolescent parenthood, and (as we will see later) inadequate government programs to meet family needs are responsible for these disheartening statistics. The poverty rate is higher among children than any other age group. And of all Western nations, the United States has the highest percentage of extremely poor children. Nearly 8 percent of U.S. children live in deep poverty (at less than half the poverty threshold, the income level judged necessary for a minimum living standard). In contrast, in Denmark, Finland, Norway, and Sweden, child poverty rates have remained at 5 percent or less for several decades, and deep child poverty is rare (UNICEF, 2007). The earlier poverty begins, the deeper it is, and the longer it lasts, the more devastating are its effects. Children of poverty are more likely than other children to suffer from lifelong poor physical health, persistent deficits in cognitive development and academic achievement, high school dropout, mental illness, and impulsivity, aggression, and antisocial behavior (Aber, Jones & Raver, 2007; Dearing, 2008; Morgan et al., 2009; Ryan, Fauth, & Brooks-Gunn, 2006).

The constant stressors that accompany poverty gradually weaken the family system. Poor families have many daily hassles—bills to pay, the car breaking down, loss of welfare and unemployment payments, something stolen from the house, to name just a few. When daily crises arise, family members become depressed, irritable, and distracted; hostile interactions increase; and children's development suffers (Conger & Donnellan, 2007; Evans, 2006). Negative outcomes are especially severe in single-parent families and families who must live in poor housing and dangerous neighborhoods—conditions that make everyday existence even more difficult, while reducing social supports that assist in coping with economic hardship (Hart, Atkins, & Matsuba, 2008; Leventhal & Brooks-Gunn, 2003).

Besides poverty, another problem—one that has become more common in the past 30 years—has reduced the life chances of many children. On any given night, approximately 350,000 people in the United States have no place to live. An estimated 23 percent of the homeless are families with children (National Coalition for the Homeless, 2008). The rise in homelessness is mostly due to two factors: a decline in the availability of government-supported low-cost housing and the release of large numbers of mentally ill people from hospitals, without an increase in community treatment programs to help them adjust to ordinary life and get better.

Most homeless families consist of women with children under age 5. Besides health problems (which affect the majority of homeless people), many homeless children suffer from developmental delays and chronic emotional stress due to their harsh, insecure daily lives (Bratt, 2002). An estimated 25 to 30 percent of those who are old enough do not go to school. Those who do enroll achieve less well than other poverty-stricken children because of poor attendance and health and emotional difficulties (Obradovic´ et al., 2009; Shinn et al., 2008).

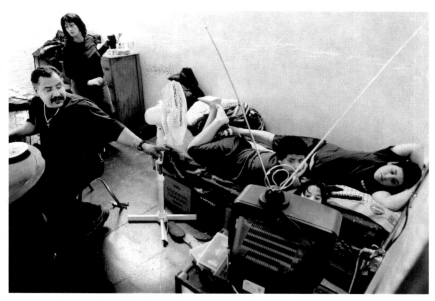

Homelessness poses enormous challenges for maintaining positive family relationships. This family has spent the last three years living in Chicago-area shelters, a circumstance that can lead to feelings of helplessness and isolation and to weakening of the family system. (AP Photo/AMY Sancetta)

Beyond the Family: Neighborhoods and Schools

As the concepts of *mesosystem* and *exosystem* in ecological systems theory make clear, connections between family and community are vital for children's well-being. From our discussion of poverty, perhaps you can see why: In poverty-stricken urban areas, community life is usually disrupted. Families move often, parks and playgrounds are in disarray, and community centers providing leisure-time activities do not exist. In such neighborhoods, family violence, child abuse and neglect, children's problem behavior, youth antisocial activity, and adult criminal behavior are especially high (Brody et al., 2003; Dunn, Schaefer-McDaniel, & Ramsay, 2010). In contrast, strong family ties to the community—as indicated by frequent contact with friends and relatives, organized youth activities, and regular church, synagogue, or mosque attendance—reduce family stress and adjustment problems (Boardman, 2004; Leventhal & Brooks-Gunn, 2003).

Neighborhoods

Let's look closely at the functions of communities in the lives of children by beginning with the neighborhood. **TAKE A MOMENT...** What were your childhood experiences like in the yards, streets, parks, and community centers surrounding your home? How did you spend your time, whom did you get to know, and how important were these moments to you?

Neighborhoods offer resources and social ties that play an important part in children's development. In several studies, low-SES families were randomly assigned vouchers to move out of public housing into neighborhoods varying widely in affluence. Compared with their peers who remained in poverty-stricken areas, children and youths who moved into low-poverty neighborhoods showed substantially better physical and mental health and school achievement (Goering, 2003; Leventhal & Brooks-Gunn, 2003).

Neighborhood resources have a greater impact on economically disadvantaged than on well-to-do young people. Higher-SES families are less dependent on their immediate surroundings for social support, education, and leisure pursuits. They can afford to transport their children to lessons and entertainment and, if necessary, to better-quality schools in distant parts of the community. In low-income neighborhoods, in-school and after-school programs that substitute for lack of other resources by providing art, music, sports, scouting, and other enrichment activities are associated with improved school performance and a reduction in emotional and behavior problems in middle childhood (Peters, Petrunka, & Arnold, 2003; Vandell & Posner, 1999; Vandell, Reisner, & Pierce, 2007). Neighborhood

These girls enjoy step-dancing lessons at a Boys and Girls Club in their California community. Neighborhood resources are especially important for economically disadvantaged children and families.
(© Tony Avelar/AP Images for Sprite)

Look and Listen:
Ask several parents to list their school-age children's regular lessons and other enrichment activities. Then inquire about home and neighborhood factors that either encourage or impede their children's participation.

organizations, such as religious youth groups and special-interest clubs, contribute to favorable development in adolescence, including increased self-confidence, school achievement, and educational aspirations (Barnes et al., 2007; Gonzales et al., 1996).

Yet in dangerous, disorganized neighborhoods, high-quality activities for children and adolescents are usually scarce. Even when they are available, crime and social disorder limit young people's access, and attendance is low (Dynarski et al., 2004). Furthermore, home and neighborhood obstacles often combine to reduce involvement. Parents overwhelmed by financial and other stressors are less likely to provide the stimulation and encouragement that motivate their children to participate (Kohen et al., 2008). In an investigation of a large sample of elementary school students diverse in SES and neighborhood residence, those living in the least stimulating homes and the most chaotic neighborhoods were least likely to participate in after-school and community-center enrichment activities (Dearing et al., 2009). Thus, the neediest children were especially likely to miss out on these development-enhancing experiences.

Just how do family–neighborhood ties reduce parenting stress and promote child development? One answer lies in their provision of *social support,* which leads to the following benefits:

- *Parental self-worth.* A neighbor or relative who listens and tries to relieve a parent's concern enhances her self-esteem. The parent, in turn, is likely to interact in a more sensitive and involved manner with her children.

- *Parental access to valuable information and services.* A friend who suggests where a parent might find a job, housing, and affordable child care and youth activities helps make the multiple roles of spouse, parent, and provider easier to fulfill.

- *Child-rearing controls and role models.* Friends, relatives, and other community members may encourage and demonstrate effective parenting practices and discourage ineffective practices.

- *Direct assistance with child rearing.* As children and adolescents participate in their parents' social networks and in neighborhood settings, other adults can influence children through warmth, stimulation, and exposure to a wider array of competent models. In this way, family–neighborhood ties can reduce the impact of ineffective parenting (Silk et al., 2004). Nearby adults can also intervene when they see young people skipping school or behaving antisocially.

The Better Beginnings, Better Futures Project of Ontario, Canada, is a government-sponsored set of pilot programs aimed at preventing the dire consequences of home and neighborhood poverty, including child and adolescent externalizing difficulties, antisocial activity, school failure, and high school dropout (Gershoff & Aber, 2006). The most successful of these efforts, using a local elementary school as its base, provided children with in-class and summer enrichment activities. Project staff also visited each child's parents regularly, informed them about community resources, and encouraged their involvement in the child's school and neighborhood life (Peters, 2005; Peters, Petrunka, & Arnold, 2003). An evaluation after four years revealed wide-ranging benefits—gains in neighborhood satisfaction, family functioning, effective parenting, and children's reading skills, along with a reduction in emotional and behavior problems.

Schools

Unlike the informal worlds of family and neighborhood, school is a formal institution designed to transmit knowledge and skills that children need to become productive members of their society. Children in the developed world spend many hours in school—6 hours a day, 5 days a week, 36 weeks a year—a total of about 14,000 hours, on average, by high school graduation. And today, because many children younger than age 5 attend "school-like" child-care centers or pre schools, the impact of schooling begins even earlier and is more powerful than these figures suggest.

Schools are complex social systems that affect many aspects of development. Schools differ in their physical environments—student body size, number of children per class, and space available for work and play. They also vary in their educational philosophies—whether teach ers regard children as passive learners to be molded by adult instruction; as active, curious beings who determine their own learning; or as collaborative partners assisted by adult experts, who guide their mastery of new skills. Finally, the social life of schools varies—for example, in the degree to which students cooperate or compete; in the extent to which students of different abilities, SES, and ethnic backgrounds learn together; and in whether classrooms, hallways, and play yards are safe, humane settings or are riddled with violence (Evans, 2006). We will discuss each of these aspects of schooling in later modules.

Schools are complex social systems that powerfully affect development. By encouraging students' active participation, this fifth-grade teacher promotes mastery of new knowledge and skills along with enthusiastic attitudes toward learning.
(© Ethan Pines/www.kippaustin.org)

Regular parent–school contact supports development at all ages. Students whose parents are involved in school activities and attend parent–teacher conferences show better academic achievement. Higher-SES parents, whose backgrounds and values are similar to those of teachers, are more likely to make phone calls and visits to school. In contrast, low-SES and ethnic minority parents often feel uncomfortable about coming to school, and daily stressors reduce the energy they have for school involvement (Grant & Ray, 2010; Jeynes, 2005; Reschly & Christenson, 2009). Parent–teacher contact is also more frequent in small towns, where most citizens know each other and schools serve as centers of community life (Peshkin, 1994). Teachers and administrators must take extra steps with low-SES and ethnic minority families and in urban areas to build supportive family–school ties.

When these efforts lead to cultures of good parenting and teaching, they deliver an extra boost to children's well-being. For example, students attending schools with many highly involved parents achieve especially well (Darling & Steinberg, 1997). And when excellent education becomes a team effort of teachers, administrators, and community members, its effects on learning are stronger and reach many more students (Hauser-Cram et al., 2006).

Look and Listen
Ask a teacher whose classroom has many students from low-SES families what percentage of parents attend parent–teacher conferences. What steps does the teacher take to promote parent–school involvement?

The Cultural Context

Child development can be fully understood only when viewed in its larger cultural context. In the following sections, we expand on this important theme by taking up the role of the *macrosystem* in development. First, we discuss ways that cultural values and practices affect environmental contexts for development. Then we consider how healthy development depends on laws and government programs that shield children from harm and foster their well-being.

Cultural Values and Practices

Cultures shape family interaction, school experiences, and community settings beyond the home—in short, all aspects of daily life. Many of us remain blind to aspects of our own cultural heritage until we see them in relation to the practices of others.

TAKE A MOMENT...Consider the question, Who should be responsible for rearing young children? How would you answer it? Here are some typical responses from my students: "If parents decide to have a baby, then they should be ready to care for it." "Most people are not happy about others intruding into family life." These statements reflect a widely held opinion in the United States—that the care and rearing of young children, and paying for that care, are the duty of parents, and only parents. This view has a long history—one in which independence, self-reliance, and the privacy of family life emerged as central American values (Halfon & McLearn, 2002). It is one reason, among others, that the public has been slow to endorse publicly supported benefits for all families, such as high-quality child care and paid employment leave for meeting family needs. And it has also contributed to the large number of U.S. children who remain poor, even though their parents are gainfully employed (Gruendel & Aber, 2007; Pohl, 2002; UNICEF, 2007).

Although the culture as a whole may value independence and privacy, not all citizens share the same values. Some belong to **subcultures**—groups of people with beliefs and customs that differ from those of the larger culture. Many ethnic minority groups in the United States have cooperative family structures, which help protect their members from the harmful effects of poverty. As the Cultural Influences box on the following page indicates, the African-American tradition of **extended-family households**, in which parent and child live with one or more adult relatives, is a vital feature of black family life that has enabled its members to survive, despite a long history of prejudice and economic deprivation. Within the extended family, grandparents play meaningful roles in guiding younger generations; adults who face employment, marital, or child-rearing difficulties receive assistance and emotional support; and caregiving is enhanced for children and the elderly. Active, involved extended families also characterize other minorities, such as Asian, Native-American, and Hispanic subcultures (Becker et al., 2003; Harwood et al., 2002).

Our discussion so far reflects a broad dimension on which cultures and subcultures differ: the extent to which *collectivism* versus *individualism* is emphasized. In **collectivist societies**, people define themselves as part of a group and stress group over individual goals. In **individualistic societies**, people think of themselves as separate entities and are largely concerned with their own personal needs (Triandis, 1995, 2005). As these definitions suggest, the two cultural patterns are associated with two distinct views of the self. Collectivist societies value an *interdependent self,* which stresses social harmony, obligations and responsibility to others, and collaborative endeavors. In contrast, individualistic societies value an *independent self,* which emphasizes personal exploration, discovery, and achievement and individual choice in relationships. Both interdependence and independence are part of the makeup of every person and occur in varying mixtures (Greenfield et al., 2003; Tamis-LeMonda et al., 2008). But societies vary greatly in the extent to which they emphasize each alternative and—as later modules will reveal—instill it in their young.

Although individualism tends to increase as cultures become more complex, cross-national differences remain. The United States is strongly individualistic, whereas most Western European countries lean toward collectivism. As we will see next, collectivist versus individualistic values have a powerful impact on a nation's approach to protecting the well-being of its children and families.

Public Policies and Child Development

When widespread social problems arise, such as poverty, homelessness, hunger, and disease, nations attempt to solve them by developing **public policies**—laws and government programs designed to improve current conditions. For example, when poverty increases and families become homeless, a country might decide to build more low-cost housing, provide economic aid to homeowners having difficulty making mortgage payments, and increase welfare benefits. When reports indicate that many children are not achieving well in school, federal and state governments might grant more tax money to school districts, strengthen teacher preparation, and make sure that help reaches children who need it most.

Nevertheless, U.S. public policies safeguarding children and youths have lagged behind policies in other developed nations. As Table 6 on page 121 reveals, the United States does not rank well on any key measure of children's health and well-being.

The problems of children and youths extend beyond the indicators in Table 6. Despite improved health-care provisions signed into law in 2010, the United States remains the only industrialized nation without a universal, publicly funded health-care system. Approximately 10 percent of U.S. children—most in low-income families—have no health insurance (Kenney, Lynch, & Cook, 2010). Further more, the United States has been slow to move toward national standards and funding for child care. Affordable care is in short supply, and much of it is substandard in quality (Lamb & Ahnert, 2006; Muenchow & Marsland, 2007). In families affected by divorce, weak enforcement of child support payments heightens poverty in mother-headed households. When they finish high school, many American non-college-bound young people lack the vocational preparation they need

TABLE 6   How Does the United States Compare to Other Nations on Indicators of Children's Health and Well-Being?

INDICATOR	U.S. RANK[a]	SOME COUNTRIES THE UNITED STATES TRAILS
Childhood poverty (among 25 industrialized nations considered)	25th	Canada, Czech Republic, Germany, Norway, Sweden, Poland, Spain[b]
Infant deaths in the first year of life (worldwide)	28th	Canada, Hong Kong, Ireland, Singapore, Spain
Teenage pregnancy rate (among 28 industrialized nations considered)	28th	Australia, Canada, Czech Republic, Denmark, Hungary, Iceland, Poland, Slovak Republic
Public expenditure on education as a percentage of gross domestic product[c] (among 22 industrialized nations considered)	12th	Belgium, France, Iceland, New Zealand, Portugal, Spain, Sweden
Public expenditure on early childhood education and child care as a percentage of gross domestic product (among 14 industrialized nations considered)	9th	Austria, Germany, Italy, Netherlands, France, Sweden
Public expenditure on health as a percentage of total health expenditure, public plus private (among 29 industrialized nations considered	29th	Austria, Australia, Canada, France, Hungary, Iceland, Switzerland, New Zealand

[a] 1 = highest, or best, rank.

[b] U.S. childhood poverty and, especially, deep poverty rates greatly exceed poverty in these nations. For example, the poverty rate is 9.5 percent in Canada, 6 percent in the Czech Republic, 4 percent in Norway, and 2.5 percent in Sweden. Deep poverty affects just 2.5 percent of children in Canada, and a fraction of 1 percent in the other countries just listed.

[c] Gross domestic product is the value of all goods and services produced by a nation during a specified time period. It provides an overall measure of a nation's wealth.

Sources: Canada Campaign 2000, 2009; OECD, 2006, 2008a, 2008b; UNICEF, 2007; U.S. Census Bureau, 2010b; U.S. Department of Education, 2010.

CULTURAL INFLUENCES

THE AFRICAN-AMERICAN EXTENDED FAMILY

The African-American extended family can be traced to the African heritage of most black Americans. In many African societies, newly married couples do not start their own households. Instead, they live with a large extended family, which assists its members with all aspects of daily life. This tradition of maintaining a broad network of kinship ties traveled to North America during the period of slavery. Since then, it has served as a protective shield against the destructive impact of poverty and racial prejudice on African-American family life. Today, more black than white adults have relatives other than their own children living in the same household. African-American parents also live closer to kin, often establish family-like relationships with friends and neighbors, see more relatives during the week, and perceive them as more important in their lives (Boyd-Franklin, 2006; Kane, 2000).

By providing emotional support and sharing income and essential resources, the African-American extended family helps reduce the stress of poverty and single parenthood. Extended-family members often help with child rearing, and adolescent mothers living in extended families are more likely to complete high school and get a job and less likely to be on welfare than mothers living on their own—factors that in turn benefit children's well-being (Gordon, Chase-Lansdale, & Brooks-Gunn, 2004; Trent & Harlan, 1994).

For single mothers who were very young at the time of their child's birth, extended-family living continues to be associated with more positive mother–child interaction during the preschool years. Otherwise, establishing

A grandmother shares a photo album chronicling family history with her son and grandchildren. Strong bonds with extended-family members have helped protect many African-American children against the destructive effects of poverty and racial prejudice.

(© Richard Lord/the Image Works)

CULTURAL INFLUENCES CONTINUED

THE AFRICAN-AMERICAN EXTENDED FAMILY

an independent household with the help of nearby relatives is related to improved child rearing. Perhaps this arrangement permits the more mature teenage mother who has developed effective parenting skills to implement them (Chase-Lansdale, Brooks-Gunn, & Zamsky, 1994). In families rearing adolescents, kinship support increases the likelihood of effective parenting, which is related to adolescents' self-reliance, emotional well-being, and reduced antisocial behavior (Hamilton, 2005; Simons et al., 2006).

Finally, the extended family plays an important role in transmitting African-American culture. Compared with nuclear-family households (which include only parents and their children), extended-family arrangements place more emphasis on cooperation and on moral and religious values. And older black adults, such as grandparents and great-grandparents, regard educating children about their African heritage as especially important (Mosely-Howard & Evans, 2000; Taylor, 2000). Family reunions—sometimes held in grandparents' and great-grandparents' hometowns in the South—are especially common among African Americans, giving young people a strong sense of their roots (Boyd-Franklin, 2006). These influences strengthen family bonds, enhance children's development, and increase the chances that the extended-family lifestyle will carry over to the next generation.

to contribute fully to society. And 8 percent of 16- to 24-year olds who dropped out of high school have not returned to earn a diploma (U.S. Department of Education, 2010).

Why have attempts to help children and youths been difficult to realize in the United States? A complex set of political and economic forces is involved. Cultural values of self-reliance and privacy have made government hesitant to become involved in family matters. Furthermore, good social programs are expensive, and they must compete for a fair share of a country's economic resources. Children can easily remain unrecognized in this process because they cannot vote or speak out to protect their own interests (Ripple & Zigler, 2003). Instead, they must rely on the goodwill of others to make them an important government priority.

Without vigilance from child advocates, policies directed at solving a particular social problem can work at cross-purposes with children's well-being, leaving them in dire straits or even worsening their con dition. For example, U.S. welfare policy aimed at returning welfare recipients to the workforce—by reducing or terminating their welfare benefits after 24 continuous months—can either help or harm children, depending on whether it lifts a family out of poverty. When welfare-to-work reduces financial strain, it relieves maternal stress, improves quality of parenting, and is associated with cognitive gains and a reduction in child behavior problems (Dunifon, Kalil, & Danziger, 2003; Gennetian & Morris, 2003; Jackson, Bentler, & Franke, 2006). In contrast, former welfare recipients who must take very low-paying jobs that perpetuate poverty often engage in harsh, coercive parenting and have poorly adjusted children (Smith et al., 2001).

Looking Toward the Future

Public policies aimed at fostering children's development can be justified on two grounds. The first is that children are the future—the parents, workers, and citizens of tomorrow. Investing in children yields valuable returns to a nation's quality of life (Heckman & Masterov, 2004).

Second, child-oriented policies can be defended on humanitarian grounds—children's basic rights as human beings. In 1989, the U.N. General Assembly, with the assistance of experts from many child-related fields, drew up the *Convention on the Rights of the Child,* a legal agreement among nations that commits each cooperating country to work toward guaranteeing environments that foster children's development, protect them from harm, and enhance their community participation and self-determination. Examples of rights include the highest attainable standard of health; an adequate standard of living; free and compulsory education; a happy, understanding, and loving family life; protection from all forms of abuse and neglect; and freedom of thought, conscience, and religion, subject to appropriate parental guidance and national law.

Although the United States played a key role in drawing up the Convention, it is one of only two countries in the world whose legislature has not yet ratified it. (The other is war-torn Somalia, which currently does not have a recognized national government.) American individualism has stood in the way. Opponents maintain that the Convention's provisions would shift the burden of child rearing from the family to the state (Melton, 2005).

Although the worrisome state of many children and families persists, efforts are being made to improve their condition. Throughout this book, we will discuss many successful programs that could be expanded. Also, growing awareness of the gap between what we know and what we do to better children's lives has led experts in child development to join with concerned citizens as advocates for more effective policies. As a result, several influential interest groups devoted to the well-being of children have emerged.

In the United States, the most vigorous is the Children's Defense Fund—a private, nonprofit organization founded by Marian Wright Edelman in 1973—which engages in research, public education, legal action, drafting of legislation, congressional testimony, and community organizing. It also publishes many reports on U.S. children's condition, government-sponsored programs that serve children and families, and proposals for improving those programs. To learn more about the Children's Defense Fund, visit its website at *www. childrensdefense.org.*

Besides strong advocacy, public policies that enhance child development depend on policy-relevant research that documents needs and evaluates programs to spark improvements. Today, more researchers are collaborating with community and government agencies to enhance the social relevance of their investigations. They are also doing a better job of disseminating their findings to the public in easily understandable, compelling ways, through television documentaries, newspaper stories, magazine articles, websites, and direct reports to government officials. In these ways, they are helping to create the sense of immediacy about the condition of children and families that is necessary to spur a society into action.

Marian Wright Edelman, founder and president of the Children's Defense Fund, speaks in support of U.S. health-care reform legislation in Washington, DC. The bill, signed into law on March 23, 2010, immediately prevented children with pre-existing health conditions from being denied insurance coverage.
(© Ryan Kelly/Congressional Quarterly/Newscom)

ASK YOURSELF

◆ **REVIEW** Links between family and community are essential for children's well-being. Provide examples and research findings from our discussion that support this idea.

◆ **APPLY** Check your local newspaper or one or two national news magazines or news websites to see how often articles on the condition of children and families appear. Why is it important for researchers to communicate with the general public about children's needs?

◆ **CONNECT** How does poverty affect the functioning of the family system, placing all aspects of development at risk?

◆ **REFLECT** Do you agree with the widespread American sentiment that government should not become involved in family life? Explain.

◇ UNTERSTANDING THE RELATIONSHIP BETWEEN HEREDITY AND ENVIRONMENT

Throughout this module, we have discussed a wide variety of genetic and environmental influences, each of which has the power to alter the course of development. Yet children who are born into the same family (and who therefore share both genes and environments) are often quite different in characteristics. We also know that some children are affected more than others by their homes, neighborhoods, and communities. In some cases, a child who is given many advantages nevertheless does poorly, while another, though exposed to unfavorable rearing conditions, does well. How do scientists explain the impact of heredity and environment when they seem to work in so many different ways?

Behavioral genetics is a field devoted to uncovering the contributions of nature and nurture to this diversity in human traits and abilities. All contemporary researchers agree that both heredity and environment are involved in every aspect of development. But for polygenic traits (those due to many genes) such as intelligence and personality, scientists are a long way from knowing the precise hereditary influences involved. Although they are making progress in identifying the multiple variations in DNA sequences associated with complex traits, so far these genetic markers explain only a

Children vary widely in mental abilities and personality traits. Most contemporary researchers seek to clarify how heredity and environment jointly contribute to individual differences in these complex characteristics.

(© Fancy/Alamy)

small amount of variation in human behavior, and a minority of cases of most psychological disorders (Plomin, 2005; Plomin & Davis, 2009). For the most part, scientists are still limited to investigating the impact of genes on complex characteristics indirectly.

Some believe that it is useful and possible to answer the question of *how much each factor contributes* to differences among children. A growing consensus, however, regards that question as unanswerable. These investigators believe that heredity and environment are inseparable (Gottlieb, Wahlsten, & Lickliter, 2006; Lerner & Overton, 2008). The important question, they maintain, is *how nature and nurture work together*. Let's consider each position in turn.

The Question, "How Much?"

To infer the role of heredity in complex human characteristics, researchers use special methods, the most common being the *heritability estimate*. Let's look closely at the information this procedure yields, along with its limitations.

Heritability

Heritability estimates measure the extent to which individual differences in complex traits in a specific population are due to genetic factors. We will take a brief look at heritability findings on intelligence and personality here and will return to them in later modules, when we consider these topics in greater detail. Heritability estimates are obtained from **kinship studies,** which compare the characteristics of family members. The most common type of kinship study compares identical twins, who share all their genes, with fraternal twins, who share only some. If people who are genetically more alike are also more similar in intelligence and personality, then the researcher assumes that heredity plays an important role.

Kinship studies of intelligence provide some of the most controversial findings in the field of child development. Some experts claim a strong genetic influence, whereas others believe that heredity is barely involved. Currently, most kinship findings support a moderate role for heredity. When many twin studies are examined, correlations between the scores of identical twins are consistently higher than those of fraternal twins. In a summary of more than 10,000 twin pairs, the average correlation was .86 for identical twins and .60 for fraternal twins (Plomin & Spinath, 2004).

Adriana and Tamara, identical twins born in Mexico, were separated at birth and adopted into different homes in the New York City area. They were unaware of each other's existence until age 20, when they met through a mutual acquaintance. The twins found that they had many similarities—academic achievement, a love of dancing, even similar taste in clothing. The study of identical twins reared apart reveals that heredity contributes to many personality characteristics. But generalizing from twin evidence to the population is controversial.

(© Jacquie Hemmerdinger/The New York Times/ Redux Pictures)

Researchers use a complex statistical procedure to compare these correlations, arriving at a heritability estimate ranging from 0 to 1.00. The value for intelligence is about .50 for child and adolescent twin samples in Western industrialized nations. This suggests that differences in genetic makeup explain half the variation in intelligence. Adopted children's mental test scores are more strongly related to their biological parents' scores than to those of their adoptive parents, offering further support for the role of heredity (Petrill & Deater-Deckard, 2004).

Heritability research also reveals that genetic factors are important in personality. For frequently studied traits, such as sociability, anxiety, agreeableness, and activity level, heritability estimates obtained on child and adolescent and young adult twins are moderate, in the .40s and .50s (Caspi & Shiner, 2006; Rothbart & Bates, 2006; Wright et al., 2008).

Twin studies of schizophrenia—a psychological disorder involving delusions and hallucinations, difficulty distinguishing fantasy from reality, and irrational and inappropriate behaviors—consistently yield high heritabilities, around .80. The role of heredity in antisocial behavior and major depression, though still apparent, is less strong, with heritabilities in the .30s and .40s (Faraone, 2008). Again, adoption studies support these results. Biological relatives of schizophrenic and depressed adoptees are more likely than adoptive relatives to share the same disorder (Plomin et al., 2001; Ridenour, 2000; Tienari et al., 2003).

Limitations of Heritability

Serious questions have been raised about the accuracy of heritability estimates, which depends on the extent to which the twin pairs studied reflect genetic and environmental variation in the population. Within a population in which all people have very similar home, school, and community experiences, individual differences in intelligence and personality would be largely genetic, and heritability estimates would be close to 1.00. Conversely, the more environments vary, the more likely they are to account for individual differences, yielding lower heritability estimates. In twin studies, most twin pairs are reared together under highly similar conditions. Even when separated twins are available for study, social service agencies have often placed them in advantaged homes that are alike in many ways (Rutter et al., 2001). Because the environments of most twin pairs are less diverse than those of the general population, heritability estimates are likely to exaggerate the role of heredity.

Heritability estimates are controversial measures because they can easily be misapplied. For example, high heritabilities have been used to suggest that ethnic differences in intelligence, such as the poorer performance of black children compared to white children, have a genetic basis (Jensen, 1969, 1998, 2001; Rushton & Jensen, 2005, 2006). Yet this line of reasoning is widely regarded as incorrect. Heritabilities computed on mostly white twin samples do not tell us what causes test score differences between ethnic groups. We have already seen that large economic and cultural differences are involved. We will discuss research indicating that when black children are adopted into economically advantaged homes at an early age, their scores are well above average and substantially higher than those of children growing up in impoverished families.

Perhaps the most serious criticism of heritability estimates has to do with their limited usefulness. Though interesting, these estimates give us no precise information on how intelligence and personality develop or how children might respond to environments designed to help them develop as far as possible (Baltes, Lindenberger, & Staudinger, 2006; Rutter, 2002). Indeed, the heritability of children's intelligence increases as parental education and income increase—that is, as children grow up in conditions that allow them to make the most of their genetic endowment. In impoverished environments, children are prevented from realizing their potential. Consequently, enhancing experiences through interventions—such as parent education and high-quality preschool or child care—has a greater impact on the development of low-SES than higher-SES children (Bronfenbrenner & Morris, 2006; Turkheimer et al., 2003).

According to one group of experts, heritability estimates have too many problems to yield any firm conclusions about the relative strength of nature and nurture (Collins et al., 2000). Although these statistics confirm that heredity contributes to complex traits, they do not tell us how environment can modify genetic influences.

The Question, "How?"

Today, most researchers view development as the result of a dynamic interplay between heredity and environment. How do nature and nurture work together? Several concepts shed light on this question.

Reaction Range

The first of these ideas is **range of reaction**—each person's unique, genetically determined response to the environment (Gottesman, 1963). Let's explore this idea in Figure 9. Reaction range can apply to any characteristic; here it is illustrated for intelligence. Notice that when environments vary from extremely unstimulating to highly enriched, Ben's intelligence increases steadily, Linda's rises sharply and then falls off, and Ron's begins to increase only after the environment becomes modestly stimulating.

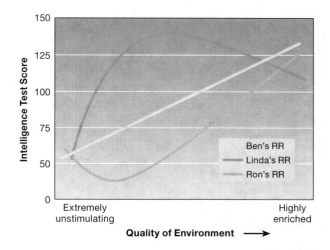

FIGURE 9   Intellectual Ranges of Reaction (RR) for Three Children in Environments that Vary from Extremely Unstimulating to Highly Enriched

Each child, because of his or her genetic makeup, responds differently to changes in quality of the environment. Ben's intelligence test score increases steadily, Linda's rises sharply and then falls off, and Ron's begins to increase only after the environment becomes modestly stimulating.

Source: Adapted from Wahlsten, 1994.

Reaction range highlights two important points. First, it shows that because each of us has a unique genetic makeup, we respond differently to the same environment. Note in Figure 9 how a poor environment results in similarly low scores for all three individuals. But when the environment provides an intermediate level of stimulation, Linda is by far the best-performing child. And in a highly enriched environment, Ben does best, followed by Ron, both of whom now outperform Linda.

Second, sometimes different genetic–environmental combinations can make two people look the same! For example, if Linda is reared in a minimally stimulating environment, her score will be about 100—average for children in general. Ben and Ron can also obtain this score, but to do so, they must grow up in a fairly enriched home. In sum, range of reaction reveals that unique blends of heredity and environment lead to both similarities and differences in behavior (Gottlieb, Wahlsten, & Lickliter, 2006).

Canalization

Another way of understanding how heredity and environment combine comes from the concept of **canalization**—the tendency of heredity to restrict the development of some characteristics to just one or a few outcomes. A behavior that is strongly canalized develops similarly in a wide range of environments; only strong environmental forces can change it (Waddington, 1957). For example, infant perceptual and motor development seems to be strongly canalized because all normal human babies eventually roll over, reach for objects, sit up, crawl, and walk. It takes extreme conditions to modify these behaviors or cause them not to appear. In contrast, intelligence and personality are less strongly canalized; they vary much more with changes in the environment.

When we look at behaviors that are constrained by heredity, we can see that canalization is highly adaptive. Through it, nature ensures that children will develop certain species-typical skills under a wide range of rearing conditions, thereby promoting survival.

Genetic–Environmental Correlation

A major problem in trying to separate heredity and environment is that they are often correlated (Plomin, 2009; Scarr & McCartney, 1983). According to the concept of **genetic–environmental correlation,** our genes influence the environments to which we are exposed. The way this happens changes with age.

Passive and Evocative Correlation. At younger ages, two types of genetic–environmental correlation are common. The first is called *passive* correlation because the child has no control over it. Early on, parents provide environments influenced by their own heredity. For example, parents who are good athletes emphasize outdoor activities and enroll their children in swimming and gymnastics. Besides being exposed to an "athletic environment," the children may have inherited their parents' athletic ability. As a result, they are likely to become good athletes for both genetic and environmental reasons.

The second type of genetic–environmental correlation is *evocative*. The responses children evoke from others are influenced by the child's heredity, and these responses strengthen the child's original style. For example, an active, friendly baby is likely to receive more social stimulation than a passive, quiet infant. And a cooperative, attentive child probably receives more patient and sensitive interactions from parents than an inattentive, distractible child. In support of this idea, the less genetically alike siblings are, the more their parents treat them differently, in both warmth and negativity. Thus, parents' treatment of identical twins is highly similar, whereas their treatment of fraternal twins and nontwin biological siblings is only moderately so. And little resemblance exists in parents' warm and negative interactions with unrelated stepsiblings (see Figure 10) (Reiss, 2003).

This mother shares her love of the piano with her daughter, who also may have inherited her mother's musical talent. When heredity and environment are correlated, they jointly foster the same capacities, and the influence of one cannot be separated from the influence of the other.
(© Lou Cypher/Corbis)

Active Correlation.   At older ages, active genetic–environmental correlation becomes common. As children extend their experiences beyond the immediate family and are given the freedom to make more choices, they actively seek environments that fit with their genetic tendencies. The well-coordinated, muscular child spends more time at after-school sports, the musically talented youngster joins the school orchestra and practices his violin, and the intellectually curious child is a familiar patron at her local library.

This tendency to actively choose environments that complement our heredity is called **niche-picking** (Scarr & McCartney, 1983). Infants and young children cannot do much niche-picking because adults select environments for them. In contrast, older children and adolescents are much more in charge of their environments.

The niche-picking idea explains why pairs of identical twins reared apart during childhood and later reunited may find, to their surprise, that they have similar hobbies, food preferences, and vocations—a trend that is especially marked when twins' environmental opportunities are similar (Plomin, 1994). Niche-picking also helps us understand why identical twins become somewhat more alike, and fraternal twins and adopted siblings less alike, in intelligence with age (Bouchard, 2004; Loehlin, Horn, & Willerman, 1997). And niche-picking sheds light on why adolescent identical twin pairs—far more often than same-sex fraternal pairs, ordinary siblings, and adopted siblings—report similar stressful life events influenced by personal decisions and actions, such as failing a course, quitting a job, or getting in trouble for drug-taking (Bemmels et al., 2008).

The influence of heredity and environment is not constant but changes over time. With age, genetic factors may become more important in influencing the environments we experience and choose for ourselves.

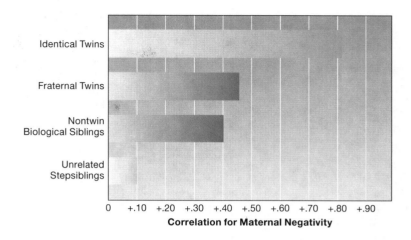

FIGURE 10   Similarity in Mothers' Interactions for Pairs of Siblings Differing in Genetic Relatedness

The correlations shown are for maternal negativity. The pattern illustrates evocative genetic–environmental correlation. Identical twins evoke similar maternal treatment because of their identical heredity. As genetic resemblance between siblings declines, the strength of the correlation drops. Mothers vary their interactions as they respond to each child's unique genetic makeup.

Source: Adapted from Reiss, 2003.

Environmental Influences on Gene Expression

Notice how, in the concepts just considered, heredity is granted priority. In range of reaction, it *determines* individual responsiveness to varying environments. In canalization, it *restricts* the development of certain behaviors. Similarly, genetic–environmental correlation is viewed as *driven* by genetics, in that children's genetic makeup causes them to receive, evoke, or seek experiences that actualize their inborn tendencies (Plomin, 2009; Rowe, 1994).

A growing number of researchers take issue with the supremacy of heredity, arguing that it does not dictate children's experiences or development in a rigid way. In one study, boys with a genetic tendency toward antisocial behavior (based on the presence of a gene on the X chromosome known to predispose both animals and humans to aggression) were no more aggressive than boys without this gene, *unless* they also had a history of severe child abuse (Caspi et al., 2002). Boys with and without the gene did not differ in their experience of abuse, indicating that the "aggressive genotype" did not increase exposure to abuse. And in a large Finnish adoption study, children whose biological mothers had schizophrenia but who were being reared by healthy adoptive parents showed little mental illness—no more than a control group with healthy biological and adoptive parents. In contrast, schizophrenia and other psychological impairments piled up in adoptees whose biological and adoptive parents were both disturbed (Tienari et al., 2003; Tienari, Wahlberg, & Wynne, 2006).

Furthermore, parents and other caring adults can *uncouple* unfavorable genetic–environmental correlations. They often provide children with positive experiences that modify the expression of heredity, yielding favorable outcomes. For example, in a study that tracked the development

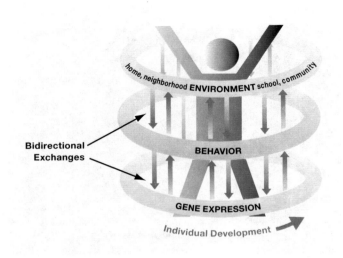

FIGURE 11 The Epigenetic Framework

Development takes place through ongoing, bidirectional exchanges between heredity and all levels of the environment. Genes affect behavior and experiences. Experiences and behavior also affect gene expression.

Source: Adapted from Gottlieb, 2007.

of 5-year-old identical twins, pair members tended to resemble each other in level of aggression. And the more aggression they displayed, the more maternal anger and criticism they received (a genetic–environmental correlation). Nevertheless, some mothers treated their twins differently. When followed up at age 7, twins who had been targets of more maternal negativity engaged in even more antisocial behavior. In contrast, their better-treated, genetically identical counterparts showed a reduction in disruptive acts (Caspi et al., 2004). Good parenting protected them from a spiraling, antisocial course of development.

Accumulating evidence reveals that the relationship between heredity and environment is not a one-way street, from genes to environment to behavior. Rather, like other system influences considered in this and the previous modules, it is *bidirectional:* Genes affect children's behavior and experiences, but their experiences and behavior also affect gene expression (Diamond, 2009; Gottlieb, 2003; Rutter, 2007a). Stimulation—both *internal* to the child (activity within the cytoplasm of the cell, hormones released into the bloodstream) and *external* to the child (home, neighborhood, school, and society)—modifies gene activity.

Researchers call this view of the relationship between heredity and environment the *epigenetic framework* (Gottlieb, 1998, 2007). It is depicted in Figure 11. **Epigenesis** means development resulting from ongoing, bidirectional exchanges between heredity and all levels of the environment. To illustrate, providing a baby with a healthy diet promotes brain growth, leading to new connections among nerve cells, which transform gene expression. This opens the door to new gene–environment exchanges—for example, advanced exploration of objects and interaction with caregivers, which further enhance brain growth and gene expression. These ongoing bidirectional influences foster cognitive and social development. In contrast, harmful environments can interfere with gene expression (see the Biology and Environment box on the following page for an example). And at times, the impact is so profound that later experiences can do little to change characteristics (such as intelligence and personality) that originally were flexible.

BIOLOGY AND ENVIRONMENT

A CASE OF EPIGENESIS: SMOKING DURING PREGNANCY ALTERS GENE EXPRESSION

A wealth of experimental research with animals confirms that environment can modify the genome in ways that have no impact on a gene's sequence of base pairs but nevertheless affect the operation of that gene (Zhang & Meaney, 2010). This epigenetic interplay, in which a gene's impact on the individual's phenotype depends on the gene's context, is now being vigorously investigated in humans.

Maternal smoking during pregnancy is among the risk factors for *attention-deficit hyperactivity disorder (ADHD)*—one of the most common disorders of childhood. ADHD symptoms—inattention, impulsivity, and overactivity—typically result in serious academic and social problems. Several studies report that individuals who are homozygous for a chromosome-12 gene (DD) containing a special repeat of base pairs are at increased risk for ADHD. Other research, however, has not confirmed any role for this gene (Fisher et al., 2002; Gill et al., 1997; Waldman et al., 1998).

Animal evidence suggests that one reason for this inconsistency is that environmental influences associated with ADHD—such as prenatal exposure to toxins—modify the gene's activity. To test this possibility, researchers recruited several hundred mothers and their 6-month-old babies, obtaining infant blood samples for genetic analysis and asking mothers whether they smoked regularly during pregnancy (Kahn et al., 2003). At a 5-year follow-up, parents responded to a widely used behavior rating scale that assesses children for ADHD symptoms.

Findings revealed that by itself, the DD genotype was unrelated to impulsivity, overactivity, or oppositional behavior. But children whose mothers had smoked during pregnancy scored higher in these behaviors than children of nonsmoking mothers. Furthermore, as Figure 12 illustrates, 5-year-olds with both prenatal nicotine exposure and the DD genetic makeup obtained substantially higher impulsivity, overactivity, and oppositional scores than all other groups—outcomes that persisted even after a variety of other factors (quality of the home environment and maternal ethnicity, marital status, and post-birth smoking) had been controlled.

BIOLOGY AND ENVIRONMENT CONTINUED

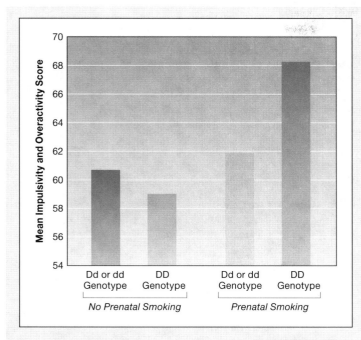

FIGURE 12 Combined Influence of Maternal Prenatal Smoking and Genotype on Impulsivity and Overactivity at age 5

In the absence of prenatal smoking, 5-year-olds who were homozygous for a chromosome-12 gene (DD) showed no elevation in impulsivity and overactivity (orange bar) compared with children of other genotypes (Dd or dd) (red bar). Among children of all genotypes, prenatal smoking was associated with an increase in these behaviors (green and purple bars). And the combination of prenatal smoking and the DD genotype greatly magnified impulsivity and overactivity (purple bar). Children's oppositional behavior followed a similar epigenetic pattern.

Source: Adapted from Kahn et al., 2003.

Another investigation following participants into adolescence obtained similar findings, suggesting that the genotype–prenatal environment effect persists (Becker et al., 2008). What processes might account for it? In animal research, tobacco smoke stimulates the DD genotype to release chemicals in the brain that promote impulsivity and overactivity (Ernst, Moolchan, & Robinson, 2001). These behaviors, in turn, often evoke harsh, punitive parenting, which can trigger defiance in children.

The DD genotype is widespread, present in more than 50 percent of people. Thus, the majority of children prenatally exposed to nicotine are at high risk for learning and behavior problems. Smoking during pregnancy has additional negative health consequences. And other genes, in epigenetic interplay with as yet unknown environmental factors, contribute to ADHD symptoms (Hudziak & Rettew, 2009).

Because his mother smoked during pregnancy, this baby may be at increased risk for developing attention-deficit hyperactivity disorder (ADHD). Prenatal exposure to nicotine seems to alter expression of a chromosome-12 gene in ways that greatly heighten impulsivity, overactivity, and oppositional behavior. (© Image Source/Getty Images)

A major reason that researchers are interested in the nature–nurture issue is that they want to improve environments so that children can develop as far as possible. The concept of epigenesis reminds us that development is best understood as a series of complex exchanges between nature and nurture. Although children cannot be changed in any way we might desire, environments can modify genetic influences. The success of any attempt to improve development depends on the characteristics we want to change, the genetic makeup of the child, and the type and timing of our intervention.

ASK YOURSELF

◆ **REVIEW** What is epigenesis, and how does it differ from range of reaction and genetic–environmental correlation? Provide an example of epigenesis.

◆ **APPLY** Bianca's parents are accomplished musicians. At age 4, Bianca began taking piano lessons. By age 10, she was accompanying the school choir. At age 14, she asked if she could attend a special music high school. Explain how genetic–environmental correlation promoted Bianca's talent.

◆ **CONNECT** Explain how each of the following concepts supports the conclusion that genetic influences on human characteristics are not constant but change over time: somatic mutation (page 102), niche-picking (page 127), and epigenesis (page 128).

◆ **REFLECT** What aspects of your own development—for example, interests, hobbies, college major, or vocational choice—are probably due to niche-picking? Explain.

◇ SUMMARY

Genetic Foundations

What are genes, and how are they transmitted from one generation to the next?

(© Rachel Epstein/Photoedit)

◆ Each individual's **phenotype,** or directly observable characteristics, is a product of both **genotype** and environment. **Chromosomes,** rodlike structures within the cell nucleus, contain our hereditary endowment. Along their length are **genes**, segments of **deoxyribonucleic acid (DNA),** that send instructions for making a rich assortment of proteins to the cytoplasm of the cell—a process that makes us distinctly human and influences our development and characteristics.

◆ **Gametes,** or sex cells, are produced through a cell division process called **meiosis. Crossing over** and chance assortment of chromosomes into gametes ensure that each receives a unique set of genes from each parent. Once sperm and ovum unite, the resulting **zygote** starts to develop into a complex human being through cell duplication, or **mitosis.**

◆ If the fertilizing sperm carries an X chromosome, the child will be a girl; if it contains a Y chromosome, a boy. **Fraternal**, or **dizygotic**, **twins** result when two ova are released from the mother's ovaries and each is fertilized. **Identical**, or **monozygotic**, **twins** develop when a zygote divides in two during the early stages of cell duplication.

Describe various patterns of genetic inheritance

◆ Traits controlled by single genes follow **dominant–recessive** and **incomplete dominance** patterns of inheritance. **Homozygous** individuals have two identical **alleles**, or forms of a gene. **Heterozygous** individuals, with one dominant and one recessive allele, are **carriers** of the recessive trait. In **incomplete dominance**, both alleles are expressed in the phenotype, resulting in a trait that combines aspects of both. **Modifier genes** enhance or dilute the effects of other genes.

◆ **X-linked inheritance** applies when recessive disorders are carried on the X chromosome and, therefore, are more likely to affect males. In **genomic imprinting**, one parent's allele is activated, regardless of its makeup.

◆ Harmful genes arise from **mutation**, which can occur spontaneously or be caused by hazardous environmental agents. Germline mutation occurs in the cells that give rise to gametes; somatic mutation can occur in body cells at any time of life.

◆ Human traits that vary continuously among people, such as intelligence and personality, result from **polygenic inheritance**—the effects of many genes. For such characteristics, scientists must study the influence of heredity indirectly.

Describe major chromosomal abnormalities, and explain how they occur

◆ Most chromosomal abnormalities are due to errors in meiosis. The most common is Down syndrome, which results in physical defects and mental retardation. Disorders of the **sex chromosomes**—XYY, triple X, Klinefelter, and Turner syndromes—are milder than defects of the **autosomes**.

Reproductive Choices

What procedures can assist prospective parents in having healthy children?

(© Joey Mcleister/Mct/
Landov)

◆ **Genetic counseling** helps couples at risk for giving birth to children with genetic abnormalities consider appropriate reproductive options. **Prenatal diagnostic methods** allow early detection of genetic problems.

◆ Reproductive technologies, such as donor insemination, in vitro fertilization, surrogate motherhood, and postmenopausal-assisted childbirth, permit many individuals to become parents who otherwise would not, but they raise serious legal and ethical concerns.

◆ Many parents who cannot conceive or who have a high likelihood of transmitting a genetic disorder decide to adopt. Although adopted children tend to have more learning and emotional problems than children in general, most fare well in the long run. Warm, sensitive parenting predicts favorable development.

Environmental Contexts for Development

Describe family functioning from the perspective of ecological systems theory, along with aspects of the environment that support family well-being and children's development

◆ The first and foremost context for child development is the family, a dynamic system characterized by bidirectional influences, in which each family member's behaviors affect those of others. Both direct and indirect influences operate within the family system, which must continually adjust to new events and changes in its members.

◆ **Socioeconomic status (SES)** profoundly affects family functioning. Higher-SES families tend to be smaller, to emphasize psychological traits, and to engage in warm, verbally stimulating interaction with children. Lower-SES families often stress external characteristics and use more commands, criticism, and physical punishment. Many affluent families are physically and emotionally unavailable, thereby impairing their children's adjustment. Poverty and homelessness undermine effective parenting and pose serious threats to children's development.

◆ Children benefit from supportive ties between the family and the surrounding environment. including stable, socially cohesive neighborhoods that provide constructive leisure and enrichment activities and that offer parents access to social support. High-quality schools with frequent parent–teacher contact are also vital.

◆ The values and practices of cultures and **subcultures** affect all aspects of children's daily lives. **Extended-family households**, which are common among many ethnic minority groups, help protect children from negative effects of poverty and other stressful conditions.

◆ **Collectivist societies**, which emphasize group needs and goals, and **individualistic societies**, which emphasize individual well-being, take different approaches to developing **public policies** to address social problems, including those affecting children. Largely because of its strongly individualistic values, the United States lags behind other developed nations in policies safeguarding children and youths.

Understanding the Relationship Between Heredity and Environment

Explain the various ways heredity and environment may combine to influence complex traits.

◆ **Behavioral genetics** is a field that examines the contributions of nature and nurture to complex traits. Researchers use **kinship studies** to compute **heritability estimates**, which show that genetic factors influence such traits as intelligence and personality. However, the accuracy and usefulness of heritability estimates have been challenged.

◆ According to the concepts of **range of reaction** and **canalization**, heredity influences children's responsiveness to varying environments. **Genetic–environmental correlation** and **niche-picking** describe how children's genes affect the environments to which they are exposed. **Epigenesis** reminds us that development is best understood as a series of complex exchanges between nature and nurture.

(© Fancy/Alamy)

◇ IMPORTANT TERMS AND CONCEPTS

allele (p. 98)
autosomes (p. 97)
behavioral genetics (p. 123)
canalization (p. 126)
carrier (p. 98)
chromosomes (p. 94)
collectivist societies (p. 120)
coparenting (p. 112)
crossing over (p. 96)
deoxyribonucleic acid (DNA) (p. 95)
dominant–recessive inheritance (p. 98)
epigenesis (p. 128)
extended-family household (p. 120)
fraternal, or dizygotic, twins (p. 97)
gametes (p. 96)

gene (p. 95)
genetic counseling (p. 105)
genetic–environmental
  correlation (p. 126)
genomic imprinting (p. 101)
genotype (p. 94)
heritability estimate (p. 124)
heterozygous (p. 98)
homozygous (p. 98)
identical, or monozygotic, twins (p. 97)
incomplete dominance (p. 99)
individualistic societies (p. 120)
kinship studies (p. 124)
meiosis (p. 96)
mitosis (p. 95)

modifier genes (p. 99)
mutation (p. 102)
niche-picking (p. 127)
phenotype (p. 94)
polygenic inheritance (p. 102)
prenatal diagnostic
  methods (p. 105)
public policies (p. 120)
range of reaction (p. 125)
sex chromosomes (p. 97)
socioeconomic status
  (SES) (p. 113)
subculture (p. 120)
X-linked inheritance (p. 101)
zygote (p. 96)

◇ REFERENCES

Aber, J. L., Jones, S. M., & Raver, C. C. (2007). Poverty and life development: New perspectives on a defining issue. In J. L. Aber, S. J. Bishop-Josef, S. M. Jones, K. T. McLearn, & D. A. Phillips (Eds.), *Child development and social policy: Knowledge for action* (pp. 149–166). Washington, DC: American Psychological Association.

Adamson, D. (2005). Regulation of assisted reproductive technologies in the United States. *Family Law Quarterly, 39,* 727–744.

Alter, J. (2008, September 29). It's not just about the boys. Get girls into school. *Newsweek,* pp. 50–51.

Anderson, P. J., Wood, S. J., Francis, D. E., Coleman, L., Anderson, V., & Boneh, A. (2007). Are neuropsychological impairments in children with early-treated phenylketonuria (PKU) related to white matter abnormalities or elevated phenylalanine levels? *Developmental Neuropsychology, 32,* 645–668.

Arcus, D., & Chambers, P. (2008). Childhood risks associated with adoption. In T. P. Gullotta & G. M. Blau (Eds.), *Family influences on childhood behavior and development* (pp. 117–142). New York: Routledge.

Baltes, P. B., Lindenberger, U., & Staudinger, U. M. (2006). Life span theory in developmental psychology. In R. M. Lerner & W. Damon (Eds.), *Handbook of child psychology: Vol. 1. Theoretical models of human development* (6th ed., pp. 569–664). Hoboken, N.J.: Wiley.

Barnes, G. M., Hoffman, J. H., Welte, J. W., Farrell, M. P., & Dintcheff, B. A. (2007). Adolescents' time use: Effects on substance use, delinquency and sexual activity. *Journal of Youth and Adolescence, 36,* 697–710.

Becker, G., Beyene, Y., Newsome, E., & Mayen, N. (2003). Creating continuity through mutual assistance: Intergenerational reciprocity in four ethnic groups. *Journal of Gerontology, 38B,* S151–S159.

Becker, K., El-Faddagh, M., Schmidt, M. H., Esser, G., & Laucht, M. (2008). Interaction of dopamine transporter genotype with prenatal smoke exposure on ADHD symptoms. *Journal of Pediatrics, 152,* 263–269.

Bellamy, C. (2004). *The state of the world's children: 2004.* New York: UNICEF.

Bemmels, H. R., Burt, A., Legrand, L. N., Iacono, W. G., & McGue, M. (2008). The heritability of life events: An adolescent twin and adoption study. *Twin Research and Human Genetics, 11,* 257–265.

Benarroch, F., Hirsch, H. J., Genstil, L., Landau, Y. E., & Gross-Tsur, V. (2007). Prader-Willi syndrome: Medical prevention and behavioral challenges. *Child and Adolescent Psychiatric Clinics of North America, 16,* 695–708.

Berkowitz, R. L., Roberts, J., & Minkoff, H. (2006). Challenging the strategy of maternal age-based prenatal genetic counseling. *Journal of the American Medical Association, 295,* 1446–1448.

Bhagavath, B., & Layman, L. C. (2007). The genetics of hypogonadotropic hypogonadism. *Seminars in Reproductive Medicine, 25,* 272–286.

Bimmel, N., Juffer, F., van IJzendoorn, M. H., & Bakermans-Kranenburg, M. J. (2003). Problem behavior of internationally adopted adolescents: A review and meta-analysis. *Harvard Review of Psychiatry, 11,* 64–77.

Bioethics Consultative Committee. (2003). *Comparison of ethics legislation in Europe.* Retrieved from www.synapse.net.mt/bioethics/euroleg1.htm

Boardman, J. D. (2004). Stress and physical health: The role of neighborhoods as mediating and moderating mechanisms. *Social Science and Medicine, 58,* 2473–2483.

Bouchard, T. J. (2004) Genetic influence on human psychological traits: A survey. *Current Directions in Psychological Science, 13,* 148–151.

Boyd-Franklin, N. (2006). *Black families in therapy* (2nd ed.). New York: Guilford.

Bradley, R. H., & Corwyn, R. F. (2003). Age and ethnic variations in family process mediators of SES. In M. H. Bornstein & R. H. Bradley (Eds.), *Socioeconomic status, parenting, and child development* (pp. 161–188). Mahwah, NJ: Erlbaum.

Bratt, R. G. (2002). Housing: The foundation of family life. In F. Jacobs, D. Wertlieb, & R. M. Lerner (Eds.), *Handbook of applied developmental science* (Vol. 2, pp. 445–468). Thousand Oaks, CA: Sage.

Brody, G. H., Ge, X., Kim, S. Y., Murry, V. M., Simons, R. L., & Gibbons, F. X. (2003). Neighborhood disadvantage moderates associations of parenting and older sibling problem attitudes and behavior with conduct disorders in African American children. *Journal of Consulting and Clinical Psychology, 71,* 211–222.

Bronfenbrenner, U., & Morris, P. A. (2006). The bioecological model of human development. In R. M. Lerner (Ed.), *Handbook of child psychology: Vol. 1. Theoretical models of human development* (6th ed., pp. 793–828). Hoboken, NJ: Wiley.

Bush, K. R., & Peterson, G. W. (2008). Family influences on child development. In T. P. Gullotta & G. M. Blau (Eds.), *Handbook of child behavioral issues: Evidence-based approaches to prevention and treatment* (pp. 43–67). New York: Routledge.

Butler, M., & Meaney, J. (Eds.). (2005). *Genetics of developmental disabilities.* Boca Raton, FL: Taylor & Francis.

Caldera, Y. M., & Lindsey, E. W. (2006). Coparenting, mother–infant interaction, and infant–parent attachment relationships in two-parent families. *Journal of Family Psychology, 20,* 275–283.

Canada Campaign 2000. (2009). 2009 Report Card on Child and Family Poverty in Canada: 1989–2009. Retrieved from www.campaign2000.ca/reportcards.html

Carr, J. (2002). Down syndrome. In P. Howlin & O. Udwin (Eds.), *Outcomes in neurodevelopmental and genetic disorders* (pp. 169–197). New York: Cambridge University Press.

Caspi, A., McClay, J., Moffitt, T. E., Mill, J., Martin, J., & Craig, I. W. (2002). Role of genotype in the cycle of violence in maltreated children. *Science, 297,* 851–854.

Caspi, A., Moffitt, T. E., Morgan, J., Rutter, M., Taylor, A., Kim-Cohen, J., & Polo-Tomas, M. (2004). Maternal expressed emotion predicts children's antisocial behavior problems: Using monozygotic-twin differences to identify environmental effects on behavioral development. *Developmental Psychology, 40,* 149–161.

Caspi, A., & Shiner, L. (2006). Personality development. In N. Eisenberg (Ed.), *Handbook of child psychology: Vol. 3. Social, emotional, and personality development* (6th ed., pp. 300–365). Hoboken, NJ: Wiley.

Catalano, R. A. (2003). Sex ratios in the two Germanies: A test of the economic stress hypothesis. *Human Reproduction, 18,* 1972–1975.

Catalano, R., Ahern, J., Bruckner, T., Anderson, E., & Saxton, K. (2009). Gender-specific selection in utero among contemporary human birth cohorts. *Paediatric and Perinatal Epidemiology, 23,* 273–278.

Catalano, R., Bruckner, T., Anderson, E., & Gould, J. B. (2005). Fetal death sex ratios: A test of the economic stress hypothesis. *International Journal of Epidemiology, 34,* 944–948.

Chase-Lansdale, P. L., Brooks-Gunn, J., & Zamsky, E. S. (1994). Young African-American multi-generational families in poverty: Quality of mothering and grandmothering. *Child Development, 65,* 373–393.

Chen, M. (2003). Wombs for rent: An examination of prohibitory and regulatory approaches to governing preconception arrangements. *Health Law in Canada, 23,* 33–50.

Christ, S. E., Steiner, R. D., Grange, D. K., Abrams, R. A., & White, D. A. (2006). Inhibitory control in children with phenylketonuria. *Developmental Neuropsychology, 30,* 845–864.

Collins, W. A., Maccoby, E. E., Steinberg, L., Hetherington, E. M., & Bornstein, M. H. (2000). Contemporary research on parenting: The case for nature and nurture. *American Psychologist, 52,* 218–232.

Conger, R. D., & Donnellan, M. B. (2007). An interactionist perspective on the socioeconomic context of human development. *Annual Review of Psychology, 58,* 175–199.

Cummings, E. M., Goeke-Morey, M. C., & Papp, L. M. (2004). Everyday marital conflict and child aggression. *Journal of Abnormal Child Psychology, 32,* 191–202.

Cummings, E. M., & Merrilees, C. E. (2010). Identifying the dynamic processes underlying links between marital conflict and child adjustment. In M. S. Schulz, M. K. Pruett, P. K. Kerig, & R. D. Parke (Eds.), *Strengthening couple relationships for optimal child development* (pp. 27–40). Washington, DC: American Psychological Association.

Cutter, W. J., Daly, E. M., Robertson, D. M. W., Chitnis, X. A., van Amelsvoort, T. A. M. J., Simmons, A., et al. (2006). Influence of X chromosome and hormones on human brain development: A magnetic resonance imaging and proton magnetic resonance spectroscopy study of Turner syndrome. *Biological Psychiatry, 59,* 273–283.

Darling, N., & Steinberg, L. (1997). Community influences on adolescent achievement and deviance. In J. Brooks-Gunn, G. Duncan, & L. Aber (Eds.), *Neighborhood poverty: Context and consequences for children: Conceptual, ethological, and policy approaches to studying neighborhoods* (Vol. 2, pp. 120–131). New York: Russell Sage Foundation.

De Souza, E., Alberman, E., & Morris, J. K. (2009). Down syndrome and paternal age, a new analysis of case-control data collected in the 1960s. *American Journal of Medical Genetics, 149A,* 1205–1208.

Dearing, E. (2008). The psychological costs of growing up poor. *Annals of the New York Academy of Sciences, 1136,* 324–332.

Dearing, E., Wimer, C., Simpkins, S. D., Lund, T., Bouffard, S. M., Caronongan, P., & Kreider, H. (2009). Do neighborhood and home contexts help explain why low-income children miss opportunities to participate in activities outside of school? *Developmental Psychology, 45,* 1545–1562.

Deković, M., & Buist, K. L. (2005). Multiple perspectives within the family: Family relationship patterns. *Journal of Family Issues, 26,* 467–490.

DeRoche, K., & Welsh, M. (2008). Twenty-five years of research on neurocognitive outcomes in early-treated phenylketonuria: Intelligence and executive function. *Developmental Neuropsychology, 33,* 474–504.

Diamond, A. (2009). The interplay of biology and the environment broadly defined. *Developmental Psychology, 45,* 1–8.

Driscoll, M. C. (2007). Sickle cell disease. *Pediatrics in Review, 28,* 259–268.

Duncan, G. J., & Magnuson, K. A. (2003). Off with Hollingshead: Socioeconomic resources, parenting, and child development. In M. H. Bornstein & R. H. Bradley (Eds.), *Socioeconomic status, parenting, and child development* (pp. 83–106). Mahwah, NJ: Erlbaum.

Dunifon, R., Kalil, A., & Danziger, S. K. (2003). Maternal work behavior under welfare reform: How does the transition from welfare to work affect child development? *Children and Youth Services Review, 25,* 55–82.

Dunn, J. R., Schaefer-McDaniel, N. J., & Ramsay, J. T. (2010). Neighborhood chaos and children's development: Question and contradictions. In G. W. Evans & T. D. Wachs (Eds.), *Chaos and its influence on children's development: An ecological perspective,* (pp. 173–189.). Washington, DC: American Psychological Association.

Dynarski, M., James-Burdumy, S., Moore, M., Rosenberg, L., Deke, J., & Mansfield, W. (2004). *When schools stay open late: The national evaluation of the 21st Century Community Learning Centers Program: New findings.* Washington DC: U.S. Department of Education.

Dzurova, D., & Pikhart, H. (2005). Down syndrome, paternal age and education: Comparison of California and the Czech Republic. *BMC Public Health, 5,* 69.

Ernst, M., Moolchan, E. T., & Robinson, M. L. (2001). Behavioral and neural consequences of prenatal exposure to nicotine. *Journal of the American Academy of Child and Adolescent Psychiatry, 40,* 630–641.

Evans, G. W. (2006). Child development and the physical environment. *Annual Review of Psychology, 57,* 424–451.

Everman, D. B., & Cassidy, S. B. (2000). Genetics of childhood disorders: XII. Genomic imprinting: Breaking the rules. *Journal of the American Academy of Child and Adolescent Psychiatry, 38,* 386–389.

Faraone, S. V. (2008). Statistical and molecular genetic approaches to developmental psychopathology: The pathway forward. In J. J. Hudziak (Ed.), *Developmental psychology and wellness: Genetic and environmental influences* (pp. 245–265). Washington, DC: American Psychiatric Publishing.

Feldman, R., Eidelman, A. I., & Rotenberg, N. (2004). Parenting stress, infant emotion regulation, maternal sensitivity, and the cognitive development of triplets: A model for parent and child influences in a unique ecology. *Child Development, 75,* 1774–1791.

Fisher, C. B., Hoagwood, K., Boyce, C., Duster, T., Frank, D. A., & Grisso, T. (2002). Research ethics for mental health science involving ethnic minority children and youths. *American Psychologist, 57,* 1024–1040.

Frith, L. (2001). Gamete donation and anonymity: The ethical and legal debate. *Human Reproduction, 16,* 818–824.

Geerts, M., Steyaert, J., & Fryns, J. P. (2003). The XYY syndrome: A follow-up study on 38 boys. *Genetic Counseling, 14,* 267–279.

Gennetian, L. A., & Morris, P. A. (2003). The effects of time limits and make-work-pay strategies on the well-being of children: Experimental evidence from two welfare reform programs. *Children and Youth Services Review, 25,* 17–54.

Gershoff, E. T., & Aber, J. L. (2006). Neighborhoods and schools: Contexts and consequences for the mental health and risk behaviors of children and youth. In L. Balter & C. S. Tamis-LeMonda (Eds.), *Child psychology: A handbook of contemporary issues* (2nd ed., pp. 611–645). New York: Psychology Press.

Gibbons, A. (1998). Which of our genes make us human? *Science, 281,* 1432–1434.

Gibbons, R., Dugaiczyk, L. J., Girke, T., Duistermars, B., Zielinski, R., & Dugaiczyk, A. (2004). Distinguishing humans from great apes with AluYb8 repeats. *Journal of Molecular Biology, 339,* 721–729.

Gill, M., Daly, G., Heron, S., Hawi, Z., & Fitzgerald, M. (1997). Confirmation of association between attention deficit hyperactivity disorder and a dopamine transporter polymorphism. *Molecular Psychiatry, 2,* 311–313.

Gillet, J.-P., Macadangdang, B., Rathke, R. L., Gottesman, M. M., & Kimchi-Sarfaty, C. (2009). The development of gene therapy: From monogenic recessive disorders to complex diseases such as cancer. *Methods in Molecular Biology, 542,* 5–54.

Goering, J. (Ed.). (2003). Choosing a better life? *How public housing tenants selected a HUD experiment to improve their lives and those of their children: The Moving to Opportunity Demonstration Program.* Washington, DC: Urban Institute Press.

Golombok, S., Lycett, E., MacCallum, F., Jadva, V., Murray, C., Rust, J., Abdalla, H., Jenkins, J., & Margar, R. (2004). Parenting of infants conceived by gamete donation. *Journal of Family Psychology, 18,* 443–452.

Gonzales, N. A., Cauce, A. M., Friedman, R. J., & Mason, C. A. (1996). Family, peer, and neighborhood influences on academic achievement among African-American adolescents: One-year prospective effects. *American Journal of Community Psychology, 24,* 365–387.

Gordon, R. A., Chase-Lansdale, P. L., & Brooks-Gunn, J. (2004). Extended households and the life course of young mothers: Understanding the associations using a sample of mothers with premature, low-birth-weight babies. *Child Development, 75,* 1013–1038.

Gottesman, I. I. (1963). Genetic aspects of intelligent behavior. In N. Ellis (Ed.), *Handbook of mental deficiency* (pp. 253–296). New York: McGraw-Hill.

Gottlieb, G. (1998). Normally occurring environmental and behavioral influences on gene activity: From central dogma to probabilistic epigenesis. *Psychological Review, 105,* 792–802.

Gottlieb, G. (2003). On making behavioral genetics truly developmental. *Human Development, 46,* 337–355.

Gottlieb, G. (2007). Probabilistic epigenesis. *Developmental Science, 10,* 1–11.

Gottlieb, G., Wahlsten, D., & Lickliter, R. (2006). The significance of biology for human development: A developmental psychobiological systems of view. In R. M. Lerner (Ed.), *Handbook of child psychology: Vol. 1. Theoretical models of human development* (6th ed., pp. 210–257). Hoboken, NJ: Wiley.

Gould, J. L., & Keeton, W. T. (1996). *Biological science* (6th ed.). New York: Norton.

Grant, K. B., & Ray, J. A. (2010). *Home, school, and community collaboration: Culturally responsive family involvement.* Thousand Oaks, CA: Sage Publications.

Greenberger, E., O'Neil, R., & Nagel, S. K. (1994). Linking workplace and homeplace: Relations between the nature of adults' work and their parenting behaviors. *Developmental Psychology, 30,* 990–1002.

Greenfield, P. M., Keller, H., Fuligni, A., & Maynard, A. (2003). Cultural pathways through universal development. *Annual Review of Psychology, 54,* 461–490.

Gruendel, J., & Aber, J. L. (2007). Bridging the gap between research and child policy change: The role of strategic communications in policy advocacy. In J. L. Aber, S. J. Bishop-Josef, S. M. Jones, K. T. McLearn, & D. A. Phillips (Eds.), *Child development and social policy: Knowledge for action* (pp. 43–58). Washington, DC: American Psychological Association.

Hagerman, R. J., Berry-Kravis, E., Kaufmann, W. E., Ono, M. Y., Tartaglia, N., & Lachiewicz, A. (2009). Advances in the treatment of fragile X syndrome. *Pediatrics, 123,* 378–390.

Hahn, S., & Chitty, L. S. (2008). Noninvasive prenatal diagnosis: Current practice and future perspectives. *Current Opinion in Obstetrics and Gynecology, 20,* 146–151.

Halfon, N., & McLearn, K. T. (2002). Families with children under 3: What we know and implications for results and policy. In N. Halfon & K. T. McLearn (Eds.), *Child rearing in America: Challenges facing parents with young children* (pp. 367–412). New York: Cambridge University Press.

Hall, J. G. (2003). Twinning. *Lancet, 362,* 735–743.

Hamilton, H. A. (2005). Extended families and adolescent well-being. *Journal of Adolescent Health, 36,* 260–266.

Hart, D., Atkins, R., & Matsuba, M. K. (2008). The association of neighborhood poverty with personality change in childhood. *Journal of Personality and Social Psychology, 94,* 1048–1061.

Harwood, R., Leyendecker, B., Carlson, V., Asencio, M., & Miller, A. (2002). Parenting among Latino families in the U.S. In M. H. Bornstein (Ed.), *Handbook of Parenting: Vol. 4. Social conditions and applied parenting* (2nd ed., pp. 21–46). Mahwah, NJ: Lawrence Erlbaum Associates.

Hauser-Cram, P., Warfield, M. E., Stadler, J., & Sirin, S. R. (2006). School environments and the diverging pathways of students living in poverty. In A. C. Huston & M. N. Ripke (Eds.), *Developmental contexts in middle childhood* (pp. 198–216). New York: Cambridge University Press.

Heath, S. B. (1990). The children of Trackton's children: Spoken and written language in social change. In J. Stigler, G. Herdt, & R. A. Shweder (Eds.), *Cultural psychology: Essays on comparative human development* (pp. 496–519). New York: Cambridge University Press.

Heckman, J. J., & Masterov, D. V. (2004). *The productivity argument for investing in young children.* Working Paper 5, Invest in Kids Working Group, Committee for Economic Development. Retrieved from jenni.uchicago.edu/Invest

Hoekstra, R. A., Bartels, M., Hudziak, J. J., Van Beijsterveldt, T. C., & Boomsma, D. I. (2008). Genetic and environmental influences on the stability of withdrawn behavior in children: A longitudinal, multi-informant twin study. *Behavior Genetics, 38,* 447–461.

Hoff, E., Laursen, B., & Tardif, T. (2002). Socioeconomic status and parenting. In M. H. Bornstein (Ed.), *Handbook of parenting: Vol. 2. Biology and ecology of parenting* (pp. 231–252). Mahwah, NJ: Erlbaum.

Hudziak, J. J., & Rettew, D. C. (2009). Genetics of ADHD. In T. E. Brown (Ed.), *ADHD comorbidties: Handbook for ADHD complications in children and adults* (pp. 23–36). Arlington, VA: American Psychiatric Publishing.

Human Genome Program. (2008). *How many genes are in the human genome?* Retrieved from www.ornl.gov/sci/techresources/Human_Genome/faq/genenumber.shtml

Isasi, R. M., Nguyen, T. M., & Knoppers, B. M. (2006) *National regulatory frameworks regarding human genetic modification technologies (somatic and germline modification).* Montréal, Québec: Centre de Recherche en Droit Public (CRDP), Université de Montréal.

Itti, E., Gaw, G. I. T., Pawlikowska-Haddal, A., Boone, K. B., Mlikotic, A., & Itti, L. (2006). The structural brain correlates of cognitive deficits in adults with Klinefelter's syndrome. *Journal of Clinical Endocrinology and Metabolism, 91,* 1423–1427.

Jackson, A. P., Bentler, P. M., & Franke, T. M. (2006). Employment and parenting among current and former welfare recipients. *Journal of Social Service Research, 33,* 13–25.

Jackson, R. A., Gibson, K. A., & Wu, Y. W. (2004). Perinatal outcomes in singletons following in vitro fertilization: A meta-analysis. *Obstetrics and Gynecology, 103,* 551–563.

Jacquet, P. (2004). Sensitivity of germ cells and embryos to ionizing radiation. *Journal of Biological Regulators and Homeostatic Agents, 18,* 106–114.

Jensen, A. R. (1969). How much can we boost IQ and scholastic achievement? *Harvard Educational Review, 39,* 1–123.

Jensen, A. R. (1998). *The g factor: The science of mental ability.* New York: Praeger.

Jensen, A. R. (2001). Spearman's hypothesis. In J. M. Collis & S. Messick (Eds.), *Intelligence and personality: Bridging the gap in theory and measurement* (pp. 3–24). Mahwah, NJ: Erlbaum.

Jeynes, W. H. (2005). A meta-analysis of the relation of parental involvement to urban elementary school student academic achievement. *Urban Education, 40,* 237–269.

Jongbloet, P. H., Zielhuis, G. A., Groenewoud, H. M., & Pasker-De Jong, P. C. (2001). The secular trends in male:female ratio at birth in postwar industrialized countries. *Environmental Health Perspectives, 109,* 749–752.

Kahn, R. S., Khoury, J., Nichols, W. C., & Lanphear, B. M. (2003). Role of dopamine transporter genotype and maternal prenatal smoking in childhood hyperactive–impulsive, inattentive, and oppositional behaviors. *Journal of Pediatrics, 143,* 104–110.

Kane, C. M. (2000). African-American family dynamics as perceived by family members. *Journal of Black Studies, 30,* 691–702.

Kenney, G. M., Lynch, V., & Cook, A. (2010). Who and where are the children yet to enroll in Medicaid and the Children's Health Insurance Program? *Health Affairs, 29,* 1920–1929.

Kesler, S. R. (2007). Turner syndrome. *Child and Adolescent Psychiatric Clinics of North America, 16,* 709–722.

King, E. M., & Mason, A. D. (2001). *Engendering development: Through gender equality in rights, resources, and voice.* Washington, DC: UNICEF.

Kliegman, R. M., Behrman, R. E., Jenson, H. B., & Stanton, B. F. (Eds.). (2008). *Nelson textbook of pediatrics e-dition* (18th ed. text with continually updated online references.) Philadelphia: Saunders.

Kohen, D. E., Leventhal, T., Dahinten, V. S., & McIntosh, C. N. (2008). Neighborhood disadvantage: Pathways of effects for young children. *Child Development, 79,* 156–169.

Kumar, S., & O'Brien, A. (2004). Recent developments in fetal medicine. *British Medical Journal, 328,* 1002–1006.

Kunisaki, S. M., & Jennings, R. W. (2008). Fetal surgery. *Journal of Intensive Care Medicine, 23,* 33–51.

Lamb, M. E., & Ahnert, L. (2006). Nonparental child care: Context, concepts, correlates, and consequences. In K. A. Renninger & I. E. Sigel (Eds.), *Handbook of child psychology: Vol. 4. Child psychology in practice* (6th ed., pp. 700–778). Hoboken, NJ: Wiley.

Lashley, F. R. (2007). *Essentials of clinical genetics in nursing practice.* New York: Springer.

Lawrence, K., Kuntsi, J., Coleman, M., Campbell, R., & Skuse, D. (2003). Face and emotion recognition deficits in Turner syndrome: A possible role for X-linked genes in amygdala development. *Neuropsychology, 17,* 39–49.

Lerner, R. M., & Overton, W. F. (2008). Exemplifying the integrations of the relational developmental system. *Journal of Adolescent Research, 23,* 245–255.

Lerner, R. M., Rothbaum, F., Boulos, S., & Castellino, D. R. (2002). Developmental systems perspective on parenting. In M. H. Bornstein (Ed.), *Handbook of parenting: Vol. 2. Biology and ecology of parenting* (2nd ed., pp. 315–344). Mahwah, NJ: Erlbaum.

Leventhal, T., & Brooks-Gunn, J. (2003). Children and youth in neighborhood contexts. *Current Directions in Psychological Science, 12,* 27–31.

LeVine, R. A., LeVine, S., Richman, A., Tapia Uribe, M. R., Sunderland Correa, C., & Miller, P. (1991). Women's schooling and child care in the demographic transition: A Mexican case study. *Population and Development Review, 17,* 459–496.

LeVine, R. A., LeVine, S. E., Rowe, M. L., & Schnell-Anzola, B. (2004). Maternal literacy and health behavior: A Nepalese case study. *Social Science and Medicine, 58,* 863–877.

LeVine, R. A., LeVine, S. E., & Schnell, B. (2001). "Improve the women": Mass schooling, female literacy, and worldwide social change. *Harvard Educational Review, 71,* 1–50.

Loehlin, J. C., Horn, J. M., & Willerman, L. (1997). Heredity, environment, and IQ in the Texas Adoption Project. In R. J. Sternberg & E. L. Grigorenko (Eds.), *Intelligence, heredity, and environment* (pp. 105–125). New York: Cambridge University Press.

Luthar, S. S., & Becker, B. E. (2002). Privileged but pressured: A study of affluent youth. *Child Development, 73,* 1593–1610.

Luthar, S. S., & Goldstein, A. S. (2008). Substance use and related behaviors among suburban late adolescents: The importance of perceived parent containment. *Development and Psychopathology, 20,* 591–614.

Luthar, S. S., & Latendresse, S. J. (2005a). Children of the affluent: Challenges to well-being. *Current Directions in Psychological Science, 14,* 49–53.

Luthar, S. S., & Latendresse, S. J. (2005b). Comparable "risks" at the socioeconomic status extremes: Preadolescents' perceptions of parenting. *Development and Psychopathology, 17,* 207–230.

Luthar, S. S., & Sexton, C. (2004). The high price of affluence. In R. V. Kail (Ed.), *Advances in child development* (Vol. 32, pp. 126–162). San Diego, CA: Academic Press.

Lytton, H., & Gallagher, L. (2002). Parenting twins and the genetics of parenting. In M. H. Bornstein (Ed.), *Handbook of parenting: Vol. 1. Children and parenting* (pp. 227–253). Mahwah, NJ: Erlbaum.

Machin, G. A. (2005). Multiple birth. In H. W. Taeusch, R. A. Ballard, & C. A. Gleason (Eds.), *Avery's diseases of the newborn* (8th ed., pp. 57–62). Philadelphia: Saunders.

Mandara, J., Varner, F., Greene, N., & Richman, S. (2009). Intergenerational family predictors of the black–white achievement gap. *Journal of Educational Psychology, 101,* 867–878.

Martin, R. (2008). Meiotic errors in human oogenesis and spermatogenesis. *Reproductive Biomedicine Online, 16,* 523–531.

McGee, G. (1997). Legislating gestation. *Human Reproduction, 12,* 407–408.

McHale, J. P., Lauretti, A., Talbot, J., & Pouquette, C. (2002). Retrospect and prospect in the psychological study of coparenting and family group process. In J. P. McHale & W. S. Grolnick (Eds.), *Retrospect and prospect in the psychological study of families* (pp. 127–165). Mahwah, NJ: Erlbaum.

McKusick, V. A. (2007). *Online Mendelian inheritance in man.* Retrieved from www.ncbi.nlm.nih.gov / sites/entrez?db=omim

Melby, J. N., Conger, R. D., Fang, S., Wichrama, K. A. S., & Conger, K. J. (2008). Adolescent family experiences and educational attainment during early adulthood. *Developmental Psychology, 44,* 1519-1536.

Melton, G. B. (2005). Treating children like people: A framework for research and advocacy. *Journal of Clinical Child and Adolescent Psychology, 34,* 646–657.

Mistry, R. S., Biesanz, J. C., Chien, N., Howes, C., & Benner, A. D. (2008). Socioeconomic status, parental investments, and the cognitive and behavioral outcomes of low-income children from immigrant and native households. *Early Childhood Research Quarterly, 23,* 193–212.

Moore, K. L., & Persaud, T. V. N. (2008). *Before we are born* (7th ed.). Philadelphia: Saunders.

Morgan, P. L., Farkas, G., Hillemeier, M. M., & Maczuga, S. (2009). Risk factors for learning-related behavior problems at 24 months of age: Population-based estimates. *Journal of Abnormal Child Psychology, 37,* 401–413.

Mosely-Howard, G. S., & Evans, C. B. (2000). Relationships and contemporary experiences of the African-American family: An ethnographic case study. *Journal of Black Studies, 30,* 428–451.

Muenchow, S., & Marsland, K. W. (2007). Beyond baby steps: Promoting the growth and development of U.S. child-care policy. In J. L. Aber, S. J. Bishop-Josef, S. M. Jones, K. T. McLearn, & D. Phillips (Eds.), *Child development and social policy: Knowledge for action* (pp. 97–112). Washington, DC: American Psychological Association.

National Center for Biotechnology Information, National Institutes of Health. (2007). *Genes and disease: Sickle cell anemia.* Retrieved from www.ncbi.nlm.nih.gov/bookshelf/br.fcgi?book=gnd&part=anemiasicklecell

National Coalition for the Homeless. (2008). *Homeless families with children.* Washington, DC: Author.

National Institutes of Health. (2008). *Genes and disease.* Retrieved from www.ncbi.nlm.nih.gov /books/bv.fcgi?rid=gnd.TOC&depth=2

Navarrete, C., Martinez, I., & Salamanca, F. (1994). Paternal line of transmission in chorea of Huntington with very early onset. *Genetic Counseling, 5,* 175–178.

Neri, Q., Takeuchi, T., & Palermo, G. D. (2008). An update of assisted reproductive technologies in the United States. *Annals of the New York Academy of Sciences, 1127,* 41-48.

Nickman, S. L., Rosenfeld, A. A., & Fine, P. (2005). Children in adoptive families: Overview and update. *Journal of the American Academy of Child and Adolescent Psychiatry, 44,* 987–995.

Nickman, S. L., Rosenfeld, A. A., Fine, P., MacIntyre, J. C., Pilowsky, D. J., & Howe, R. A. (2005). Children in adoptive families: Overview and update. *Journal of the American Academy of Child and Adolescent Psychiatry, 44,* 987–995.

Obradović, J., Long, J. D., Cutuli, J. J., Chan, C. K., Hinz, E., Heistad, D., & Masten, A. S. (2009). Academic achievement of homeless and highly mobile children in an urban school district: Longitudinal evidence on risk, growth, and resilience. *Development and Psychopathology, 21,* 493–518.

OECD (Organisation for Economic Cooperation and Development). (2006). *Starting strong II: Early childhood education and care.* Paris: OECD Publishing. Retrieved from www.sourceoecd.org/education/9264035451

OECD (Organisation for Economic Cooperation and Development). (2008a). *Education at a glance 2008: OECD indicators.* Paris: Author. Retrieved from www.oecd.org/infobycountry/0,3380,en_2649_33715_1_1_1_1_1,00.html

OECD (Organisation for Economic Cooperation and Development). (2008b). OECD Health data: 2008. Retrieved from secure.cihi.ca/cihiweb /dispPage.jsp?cw_page=media_ 26jun2008_e

Parke, R. D., & Buriel, R. (2006). Socialization in the family: Ethnic and ecological perspectives. In N. Eisenberg (Ed.), *Handbook of child psychology: Vol. 3. Social, emotional, and personality development* (6th ed., pp. 429–504). Hoboken, NJ: Wiley.

Pauli, S. A., Berga, S. L., Shang, W., & Session, D. R. (2009). Current status of the approach to assisted reproduction. *Pediatric Clinics of North America, 56,* 467–488.

Peña, R., Wall, S., & Person, L. (2000). The effect of poverty, social inequality, and maternal education on infant mortality in Nicaragua, 1988–1993. *American Journal of Public Health, 90,* 64–69.

Peshkin, A. (1997). *Places of memory: Whiteman's schools and Native American communities.* Mahwah, NJ: Erlbaum.

Peters, R. D. (2005). A community-based approach to promoting resilience in young children, their families, and their neighborhoods. In R. D. Peters, B. Leadbeater, & R. J. McMahon (Eds.), *Resilience in children, families, and communities: Linking context to practice and policy* (pp. 157–176). New York: Kluwer Academic.

Peters, R. D., Petrunka, K., & Arnold, R. (2003). The Better Beginnings, Better Futures Project: A universal, comprehensive, community-based prevention approach for primary school children and their families. *Journal of Clinical Child and Adolescent Psychology, 32,* 215–227.

Petrill, S. A., & Deater-Deckard, K. (2004). The heritability of general cognitive ability: A within-family adoption design. *Intelligence, 32,* 403–409.

Pinderhughes, E. E., Dodge, K. A., Bates, J. E., Pettit, G. S., & Zelli, A. (2000). Discipline responses: Influences of parents' socioeconomic status, ethnicity, beliefs about parenting, stress, and cognitive-emotional processes. *Journal of Family Psychology, 14,* 380–400.

Plomin, R. (1994). *Genetics and experience: The interplay between nature and nurture.* Thousand Oaks, CA: Sage.

Plomin, R. (2005). *Finding genes in child psychology and psychiatry: When are we going to be there?* Unpublished manuscript. London: King's College.

Plomin, R. (2009). The nature of nurture. In K. McCartney & R. A. Weinberg (Eds.), *Experience and development: A festschrift in honor of Sandra Wood Scarr* (pp. 61–80). New York: Psychology Press.

Plomin, R., & Davis, O. S. P. (2009). The future of genetics in psychology and psychiatry: Microarrays, genome-wide association, and non-coding RNA. *Journal of Child Psychology and Psychiatry, 50,* 63–71.

Plomin, R., DeFries, J. C., McClearn, G. E., & McGuffin, P. (2001). *Behavioral genetics* (4th ed.). New York: Worth.

Plomin, R., & Spinath, F. M. (2004). Intelligence: Genetics, genes, and genomics. *Journal of Personality and Social Psychology, 86,* 112–129.

Pohl, R. (2002). *Poverty in Canada.* Ottawa: Innercity Ministries.

Punamaki, R. L. (2006). Ante- and perinatal factors and child characteristics predicting parenting experience among formerly infertile couples during the child's first year: A controlled study. *Journal of Family Psychology, 20,* 670–679.

Reiss, D. (2003). Child effects on family systems: Behavioral genetic strategies. In A. C. Crouter & A. Booth (Eds.), *Children's influence on family dynamics* (pp. 3–36). Mahwah, NJ: Erlbaum.

Reschly, A. L., & Christenson, S. L. (2009). Parents as essential partners for fostering students' learning outcomes. In R. Gilman & E. Scott Huebner (Eds.), *Handbook of positive psychology in schools* (pp. 257–272). New York: Routledge.

Resta, R., Biesecker, B. B., Bennett, R. L., Blum, S., Hahn, S. E., Strecker, M. N., & Williams, J. L. (2006). A new definition of genetic counseling: National Society of Genetic Counselors' Task Force Report. *Journal of Genetic Counseling, 15,* 77–83.

RESULTS. (2006). *The abolition of public school fees.* Retrieved from www.results.org/website /article. asp?id=1718

Ridenour, T. A. (2000). Genetic epidemiology of antisocial behavior. In D. H. Fishbein (Ed.), *The science, treatment, and prevention of antisocial behaviors: Application to the criminal justice system* (pp. 7.1–7.24). Kingston, NJ: Civic Research Institute.

Ripple, C. H., & Zigler, E. (2003). Research, policy, and the federal role in prevention initiatives for children. *American Psychologist, 58,* 482–490.

Rothbart, M. K., & Bates, J. E. (2006). Temperament. In N. Eisenberg (Ed.), *Handbook of child psychology: Vol. 3. Social, emotional, and personality development* (6th ed., pp. 99–166). Hoboken, NJ: Wiley.

Rowe, D. (1994). *The limits of family influence: Genes, experience, and behavior.* New York: Guilford.

Rushton, J. P., & Jensen, A. R. (2005). Thirty years of research on race differences in cognitive ability. *Psychology, Public Policy, and Law, 11,* 235–294.

Rushton, J. P., & Jensen, A. R. (2006). The totality of available evidence shows the race IQ gap still remains. *Psychological Science, 17,* 921–922.

Russell, R. B., Petrini, J. R., Damus, K., Mattison, D. R., & Schwarz, R. H. (2003). The changing epidemiology of multiple births in the United States. *Obstetrics and Gynecology, 101,* 129–135.

Rutter, M. (2002). Nature, nurture, and development: From evangelism through science toward policy and practice. *Child Development, 73,* 1–21.

Rutter, M. (2007a). Gene–environment interdependence. *Developmental Science, 10,* 12–18.

Rutter, M., Pickles, A., Murray, R., & Eaves, L. (2001). Testing hypotheses on specific environmental causal effects on behavior. *Psychological Bulletin, 127,* 291–324.

Ryan, R. M., Fauth, R. C., & Brooks-Gunn, J. (2006). Childhood poverty: Implications for school readiness and early childhood education In B. Spodek & O. N. Saracho (Eds.), *Handbook of research on the education of young children* (2nd ed., pp. 323–346). Mahwah, NJ: Erlbaum.

Saitta, S. C., & Zackai, E. H. (2005). Specific chromosome disorders in newborns. In H. W. Taeusch, R. A. Ballard, & C. A. Gleason (Eds.), *Avery's diseases of the newborn* (8th ed., pp. 204–215). Philadelphia: Saunders.

Scarr, S., & McCartney, K. (1983). How people make their own environments: A theory of genotype–environment effects. *Child Development, 54,* 424–435.

Schacht, P. M., Cummings, E. M., & Davies, P. T. (2009). Fathering in family context and child adjustment: A longitudinal analysis. *Journal of Family Psychology, 23,* 790–797.

Schonberg, R. L., & Tifft, C. J. (2007). Birth defects and prenatal diagnosis. In M. L. Batshaw, L. Pellegrino, & N. J. Roizen (Eds.), *Children with disabilities* (6th ed., pp. 83–96). Baltimore: Paul H. Brookes.

Schwarte, A. R. (2008). Fragile X syndrome. *School Psychology Quarterly, 23,* 290–300.

Schweiger, W. K., & O'Brien, M. (2005). Special needs adoption: An ecological systems approach. *Family Relations, 54,* 512–522.

Sekido, R., & Lovell-Badge, R. (2009). Sex determination and SRY: Down to a wink and a nudge? *Trends in Genetics, 25,* 19–29.

Sermon, K., Van Steirteghem, A., & Liebaers, I. (2004). Preimplantation genetic diagnosis. *Lancet, 363,* 1633–1641.

Sherman, S. L., Allen, E. G., Bean, L. H., & Freeman, S. B. (2007). Epidemiology of Down syndrome. *Mental Retardation and Developmental Disabilities Research Reviews, 13,* 221–227.

Sherman, S. L., Freeman, S. B., Allen, E. G., & Lamb, N. E. (2005). Risk factors for nondisjunction of trisomy 21. *Cytogenetic Genome Research, 111,* 273–280.

Shinn, M., Schteingart, J. S., Williams, N. C., Carlin-Mathis, J., Bialo-Karagis, N., Becker-Klein, R., & Weitzman, B. C. (2008). Long-term associations of homelessness with children's well-being. *American Behavioral Scientist, 51,* 789–809.

Silk, J. S., Sessa, F. M., Morris, A. S., Steinberg, L., & Avenevoli, S. (2004). Neighborhood cohesion as a buffer against hostile maternal parenting. *Journal of Family Psychology, 18,* 135–146.

Simons, L. G., Chen, Y. F., Simons, R. L., Brody, G., & Cutrona, C. (2006). Parenting practices and child adjustment in different types of households: A study of African-American families. *Journal of Family Issues, 27,* 803–825.

Simpson, J. A., Rholes, W. S., Campbell, L., Tran, S., & Wilson, C. L. (2003). Adult attachment, the transition to parenthood, and depressive symptoms. *Journal of Personality and Social Psychology, 84,* 1172–1187.

Slonims, V., & McConachie, H. (2006). Analysis of mother–infant interaction in infants with Down syndrome and typically developing infants. *American Journal of Mental Retardation, 111,* 273–289.

Smith, J. R., Brooks-Gunn, J., Kohen, D., & McCarton, C. (2001). Transitions on and off AFDC: Implications for parenting and children's cognitive development. *Child Development, 72,* 1512–1533.

Stams, G. J. M., Juffer, F., & van IJzendoorn, M. H. (2002). Maternal sensitivity, infant attachment, and temperament in early childhood predict adjustment in middle childhood: The case of adopted children and their biologically unrelated parents. *Developmental Psychology, 38,* 806–821.

Steinberg, L., & Silk, J. S. (2002). Parenting adolescents. In M. H. Bornstein (Ed.), *Handbook of parenting: Vol. 1. Children and parenting* (pp. 103–134). Mahwah, NJ: Erlbaum.

Stormshak, E. A., Bierman, K. L., McMahon, R. J., Lengua, L. J., & the Conduct Problems Prevention Research Group. (2000). Parenting practices and child disruptive behavior problems in early elementary school. *Journal of Clinical Child Psychology, 29,* 17–29.

Stromquist, N. P. (2007). Gender equity education globally. In S. S. Klein, B. Richardson, D. A. Grayson, L. H. Fox, & C. Kramarae (Eds.), *Handbook for achieving gender equity through education* (2nd ed., pp. 33–42). Mahwah, NJ: Erlbaum.

Tamis-LeMonda, C. S., Way, N., Hughes, D., Yoshikawa, H., Kalman, R. K., & Niwa, E. Y. (2008). Parents' goals for children: The dynamic coexistence of individualism and collectivism in cultures and individuals. *Social Development, 17,* 183–209.

Taylor, R. L. (2000). Diversity within African-American families. In D. H. Demo & K. R. Allen (Eds.), *Handbook of family diversity* (pp. 232–251). New York: Oxford University Press.

Thomas, K. A., & Tessler, R. C. (2007). Bicultural socialization among adoptive families: Where there is a will, there is a way. *Journal of Family Issues, 28,* 1189–1219.

Tienari, P., Wahlberg, K. E., & Wynne, L. C. (2006). Finnish adoption study of schizophrenia: Implications for family interventions. *Families, Systems, and Health, 24,* 442–451.

Tienari, P., Wynne, L. C., Laksy, K., Moring, J., Nieminen, P., Sorri, A., et al. (2003). Genetic boundaries of the schizophrenia spectrum: Evidence from the Finnish adoptive family study of schizophrenia. *The American Journal of Psychiatry, 160,* 1587–1594.

Trent, K., & Harlan, S. L. (1994). Teenage mothers in nuclear and extended households. *Journal of Family Issues, 15,* 309–337.

Triandis, H. C. (1995). *Individualism and collectivism.* Boulder, CO: Westview Press.

Triandis, H. C. (2005). Issues in individualism and collectivism research. In R. M. Sorrentino, D. Cohen, J. M. Olson, & M. P. Zanna (Eds.), *Culture and social behavior: The Ontario Symposium* (Vol. 10, pp. 207–225). Mahwah, NJ: Erlbaum.

Tudge, J. R. H., Hogan, D. M., Snezhkova, I. A., Kulakova, N. N., & Etz, K. E. (2000). Parents' child-rearing values and beliefs in the United States and Russia: The impact of culture and social class. *Infant and Child Development, 9,* 105–121.

Turkheimer, E., Haley, A., Waldron, M., D'Onofrio, B., & Gottesman, I. I. (2003). Socioeconomic status modifies heritability of IQ in young children. *Psychological Science, 14,* 623–628.

UNICEF (United Nations Children's Fund). (2007). *An overview of child well-being in rich countries, Innocenti Report Card 7.* Florence, Italy: UNICEF Innocenti Research Centre.

UNICEF (United Nations Children's Fund). (2009a). *All children everywhere: A strategy for basic education and gender equality.* New York: Author.

UNICEF (United Nations Children's Fund). (2010). *Young champions for education: A progress review.* Retrieved from www.ungei.org/resources/1612_2341.html

United Nations. (2006). *World population prospects: The 2006 revision. Population database.* Retrieved from esa.un.org/unpp/index.asp?panel=2

U.S. Census Bureau. (2010b). *Statistical abstract of the United States* (129th ed.). Washington, DC: U.S. Government Printing Office.

U.S. Department of Education. (2010). *Digest of education statistics, 2009.* Washington, DC: U.S. Government Printing Office.

U.S. Department of Health and Human Services. (2009d). *Down syndrome.* Retrieved from www.cdc.gov/ncbddd/birthdefects/DownSyndrome.htm

U.S. Department of Health and Human Services. (2010c). *Vital statistics—mortality.* Retrieved from www.cdc.gov/nchs/data_access/vitalstats/VitalStats_Mortality.htm

Van Eyk, J., & Dunn, M. J. (Eds.). (2008). *Clinical proteomics.* Weinheim, Germany: Wiley-VCH.

van IJzendoorn, M. H., Juffer, F., & Poelhuis, C. W. K. (2005). Adoption and cognitive development: A meta-analytic comparison of adopted and nonadopted children's IQ and school performance. *Psychological Bulletin, 131,* 301–316.

Vandell, D. L., & Posner, J. K. (1999). Conceptualization and measurement of children's after-school environments. In S. L. Friedman & T. D. Wachs (Eds.), *Measuring environment across the life span* (pp. 167–196). Washington, DC: American Psychological Association.

Vandell, D. L., Reisner, E. R., & Pierce, K. M. (2007). *Outcomes linked to high-quality after-school programs: Longitudinal findings from the Study of Promising After-School Programs.* Retrieved from www.gse.uci.edu/childcare/pdf/afterschool/PP%20Longitudinal%20Findings%20Final%20Report.pdf

Verhulst, F. C. (2008). International adoption and mental health: Long-term behavioral outcome. In M. E. Garralda & J. P. Raynaud (Eds.), *Culture and conflict in adolescent mental health* (pp. 83–105). Lanham, MD: Jason Aronson.

Verissimo, M., & Salvaterra, F. (2006). Maternal secure-base scripts and children's attachment security in an adopted sample. *Attachment and Human Development, 8,* 261–273.

Vernon-Feagans, L., Pancsofar, N., Willoughby, M., Odom, E., Quade, A., & Cox, M. (2008). Predictors of maternal language to infants during a picture book task in the home: Family SES, child characteristics and the parenting environment. *Journal of Applied Developmental Psychology, 29,* 213–226.

Waddington, C. H. (1957). *The strategy of the genes.* London: Allen & Unwin.

Wagenaar, K., Huisman, J., Cohen-Kettenis, P. T., & Delemarre-van de Waal, H. A. (2008). An overview of studies on early development, cognition, and psychosocial well-being in children born after in vitro fertilization. *Journal of Developmental and Behavioral Pediatrics, 29,* 219–230.

Wahlsten, D. (1994). The intelligence of heritability. *Canadian Psychology, 35,* 244–259.

Waldman, I. D., Rowe, D. C., Abramowitz, A., Kozel, S. T., Mohr, J. H., & Sherman, S. L. (1998). Association and linkage of the dopamine transporter gene and attention-deficit hyperactivity disorder in children: Heterogeneity owing to diagnostic subtype and severity. *American Journal of Human Genetics, 63,* 1767–1776.

Weiss, K. M. (2005). Cryptic causation of human disease: Reading between the germ lines. *Trends in Genetics, 21,* 82–88.

Whiteside-Mansell, L., Bradley, R. H., Owen, M. T., Randolph, S. M., & Cauce, A. M. (2003). Parenting and children's behavior at 36 months: Equivalence between African-American and European-American mother–child dyads. *Parenting: Science and Practice, 3,* 197–234.

Williams, C. (2006). Dilemmas in fetal medicine: Premature application of technology or responding to women's choice? *Sociology of Health and Illness, 28,* 1–20.

Wiseman, F. K., Alford, K. A., Tybulewicz, V. L. J., & Fisher, E. M. C. (2009). Down syndrome—recent progress and future prospects. *Human Molecular Genetics, 18,* R75–R83.

Wright, M. J., Gillespie, N. A., Luciano, M., Zhu, G., & Martin, N. G. (2008). Genetics of personality and cognition in adolescents. In J. J. Hudziak (Eds.), *Developmental psychology and wellness: Genetic and environmental influences* (pp. 85–107). Washington, DC: American Psychiatric Publishing.

Zhang, T.-Y., & Meaney, M. J. (2010). Epigenetics and the environmental regulation of the genome and its function. *Annual Review of Psychology, 61,* 439–466.

Name: _____   Date: _____

MODULE 4-B

ACTIVITY

◇ **PARENTAL ETHNOTHEORIES**

Sara Harkness and Charles M. Super (1996; 2006) have written extensively on parents' cultural beliefs systems or what they term *parental ethnotheories*. Goodnow (1996) points out that there are several reasons why it is useful to study parents' cultural beliefs. These beliefs (1) provide insight into the cognition and development of adults, (2) help us understand parenting behavior, (3) are one aspect of the context in which children develop, and (4) when studied across generations, can provide clues about cultural transmission and change. This activity will allow you to explore a variety of parental ethnotheories and examine the cultural basis for your own beliefs about childrearing.

Directions: Circle the number to indicate your view on each of the parental ethnotheories below.

1. Everyone in the household has responsibility for keeping an eye on a crawling child or toddler.

STRONGLY DISAGREE								STRONGLY AGREE
1	2	3	4	5	6	7	8	9

2. Praising a child for accomplishing a task leads to disobedience and selfishness.

STRONGLY DISAGREE								STRONGLY AGREE
1	2	3	4	5	6	7	8	9

3. It is cruel and neglectful to put a baby alone in a room to sleep.

STRONGLY DISAGREE								STRONGLY AGREE
1	2	3	4	5	6	7	8	9

Taken from *Cross-Cultural Explorations: Activities in Culture and Psychology*, Second Edition, by Susan Goldstein.

4. An infant can be well cared for by spending significant amounts of time being passed among many different adults, staying with no one person for more than several minutes at a time.

STRONGLY DISAGREE								STRONGLY AGREE
1	2	3	4	5	6	7	8	9

5. Parents need to train their children in specific skills to prepare them for starting school.

STRONGLY DISAGREE								STRONGLY AGREE
1	2	3	4	5	6	7	8	9

6. Babies should be encouraged to "sleep through the night" as soon as possible.

STRONGLY DISAGREE								STRONGLY AGREE
1	2	3	4	5	6	7	8	9

7. Lactating women should freely nurse each other's children.

STRONGLY DISAGREE								STRONGLY AGREE
1	2	3	4	5	6	7	8	9

8. Parents should respond immediately when their infant begins to cry.

STRONGLY DISAGREE								STRONGLY AGREE
1	2	3	4	5	6	7	8	9

9. The role of parents is to protect and nurture their children, rather than stimulate their intellect.

STRONGLY DISAGREE								STRONGLY AGREE
1	2	3	4	5	6	7	8	9

10. Children are happiest and most well behaved when parents keep to a set daily routine.

STRONGLY DISAGREE								STRONGLY AGREE
1	2	3	4	5	6	7	8	9

11. It is important for babies' later development that they receive verbal and visual stimulation.

STRONGLY DISAGREE								STRONGLY AGREE
1	2	3	4	5	6	7	8	9

12. By age six or seven, children are capable of caring for younger siblings.

STRONGLY DISAGREE								STRONGLY AGREE
1	2	3	4	5	6	7	8	9

13. A parent who doesn't use physical punishment doesn't fully love his or her child.

STRONGLY DISAGREE								STRONGLY AGREE
1	2	3	4	5	6	7	8	9

14. Parenting difficulties are best addressed by consulting medical or psychological experts or books written by such experts.

STRONGLY DISAGREE								STRONGLY AGREE
1	2	3	4	5	6	7	8	9

Reactions:

1. With which parental ethnotheories did you most strongly agree? Why?

2. With which parental ethnotheories did you most strongly disagree? Why?

3. Meredith Small (1998) includes an *eco-cultural* perspective (Berry, 1976) in her approach to understanding childrearing. She describes the many ways in which parenting beliefs and practices evolve in response to environmental as well as sociocultural demands. For example, she cites the case of the Ache of Paraguay who carry their children, rather than allowing them to crawl or walk - first in slings, then in baskets, and then piggyback—until they are 5 years old. This practice makes sense considering the hazards for a small child crawling or walking in the forest environment of the Ache. How have the parental ethnotheories of your culture evolved in response to the physical or sociocultural environment? Please give an example below.

◇ REFERENCES

Berry, J. W. (1976). Human ecology and cognitive style: Comparative studies in cultural and psychological adaptation. New York: Sage/Halsted.

Goodnow, J. J. (1996). From household practices to parents' ideas about work and interpersonal relationships. In S. Harkness & C. M. Super (Eds.), Parents' cultural belief systems: Their origins, expressions, and consequences (pp. 313-344). New York: Guilford.

Harkness, S., & C. M. Super (1996). Parents' cultural belief systems: Their origins, expressions, and consequences. New York: Guilford.

Harkness, S., & C. M. Super (2006). Themes and variations: Parental ethnotheories in Western cultures. In K. R. Rubin & O. B. Chung (Eds.), Parenting beliefs, behaviors, and parent-child relations: A cross-cultural perspective (pp. 61 - 79). New York: Taylor & Francis.

Small, M. F. (1998). Our babies, ourselves: How biology and culture shape the way we parent. New York: Anchor Books.

SECTION 5

MARRIAGE AND THE FAMILY

MODULE 5-A

MARRIAGE AND THE FAMILY

A bride and groom smile as they take part in a mass wedding ceremony in Baghdad's impoverished Sadr City 06 August 2005. The Iraqi Martyr Association for Humanitarian Services organized the mass wedding of 100 Shiite Muslim couples, giving each a 500 US dollar check as a wedding gift.
(Newscom/Ali al-Saadi/AFP/Getty Images/Newscom)

Preview

- How do anthropologists define marriage and family?

- What are the characteristics of nuclear and extended families?

- How do residency patterns relate to other aspects of a culture?

- How do marriage rules extend kinship while observing incest taboos?

- What are some theories about the origins of the incest taboo?

- How is marriage a rite of passage?

- What are some social functions of marriage?

- What forms of marriage are known to exist?

- How is marriage a form of political alliance and economic exchange?

A woman had an only son who became grown up and had not been married yet. She wanted to find him a bride, but he always told her, "Later, not now...." One day his mother said to him, "Listen, my son, I've grown old and become tired of household work. You must get married before I die."

He said to her, "Well! Find me a good girl from a good house."

She...found him a girl from one of the most notable houses in their town and he married her.

When the wedding [party] was over and after seven days or so, he went back to his shop to work, while his mother stayed with his wife. "Listen, in this house [you] don't open what is closed or close what is opened, nor uncover what is covered or cover what is uncovered, nor unwrap what is wrapped or wrap what is unwrapped, nor unfold what is folded or fold what is unfolded. Do you understand?"

The girl, his wife, said, "Yes."

Taken from *Cultural Anthropology*, Third Edition, by Nancy Bonvillain.

Days passed with things like that. His mother is everything in the house; his wife works all day while his mother orders her around. When the man returns home, his mother would set the dinner for him and if he would say "[Let us] call [his wife] to eat with me," his mother would answer him, "This can't be. She is still new in the house. She would get bold with us. Wait for a few more days."

After a few more days her son would say, "Let her come and eat with me."

His mother would say, "She hasn't been broken to our house yet. She does not need to eat for she has been eating all day."

He would say to his mother, "May God extend his grace upon us. Let her eat as much as she wants," and [he] used to eat only until he was half-full and leave some of the best food to his wife. His mother would hide it and would give her only hard bread and water.

The girl grew sicker and weaker by the day. Whenever her husband asked her, "What is the matter with you?" she would answer, "Nothing."

One day he said to one of his friends at the store, "By God, my wife is becoming sick. Every day she is getting thinner and paler. I am afraid she doesn't want me. Ever since she set foot in my house, she doesn't speak to me, and she is always sad."

His friend said to him, "I'll tell you what to do to see whether she wants you and wants to stay in your house, or whether she hates you and would like to return to her father's house. After dinner swear by God that she joins you and your mother for the coffee, then break wind. If she laughs at you, she doesn't care for you and you should send her back to her father's home. If she doesn't, then she is ill."

That same day after the man ate his supper and thanked his God, he said to his mother, "Call [his wife] to have coffee with us." He swore by God, and his mother went to call her. As they were drinking their coffee, he broke wind. His mother laughed, but his wife didn't and kept on drinking until she finished her cup....

The following day he told his friend about what had happened. His friend said to him, "Your wife is hungry. Your mother is starving your wife."

He built a new house for his wife and moved out of the old one and got his mother a servant.

Excerpts from Richard Dorson, *Folktales Told around the World*, pp. 166–168. © 1975.
Reprinted by permission of the University of Chicago Press.

This narrative from Iraq tells of the conflict and tensions between a new bride and her mother-in-law. In the story, the young husband is beset with divided loyalties. His respect for his mother is tempered by his concern for his wife. The wife is obedient and deferential to the older woman. The narrative raises issues of power for women in patrilineal and patriarchal households. The mother tries to exert power over her daughter-in-law, but in the end she has less authority than her son because he is the man, the recognized head of the family. He chooses to protect his wife's interests and allies himself with her.

This Iraqi family unit was formed not only through rules of descent but also through marriage rules. The family unit at the household level consisted of a man, his widowed mother, his wife, any children borne by his wife, and the man's unmarried siblings. This module explores marriage and the family and how they interrelate with other elements of culture in a society.

Kinship systems and family arrangements are basic elements in all societies. They are among the topics of central concern in anthropology because they help structure people's daily lives and lay the foundations for how they are integrated into their communities. However, societies differ greatly in how families are formed, about who constitutes a family, and about the rights and obligations of family members toward one another. As we shall see, variations in family organization are not random but are consistent with economic and social needs. Thus, different types of families are preferred in different types of societies.

◇ DEFINING MARRIAGE AND FAMILY

People are social beings. We live together in groups, work with others, and form emotional bonds with other people. Although some individuals live alone at any given time in every society, most people live with others during all or most of their lives. Most people who live together are members of families. In everyday speech, we use the word *family* casually to refer to our relatives without specifying how we are related to these people. Even anthropologists do not agree on a single or concise definition of family.

Anthropologists tend to make a distinction between family and household, although the two words are often used interchangeably. A **household** refers to a group of people occupying a common dwelling. The Iraqi man, his wife, and his mother are members of a household. The term *homestead* refers to multiple dwellings occupied by related and interacting people.

Members of families are related either through descent (consanguines) or marriage (affines). For example, one's grandparents, parents, aunts and uncles, siblings, children, and cousins are all consanguineal relatives, whereas one's spouse and all the people called in-laws are affinal relatives. North Americans differ in the ways they apply the word *family* to many of these relatives. Some people use the word to encompass all their relations, but others restrict the term to refer to close relatives with whom they interact regularly.

A useful starting definition of **family** is one given by anthropologist Kathleen Gough (1975, 52). She defines the family as a "married couple or other group of adult kinfolk who co-operate economically and in the upbringing of children, and all or most of whom share a common dwelling." In this definition, a family is more than just a couple. Gough's definition includes several important features of family, stressing the cooperative links among members who share social and economic responsibilities. On this basis, the Iraqi man, his wife, and his mother constitute a family.

There are other definitions of family, however, and family members need not occupy the same household. Some members of polygynous families may occupy different households within an area. In addition, although marriage is the most common bond that creates families, marriage itself is not a required component of family. Heterosexual or gay couples who are not married also constitute families. The single-parent family of parent and child is perhaps the smallest family unit (Fox 1984).

Although issues of family composition, family life, and "family values" are controversial in the current climate of North American social and political discourse, the American Anthropological Association has taken a strong position supporting the legitimacy and viability of all family types. In its statement, issued in 2003, the association said the following:

> More than a century of anthropological research on households, kinship relationships, and families, across cultures and through time, provide no support for the view that either civilization or viable social orders depend upon marriage as an exclusively heterosexual institution. Rather, a vast array of family types can contribute to stable and humane societies.

The family is a basic unit of economic cooperation and stability. Members of families usually perform at least somewhat different economic tasks, a pattern that highlights the interdependent relationships among family members. They also pool all or at least some of their resources for the survival of the group.

The family serves social needs as well, providing members with companionship, emotional support, and assistance. Families also function in the propagation and survival of society. They provide the context for biological reproduction and for the training and enculturation of children. Families function universally as vehicles for socialization into expected roles and goals of their own or adopted children. Children

household
A group of people occupying a common dwelling.

family
A married couple or other group of adult kinfolk who cooperate economically and in the upbringing of children, and all or most of whom share a common dwelling.

These roommates share a household. Unlike family households, roommates typically do not share all economic resources and have no expectations of mutual obligations or an enduring relationship.
(Alamy Limited/Blend Images/Alamy)

These indigenous Mexican families in Tzintzuntzan are celebrating the Day of the Dead.
(Glow Images, Inc./Heeb Christian/Glow Images, Inc.)

learn what is appropriate by observing adults and by overt learning and practicing of skills for roles they will assume as adult women and men. In the context of their families, children learn their gender identity and their role in households and communities. Through observation of social relations between their parents or among all adults in their households, they learn whether men and women have equal rights to contribute to discussions and decision making. They also deduce social rights through the ways that conflicts are resolved. Girls and boys also learn whether they can expect emotional and economic support from their natal kin groups once they reach adulthood and form their own families.

In addition, families are decision-making groups. Members of families consult with one another, make decisions together, and may function as political units with others in their communities to establish and provide leadership. In some societies, positions of leadership are inherited within families. Everywhere, inheritance of property and the transmission of cultural knowledge take place within family units.

All societies contain units recognized as families, but there are differences in the ways in which families are formed. Throughout the world, most families are formed through marriage. *Marriage* is another word that we use casually with reference to a union between two people, but anthropologists have not settled on an uncontested definition of marriage. There is even some debate in the field about whether marriage and the family are universal constructs. Still, even if we accept that marriage is a recognized social status in most, if not all, cultures, there are differences in the ways that marriages are contracted and in the relationships between the spouses.

Marriage is generally understood as a socially recognized, enduring, stable bond between two people who each have certain rights and obligations toward one another. These rights and obligations vary from culture to culture, but are likely to include some common features. For example, married partners have the right to expect to have a sexual relationship with each other, although the number of partners may vary. In plural marriages, for example, a person may have more than one spouse. In most societies, spouses have obligations to assist one another in rearing children and providing for their household. They share economic resources and provide shelter, clothing, and household equipment. Marriage also establishes bonds between groups of kin (the relatives of each spouse), who also have rights and obligations toward one another.

Through marriage, men and their kinship groups may claim rights to children. For this reason, there is a fundamental difference in the emphasis on marriage in patrilineal groups, where descent and inheritance are traced through men, and matrilineal groups, where they are traced through women. In matrilineal societies, kinship groups obtain new members when the women of the group give birth to children. A mother's child automatically becomes a member of her own kin group, whether she is married or not. In contrast, patrilineal kinship units cannot obtain children from their own women because a child does not belong to its mother's kin group but to its father's. In this case, marriage serves the purpose of securing a stable relationship between men and women from outside their kin group. Marriage also provides for the establishment of what Kathleen Gough calls "social fatherhood." **Social fatherhood** may or may not be the same as biological paternity. One's social father is the man who fulfills the responsibilities of parenting, just as stepparents and adoptive parents are social parents.

Based on your experience in your family, what are some specific expressions of the functions of the family as a social institution?

What do you think might be some sources of disagreements about the definitions of marriage and family?

marriage
A socially recognized, stable, and enduring union between two adults who publicly acknowledge their rights and obligations and form a new alliance between kin groups.

social fatherhood
The status of a man who fulfills the responsibilities of parenting, a role that may or may not be the same as biological paternity.

REVIEW

A family is a group of people related by blood or by marriage who live together, raise children, and share economic and other social responsibilities. A household consists of relatives and, often, nonrelatives who live together and share economic responsibilities. In all societies, enculturation of children and the inheritance of property and status take place within families. In most societies, families are formed through marriage, a public acknowledgment of a couple's commitment and a new alliance between kin groups. Marriage enables men in patrilineal societies to add children to their kin group, whereas children in matrilineal societies are automatically in their mother's group. Marriage also allows for social fatherhood.

◇ FAMILIES AND IDEAL TYPES

Anthropologists differentiate between one's family of orientation (the family one grows up in) and one's family of procreation (the family one founds as an adult). In addition, anthropologists have long used a classification of ideal family types that is generally descriptive of different family structures.

Many real families diverge from these types in some way or to some degree. Nevertheless, the types are useful because they broadly correlate with other aspects of culture. The nuclear family, extended family, joint family, and single-parent family are some of these types.

Nuclear Families

Among nomadic foragers and members of industrial societies, most families are of the type that anthropologists call "nuclear." A **nuclear family** consists of one or both parents and their children, although another relative, such as a grandparent or an unmarried sibling of one of the parents, may reside in the same household for a time. The nuclear family is the characteristic family form of societies with bilateral descent, which, are typically either foraging or industrial societies.

A nuclear family structure provides certain benefits. For instance, it has the advantage of mobility. The relatively small number of people in a nuclear family unit can easily separate themselves from the larger community in which they live. In foraging societies, nuclear families aid in survival in conditions of scarcity. If there are insufficient resources to support a large group, nuclear families can go their own way, dispersing into a large territory and exploiting meager resources. In industrial societies, nuclear families allow for economic independence and promote the loosening or weakening of wider kinship bonds. This pattern is advantageous for societies where competition and individual advancement are goals.

Comparatively, small families are an advantage for people in both foraging and industrial societies. Family size is limited among foragers in order not to exceed the carrying capacity of the environment. In addition, infants and young children need to be carried when traveling, which favors the spacing of births. Because foragers lack grains and animal milk as foods for babies, mothers nurse their children for as long as three or four years. Therefore, closely spaced children have a low chance of survival. As well, frequent pregnancies and deliveries have a negative impact on the health and long-term survival of mothers. In industrial societies, small nuclear families have the mobility necessary for leaving larger kin groups and moving from job to job and region to region. Distant relatives are unlikely to make claims for assistance, and if they do, families can easily avoid contact with them or deny their requests for aid. Small families are an advantage because dependent children are economic liabilities in industrial economies where work requires strength, stamina, and skilled training and where laws forbid or restrict child laborers.

Nuclear families risk social isolation. Family reunions in industrial societies may be seen as equivalent to seasonal gatherings of larger kin units among nomadic foragers. **Single-parent families** in industrial societies are formed as the result of divorce or the death of a spouse and parent. Others develop when the parents do not marry or live together. In the United States, most single-parent households consist of mother and children. According to U.S. Census statistics for 2009, 12 percent of all households were headed by a single mother and 4 percent had a single father as head. Single-parent households, especially those headed by women, are more likely to have incomes near or below the poverty line. Their economic difficulties stem from a common problem of nuclear families: Economic independence accrues only to people with resources and jobs. For people with meager incomes, the isolation of single-parent families increases the difficulty of seeking support from kin. In contrast, in extended family systems, people who lose or lack a spouse can rely on a large network of relatives for assistance.

Extended and Joint Families

Family systems based on an extended family principle are more common worldwide. Extended family arrangements are especially prevalent in farming and pastoral economies. **Extended families** consist of three or more generations of people, extending the family

This Japanese nuclear family is enjoying a day out.
(The Image Works/Elizabeth Crews/The Image Works)

nuclear family
Family consisting of parents and their children.

single-parent family
Family consisting of one parent (either mother or father) and her or his children.

This four-generation extended Polish family, grouped around their 96-year-old matriarch, is characterized by vertical ties between generations.
(The Image Works/David Grossman/The Image Works)

extended family
Family formed with three or more generations—for example, parents, children, and grandparents.

joint family
Family consisting of siblings with their spouses and children, sharing work and resources.

Which ideal type best characterizes your family? What are some benefits and challenges of life in this type of family in relation to the larger culture?

vertically. Typically, an extended family unit is composed of an elder parent or couple, their unmarried children, some of the married children, and the children's spouses and children. Rules of descent determine which adult married children remain with the parents. That is, in patrilineal systems where descent and inheritance are traced through men, more often the sons remain with their parents, whereas daughters leave home after marriage to reside with their husbands' families. In matrilineal societies, daughters remain with their parents after marriage, but married sons leave to join their wives' families.

A family that is extended laterally rather than vertically is referred to as a joint family, which is much less common. A **joint family** typically consists of siblings who combine their families to share work and resources, such as two or three brothers, their wives, and their children.

Extended and joint family systems have the advantage of establishing a more or less stable group of people who can share resources, household tasks, and subsistence work, and provide emotional support and material aid. However, because many people live together, conflicts may develop. Intergenerational tensions may arise because of the authority of the eldest couple over their adult children, or sibling rivalry may develop in a joint family compound. Conflicts over authority, inheritance, and loyalty are common. In addition, extended and joint family systems may lead to social difficulties for in-marrying spouses. Women moving in with their husbands' kin, for example, may face demanding mothers-in-law. Economic cooperation and interdependence is a prominent feature of extended and joint families. For this reason, people in industrial societies may form this type of family unit on a temporary or permanent basis when they are unemployed or otherwise lack resources. For example, according to the U.S. Census Bureau, in the current economic crisis experienced by many American families, the number of "multifamily households" rose sharply, by 11.7 percent from 2008 to 2010. In 2010, there were 15.5 million such households, accounting for 13.2 percent of all households and including 54 million people (Luo 2010). However, this dramatic increase does not reflect the full scope of the problem since the Census Bureau defines a multifamily household as one consisting of at least two nuclear families, excluding arrangements when adult siblings reside together or a childless adult moves in with his or her parents.

REVIEW

Ideal family types include nuclear, single-parent, extended, and joint families. A nuclear family consists of parents and their offspring and occasionally another relative. Single-parent families have a mother or a father and children. Women head most single-parent families. Extended families consist of parents, their unmarried children, married children and their spouses, and their grandchildren. Joint families extend the family unit horizontally among siblings rather than vertically across generations.

CULTURE CHANGE

THE CHANGING AMERICAN FAMILY

Family types are responsive to changes in productive modes and general social values. In the United States, the percentage of family units conforming to the idealized model of husband, wife, and children has declined since the mid-twentieth century. The idealized nuclear family model is itself a product of economic needs and adjustments made during the nineteenth and twentieth centuries as capitalist and industrial production dominated North American society. Other kinds of family units have now become more common. The number of blended families, based on remarriages and the combining of children from previous marriages, has also increased.

Growing rates of divorce have also increased the number of single-parent households. As women have gained more economic independence, the financial need to remarry after divorce or the death of a spouse has declined. More people also never marry. Many households consist of a man and woman involved in a long-term relationship who choose not to marry. Such couples may or may not have children. Another less common but not unusual type of household consists of two people of the same gender who share a sexual relationship, economic responsibilities, and other attributes of family life such as child rearing.

Census statistics indicate changes in U.S. household composition, marital status, and numbers of children over the last several decades. Tables 1 through 4 present some of the relevant data.

As the figures in Table 1 indicate, the percentages of people "Never Married" and "Divorced" have risen between 1980 and 2009, whereas the percentage of people "Married" has declined.

The size of families has also decreased between 1980 and 2009. More couples are having fewer children than in the past. Indeed, the number of childless couples has increased, as Table 2 demonstrates. Table 3 shows that the composition of households also changed from 1990 to 2009.

The number of cohabitating unmarried couples has also increased. In 1980, there were 1,589,000 such couples, but by 2000, there were 4,486,000 unmarried couples, and the number rose to 6,214,000 by 2008 (U.S. Census Bureau, *Statistical Abstract of the United States, 2001*, Table 52; 2009, Table 63).

TABLE 1 Marital Status of the U.S. Population, 1980–2009 (as percentage of total, by sex)

	1980		1990		2000		2009	
	Male	*Female*	*Male*	*Female*	*Male*	*Female*	*Male*	*Female*
Never Married	27.3	21.1	32.1	22.5	32.3	23.4	29.5	22.8
Married	67.1	64.3	60.9	62.4	59.7	60.7	58.9	56.0
Widowed	1.6	7.1	1.5	6.5	1.6	6.5	2.6	9.8
Divorced	4.0	7.6	5.5	8.5	6.4	9.3	9.0	11.4

Source: U.S. Census Bureau, *Statistical Abstract of the United States, 2001*, Table 49; *2011*, Table 56.

TABLE 2 Number of Children per Household

NUMBER OF CHILDREN	1980	1990	2000	2009
No children	48%	51%	52%	55%
One child	21	20	20	19
Two children	19	19	18	17
Three or more children	12	10	10	9

Source: U.S. Census Bureau, *Statistical Abstract of the United States, 2001*, Table 58; *2003*, Table 71; *2011*, Table 64.

TABLE 3 Composition of Households

TYPE OF HOUSEHOLD	1990	2000	2009
Family Household	71%	69%	67%
Married couple family	56	53	50
Single father	3	4	4
Single mother	12	12	12
Nonfamily Household	29	31	33
Living alone	25	26	27
Males	10	11	12
Females	15	15	15

Source: U.S. Census Bureau, *Statistical Abstract of the United States, 2001*, Table 53; *2011*, Table 61.

(*continued*)

CULTURE CHANGE CONTINUED

TABLE 4 Number of People per Family

SIZE OF FAMILY	1980	1990	2000	2009
Two people	39%	42%	44%	33.4%
Three people	23	23	22	15.9
Four people	21	21	20	13.7
Five people	10	9	9	6.1
Six people	4	3	3	2.2
Seven or more people	3	2	2	1.3

Source: U.S. Census Bureau, *Statistical Abstract of the United States, 2003,* Table 67; *2011,* Table 62.

Finally, as Table 4 indicates, the number of people per family has declined since 1980.

More families with children consist of single parents. In 1990, 71.9 percent of all families with children contained two parents; by 2005, the percentage had dropped to 67.4 percent. In 2005, mothers headed 26.4 percent of all families with children, whereas fathers headed 6.2 percent (U.S. Census Bureau, *Statistical Abstract of the United States, 2011,* Table 63). In addition, although the actual numbers remain small, the growth of stay-at-home fathers reflects changes in gender expectations. In 2009, of all married couple families with children under 15 years old, 22.6 percent had stay-at-home mothers while 0.7 percent had stay-at-home fathers. This represents a more than doubling of stay-at-home fathers since 1995 and a decline in the numbers of stay-at-home mothers (U.S. Census Bureau, *Statistical Abstract of the United States, 2011,* Table 68).

Census figures also indicate a sharp increase in the number of same-sex households between 1990 and 2009. This may reflect both real growth in same-sex households and a greater likelihood that their members self-report. In 2006, 776,943 households consisted of same-sex partners. Of these, 413,095 were male couples and 363,848 were female couples (U.S. Census Bureau, *Statistical Abstract of the United States, 2006,* Table 62). Taking a different perspective on the data, in 2009 of all households with unmarried partners, 0.24 percent consisted of two men while 0.26 percent consisted of two women (U.S. Census Bureau, *Statistical Abstract of the United States, 2011,* Table 63).

Although same-sex marriages are legal in Massachusetts, Connecticut, Iowa, Vermont, New Hampshire, and New York State, the U.S. Census Bureau reclassifies legally married same-sex couples as "unmarried, same-sex partners" in compliance with the Defense of Marriage Act.

Data for 2009 reveal that 69.8 percent of all children live with two parents (U.S. Census Bureau, *Statistical Abstract of the United States, 2009,* Table 69). Although this is a decline from the 85 percent in 1970, it is still a sizable majority. In 2009, 22.8 percent of children lived with their mother only (up from 11 percent in 1970) while 3.4 percent lived only with their father. Comparative evidence shows that the figures on children and household composition have remained fairly steady since 1990, indicating that the familial effects of social changes in the 1960s and 1970s have leveled off. Only 4.0 percent of the nation's children live in households without either parent, and about 2 percent are living with their grandparents only. There are marked disparities in children's experiences for different racial and ethnic groupings; for example, 85.2 percent of Asian children, 75.8 percent of non-Hispanic white children, 68.7 percent of Hispanic children, but only 38.1 percent of African American children live with two parents.

All of these data are consistent with quantitative and qualitative studies soliciting Americans' attitudes toward marriage and family life. Several large-scale research projects from the 1960s through the late 1990s reveal that, although most Americans "... value marriage, children, and family life, these institutions are now much more voluntary and less obligatory...leading to more individual freedom in these areas" (Thornton and Young-DeMarco 2001, 1031). Examples of these shifts include more acceptance of divorce, of unmarried couples living together, and of unmarried women having children.

◇ ENDOGAMY, EXOGAMY, AND THE INCEST TABOO

Marriage serves as a means of extending kinship within a particular group (*endogamy*) or extending kinship to other groups (*exogamy*). All societies ban marriage—and condemn sexual relations—within the nuclear family, particularly between parents and children and also, with very few exceptions, between brothers and sisters. This ban is referred to as the **incest taboo.** The incest taboo is essentially a rule of nuclear family exogamy, forcing people to marry outside their families. The incest taboo is universal, but beyond the nuclear family the "forbidden" relatives are different in different societies. For example, one set of cousins is preferred for marriage in some societies, whereas other sets of cousins are forbidden under the incest taboo.

incest taboo
A ban on sexual relations or marriage between parents and their children or between siblings.

Effects of Exogamy on Social Organization

The marriage rules of endogamy and exogamy are predicated on the incest taboo. Both exogamy and endogamy reflect and reinforce the structure and organization of a society. For example, village exogamy is the norm in societies in which people contract marriages with residents of other villages. Through intervillage marriages, people create alliances over a broader geographic area, thereby widening their networks of allies and supporters. In areas of frequent warfare, such marriages also give some protection against raids because people are less likely to attack villages where they have relatives.

In addition, some stratified societies practice exogamy, stipulating that members of identifiable social groups or strata need to marry outside their own group or **class,** a social grouping whose membership is usually based on a combination of birth and achievement. For example, the Natchez of the south-central United States were divided into two major classes—nobles and commoners. These groups had different, unequal access to resources, services, and power. The nobility consisted of three graded ranks: Suns, Nobles, and Honored Persons. Descent was

class
Social grouping usually determined on the basis of a combination of birth and achievement.

CONTROVERSIES

EXPLAINING THE INCEST TABOO

The origins of the incest taboo are much debated. One theory proposes that the incest taboo arose out of an instinctive aversion toward sexual relations within the nuclear family. However, incest occurs fairly widely in human societies, so avoiding it is not instinctual. Another biological theory suggests that the incest taboo is a learned, cultural response to the possible biological consequences of inbreeding, which can increase the incidence of undesirable or harmful (as well as desirable and beneficial) genetic traits in a population. This theory assumes that ancestral humans understood the relationship between mating and the variability of traits in their population, and that this cultural adaptation then spread to all human societies through diffusion or contact to become a universal element of culture or, alternatively, that human societies in different areas independently invented an incest taboo.

A theory championed by anthropologist Bronislaw Malinowski, based on the work of Sigmund Freud, focused on the origin of the incest taboo as a response to the need to lessen sexual competition within the nuclear family unit. This psychological theory might account in part for the ban on sexual relations between parents and their children, which would strain the marriage bond between husband and wife. However, it does not explain the near-universal prohibition on marriage between siblings. Sibling marriage occurred among the monarchs of ancient Peru, Egypt, and Hawaii but was not defined as incest. Marriage between a brother and sister at the highest level of the state consolidated power and minimized struggles over succession. However, sibling marriage was not permitted among ordinary citizens.

Many anthropologists favor understanding the incest taboo as a means of ensuring survival by forcing people to make alliances with others outside the nuclear family. This "marry out or die out" theory emphasizes that marriage within a small unit will over time lead to the isolation and genetic homogeneity of the group, which makes the unit more vulnerable to population loss or even extinction. Mating outside the nuclear family reduces this risk and also creates social alliances and bonds of reciprocity with other people that can be critical in times of scarcity and other dangers to survival.

We may never know why the incest taboo started, but the fact that it is universal indicates its importance. All these theories add interesting dimensions and clues to the debate.

CRITICAL THINKING QUESTION

Which theory or combination of theories about the origin of the incest taboo do you favor, and why?

Brahmans, like the one in this photograph, are the highest of four main castes identified in ancient Hindu sacred writings.
(Alamy Limited/Melvyn Longhurst/Alamy)

matrilineal. The chief was the highest-ranked member of the highest-ranked matrilineage, the Suns. The Suns were never able to consolidate their power and wealth, however, because the Natchez social system required that all members of the nobility practice class exogamy. That is, they had to marry commoners. The Sun matrilineage was perpetuated through children of Sun women who were Suns themselves, but children of Sun men, including children of the Great Sun, were not members of that chiefly lineage. The children and more distant relatives of Sun men became Nobles and Honored Persons, whose male children were commoners through membership in their mothers' lineage. On the other hand, children of male commoners became members of the nobility if their fathers married noble women. Commoners could also raise their status through exemplary services to the nation, such as serving in the military, which raised wives' status as well (Bonvillain 2001, 132–33).

GLOBALIZATION

Increases in rates of multiracial marriage and in numbers of mixed-race children in many parts of the world can be seen as an extension of the process of globalization. In many countries, including the United States, interethnic marriage also contributes to the spread of English.

caste
Social grouping whose membership is determined at birth and is generally inflexible.

Effects of Endogamy on Social Organization

Many stratified societies also practice endogamy, in which people marry within their class or rank to maintain social, economic, and political distinctions. Endogamous marriages solidify and preserve the privilege of elites by consolidating wealth and power.

A strong form of endogamy occurs in caste systems. **Caste** is an ascribed social category identifying a group by status or by occupation. At birth, people automatically become members of the caste of their parents and remain in that caste throughout life. In India, for example, people traditionally must marry other members of their own caste. Caste exogamy (marrying someone of another caste) is, in principle, forbidden, although it does occur.

Informal class endogamy is widespread in stratified societies, simply because people with similar backgrounds tend to associate with one another and marry within their group. Members of the same class tend to socialize together, attend the same schools, live in the same neighborhoods, perform the same social activities, and so on. Therefore, even in the absence of a strong marriage rule, proximity and informal sanctions against marrying down tend to lead to class endogamy. Other marriage preferences that follow informal social norms include the tendency for people in pluralistic societies to marry within their own racial or ethnic group and to choose partners who speak the same language and observe the same religion.

REVIEW

The universal incest taboo is a general ban against sexual relations between individuals within a nuclear family. Explanations for its origins include biological and psychological explanations and hypotheses based on cultural adaptations to survival factors. Marriage rules affect the organization of a society. Examples of impacts of endogamy on social systems include the caste system of India, alliances created through cross-cousin marriage, and class systems with preferential marriage based on shared membership in a social, racial, or ethnic group.

monogamy
Marriage rule that stipulates a union between two people.

polygamy
Marriage in which the marital unit consists of three or more people.

◈ FORMS OF MARRIAGE

Marriage rules define the forms that marriages can take, and these forms vary. For example, norms concerning the number of spouses that can constitute the marital unit differ in different societies. In most societies, marriage is a union between two people—**monogamy.** However, in some societies the marital unit may consist of three or more people—**polygamy,** or plural marriage. Monogamy is the most common form of union today, even in societies where plural marriages are possible.

Societies that permit remarriage after the death of a spouse or divorce practice **serial monogamy,** meaning that a person can be married to only one person at a time, although individuals may have two or more spouses during their lifetime.

Polygyny and Polyandry

There are two forms of polygamy. **Polygyny** is marriage between a man and two or more women, and **polyandry** is marriage between a woman and two or more men. Polygyny is far more common than polyandry as a form of plural marriage, but most couples live in monogamous unions, even in societies where plural marriages are possible. A common type of polygyny is a pattern in which a man marries two or more sisters, usually wedding one first and the other years later. This system is called **sororal polygyny.** Sororal polygyny has the advantage of minimizing potential conflicts between wives because the women have close emotional and supportive bonds as sisters. When co-wives are not related, they may have tensions between them, each vying for favoritism from their common husband to benefit themselves and their children. Different societies favor different kinds of residence patterns for plural marriages. In some, the entire unit of husband and several wives lives together in one dwelling. In others, each wife of a polygynous homestead has a separate hut for herself and her children.

Polyandry may also take several forms. In some cases, a woman may marry unrelated men whereas, in others, several brothers may be married to the same woman, a form called fraternal polyandry. The best documented examples of polyandry occur in South Asia, especially in India, Tibet, and Nepal. Polyandry has also been reported elsewhere in the past, including among the Inuit of Arctic Canada and the Iroquois of New York State.

Polyandrous marriages may occur in societies where there are shortages of women. For example, in some communities in the Indian Himalayas and Chinese Tibet, such as the Nyinba and the Pahari, brothers may jointly contract for a wife. This fraternal polyandry permits all men to be married, and also promotes economic cooperation among brothers for their mutual benefit. Rather than fragmenting a family's property through inheritance by numerous and possibly conflicting heirs, polyandrous unions solidify wealth, property, and social status and raise people's overall standard of living (Levine 1988). However, the shortage of women in Nyinba society derives from social attitudes that devalue females. Because sons are preferred, they are better fed and cared for than are daughters. The neglect of females leads to higher rates of infant and child mortality, resulting in a gender imbalance. Currently, in traditional Nyinba communities, the sex ratio is 118 men to 100 women (Stone 2006, 201). Polyandry permits all men to marry while at the same time limiting population growth, an adaptive strategy in a region of scarce resources.

Finally, Nyinba men are often away from their households pursuing economic activities. Men's work includes herding their households' animals, especially goats and sheep. They are also involved in trading grains and other products, traveling from Tibet into northern India (Stone 2006, 195). Polyandry ensures that households will likely have at least one man at home to accomplish male economic tasks.

Fraternal polyandrous marriages were also common in villages of the Lahaul Valley in India, close to its border with Tibet. Such arrangements solved the problem of splintering small family farms among brothers and instead allowed the continued consolidation of scant acreage. In addition, in the words of a 60-year old man living in a polyandrous household, "If you marry a different woman, then there are more chances of family disputes. Family property is divided, and problems arise" (Polgreen 2010). Finally, polyandry helps to limit population growth, an economic necessity in an environment of scarce farmland. Familial relationships were also regulated by kinship practices in which children used the term meaning "father" for the eldest brother married to their mother. The other brothers were called "uncle." Although descent followed patrilineal principles, women had high status in their households.

Explanations of Polygyny

Polygyny develops in different societies for different reasons. Care must therefore be taken in interpreting its meanings and functions depending on the

serial monogamy
Marriage pattern that stipulates that a person can be married to only one person at a time, although individuals may have two or more spouses during their lifetime. Subsequent marriages may be formed after the death of one spouse or after divorce.

polygyny
Marriage between a man and two or more women.

polyandry
Marriage between a woman and two or more men.

sororal polygyny
Marriage between a man and two or more women who are sisters.

In this West African family, each co-wife has her own hut, which she occupies with her children.
(The Image Works/Lauren Goodsmith/The Image Works)

cultural and historical contexts in which polygyny occurs. In communities where women significantly outnumber men, polygyny helps correct imbalances in the sex ratio. Among the Innu of eastern Canada in earlier centuries, for example, polygyny, limited to two or three wives, ensured marriage for all women in a society with a scarcity of men. Male mortality rates were comparatively higher than female mortality rates because of the dangers for men in hunting and warfare. After lecturing the Innu about the evils of plural marriage, the seventeenth-century French Jesuit missionary Paul LeJeune observed: "Since I have been preaching among them that a man should not have more than one wife, I have not been well received by the women; for, since they are more numerous than the men, if a man can only marry one of them, the others will have to suffer. Therefore this doctrine is not to their liking" (Thwaites 1906, vol. 12, 165). In the case of the Innu, polygyny prevented population decline by maintaining an effective rate of reproduction.

Polygyny occurs in some strongly patriarchal societies in which women are viewed as property and a source of status. Men who can afford to support a greater number of wives and dependents are seen to have greater wealth, power, and prestige in their communities. Historically, hereditary high chiefs of polygynous Central African kingdoms boasted hundreds of wives and concubines. In pre-Communist imperial China, wealthy men measured their status and good fortune in the number of wives they accumulated. Daughters became mediums of exchange between men seeking to form alliances with each other.

Polygyny also develops as an adaptation to economic needs or goals because of the important economic roles women serve. For example, as the economy of the Plains Indians shifted to dependence on the buffalo by the middle of the nineteenth century, men wanted to obtain the economic services of more than one wife because women were responsible for tanning the buffalo hides and thus turning a raw product into a marketable item. To advance themselves in trade networks that were supplied by the labor of women, men wanted several wives.

In some farming societies, polygyny serves the purpose of supplying additional labor of women and their children. For example, among the Tswana and Herero, two cattle-herding and horticultural societies of southern Africa, men with more than one wife were able to accumulate greater farm surpluses because of women's key roles as subsistence farmers. Also, the more wives a man had, the more children he acquired. His children raised his social standing because they contributed to the growth of his patrilineage and patriclan. A man's sons helped care for his cattle, and his daughters brought cattle to the family as wedding gifts from their husbands' kin.

Men living in foraging societies may reap benefits from the labor of more than one wife. Among the Tiwi of Australia, men want to have several wives because the Aboriginal foraging economy centers on the collection of wild plant resources, work that women generally do. As one Tiwi reported, "If I had only one or two wives I would starve, but with my present ten or twelve wives I can send them out in all directions in the morning and at least two or three of them are likely to bring something back with them at the end of the day, and then we can all eat" (Hart and Pilling 1960, 34).

Tiwi husbands benefit from polygyny both economically and socially. A man with several wives can accumulate enough food surplus to give to others, raising his prestige by his generosity. Australian Aborigine men also value their wives because of their desire to have many children, a condition of marriage. The Tiwi traditionally practiced reciprocal polygyny, with men sometimes agreeing to marry each other's sisters or each other's daughters.

Specialized Adaptive Forms of Marriage

Cultures demonstrate a great deal of variety in the ways that people think of sexual relations, marriage, and family. Marriage might even be entirely symbolic and not involve procreation. Yet, even in rare forms of marriage, principles of descent, patterns of residence and household composition, and ways of establishing bonds with others form systems of relationships and meaning that integrate individuals into families and communities. So, although these forms of marriage were restricted to only a few societies, they shed light on the various social and economic functions of marriage.

In some African societies with patrilineal descent, marriages can be contracted in ways that emphasize the importance of descent and the continuity of patrilineal kin groups. Among the Nuer, for example, if a married man died without sons, one of his younger brothers married his widow. The children of the new couple, though, were considered heirs of the deceased (Evans-Pritchard

1955). Nuer **ghost marriage** thus permitted an elder brother to maintain his patrilineage even after his death. In Nuer society, seniority in a lineage was an important criterion for determining relative social status, so allowing descent to follow from an elder sibling, dead or alive, was a strategic practice. In this way, children born to the younger brother but claimed by the dead older brother would have seniority over members of junior lineages.

Another Nuer marital option was allowed when a lineage failed to produce a male heir. In that event, a woman in the lineage could take the role of husband and be married to another woman. The woman who became a husband refrained from having sex because husbands cannot conceive. The "wife" conceived by having sex with a chosen man from any lineage other than her own. The children borne to the "wife" belonged to the "husband's" lineage, thus supplying the line with heirs (Evans-Pritchard 1955, 108).

In marriages between women, the woman who acted as husband was transformed into a legal man. As a "man," she could receive bridal payments given in marriages for her kinswomen, and she could inherit cattle from her father. She could also be compensated with cattle if her "wife" had an adulterous affair without her consent. Nuer practices of marriage between women and "ghost marriage" both create social fatherhood for the purpose of securing the continuation of patrilineages.

In another rare form, the matrilineal Kwakwaka'wakw (Kwakiutl) of British Columbia developed a marriage option that created daughters for men who had none. Such a strategy was necessary because status, wealth, and named titles were transmitted from men to men through women. In practice, men needed daughters because wealth and titles passed from a father to his daughter's children. To accommodate men who had no daughters, several types of marriage could be arranged. According to George Hunt, a Kwakiutl chief, a man "turned the left side of his son's body into a woman and gave ['her'] the name belonging to the oldest daughter of his line" (quoted in Boas 1966, 55). Then another man proposed marriage to the first man's "daughter." After they were married, the first man was able to acquire the titles belonging to "her" lineage and could pass these on to children whom he had with a subsequent wife. If a man had no children at all, according to Hunt, "the father may call his foot or one side of his body, his daughter. The marriage ceremony is performed as though these were the women married, and the names are transferred in the usual manner." This was called "taking hold of the foot" (Boas 1897, 359). These marital options allowed for the transmission of wealth and status in a society where men controlled wealth but the wealth passed through women.

The Nayar, a matrilineal people living in Kerala, South India, had concepts of marriage that differ from most peoples' (Gough 1961; Mencher 1965). Although contemporary Nayar no longer practice these marriage options, they demonstrate possible societal options. Nayar kinship centers on matrilineal relatives, organized into matrilineal descent and residence groups called *taravad*. The *taravad* consists of sisters and brothers, the sisters' children, the sisters' daughters' children, and so on, all descended from a female ancestor. They hold land and other property in common, managed by the senior man. They also care collectively for children born to their female members. In the past, shortly before a girl reached puberty, she was married to a man chosen by her family. After the marriage ceremony, the couple stayed together for three days. If they wanted, they were permitted to have sexual intercourse but that was not a requirement. On the fourth day, they separated and need not ever see each other again. The man and woman had no social or economic responsibilities toward one another and did not live together. However, the bond between them was symbolized when the man died because the woman honored him in mourning ceremonies.

Thereafter, the man and woman had a succession of lovers over the years. These unions were referred to as "joining together" (Stone 2006, 143). A lover acknowledged and legitimized his sexual relationship with a particular woman by giving her gifts three times a year for as long as the liaison lasted. Children produced from these unions belonged to the *taravad* of the mother, and her family took responsibility for the economic care of children. Fathers had no economic obligations for their children, but establishment of paternity was critical to the social standing of mother and child. Her "husbands" publicly declared themselves possible fathers of a child by giving gifts to the mother and to the midwife who assisted in the birth.

Today, distinctive Nayar marriage practices have largely disappeared, replaced by monogamous marriages and nuclear family residence patterns. Although matrilineal kinship groups continue to delineate relationships for some people, the Nayar have shifted toward patrilineal preferences consistent with the loss of property rights previously held by matrilineal groups because contemporary wage work, especially performed by men, has led to the separateness and mobility of the family unit.

ghost marriage
Marriage practice among the Nuer of Sudan in which a widow marries her dead husband's brother and in which the children ensuing from the second marriage are said to be the children of the first, dead husband.

In May 2004, Massachusetts became the first state to legalize gay marriage. Other states permitting same-sex marriage include Vermont, Iowa, New Hampshire, the District of Columbia, and New York State. Pictured here is a couple preparing to marry in New York City in 2011.
(Newscom/SIPA USA/SIPA/Newscom)

same-sex marriage
Marriage between two men or two women.

The Na, an ethnic group of Yunnan province in southern China, do not recognize marital ties or obligations at all (Hua 2001). Households consist of siblings and the children of female members. Men or women can propose sexual encounters, termed "visits," but they always take place at night in the woman's house. They have no mutual obligations or rights and do not expect to have exclusive sexual access to one another. Nor do they contribute to a joint household. Children belong to the kin group of the mother, but they do not acknowledge paternity or social fatherhood. Instead, children are raised by their mother and her male and female kin.

Same-Sex Marriage

Although most marriages in most cultures are unions between men and women, some societies allow marriage between individuals of the same sex. This is not the same as the **same-sex marriages** practiced by the Nuer, in which a woman is legally defined as a man for purposes of marriage to another woman. In this case, the couple does not have sexual relations. Rather, the female wife has sex with a man in order to bear children for her female husband.

Same-sex marriage was an option in many Native American societies as late as the early decades of the twentieth century. Especially in cultures of the Great Plains, the Southwest, and California, two women or two men might marry, have sexual relations, and share household and family responsibilities. These people, now often referred to as "Two-Spirits," were publicly recognized as forming legitimate couples.

In North America today, growing numbers of lesbian and gay couples advocate for the right to marry in ceremonies that have legal standing. Advocates note that same-sex couples fulfill all of the same obligations and responsibilities toward one another as do heterosexual couples. They share their resources, make joint decisions, and make commitments to exclusive sexual relationships. Many also raise children together. Opponents of lesbian and gay marriage claim that the traditional cultural concept of marriage, based on religious precepts, applies only to the union of one man and one woman. Growing tolerance for homosexual marriages in the United States and Canada is a measure of social and culture change. In the United States, Vermont was the first state to permit the legal recognition of civil unions between homosexuals, so long as they did not call it "marriage." In 2004, Massachusetts became the first state to legalize same-sex marriage, not simply to recognize same-sex civil unions, followed in 2008 by California and Connecticut. However, in 2008, voters in California approved a ballot initiative banning same-sex marriages. Then in 2009, Vermont, Iowa, and Maine recognized same-sex marriages but Maine voters rejected the law in 2010 and in 2010, same-sex marriage was legalized in New Hampshire and the District of Columbia. Finally, in 2011, the New York State legislature enacted a bill to legalize same-sex marriage, as did the Tribal Council of the Suquamish Tribe in the state of Washington. The inconsistencies in legislative action and voter responses demonstrate that the issue remains deeply controversial. In 2003, the Supreme Court of Canada ruled that Canadian marriage laws allow homosexuals to wed. Belgium, the Netherlands, Norway, Spain, South Africa, Sweden, and Argentina also allow same-sex couples to marry.

REVIEW

Monogamy is the marriage of one man and one woman, either for life or for a given time (serial monogamy). Polygamy, or plural marriage, can be in two forms: polygyny or polyandry. Polygyny is marriage between one man and two or more women. Marriage between a man and two or more sisters is called sororal polygyny. Explanations for the development of polygyny relate to population sex ratios, the status of women, and economic adaptations. Polyandry, marriage between one woman and two or more men, often brothers, is rarer. Other rare forms of marriage include ghost marriages, foot marriages, and same-sex marriages.

◇ MARRIAGE AS ALLIANCE AND ECONOMIC EXCHANGE

The relationship established through marriage is not only social but economic as well. Each spouse usually has certain obligations to the other and to their children to supply basic needs such as food, clothing, and shelter. The economic factor in marriage may also be expressed through exchanges of goods and services prior to, during, or after marriage rites. In most Native American cultures, for instance, gifts were mutually exchanged before and during a marriage ceremony. Relatives of the bride and groom gave each other foods, clothing, and ornaments as a sign of their mutual respect and support. The reciprocal exchange of gifts is common in egalitarian societies in which the families of bride and groom demonstrate an equality of relationship and obligation.

Some of these Botswana cattle may become bridewealth for sons from the owner's family to give to the parents of their prospective wives.
(Corbis/Peter Johnson/Corbis)

Bridewealth and Brideservice

In some places, substantial gifts and/or services may be given, not mutually by both sides, but more often by one side to the other. In patrilineal societies, for example, **bridewealth** is given from the husband's group to that of the wife. Among the Nuer and most of the cattle-herding societies of eastern Africa, bridewealth was primarily in the form of cattle. In the plains of North America, people gave horses as bridewealth. The number of cattle or horses given was taken to be a reflection of the wealth and prestige of the husband's kin and an indication of the esteem in which they held the bride and her family. Offering too little, then, could be an insult.

In societies where a married couple lived with the husband's kin, the transfer of goods from the husband's group to that of the wife was symbolic compensation for the woman's loss to her family. Bridewealth was also recognition that, after the wedding, the husband's family benefited from the bride's labor while her own kin would be deprived of it. In addition, bridewealth was a means of legitimizing the couple's children and their membership in the husband's patrilineal group, patrilineal kinship groups obtain new members by monopolizing the reproductive potential of women who their men marry. Bridewealth typically was returned if a couple divorced, so the wife's kin often had a large stake in discouraging the dissolution of the marriage.

Patterns and amounts of bridewealth payments may change as societies undergo economic and social transformations. For example, among the Nuer of the Southern Sudan, the number of cattle expected as gifts from the husband's family to that of the wife has fluctuated in the last 50 years in response to conditions that affected the size of herds. When drought or cattle diseases decimated herds, the number of cattle given as bridewealth declined. During the first civil war in Sudan, which lasted from 1963 until 1972, bridewealth rates also declined sharply (Hutchinson 1996, 81). Thereafter, the expected number of cattle increased in the 1980s during a period of relative stability.

A second change in bridewealth practices among the Nuer was the introduction of money. Although some families are willing to accept some money, cattle remain the preferred tokens of bridewealth. As the Nuer say, "Money has no blood" (Hutchinson 1996, 74).

Finally, some young Nuer men now attempt to free themselves from family ties by purchasing cattle for their own bridewealth payments with funds that they have earned from work. This is a significant break with past practices where the circulation of cattle among families in bridewealth payments secured and symbolized larger social bonds, linking individuals to the support networks of their kin who contributed cattle for their bridewealth payments and linking families to other kinship groups.

In another form of gift giving related to marriage, called **brideservice,** men are obligated to perform services for their wife's parents. A period of brideservice may predate the marriage ceremony, or the period may extend for many years after marriage. During this period, the future or

bridewealth
Presents given by the husband's family to the wife's kin before, during, or after the wedding ceremony.

brideservice
A period of months or years before or after marriage during which the husband performs labor for his wife's parents.

newly married husband contributes his labor to his parents-in-law. Depending on the subsistence strategies employed, he may give all or a portion of animals he has caught and help with planting and harvesting crops. In addition, the husband may help construct his parents-in-law's dwellings, fetch wood or water, and perform other domestic tasks.

Groom-Service and Groom-Wealth

groom-service
Obligation for a future bride to perform service for her future husband and his family.

Although less common than brideservice and bridewealth, in some societies, a future bride is obligated to perform service for her future husband and his family. Such **groom-service** might include preparation of food or production of household items deemed expected of the work of wives. A bride might go to stay at her future in-laws' dwelling to perform these services and remain there until they are completed

Instead of, or in addition to, rendering service, the bride's parents and relatives may donate goods to the groom's parents and relatives. **Groom-wealth** might include clothing, ornaments, and household supplies. The gifts given are then distributed among the relevant kin.

groom-wealth
Gifts such as clothing, ornaments, and household supplies given by the parents and relatives of the bride to the parents and relatives of the groom.

From the parents' perspective, both brideservice and groom-service provide demonstrations of the "suitability" of a future son-in-law or daughter-in-law as a "marriage partner and a household member" (Huber, Danaher, and Breedlove 2011, 5). These are also opportunities for the groom or bride to demonstrate and practice the skills that will be expected of them in their roles as husband or wife.

Dowry

dowry
Gifts given by the wife's family to the married couple or to the husband's kin before, during, or after the wedding ceremony.

In some societies, the bride's family gives goods of value to the bride, although these gifts do not usually remain as the property of the bride but rather are given to the newly married couple and/or to the husband's kin prior to or upon the marriage. This type of exchange is called **dowry**. Dowries are prevalent in some patriarchal cultures that stress the prestige of men and their families. In theory, dowries are a kind of insurance that protects the interests of a wife in a patrilineal and patriarchal society. In practice, however, dowry wealth is often appropriated by the husband and his family.

In Europe, from medieval times until well into the nineteenth century, well-to-do families bestowed dowries on their daughters when they married. The ability to give large amounts of money, property, and annual incomes was a sign of a family's wealth, enhancing their prestige as well. In turn, fathers who could afford handsome dowries could bargain for wealthy and powerful sons-in-law. Through marriage exchanges of dowries for husbands with property and status, men acquired a host of affinal relatives as personal and political allies. The legacy of the European dowry system is preserved today in the custom of collecting fine clothes and linens in a bridal hope chest.

Dowry as property given by the bride's parents is the most common form, but in some societies it is the groom's parents who transfer wealth to the new couple (Huber, Danaher, and Breedlove 2011, 6). In others, both sets of relatives give property to the bride and groom.

Marriages are economic transactions, but they are also occasions for celebration. What is celebrated is not simply the union of two people, but the alliances formed between two families, lineages, or clans. When marriage takes place between a man and a woman who come from different villages, the wedding may symbolize extended networks and alliances between two communities.

REVIEW

As well as creating alliances among families and larger social units, marriage has important economic functions, and economic exchange is a common feature of marriage arrangements. Gifts are exchanged in many societies to represent the new economic obligations the spouses now have to one another and their in-laws. Bridewealth, found in patrilineal societies, consists of forms of wealth or objects of value given to the bride's family by the groom's family. Brideservice consists of work that the groom does for his in-laws. In the dowry system, the family of the bride pays or promises to pay wealth to the family of the groom in exchange for the marriage of their daughter.

CULTURE CHANGE

DOWRY IN INDIA

Dowry was the traditional marital exchange in India. A woman's family had to present wealth in jewelry, fine cloth, and money to the husband's family before the marriage took place. The amount of wealth given was an indication of both the bride's status and the esteem of the husband's kin. Wealthy parents gave a lot of property, but even poor families tried to collect as many valuables as they could so as not to shame their daughter and themselves.

The economic burden of dowry contributed to a preference for sons over daughters because girls were a financial liability whereas boys brought in dowry wealth when they married. Thus, the custom of dowry contributed to female infanticide and the neglect of the health of daughters in India and Bangladesh. However, dowry was not the only factor involved in preferences for sons and the consequences of such preferences. Rather, a constellation of behaviors and attitudes place value on men and undermine the worth of women: kinship based on patrilineal descent and inheritance, subsistence strategies emphasizing intensive agriculture done primarily by men, and male control over land.

Although outlawed by the Dowry Prohibition Act (1961, amended in 1984 and 1986), a husband's family often still demands specific amounts of cash or goods to contract a marriage (Ghadially and Kumar 1988, 175). Young men of high status, good education, and favorable employment prospects command large sums. Dowry demands are often made after a marriage is contracted and even after a wedding.

The deaths of young wives whose families have not satisfied the dowry demands of their in-laws have led to controversy. Of a registered 179 "unnatural deaths" of young married women in Delhi between 1981 and 1982, 12 percent to 16 percent were reportedly dowry-related (Ghadially and Kumar 1988, 167). In two-thirds of these cases, young women committed suicide; their in-laws murdered the remaining third. The families involved were of all social classes, educational levels, and occupations.

Ghadially and Kumar (1988) also report that, in the Indian state of Maharashtra, dowry deaths rose from 120 in 1984 to 211 in 1985, an increase of 64 percent. By the mid-1990s, dowry deaths, including bride burnings, had climbed to an estimated 5,800 incidents a year. Many "unnatural deaths" of women are classified as "kitchen/cooking accidents" and "stove bursts," a common method of killing unprofitable daughters-in-law. Retaliation against wives whose families fail to meet dowry demands takes many forms, from verbal abuse to beatings, burns, hanging, poisoning, and strangulation.

A disturbing finding in studies of dowry abuse and death is that the wife's parents are sometimes aware of the violence perpetrated against their daughter but tell her to endure her situation rather than stir controversy that would sully her family's reputation.

Dowry and the related mistreatment and deaths of women gave impetus to the birth of the feminist movement in India. Beginning in 1979, women's groups staged public protests to publicize the issue of dowry harassment. As a result, many families of abused daughters came forward to give testimony and ask for redress. In 1980, the government mandated police investigation of the death of any woman who had been married less than five years at the time of her death. In 1983, legislation made "cruelty to a wife a cognizable, non-bailable offense" and stipulated that "cruelty" included both mental and physical harassment (Kumar 1995, 68). Cases reported as suicides (frequently involving death by dousing and burning) could be investigated as "abetment to suicide," shifting the burden of proof to the woman's husband and his family, and women who died within seven years of marriage had to have autopsies.

The latest studies, however, indicate increases in dowry demands. For example, the All India Democratic Women's Association surveyed 10,000 people in eighteen of India's twenty-six states and found "an across-the-board increase in dowry demands" (Brooke 2003). Government statistics report that, in 2001, husbands or in-laws angry over small dowries killed nearly 7,000 women. In 2003, a well-publicized case brought the issue of dowry demands to national attention. A bride called police on her wedding day when her father refused to pay her in-laws an additional $25,000 they demanded, and a scuffle broke out. The husband eventually served fourteen days in jail for violating laws against dowry (Brooke 2003). Government statistics indicate that dowry deaths rose 46 percent from 1995 to 2005 (Government of India 2006, 171).

■ CASE STUDY

A WEDDING IN NEPAL

In larger communities and settled populations, especially where lineages are important kinship, economic, and political units, marriages may be complex, lengthy procedures. Among the Lohorung Rai of eastern Nepal, marriage involves a ten-step process (Hardman 2000). The most complex aspect of the marriage is the negotiation between the families of the intended husband and wife. These negotiations underscore the social and economic as well as spiritual alliances created between two families, their clans, and their villages.

Most Lohorung Rai marriages are arranged when the boy and girl are young, beginning with a gift of liquor brought from the boy's kin to the girl's parents. The boy's emissaries recount his good qualities and those of his family. The girl's family often refuse the initial request, returning the gift to the boy's relatives, and several trips may be needed before the girl's parents drink the liquor and tell the boy's relatives how much meat they will need to distribute to their kin.

Subsequently, the boy's kin bring more gifts to those of the girl. Eventually, they present the final gift of a live pig, some rice, and liquor to the girl's kin. This final gift, referred to as a "ransom," marks the formal betrothal of the couple and commits the families to the marriage. The wedding, lasting all night, takes place at the bride's home. The groom proceeds there accompanied by his cousin (father's sister's son). The rite not only celebrates a marriage but also marks the transition of a male from boyhood to manhood.

After the wedding, the bride accompanies her husband to his parents' home, but the following day she returns to her own parents' home, bringing additional gifts from her husband's family. She returns to her husband's home sixteen days later but remains for only a few days, not finally taking up residence there for perhaps a year. Several years later, usually after the birth of her first child, she returns to her parents' home for a final rite of separation, receiving gifts from her brothers.

The lengthy and complex Lohorung Rai marriage process not only solidifies an alliance between two families but also symbolizes and enacts the difficulty of a young woman's separation from her family in a society where postmarital residence is in the husband's locality and usually involves village exogamy. The woman's family demonstrates their reluctance to lose her by hesitating to accept the initial gifts, and she shows her reluctance to leave by repeatedly returning to her parents' home.

At this Nepalese wedding, the bride's relatives accept gifts of gold, clothing, and jewelry that symbolize the marriage.
(Corbis/John Van Hasselt/Corbis)

◇ MARRIAGE AS A RITE OF PASSAGE

For individuals, families, kin groups, and communities, marriages are crucial rites of passage. Because of the importance of the alliances formed by marriage, one's parents or other relatives arrange marriages, especially first marriages, in many societies. A proposal of marriage may be made from one side or the other, although it is more common worldwide for the future husband's kin to approach the family of the intended wife. This is true whether the people follow patrilineal or matrilineal rules of descent.

A proposal of marriage may be a simple, short process, or it may be a long, drawn-out, ritualized exchange of greetings, proposals, counterproposals, and gift exchanges before the hoped-for marriage is finally settled upon. Among the Lohorung Rai of Nepal, for example, the marriage proposal process may take many years to accomplish. After the husband's family makes the initial contact, numerous exchanges of refusal and counterproposal follow before a final date is set for the wedding.

IN THEIR OWN VOICES

"I HEAR THAT I'M GOING TO GET MARRIED!"

Florence Edenshaw Davidson, a Haida woman from Vancouver Island, British Columbia, Canada, was 14 when her parents told her that she would be married to Robert Davidson. As was proper in this matrilineal society, Robert's kin made the proposal to Florence's parents. Her father deferred to his wife's brother (Florence's mother's brother), who was a senior member of Florence's matriclan. These are Florence's recollections about how she came to be married to her husband.

I was still going to school yet when several people came into my dad's house to propose for my husband-to-be. I was wondering what was going on when all these people came in. The women all belonged to C'al'lanas, my husband's tribe [lineage], and the men all belonged to my husband's dad's tribe, Stl'ang'lanas, except for my husband's brother. They were all streaming in and I didn't know what was going on....

"Don't say anything when I tell you something," my mother said to me. "Those who came in last week proposed to you." I didn't know what to say. Propose! Why? I thought. I was just a kid yet. I didn't know what to say and mother advised me not to say anything about the proposal because they were high-class [y'a Yet] people....

"They want you to marry Robert Davidson." "Did you say yes?" I asked her. "No, your dad sent them to your uncle [Florence's mother's brother]. Your dad says he's got nothing to do with it; it has to go through your uncle. You have more respect for your uncle than for us," she told me. "That's the only brother I have." "You're going to make me marry," I said. "Yes, you're going to marry him." "I'm not going to marry him," I said. "Don't say that, Florence, he's a real prince [y'a Yet]."

It bothered me so much....Every day I bothered my mother. "I'm not going to marry that old man. I'm not. If you make me marry him, summertime I'll run away. You won't see me again." My mother didn't say anything....My dad didn't say a word to me about it. Finally, my mother said, "Don't say anything dear. Your uncle thinks it's best for you to marry him. He's a prince. He's going to respect you all your life and if you don't want to marry him you're going to feel bad all your life. He belongs to clever people; you're not going to be hard up for anything. We need a young man's help, too. You must remember that. We belong to chiefs too and you're not supposed to talk any old way. You have to respect yourself more than what you worry about."...I made up my mind not to say anything much as I disliked it.

From Margaret Blackman, *During My Time: Florence Edenshaw Davidson, a Haida Woman*, pp. 95–96. © 1982. Reprinted by permission of the University of Washington Press.

And these are the recollections of James Sewid, a Kwakwaka'wakw man from Alert Bay, British Columbia. He, too, was married when he was nearly 14 to a girl he knew only by sight.

And that's when the big day came....I had been out late that night to a dance with my friends and when I came in I lay down on the couch. That was when I heard Jim and Mary Bell talking about me to Ed and Rachel Whanock and my mother and stepfather. One of them was saying, "You might as well go and see her parents because I think he should get married because we don't want him running around like this."...I lay there and pretended that I was sleeping and pretty soon my grandparents walked out. So as soon as they had gone I got up and said to my stepfather, "Let's go take a walk. It's pretty warm in here."...When we got outside...I asked him, "What was going on in there? I heard the people talking about me." "Well," he said, "you're going to get married." "Well," I said, "I can't get married! I'm too young!" "Oh that's all right," he said. "We'll look after you. I think it is the best way for you, to get married now, because if you're not going to get married now you might go haywire." "Well," I said, "who is this girl anyway?" And just then we happened to be passing by the house where Moses Alfred lived, and David said, "It is the girl that lives here." I didn't know what to say. I used to see her around the village but I didn't know her.

Well, it was the Indian custom for someone to go to the parents of the girl and ask their consent. That is where my grandparents had gone that night when they walked out of the house. So I just waited for the answer that this girl's parents would give to the old people who went to talk with them. I was careful after that not to listen anymore because I didn't like to butt in on what was going on. A few days after that I was alone with my mother....I said to her, "I hear that I'm going to get married. You know that I'm too young to get married." "Oh, no!" she said. "Don't talk like that. We want you to get married. You are going to marry Flora Alfred. It has already been arranged with her parents and it's all right. Now you have to go and see the minister so it can be announced in the church and published in the band." "Well," I said, "I don't think I should get married. It isn't that I don't want to get married, but what am I going to do if I have children?" "Well," my mother said, "we'll look after you some."

IN THEIR OWN VOICES CONTINUED

After that I went to see my old grandmother, Lucy. She had already heard about it. I went in and sat down and said, "Well, they say I'm going to get married." "Yes," she said, "I heard about that and I think it's a wonderful thing. I would really like to see it. I want to see you get married and have children before I die...." Well, that is what made me kind of give in. I didn't want to get married but of course...I had no business to try and argue or anything like that because I knew that the older people knew what was right for me; that's what I figured. I never did like to argue with anybody that was older than me but I always liked to respect what they said to me.

From James Spradley, *Guests Never Leave Hungry: The Autobiography of James Sewid, a Kwakiutl Indian*, pp. 66–67. © 1972. Reprinted by permission of Yale University Press.

Although both Florence and James voiced reservations about their arranged marriages, especially concerning their young age and fears about taking on adult responsibilities, they gave up in the interests of their families. As it turned out, they both had long and loving relationships with their spouses.

CRITICAL THINKING QUESTION

Would you be willing to have your family arrange your marriage? Why, or why not?

arranged marriages
Marriages that are arranged by the parents or other relatives of the bride and groom.

courtship
Period prior to marriage when a couple tests attraction to and compatibility with each other.

Arranged marriages symbolically emphasize the fact that such unions are not simply relationships between a woman and a man but are more fundamentally alliances between families. Each side measures their own worthiness in relation to the social standing and resources of the other side. Their willingness to promote a marital union is an indication of their trust in their future affines.

Weddings are rites of passage in which the participants change their status from single to married. In societies without arranged marriages, preparation for marriage usually involves some form of **courtship,** in which a couple tests their attraction and compatibility as well as the acceptability of their union to others who are important in their lives. Mate selection is the common goal of courtship, and weddings mark the passage from courtship to marriage. The bases on which people choose their mates may include personal compatibility, desired personality traits, likelihood of reliability and economic contributions, and physical attraction. In most societies, the Western concept of romantic love is not a prerequisite for courtship or marriage, although these feelings may develop when people begin to live together, adjusting to one another and sharing their lives.

In foraging and horticultural societies, a wedding ceremony is usually a simple affair. Among the Mohawk, a young man's family traditionally proposed a marriage to the family of the intended bride, or a couple announced their plans to marry. Before the wedding, the couple separately presented gifts to their future mothers-in-law. The future husband gave his bride's mother a gift of deer meat, and the future bride gave her husband's mother a gift of cornbread. These presents were symbolic of the economic roles of men as hunters and women as farmers, thus representing the interdependence of spouses and households.

A Mohawk wedding involved a feast sponsored by the bride's family for relatives, clan members, and villagers. The father of the bride made a formal announcement of the couple's marriage and bestowed the family's approval. Then followed speeches from a number of respected elder guests who exhorted the couple to behave properly, responsibly, and kindly to each other.

In contrast, in societies where the accumulation of wealth is valued, typically in agrarian or industrial societies, weddings may be elaborate affairs, attended by hundreds of people. These rituals include displays of family wealth and transfers of gifts and property to the couple and/or to their relatives.

This couple married through mutual consent after declaring their love for one another, and their families were the last to know about their plans.
(The Image Works/Bob Daemmrich/ The Image Works)

REVIEW

Weddings are rites of passage that publicly confirm the changes in marital and kinship status of the participants. Societies that place high value on kinship and community relations often have arranged marriages. In others, individuals choose their own marriage partners. Weddings also extend the alliance and economic transaction functions of marriage.

◇ PATTERNS OF RESIDENCE AFTER MARRIAGE

The elaborate Nepalese wedding process described in the Case Study is partly a result of postmarital residence patterns that call for a bride to separate herself from her relatives. In all societies, newly married couples follow norms dictating where they should live. They may live with or near the husband's or the wife's family; they may alternate their residences between families; or they may establish a place of their own apart from any of their relatives. Their choice may depend on factors such as the amount of resources available or the composition of existing households. Societies vary in the patterns of postmarital residence that they encourage. Particular postmarital **residence rules** are often associated with different descent systems and specific economic strategies.

residence rules
Rules that stipulate where a couple will reside after their marriage.

Matrilocal and Patrilocal Residence

Arrangements in which a married couple lives with or near the wife's family are termed **matrilocal residence.** Usually (but not always), matrilocal residence is associated with matrilineal descent. That is, societies that reckon descent matrilineally usually prefer that couples live with the wife's family. Because children resulting from marriage belong to the lineage of the mother, matrilocal residence ensures that kin group members remain together. Matrilocal households typically consist of an elder couple, their daughters, their daughters' husbands and children, and their unmarried sons. Married sons live with their wives' kin. This kind of residence pattern is also called **uxorilocal**—living with the wife's family.

matrilocal residence
Pattern for residence after marriage in which the couple lives with or near the wife's family.

uxorilocal
Living with or near the wife's parents.

   Patrilocal residence refers to arrangements in which a married couple lives with or near the husband's family. Patrilocal residence usually occurs in societies that reckon descent patrilineally. Because children resulting from marriage belong to the father's lineage, patrilocal residence creates stable, interacting groups of patrilineally related kin. Patrilocal households, therefore, consist of an elder couple, their sons, their sons' wives and children, and their unmarried daughters. Married daughters live with their husbands' relatives. This kind of residence pattern is also called **virilocal**—living with the husband's family.

patrilocal residence
Pattern of residence after marriage in which the couple lives with or near the husband's relatives.

virilocal
Living with or near the husband's parents.

Avunculocal Residence

In some societies with matrilineal descent and inheritance, an arrangement called **avunculocal residence** is preferred (from the Latin word *avunculus* meaning "mother's brother" and origin of the English word *uncle*). In these cases, a married couple lives with the husband's mother's brother. Avunculocal residence is found in societies where inheritance follows matrilineal descent but in which men hold wealth, property, and social status. According to rules of matrilineal descent, a man's wealth and status cannot be passed to his own son because his son is a member of his wife's kinship group, not his own. Wealth, therefore, passes from a man to his sister's son. From the inheritor's point of view, a man gains wealth and status from his mother's brother. Avunculocal residence establishes a residential and emotional bond between a man and the person from whom he will inherit.

avunculocal residence
Patterns of residence after marriage in which the couple lives with or near the husband's mother's brother.

Bilocal and Neolocal Residence

In **bilocal residence,** married couples live alternately with the husband's and the wife's families. Bilocality has the advantage of flexibility, adapting residence to economic and resource conditions. When resources are scarce, couples can make adjustments by relocating from one household to another. Bilocal patterns are also adaptive in realigning living arrangements depending on the composition of households. That is, if households grow too large by the addition of in-marrying spouses and their children, then some people can leave and align themselves with their spouse's kin.

bilocal residence
Patterns of residence after marriage in which the couple alternates between living with the wife's kin and the husband's kin.

   In societies with **neolocal residence,** a married couple establishes a new household independently of the residence of either the husband's or the wife's kin. Such systems typically are found in industrial and postindustrial societies, where couples tend to form new households immediately after marriage or within a year or two. Neolocal residence has the feature of independence, another reflection of the loosening of kinship bonds advantageous in capitalist economies. Neolocal residence separates people from larger kinship groups, allowing them to ignore claims from relatives who might want to share their resources.

neolocal residence
Pattern of residence after marriage in which the couple establishes a new, independent household separate from their relatives.

Correlates of Residence Patterns

What residence rule is observed in your culture? Are there different historical patterns in residence that relate to people's cultures of origin?

Among foragers, postmarital residence tends to be fairly diverse. Although couples generally live with relatives, the choice of the wife's or husband's family depends on the composition of the households, the availability of resources, and personal preferences. According to Kathleen Gough (1975), approximately 60 percent of foraging societies tended to live patrilocally, whereas 16 percent to 17 percent preferred matrilocal residence. An additional 15 percent to 17 percent were bilocal, choosing location with the family of either spouse. In farming societies with unilineal descent systems, postmarital residence tends to be consistent with principles of descent. Societies with matrilineal descent usually prefer matrilocal residence, whereas those with patrilineal descent prefer patrilocal residence. In societies whose economies are based on intensive agriculture, descent is nearly always patrilineal, and residence is nearly always patrilocal. The patterns are consistent with men's primary responsibility for farming and their control over the allocation and use of land.

internal warfare
Warfare between closely situated villages or communities.

external warfare
Warfare that takes place at some distance from home communities, requiring warriors' absence from their homes for extended periods of time.

Residence patterns have been observed to correlate with other cultural patterns. For example, in a classic study, anthropologists found that in societies with frequent **internal warfare,** household groups are likely to be organized patrilocally (Ember and Ember 1971). Internal warfare is characterized by frequent raiding among neighboring or nearby settlements. Because men act as warriors who defend their households and communities against the threat of attack by others, living near male relatives they trust is advantageous for them. In contrast, **external warfare,** fought against people from other societies, does not favor a particular residence rule, though external warfare that takes warriors away from home for extended periods may shift economic burdens to women in a way that favors matrilocal residence.

The Iroquois of North America and the Yanomamo of South America provide contrasting examples of the connection between types of warfare and postmarital residence patterns. Iroquois society was based on matrilineal descent, with people organized into matriclans. Iroquois economy centered on horticulture, an occupation for women, supplemented by hunting and fishing, performed by men. By the seventeenth and eighteenth centuries, men were involved in frequent and prolonged external warfare with Europeans and with other native peoples, spending many months away from home. Matrilocal residence, the traditional preferred pattern, was strengthened by men's absence from home communities. In contrast, the Yanomamo reckon descent patrilineally. They are horticulturalists whose subsistence is provided almost entirely by men. Yanomamo men engage in frequent internal warfare, raiding neighboring villages and defending their own homes against attacks by others. Consistent with the Embers's predictions, postmarital residence is strongly patrilocal.

Like the Yanomamo of the Amazon, the Dani of the New Guinea highlands were patrilineal horticulturalists who engaged in frequent internal warfare.
(Anthro-Photo File/Adrian Arbib/Anthro-Photo File)

REVIEW

Residence rules tend to ensure that people belonging to the same kin group remain close to one another. Matrilocal patterns, in which the couple lives with or near the wife's parents, are common in matrilineal societies. Patrilocal patterns, in which the couple lives with or near the husband's parents, is common in patrilineal societies. In avunculocal residence, the couple moves in with the husband's mother's brother. Bilocal residency allows the couple to live with either the husband's or wife's family, depending on the resources available. Neolocal residency allows the couple to establish their own independent household.

CASE STUDY

RESIDENCE IN RURAL NORTH INDIA AND WESTERN BORNEO

RURAL NORTH INDIA

Households consist of large extended or joint families. Village economies center on farming, although villagers may have other occupations. Descent follows patrilineal principles; that is, people belong to the kinship group of their father. Parents arrange marriages. Men typically marry in their early twenties to women in their teens. Girls may be betrothed as young children. Postmarital residence is generally patrilocal. Residential groups, therefore, consist of a couple, their sons and sons' families, and their unmarried daughters. Women move to their husbands' homes upon marriage and have infrequent contact with their own kin. Because girls usually marry shortly after puberty, a wife's subordination is based on age as well as gender. She is thus easily dominated by her husband and especially by his mother. As many researchers have noted, Indian wives often experience their greatest difficulties from their mothers-in-law rather than their husbands (Chitnis 1988).

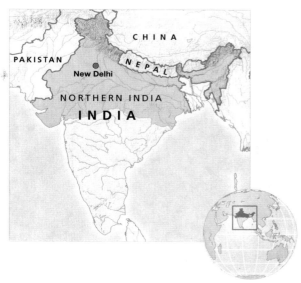

The domination by mothers-in-law is due, in part, to the uncertain quality of relationships between spouses. Rarely are newlywed couples acquainted before marriage, and unions are arranged without consent from either the bride or the groom. Once married, couples have little interaction. The husband is himself young and lives under his father's authority. As a subordinate in his father's household, he takes care not to shift away from his first allegiance to his parents. Because wives are perceived as potentially destabilizing to established familial order, married sons refrain from showing too much affection or even concern for them, especially early in their married life. Couples rarely interact publicly or have extended conversation when other family members are present. A wife thus spends most of her time with other women in the household. These women, unmarried daughters and in-marrying wives, are all under the supervision of the elder woman. A new daughter-in-law is typically met with some hostility by her husband's mother and sisters. As a result, authoritative statuses are immediately established and reinforced.

WESTERN BORNEO

Iban of Western Borneo

The Iban are rice farmers living along rivers in Western Borneo, especially in the province of Sarawak, Malaysia. Their social system centers on an autonomous unit called a "bilek" or family whose members are related through bilateral ties. The bilek controls land collectively and owns ritual property. Members of the family work cooperatively in economic tasks, especially but not limited to farming the rice fields that supply their basic subsistence. The bilek also owns and occupies a section of the longhouse dwelling that typifies Iban society. An Iban settlement contains one longhouse that is structurally divided into several apartment-like units. Most longhouses contain between ten and twenty bilek units (Freeman 1970, 184).

A bilek itself consists of three generations: an elder couple, one of their married sons or daughters, his or her spouse and children, and the elder couple's unmarried children. Siblings have equal rights as to who will remain with their parents. The Iban show no preference based on gender or seniority. Decisions about where a new couple resides are made on the basis of personal choice and negotiation about access to resources. The son or daughter who remains has full rights to bilek land and other property, whereas sons or daughters who leave to reside with the families of their spouses give up their ancestral rights and instead gain access to the land and property of their spouse's family. That is, residence, not genealogy alone, confers social, economic, and ritual rights.

When more than one sibling and spouse claim the natal bilek unit, one of the siblings will eventually leave and set up his own bilek unit (with spouse and children), beginning the process of descent and affiliation anew. Looked at as a structure over time, the bilek family persists, but its members change as generations succeed generations and as siblings unite and then separate to form their own families.

The separate families that together occupy a longhouse form a community distinct from similar communities. Longhouses are dispersed at irregular intervals along river banks (Freeman 1970, 184).

██████████ **CASE STUDY** CONTINUED ────────────────────

They are the residential bases of a community. The residents have ritual responsibilities toward one another and ensure their collective well-being through the proper performance of rituals. Each longhouse has a headman who can help resolve disputes and advise residents on appropriate behavior in keeping with customs and beliefs. When a headman dies or retires, any male resident of the longhouse can succeed him. The choice is made by community consensus.

A few closely related families form the core of the longhouse. The other resident families can claim ties to one of the core groups through either blood or marriage. Indeed, although marriages between siblings are banned, marriage between first or second cousins is preferred because it "...constantly reinforces the network of cognatic ties linking individual Iban, and kin" (Freeman 1970, 190). However, people are free to choose their own spouse. Relationships between husband and wife are based on mutual respect and equality. Although women's and men's economic and ritual roles are distinct, they treat each other and are viewed by others as equals.

Finally, the core group of families in each longhouse generally remains stable until the death of an elder couple leads to fragmentation. However, other families may move to another longhouse in cases of serious conflict. Because people have consanguineous or affinal ties to many other communities, relocation is usually easy.

Today, the Iban (also known as "Dayak") are an indigenous minority within Malaysia, dominated by ethnic Malays who differ in their language, religion, and cultural practices. Many Iban have been educated in British and American schools. They have used their education to advance the rights of their people. Nearly half of the 1.4 million inhabitants of Sarawak are Iban. Another quarter are Moslem Malays, and most of the remainder are ethnic Chinese (Crossette 1987). According to Iban anthropologist James Masing, the Iban are attempting to strengthen their own communities and identities: "Our priority now is to organize the Dayak community and make them a strong political force" (Crossette 1987).

── ■

◇ WIDOWHOOD AND DIVORCE

All societies have strategies intended to preserve kin ties, marriage bonds, and household units. All cultures have patterns of beliefs and behaviors for dealing with widows and orphans, for example, and for regulating divorce and remarriage. These cultural patterns reveal the underlying principles of kinship, marriage, and family that are most important in a society. For example, the importance of family alliances is highlighted by marriage preference patterns that anthropologists refer to as "levirate" and "sororate."

The Levirate and Sororate

levirate
Marriage preference rule in which a widow marries her deceased husband's brother.

In the levirate and sororate marriage patterns, if a spouse dies, the deceased's family of origin supplies a younger sibling to marry the surviving spouse. So, for example, in the **levirate,** if a husband dies, his (usually younger) brother will marry the surviving widow. In the **sororate,** a younger sister of a deceased wife will marry the surviving widower. These kinds of marriages symbolically stress family alliances because they say in effect that once two families are joined through marriage, maintaining the established alliance is in the families' interests. Because the death of a husband or wife potentially disrupts the bond between families, a sibling of the deceased spouse perpetuates the alliance by marrying the survivor. The "ghost marriage" of the Nuer is a type of levirate because a younger brother marries the widow of his elder brother. It differs from the more common pattern only in that children of the subsequent union are considered the offspring of the dead brother.

sororate
Marriage between a widower and his deceased wife's sister.

Divorce

Societies vary in their views about the dissolution of marriages. In some societies, divorce is a common outcome of an unhappy union, whereas in others, it rarely occurs because of social or religious restrictions. In some societies, either husband or wife may seek divorce; in others, only one of the parties (usually the husband) may initiate a breakup of the marriage. The ways in which marriages are dissolved also vary across cultures.

In general, matrilineal societies have more lenient attitudes toward divorce than do patrilineal societies because of the differences in principles of descent and the resulting claims that kinship groups have over children. Nearly universally (although there are exceptions), young children continue to live with their mothers after a divorce. Because children belong to the kin group of their mother in matrilineal societies, divorce does not cause a contradiction between location and kinship. In contrast, the dissolution of a marriage in patrilineal societies causes a problem because patrilineal descent groups are able to make claims over children produced by the wives of their male members through marriage. In addition, patrilineal societies generally exert more control over women's sexual behavior than do matrilineal societies because they need to establish paternity to ensure a child's legitimate place in the father's kinship group.

Foraging and horticultural societies often have flexible attitudes toward divorce, regardless of the type of descent system in their culture. In native North America, for example, with few exceptions, either husband or wife could initiate a breakup of their marriage. Divorce was fairly common, especially in the early years of a marriage and especially if the couple had no children. Acceptable grounds for divorce included adultery, failure to provide or fulfill domestic obligations, or simply personal incompatibility. Few societies had formal procedures for divorce. Rather, the couple would separate, each returning to his or her natal family, or the in-marrying spouse would leave. A divorce could be the result of a joint decision by husband and wife, or one or the other could initiate it.

In some Native American societies, there were publicly recognized ways to signal one's wishes for divorce. For example, among both the Mohawk and the Diné, two matrilineal, matrilocal societies, if a woman wanted a divorce, she might remove her husband's personal belongings from the house when he was away and place them outside. When the husband returned, he would collect his belongings and go back to the home of his mother or sister. If the husband initiated the divorce, he would simply take his possessions and leave. No social stigma was attached to either husband or wife after a divorce.

In Saudi culture, children belong to the father, his patrilineage, and his patriclan.
(The Image Works/Peter Sanders/HAGA/ The Image Works)

Among the Lakota and some other peoples of the Great Plains, both parties could jointly agree upon a divorce. However, a man had a public way of signaling his wishes to end their marriage that was not available to a woman. He would beat a drum at a warrior society dance and proclaim that he wished to "throw away [his] wife" (Hassrick 1964, 130). Through this strategy, a man not only ended his marriage but publicly humiliated his wife as well. Although men did not suffer social criticism if their marriages ended, divorced women were shamed.

There are economic deterrents to divorce. For example, exchanges of bridewealth tend to lessen rates of divorce. The husband's kinship group does not favor divorce because a couple's children, although belonging to the husband's kin group in patrilineal societies, usually stay with their mother and therefore leave the husband's household if divorce occurs. A wife's family may also be reluctant to sanction a divorce because when couples break up, the wife's kin must return the goods that they received as bridewealth. Therefore, they may pressure an unhappy wife to remain with her husband. Conflicts over bridewealth and its return in cases of divorce may not only result in the end of family alliances but lead to interfamilial tension and conflict.

In extreme patriarchal societies, such as in some villages in India, in prerevolutionary China, and in many Middle Eastern nations, women rarely have the right to divorce, whereas men are free to break up their marriages, usually on grounds of their wives' disobedience, laziness, or adultery. In some societies, a woman's failure to produce sons might also be a cause for divorce. In such cases, great social criticism is heaped on a divorced woman and on her family as well, although little if any criticism is leveled at the husband.

In some cultures, religious beliefs are used to strongly condemn and even outlaw divorce. Today, Roman Catholicism, Islam, and Orthodox Judaism place barriers to the breakup of marriages. In these belief systems, people have no right to dissolve a union because a marriage was sanctified in the wedding ceremony. In strict Islamic and Orthodox Jewish communities, it is very difficult for women to initiate divorce, but men may seek divorce in religious councils if they cite acceptable grounds.

REVIEW

The levirate and the sororate marriage patterns maintain alliances between families after the death of a spouse. Marriage is not only a relationship but also an economic obligation to the other party. Patrilineal societies generally have more strict rules concerning divorce than do matrilineal societies.

CASE STUDY

MARRIAGE AND DIVORCE AMONG THE KPELLE OF LIBERIA

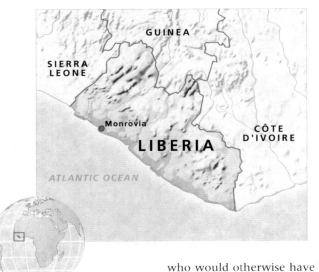

Marriage patterns among the Kpelle, a farming society, provide several options of payment and service that lead to differences in the strength of bonds between couples and the rights that a man exercises over his children (Gibbs 1965). The idea and standard form of marriage involves transfer of bridewealth from a husband's kin group to that of his wife. It permits a husband and his lineage to claim children produced by the marriage. A second form involves performance of brideservice rather than payment of bridewealth. In this type of marriage, a couple resides with the wife's family for a fixed time agreed upon by the parties concerned. During this period, the husband performs labor for his in-laws. Children born to the couple during the years of service belong to the wife's lineage rather than to the husband's. Once the period of brideservice is completed, the children become members of the father's patrilineage.

A third marital option is "male concubinage." In this option, the status of the couple is ambiguous. It involves an economic and sexual union between a poor man and one of the wives of a chief or wealthy man. Although the woman remains the legal wife of the patron, her relationship with the client is publicly recognized and sanctioned. Such a marriage enables a poor man who would otherwise have few marital prospects to marry and ally himself with the wealthy person. A wealthy man who is either already a chief or wishes to become one can gain the political support of a dependent client. Because the client and the patron's wife farm land the patron controls, the latter obtains products of their labor that he can sell for cash or distribute to others and thereby gain their support as well. Finally, because the woman remains the legal wife of the patron, children born to the client couple belong to the patron's lineage rather than to that of their biological father.

Kpelle marriages, then, are basically differentiated in terms of the legal status of women and the rights that husbands and their lineages may claim over a woman's children. If a woman is a full legal wife, that is, in a standard marriage with payment of bridewealth, her children belong to her husband's patrilineage. If a woman's legal status is in transition, as during the period of brideservice, her children belong to her patrilineage and her husband cannot claim them. And if the woman is the legal wife of a patron even though she lives with another man, her children belong to the patron.

Although marriage is the usual and preferred state for adults, rates of divorce are "moderately high" (Gibbs 1965). Divorces are granted by formal courts under the jurisdiction of local chiefs. Proceedings involve public hearings to determine the party at fault. Women usually initiate divorce, in part because the initiator usually ascribes blame, and men are reluctant to be publicly criticized for ending their marriages. Even though women are characteristically blamed for failed marriages, their request for divorce is usually granted. A man who wishes a divorce may mistreat his wife, so that she will seek a formal divorce in court. In this manipulative manner, he obtains his objective but is not publicly faulted.

Kpelle divorce benefits both wife and husband in an unhappy marriage. A wife who seeks to divorce is given her freedom and thus is personally satisfied. A husband, whether or not he wants to be divorced, receives the return of bridewealth that he had given to his wife's kin when he married, and retains rights as father to his children, including the privilege of receiving bridewealth for his daughters when they marry.

This description of Kpelle practices remains accurate for those in relatively isolated villages. However, in areas where economic transformations have affected subsistence patterns, marriage and divorce have also changed. In traditional villages, household farming, especially of rice, is the basis of subsistence. In villages close to main roads or larger towns, some people also produce cash crops, whereas others work in towns and cities. Both cash crops and wage work provide money to purchase food and other goods previously produced in the household. These changes have affected bridewealth payments. Previously, a prospective husband and his family often needed to spend years accumulating the goods or funds needed for bridewealth. If they did not have the funds themselves, they needed to borrow from others, thus becoming clients financially and socially of people more prosperous than themselves. Men are now often able to amass bridewealth while they are relatively young and are therefore less dependent on other members of their families, including their parents. This has loosened family ties.

Women can also benefit from changed circumstances. Young women can postpone marriage and maintain their independence by selling crops they have grown or other goods in markets in towns, or through wage work, even though women have fewer jobs available than do men. Older women who are divorced or widowed can decide not to remarry if they have independent sources of income. Studies conducted in the 1970s document the beginnings of trends still operative today; for example, women residing in "modern towns" are more likely to "marry later, divorce more often, and remarry less frequently" than women living in traditional villages (Bledsoe 1976, 380).

Conversations with Kpelle living in small villages or larger towns revealed complicated attitudes toward marriage and divorce. Although young men and women favored the severing of responsibilities toward their elders, exemplified for men by amassing their own bridewealth payments and for women by postponing marriage, older men and women regretted the breakdown of family obligations that had kept younger people dependent on them. In Bledsoe's view, ". . . the distinction between the old and the young is probably more important in understanding individuals' goals and strategies in African societies, than the distinction between men and women" (1976, 387). Men and women have, however, used different strategies to reach their goals.

ANTHROPOLOGY APPLIED

ANTHROPOLOGISTS AS EXPERT WITNESSES

Testifying in court is not associated with cultural anthropology. However, cultural anthropologists are often called to testify in cases involving possible cultural misunderstandings on issues ranging from landownership to family law and child custody. They also testify as expert witnesses in cases about tribal rights, criminal investigation, and forensic science.

In her article "Infighting in San Francisco: Anthropology in Family Court, Or: A Study in Cultural Misunderstanding," anthropologist Barbara Jones (1998) outlines a custody dispute in which she was an expert witness. The dispute was between a mother seeking custody and the father, with whom the child was living. The mother had remarried a fourth time, was pregnant, and planned to leave the country. The father was single but closely tied to an extended family network. A psychologist, hired by the court and assumed to be unbiased, examined both households and concluded that the mother should have sole custody of the child. Jones believed that the psychologist did not understand the benefits that the father and his extended family could offer the child.

She told the court that the child had been interacting almost daily with loving grandparents, cousins, aunts, and uncles. The father had also hired a full-time nanny to care for his daughter while he worked. Contrary to the psychologist, Jones concluded that the father's extended family provided greater benefits to the child than the mother's situation would allow.

(Corbis/Tony Savino/Sygma/Corbis)

(Corbis/Reuters/Corbis)

CRITICAL THINKING QUESTION
What perspectives do anthropologists have that might make them valuable contributors to legal cases?

◇ MODULE SUMMARY

Defining Marriage and Family

- Families serve economic and social functions. Members of families usually reside together and provide for biological reproduction and the training and enculturation of children. Families provide people with companionship, emotional support, and assistance, and are the basic unit of economic cooperation and interdependence. Families, particularly households, work together to complete the daily tasks necessary for survival. They are also decision-making groups. In many societies, families perform religious functions and rituals that celebrate significant events in members' lives.

- Marriage is the most common way in which families are formed. Marriage is a socially recognized, enduring, stable bond between people who each have certain rights and obligations with respect to one another. Husbands and wives can expect to have an exclusive sexual relationship and assist one another in raising children and in provisioning their household. Through the marriage bond, men are able to claim "social fatherhood" by establishing themselves as the husband of the mother.

Families and Ideal Types

- Although the family is a universal cultural construct, the types of families found in different kinds of societies vary. Nuclear families consist of parents and their children, whereas extended families usually contain at least three generations. Nuclear families are often found in industrial societies, which stress economic independence, and in many foraging societies, because they are adaptive to survival when resources are scarce.

- Extended families are more common in farming and pastoral societies. They have the advantage of perpetuating the social unit, sharing resources and work, and providing emotional support and material aid.

- Family types are responsive to changes in productive modes and general social values. In many countries, the idealized model of husband, wife, and children has declined, as has the number of children per household.

Endogamy, Exogamy, and the Incest Taboo

- The incest taboo universally forbids marriage between parents and their children and between siblings. In some societies, it also forbids marriage between other relatives.

- Theories about the origin of the incest taboo include an instinctual revulsion and aversion toward sexual relations within the nuclear family, the biological consequences of inbreeding, a reduction in the fitness of a population through genetic homogeneity, a response to the need to diminish sexual competition within the nuclear family unit, and a means of forcing people to make alliances with others.

Forms of Marriage

- Different societies allow people to have different numbers of spouses at any one time. Marriage between one man and one woman is called monogamy; marriage between more than two people is called polygamy. Polygyny is the marriage between one man and two or more women. Polyandry is the marriage between one woman and two or more men.

Marriage as Alliance and Economic Exchange

- Marriage often involves an economic exchange. Bridewealth is a gift a husband or his family gives to the family of his intended wife. Similarly, groom-wealth is given by a wife or her family to the family of her intended husband. Brideservice or groom-service requires the husband or wife to perform some services for the parents of his or her spouse. Dowry is the economic goods or wealth the bride's family gives to the new couple or to the husband's kin.

Marriage as a Rite of Passage

- Marriages may be arranged by parents or by the couple themselves through courtship. The marriage ceremony publicly sanctions marriage and symbolizes the rights and duties of couples to each other and to their families.

Patterns of Residence after Marriage

- In some societies, a married couple resides with or near the husband's relatives (patrilocal residence). In others, they reside with or near the wife's kin (matrilocal residence). In bilocal residence, married couples live alternately with the husband's and the wife's families. In societies with matrilineal descent and inheritance, a couple may live with the husband's mother's brother (avunculocal residence). In neolocal residence, couples establish a new household, separate from either group of kin.

Widowhood and Divorce

- Marriage preference patterns, called levirate and sororate, emphasize marriage as an alliance between families. In the levirate, a deceased husband's brother (usually younger) marries the surviving widow; in the sororate, a younger sister of the deceased wife marries the surviving widower.

◇ REVIEW QUESTIONS

1. What definition of marriage would cover all the marriage types discussed in this module?

2. How is subsistence related to family forms? How can changes in marriage and family reflect adaptations to changes in subsistence?

3. How do endogamy and exogamy affect a society's social organization?

4. What are some hypotheses about the origins of the incest taboo?

5. What are the benefits of polygamous marriages? What are the drawbacks?

6. What are common forms of political and economic exchange in marriage, and what types of kinships are associated with those forms?

7. How are postmarital residence patterns related to kinship? How are residence rules related to women's and men's status in a society?

8. What are some reasons that marriages are arranged? Why is divorce discouraged in arranged marriages?

9. How are levirate and sororate different? Why do societies have these practices?

◇ REFERENCES

Blackman, Margaret. 1982. *During My Time: Florence Edenshaw Davidson, a Haida Woman*. Seattle: University of Washington Press.

Bledsoe, Caroline. 1976. "Women's Marital Strategies among the Kpelle of Liberia." *Journal of Anthropological Research* 32:372–89.

Boas, Franz. 1897. *The Social Organization and the Secret Societies of the Kwakiutl Indians*. Report of the U.S. National Museum of 1895. Washington, DC, pp. 311–738.

Boas, Franz. 1966. *Kwakiutl Ethnography*, ed. H. Codere. Chicago: University of Chicago Press.

Bonvillain, Nancy. 2001. *Native Nations: Cultures and Histories of Native North America*. Upper Saddle River, NJ: Prentice Hall.

Brooke, James. 2003. "Dowry Too High, Lose Bride and Go to Jail." *New York Times*, February 3.

Chitnis, Suma. 1988. "Feminism: Indian Ethos and Indian Convictions." In *Women in Indian Society*, ed. R. Ghadially, 81–95. Newbury Park, CA: Sage.

Crossette, Barbara. 1987. "New Generation Finds Strength in Borneo's Past." *New York Times*, October 18.

Dorson, Richard. 1975. *Folktales Told around the World*. Chicago: University of Chicago Press.

Ember, Melvin, and Carol Ember. 1971. "The Conditions Favoring Matrilocal vs. Patrilocal Residence." *American Anthropologist* 73:571–94.

Evans-Pritchard, E. E. 1955. *Kinship and Marriage Among the Nuer*. Oxford: Clarendon.

Fox, Robin. 1984. *Kinship and Marriage: An Anthropological Perspective*. New York: Cambridge University Press.

Freeman, Derek. 1970. "The Iban of Western Borneo." In *Cultures of the Pacific*, ed. Thomas Harding and Ben Wallace, 180–200. New York: The Free Press.

Ghadially, Rehana, and Pramod Kumar. 1988. "Bride Burning: The Psycho-Social Dynamics of Dowry Deaths." In *Women in Indian Society*, ed. R. Ghadially, 167–77. Newbury Park, CA: Sage.

Gibbs, James. 1965. "The Kpelle of Liberia." In *Peoples of Africa*, ed. J. Gibbs. New York: Holt, Reinhart & Winston, 197–240.

Gough, Kathleen. 1961. "Nayar: Central Kerala." In *Matrilineal Kinship*, ed. David Schneider and Kathleen Gough, 298–384. Berkeley: University of California Press.

Gough, Kathleen. 1975. "The Origin of the Family." In *Toward an Anthropology of Women*, ed. R. Reiter, 51–76. New York: Monthly Review Press.

Government of India. 2006. Crime in India, Chapter Three: Violent Crimes. www.mppolice.gov.in/ mpphq/crimeinindia/ table-htm.

Hardman, Charlotte. 2000. "Rites of Passage among the Lohorung Rai of East Nepal." In *Indigenous Religions*, ed. G. Harvey, 204–18. London: Cassell.

Hart, C. W. M., and Arnold Pilling. 1960. *The Tiwi of Northern Australia*. New York: Holt, Rinehart & Winston.

Hassrick, Royal. 1964. *The Sioux, Life and Customs of a Warrior Society*. Norman: University of Oklahoma Press.

Hua, Cai. 2001. *A Society without Fathers or Husbands: The Na of China*. Cambridge, MA: Zone Books/MIT Press.

Huber, Brad, William Danaher and William Breedlove. 2011. "New Cross-Cultural Perspectives on Marriage Transactions." Cross-Cultural Research, online version May 16, 2011 (http://ccr.sagepub.com/ content/early/2011/05/12/1069397111402466)

Hutchinson, Sharon. 1996. *Nuer Dilemmas: Coping with Money, War, and the State*. Berkeley: University of California Press.

Jones, Barbara. 1998. "Infighting in San Francisco: Anthropology in Family Court, Or: A Study in Cultural Misunderstanding." *High Plains Applied Anthropologist 18*(1):37–41.

Kumar, Radha. 1995. "From Chipko to Sati: The Contemporary Indian Women's Movement." In *The Challenge of Local Feminisms: Women's Movement in Global Perspective*, ed. A. Basu. Boulder, CO: Westview.

Levine, Nancy E. 1988. *The Dynamics of Polyandry. Kinship, Domesticity, and Population on the Tibetan Border*. Chicago: University of Chicago Press.

Luo, Michael. 2010. "'Doubling Up' in Recession-Strained Quarters." *New York Times*, December 28, A1.

Mencher, Joan. 1965. "The Nayars of South Malabar." In *Comparative Family Systems*, ed. M. E. Nimkoff, 162–91. Boston: Houghton Mifflin.

Polgreen, Lydia. 2010. "One Bride for 2 Brothers: A Custom Fades in India." *New York Times*, July 17, A4.

Spradley, James. 1972. *Guests Never Leave Hungry: The Autobiography of James Sewid, a Kwakiutl Indian*. Montreal: McGill Queens University Press.

Stone, Linda. 2006. *Kinship and Gender*, 3rd ed. Boulder Colorado: Westview Press.

Thornton, Arland, and Linda Young-DeMarco. 2001. "Four Decades of Trends in Attitudes Toward Family Issues in the United States: The 1960s Through the 1990s." *Journal of Marriage and Family* 63: 1009–37.

Thwaites, R. G., ed. 1906. *Jesuit Relations and Allied Documents, 1610–1791*. 73 vols. Cleveland, OH: Burrows Brothers.

U.S. Bureau of the Census. 2001, 2003. *Statistical Abstracts*.

Name: _____   Date: _____

MODULE 5-B

ACTIVITY

◇ LOVE AND MARRIAGE

This activity explores cultural differences in beliefs about love and marriage. Once you have completed this activity, you should have a better understanding of the cultural context of your own beliefs about love and marriage.

Directions: Robert Levine and colleagues (1995) asked college students in 11 cultures (India, Pakistan, Thailand, Mexico, Brazil, Japan, Hong Kong, Republic of the Philippines, Australia, England, and the United States) to complete the questions below. First, answer these questions based on your own beliefs. Then respond to the reaction questions that follow in order to better understand the cultural influences on your beliefs.

The questions below ask for your thoughts about marriage. Since only heterosexual couples may legally marry in most parts of the world, you may also think about these questions in terms of making a lifelong commitment.

1. If a man (woman) had all the other qualities you desired, would you marry this person if you were not in love with him (her)?

No _____   Yes _____

Please explain:

Taken from *Cross-Cultural Explorations: Activities in Culture and Psychology*, Second Edition, by Susan Goldstein.

2. If love has completely disappeared from a marriage, I think it is probably best for the couple to make a clean break and start new lives.

Agree _____   Disagree _____

Please explain:

3. In my opinion, the disappearance of love is not a sufficient reason for ending a marriage and should not be viewed as such.

Agree _____   Disagree _____

Please explain:

Reactions:

1. Levine and colleagues found that members of individualist cultures were more likely than members of collectivist cultures to view love as important in decisions about marriage. In fact, in some collectivist cultures, intense romantic love is viewed as immature and threatening to the family structure. How might you explain this finding?

2. Levine and colleagues also reported a distinction among collectivist cultures, with members of more economically developed countries (such as Japan and Hong Kong) attributing greater importance to love than less economically developed collectivist cultures (such as India, Pakistan, Thailand, and the Philippines). How might you explain this finding?

3. In a 1967 study of American college students, Kephart reported that 65% of males and 24% of females answered "*no*" to the question about marrying someone who had the qualities you desired, but with whom you are not in love. No such gender differences were found by Levine and colleagues. Approximately 80% of males and females in their sample of Americans answered "*no*" to the same question. How might you explain the dramatic change in response of American females between 1967 and 1995? Why do you think the scores of males show increased importance attributed to love over that same period of time?

4. The few valid studies that have compared the marital satisfaction of arranged marriages versus autonomous marriages ("love matches") have had conflicting results. It is particularly difficult to compare divorce rates since societies vary greatly in terms of the ease with which marital partners, particularly women, can divorce (Hatfield & Rapson, 2005). We do know that there appears to be a global trend away from arranged marriages (Dion & Dion, 2005). Do you think this trend will ultimately be harmful or beneficial to relationships? Please explain.

5. What cultural messages may have influenced your own beliefs about the importance of love in marriage or lifelong commitments?

◇ SOURCE

Adapted from Kephart, W. M. (1967). Some correlates of romantic love. *Journal of Marriage and the Family, 29,* 470-474, and Levine, R., Sato, S., Hashimoto, T., & Verma, J. (1995). Love and marriage in eleven cultures. *Journal of Cross-Cultural Psychology, 26,* 554-571.

◇ REFERENCES

Dion, K. L., & Dion, K. K. (2005). Culture and relationships: The downside of self-contained individualism. In R. M. Sorrentino, D. Cohen, J. M. Olson, & M. P. Zanna (Eds.), *Cultural and social behavior: The Ontario Symposium* (Vol. 10, pp. 77-94). Mahwah, NJ: Erlbaum,

Hatfield, E., & Rapson, R. L. (2005). *Love and sex: Cross-cultural perspectives.* Lanham, MD: University Press of America.

SECTION 6
LANGUAGE

MODULE 6-A

LANGUAGE AND CULTURAL MEANING

Compare the different ways that speakers of English and Navajo express their intentions and actions (note that Navajo utterances have been translated into English):

ENGLISH SPEAKER: I must go there.

NAVAJO SPEAKER: It is only good that I shall go there.

ENGLISH SPEAKER: I make the horse run.

NAVAJO SPEAKER: The horse is running for me.

In their use of language, speakers of English and Navajo express different views of events and experiences. By framing their intentions or activities with contrasting words and grammatical forms, they show in these examples that they have different attitudes about people's rights and obligations. English speakers encode the rights of people to control other beings (people or animals) or to be controlled or compelled themselves. In contrast, Navajo speakers give all beings the ability to decide for themselves, without compulsion or control from others.

The words used by speakers of English and Navajo express and reflect attitudes about the world that come from their own cultures. Although the attitudes indicated by these examples are specific, the process of encoding values, ideas, and emotions in language is universal. Such culturally shared attitudes, or *cultural models,* are based on people's ideas about the world they live in. Cultural models are expressed in several ways, but language is key to their transmission. Cultural models may be stated overtly, as in proverbs such as "don't cry over spilt milk" or "the early bird catches the worm," and either direct one's actions and attitudes or provide explanations for one's circumstances. Beliefs about the world may also be conveyed through accepted myths and legends, whether religious or secular, for example, the depiction of events in the Garden of Eden or the story of George Washington and the cherry tree. Such accounts guide human thought and action by providing moral lessons for individual behavior. More frequently, however, cultural models are covertly expressed throughout daily communicative interaction. The words we use have many layers of meaning, including concrete reference to objects and events and metaphoric or symbolic significance. Taken together, cultural meanings and models form a unique worldview, providing both an understanding of the world as it is thought to be and a blueprint for the way one ought to behave. Reality is not absolute or abstract; it is lived within familiar contexts of social behavior and cultural meanings.

In this module, we examine some linguistic means used to express models of the physical and social universe, including ideas about the shape and content of the environment, the kinds of forces affecting humans, and the ways people are expected to interact. We also explore the role of language in helping to construct and reinforce these models. All these issues are addressed in the field of linguistic anthropology. Studies examine the *lexicon,* or vocabulary, of a language in order to discover direct and indirect meanings of words. Issues raised include the degree of specialization in

Taken from *Language, Culture and Communication: The Meaning of Messages,* Seventh Edition, by Nancy Bonvillain.

various areas of meaning; the extent to which the words available in a language influence people's perceptions of their world; and the ways that words encode and transmit cultural, emotional, and symbolic meanings and values.

Researchers also seek to understand whether grammatical categories and structure affect speakers' worldviews. These studies raise questions concerning how the grammatical requirements of a language influence, direct, and reflect people's thought.

◇ FOUNDATIONS OF LINGUISTIC ANTHROPOLOGY

The two most influential figures in the development of linguistic anthropology were Edward Sapir (1884–1939) and Benjamin Whorf (1897–1941). Both men studied the languages and cultures of several Native American peoples. Among Sapir's many interests and contributions to the field were his discussions of the importance of analyzing vocabulary in order to uncover the physical and social environment in which people live. According to Sapir, "The complete vocabulary of a language may indeed be looked upon as a complex inventory of all the ideas, interests and occupations that take up the attention of the community" (1949a:90–91). Sapir argued that all human experience is, to some extent, mediated through culture and language. Objects or forces in the physical environment become labeled in language only if they have cultural significance—that is, if they "take up the attention of the community." And once a language provides a word for an object or activity, that object or event becomes culturally significant. The relationship of vocabulary and cultural value is multidirectional. Speakers give names (words) to important entities and events in their physical and social worlds, and those entities and events, once named, become culturally and individually noticed and experienced. Through this interdependent process, unique cultural models are created and reinforced. As Sapir noted, "The worlds in which different societies live are distinct worlds, not merely the same world with different labels attached" (1949b:162).

Sapir's statement applies most concretely to geographic features, which can either be named in minute detail or glossed over with general terms. People name details when their survival depends directly on their environment. For example, in the language of Paiute people living in semidesert areas of Arizona, Utah, and Nevada, among the geographic terms translated by Sapir are the following: "divide, ledge, sand flat, semicircular valley, circular valley or hollow, spot of level ground in mountains surrounded by ridges, plain valley surrounded by mountains, plain, desert, knoll, plateau, canyon without water, canyon with creek, wash or gutter, gulch, slope of mountain or canyon wall receiving sunlight, shaded slope of mountain or canyon wall, rolling country intersected by several small hill-ridges" (1949a:91). The English language is able to express these numerous topographical features in a descriptive way, as shown by Sapir's translations, but it lacks separate words unique to each. The Paiute language labels each feature with a separate name and thereby gives it distinctive value. A motivating force behind the strategies of both English and Paiute is the relative interest and importance that speakers attribute to environmental conditions. Vocabularies in different languages can therefore be compared and conclusions can be drawn about cultural attitudes from the degree of specialization within sectors of vocabulary.

One caution is worth noting concerning relationships between cultural interest and elaboration of vocabulary. Because cultures often change more rapidly than do languages, a "linguistic lag" can account for the fact that words or contrasts may reflect previous rather than current cultural interests. In time, as linguistic change catches up with cultural change, such words are likely to shift in meaning or to disappear.

Benjamin Whorf, who had been a student of Sapir, investigated whether grammatical structures provide frameworks for orienting speakers' thoughts and behaviors. He believed that the influence of language can be seen both through vocabulary and through more complex grammatical relations. For example, while Whorf was working for a fire insurance company, he noticed that fires were often caused by a person's inappropriate behavior motivated by labels given to objects. He found that workers occasionally threw matches and cigarette stubs into "empty" gasoline drums even though the drums contained combustible vapors and invisible traces of gasoline. Whorf concluded that the men's behavior resulted from their misinterpretation of the word "empty," which usually refers to "null and void, negative, inert" (1956b:135).

Whorf also wrote extensive analyses of the language spoken by Hopi people in Arizona, focusing on its distinctive underlying grammatical categories. One important issue raised through this research is the role that grammar plays in influencing the kinds of relations that speakers perceive in their world. In Hopi, there are three words translated as "that" in English. Each Hopi word signals a different relationship between clauses in a sentence (1956a:85). Compare the following:

1. I see that it is red.
2. I see that it is new.
3a. I hear that it is red.
3b. I hear that it is new.

In the first sentence, a speaker makes deductions based on direct sensory (in this case, visual) awareness. In the second sentence, a speaker makes inferences about "newness" based on evaluations of data (possibly including that "it" is shiny, clean, etc.). In sentences 3a and 3b, a speaker repeats or reports a fact provided by someone else, not directly experienced by the speaker herself. Comparing Hopi forms with English, we can conclude that because Hopis must choose among the various words, they are directed by grammatical requirements of their language to notice underlying causes of their knowledge of things (through direct senses, through inference, or through reported facts), whereas speakers of English need not pay attention to such differences. This does not mean that English speakers cannot become aware of different sources of knowledge; it simply means that they are not habitually led to making such distinctions.

In a comparison of Hopi and a language like English (which Whorf categorized as Standard Average European [SAE] to emphasize that European languages share basic grammatical characteristics), Whorf concluded that Hopi and English have different ways of conceptualizing time, number, and duration (1956b). He felt that these concepts are fundamental in creating a culture's metaphysics or view of the universe. According to Whorf, the Hopi language emphasizes continuity, cyclicity, and intensity in events, whereas SAE emphasizes the boundedness and objectification of entities. For example, English uses nouns to refer to phases in a cycle of time, such as "summer" or "morning." Hopi, though, treats phases as continuing events (or "eventings"). Words like "morning" are translated into Hopi as kinds of adverbs such as "while morning-phase is occurring" (ibid.:142–143). Contrasting the verb systems of English and Hopi, Whorf noted that English tenses divide time into three distinct units of past, present, and future, whereas Hopi verbs do not indicate the time of an event as such but instead focus on the manner or duration of an event. Whorf concluded that "concepts of 'time' and 'matter' are not given in substantially the same form by experience to all [people] but depend upon the nature of the language or languages through the use of which they have been developed" (ibid.:158).

The opinions of Sapir and Whorf on relationships among language, thought, and behavior have been the subject of research and debate. Several key variations of their ideas are advocated differently in various writings. One version is that some elements of language, for example, in vocabulary or grammatical systems, influence speakers' perceptions and can affect their attitudes and behavior. Another version suggests that language is ultimately directive in this process. The difference between the two versions seems to be the degree of control that language exerts. In fact, both Sapir and Whorf wavered in their statements on the issue of causal or directional relationship between language and thought. To quote Sapir,

> Human beings do not live in the objective world alone, nor alone in the world of social activity as ordinarily understood, but are very much at the mercy of the particular language which has become the medium of expression for their society. The fact of the matter is that the "real world" is to a large extent unconsciously built up on the language habits of the group. (1949b:162)

However, in the very next paragraph, Sapir stated that "we see and hear and otherwise experience very largely as we do because the language habits of our community predispose certain choices of interpretation" (ibid.). There is a difference between being "at the mercy" of one's language and being predisposed to "choices of interpretation," the latter implying options of thought.

In answer to one of Whorf's own questions about whether there are "traceable affinities between (a) cultural and behavioral norms and (b) large-scale linguistic patterns," Whorf answered that "there are connections but not correlations or diagnostic correspondences" (1956b:159). Discussing the historical development of the "network of language, culture and behavior," Whorf asked, "Which was first: the language patterns or the cultural norms?" And he answered: "In the main they have grown up together, constantly influencing each other. But in this partnership the nature of the language is the factor that limits free plasticity and rigidifies channels of development in the more autocratic way" (ibid.:156).

Sapir also discussed historical processes and asserted that "culture and language may be conceived of as in a constant state of interaction and definite association for a considerable lapse of time. This state of correlation, however, cannot continue indefinitely." Because cultures change more rapidly than do languages, "the forms of language will in course of time cease to symbolize those of culture" (1949b:102).

A review of the writings of Sapir and Whorf indicates that neither thought of the relationships among language, culture, and human thinking as rigid and mechanistic but rather as coexisting in fluid and dynamic interactions.

A Contemporary Comment

Working in an entirely different tradition, but overlapping historically with Sapir and Whorf, the Soviet linguist V. N. Volosinov expressed quite similar views about relationships of language, thought, and experience. Like the American researchers, Volosinov believed that language and speakers' perceptions of experience are intertwined. There exists an inner and external element in expression, a process by which the experiential is translated into a form where it embodies signs and obtains meaning. The inner element is the thought or idea that seeks expression to the external, to its "outward objectification." This external element requires that what is expressible be organized into a fixed medium or material. As the inner element is translated for delivery to the external it is transformed. Thus, compromises are made in order for the inner expression to be manifested outwardly. Volosinov stressed, "It is not experience that organizes expression, but the other way around . . . *expression organizes experience*. Expression is what first gives experience its form and specificity of direction [emphasis in original]." (1973: 84, 85). He stated:

Volosinov believed that an individual's thought is guided by possibilities offered by his or her language:

> It is a matter not so much of expression accommodating itself to our inner world but rather of our inner world accommodating itself to the potentialities of our expression, its possible routes and directions. (ibid.:91)

Finally, Volosinov stressed the social nature of inner personal experience: "The structure of experience is just as social as is the structure of its outward objectification. The degree to which an experience is perceptible, distinct and formulated is directly proportional to the degree to which it is socially oriented" (ibid.:87).

There are no indications that the American and Soviet scholars knew of each other's work, but their contemporaneous intellectual interests and conclusions were compatible.

Reexamination of Linguistic Relativity

Recent research has examined issues earlier introduced by Sapir and Whorf about the relationships among language, culture, and thought. To pursue these investigations, a comparative approach is vital. Comparison of lexical forms and grammatical structures from different languages allows researchers to disentangle the interrelated factors of language structure, cultural influences, and thought processes. In addition, some studies attempt to develop experimental designs focusing on memory and perception tasks that can lead to understanding how speakers of various languages use different cognitive resources to classify objects and events.

Studies in linguistic relativity also consider the functions and uses of language to investigate the full range of meanings produced when people speak. Using a comparative perspective in the analysis of discourse provides a framework for understanding the interrelationships of linguistic and cultural factors. Discourse analysis also contributes an emphasis on analyzing both the production and interpretation of speech in the context of use and evaluation. These studies move away from the analysis of context-free words and grammatical structures toward investigating language in use.

To examine the possible interplay of language and cognitive processes, John Lucy (1996) developed an analytic and experimental design studying the effects of grammatical requirements on memory and sorting tasks with speakers of English and Yucatec, a Mayan language spoken in Mexico. Lucy focused on two grammatical features distinguishing the two languages: marking for plural number and use of numerals that modify nouns. The first feature is that English requires an obligatory marker of plural number on the vast majority of its lexicon, including nouns referring to animate beings (humans and animals) and most inanimate objects. Plural marking does not occur with amorphous substances such as sugar, mud, water, and so on. In contrast, Yucatec allows for, but does not require, plural marking for only a very small number of nouns. Plural marking is more likely to occur with animate beings, but even with these, it is not obligatory.

Lucy devised experiments presenting pictures of scenes of Yucatec village life to speakers of Yucatec and English and asked them to perform a number of tasks requiring recalling and recognizing the pictures and sorting depicted objects as similar or different. The results indicated a strong effect of language structure on memory and classifying tasks. In remembering and sorting, speakers of English paid attention to number for animate beings and objects but ignored number for substances (ibid.:49). Speakers of Yucatec paid attention to number only for animate beings, ignoring number for everything else.

A second distinction between English and Yucatec concerns use of numerals. In English, count nouns are preceded directly by a numeral modifier (e.g., one dog, two cats). In contrast, Yucatec numerals are used in conjunction with a classifier that provides information about the shape, texture, or other material properties of the noun referent. For instance, the utterance translated from Yucatec as "one candle" is better understood as meaning "one long thin candle" (ibid.:50). As Lucy explains, the meaning of English nouns includes their form or unit, but the meaning of Yucatec nouns focuses on their substance rather than their form. So, for example, "one long thin candle" is better translated as "one long thin wax," with the cultural presupposition that wax occurring in a long thin shape is a candle. Note that English does use numeral classifiers with noncount nouns, for example, "a glass of water," providing information about the shape or unit in which the substance is contained.

To investigate the effect of numeral structure on cognition, Lucy provided speakers of English and Yucatec with sets of three test objects and asked the subjects to classify one of the objects as more like another (i.e., "Is item X more like A or more like B?"). Results of this experiment revealed that English speakers classified objects on the basis of shape, whereas Yucatec speakers classified objects on the basis of their material composition.

Both types of experiments confirm the strength of linguistic structuring and meaning in interaction with cultural patterning and cognitive processes. Further research with young speakers of English and Yucatec indicated that children younger than 7 years tended to classify objects as similar on the basis of shape rather than material, but that at about the age of 8 years, Yucatec children shifted to a preference for material as their basis for sorting objects (ibid.:51). Studies such as this suggest the significance of conducting future research that includes additional comparative and longitudinal data.

In a study investigating temporal concepts in English and Mandarin Chinese, Lera Boroditsky (2001) questioned whether speakers of languages that differ in the ways they talk about time also think about time differently. According to Boroditsky, concepts of time have both universal and language-specific features. From experience, time is "a phenomenon in which we, the observer, experience continuous unidirectional change that may be marked by appearance and disappearance of objects and events" (ibid.:4). But languages may vary in the way in which they develop metaphors and abstract conceptualizations of time. Many languages use metaphors derived from spatial concepts to express notions of time. For example, English talks about time in terms of horizontal space (e.g., "he took three steps *forward*" or "the dumpster is *behind* the store"). While speakers of Mandarin may also use horizontal front/back expressions for time, they also commonly use vertical or up/down metaphors when talking about the order of events, weeks, months, and so on. In these constructions, earlier events are expressed as "up" (or *shang* in Mandarin) while later events are "down" (or *xia* in Mandarin). For instance, /shang ge yue/ (up month) refers to "last (or previous) month" and /xia ge yue/ (down month) is used to indicate "next (or following) month" (ibid.:4–6).

To test whether the different metaphors for time in English and Mandarin have an effect on the ways speakers think about time, Boroditsky conducted several experiments with native speakers of English and Mandarin who were all students at Stanford University, completing the tests in English. Participants were given test questions after seeing primes depicting either horizontal or vertical spatial metaphors applied to time (see Figures 1a and b and 2a and b). The participants were asked to

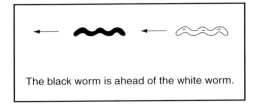

FIGURE 1A   Example of a Horizontal Spatial Prime (Boroditsky 2001)

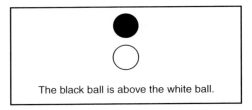

FIGURE 1B   Example of a Vertical Spatial Prime (Boroditsky 2001)

FIGURE 2A   Example of a Horizontal Spatial Prime
(Lera Boroditsky: "Does Language Shape Thought?: Mandarin and English Speakers' Conceptions of Time," 2001, *Cognitive Psychology,* vol. 43: 1–22.)

FIGURE 2B   Example of a Vertical Spatial Prime
(Lera Boroditsky: "Does Language Shape Thought?: Mandarin and English Speakers' Conceptions of Time," 2001, *Cognitive Psychology,* vol. 43: 1–22.)

respond true or false to statements such as "March comes *before* April." They were also given questions of purely temporal constructions such as "March comes *earlier* than April." Their response times were noted as a measure of their comprehension of horizontal spatial metaphors. The results demonstrated that English and Mandarin speakers had faster response times for *before/after* after horizontal primes than after vertical primes. However, English speakers answered purely temporal questions (earlier/later) faster after horizontal primes, while Mandarin speakers answered these questions faster after vertical primes.

Another experiment tested the effect of English learning on native Mandarin speakers' responses. Results showed that the older a person was when starting to learn English, the greater was the effect of Mandarin on one's thinking vertically about time. However, the length of exposure to English had no effect. Rather, age of acquisition was the significant factor.

According to Boroditsky, the results of these experiments demonstrated that "language shapes thought. . . . One's native language appears to exert a strong influence over how one thinks about abstract domains like time" (2001:18). In the absence of experiential data (through the senses of sight, sound, etc.), language may play a critical role in shaping the way that speakers conceptualize abstract notions like time.

Issues of language and perception can also be addressed by examining differences in conversational style favored by speakers of different languages. Much of the work of John Gumperz and his associates focuses on analyzing the role of what Gumperz calls "conversational inference," defined as "the situated and presupposition-bound interpretive processes by which interlocutors assess what they perceive at any one point in a verbal encounter and on which they base their responses" (1996:375). That is, when people interact verbally with one another, they continually interpret and evaluate their co-participant's speech in order to ascertain not only its meaning but also its intention. On the basis of these interpretations, each speaker responds to what he or she perceives as the other person's meaning. However, when people learn second or third (or more) languages, they may learn to properly use the pronunciations, words, and grammatical patterns of their additional language, but they may unconsciously transfer the conversational inferences they learned with their native language into verbal encounters in which they speak a nonnative tongue. Therefore, they may misinterpret the meanings and intentions of their co-participants regardless of the fact that they may understand the literal meaning of the words spoken to them.

Communicative practices that are considered appropriate within a particular community foster feelings of identity and group membership. Among the kinds of practices that may signal group membership are features of intonation (pitch, rhythm, velocity), pausing, and stylistic and rhetorical choices. Because people rely on these patterns without consciously reflecting on their meaning, they are usually unaware that they are making a communicative choice but instead believe that their conversational practices are natural. Therefore, people are also not consciously aware of making particular interpretations and evaluations of other people's speaking styles, instead assuming that their reactions are natural as well.

People with different cultural backgrounds may assume that different styles of speaking are appropriate in particular settings, resulting in a kind of miscommunication. For example, research with South Asian immigrants in Great Britain reveals contrasting discourse norms both in production and interpretation. In the following extract from an interview between a native Pakistani applicant for admission to a paid training course (ibid.:390–391), the applicant and the British interviewer misinterpret each other's communicative cues (/*/ indicates word said with strong stress):

INTERVIEWER (I):   [A]nd you put here that you want to apply for that course, because there are more jobs in the *trade.

APPLICANT (A):   Yeah.

I: So perhaps you could explain *apart from that reason, *why else you want to apply for *electrical work.

A: I think I like this job in my as a profession.

I: And *why do you think you'll *like it?

A: Why?

I: Could you explain to me *why?

A: I why do I like it? Well, I think is ah more job prospect!

In this encounter, the interviewer is using British norms by indirectly asking the applicant to expand on his interests and past experiences, but the applicant, unfamiliar with these norms, interprets the interviewer's words literally and simply rephrases his statements. Here we find a demonstration of people thinking differently about what is going on in their interaction. Each one misinterprets the other's contribution. And both find it difficult to move beyond their own interpretation, becoming increasingly annoyed and frustrated. They do not realize that their sense of what is happening is derived from their own culturally specific patterns of discourse production and interpretation.

◇ LEXICAL AND CULTURAL CATEGORIES

Building on the pioneering foundations of the first half of the twentieth century, modern researchers have broadened the exploration of topics in language and culture. Some study taxonomic systems in vocabulary and raise questions about possible universality of linguistic and cognitive processes. Other research investigates how cultural values and symbols are encoded in words or expressions and are then used by speakers to transmit emotional, attitudinal, and symbolic meanings.

Domains

Studies of categories and taxonomies in vocabulary often focus on analyses of semantic domains. A *semantic domain* is an aggregate of words, all sharing a core meaning, related to a specific topic—for example, kinship terms, body part words, and colors. Words within a domain are united by similarities and contrasts. The words share certain features of meaning because they refer to the same type of object, person, or event, but each word contrasts with all others in the set and labels a distinctive entity. By discovering systematic principles of similarity and contrast in a given domain, we can make inferences about how speakers experience their world. The number of distinctions made within a domain reflects the degree of cultural interest, as shown, for instance, by comparing the English and Paiute topographical terms given earlier from Sapir's research.

Cultural focus can also be seen in distinctions made by English terms for animals. For certain animals, we note age and sex, whereas for others we ignore such factors. For instance, within the species of "horse," we have separate words for female and male adults (*mare* and *stallion*), for babies (*foal*), and for female and male preadults (*filly* and *colt*). Age and sex of cattle are similarly distinguished: *cow, bull, calf, heifer,* and *bullock*. Also, we have numerous words for different breeds of these animals. In contrast, we treat other animals in much more generalized ways, using only one term for all individuals—for example, *chipmunk, otter,* and *moose*. These differences in linguistic treatment obviously parallel, and are based on, our cultural interest in various kinds of animals because of our economy, eating habits, or other needs.

Cultural interest is not static; it changes over time as new items and practices are introduced. When innovations are adopted, words are required to label these new entities and activities. Speakers can either create new words or extend the semantic range of existing words to include new items. In some cases, innovations replace indigenous objects, resulting in changes in meanings or functions of native words. For instance, shifts have occurred in meanings of the word *ăh* (now meaning "sheep") in a dialect of Tzeltal, spoken by native people in Mexico (Witkowski and Brown 1983:571). When sheep were introduced to the Tzeltal people by the Spanish in the sixteenth century, Tzeltal speakers applied their indigenous word for "deer," *ăh*, to this new animal, adding a descriptor, "cotton," *tunim*, so that "sheep" were called *tunim ăh* ("cotton deer"). Over the centuries, sheep have been incorporated into the Tzeltal economy while at the same time, deer have become of peripheral interest. Now the word *ăh* is used exclusively for "sheep," whereas "deer" is labeled as *te?tikil ăh*, literally "wild sheep." In this process, special marking for "sheep" has disappeared, emerging instead on "deer" in the modifier "wild."

In many languages of native North and South America, replacement of indigenous items and changes in cultural importance are reflected in marking older entities with attributes such as "native," "real," or other descriptive terms. When new items are introduced, speakers associate them with already existing entities and name them with indigenous words. Then, when older entities become eclipsed in importance by innovations, shifts occur in meanings so that the new item is the neutral term and the indigenous one receives modification. These processes can be seen in the following examples (ibid.:572–575):

1. Huastec (Mexico):
   precontact: *bičim*   "deer"
   contemporary: *bičim*   "horse"
                            tenek bičim   "deer"   (lit. native horse)
2. Biloxi (southeast United States):
   kcixka   "pig"
   kcixka yoka   "opossum"   (lit. swamp pig)

3. Comanche (US Plains):
   kahnI   "house"
   nïmïkahnI   "teepee"   (lit. Indian house)

Lexical Components

In some domains of vocabulary, cross-cultural comparisons uncover basic differences in the ways that people perceive their universe. For example, study of kinship terms (words used to name relatives) can reveal people's perceptions of their social relations. Americans generally use the following words for relatives: *grandmother, grandfather, mother, father, aunt, uncle, sister, brother, cousin, daughter, son, niece, nephew, granddaughter,* and *grandson.* By analyzing the kinds of contrasts made with these words, we can discover systematic components of meaning that are used to name relatives. First, we distinguish between generations: grandmother/mother/daughter/granddaughter. Second, we note the sex of relatives: mother/father; sister/brother. Third, we distinguish between direct or lineal relatives and collateral relatives: mother/aunt; son/nephew. These three sets of contrasts—that is, generation, sex of relative, and lineality—define the features of our kin that we consider meaningful. Another interesting aspect of English terminology is the reciprocity between alternate generations. The same combining form /grand-/ is used when skipping up one generation or downward: grandparent/grandchild.

The procedure used to determine significant contrasts is called *componential analysis* and was developed by Ward Goodenough in studies of American kinship (1956, 1965). Words in a domain are viewed as being composed of isolable "components" of meaning that co-occur in different combinations, for example, younger generation + female + lineal fi "daughter." Comparisons of distinctive components used in any system of terms allow linguists and anthropologists to understand better the *ethnosemantics,* or indigenous systems of meaning, of a culture and its members.

Underlying principles or components in the English system are not necessarily used in all languages. Other languages and therefore their speakers employ different sets of contrasts. In languages of Iroquoian peoples (indigenous inhabitants of present-day New York State and Ontario and Quebec, Canada), the following kinds of relatives are named (examples are from Seneca, one of the Iroquoian languages; Lounsbury 1964):

grandmother (and her sisters): *ʔakso:t*

grandfather (and his brothers): *hakso:t*

mother and mother's sister: *noʔyẽh*

father and father's brother: *haʔnih*

mother's brother: *hakhnoʔsẽh*

father's sister: *ake:hak*

older sister: *ahstiʔ*

younger sister: *kheʔkẽ:ʔ*

older brother: *hahtsiʔ*

younger brother: *heʔkẽ:ʔ*

cousin: *akya:ʔse:ʔ*

daughter: *khe:awak*

son: *he:awak*

niece: *khehsõʔneh* (female speaker); *kheye :wõ:tẽʔ* (male speaker)

nephew: *hehsõʔneh* (female speaker); *hey :wõ:tẽʔ* (male speaker)

granddaugther: *kheya:teʔ*

grandson: *heya:teʔ*

This system is organized around several key principles, some similar to English terminology and others that differ. Both systems use notions of generation and the sex of relative. However, Iroquoian speakers have separate terms for older and younger siblings (older sister/younger sister and older brother/younger brother). A major contrasting feature between the two languages is their treatment of lineal and collateral relatives. In English, sisters of one's mother and father are lumped together with one term, "aunt," as are brothers of one's mother and father, "uncle." In the Iroquoian system, one's mother's sisters are called by the same word as one's own mother, whereas one's father's sister is named separately. Similarly, one's father's brother is called "father," whereas one's mother's brother is distinguished. This principle of associating mother and father with their same-sex sibling is carried logically through succeeding generations and results in merging some relatives who we would call "cousin" into categories of sister/brother:

mother's sister's daughter = sister

mother's sister's son = brother

father's brother's daughter = sister

father's brother's son = brother

The logic here is based on the fact that a child of one's mother or father is one's sibling; therefore, a child of anyone called "mother" or "father" is called "sister" or "brother."

Differences in kinship terminologies are not merely linguistic; they reflect societal attitudes toward one's relatives. Individuals called by each kin term are understood by speakers to stand in particular social relationships and to have certain rights and obligations vis-à-vis speakers. The meanings of words, then, reflect one's social universe.

Lexical Classifications

Research in vocabularies reveals that, in some domains, distinctions are clear and unequivocal, whereas in others, components and categories are more complex. In a domain such as kinship, people are easily differentiated from one another; for example, a person is either female or male, either younger or older than the speaker. But in other domains, items cannot be classified absolutely. In addition, speakers may disagree about whether to include or exclude particular items in any given category. And they need to know which aspects of an entity are critical in determining the category to which the entity belongs.

To classify words, speakers need to know the defining characteristics of each class. For example, in the United States, many people include a whale in the category of "fish" because whales live in the ocean and move by swimming, even though they are biologically mammals, giving birth to live young. The "mistake" of classifying a whale as a fish reveals that definitional criteria of category membership do not all have equal weight. Certain traits are considered by speakers to be more important than others. The most obvious facts about whales are that they look like fish, swim in the ocean, and do not come ashore (unlike seals and walrus, which do come ashore). Because whales share some key diagnostic criteria of the "fish" category, they can be thought of as "fishlike."

Category membership, then, is not always absolute but frequently involves questions of degree or "fuzziness." Fuzzy sets or categories are based on the idea that "instead of just being in the set or not, an individual is in the set to a certain degree" (Lakoff 1972:185). Fuzzy category membership is often signaled linguistically in English by use of *hedges*, "words whose meaning implicitly involves fuzziness," such as "sort of, loosely speaking, somewhat, essentially" (ibid.:195–196). In the case of whales, one can say

a. Strictly speaking, a whale is a mammal.
b. Loosely speaking, a whale is a fish.

In (a), a speaker focuses on primary diagnostic criteria of biological traits, whereas in (b), the speaker ignores these and instead focuses on secondary criteria of habitat and behavior. Both (a) and (b) are true statements, although

c. Strictly speaking, a whale is a fish.
d. Loosely speaking, a whale is a mammal.

are false.

Inherent fuzziness of hedges can also be shown by the falseness of either of the following:

a. Strictly speaking, a robin is a bird.
b. Loosely speaking, a robin is a bird.

Because a robin is unquestionably a bird, the sort of hedge that implies uncertainty cannot be used in this case because the entity is a typical example of its category.

Criteria used for classification are different in different languages. For example, some languages organize noun categories on the basis of gender (masculine/feminine/neuter) or animate/inanimate distinctions. Others employ semantic criteria of form or use (Swahili, Swati) or shape and texture (Navajo). However, labels used by linguists to refer to noun classes may be misleading because they may reflect Western thinking about attributes of referents rather than accurately capture indigenous worldviews. This point has been discussed by Mo Kaa (1976) in an analysis of Algonkian languages (spoken in eastern and central North America).

Linguists usually claim that Algonkian languages (Ojibwa, Cree, Blackfoot, Cheyenne) base noun classes on a distinction between animates and inanimates. Leonard Bloomfield's influential grammar of Algonkian noted the following members of the "animate" category: "all persons, animals, spirits, and large trees, and some other objects, such as tobacco, maize, apple, raspberry, calf of leg, stomach, spittle, feather, bird's tail, horn, kettle, pipe for smoking, snowshoe" (1946:94). Although this list may seem haphazard from a Euro-American sense of "animate" (to be "alive"), Kaa suggested that the problem is not with Algonkian inconsistencies but with the failure of Western terminology to express native meanings adequately.

Kaa offered an alternative statement of Algonkian "animate" that may be less concise but more attuned to the Algonkian people's perspective: "Animate" entities are "more spiritually relevant and personalized beings, things, and phenomena" (ibid.:92). This definition embodies several important aspects of the Algonkian worldview. First, it states criteria in relative rather than absolute terms, thus avoiding Western tendencies to think in polarities. Second, because the definition is relative, it recognizes that noun classifications are sensitive to contextual and individual variation, accounting for the fact that some nouns are categorized differently by different speakers. Third, it emphasizes the similarity among "beings, things, and phenomena" rather than their oppositions.

A conversation between an Ojibwa speaker and A. Irving Hallowell corroborated Kaa's description of Algonkian "animates." Hallowell was interested in discovering Ojibwa concepts of "personhood," understanding that "this category of being is by no means limited to *human* beings" (emphasis in original) (1960:22). Hallowell noted that "stones" are classed grammatically as "animates," so he asked an Ojibwa speaker: "Are *all* the stones we see about us here alive?" "No! But *some* are" was the reply (ibid.:26). In the Ojibwa worldview, stones have potential for motion and can occasionally take on other animate attributes. They are most apt to do so in religious contexts, especially related to rituals associated with *Midewiwin*, an Ojibwa ceremonial and curing society. Stones therefore can have agency and perform actions or, to quote Kaa again, they are "spiritually relevant and personalized."

Ethnoscience

Ethnoscience refers to systems of classification that people construct to organize knowledge of their universe. The term *ethnoscience* is derived from the Greek word *ethnos,* meaning "people" or "a division of people." Such systems are based on taxonomic hierarchies in which some entities are ordered hierarchically (e.g., a "spaniel" is a kind of "dog") and other entities are contrasted taxonomically (e.g., "dog" and "cat").

Studies of ethnoscientific domains in different cultures demonstrate the variety of underlying assumptions that can be used to group entities. Analysts of comparative data from many languages proposed the following universal taxonomy for living things (Berlin, Breedlove, and Raven 1974:25–27): Unique Beginner (most general and abstract term that subsumes all of the other categories, e.g., *plant, animal*); Life Forms (perhaps five or ten terms, each named by a separate, independent word, e.g., *tree, grass, bird, mammal*); Generics (many terms, usually named by separate words, e.g., *oak, pine, robin, blue jay, dog, horse*); Specifics (items within generic categories, often named by identifying modifiers, e.g., *blue spruce, white birch*); and Varietals (items within specific categories, e.g., *baby lima bean, butter lima bean*).

Grouping of items within a particular category is based on perceived similarities or shared parameters of meaning. Distinctions between categories are based on perceived contrasts. For example, the Digo, an indigenous people living in coastal regions of Kenya and Tanzania whose language belongs to the Bantu linguistic family, have a system of botanical terms that makes culturally relevant categories of form and function (Nicolle 2001). Most Digo consultants begin their taxonomy of plant terms with three "life form" labels: *linyasi* ("grass"); *mmea* ("plant"), and *muhi* ("tree"). Although they did not use a "unique beginner" term, they consider these three "life forms" as belonging to a related abstract category. While these life forms are distinct taxa, there may be some overlap in their application to particular specimens. For example, the term *mmea* ("plant") could be applied to any young plant, including a tree seedling, even though a mature tree would be in the category of *muhi* ("tree"). However, a tree seedling could also be considered *muhi*. The term *mmea*, then, may encompass any young member of the (unnamed) plant family (Nicolle 2001:38).

Digo speakers employ several contrastive parameters to distinguish specific botanical entities. Attention to these parameters allows speakers to decide whether something is a member of the category of *muhi* ("tree") or *mmea* ("plant"). The parameters include the entity's size and whether it is cultivated, where it is located, and whether it bears fruit. For instance, members of the category of *muhi* ("tree") are typically large (two meters or more in height), not cultivated, located in the bush outside villages, and may bear fruit that is edible. In contrast, members of the category of *mmea* ("plant") are small, cultivated in farms or gardens, and do not bear fruit. In addition to these parameters, the categories are distinguished on the basis of their uses. That is, *muhi* may be used for medicines but not for food (except for their edible fruits); *mmea* are used as foods or spices (Nicolle 2001:40).

Although there is general agreement about the distinctions among the life forms, speakers vary in the assignment of any particular exemplar to one or another category. Variations among speakers arise from the proportionate weight given to each of the parameters used to contrast category membership (Nicolle 2001:40). For instance, consultants disagreed about whether to place "cucumber tree" (*Averrhoa bilimbi*) among the *muhi* or *mmea*. The fact that "cucumber tree" is cultivated should place it among the *mmea*, but because of its size (usually more than two meters in height) and the fact that it bears edible fruit, it may be called *muhi*. In some cases, consultants did agree on the placement of potentially ambiguous exemplars. For example, "pigeon pea" (*Cajanus cajun*) is considered a member of the *mmea* group because it is one of the most important cultigens in Digo subsistence and economy, functioning in household consumption and commercial sale. These characteristics outweigh other features that might lead it to be called *muhi*; that is. it may grow to more than two meters, it bears edible fruit, and its leaves are used as an eye medicine.

This analysis of Digo plant categories illustrates the important point that traits used to assign any particular entity to specific categories depends on speakers' consideration of various distinguishing features and the relevant weight given to each. It also illustrates the fact that there may be disagreements within communities about specific assignments and category membership.

Universal Processes: Color Terms

Rather than emphasizing linguistic and cultural differences in systems of categorization, many linguists are discovering universal principles of classification. Much attention has been given to the domain of color terminology. In a groundbreaking and influential study, *Basic Color Terms* (1969), Brent Berlin and Paul Kay presented a theory of universal color categories and their sequential development. In their study, Berlin and Kay collected color-term data from 98 languages by asking speakers to sort 329 color chips into categories that could not be subsumed within any other class. This testing procedure resulted in terms such as "red" but not "scarlet" or "maroon" because the latter two are recognized as "kinds of" red. On the basis of consultants' responses, Berlin and Kay postulated 11 basic color terms: *white, black, red, green, yellow, blue, brown, purple, pink, gray,* and *orange*. Not all languages contain all 11 terms. By examining the content of various color systems, Berlin and Kay proposed the following evolutionary sequence, which starts on the left and incrementally incorporates colors to the right.

white →	red →	green →	blue →	brown →	purple
black		yellow			pink
					orange
					gray

Note that no language distinguishes less than two colors. A one-color system would actually be impossible because a classification scheme, by definition, must contain at least two members; that is, two items must be seen to contrast with each other. Berlin and Kay's sequence accounts for the instance when a language contains only two color terms: They are always "white" and "black." Additional terms are added in the order of development presented with examples in the following table:

NUMBER OF TERMS	COLOR TERMS	LANGUAGE
Two	white, black	Jale (New Guinea), Ngombe (Africa)
Three	white, black, red	Arawak (Caribbean), Swahili (southern Africa)
Four	white, black, red, yellow	Ibo (Nigeria), Tongan (Polynesia)
Five	white, black, red, yellow, green	Tarascan (Mexico), !Kung (southern Africa)
Six	white, black, red, yellow, green, blue	Tamil (India), Mandarin (China)
Seven	white, black, red, yellow, green, blue, brown	Nez Percé (Montana), Javanese
Eight to eleven	white, black, red, yellow, green, blue, brown, purple and/or pink and/or orange and/or gray	English, Zuni (New Mexico), Dinka (Sudan), Tagalog (Philippines), among others

Source: Compiled from Berlin and Kay 1969:152–156.

Kay (1975) later revised the original sequence somewhat in order to account for the fact that certain languages—for example, Japanese, Inuktitut (Arctic Canada), Aguaruna (Peru)—encode a color of "green-blue" that may occur before labeling "yellow." Kay called this color category "GRUE" and placed it either preceding or following "yellow" in development. He noted that the category "GRUE" never splits separately into both "green" and "blue" before the naming of "yellow." The revised sequence, then, is given below:

A few languages seem to necessitate further minor modifications. For example, Russian does not have a word for a single color "blue" but rather distinguishes "dark blue" and "light blue." However, Berlin and Kay's sequence has essentially been substantiated.

Although there may be universal patterns in the development of systems of color-term classification, languages differ in the symbolic meanings embodied in color terms. Words for colors may be used to call forth emotional and ideological responses, for example, black for mourning, white for purity, and red for passion. But these meanings and uses vary cross-culturally.

Focal Meaning and Prototypes

Berlin and Kay's work in color systems has proven to be of great significance because it raised important questions concerning universal cognitive and linguistic processes. It also uncovered complexities in the organization of classes and in understanding how speakers make discriminations. These discoveries are not limited to color terms but have wider applicability in language.

The concept of focal meaning within classes has become relevant in ethnolinguistic studies. The *focal meaning* of a word is its central sense within the whole range of meanings that it has. A word's focal meaning refers to the "best example" or "most typical example" of possible meanings that it encompasses. For instance, in color terminology, each word covers a graded range of different hues along a continuum rather than a discrete and absolute quality, but each word also has a central meaning, a "best example." Speakers in a community agree on the focal meaning of a word, although they may well disagree about including or excluding peripheral cases in given categories. So, if asked to pick out the "best example" of "red," speakers agree on a color sometimes called "scarlet" or, colloquially, "fire-engine red." In their study, Kay and McDaniel found that focal meanings of basic color terms were substantially similar in all languages, suggesting a universal color system based on physical stimuli (Kay and McDaniel 1978).

The concept of prototypes can also be generally applied in semantic analyses. A *prototype* is an idealized, internalized conceptualization of an object, quality, or activity. Real-life objects and activities are measured against these internalized concepts and are named according to how well they approximate the ideal. As Charles Fillmore stated, a prototype approach to semantics "seeks to represent the meaning of a linguistic expression, not through a statement of the necessary and sufficient conditions for membership in a category...but rather through the analysis of instances (or near instances) of the category in terms of approximations to the prototype" (1982:32). For example, a category such as "bird" "is identified in terms of a fixed set of conditions, but the best examples are those that are close to an idealization of that category" (ibid.:33). Therefore, although a robin, penguin, and ostrich are all kinds of birds, speakers (in our culture) agree that "robin" is closest to the prototype or idealization or, as Fillmore said, "is somehow 'birdier' than the other two" (ibid.).

In classifying concrete objects, speakers may disagree about whether to place items in given categories because they disagree about whether the items approximate enough prototypical characteristics. For instance, "prototypical" or "best example" of "chair" in North American culture is an object with four legs, a seat, back, and two armrests. Although speakers generally include an object fitting such a description in the category "chair," they may disagree about whether to include objects lacking one or another defining property.

People categorize objects based on their use as well as on physical properties. In an experimental study, William Labov showed subjects drawings of cups and cuplike containers and asked them to provide names for these objects, such as cup, mug, bowl, dish, pitcher (1973:353–355). People were then asked to imagine the same series of objects containing coffee, mashed potatoes, or flowers. Respondents were most likely to label borderline or peripheral (i.e., untypical) objects as "cups" if they contained coffee and least likely to do so if they held flowers. Labov concluded that "language is essentially a categorical device" and that in order to understand it, processes of categorization must be studied "at work" (ibid.:368).

People and activities can also be evaluated with reference to prototypical constructs. In these cases, of course, speakers depend on cultural models consisting of expectations for and evaluations of behavior. A social category of this type, illustrated by the word *bachelor*, "is defined in terms of a set of conditions, but the best examples are those which are situated in a standard or prototype background setting" (Fillmore 1982:34). Although "bachelor" can be defined as an unmarried adult male, not all unmarried men would appropriately be called bachelors; a man living in a stable, conjugal relationship; a boy abandoned in a jungle and grown to maturity alone; a brain-damaged boy grown to adulthood in a coma; or the pope are examples (Quinn and Holland 1987:23). The point here is that categories like these cannot be defined abstractly; rather, they are appropriately understood only in the context of culturally shared expectations. This is what Fillmore termed a *background setting*.

Prototypes can also be used as guides in evaluating one's own or another's behavior. Because all communication occurs in cultural contexts, speakers' understanding of what is happening is often measured against prototypical constructs. Speech events, that is, instances of communicative interaction, form a domain that encompasses many kinds of genres, including conference, argument, negotiation, debate, lecture, confession, and apology. Participants evaluate ongoing behavior and form conclusions about what kind of interaction is taking place. Consensus among participants may or may not exist, depending on their perceptions of how the encounter conforms to a prototype model. Lack of consensus can also result when participants are motivated to define encounters in particular ways given their own goals and purposes—for example, people can disagree about whether they're having an argument.

These examples illustrate the importance of situating our understanding of the meaning of words and their usage in the context of culture.

Concepts of Space and Location

One of the universal sets of concepts that all people must have consists of notions of space, spatial relations, and location. These concepts are presumed by linguists and psychologists working in the field to be features of basic cognitive conceptual structure inherent in all human beings as part of our cognitive makeup (Jackendoff 1996; Levinson 1996). Developing and mastering concepts of space and location are critical to human life and are interrelated with visual and motor skills. People need to locate and manipulate objects and to be mobile within a spatial environment. While conceptual structure is universal, the way it is encoded in languages differs dramatically. These differences may be manifest in the lexicon and/or in syntax. Semantic features of words may encode specific reference to spatial concepts, and syntactic requirements may mandate the expression of certain kinds of spatial notions.

According to Jackendoff (1996:8–9), spatial representation must include the encoding of object shapes, dimensions, and variations and of the relations of objects and scenes. In addition, basic conceptual structure includes ideas of place or location and path or trajectory, as exemplified, for instance, in the following sentences: "The book is lying *on the table*" (place); "The arrow flew *through the air past my head*" (trajectory) (ibid.:9–10). Finally, conceptual structure contains notions of physical motion, enabling people to keep track of moving objects.

Languages have lexical and/or syntactic devices that allow speakers to describe spatial relations between objects and grounds. There seem to be two basic distinctions in emphases utilized by various languages. Some languages focus on systems that place objects in space by reference to intrinsic or object-internal orientations (e.g., "its back"), while others focus on contingent or reference-point relations (e.g., "at," "near," "here") (Lucy 1998:107). Languages also use techniques to coordinate these two types of concepts. These techniques emphasize either absolute systems of coordination, relative systems of coordination, or deictic systems of reference. Absolute systems describe a reference point and its placement within a presupposed orienting axis (e.g., a feature of local topography or cardinal directions), while relative systems extract intrinsic properties from the reference objects and project them over space (ibid.). Deictic or egocentric systems of spatial reference describe objects from the point of view of the speaker (e.g., noting an object's location to the left or right of the speaker) (Peterson et al. 1996).

While all languages have ways of indicating both intrinsic and contingent concepts and may utilize absolute, relative, and deictic systems, languages differ in their preference and frequency of usage. English emphasizes relativistic space, locating one object by reference to another object or spatial field. These relations are encoded in locative or directional prepositions (*at, near, away from, toward, in front of,* etc.). Other languages emphasize absolute space, locating objects in reference to absolute directions or topographical features. For example, the indigenous Australian language Guugu Yimithirr, spoken in North Queensland, specifies locations according to cardinal directions of east, west, north, and south. Therefore, an object is located as "to the north of," "to the south of," and so forth (Levinson 1996:180). To apply such a system correctly, speakers must constantly be aware of their absolute orientation in space. In experimental research, Guugu Yimithirr speakers were able to estimate locations within an average error of less than 14° (ibid.:181). And they remember spatial arrays in terms of their distribution relative to cardinal directions. In utilizing such a system, Guugu Yimithirr speakers have to access fundamentally different orientations to space and objects than do speakers of English.

Speakers of Tzeltal, a Mayan language of Mexico and Guatemala, employ a type of system of absolute spatialization, but one that differs from that of Guugu Yimithirr. In the Tzeltal language, a primary system of spatial reference is based on a fixed uphill/downhill inclined plane that roughly corresponds to the south/north axis of their landscape. This system is used for all referents regardless of whether they are located on inclined or flat surfaces. For example, two objects can be differentiated by referring to the northerly one as "downhill" of the other, even if both are on a flat surface (ibid.:181). A secondary system of spatial reference denotes objects that are in actual contact with others, but distinctions are made based on the kind of contact that they have. In addition, these two systems are supplemented by differentiation of objects according to nonlocational features such as shape, position of the figure, adhesion, and manner in which the position was obtained (ibid.:182).

Finally, spatial reference is modified by a distinction between describing motion and describing location. Motion is encoded through a small set of motion verb roots, while location is encoded through a larger set of stative predicates with functions similar to English adjectives.

An additional significant contrast between Tzeltal and English is the way that each language distinguishes figures and grounds. English describes in great detail the nature of the ground while presupposing features of the figure, but Tzeltal focuses on details in the description of the figure while assuming the nature of the ground. For instance, to locate objects, English describes where to look, while Tzeltal describes what to look for (ibid.:185).

Intriguing questions remain concerning how these differences in lexical and syntactic patterning and in spatial and locational emphases are related to underlying cognitive structures in speakers of disparate languages. Summing up cross-cultural research in this field, Peterson and her associates observe, "It seems clear that different languages and/or cultures can utilize different cognitive skills to different degrees" (1996:570). Evidence from experimental research on problem solving and memory tasks supports the conclusion that speakers of languages that encode spatial relations differently have distinct perceptions about the way that objects relate to one another and to their environmental background. Therefore, it is not claimed that speakers of different languages have different underlying cognitive conceptual structures, but rather that particular cognitive structures may be more or less salient depending on the linguistic resources that speakers have to express basic notions. These linguistic resources are not absolutely constraining. Instead, they lead speakers into certain habitual ways of expressing concepts and therefore of thinking about underlying relationships.

Studies in children's acquisition of spatial concepts indicate that the way their language structures space and location influences their perceptual processes. As Melissa Bowerman (1996:386) notes, some form of spatial understanding predates mastering linguistic skills, but specific linguistic input has a very early (as early as 18 months) impact on children's perception. Although spatial knowledge is necessary to all humans, dividing space into categories and manipulating their meanings and relationships is learned linguistic behavior. Children build on basic prelinguistic knowledge as they acquire the words and syntactic patterns that their language requires to talk about spatial concepts. In morphologically analytic languages like English, separate words, often in the form of prepositions or postpositions, are used to describe relationships between objects or between an object and its ground, while in morphologically complex languages, nominal or verbal morphemes are used to express these relationships. Cross-linguistic research suggests that children acquire the means of expressing these notions in roughly the same order. First learned are concepts of containment or support, proximity, separation, surrounding, and order (ibid.:388). In English, such concepts are expressed through prepositions such as *in* (containment); *on* (support and contiguity); *under* (occlusion); *next to, beside,* and *between* (proximity), and *in front of* and *behind* (projective order). Of course, different languages may have words with similar translations in their lexicon, but these words may have ranges of meaning that do not translate exactly from one language to another. For instance, note the different concepts that the English word *in* expresses (Levinson 1996:187):

    a. The peaches are in the can. (enclosed)
    b. The peaches are in the bowl. (partially enclosed)
    c. The dog is in the yard. (bounded in two dimensions)
    d. The shuttle is in outer space. (unbounded)

Now examine some differences in how English, Finnish, Dutch, and Spanish treat some spatial relationship concepts, as illustrated in the diagrams in Figure 3 (Bowerman 1996:394).

Comparing English and Tzeltal, we find that while the English preposition *in* encodes containment of any object into any container, Tzeltal has numerous locative expressions depending on the distinct type of object and the distinct type of containment. For example, the following uses of the English *in* are differentiated in Tzeltal (Brown 1994):

    a. A man is in a house. (be inside)
    b. An apple is in a bowl. (in a bowl-shaped container)
    c. Water is in a bottle. (in a taller-than-wide or cylindrical container)
    d. An apple is in a bucket of water. (immersed in liquid)
    e. A bag of coffee is in a pot. (inserted singly into a closely fitting container)
    f. Pencils are in a cup. (long/thin objects inserted carefully into a bounded object)
    g. A bull is in a corral. (inserted into container with a narrow opening)

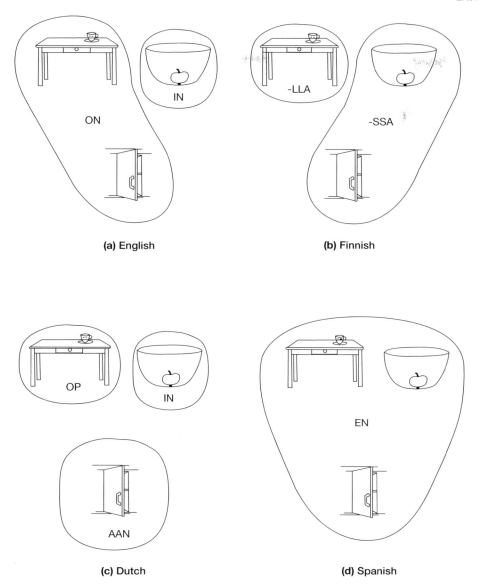

FIGURE 3   Classification of Three Static Spatial Situations in English, Finnish, Dutch, and Spanish

Source: Bowerman, M. 1996. Learning how to structure space for language: A cross linguistic perspective. In *Language and Space*, Bloom, P., et al., eds., pp. 385–436, MIT Press. *International Journal of American Linguistics*. Copyright © University of Chicago Press.

Speakers of English can, of course, express the meanings that Tzeltal distinguishes, but they are not compelled by the requirements of their language to notice the contrasts in types of objects and types of containers that speakers of Tzeltal must be aware of every time they talk about containment. These facts raise critical questions about people's basic assumptions of similarities and differences among objects and their relationships. That is, English speakers may feel that certain spatial relationships are "the same" because they use the same words to describe them, whereas speakers of other languages may perceive other kinds of relationships as similar.

People tend to classify objects and events in their minds according to the resources available in their languages to express those objects and events. As Bowerman concludes, "A perceptual or action-based understanding of what is going on in given spatial situations is probably a necessary condition for learning to talk about space, but this knowledge alone does not buy children knowledge of how to *classify* space in their language" (1996:399). And finally, experimental observation comparing spatial descriptions elicited from American, Dutch, and Korean adults and children in three cohorts (2,0–2,5; 2,6–2,11; and 3,0–3,5) indicated that the languages spoken strongly influenced the way that people classified space and location (ibid.:410, 415). Although there were differences between the linguistic skills of children and adults, especially in some overgeneralizations and lack of refinement in children's descriptions, speakers of each language were more similar to each other than they were to their age cohorts who spoke other languages. Significantly, even the youngest children classified spatial actions in ways more similar to adults speaking their own language than to children of the same age who spoke different languages.

In sum, research concerning language and spatial concepts and their acquisition hints at both the role of prelinguistic cognitive concepts and of language in structuring and classifying those concepts. Although languages can express any given notion, the ease with which concepts are expressed and are retrievable varies with the linguistic resources available and required in any given language through which the concepts are classified and encoded.

◇ CULTURAL PRESUPPOSITION

The vocabulary of a language is not merely an inventory of arbitrary labels referring to objects, entities, or events. Words also convey many kinds of cultural meanings that add to, transform, or manipulate basic senses of words. Research into these areas of meaning and usage includes investigation of cultural presuppositions, associational or extensional meanings, and uses of words to carry symbolic or ideological content.

The concept of *cultural presupposition* refers to the fact that participants in speech interactions come to encounters with an array of knowledge and understandings (models) of their culture as expressed and transmitted through language. The relevance of some of this shared knowledge is fairly obvious. For instance, if a speaker mentions the World Series, he or she assumes that listeners understand that the reference is to baseball, that teams compete throughout a season, and that winners of league competitions play each other for the championship. For conversation to run smoothly, much of what speakers say depends on their accurate assessment of hearers' knowledge. These presuppositions are collected by people during their lifetime of involvement in and learning through their experiences, that is, their enculturation. Because all human experiences are cultural, a tremendous amount of accumulated but unstated knowledge is continuously carried with us.

Other kinds of cultural presuppositions are more complex, and their incorporation into meanings of words is more subtle. For example, as shown in the four sentences that opened this module, English and Navajo express different concepts presupposing people's (and other animate beings') rights to individual autonomy (Young 1978). English has many terms expressing various types of coercion: *cause, force, oblige, make, compel, order, command, constrain, must, have to,* and *ought to*. In contrast, the Navajo language, spoken in New Mexico and Arizona, does not contain verbs of this sort. Rather than saying "I *must* go there" or "I *have to* go there," a Navajo speaker says *ákǫ́ǫ́ deesháałgo t'éiyá yáʔ át'ééh* ("it is only good that I shall go there"). This construction "lacks the force of compelling necessity" (ibid.:168). Whereas English readily expresses the idea that a person has a right to impose her or his will on another animate being, Navajo again does not express direct compulsion, as seen in the contrasting sentences in English (I *make* the horse run) and Navajo (*łį́ʼ́ į́ʼ́ shá yilghoł* ["the horse is running for me"]). The Navajo sentence "implies an action on the part of the horse that is essentially voluntary,...lacking the important overtone of coercive authority" (ibid.). These examples reflect the contrast in language ideologies as expressed through word choice and grammar, encapsulating differing views of speakers' rights in relation to others.

To use and interpret words appropriately, speakers make assumptions about each other's intentions, desires, or goals. For example, "joking" and "insulting" speech share certain important features; a speaker may "joke" or "insult" an addressee by pointing out the latter's mistakes, weaknesses, or inappropriate behavior. The difference between jokes and insults lies primarily in the speaker's perceived intent that she or he must make clear through choice of word, tone of voice, and/or facial expression. Interpretations of intent rely on cultural and social norms as well because appropriate topics or targets of joking are determined by culture. In some societies, people never joke with or tease their parents, whereas in other societies such behavior could be acceptable in certain contexts but not in others.

Cultural norms of communicative behavior also involve presuppositions. In our society, when two acquaintances meet, they may use greetings such as "Hi! How are you?" or "What's happening?" If speakers use the greeting "How are you?" do they actually want a substantive answer to this question? In casual encounters between acquaintances, a response that reveals personal problems or serious illness would be considered highly inappropriate. For participants to behave in an acceptable manner, they have to know the social purposes of particular words or utterances. In this example, speakers must know that an utterance that has been expressed in interrogative form is actually not intended as a question, that is, a request for information. Rather, it is a routinized request for a routinized response.

Words can also be used to convey symbolic meanings expressing cultural values and shared assumptions. For example, describing a group of people as "terrorists" expresses a strongly negative judgment against them. The power of language is not only that the values attached to words reveal the attitudes of speakers, but also that words are used to create compatible attitudes in hearers. Labeling someone as a terrorist is, in part, an attempt to influence hearers' opinions about this person because terrorism is an act that is socially condemned. In contrast, describing a person as a freedom fighter attempts to create a positive response.

Advertisers of products in our society (and presumably in many others as well) use an interrelated constellation of words and symbols that rely on and reinforce underlying cultural presuppositions. Advertisements often describe products as "new," "bigger," and "improved." These seemingly innocuous words reveal central themes of change and progress. An unstated assumption links concepts of newness and bigness with advances over items previously produced by both the same company and its competitors.

These are concepts implicit in commodity production, marketing, and consumerism. They are also interconnected with philosophical ideas of evolution. Life-forms are dynamic and ever-changing and lead naturally to better ("improved") versions. Change is conceived of as competitive based on analogies with biological processes—that is, organisms compete for econiches, resulting in "survival of the fittest." These ideas of change are so commonplace in our society that we take them to be *natural*, inherent in entities and processes themselves, rather than understanding that they are cultural constructs. Because change is "naturally" an advance, innovations are assumed to be desirable improvements. Advertisements that stress the diversity of products within a competitive environment have not created this imagery but exploit it. Repetitive exposure to such use of language reinforces overt and covert cultural and ideological messages implied and presupposed by the words. In this case, advertisements convey economic and philosophical presuppositions through word choice.

All language use has a manipulative aspect to it in the sense that speakers employ words in order to have an effect on hearers, such as to convey information, ask questions, or issue commands. But the words chosen are often not neutral in their connotations. They have associated senses that presuppose culturally shared symbolic meanings. Cultural symbols are transmitted through language and obtain their strength because speakers and hearers nonconsciously accept their indirectly expressed assumptions. The power of language to convey social messages is recognized, for instance, by many American women who object to being called "girl" or by African-American men who object to being called "boy."

Because of the covert symbolic aspect of language, it is difficult to understand the full range of meanings expressed by speakers in another culture. To gain insights into a people's worldview or system of values, it is necessary to ascertain the cultural symbols embedded in their words. This is one reason that translation from one language into another is never completely accurate. Words in isolation can be translated, but the full sense of those words in context cannot be conveyed easily or succinctly.

As difficult as it is to translate the meaning of words, it is an even more complex task to transfer the meanings conveyed by the structure and use of discourse from one language or culture to another. Discourse practices are taken for granted; these practices become part of a speaker's production and interpretation of speech without her or his conscious reflection on the presupposed meanings of particular choices. The practices become "naturalized," that is, thought of as natural rather than as culturally produced and evaluated. Differences in patterns of discourse include the kinds of meanings focused on, the way conversations or arguments are structured, the allocation of the right to speak, and a vast array of unstated assumptions about the world and about people's rights and powers.

◇ EXTENDED AND TRANSFERRED MEANING

Metaphor and Metonymy

Cultural meanings are also expressed through complex processes of semantic extension and transfer. One such process is that of *metaphor*. Metaphors are based on unstated comparisons between entities or events that share certain features. The comparisons implicitly highlight similarities while ignoring contrasts. According to George Lakoff and Mark Johnson, "[T]he essence of metaphor is understanding and experiencing one kind of thing in terms of another" (1980:5). Analysis of recurring metaphors in a language reveals underlying concepts that help construct the reality or worldview of speakers. In a statement consistent with the writings of Sapir and Whorf, Lakoff and Johnson explain that "[c]ultural assumptions, values and attitudes are not a conceptual overlay that we may or may not place upon experience as we choose. It would be more correct to say that all experience is cultural...we experience our 'world' in such a way that our culture is already present in the very experience itself" (ibid.:57). They also argue that analyses of metaphor provide insights into cultural constructions of reality because "our ordinary conceptual system, in terms of which we both think and act, is fundamentally metaphorical in nature" (ibid.:3).

An example from their work that illustrates a frequent construct in English is the pervasive theme "Time is money" (ibid.:7–9). This concept is embedded in these statements:

You don't use your time *profitably.*

How do you *spend* your time these days?

This gadget will *save* you hours.

These expressions are based on metaphors that treat intangible entities or qualities as though they were concrete objects. In our conceptual model, we conceive of time as a particular kind of object or commodity. "Time in our culture is a valuable commodity. It is a limited resource that we use to accomplish our goals.... Thus we understand and experience time as the kind of thing that can be spent, wasted, budgeted, invested wisely or poorly, saved or squandered" (ibid.:8).

Another recurring metaphorical construct discussed by Lakoff and Johnson is the opposition between "up" and "down." Activities or states viewed positively are expressed as "up"; those evaluated negatively are expressed as "down" (ibid.:15–17). The following list presents some of these comparisons:

	UP	*DOWN*
Emotions:	You're in *high* spirits.	He's feeling *low* today.
Consciousness:	Wake *up*!	She *sank* into a coma.
Health:	He's in *top* shape.	Her health is *declining.*
Control:	I'm *on top* of the situation.	He *fell* from power.
Status:	She'll *rise* to the top.	He's at the *bottom* of society.
Virtuousness:	He's *high* minded.	I wouldn't *stoop* that low.

The English language characteristically employs lineal metaphors to describe many different kinds of events. Common expressions include *trace a relationship, follow a line of thought, set a course of action, follow the direction of an argument,* and *bridge a gap in conversation.* Certain ways of talking indicate that lineal order is positively valued in our society: *line up support for one's cause, set the record straight, keep someone in line, straighten up.* Contrasting expressions reveal cultural attitudes: *keeping to the straight and narrow* is virtuous, whereas *wandering from the path* is suspect. Similarly, in conversation, *getting straight to the point* is desirable in our society, but *talking around an issue* or *beating around the bush* indicates deception.

Another type of metaphoric construction common in English is the use of container images when depicting nonphysical entities or processes. This pattern is consistent with tendencies in English to make objects out of intangibles. Once a nonconcrete entity is transformed into an object, it can be contained, entered, left, held, or the like. Use of locative prepositions (prepositions that denote location, direction, or movement in regard to an object) often signals this type of metaphor: He's *out of* his mind; They're *in* love; I feel *under* the weather. In these expressions, subjects are depicted "as if" they were in some physical relation to a defined and contained space, for example, to be *in* love. Here, "love," an internal emotion, is transformed into a tangible object and then treated "as if" it were an objectified and tangible place on the model of actual physical space, such as "they're in the house."

Every language has characteristic conceptual metaphors that structure not only the language itself but also particular views of reality that speakers share and unconsciously assume. For example, in the Navajo language, the categorization of motion is a major focus of the verb system. Dozens of verbs denote specific aspects of movement and/or of objects affected by motion. Most important, many kinds of events are described with verbs having the theme of movement as their focal meaning. That is, Navajo uses metaphors of motion in "understanding and experiencing" the world. This pervasive metaphor is most clearly demonstrated by examining verbs with their Navajo meanings. In the act of dressing "one moves into clothing (*ʔé:h-há:h*)," to sing is "to move words out of an enclosed space (*ha-di-ʔà:h*)," and a youth is described as "one moves about newly (*ʔánˊ,ı:-nà há*)." (Hoijer 1951:116–117)

A special type of metaphor occurring in many languages is *personification*—the process of attributing animate or human qualities to nonliving entities or events. Here are some examples from English:

High prices are *eating up* my paycheck.

Anxiety is *killing* him.

The window *looks out* over the mountains.

These sentences are semantically inconsistent or anomalous in a literal sense, but they are transformed into culturally acceptable expressions through metaphor. In the last sentence, an inanimate object, window, is interpreted "as if" it were capable of an action, looking, which is inherently possible only for animate beings. In the other expressions, intangible processes are likewise treated as though they were concrete animate beings and therefore able to eat or kill.

Metonymy, another type of semantic transfer, is the substitution of one entity by another based on their shared occurrence in context rather than on the similarity of their attributes. It is a process of replacing one entity with another, not because one is treated "as if" it were another (metaphor), but because one is taken to "stand for" the other on the basis of some contextual relationship. Metonymic transfers highlight one aspect of an entity by decomposing the totality of the object or person and singling out one of its (or his or her) attributes. Associations between two entities may be of various kinds, including substitution of part of an object to represent the whole, the producer for the object produced, or the object used or owned by someone for the user/owner. Some examples from English are the following:

This business needs some new blood.

(part for whole: blood for person)

She likes to read Thomas Hardy.

(producer for product: author for books written by him)

Use of metonymy may stress a speaker's particular interest in an entity. Whereas metaphor adds to the meaning of words by increasing their semantic range through comparisons with other entities, metonymy narrows the semantic focus by highlighting only one aspect of an entity and ignoring its other attributes.

Metaphors of Kinship

In an analysis of extended and transferred meanings, each association of linguistic form and cultural content necessitates its own culturally based interpretation. However, certain domains tend to be extended metaphorically and/or metonymically in many languages. Kinship terminology is one such domain. *Kin terms* are frequently used to refer metaphorically to nonrelatives. In our society, in some families children call close friends of their parents by kin terms, usually *aunt* or *uncle*. For these families, it is considered impolite for a child to call an adult by her or his first name. But calling one's parents' close friend by a title and his or her last name, such as "Ms. Smith" or "Mr. Jones," appears highly formal and distant. The compromise of extending kin terms, such as "Aunt Susan" or "Uncle John," expresses informality and intimacy of a relationship without being rude. An adult is spoken about (or spoken to) "as if" she or he were a relative. For some speakers, the kin terms *brother* and *sister* are used in political, social, or religious contexts. Sisters and brothers are equals, share experiences of life, and owe each other reciprocal respect and support.

Another example of metaphoric extension of kin terms comes from the Navajo language. The morpheme for "mother" {-ma} is used to refer to the following entities: mother, the earth, agricultural fields, corn, sheep, and Changing Woman (a major Navajo deity) (Witherspoon 1975:15–16). These meanings are connected by a constellation of symbols of motherhood. In Navajo culture, the primary social and emotional bond is that between mother and child. Mother and child are linked through birth and nurturance. A mother gives life to her child and then continually safeguards that life with physical and emotional support.

The metaphor of motherhood is extended to the earth and agricultural fields because they share an essential attribute of mothers; they are fertile and bring forth life in the form of plants and foods. Metaphoric reference to corn and sheep is based on their economic importance to Navajos. Corn is their most important crop and forms the basis of traditional subsistence. Sheep are of great cultural significance, both as source of income and as measurement of personal wealth. For all these reasons, then, corn and sheep sustain Navajo people "as if" they were mothers. Finally, metaphoric use of *mother* to refer to the deity Changing Woman combines fertility and nurturing themes of motherhood. In Navajo myths, Changing Woman came into being at a time of chaos when people were not able to reproduce. The first puberty rite was conducted for her so that she could menstruate and become fertile. Afterward, she created the original Navajo clans from pieces of her skin. And she gave corn to the people, thus contributing to their daily sustenance. This myth expresses complex meanings linking Changing Woman's being, her fertility, and her actions to the birth and survival of Navajo people. Thus, she is a quintessential metaphor of motherhood.

Kinship terms (as well as other words) can be affected by multiple processes of semantic transfer, demonstrating the richness of language's creative possibilities. Meanings of the word *amma* (mother) in Kannada, a Dravidian language spoken by some 26 million people in India, are interconnected by complex processes of extension and transfer (Bean 1975). *Amma* has the focal meaning of "mother" but is extended through metaphor to refer to any adult woman and to goddesses. *Amma* is also used as a metonym in reference to smallpox. To appreciate the consistency of these meanings of *amma*, we need to understand the cultural implications of adulthood and the belief systems of Hindus.

According to Susan Bean, the word *amma* is extended to any adult woman, especially in polite speech, because in rural Indian society all adult women are assumed to be married and therefore are assumed to be mothers (ibid.:320–321). All women, therefore, are addressed "as if" they were mothers. The metaphor of "mother" is also extended to Hindu goddesses, who are either benevolent and nurturing or fierce and dangerous (ibid.:323–324). Benevolent goddesses are "like" one's mother; dangerous goddesses are spoken of "as if" they were mother in order to appease and placate them so that, by treating them respectfully, they will respond with kindness (like a mother). Finally, the word *amma* can be used in a metonymic transfer to refer to smallpox. The metonym results from a believed association between certain goddesses and smallpox (ibid.:324). Because the deities can cause and cure smallpox, they have become linguistically linked to the disease. The word *amma*, which was first extended through metaphor to "goddess," is then substituted through metonymy for "smallpox."

Metaphors of the Body

Another underlying metaphor found commonly in languages is the use of body-part terms to describe actions or states or to label inanimate objects. The latter process can entail personification, as in "leg of a table" or "arm of a chair." These items of furniture are depicted "as if" their physical structure were analogous to a human body. In English, we also use body-part imagery in more complex verbal expressions, such as:

Let's get to the *heart* of the matter.
She's willing to *face* her problem.

She *shoulders* many responsibilities.

The criminal *fingered* his accomplice.

Widespread use of corporeal metaphors probably results from the fact that human beings give central importance to their own bodies. We extend the imagery of body to inanimate objects and to descriptions of activities. It is a process of observing and experiencing the world through human eyes and, by analogy, with human form.

Many languages use body-part terms to describe activities or noncorporeal entities. In Zapotec, a language spoken in Oaxaca, Mexico, the human body provides the prototypical model for describing parts of any animate being or inanimate object (MacLaury 1989). The bodies of all animals are named from the perspective of human anatomy. For example, the front leg of a four-legged animal is called "hand" and the hind leg is called "foot." An animal is described "as if" it were a person walking on all fours (ibid.:121). In addition, human body-part names are extended metaphorically to describe inanimate objects by the following analogies:

top = head (*gɨk*)

front = belly (*là²áyn*)

upper front = face (*loō*)

lower front = foot (*ye²e*)

back = back (*tîč*)

side = side (*ko²o*)

underneath = bottom, buttocks (*gɨ-t*)

entrance, opening = mouth, lips (*ro²o*)

inside = stomach (*la²ayn*)

Note: The pitch markings on vowels follow these conventions: (´) extra high; (`) high; (¯) low; (unmarked) extra low; (ˆ) extra high-high.

Figures 4, 5, and 6 illustrate Zapotec human body-part terms and their analogous meanings related to various animate and inanimate entities. Figure 4 shows the words for human body parts, and Figure 5 shows their application to an animal. Body-part terms are applied to containers in Figure 6. The top of a box is called "head," front is "face," back is "back," inside is "stomach," and bottom is "foot."

Nearby indigenous languages belonging to the Mixtecan family also extend body-part terms, endowing them with many complex meanings (Hollenbach 1995). As in the semantic processes demonstrated in Zapotec, the words for "face" and "foot" are used for analogous parts of inanimate objects and for the space that "projects out from that part," or what Hollenbach calls "projecting space" (ibid.:171). Examples of "projecting space" for "face" include "the *front surface* of the house," "the *area in front* of the house"; examples for "foot" include "the *base* of the tree," "the *space near the foot* of the tree." In addition, words for "face" and "foot" are extended into temporal domains. That is, the spatial use of "face" to refer to "place (where)" has become the temporal "time (when)" and the spatial use of "foot" to refer to "bottom of" has become the temporal "beginning of" (ibid.:172).

The Mohawk language frequently uses the noun morpheme for "body," {-*ya²t-*}, in verbs with metaphoric meaning. Some examples are the following (Bonvillain 1989: 346–347):

I had a nightmare: it pressed, squeezed my body.
ũ-k-ya²t-ò:lalak-e²
DEF-I-body-press, squeeze-ASP
He judged it, weighed it: he cut the body in half.
wa²-t-ha-ya²t-ò:leht-e²
DEF-two-he-body-cut in half-ASP

Other metaphoric constructions in Mohawk employ specific body-part terms, such as (Bonvillain 1990):

You're crazy: Your brain is stirred, mixed.
te-se-nũ²wal-awɨ:lye-²
two-you-brains-stir, mix-ASP

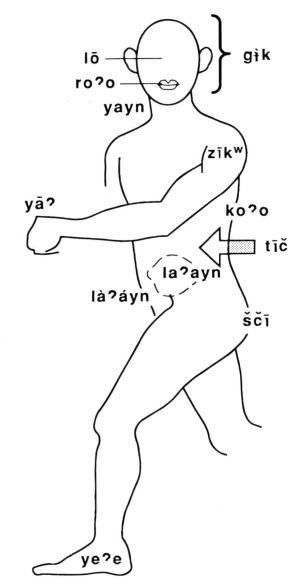

FIGURE 4 Zapotec Body Part Terms

(MacLaury, *International Journal of American Linguistics* 55 (1989) 122. Copyright © University of Chicago Press.)

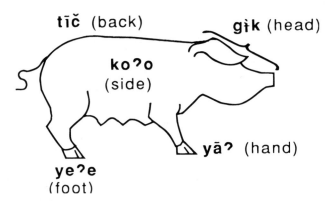

FIGURE 5 Zapotec Terms Applied to Animals

(MacLaury, *International Journal of American Linguistics* 55 (1989) 123. Copyright © University of Chicago Press.)

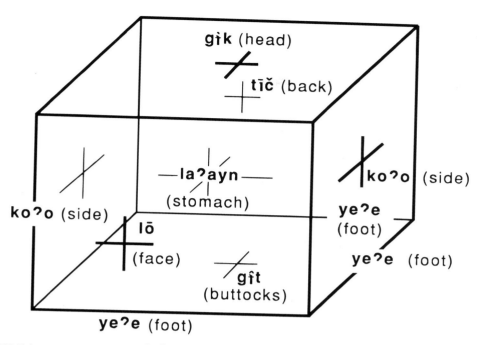

FIGURE 6 Zapotec Terms Applied to Boxes

I choked her: I broke her breath in two pieces.
   wa²-khe-hǜl-ya²k-e²
   DEF-I:her-breath-break in two-ASP
I take her advice: I stand up my inner ear to her.
   khey-at-ahǖ hsa-t-e²
   I:her-self-inner ear-stand up-ASP

Human senses frequently provide the basis for metaphoric constructs. In English, the visual sense is particularly prone to such uses, as in "I see what you mean" or "that was an insightful remark"; or in a nice combination of visual, lineal, and bodily metaphors: "I can see where this argument is heading." The term *worldview* also derives from this same underlying sensory concept.

◇ SUMMARY

Cultural models provide frameworks for understanding the physical and social worlds we live in. These models are implicitly and explicitly transmitted through language. Therefore, linguistic analyses, particularly of words and expressions, reveal underlying assumptions, interests, and values.

Several different kinds of ethnolinguistic evidence contribute to an understanding of associations between language and cultural meaning. First, degrees of specialization and principles of classification within semantic domains indicate cultural interest and discrimination. Second, focal meanings of words and prototypes of categories demonstrate the ways that people make sense of the multitude of objects and events in their world. Third, the symbolic content of language, expressed in words and in metaphoric extensions, transmits and reinforces complex social and cultural messages. Finally, patterns of discourse in communicative interactions reflect cultural assumptions about appropriate use of language in context, about the rights and powers of participants, and about the meaning of communication itself.

✛ REFERENCES

Bean, Susan. 1975. Referential and indexical meanings of *amma* in Kannada: Mother, woman, goddess, pox and help! *Journal of Anthropological Research* 31:313–330.

Berlin, Brent, and Paul kay. 1969. *Basic Color Terms: Their Universality and Evolution.* Berkeley: University of California Press.

Berlin, Brent, Dennis Beedlove, and Peter Raven. 1974. Principles of Tzeltal Plant Classification. New York: Academic Press.

Bloomfield, Leonard. 1946. Algonquian. In *Linguistic Structures of Native America,* ed. H. Hoijer. Publications in Anthropology No. 6. New York: Viking Fund, pp. 85–129.

Bonvillain, Nancy. 1989. Body, mind and idea: Semantics of noun incorporation in Akwesasne Mohawk. *International Journal of American Linguistics* 55:341–358.

Bonvillain, Nancy. 1990. Noun incorporation and metaphor: Semantic process in Akwesasne Mohawk. *Anthropological Linguistics* 32:173–194.

Boroditsky, Lera. 2001. Does language shape thought? Mandarin and English speakers' conceptions of time. *Cognitive Psychology* 43:1–22.

Bowerman, Melissa. 1996. Learning how to structure space for language: A crosslinguistic perspective. In *Language and Space,* ed. P. Bloom, M. Petersen, L. Nadel, and M. Garrett. Cambridge, MA: MIT Press, pp. 385–436.

Brown, Penelope. 1994. The ins and ons of Tzeltal locative expressions: The semantics of static description of location. *Linguistics* 32:743–790.

Fillmore, Charles. 1982. Towards a descriptive framework for spatial deixis. In *Speech, Place and Action,* ed. R. J. Jarvella and W. Klein. New York: Wiley, pp. 31–59.

Goodenough, Ward. 1956. Componential analysis and the study of meaning. *Language* 32:195–216.

Goodenough, Ward. 1965. Yankee kinship terminology: A problem in componential analysis. In *Formal Semantic Analysis,* ed. E. Hammel. *American Anthropologist* 67:259–287.

Gumperz, John. 1996. The linguistic and cultural relativity of conversational inference. In *Rethinking Linguistic Relativity,* ed. J. Gumperz and S. Levinson. New York: Cambridge University Press, pp. 374–406.

Hallowell, A. Irving. 1960. Ojibwa ontology, behavior and world view. In *Culture in History: Essays in Honor of Paul Radin,* ed. S. Diamond. New York: Columbia University Press, pp. 19–52.

Hoijer, Harry. 1951. Cultural implications of some Navaho linguistic categories. *Language* 27: 111–120.

Hollenbach, Barbara. 1995. Semantic and syntactic extensions of body-part terms in Mixtecan. *International Journal of American Linguistics* 61, no. 2:168–190.

Jackendoff, Ray. 1996. The architecture of the linguistic-spatial interface. In *Language and Space,* ed. P. Bloom, M. Petersen, L. Nadel, and M. Garrett. Cambridge, MA: MIT Press, 1–30.

Kaa, Mo. 1976. The logic of non-European linguistic categories. In *Universalism versus Relativism in Language and Thought: Proceedings of a Colloquium on the Sapir-Whorf Hypothesis,* ed. R. Pinxten. The Hague: Mouton, pp. 85–96.

Kay, Paul. 1975. Synchronic variability and diachronic change in basic color terms. *Language in Society* 4:257–270.

Kay, Paul, and Chad McDaniel. 1978. The linguistic significance of the meanings of basic color terms. *Language* 54:610–646.

Labov, William. 1973. The boundaries of words and their meanings. In *New Ways of Analyzing Variation in English,* ed. C. Bailey and R. Shuy. Washington, DC: Georgetown University Press, pp. 340–373.

Lakoff, George. 1972. Hedges: A study in meaning criteria and the logic of fuzzy concepts. *Papers from the 8th Regional Meeting of the Chicago Linguistic Society.* Chicago, IL: Chicago Linguistic Society, pp. 183–228.

Lakoff, George, and Mark Johnson. 1980. *Metaphors We Live By.* Chicago, IL: University of Chicago Press.

Levinson, Stephen. 1996. Relativity in spatial conception and description. In *Rethinking Linguistic Relativity,* ed. J. Gumperz and S. Levinson. New York: Cambridge University Press, pp. 177–202.

Lounsbury, Floyd. 1964. The structural analysis of kinship semantics. In *Proceedings of the IXth International Congress of Linguists,* ed. H. Lunt. The Hague: Mouton, pp. 1073–1093.

Lucy, John. 1996. The scope of linguistic relativity: An analysis and review of empirical research. In *Rethinking Linguistic Relativity,* ed. J. Gumperz and S. Levinson. New York: Cambridge University Press, pp. 37–70.

Lucy, John. 1998. Space in language and thought: Commentary and discussion. *Ethos* 26, no. 1:105–111.

MacLaury, Robert. 1989. Zapotec body-part locatives: Prototypes and metaphoric extensions. *International Journal of American Linguistics* 55:119–154.

Nicolle, Steve. 2001. A comparative study of ethnobotanical taxonomies: Swahili and Digo. *SIL (Summer Institute of Linguistics), Notes on Anthropology,* vol. 5, pp. 33–43.

Peterson, Mary, Lynn Nadel, Paul Bloom, and Merrill Garrett. 1996. Space and language. In *Language and Space,* ed. P. Bloom, M. Petersen, L. Nadel, and M. Garrett. Cambridge, MA: MIT Press, pp. 553–577.

Quinn, Naomi, and Dorothy Holland. 1987. Culture and cognition. In *Cultural Models of Language and Thought,* ed. D. Holland and N. Quinn. New York: Cambridge University Press, pp. 3–40.

Sapir, Edward. 1949a (1912). Language and environment. In *Selected Writings of Edward Sapir,* ed. D. Mandelbaum. Berkeley: University of California Press, pp. 89–103.

Sapir, Edward. 1949b (1929). The status of linguistics as a science. In *Selected Writings of Edward Sapir,* ed. D. Mandelbaum. Berkeley: University of California Press, pp. 160–166.

Volosinov, V. N. 1973 (1929). *Marxism and the Philosophy of Language.* Cambridge, MA: Harvard University Press.

Whorf, Benjamin. 1956a (1941). A linguistic consideration of thinking in primitive communities. In *Language, Thought and Reality,* ed. J. B. Carroll. Cambridge, MA: MIT Press, pp. 65–86.

Whorf, Benjamin. 1956b (1941). The relation of habitual thought and behavior to language. In *Language, Thought and Reality,* ed. J. B. Carroll. Cambridge, MA: MIT Press, pp. 134–159.

Witherspoon, Gary. 1975. *Navajo Kinship and Marriage.* Chicago, IL: University of Chicago Press.

Witkowski, Stanley, and Cecil Brown. 1983. Marking-reversals and cultural importance. *Language* 59: 569–582.

Young, Robert. 1978. English as a second language for Navajos. In *A Pluralistic Nation,* ed. M. Lourie and N. Conklin. Rowley, MA: Newbury House, pp. 162–172.

Name: _____ Date: _____

MODULE 6-B

ACTIVITY

◇ **NONVERBAL COMMUNICATION**

Is it possible to be in the same room as another person and not communicate? Even if we do not speak, we communicate through our facial expressions and gestures. Even if we do not move, we communicate through our posture, use of space, and appearance. Nonverbal behaviors serve several functions including repeating, complementing, or accenting a verbal message, contradicting verbal cues, substituting for a verbal message, and regulating the flow of conversation (Ekman & Friesen, 1969). The ability to comprehend nonverbal communication seems to be an important component of intercultural competence (Molinsky, Krabberhoft, Ambady, & Choi, 2005).

Some aspects of nonverbal behavior appear to be universal. For example, Caroline Keating and E. Gregory Keating (cited in Keating, 1994) found that in a variety of cultures tested, interpersonal distances (called *proxemics*) were closer between people who were acquainted than among strangers. In addition, the experience of crowding appears to be equally stressful across ethnic groups studied (Evans, 2000). On the other hand, there are also significant cultural differences in nonverbal behavior. Although it may be universal that acquaintances prefer smaller interpersonal distances than strangers and that people find overcrowding stressful, the preferred distance between people varies quite dramatically across cultures. According to Edward T. Hall (1966), members of low contact cultures, such as Japan, tend to prefer significantly larger interpersonal distances than Americans and Canadians, who in turn prefer larger interpersonal distances than people in high contact cultures such as many Arabs, Greeks, and Southern Italians. Individuals dealing with someone from a lower contact culture than themselves may feel rejected. Individuals dealing with someone from a higher contact culture than themselves may feel intruded upon.

Often when we think of nonverbal communication, we think of gestures that correspond to specific meanings (called *emblems*). Although the existence of emblems appears to be universal, as any traveler knows there are many cross-cultural differences in meaning. For example, the ring gesture, made by touching one's index finger to one's thumb, is used in different parts of the world with such diverse meanings as okay, a body orifice, zero or nothing, money, and Thursday (Morris, Collett, Marsh, & O'Shaughnessy, 1979). The purpose of this activity is to better understand the function of nonverbal communication and the ways it differs from verbal communication.

Taken from *Cross-Cultural Explorations: Activities in Culture and Psychology*, Second Edition, by Susan Goldstein.

Directions: In the space provided below, list all of the words or meanings that you know how to express nonverbally. Then answer the questions that follow.

1. Think about the nonverbal expressions you listed above. How is nonverbal communication similar to verbal communication?

2. How is nonverbal communication different from verbal communication?

3. Do you think the potential for intercultural misunderstanding is greater in verbal or nonverbal communication? Please explain.

4. How would you go about learning the nonverbal behavior of another culture?

5. Look back to your list of nonverbal expressions. In the space provided below, write/draw a dictionary entry for one of these expressions. It may be helpful to refer to a print dictionary for ideas about the format and content of your entry.

◇ REFERENCES

Ekman, P. & Friesen, W. (1969). The repertoire of nonverbal behavior: Categories, origins, usage, and coding. *Semiotica, 1*, 49-98.

Evans, G. W. (2000). Cross-cultural differences in tolerance for crowding: Fact or fiction? *Journal of Personality and Social Psychology, 79*, 204-210.

Hall, E. T. (1966). *The silent language.* Garden City, NY: Doubleday.

Keating, C. F. (1994). World without words: Messages from face and body. In W. J. Lonner, & R. S. Malpass (Eds.), *Psychology and culture* (pp. 175-182). Boston: Allyn & Bacon.

Molinsky, A. L., Krabberhoft, M. A. Ambady, N., & Choi, S. Y. (2005). Cracking the nonverbal code: Intercultural competence and gesture recognition across cultures. *Journal of Cross-Cultural Psychology, 36*, 380-395.

Morris, D., Collett, P., Marsh, P., & O'Shaughnessy, M. (1979), *Gestures.* New York: Stein and Day.

SECTION 7

COGNITIVE DEVELOPMENT AND INTELLIGENCE

MODULE 7-A

COGNITIVE GROWTH:
PIAGET AND VYGOTSKY

(Michael Ventura/Alamy)

LEARNING OBJECTIVES

Part 1

L01 What is cognitive development, and how did Piaget revolutionize its study?

L02 What theoretical elements underlie Piaget's theory?

Part 2

L03 What are the key features—and criticisms—of Piaget's theory?

L04 What are some alternate approaches to Piaget's view of cognitive development?

Part 3

L05 What are the key features—and criticisms—of Vygotsky's theory?

Taken from *Life Span Development: A Topical Approach,* Second Edition, by Robert S. Feldman, Ph.D.

Preview (Continued)

Developmental Diversity and your life:

A Walk Through a Cultural Landscape

Review and Apply

PROLOGUE: BABY-TALK

Amelie Hawkins raises her eyebrows and grins broadly, leaning into her three-month-old daughter while shaking a baby rattle and cooing in a sing-song voice, "Oooo, you like that! Yes you do! Yes you do-oo-oo! Rattle! That's a rattle!" Amelie's daughter giggles and grins, flapping her arms and kicking her legs, but that's as coherent as it gets. For now.

"I know she can't understand me, but she hears the sounds. She's learning. I can see it in her eyes. She's taking it in. She doesn't know what any of it means yet," Amelie laughs, pausing thoughtfully. "But she's aware. One day she'll say something back—that will be a very exciting day!"

Children experience cognitive advances that develop at breathtaking speed throughout childhood. (StockLite/Shutterstock)

LOOKING AHEAD

How much of the world do infants understand? How do social interactions influence cognitive development? In this module we consider cognitive development during childhood and adolescence in general from two important theoretical perspectives. After reviewing the basics of cognitive development, we examine in detail the work of Swiss psychologist Jean Piaget, whose stage theory of development has served as a highly influential impetus for a considerable amount of work on cognitive development. We'll look at the foundations of Piaget's theory in the use of schemes and in the processes of assimilation and accommodation, and we will trace cognitive development through the four stages that Piaget identified and defined through his observations of children and adolescents.

Next we will evaluate Piaget's theory, considering both its enormous contributions to developmental research and the many criticisms of his approach that have been voiced by researchers in the field.

Finally, we will conclude the module with a discussion of the work of Lev Vygotsky, a Russian psychologist. Vygotsky's views on the importance of culture to cognitive development have become increasingly influential, particularly in his focus on the social and cultural aspects of development and learning. Our discussions of Piaget and Vygotsky pave the way for consideration of the information processing approaches to cognitive development to which we turn in the next module.

PART 1   PIAGET'S APPROACH TO COGNITIVE DEVELOPMENT

LEARNING OBJECTIVES

LO 1   What is cognitive development, and how did Piaget revolutionize its study?
LO 2   What theoretical elements underlie Piaget's theory?

◇ PIAGET: THE MASTER OBSERVER OF CHILDREN

Action = Knowledge.

If a simple equation could summarize a comprehensive theory of cognitive development, this one might encapsulate the ideas of Swiss psychologist Jean Piaget (1896–1980) about how we begin to understand the world. Unlike previous theorists, Piaget argued that infants do not acquire knowledge from facts communicated by others, nor through sensation and perception. Instead, Piaget suggested that knowledge is the product of direct motor behavior. Although many of his basic explanations and propositions have been challenged by subsequent research, as we'll discuss later, the view that in significant ways infants learn by doing remains unquestioned (Piaget, 1952, 1962, 1983; Bullinger, 1997).

Piaget's background and training influenced both the development of his theory and the methods he used to investigate it. Piaget was educated as a biologist and philosopher, and he received a Ph.D. in zoology. His initial work was aimed at producing an account of how knowledge was related to biology, which ultimately led to a theory of how children's understanding of the world develops. In doing research, Piaget relied on methods that are common among investigations of nonhuman species. For instance, his studies would often intensively focus on only a few children, including his own offspring. Furthermore, he frequently would observe children in their "natural habitat," such as while they were playing games. His goal was to understand *how* children think, rather than characterizing whether their thinking was right or wrong at a given age.

Key Elements of Piaget's Theory

Piaget's theory is *based on a stage approach to development. He assumed that all children pass through a series* of four universal stages in a fixed order from birth through adolescence: sensorimotor, preoperational, concrete operational, and formal operational. He also suggested that movement from one stage to the next occurs when a child reaches an appropriate level of physical maturation and is exposed to relevant experiences. Without such experience, Piaget assumed that children were incapable of reaching their cognitive potential. Some approaches to cognition focus on changes in the content of children's knowledge about the world, but Piaget argued that it was critical to also consider the changes in the quality of children's knowledge and understanding as they move from one stage to another.

For instance, as they develop cognitively, infants experience changes in their understanding about what can and cannot occur in the world. Consider a baby who participates in an experiment during which she is exposed to three identical versions of her mother all at the same time, thanks to some well-placed mirrors. A three-month-old infant will interact happily with each of these images of mother. However, by five months of age, the child becomes quite agitated at the sight of multiple mothers. Apparently by this time the child has figured out that she has but one mother, and viewing three at a time is thoroughly alarming (Bower, 1977). To Piaget, such reactions indicate that a baby is beginning to master principles regarding the way the world operates, indicating that she has begun to construct a mental sense of the world that she didn't have two months earlier.

Piaget believed that the basic building blocks of the way we understand the world are mental structures called **schemes**, organized patterns of functioning, that adapt and change with mental development. At first, schemes are related to physical, or sensorimotor, activity, such as picking up or reaching for toys. As children develop, their schemes move to a mental level, reflecting thought. Schemes are similar to computer software: They direct and determine how data from the world, such as new events or objects, are considered and dealt with (Rakison & Oakes, 2003; Rakison & Krogh, 2012).

If you give a baby a new cloth book, for example, he or she will touch it, mouth it, perhaps try to tear it or bang it on the floor. To Piaget, each of these actions represents a scheme, and they are the infant's way of gaining knowledge and understanding of this new object.

Piaget suggested that two principles underlie the growth in children's schemes: assimilation and accommodation. **Assimilation** is the process by which people understand an experience in terms of their current stage of cognitive development and way of thinking. Assimilation occurs, then, when a stimulus or an event is acted upon, perceived, and understood in accordance with existing patterns of thought. For example, an infant who tries to suck on any toy in the same way is assimilating the objects to her existing sucking scheme. Similarly, a child who encounters a flying squirrel at a zoo and calls it a "bird" is assimilating the squirrel to his existing scheme of bird.

In contrast, **accommodation** refers to changes in existing ways of thinking, understanding, or behaving in response to encounters with new stimuli or events. For instance, when a child sees a flying squirrel and calls it "a bird with a tail," he is beginning to accommodate new knowledge, modifying his scheme of bird.

Piaget believed that the earliest schemes are primarily limited to the reflexes with which we are all born, such as sucking and rooting. Infants start to modify these simple early schemes almost immediately, through the processes of assimilation and accommodation, in response to their exploration of the environment. Schemes quickly become more sophisticated as infants become more advanced in their motor capabilities—to Piaget, a signal of the potential for more advanced cognitive development.

Swiss psychologist Jean Piaget. (Bill Anderson/Photo Researchers, Inc.)

scheme
an organized pattern of sensorimotor functioning

assimilation
the process in which people understand an experience in terms of their current stage of cognitive development and way of thinking

accommodation
changes in existing ways of thinking that occur in response to encounters with new stimuli or events

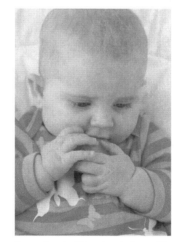

According to Piaget, a baby will use a sensorimotor scheme, such as mouthing or banging, to understand a new object. (Vanessa Davies/Dorling Kindersley, Ltd.)

◈ COGNITIVE DEVELOPMENT IN INFANCY

Olivia's dad is wiping up the mess around the base of her high chair—for the third time today! It seems to him that fourteen-month-old Olivia takes great delight in dropping food from the high chair. She also drops toys, spoons, anything it seems, just to watch how it hits the floor. She almost appears to be experimenting to see what kind of noise or what size of splatter is created by each different thing she drops.

Piaget probably would have said that Olivia's dad is right in theorizing that Olivia is conducting her own series of experiments to learn more about the workings of her world. As we noted at the beginning of this module, Piaget's views of the ways infants learn can be summed up in a simple equation: Action = Knowledge.

Piaget argued that infants acquire knowledge through direct motor behavior. Although many of his basic explanations and propositions have been challenged by subsequent research, the view that in significant ways infants learn by doing remains unquestioned (Piaget, 1952, 1962, 1983; Bullinger, 1997).

Piaget's theory, as noted earlier, is based on a stage approach to development, with children and adolescents passing through four universal stages in a predetermined sequence: sensorimotor, preoperational, concrete operational, and formal operational.

sensorimotor stage (of cognitive development)
Piaget's initial major stage of cognitive development, which can be broken down into six substages

The Sensorimotor Period: The Earliest Stage of Cognitive Growth (Birth to 2 Years)

Piaget suggests that the **sensorimotor stage**, the initial major stage of cognitive development, can be broken down into six substages. These are summarized in Table 1. It is important to keep in mind

TABLE 1 Piaget's Six Substages of the Sensorimotor Stage

SUBSTAGE	AGE	DESCRIPTION	EXAMPLE
Substage 1: Simple reflexes	First month of life	During this period, the various reflexes that determine the infant's interactions with the world are at the center of the infant's cognitive life.	The sucking reflex causes the infant to suck at anything placed in his lips.
Substage 2: First habits and primary circular reactions	From 1 to 4 months	At this age infants begin to coordinate what were separate actions into single, integrated activities.	An infant might combine grasping an object with sucking on it, or staring at something with touching it.
Substage 3: Secondary circular reactions	From 4 to 8 months	During this period, infants take major strides in shifting their cognitive horizons beyond themselves and begin to act on the outside world.	A child who repeatedly picks up a rattle in her crib and shakes it in different ways to see how the sound changes is demonstrating her ability to modify her cognitive scheme about shaking rattles.
Substage 4: Coordination of secondary circular reactions	From 8 to 12 months	In this stage infants begin to use more calculated approaches to producing events, coordinating several schemes to generate a single act. They achieve object performance during this stage.	An infant will push one toy out of the way to reach another toy that is lying, partially exposed, under it.
Substage 5: Tertiary circular reactions	From 12 to 18 months	At this age infants develop what Piaget regards as the deliberate variation of actions that bring desirable consequences. Rather than just repeating enjoyable activities, infants appear to carry out miniature experiments to observe the consequences.	A child will drop a toy repeatedly, varying the position from which he drops it, carefully observing each time to see where it falls.
Substage 6: Beginnings of thought	From 18 months to 2 years	The major achievement of Substage 6 is the capacity for mental representation or symbolic thought. Piaget argued that only at this stage can infants imagine where objects that they cannot see might be.	Children can even plot in their heads unseen trajectories of objects, so that if a ball rolls under a piece of furniture, they can figure out where it is likely to emerge on the other side.

that although the specific substages of the sensorimotor period may at first appear to unfold with great regularity, as though infants reach a particular age and smoothly proceed into the next substage, the reality of cognitive development is somewhat different. First, the ages at which infants actually reach a particular stage vary a good deal among different children. The exact timing of a stage reflects an interaction between the infant's level of physical maturation and the nature of the social environment in which the child is being raised.

Piaget viewed development as a more gradual process than the notion of different stages might seem to imply. Infants do not go to sleep one night in one substage and wake up the next morning in the next one. Instead, there is a rather steady shifting of behavior as a child moves toward the next stage of cognitive development. Infants also pass through periods of transition, in which some aspects of their behavior reflect the next higher stage, while other aspects indicate their current stage (see Figure 1).

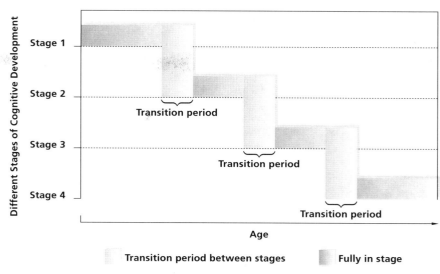

FIGURE 1 Transitions

Infants do not suddenly shift from one stage of cognitive development to the next. Instead, Piaget argues that there is a period of transition in which some behavior reflects one stage, while another behavior reflects the more advanced stage. Does this gradualism argue against Piaget's interpretation of stages?

Substage 1: Simple Reflexes (First Month)

The first substage of the sensorimotor period is Substage 1: Simple reflexes, encompassing the first month of life. During this time, various inborn reflexes are at the center of infants' physical and cognitive lives, determining the nature of their interactions with the world. At the same time, some of the reflexes begin to accommodate the infant's experience with the nature of the world. For instance, an infant who is being breast-fed, but who also receives supplemental bottles, may start to change the way he or she sucks, depending on whether a nipple is on a breast or a bottle.

Substage 2: First Habits and Primary Circular Reactions (1 to 4 Months)

goal-directed behavior behavior in which several schemes are combined and coordinated to generate a single act to solve a problem

The first habits and primary circular reactions substage occurs from one to four months of age. In this period, infants begin to coordinate what were separate actions into single, integrated activities. For instance, an infant might combine grasping an object with sucking on it, or staring at something while touching it.

If an activity engages a baby's interests, he or she may repeat it over and over, simply for the sake of continuing to experience it. This repetition of a chance motor event helps the baby start building cognitive schemes through a process known as a circular reaction. Primary circular reactions are schemes reflecting an infant's repetition of interesting or enjoyable actions, just for the enjoyment of doing them, which focus on the infant's own body.

Substage 3: Secondary Circular Reactions (4 to 8 Months)

Secondary circular reactions are more purposeful. According to Piaget, this third stage of cognitive development in infancy occurs from four to eight months of age. During this period, a child begins to act upon the outside world. For instance, infants now seek to repeat enjoyable events in their environments if they happen to produce them through chance activities. A child who repeatedly picks up a rattle in her crib and shakes it in different ways to see how the sound changes is demonstrating her ability to modify her cognitive scheme about shaking rattles. She is engaging in what Piaget calls secondary circular reactions, which are schemes regarding repeated actions that bring about a desirable consequence.

Infants in Substage 4 can coordinate their secondary circular reactions, displaying an ability to plan or calculate how to produce a desired outcome.
(Dave King/Dorling Kindersley, Ltd.)

object permanence
the realization that people and objects exist even when they cannot be seen

From A CAREGIVER'S Perspective:
In general, what are some implications for childrearing practices of Piaget's observations about the ways children gain an understanding of the world? Would you use the same approaches in childrearing for a child growing up in a non-Western culture? Why or why not?

👁️─Watch a video of an infant demonstrating the principle of object permanence in www.pearsoncustom.com/mi/msu_mylab

Substage 4: Coordination of Secondary Circular Reactions (8 to 12 Months)

Some major leaps forward occur in Substage 4: coordination of secondary circular reactions, which lasts from around 8 months to 12 months. In Substage 4, infants begin to employ **goal-directed behavior**, in which several schemes are combined and coordinated to generate a single act to solve a problem. For instance, they will push one toy out of the way to reach another toy that is lying, partially exposed, under it.

Infants' newfound purposefulness, their ability to use means to attain particular ends, and their skill in anticipating future circumstances owe their appearance in part to the developmental achievement of object permanence that emerges in Substage 4. **Object permanence** is the realization that people and objects exist even when they cannot be seen. It is a simple principle, but its mastery has profound consequences.

Consider, for instance, seven-month-old Chu, who has yet to learn the idea of object permanence. Chu's mother shakes a rattle in front of him, then takes the rattle and places it under a blanket. To Chu, who has not mastered the concept of object permanence, the rattle no longer exists. He will make no effort to look for it.

Several months later, when he reaches Substage 4, the story is quite different (see Figure 2). This time, as soon as his mother places the rattle under the blanket, Chu tries to toss the cover aside, eagerly searching for the rattle. Chu clearly has learned that the object continues to exist even when it cannot be seen. For the infant who achieves an understanding of object permanence, then, out of sight is decidedly not out of mind.

The attainment of object permanence extends not only to inanimate objects, but to people, too. It gives Chu the security that his father and mother still exist even when they have left the room. 👁️

Substage 5: Tertiary Circular Reactions (12 to 18 Months)

Substage 5: Tertiary circular reactions is reached at around the age of 12 months and extends to 18 months. As the name of the stage indicates, during this period infants develop these reactions, which are schemes regarding the deliberate variation of actions that bring desirable consequences. Rather than just repeating enjoyable activities, as they do with secondary circular reactions, infants appear to carry out miniature experiments to observe the consequences.

For example, Piaget observed his son Laurent dropping a toy swan repeatedly, varying the position from which he dropped it, carefully observing each time to see where it fell. Instead of just repeating the action each time, Laurent made modifications in the situation to learn about their consequences. As you may recall from our discussion of research methods, this behavior represents

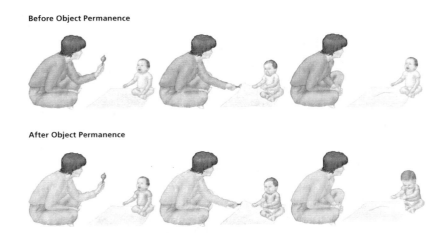

Before Object Permanence

After Object Permanence

FIGURE 2 Object Permanence

Before an infant has understood the idea of object permanence, he will not search for an object that has been hidden right before his eyes. But several months later, he will search for it, illustrating that he has attained the concept of object permanence. Why would the concept of object permanence be important to a caregiver?

the essence of the scientific method: An experimenter varies a situation in a laboratory to learn the effects of the variation.

What is most striking about infants' behavior during Substage 5 is their interest in the unexpected. Unanticipated events are treated not only as interesting, but also as something to be explained and understood. Infants' discoveries can lead to newfound skills, some of which may cause a certain amount of chaos. For instance, an infant may pull at a tablecloth in order to reach a plate of cookies or throw a water toy into the tub with increasing vigor to see how high the water splashes.

mental representation
an internal image of a past event or object

deferred imitation
an act in which a person who is no longer present is imitated by children who have witnessed a similar act

Substage 6: Beginnings of Thought (18 Months to 2 Years)

The final stage of the sensorimotor period is Substage 6: beginnings of thought, which lasts from around 18 months to 2 years. The major achievement of Substage 6 is the capacity for mental representation, or symbolic thought. A **mental representation** is an internal image of a past event or object. Piaget argued that by this stage infants can imagine where objects might be that they cannot see. They can even plot in their heads unseen trajectories of objects, so if a ball rolls under a piece of furniture, they can figure out where it is likely to emerge on the other side.

Because of children's new abilities to create internal representations of objects, their understanding of causality also becomes more sophisticated. For instance, consider Piaget's description of his son Laurent's efforts to open a garden gate:

> Laurent tries to open a garden gate but cannot push it forward because it is held back by a piece of furniture. He cannot account either visually or by any sound for the cause that prevents the gate from opening, but after having tried to force it he suddenly seems to understand; he goes around the wall, arrives at the other side of the gate, moves the armchair which holds it firm, and opens it with a triumphant expression. (Piaget, 1954, p. 296)

Infants begin to use goal-directed behavior in Substage 4 of the sensorimotor stage. (Aphichart/Shutterstock)

The attainment of mental representation also permits another important development: the ability to pretend. Using the skill of what Piaget refers to as **deferred imitation**, in which a person who is no longer present is imitated later, children are able to pretend that they are driving a car, feeding a doll, or cooking dinner long after they have witnessed such scenes played out in reality.

◇ COGNITIVE DEVELOPMENT IN THE PRESCHOOL YEARS

> *Three-year-old Sam was talking to himself in two very different voices. "Find your shoes," he said in a low voice. "Not today. I'm not going. I hate the shoes," he said in a higher-pitched voice. The lower voice answered, "You are a bad boy. Find the shoes, bad boy." The higher-voiced response was "No, no, no."*
>
> *Sam's parents realized that he was playing a game with his imaginary friend, Gill—a bad boy who often disobeyed his mother. In fact, according to Sam's musings, Gill often was guilty of the very same misdeeds for which his parents blamed Sam.*

Piaget saw the preschool years as a time of both stability and change. He placed the preschool years into a single stage of cognitive development—the preoperational stage—which lasts from two until around seven.

preoperational stage
according to Piaget, the stage from approximately age two to age seven in which children's use of symbolic thinking grows, mental reasoning emerges, and the use of concepts increases

Piaget's Stage of Preoperational Thinking (Ages Two to Seven)

During the **preoperational stage**, children's use of symbolic thinking grows, mental reasoning emerges, and the use of concepts increases. Seeing Mom's car keys may prompt a question, "Go to store?" as the child comes to see the keys as a symbol of a car ride. In this way, children become better at representing events internally and less dependent on sensorimotor activity to understand the world around them. Yet they are still not capable of **operations**: organized, formal, logical mental processes.

According to Piaget, a key aspect of preoperational thought is **symbolic function**, the ability to use a mental symbol, a word, or an object to stand for or represent something that is not physically present. For example, preschoolers can use a mental symbol for a car (the word "car"), and they understand that a small toy car is representative of the real thing. They have no need to get behind the wheel of an actual car to understand its basic purpose and use.

operations
organized, formal, logical mental processes

symbolic function
the ability to use a mental symbol, a word, or an object to stand for or represent something that is not physically present

The Relation between Language and Thought

Symbolic function is at the heart of one of the major advances of the preoperational period: the increasingly sophisticated use of language. Piaget suggests that the advances in language during the preschool years reflect improvements over the type of thinking that is possible during the earlier sensorimotor period. Instead of slow sensorimotor-based thinking, symbolic thought, which relies on improved linguistic ability, allows preschoolers to represent actions virtually, at much greater speed.

Even more important, language allows children to think beyond the present to the future. Rather than being grounded in the here-and-now, preschoolers can imagine future possibilities through language in the form of fantasies and daydreams.

Centration: What You See Is What You Think

Place a dog mask on a cat and what do you get? According to three- and four-year-old preschoolers, a dog. To them, a cat with a dog mask ought to bark like a dog, wag its tail like a dog, and eat dog food. In every respect, the cat has been transformed into a dog (deVries, 1969).

centration

the process of concentrating on one limited aspect of a stimulus and ignoring other aspects

To Piaget, the root of this belief is **centration**, a key element, and limitation, of thinking in the preoperational period. Centration is the process of concentrating on one limited aspect of a stimulus—typically its superficial elements—and ignoring others. These elements come to dominate preschoolers' thinking, leading to inaccuracy.

Centration is the cause of the error illustrated in Figure 3. Asked which row contains more buttons, children who are four or five usually choose the row that looks longer rather than the one that actually contains more buttons. This occurs even though children of this age know quite well that 10 is more than 8. Rather than taking into account their understanding of quantity, they focus on appearance.

Preschoolers' focus on appearances might be related to another aspect of preoperational thought, the lack of conservation.

Conservation: Learning That Appearances Are Deceiving

Consider the following scenario:

> Four-year-old Jaime is shown two drinking glasses. One is short and broad; the other, tall and thin. A teacher half-fills the short, broad glass with apple juice. The teacher then pours the juice into the tall, thin glass. The juice fills the tall glass almost to the brim. The teacher asks Jaime a question: Is there more juice in the second glass than there was in the first?

If you view this as an easy task, so do children like Jaime. The problem is that they almost always get it wrong.

Most four-year-olds say that there is more apple juice in the tall, thin glass than there was in the short, broad one. In fact, if the juice is poured back into the shorter glass, they are quick to say that there is now less juice than there was in the taller.

The reason is that children of this age have not mastered conservation. **Conservation** is the knowledge that quantity is unrelated to the arrangement and physical appearance of objects. Some other conservation tasks are shown in Figure 4.

FIGURE 4 Which Glass Contains More?

Most four-year-old children believe that the amount of liquid in the two glasses differs because of the differences in the containers' shapes, even though they may have seen equal amounts of liquid being poured into each.
(Tony Freeman/PhotoEdit, Inc.)

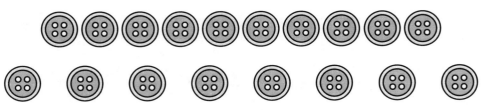

FIGURE 3 Which Row Contains More Buttons?
When preschoolers are shown these two rows and asked which row has more buttons, they usually respond that the lower row of buttons contains more because it looks longer. They answer in this way even though they know quite well that 10 is greater than 8. Do you think preschoolers can be taught to answer correctly?

Why do children in the preoperational stage make conservation errors? Piaget suggests that the main reason is that their tendency toward centration prevents them from focusing on the relevant features of the situation. Furthermore, they cannot follow the sequence of transformations that accompanies changes in the appearance of a situation.

Incomplete Understanding of Transformation

A preoperational, preschool child who sees several worms during a walk in the woods may believe that they are all the same worm. The reason: She views each sighting in isolation, unable to understand that a transformation would be necessary for a worm to move quickly from one location to the next.

As Piaget used the term, **transformation** is the process in which one state is changed into another. For instance, adults know that if a pencil that is held upright is allowed to fall down, it passes through a series of successive stages until it reaches its final, horizontal resting spot. In contrast, children in the preoperational period are unable to envision or recall the successive transformations that the pencil followed in moving from the upright to the horizontal position.

Egocentrism: The Inability to Take Others' Perspectives

Another hallmark of the preoperational period is egocentric thinking. **Egocentric thought** is thinking that does not take into account the viewpoints of others. Preschoolers do not understand that others have different perspectives. Egocentric thought takes two forms: lack of awareness that others see things from a different physical perspective; and failure to realize that others may hold thoughts, feelings, and points of view that differ from theirs. (Note what egocentric thought does *not* imply: that preoperational children intentionally think in a selfish or inconsiderate manner.)

Egocentric thinking lies behind children's lack of concern over their nonverbal behavior and the impact it has on others. For instance, a four-year-old who receives a gift of socks may frown as he opens the package, unaware that his face can be seen by others and reveals his true feelings (Feldman, 1992; Nilsen & Graham, 2009).

Egocentrism largely explains why many preschoolers talk to themselves, even in the presence of others, and often ignore what others are telling them. This behavior illustrates the egocentric nature of preoperational children's thinking: the lack of awareness that their behavior acts as a trigger to others' reactions and responses. Consequently, much of preschoolers' verbal behavior has no social motivation but is meant purely for their own consumption.

Egocentrism can also be seen in hiding games. In hide-and-seek, three-year-olds may "hide" by covering their faces with a pillow—even though they remain in plain view. Their reasoning: If they cannot see others, others cannot see them. They assume that everyone else shares their view.

The Emergence of Intuitive Thought

Because Piaget labeled this the "preoperational period" and focused on cognitive deficiencies, it is easy to assume that preschoolers are marking time, but during this period they are far from idle. Cognitive development proceeds steadily, and new abilities emerge, including intuitive thought.

Intuitive thought refers to preschoolers' use of primitive reasoning and their avid acquisition of world knowledge. From about age four through seven, curiosity blossoms. Children ask "Why?" questions about nearly everything. At the same time, they may act as if they are authorities on particular topics, certain that they have the final word on an issue. Their intuitive thought leads them to believe that they know answers to all kinds of questions, with little or no logical basis for this confidence.

In the late stages of the preoperational period, children's intuitive thinking prepares them for more sophisticated reasoning. For instance, preschoolers come to understand that pushing harder on the pedals makes a bicycle move faster, or that pressing a button on a remote control makes the television change channels. By the end of the preoperational stage, preschoolers begin to grasp functionality, the idea that actions, events, and outcomes are related to one another in fixed patterns. They also become aware of identity, the understanding that certain things stay the same, regardless of changes in shape, size, and appearance—for instance, that a lump of clay contains the same amount of clay whether it is clumped into a ball or stretched out like a snake. Comprehension of identity is necessary for children to develop an understanding of conservation (the understanding, as we discussed earlier,

conservation
the knowledge that quantity is unrelated to the arrangement and physical appearance of objects

transformation
the process in which one state is changed into another

egocentric thought
thinking that does not take into account the viewpoints of others

intuitive thought
thinking that reflects preschoolers' use of primitive reasoning and their avid acquisition of knowledge about the world

that quantity is not related to physical appearances). For suggestions on promoting cognitive development in preschooler, see the *Are You an Informed Consumer of Development?* box on below.

◇ COGNITIVE DEVELOPMENT IN THE SCHOOL YEARS AND ADOLESCENCE

As we have seen, from Piaget's perspective preschoolers think preoperationally. They are largely egocentric and lack the ability to use *operations*—organized, formal, logical mental processes.

The Rise of Concrete Operational Thought (Ages 7 to 12)

All this changes during the school years in what Piaget calls the concrete operational stage. Occurring between ages 7 and 12, this stage is characterized by the active, and appropriate, use of logic. Concrete operational thought applies logical operations to concrete problems. For instance, when children in this stage confront a conservation problem (such as determining whether the amount of liquid poured from one container to another of a different shape stays the same), they use cognitive and logical processes to answer, no longer judging solely by appearance. They are able to reason correctly that since none of the liquid has been lost, the amount stays the same. Being less egocentric, they can consider multiple aspects of a situation, an ability known as decentering.

The shift from preoperational to concrete operational thought takes time. Children shift between these modes of thought before concrete operations take a firm hold, able to answer conservation problems but unable to explain why. When asked for their reasoning, they may simply respond, "Because."

Once concrete operations take hold, however, children make several cognitive leaps, such as the concept of reversibility—the notion that transformations to a stimulus can be reversed. Grasping this notion, children realize that a ball of clay squeezed into a long, thin rope can become a ball

ARE YOU AN INFORMED CONSUMER OF DEVELOPMENT?

PROMOTING COGNITIVE DEVELOPMENT IN PRESCHOOLERS:
FROM THEORY TO THE CLASSROOM

Piaget's theory has had enormous influence on educational practice, particularly during the preschool years. Among the suggestions for parents and preschool teachers that arise out of the Piagetian approach are the following:

- Both parents and teachers should be aware of which general stage of cognitive development, with its capabilities and limitations, each individual child has reached. Unless they are aware of a child's current level of development, it will be impossible to provide appropriate materials and experiences.

- Instruction should be at a level that reflects—but is just slightly higher than—each student's current level of cognitive development. For instance, Piaget suggests that cognitive growth is more likely to occur when information and material are of moderate novelty. With too little novelty, children will be bored; with too much, they will be confused.

- Instruction should be individualized as much as possible. Because children of the same age may hover around different levels of cognitive development, curriculum materials that are prepared individually stand a better chance of success.

- Students should be kept actively engaged in learning, and they should be allowed to pace themselves as they move through new material.

- Opportunities for social interaction—both with other students and with adults—should be provided. By receiving feedback from others and observing how others react in given situations, children learn new approaches and ways of thinking about the world.

- Students should be allowed to make mistakes. Cognitive growth often flows from confronting errors.

- Because cognitive development can occur only when children have achieved the appropriate level of maturation, children should not be pushed too far ahead of their current state of cognitive development. For instance, although it may be possible through intensive training to get preoperational children to recite, in a rote manner, the correct response to a conservation problem, this does not mean that they will have true comprehension of what they are verbalizing.

again. More abstractly, this concept allows children to understand that if 3 + 5 equals 8, then 5 + 3 also equals 8—and, later, that 8 − 3 equals 5.

Concrete operational thinking also permits children to grasp such concepts as the relationship between time and speed. For instance, consider the problem in which two cars traveling different-length routes start and finish at the same points in the same amount of time. Children entering the concrete operational period reason that the cars' speed is the same. However, between ages 8 and 10, children begin to understand that for both cars to arrive simultaneously at the finish point, the car traveling the longer route must be moving faster.

Despite these advances, children still have one critical thinking limitation. They remain tied to concrete, physical reality. Furthermore, they cannot understand truly abstract or hypothetical questions, or questions involving formal logic, such as the concept of free will or determinism.

The ability to think beyond the concrete, current situation to what might or could be distinguishes adolescents' thinking from that of younger children. Adolescents are able to consider a variety of abstract possibilities; they can see issues in relative, as opposed to absolute, terms. When problems arise, they can perceive shadings beyond the black-and-white solutions of younger days (Keating, 1980, 1990; Lehalle, 2006).

Like scientists who form hypotheses, adolescents in the formal operational stage use systematic reasoning. They start with a general theory about what produces a particular outcome and then deduce explanations for specific situations in which they see that particular outcome. (Kevin Radford/SuperStock)

Mrs. Kirby smiled as she read a highly creative paper. As part of her eighth-grade American Government class, she asked students to write about what their lives would be like if America had not won its war for independence from Britain. She had tried a similar task with her sixth-graders, but many of them were unable to imagine anything other than what they knew. Her eighth-graders, however, were inventing some very interesting scenarios. One boy imagined himself as Lord Lucas; a girl imagined that she would serve a rich landowner; another that she would plot to overthrow the government.

There are several explanations for adolescents' cognitive development. According to Piaget, with adolescence comes the formal operational stage.

Piaget's Formal Operational Stage (Ages 12 to 15)

Leigh, age 14, is asked to solve the problem: What determines the speed at which a pendulum moves back and forth? Leigh is given a weight hanging from a string and told that she can vary several things: the length of the string, the weight of the object, the amount of force used to push the string, and the height to which the weight is raised in an arc before it is released.

Leigh doesn't remember, but she was asked to solve the same problem at age eight as part of a longitudinal research study. She was then in the concrete operational period, and her efforts were not very successful. Her haphazard approach showed no systematic plan of action. For instance, she simultaneously tried to push the pendulum harder and shorten the length of the string and increase the weight on the string. Because she varied so many factors at once, when the pendulum's speed changed, she had no way of knowing what had made the difference.

Now, Leigh is more systematic. Rather than immediately pushing and pulling at the pendulum, she stops to think about which factors to consider. She ponders how she might test which factor is important, forming a hypothesis. Then, as a scientist conducts an experiment, she varies only one factor at a time. By examining each variable separately and systematically, she comes to the correct solution: The length of the string determines the speed of the pendulum.

© Mick Stevens/Conde Nast Publications/www.cartoonbank.com. Published in The New Yorker May 29, 2000

Using Formal Operations to Solve Problems

Leigh's approach to the pendulum question, a problem devised by Piaget, shows she has moved into the formal operational period of cognitive development (Piaget & Inhelder, 1958). In the formal operational stage, people develop the ability to think abstractly. Piaget suggested that people reach this stage at the start of adolescence, around age 12.

Adolescents can consider problems in abstract rather than concrete terms by using formal principles of logic. They can test their understanding by systematically conducting rudimentary experiments and observing the results. Thus, the adolescent Leigh could think about the pendulum problem abstractly, and she understood how to test her hypotheses.

Adolescents are able to use formal reasoning, starting with a general theory about what causes a certain outcome, and then deducing explanations for the situations in which that outcome occurs. Like the scientists who form hypotheses, they can test their theories. What distinguishes this kind of thinking from earlier stages is the ability to start with the abstract and move to the concrete; in previous stages, children are tied to the concrete present. At age eight, Leigh just moved things around to see what would happen in the pendulum problem, a concrete approach. At age 12, she began with the abstract idea that each variable should be tested separately.

Adolescents also can use propositional thought during this stage. Propositional thought is reasoning that uses abstract logic in the absence of concrete examples. Such thinking allows adolescents to understand that if certain premises are true, then a conclusion must also be true. For example:

All men are mortal. [*premise*]

Socrates is a man. [*premise*]

Therefore, Socrates is mortal. [*conclusion*]

Adolescents understand that if both premises are true, then so is the conclusion. They are capable of using similar reasoning when premises and conclusions are stated more abstractly, as follows:

All As are B. [*premise*]

C is an A. [*premise*]

Therefore, C is a B. [*conclusion*]

Although Piaget proposed that the formal operational stage begins at the onset of adolescence, he also hypothesized that—as with all the stages—full cognitive capabilities emerge gradually through a combination of physical maturation and environmental experiences. It is not until around age 15, Piaget says, that adolescents fully settle into the formal operational stage.

In fact, evidence suggests that many people hone these skills at a later age, and some never fully employ them at all. Most studies show that only 40 to 60 percent of college students and adults achieve formal operational thinking completely, with some estimates as low as 25 percent. But many adults who do not use formal operational thought in every domain are fully competent in some aspects of their lives (Keating & Clark, 1980; Sugarman, 1988; Commons & Richards, 2003).

The culture in which they are raised affects how adolescents use formal operations. People with little formal education, who live in isolated, technologically unsophisticated societies, are less likely to use formal operations than formally educated persons in more sophisticated societies (Jahoda, 1980; Segall et al., 1990; Oesterdiekhoff, 2007).

It is not that adolescents (and adults) from cultures using few formal operations are incapable of attaining them. It is more likely that what characterizes formal operations—scientific reasoning—is not equally valued in all societies. If everyday life does not require or promote a certain type of reasoning, it is not likely that people will use such reasoning when confronting a problem (Greenfield, 1976; Shea, 1985; Gauvain, 1998; Smorti, 2008).

Adolescents' ability to reason abstractly leads them to question accepted rules and explanations. (Marmaduke St. John/Alamy)

The Consequences of Adolescents' Use of Formal Operations

The ability to reason abstractly, to use formal operations, changes adolescents' everyday behavior. Whereas earlier they may have blindly accepted rules and explanations, their increased abstract reasoning abilities may lead to strenuous questioning of their parents and other authority figures.

In general, adolescents become more argumentative. They enjoy using abstract reasoning to poke holes in others' explanations, and their increased critical thinking abilities zero in on parents' and teachers' perceived shortcomings. For instance, they may see their parents' arguments against using drugs as inconsistent if their parents used drugs in adolescence without consequence. But adolescents can be indecisive, too, as they are able to see the merits of multiple sides to issues (Elkind, 1996; Kuhn & Franklin, 2006).

Coping with these new critical abilities can be challenging for parents, teachers, and other adults who deal with adolescents. But it makes adolescents more interesting, as they actively seek to understand the values and justifications they encounter.

REVIEW AND APPLY

REVIEW

- Cognitive developmentalists study both continuity and change linked to changes in a person's intellectual abilities.
- Jean Piaget argued that infants acquire knowledge directly through motor behavior, organizing their world into mental structures called schemes and subsequently either assimilating experiences into their current level of understanding or accommodating their ways of thinking to include the new experience.

- Piaget's theory is based on a stage approach to development in which children pass through a series of stages in a fixed order from birth through adolescence: sensorimotor, preoperational, concrete operational, and formal operational.

- The key way in which Piaget differs from many theorists who preceded him is in his observation that children experience qualitative changes in knowledge and understanding as they move from stage to stage, not just quantitative changes.

- Piaget's theory of human cognitive development involves a succession of stages through which children progress from birth to adolescence. As people move from one stage to another, the way they understand the world changes.

- The sensorimotor stage, from birth to about two years, involves a gradual progression through simple reflexes, single coordinated activities, interest in the outside world, purposeful combinations of activities, manipulation of actions to produce desired outcomes, and symbolic thought. These are the six substages of the sensorimotor stage.

- According to Piaget, children in the preoperational stage develop symbolic function, a change in their thinking that is the foundation of further cognitive advances, but they are hampered by a tendency toward egocentric thought.

- Individuals in middle childhood are in the concrete operational stage of cognitive development, characterized by the application of logical processes to concrete problems and by "decentering"—the ability to take multiple aspects of a situation into account.

- As they enter Piaget's formal operational stage, adolescents begin to think abstractly, use logic, and perform systematic experiments to answer questions

APPLY

- Think of a common young children's toy with which you are familiar. How might its use be affected by the principles of assimilation and accommodation?

- Do you think it is possible to break a preschooler's habit of egocentric thought by directly teaching him to take another person's point of view? Would showing him a picture of himself "hidden" behind a chair change his thinking? Why?

PART 2 APPRAISING PIAGET: SUPPORT, CHALLENGES, AND ALTERNATIVES

LEARNING OBJECTIVES

LO 3 What are the key features—and criticisms—of Piaget's theory?
LO 4 What are some alternate approaches to Piaget's view of cognitive development?

Most developmental researchers would probably agree that in many significant ways, Piaget's descriptions of how cognitive development proceeds are largely accurate. Yet, there is substantial disagreement over the validity of the theory and many of its specific predictions (Marcovitch, Zelazo, & Schmuckler, 2003; Demetriou & Raftopoulos, 2004).

Appraising Piaget: Research on babies in non-Western cultures suggests that Piaget's stages are not universal, but are to some degree culturally derived.
(Anthro-Photo File)

Let's start with what is clearly correct about the Piagetian approach. Piaget was a virtuoso observer and masterly reporter of children's behavior, and his descriptions of growth remain a monument to his powers of observation. His many books contain brilliant, careful observations of children at work and play.

Furthermore, literally thousands of studies have supported Piaget's view that children learn much about the world by acting on objects in their environment. Finally, the broad outlines sketched out by Piaget of the sequence of cognitive development and the increasing cognitive accomplishments that occur during infancy and the preschool years, in particular, are generally accurate (Kail, 2004; Schlottmann & Wilkening, 2012). His theories have had powerful educational implications, and many schools use his principles to guide instruction (Flavell, 1996; Siegler & Ellis, 1996; Brainerd, 2003).

◇ THE CRITICS WEIGH IN

Despite the powerful influence of Piaget's work, specific aspects of his theory have come under increasing scrutiny—and criticism—in the decades since he carried out his pioneering work. For example, some researchers question the concept of stages that forms the basis of Piaget's theory. Although even Piaget acknowledged that children's transitions between stages are gradual, critics, particularly those who favor the information processing approach, contend that development proceeds in a much more continuous fashion. Rather than showing major leaps of competence at the end of one stage and the beginning of the next, improvement comes in more gradual increments, growing step by step in a skill-by-skill manner (Siegler, 2003; Lavelli & Fogel, 2005).

Regarding infants in particular, some critics dispute Piaget's notion that cognitive development is grounded in motor activities. They charge that Piaget overlooked the importance of the sensory and perceptual systems that are present from a very early age in infancy—systems about which Piaget knew little, since so much of the research illustrating how sophisticated they are even in infancy was done relatively recently (Butterworth, 1994; Johnson, 2009).

- **Timing of Mastery of Object Permanence.** Piaget's critics also point to more recent studies that cast doubt on Piaget's view that infants are incapable of mastering the concept of object permanence until they are close to a year old. For instance, some work suggests that younger infants did not appear to understand object permanence because the techniques used to test their abilities were not sensitive enough to their true capabilities (Aguiar & Baillargeon, 2002; Baillargeon, 2004; Krojgaard, 2005).

  It may be that a four-month-old doesn't search for a rattle hidden under a blanket because she hasn't learned the motor skills necessary to do the searching—not because she doesn't understand that the rattle still exists. Similarly, the apparent inability of young infants to comprehend object permanence may reflect more about their memory deficits than their lack of understanding of the concept: The memories of young infants may be poor enough that they simply do not recall the earlier concealment of the toy. In fact, when more age-appropriate tasks are employed, some researchers have found indications of object permanence in children as young as three months (Aguiar & Baillargeon, 2002; Wang, Baillargeon, & Paterson, 2005; Ruffman, Slade, & Redman, 2006).

  Many researchers contend that Piaget underestimated children's capabilities generally, in part due to the limitations of the mini-experiments he conducted. Subjected to a broader array of experimental tasks, children show less consistency within stages than Piaget predicted. Increasing evidence suggests that children's cognitive abilities emerge earlier than supposed; for example, some children demonstrate concrete operational thinking before age seven, the age at which Piaget suggested these abilities first appear (Bjorklund, 1997b; Dawson-Tunik, Fischer, & Stein, 2004).

- **Children's Understanding of Numbers.** Piaget may also have erred in asserting that preschoolers have little understanding of numbers, as shown by their inability to grasp conservation and reversibility (the understanding that a transformation can be reversed to return something to its original state). Recent experimental work calls that assertion into question. For instance, developmental psychologist Rochel Gelman has found that children as young as three can easily tell the difference between rows of two and three toy animals, regardless of the animals' spacing. Older children are able to identify which of two numbers is larger and show a rudimentary understanding of addition and subtraction (Vilette, 2002; Brandone et al., 2012).

Gelman concludes that children have an innate ability to count, akin to the ability to use language that some theorists see as universal and genetically determined. This is clearly at odds with Piagetian notions, which suggest that children's numerical abilities do not blossom until after the preoperational period (i.e., after about age seven).

- **Conservation.** There are further difficulties with Piaget's contention that conservation does not emerge until the end of the preoperational period. This contention has not stood up to experimental scrutiny. Children can learn to answer conservation tasks correctly if they are given certain training and experiences. The fact that one can improve children's performance argues against the Piagetian view that children in the preoperational period have not reached a level of cognitive maturity to understand conservation (Halford & Andrews, 2006).

- **Cultural Issues.** Piaget's work also seems to describe children from developed, Western countries better than those in non-Western cultures. For instance, some evidence suggests that cognitive skills emerge on a different timetable for children in non-Western cultures than for children living in Europe and the United States. Infants raised in the Ivory Coast of Africa, for example, reach the various substages of the sensorimotor period at an earlier age than infants reared in France (Dasen et al., 1978; Mistry & Saraswathi, 2003; Tamis-LeMonda et al., 2012).

Despite these criticisms—which research has shown to be valid—we cannot dismiss Piaget. Although some early cross-cultural research implied that children in certain cultures remain preoperational, failing to master conservation and develop concrete operations, more recent research suggests otherwise. For instance, with proper training in conservation, children in non-Western cultures who do not conserve learn to do so. In one study, urban Australian children—who develop concrete operations on Piaget's timetable—were compared to rural Aborigine children, who typically do not conserve at the age of 14 (Dasen, Ngini, & Lavallee, 1979; Maynard & Greenfield, 2003). With training, the rural Aborigine children showed conservation skills similar to those of their urban counterparts, although about three years later (see Figure 5).

When children are interviewed by researchers from their own culture, who share their language and customs, and whose reasoning tasks relate to important cultural domains, the children are much more likely to display concrete operational thinking. Such research suggests that Piaget was right in arguing that concrete operations are universally achieved during middle childhood. Performance differences between Western and some non-Western children on Piagetian measures of conservation and concrete operations probably reflect a difference in experiences. The progress of cognitive development cannot be understood without considering a child's culture (Jahoda, 1983; Mishra, 2001; Lau, Lee, & Chiu, 2004).

A Final Summation

Even Piaget's most passionate critics concede that he has provided us with an ingenious description of the broad outlines of cognitive development during infancy. His failings seem to be in underestimating the capabilities of younger infants and in his claims that sensorimotor skills develop in a consistent, fixed pattern.

Still, his influence has been enormous. Piaget's theories have inspired countless studies on the development of thinking capacities and processes, and they have spurred much classroom reform. His bold statements about the nature of cognitive development sparked opposition that brought forth new approaches, such as the information processing perspective we examine next. Piaget remains a towering, pioneering figure in the field of development (Roth, Slone, & Dar, 2000; Kail, 2004).

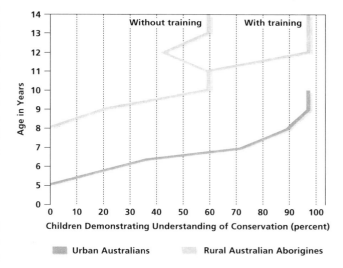

FIGURE 5 Conservation

Training Rural Australian Aborigine children trail their urban counterparts in the development of their understanding of conservation; with training, they later catch up. Without training, around half of fourteen-year-old Aborigines do not have an understanding of conservation. What can be concluded from the fact that training influences the understanding of conservation?

(*Source:* Based on Dasen, Ngini, & Lavallee, 1979.)

◇ BEYOND PIAGET

As we've seen, Piaget, for all his brilliance and influence, has drawn his share of criticism. Let's look at several contemporary approaches that differ from Piaget's on the question of when cognitive development comes to an end. The developmentalists who espouse these approaches all agree on one thing: that Piaget underestimated the portion of the life span during which cognitive development occurs.

Consider the following scenario drawn from research by Adams and Labouvie-Vief (1986).

Ben is known to be a heavy drinker, especially when he goes to parties. Tyra, Ben's wife, warns him that if he comes home drunk one more time, she will leave him and take the children. Tonight Ben is out late at an office party. He comes home drunk. Does Tyra leave Ben?

The nature of thought changes qualitatively during early adulthood.
(Kaiser/Caro/Alamy)

To the typical adolescent this case is open-and-shut: Tyra leaves Ben. But in early adulthood, the answer is less clear. People become less concerned with sheer logic and instead take into account real-life concerns that may influence and temper behavior.

To Piaget, the first stage of development is the sensorimotor stage, achieved in infancy, and the final stage is the formal operations stage, reached in adolescence. If we subscribed to the traditional Piagetian view of cognitive development, we would expect to find little intellectual growth in early adulthood.

Piaget argued that by the time people left adolescence, their thinking, at least qualitatively, had largely become what it would be for the rest of their lives. They might gather more information, but the ways in which they thought about it would not change. But this view of development seems overly limited. Does development really stop in adolescence?

Labouvie-Vief and Postformal Thought

Gisela Labouvie-Vief and several other modern developmentalists have begun to conclude that the answer is No. They have found that cognitive development continues beyond adolescence because people are faced with dealing with the complexities of life throughout adulthood.

Labouvie-Vief suggests that the nature of thinking changes during early adulthood. She asserts that thinking based solely on formal operations is insufficient to meet the demands placed on young adults. The complexity of society, which requires specialization, and the challenge of finding one's way through that complexity require thought that transcends logic to include practical experience, moral judgments, and values (Labouvie-Vief, 2006, 2009).

For example, imagine a young, single woman in her first job. Her boss, a married man whom she respects greatly and who is in a position to help her career, invites her to go with him to make an important presentation to a client. When the presentation, which has gone very well, is over, he suggests they go out to dinner and celebrate. Later that evening, after sharing a bottle of wine, he attempts to accompany her to her hotel room. What should she do?

Logic alone doesn't answer such questions. Labouvie-Vief suggests that young adults' thinking must develop to handle ambiguous situations like these. She suggests that young adults learn to use analogies and metaphors to make comparisons, confront society's paradoxes, and become comfortable with a more subjective understanding. This requires weighing all aspects of a situation according to one's values and beliefs. It allows for interpretive processes and reflects the fact that the reasons behind events in the real world are painted in shades of gray rather than black and white (Labouvie-Vief, 1990; Thornton, 2004).

To demonstrate how this sort of thinking develops, Labouvie-Vief presented experimental subjects, ranging in age from 10 to 40, with scenarios similar to the Ben and Tyra scenario above. Each story had a clear, logical conclusion, but it could be interpreted differently if real-world demands and pressures were taken into account.

In responding to the scenarios, adolescents relied heavily on the logic of formal operations. They tended to predict that Tyra would immediately pack up her bags and leave with the children when Ben came home drunk. After all, that's what she said she would do. In contrast, young adults were more apt to consider various real-life possibilities: Would Ben be apologetic and beg Tyra not to leave? Did Tyra really mean it when she said she would leave? Does Tyra have some place to go?

Young adults exhibited what Labouvie-Vief calls postformal thinking. **Postformal thought** is thinking that goes beyond Piaget's formal operations. Rather than being based on purely logical

postformal thought
thinking that acknowledges that adult predicaments must sometimes be solved in relativistic terms

processes, with absolutely right and wrong answers to problems, postformal thought acknowledges that adult predicaments must sometimes be solved in relativistic terms.

Postformal thought also encompasses *dialectical thinking,* an interest in and appreciation for argument, counterargument, and debate (Basseches, 1984; Sinnott, 2003). Dialectical thinking accepts that issues are not always clear-cut and that answers to questions must sometimes be negotiated. According to psychologist Jan Sinnott (1998), postformal thinkers shift back and forth between an abstract, ideal solution and real-world constraints that might prevent implementation of that solution. Postformal thinkers understand that just as there can be multiple causes of a situation, there can be multiple solutions.

From An EDUCATOR'S Perspective:

Can you think of situations that you would deal with differently as an adult than as an adolescent? Do the differences reflect postformal thinking?

Perry's Approach to Postformal Thinking

To psychologist William Perry (1970, 1981), the developmental growth of early adulthood involves mastering new ways of understanding the world. To examine intellectual and moral growth during college, Perry interviewed studentheads at Harvard University. He found that students entering college tended to use dualistic thinking in their views of the world: Something was either right or wrong; people were either good or bad; others were either for them or against them.

However, as these students encountered new ideas and points of view from other students and their professors, their dualistic thinking declined. Consistent with postformal thinking, they understood that it is possible to hold multiple perspectives on an issue. Their attitude toward authorities also changed: Instead of assuming that experts had all the answers, they began to realize that their own thinking had validity if their position was well thought out and rational.

In fact, according to Perry, they had reached a stage in which knowledge and values were regarded as relativistic. Rather than seeing the world as having absolute standards and values, they argued that different societies, cultures, and individuals could have different standards and values, and all of them could be equally valid.

It's important to keep in mind that Perry's theory is based on a sample of interviews conducted with well-educated students attending an elite college. His findings may not apply as well to people who have never learned how to examine multiple points of view.

Schaie's Stages of Cognitive Development

Developmental psychologist K. Warner Schaie offers another perspective on postformal thought. Taking up where Piaget left off, Schaie suggests that adults' thinking follows a set pattern of stages (illustrated in Figure 6). But Schaie focuses on the ways in which information is used during adulthood, rather than on changes in the acquisition and understanding of new information, as in Piaget's approach (Schaie & Willis, 1993; Schaie & Zanjani, 2006).

Schaie suggests that before adulthood, the main cognitive developmental task is acquisition of information. Consequently, he labels the first stage of cognitive development, which encompasses all of childhood and adolescence, the **acquisitive stage**. Information gathered before we grow up is

acquisitive stage
according to Schaie, the first stage of cognitive development, encompassing all of childhood and adolescence, in which the main developmental task is to acquire information

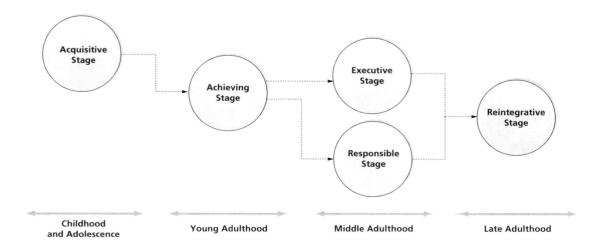

FIGURE 6 Schaie's Stages of Adult Development

(*Source:* Schaie, 1977–1978.)

According to Schaie, children in the acquisitive stage gather information that helps prepare them for future activities. How might the girl in the photo use her current play in the future?
(Studio M/Stock Connection)

achieving stage
the point reached by young adults in which intelligence is applied to specific situations involving the attainment of long-term goals regarding careers, family, and societal contributions

responsible stage
the stage where the major concerns of middle-aged adults relate to their personal situations, including protecting and nourishing their spouses, families, and careers

executive stage
the period in middle adulthood when people take a broader perspective than earlier, including concerns about the world

reintegrative stage
the period of late adulthood during which the focus is on tasks that have personal meaning

largely squirreled away for future use. Much of the rationale for education during childhood and adolescence, then, is to prepare people for future activities.

The situation changes considerably in early adulthood when the focus shifts from the future to the here-and-now. According to Schaie, young adults are in the **achieving stage**, applying their intelligence to attain long-term goals regarding their careers, family, and contributions to society. During the achieving stage, young adults must confront and resolve several major issues, and the decisions they make—such as what job to take and whom to marry—have implications for the rest of their lives.

During the late stages of early adulthood and in middle adulthood, people move into the responsible and executive stages. In the **responsible stage**, middle-aged adults are mainly concerned with protecting and nourishing their spouses, families, and careers.

Sometime later, further into middle adulthood, many people (but not all) enter the **executive stage** in which they take a broader perspective, becoming more concerned about the larger world. People in the executive stage put energy into nourishing and sustaining societal institutions. They may become involved in town government, religious congregations, service clubs, charitable groups, factory unions—organizations that have a larger purpose in society (Sinnott, 1997, 2003).

Finally, the **reintegrative stage** is the period of late adulthood during which people focus on tasks that have personal meaning. They no longer focus on acquiring knowledge to solve potential problems that they may encounter. Instead, they acquire information about issues that specifically interest them. Furthermore, they have less interest in—and patience for—things that they do not see as having some immediate application to their lives.

REVIEW AND APPLY

REVIEW

- Recent developmentalists, while acknowledging Piaget's acute observational ability and his pioneering contributions to cognitive development, have questioned many of his conclusions, including the boundaries between his stages, the severe limits he attached to preschoolers' abilities, the universality of cognitive development across cultures, and his judgment that cognitive development is essentially complete by the end of adolescence.

- In contrast to Piaget, Gisela Labouvie-Vief maintains that adults engage in postformal thought, in which predicaments must sometimes be solved in relativistic terms, rather than as absolute rights and wrongs.

- William Perry suggests that people move from dualistic thinking to relativistic thought during early adulthood.

- K. Warner Schaie argues that adults pass through five stages of information: acquisitive, achieving, responsible, executive, and reintegrative.

APPLY

- Do adults use schemes to organize their environment? Do the principles of assimilation and accommodation apply to adult learning as well as children's learning? How?

- When faced with complex problems, do adults routinely use formal operations? What aspects of a culture might encourage or discourage the use and application of formal operational approaches?

PART 3   VYGOTSKY'S VIEW OF COGNITIVE DEVELOPMENT: TAKING CULTURE INTO ACCOUNT

LEARNING OBJECTIVE

LO 5   What are the key features—and criticisms—of Vygotsky's theory?

> *As her daughter watches, a member of the Chilcotin Indian tribe prepares a salmon for dinner. When the daughter asks a question about a small detail of the process, the mother takes out another salmon and repeats the entire process. According to the tribal view of learning, understanding and comprehension can come only from grasping the total procedure, and not from learning about the individual subcomponents of the task. (Tharp, 1989)*

The Chilcotin view of how children learn about the world contrasts with the prevalent view of Western society, which assumes that only by mastering the separate parts of a problem can one fully comprehend it. Do differences in the ways particular cultures and societies approach problems influence cognitive development? According to Russian developmental psychologist Lev Vygotsky, who lived from 1896 to 1934, the answer is a clear Yes.

Vygotsky viewed cognitive development as the product of social interactions. Instead of concentrating on individual performance, Vygotsky's increasingly influential view focuses on the social aspects of development and learning.

Vygotsky sees children as apprentices, learning cognitive strategies and other skills from adult and peer mentors who not only present new ways of doing things, but also provide assistance, instruction, and motivation. Consequently, he focuses on the child's social and cultural world as the source of cognitive development. According to Vygotsky, children gradually grow intellectually and begin to function on their own because of the assistance that adult and peer partners provide (Vygotsky, 1926/1997; Tudge & Scrimsher, 2003).

Vygotsky contends that culture and society establish the institutions, such as preschools and play groups, which promote development by providing opportunities for cognitive growth. Furthermore, by emphasizing particular tasks, culture and society shape the nature of specific cognitive advances. Unless we look at what is important and meaningful to members of a given society, we may seriously underestimate the nature and level of cognitive abilities that ultimately will be attained (Tappan, 1997; Schaller & Crandall, 2004; Balakrishnan & Claiborne, 2012).

For example, children's toys reflect what is important and meaningful in a particular society. In Western societies, preschoolers commonly play with toy wagons, automobiles, and other vehicles, in part reflecting the mobile nature of the culture. In this way, a society subtly communicates to children a great deal about its expectations and characteristics.

In much the same way, societal expectations about gender play a role in how children come to understand the world. For example, one study conducted at a science museum found that parents provided more detailed scientific explanations to boys than to girls at museum displays. Such differences in level of explanation may lead to more sophisticated understanding of science in boys and ultimately may produce later gender differences in science learning (Crowley et al., 2001).

Vygotsky's approach is therefore quite different from Piaget's. Where Piaget looked at children and saw junior scientists, working by themselves to develop an independent understanding of the world, Vygotsky saw cognitive apprentices, learning from master teachers the skills valued in the child's culture (Kitchener, 1996; Fernyhough, 1997; Halford, 2005; Karpov, 2006).

◇ THE ZONE OF PROXIMAL DEVELOPMENT

Vygotsky proposed that children's cognitive abilities increase through exposure to information that is new enough to be intriguing, but not too difficult to contend with. He called this the **zone of proximal development, or ZPD**, the level at which a child can almost, but not fully, perform a task independently, but can do so with the assistance of someone more competent. For cognitive

zone of proximal development or ZPD
according to Vygotsky, the level at which a child can *almost*, but not fully, perform a task independently, but can do so with the assistance of someone more competent

Students working in cooperative groups benefit from the insights of others.
(Michael Newman/PhotoEdit, Inc.)

scaffolding
the support for learning and problem solving that encourages independence and growth

Watch a teacher use the scaffolding technique with preschoolers in www.pearsoncustom.com/mi/msu_mylabs

development to occur, new information must be presented—by parents, teachers, or more skilled peers—within the zone of proximal development. For example, a preschooler might not be able to figure out by herself how to stick a handle on the clay pot she's making, but she can do it with advice from her child-care teacher (Blank & White, 1999; Chaiklin, 2003; Kozulin, 2004).

The concept of the zone of proximal development suggests that even though two children might be able to achieve the same amount without help, if one child receives aid, he or she may improve substantially more than the other. The greater the improvement that comes with help, the larger the zone of proximal development.

The assistance or structuring provided by others has been termed **scaffolding**, after the temporary scaffolds that aid in building construction. Scaffolding is the support for learning and problem solving that encourages independence and growth (Puntambekar & Hübscher, 2005). As in construction, the scaffolding that older people provide, which facilitates the completion of identified tasks, is removed once children can solve a problem on their own (Rogoff, 1995; Warwick & Maloch, 2003).

To Vygotsky, scaffolding not only helps children solve specific problems, it also aids in the development of their overall cognitive abilities. In education, scaffolding involves, first of all, helping children think about and frame a task appropriately. In addition, a parent or teacher is likely to provide clues to task completion that fit the child's level of development and to model behavior that can lead to task completion.

To illustrate how scaffolding operates, consider the following conversation between mother and son:

Mother: Do you remember how you helped me make the cookies before?
Child: No.
Mother: We made the dough and put it in the oven. Do you remember that?
Child: When Grandma came?
Mother: Yes, that's right. Would you help me shape the dough into cookies?
Child: OK.
Mother: Can you remember how big we made the cookies when Grandma was here?
Child: Big.
Mother: Right. Can you show me how big?
Child: We used the big wooden spoon.
Mother: Good boy, that's right. We used the wooden spoon, and we made big cookies. But let's try something different today by using the ice cream scoop to form the cookies.

Although this conversation may not appear to be a particularly sophisticated specimen of teaching and learning, it illustrates the practice of scaffolding. The mother is supporting her son's efforts, and she gets him to respond conversationally. In the process, she not only expands her son's abilities by using a different tool (the scoop instead of the spoon), she models how conversations proceed.

In some societies parental support for learning differs by gender. In one study, Mexican mothers were found to provide more scaffolding than fathers. A possible explanation is that mothers may be more aware of their children's cognitive abilities than are fathers (Tenenbaum & Leaper, 1998; Tamis-LeMonda & Cabrera, 2002; also see the *From Research to Practice* box on next page).

◆ CULTURAL TOOLS

One key aspect of the aid that more accomplished individuals provide to learners comes in the form of cultural tools. Cultural tools are actual, physical items (e.g., pencils, paper, calculators, computers, and so forth), as well as an intellectual and conceptual framework for solving problems. The framework includes the language that is used within a culture, its alphabetical and numbering schemes, its mathematical and scientific systems, and even its religious systems. These cultural tools provide a structure

FROM RESEARCH TO PRACTICE

INFANTS LEARN FROM ADULTS, NOT VIDEOS

The advertisements are certainly compelling—proud parents giving gushing testimonials about the effectiveness of the latest "baby genius" DVD and how it helped their toddler's vocabulary "blossom." The word has gotten out that an intellectually stimulating environment best supports young children's rapidly developing cognitive abilities, and many parents are drawn to the idea of providing such enrichment even during down-times when they themselves are unavailable for interaction. But are such baby media products really beneficial?

Quite a bit of research shows that they're not. One recent study examined the effectiveness of a baby DVD that teaches vocabulary by having groups of parents use the product in their homes for four weeks, either while actively engaging their children or while just passively watching. The researchers intentionally chose a best-selling DVD, allowed a lengthy exposure time, created real-world conditions by doing the study in people's homes, ensured that parents followed the directions closely, and monitored for compliance, all to give the DVD the best possible chance of actually working.

Another group of parents attempted to teach their children the same vocabulary words themselves without the DVD, and a control group used no vocabulary training at all. The findings were clear: whether parents actively engaged their children with the DVD or just passively watched it, those children didn't learn the words significantly better than the control group. Only the children who were learning the words from their parent (with no DVD) learned them better than the control group (DeLoache et al., 2010).

Other research on infants' early language production helps explain this finding: infants learn vocabulary best in an interactive setting where adults are responding to the sounds the infant is making. According to research by Michael Goldstein, babies learn vocabulary best when they initiate the learning and when they choose the object to be labeled. For instance, if an infant babbles while looking at an object, the best approach is to name the object (even if the babbling sounds like a different word). In this way, the "lesson" coincides with the infant's natural exploration of the world rather than trying to impose an experience on the child, as videos do (Goldstein et al., 2010; Klass, 2010; Bergelson & Swingley, 2012).

- According to Goldstein, if an infant is looking at an apple and saying "ba-ba-ba," it's better for parents to name the apple rather than find a word that fits the babble (such as banana or bottle). Why do you think this is so?
- Goldstein's research shows that parents who liked educational DVDs best believed that it improved their child's vocabulary significantly, even though that was rarely the case. Why might parents acquire this false belief?

that can be used to help children define and solve specific problems, as well as an intellectual point of view that encourages cognitive development.

For an example of the pervasive influence of culture on thinking and action, consider the *Developmental Diversity* feature.

◇ EVALUATING VYGOTSKY'S CONTRIBUTIONS

Vygotsky's view has become increasingly influential, which is surprising given that he died over 70 years ago at the age of 37 (Van Der Veer & Valsiner, 1993, 1994; Winsler, 2003). His influence has grown because his writings are only now becoming widely disseminated in the United States due to the growing availability of good English translations. For most of the twentieth century Vygotsky was not widely known even within his native land. His work was banned for some time, and it was not until the breakup of the Soviet Union in the 1990s that it became freely available in the formerly Soviet countries. Thus, Vygotsky, long hidden from his fellow developmentalists, didn't emerge onto the scene until long after his death (Wertsch, 2008).

Even more important, though, is the quality of Vygotsky's ideas. They represent a consistent theoretical system and help explain a growing body of research on the importance of social interaction in promoting cognitive development. The idea that children's comprehension of the world flows from their interactions with their parents, peers, and other members of society is increasingly well supported. It is also consistent with a growing body of multicultural and cross-cultural research, which finds evidence that cognitive development is shaped, in part, by cultural factors (Daniels, 1996; Scrimsher & Tudge, 2003).

Of course, not every aspect of Vygotsky's theorizing has been supported, and he can be criticized for a lack of precision in his conceptualization of cognitive growth. For instance, such broad concepts as the zone of proximal development are not terribly precise, and they do not always lend themselves to experimental tests (Wertsch, 1999; Daniels, 2006).

DEVELOPMENTAL DIVERSITY AND YOUR LIFE

A WALK THROUGH A CULTURAL LANDSCAPE

> *"Dad, how far is it to school?"*
>
> *"It's about three blocks past the supermarket."*
>
> *"School is about a 20-minute ride downtown on the subway that stops across the street from our apartment."*
>
> *"If you walk to the public well, and then walk that distance again, and then again, you will reach the school."*
>
> *"You know how the boys and girls all race to that tall tree in the grove by the river? The school is maybe two of those races from our house, in the direction of the morning sun."*

Our culture is all around us, as invisible and as much taken for granted as water is to fish. No matter what we do or think about, we are expressing ourselves in terms of our culture.

Consider the cultural differences in how people talk about distance. In cities, distance is usually measured in blocks ("the store is about 15 blocks away"). To a child from a rural background, more culturally meaningful terms are needed, such as yards or miles, such practical rules of thumb as "a stone's throw," or references to known distances and landmarks ("about half the distance to town"). To make matters more complicated, "how far" questions are sometimes answered in terms not of distance, but of time ("it's about 15 minutes to the store"), which will be understood variously to refer to walking or riding time, depending on context—and, if riding time, to different forms of riding—by ox cart, bicycle, bus, canoe, or automobile, again depending on cultural context.

In short, not only is the nature of the tools available to children to solve problems and perform tasks highly dependent on the culture in which they live, but also the ways they think about problems and questions, and the ways they use those tools. ∎

Furthermore, aside from his observations about the social function that children's private speech serves and his approach to the development of intelligence, Vygotsky was largely silent on how basic cognitive processes such as attention and memory develop and how children's natural cognitive capabilities unfold. Because of his emphasis on broad cultural influences, he did not focus on how individual bits of information are processed and synthesized. These processes, essential to a complete understanding of cognitive development, are more directly addressed by information processing theories.

Still, Vygotsky's melding of the cognitive and social worlds of children has marked an important advance in our understanding of cognitive development.

REVIEW AND APPLY

REVIEW

- Lev Vygotsky proposed that the nature and progress of children's cognitive development are dependent on the children's social and cultural context.

- According to Vygotsky, culture and society determine how people engage in thought and set the agenda for education and the cognitive abilities that their members are expected to attain.

- Vygotsky's theory features the concepts of the zone of proximal development and scaffolding.

- Vygotsky suggests that schoolchildren should have the opportunity to experiment and participate actively with their peers in their learning.

- Vygotsky's ideas have influenced educational practices in the United States and other nations. In particular, the practice of cooperative learning and the technique of reciprocal teaching owe their development to his insights about how teachers can best help students learn.

- Despite a lack of precision about basic cognitive processes, Vygotsky has become in the years since his death an influential figure in the study of cognitive development and the practice of education.

APPLY

- If children's cognitive development is dependent on interactions with others, what obligations does society have regarding such social settings as preschools and neighborhoods?

- In what ways have educators and others begun to apply Vygotsky's ideas in schools and communities? Should governments take an active role in this endeavor?

LOOKING BACK

LO 1 What is cognitive development and how did Piaget revolutionize its study?

- Cognitive development focuses on changes in behavior that correspond to changes in an individual's intellectual abilities, with special attention to intelligence, language, and similar topics.

- Piaget differed from earlier psychologists in arguing that infants learn by doing, not by listening to the teaching of adults or through sensation and perception.

- Piaget's background as a biologist led him to use observational techniques to study children one or two at a time in their "natural habitat."

LO 2 What theoretical elements underlie Piaget's theory?

- Piaget theorized that the foundations of the way we understand the world are mental structures called schemes, organized patterns of functioning, that adapt and change with mental development.

- Two underlying principles explain how children's schemes grow. Assimilation consists of fitting stimuli or events into existing patterns of thought, while accommodation consists of expanding existing patterns of thought to fit stimuli or events.

- Piaget has been criticized for neglecting any consideration of development beyond the end of adolescence. Several cognitive researchers extend the stage approach to adulthood.

LO 3 What are the key features—and criticisms— of Piaget's theory?

- Piaget's theory is based on a stage approach to development, with children and adolescents passing through four universal stages in a predetermined sequence: sensorimotor, preoperational, concrete operational, and formal operational.

- In the six substages of the sensorimotor period, simple reflexes at first determine behaviors, then the infant's earliest habits become circular reactions, which eventually become goal-oriented problem-solving activities. In the next substage, infants deliberately vary their actions as if conducting experiments, and in the final substage, they begin to produce mental representations of events or objects.

- The preoperational stage occurs during the preschool years, as children's use of symbolic thinking, reasoning, and concepts increases. The preoperational stage has several limitations, including centration, a failure to conserve, an incomplete understanding of transformation, and egocentrism.

- Concrete operational thought develops during the early adolescent years. This stage is characterized by the active and appropriate use of logic. However, individuals in this stage are still limited to concrete reality and unable to deal with abstract or hypothetical questions.

- Piaget's final stage, the formal operational period, occurs in later adolescence as people develop the ability to think abstractly.

LO 4 What are some alternate approaches to Piaget's view of cognitive development?

- Despite Piaget's great influence on the field, specific aspects of his theory have been criticized, including the concept of stages that forms the basis of his theory and what many critics perceive as his persistent underestimation of children's abilities. We have also noted the criticism that his theory neglects ongoing cognitive development in adulthood.

- Gisela Labouvie-Vief maintains that postformal thought develops in young adulthood. Postformal thinking surpasses logic to encompass interpretive and subjective thinking.

- William Perry suggests that people move from dualistic thinking to relativistic thought during early adulthood, and K. Warner Schaie argues that adults pass through the acquisitive, achieving, responsible, executive, and reintegrative stages in the way they use information.

LO 5 What are the key features—and criticisms— of Vygotsky's theory?

- In Vygotsky's view, cognitive development is the product of culture and of social interactions.

- Vygotsky notes that children learn best by participating in active learning through child–adult and child–child interactions that fall within each child's zone of proximal development.

- He also observes that learners need support—a process called scaffolding—to encourage their learning and problem solving until they achieve independence and growth.

- Vygotsky's views are respected because they represent a consistent theoretical system and are consistent with modern research on learning and cognitive development.

- Critics contend that Vygotsky's theories lack precision and lend themselves only with difficulty to experimental tests. Furthermore, Vygotsky never addressed some of the major topics in cognitive development, such as attention and memory, and dealt only slightly with intelligence.

✧ KEY TERMS AND CONCEPTS

scheme (p. 221)
assimilation (p. 221)
accommodation (p. 221)
sensorimotor stage (of cognitive development) (p. 222)
goal-directed behavior (p. 224)
object permanence (p. 224)
mental representation (p. 225)
deferred imitation (p. 225)

preoperational stage (p. 225)
operations (p. 225)
symbolic function (p. 225)
centration (p. 226)
conservation (p. 226)
transformation (p. 227)
egocentric thought (p. 227)
intuitive thought (p. 227)
postformal thought (p. 234)

acquisitive stage (p. 235)
achieving stage (p. 236)
responsible stage (p. 236)
executive stage (p. 236)
reintegrative stage (p. 236)
zone of proximal development or ZPD (p. 237)
scaffolding (p. 238)

◆ EPILOGUE

We have examined the work of two major cognitive development researchers, Jean Piaget and Lev Vygotsky, as well as several critics of their approaches. We have seen the weighty influence of Piaget's work on subsequent theoretical approaches and experimental work, and we have marveled at the posthumous ability of a Russian psychologist to construct a structure of theory and thought that has recently gained a strong footing in American education.

Turn back to the prologue of this module, about Amelie Hawkins's conversations with her three-month-old daughter, and answer the following questions.

1. Is Amelie correct that her daughter is learning from the baby talk that Amelie directs at her?

2. What milestones in cognitive development can Amelie expect her daughter to achieve in the coming year?

◆ WWW.PEARSONCUSTOM.COM/MI/MSU_MYLABS VIDEO SERIES

For videos related to this module's content, log into www.pearsoncustom.com/mi/msu_mylabs to view the entire www.pearsoncustom.com/mi/msu_mylabs Video Series.

MYVIRTUALLIFE

- **What decisions would you make while raising a child?**
- **What would the consequences of those decisions be?**

Find out by accessing

WWW.PEARSONCUSTOM.COM/MI/MSU_MYLABS

to raise a virtual child and live your own virtual life.

◆ REFERENCES

Aguiar, A., & Baillargeon, R. (2002). Developments in young infants' reasoning about occluded objects. *Cognitive Psychology, 45,* 267–336.

Baillargeon, R. (2004). Infants' physical world. *Current Directions in Psychological Science, 13,* 89–94.

Balakrishnan, V., & Claiborne, L. (2012). Vygotsky from ZPD to ZCD in moral education: Reshaping Western theory and practices in local context. *Journal of Moral Education, 41,* 225–243.

Basseches, M. (1984). *Dialectical thinking and adult development.* Norwood, NJ: Ablex.

Bergelson, E., & Swingley, D. (2012). At 6–9 months, human infants know the meanings of many common nouns. *PNAS Proceedings of the National Academy of Sciences of the United States of America, 109,* 3253–3258.

Bjorklund, D. F. (1997). The role of immaturity in human development. *Psychological Bulletin, 122,* 153–169.

Blank, M., & White, S. J. (1999). Activating the zone of proximal development in school: Obstacles and solutions. In P. Llyod & C. Fernyhough (Eds.), *Lev Vygotsky: Critical assessments: The zone of proximal development Vol. III.* New York: Routledge.

Bower, T. G. R. (1977). *A primer of infant development.* San Francisco: Freeman.

Brainerd, C. (2003). Jean Piaget, learning research, and American education. In B. Zimmerman (Ed.), *Educational psychology: A century of contributions.* Mahwah, NJ: Lawrence Erlbaum.

Brandone, A. C., Cimpian, A., Leslie, S., & Gelman, S. A. (2012). Do lions have manes? For children, generics are about kinds rather than quantities. *Child Development, 83,* 423–433.

Bullinger, A. (1997). Sensorimotor function and its evolution. In J. Guimon (Ed.), *The body in psychotherapy* (pp. 25–29). Basil, Switzerland: Karger.

Butterworth, G. (1994). Infant intelligence. In J. Khalfa (Ed.), *What is intelligence? The Darwin College lecture series* (pp. 49–71). Cambridge, England: Cambridge University Press.

Chaiklin, S. (2003). The zone of proximal development in Vygotsky's analysis of learning and instruction. In A. Kozulin & B. Gindis (Eds.), *Vygotsky's educational theory in cultural context.* New York: Cambridge University Press.

Commons, M. L., & Richards, F. A. (2003). Four postformal stages. In J. Demick & C. Andreoletti (Eds.), *Handbook of adult development* (pp. 199–219). New York: Kluwer Academic/Plenum Publishers.

Crowley, K., Callaman, M. A., Tenenbaum, H. R., & Allen, E. (2001). Parents explain more often to boys than to girls during shared scientific thinking. *Psychological Science, 12,* 258–261.

Daniels, H. (2006, February). The 'Social' in post-Vygotskian theory. *Theory & Psychology, 16,* 37–49.

Daniels, H. (Ed.). (1996). *An introduction to Vygotsky.* New York: Routledge.

Dasen, P., Inhelder, B., Lavallee, M., & Retschitzki, J. (1978). *Naissance de l'intelligence chez l'enfant Baoule de Cote d'Ivoire.* Berne, IN: Hans Huber.

Dasen, P., Ngini, L., & Lavallee, M. (1979). Cross-cultural training studies of concrete operations. In L. H. Eckenberger, W. J. Lonner, & Y. H. Poortinga (Eds.), *Cross-cultural contributions to psychology.* Amsterdam: Swets & Zeilinger.

Dawson-Tunik, T., Fischer, K., & Stein, Z. (2004). Do stages belong at the center of developmental theory? A commentary on Piaget's stages. *New Ideas in Psychology, 22,* 255–263.

DeLoache, J. S., Chiong, C., Sherman, K., Islam, N., Vanderborght, M., Troseth, G. L., et al. (2010). Do babies learn from baby media? *Psychological Science, 21,* 1570–1574.

Demetriou, A., & Raftopoulos, A. (2004). *Cognitive developmental change: Theories, models and measurement.* New York: Cambridge University Press.

deVries, R. (1969). Constancy of genetic identity in the years 3 to 6. *Monographs of the Society for Research in Childhood Development, 34,* (3, Serial No. 127).

Elkind, D. (1996). Inhelder and Piaget on adolescence and adulthood: A postmodern appraisal. *Psychological Science, 7,* 216–220.

Feldman, R. S. (Ed.). (1992). *Applications of nonverbal behavioral theories and research.* Hillsdale, NJ: Lawrence Erlbaum.

Fernyhough, C. (1997). Vygotsky's sociocultural approach: Theoretical issues and implications for current research. In S. Hala (Ed.), *The development of social cognition* (pp. 65–92). Hove, England: Psychology Press/Lawrence Erlbaum, Taylor & Francis.

Flavell, J. H. (1996). Piaget's legacy. *Psychological Science, 7,* 200–203.

Gauvain, M. (1998). Cognitive development in social and cultural context. *Current Directions in Psychological Science, 7,* 188–194.

Goldstein, M. H., Schwade, J., Briesch, J., & Syal, S. (2010). Learning while babbling: Prelinguistic object directed vocalizations indicate a readiness to learn. *Infancy, 15,* 362–391.

Greenfield, P. M. (1976). Cross-cultural research and Piagetian theory: Paradox and progress. In K. F. Riegel & J. A. Meacham (Eds.), *The developing individual in a changing world: Vol. 1.* The Hague, The Netherlands: Mouton.

Halford, G. (2005). Development of Thinking. In *The Cambridge handbook of thinking and reasoning.* New York: Cambridge University Press.

Halford, G., & Andrews, G. (2006). Reasoning and problem Solving. In *Handbook of child psychology: Vol 2, Cognition, perception, and language (6th ed.).* Hoboken, NJ: John Wiley & Sons Inc.

Jahoda, G. (1980). Theoretical and systematic approaches in mass-cultural psychology. In H. C. Triandis & W. W. Lambert (Eds.), *Handbook of cross-cultural psychology* (Vol. 1). Boston: Allyn & Bacon.

Jahoda, G. (1983). European "lag" in the development of an economic concept: A study in Zimbabwe. *British Journal of Developmental Psychology, 1,* 113–120.

Johnson, S. (2009). Developmental origins of object perception. In *Learning and the infant mind.* New York: Oxford University Press.

Kail, R. V. (2004). Cognitive development includes global and domain-specific processes. *Merrill-Palmer Quarterly, 50* [Special issue: 50th anniversary issue: Part II, the maturing of the human development sciences: Appraising past, present, and prospective agendas], 445–455.

Karpov, Y. (2006). Neo-Vygotskian activity theory: Merging Vygotsky's and Piaget's theories of cognitive development. *Frontiers in: Cognitive psychology.* Hauppauge, NY: Nova Science Publishers.

Keating, D. P. (1980). Thinking processes in adolescence. In J. Adelson (Ed.), *Handbook of adolescent psychology.* New York: Wiley.

Keating, D. P. (1990). Adolescent thinking. In S. S. Feldman & G. R. Elliott (Eds.), *At the threshold.* Cambridge, MA: Harvard University Press.

Keating, D. P., & Clark, L. V. (1980). Development of physical and social reasoning in adolescence. *Developmental Psychology, 16,* 23–30.

Kitchener, R. F. (1996). The nature of the social for Piaget and Vygotsky. *Human Development, 39,* 243–249.

Klass, P. (2010, October 11). Understanding 'bababa' as a key to development. *The New York Times,* p. D5.

Kozulin, A. (2004). Vygotsky's theory in the classroom: Introduction. *European Journal of Psychology of Education, 19,* 3–7.

Krojgaard, P. (2005). Infants' search for hidden persons. *International Journal of Behavioral Development, 29,* 70–79.

Kuhn, D., & Franklin, S. (2006). The second decade: What develops (and how). *Handbook of child psychology: Vol 2, Cognition, perception, and language (6th ed.).* Hoboken, NJ: John Wiley & Sons Inc.

Labouvie-Vief, G. (1990). Modes of knowledge and the organization of development. In M. L. Commons, C. Armon, L. Kohlberg, F. A. Richards, T. A. Grotzer, & J. Sinnott (Eds.), *Adult development (Vol. 2). Models and methods in the study of adolescent thought.* New York: Praeger.

Labouvie-Vief, G. (2006). Emerging structures of adult thought. In J. J. Arnett & J. L. Tanner (Eds.), *Emerging adults in America: Coming of age in the 21st century.* Washington, DC: American Psychological Association.

Labouvie-Vief, G. (2009). Cognition and equilibrium regulation in development and aging. *Restorative Neurology and Neuroscience, 27,* 551–565.

Lau, I., Lee, S., & Chiu, C. (2004). Language, cognition, and reality: Constructing shared meanings through communication. In M. Schaller & C. Crandall (Eds.), *The psychological foundations of culture.* Mahwah, NJ: Lawrence Erlbaum.

Lavelli, M., & Fogel, A. (2005). Developmental changes in the relationship between the infant's attention and emotion during early face-to-face communication: The 2-month transition. *Developmental Psychology [serial online], 41,* 265–280.

Lehalle, H. (2006). Moral development in adolescence: How to integrate personal and social values? In *Handbook of adolescent development.* New York: Psychology Press.

Marcovitch, S., Zelazo, P., & Schmuckler, M. (2003). The effect of the number of A trials on performance on the A-not-B task. *Infancy, 3,* 519–529.

Maynard, A., & Greenfield, P. (2003). Implicit cognitive development in cultural tools and children: Lessons from Maya Mexico. *Cognitive Development, 18,* 489–510.

Mishra, R. (2001). Cognition across Cultures. In *The handbook of culture and psychology.* New York: Oxford University Press.

Mistry, J., & Saraswathi, T. (2003). The cultural context of child development. In R. Lerner & M. Easterbrooks (Eds.), *Handbook of psychology: Developmental psychology* (Vol. 6, pp. 267–291). New York: Wiley.

Nilsen, E., & Graham, S. (2009). The relations between children's communicative perspective-taking and executive functioning. *Cognitive Psychology, 58,* 220–249.

Oesterdiekhoff, G. (2007). The reciprocal causation of intelligence and culture: A commentary based on a Piagetian perspective. *European Journal of Personality, 21,* 742–743.

Perry, W. G. (1970). *Forms of intellectual and ethical development in the college years.* New York: Holt.

Perry, W. G. (1981). Cognitive and ethical growth: The making of meaning. In A. W. Chickering and Associates (Eds.), *The Modern American College.* San Francisco: Jossey-Bass.

Piaget, J. (1952). *The origins of intelligence in children.* New York: International Universities Press.

Piaget, J. (1962). *Play, dreams and imitation in childhood.* New York: Norton.

Piaget, J. (1983). Piaget's theory. In W. Kessen (Ed.), P. H. Mussen (Series Ed.), *Handbook of child psychology: Vol 1. History, theory, and methods* (pp. 103–128). New York: Wiley.

Piaget, J., & Inhelder, B. (1958). *The growth of logical thinking from childhood to adolescence* (A. Parsons & S. Seagrin, Trans.). New York: Basic Books.

Puntambekar, S., & Hübscher, R. (2005). Tools for scaffolding students in a complex learning environment: What have we gained and what have we missed? *Educational Psychologist, 40,* 1–12.

Rakison, D. H., & Krogh, L. (2012). Does causal action facilitate causal perception in infants younger than 6 months of age? *Developmental Science, 15,* 43–53.

Rakison, D., & Oakes, L. (2003). *Early category and concept development: Making sense of the blooming, buzzing confusion.* London: Oxford University Press.

Rogoff, B. (1995). *Observing sociocultural activity on three planes: Participatory appropriation, guided participation, and apprenticeship.* New York: Cambridge University Press.

Roth, D., Slone, M., & Dar, R. (2000). Which way cognitive development? An evaluation of the Piagetian and the domain-specific research programs. *Theory & Psychology, 10,* 353–373.

Ruffman, T., Slade, L., & Redman, J. (2006). Young infants' expectations about hidden objects. *Cognition [serial Online], 97,* B35-b43.

Schaie, K. W. (1977–1978). Toward a stage of adult theory of adult cognitive development. *Journal of Aging and Human Development, 8,* 129–138.

Schaie, K. W., & Willis, S. L. (1993). Age difference patterns of psychometric intelligence in adulthood: Generalizability within and across ability domains. *Psychology and Aging, 8,* 44–55.

Schaie, K. W., & Zanjani, F. A. K. (2006). Intellectual development across adulthood. In C. Hoare (Eds.), *Handbook of adult development and learning.* New York: Oxford University Press.

Schaller, M., & Crandall, C. S. (Eds.). (2004). *The psychological foundations of culture.* Mahwah, NJ: Lawrence Erlbaum.

Schlottmann, A., & Wilkening, F. (2012). Judgment and decision making in young children. In M. K. Dhami, A. Schlottmann, & M. R. Waldmann (Eds.), *Judgment and decision making as a skill: Learning, development and evolution.* New York: Cambridge University Press.

Scrimsher, S., & Tudge, J. (2003). The teaching/learning relationship in the first years of school: Some revolutionary implications of Vygotsky's theory. *Early Education and Development, 14* [Special issue], 293–312.

Segall, M. H., Dasen, P. R., Berry, J. W., & Poortinga, Y. H. (1990). *Human behavior in global perspective.* Boston: Allyn & Bacon.

Shea, J. D. (1985). Studies of cognitive development in Papua New Guinea. *International Journal of Psychology, 20,* 33–61.

Siegler, R. S. (2003). Thinking and intelligence. In M. Bornstein & L. Davidson (Eds.), *Well-being: Positive development across the life course* (pp. 311–320). Mahwah, NJ: Lawrence Erlbaum.

Siegler, R. S., & Ellis, S. (1996). Piaget on childhood. *Psychological Science, 7,* 211–215.

Sinnott, J. D. (1997). Developmental models of midlife and aging in women: Metaphors for transcendence and for individuality in community. In J. Coyle (Ed.), *Handbook on women and aging* (pp. 149–163). Westport, CT: Greenwood.

Sinnott, J. D. (2003). Postformal thought and adult development: Living in balance. In *Handbook of adult development.* New York: Kluwer Academic/Plenum Publishers.

Sinnott, J. D. (1998b). *The development of logic in adulthood: Postformal thought and its applications.* New York: Plenum.

Smorti, A. (2008). Everyday life reasoning, possible worlds and cultural processes. *Integrative Psychological & Behavioral Science, 42,* 224–232.

Sugarman, S. (1988). *Piaget's construction of the child's reality.* Cambridge, England: Cambridge University Press.

Tamis-LeMonda, C. S., & Cabrera, N. (2002). *Handbook of father involvement: Multidisciplinary perspectives.* Mahwah, NJ: Lawrence Erlbaum.

Tamis LeMonda, C. S., Song, L., Leavell, A., Kahana Kalman, R., & Yoshikawa, H. (2012). Ethnic differences in mother–infant language and gestural communications are associated with specific skills in infants. *Developmental Science, 15,* 384–397.

Tappan, M. B. (1997). Language, culture and moral development: A Vygotskian perspective. *Developmental Review, 17,* 199–212.

Tenenbaum, H. R., & Leaper, C. (1998). Gender effects on Mexican-descent parents' questions and scaffolding during toy play: A sequential analysis. *First Language, 18,* 129–147.

Tharp, R. G. (1989). Psychocultural variables and constants: Effects on teaching and learning in schools: Special issue: Children and their development: Knowledge base, research agenda, and social policy application. *American Psychologist, 44*, 349–359.

Thornton, J. (2004). Life-span learning: A developmental perspective. *International Journal of Aging & Human Development, 57*, 55–76.

Tudge, J., & Scrimsher, S. (2003). Lev S. Vygotsky on education: A cultural-historical, interpersonal, and individual approach to development. In B. Zimmerman (Ed.), *Educational psychology: A century of contributions*. Mahwah, NJ: Lawrence Erlbaum.

Van Der Veer, R., & Valsiner, J. (1993). *Understanding Vygotsky.* Oxford, England: Blackwell.

Vilette, B. (2002). Do young children grasp the inverse relationship between addition and subtraction? Evidence against early arithmetic. *Cognitive Development, 17*, 1365–1383.

Vygotsky, L. S. (1926/1997). *Educational psychology.* Delray Beach, FL: St. Lucie Press.

Wang, S-H., Baillargeon, R., & Paterson, S. (2005). Detecting continuity violations in infancy: A new account and new evidence from covering and tube events. *Cognition, 95*, 129–173.

Warwick, P., & Maloch, B. (2003). Scaffolding speech and writing in the primary classroom: A consideration of work with literature and science pupil groups in the USA and UK. *Reading: Literacy & Language, 37*, 54–63.

Wertsch, J. V. (1999). The zone of proximal development: Some conceptual issues. In P. Lloyd & C. Fernyhough (Eds.), *Lev Vygotsky: Critical assessments, Vol. 3: The zone of proximal development.* New York: Routledge.

Wertsch, J. V. (2008). From social interaction to higher psychological processes: A clarification and application of Vygotsky's theory. *Human Development, 51*, 66–79.

Winsler, A. (2003). Introduction to special issue: Vygotskian perspectives in early childhood education. *Early Education and Development, 14 [Special issue]*, pp. 253–269.

MODULE 7-B

INTELLIGENCE

(Sergey Peterman/Fotolia)

Preview

Part 1

Intelligence: Determining Individual Strengths

- Intelligence Benchmarks: Differentiating the Intelligent from the Unintelligent
- Measuring IQ: Present-Day Approaches to Intelligence

NEUROSCIENCE AND DEVELOPMENT: When Song Is Silent: Why Amusia Sufferers Can't Hear a Tune

- Smart Thinking: The Triarchic Theory of Intelligence

Review and Apply

LEARNING OBJECTIVES

Part 1
L01 What is intelligence, and how has it been measured over the years?
L02 What are newer conceptions of intelligence?

Taken from *Life Span Development: A Topical Approach*, Second Edition, by Robert S. Feldman, Ph.D.

Understanding precisely what is meant by the concept of intelligence has proven to be a major challenge for researchers.
(Radius Images/Glow Images)

PROLOGUE: STRIVING FOR THE BEST

Paul Galesko was a talented student in high school—popular with his classmates, a member of the drama society and the marching band, and at the top of all his classes. In fact, Paul had been a driven student since his first year, challenging himself each semester with the most advanced classes he could take—usually at the honors level. Paul's parents had instilled in him the value of education as a means to a better life; he could see for himself how his parents had to endure difficult lives because of their own lack of higher education and their decision to start having children when they were both young and not yet financially established. Paul was excited to be accepted at his first choice college, and during his first semester of college, he again earned terrific grades.

LOOKING AHEAD

Paul's academic achievements in high school and college raise a number of issues, addressed in this module, about the nature of intelligence. How can we define intelligent behavior? Are people like Paul smarter than others, or does he simply work harder or has more motivation to excel? What makes one person more, or less, intelligent than others.

To answer these questions, we first consider the ways that have been developed to differentiate children on the basis of intelligence. We discuss traditional measures of intelligence—IQ tests—and examine newer alternatives such as those suggested by Lev Vygotsky and information processing approaches to intelligence.

We then explore some of the controversial issues in the realm of intelligence. We consider how to measure intelligence in infancy and the meaning of racial differences in IQ scores. We also look at the contested topic of intelligence among adults and examine whether the picture of declining cognitive competence is an empty stereotype or has some truth in it. We then suggest ways that adults can maintain their cognitive functioning.

The module ends with an examination of the two groups that show the extremes of intelligence: people with intellectual disabilities and gifted people. We consider the nature of the exceptionality of each of these populations and focus on the question of how exceptional children should best be integrated into society.

PART 1   INTELLIGENCE: DETERMINING INDIVIDUAL STRENGTHS

LEARNING OBJECTIVES

LO 1   What is intelligence, and how has it been measured over the years?
LO 2   What are newer conceptions of intelligence?

"Why should you tell the truth?" "How far is Los Angeles from New York?" "A table is made of wood; a window of ____."

As ten-year-old Hyacinth sat hunched over her desk, trying to answer a long series of questions like these, she tried to guess the point of the test she was taking in her fifth-grade classroom. Clearly, the test didn't cover material that her teacher, Ms. White-Johnston, had talked about in class.

"What number comes next in this series: 1, 3, 7, 15, 31, ____?"

As she continued to work her way through the questions, she gave up trying to guess the rationale for the test. She'd leave that to her teacher, she sighed to herself. Rather than attempting to figure out what it all meant, she simply tried to do her best on the individual test items.

Hyacinth might be surprised to learn that she was not alone in questioning the meaning and import of the items on the test she was taking. For although the test items were painstakingly developed, many developmentalists would admit to harboring their own doubts as to whether questions such as these are appropriate to the task of assessing what they are designed to measure: intelligence.

Understanding precisely what is meant by the concept of intelligence has proven to be a major challenge for researchers interested in delineating what separates intelligent from unintelligent behavior. Although nonexperts have their own conceptions of intelligence (one survey found, for instance, that laypersons believe that intelligence consists of three components: problem-solving ability, verbal ability, and social competence), it has been more difficult for experts to concur (Sternberg et al., 1981; Weinberg, 1989). Still, a general definition of intelligence is possible: **Intelligence** is the capacity to understand the world, think with rationality, and use resources effectively when faced with challenges.

Part of the difficulty in defining intelligence stems from the many—and sometimes unsatisfactory—paths that have been followed over the years in the quest to distinguish more intelligent people from less intelligent ones. To understand how researchers have approached the task of devising batteries of assessments called *intelligence tests*, we need to consider some of the historical milestones in the area of intelligence. ◉

intelligence
the capacity to understand the world, think with rationality, and use resources effectively when faced with challenges

Watch "Intelligence Testing, Then and Now" in to see a psychologist discuss the history and current uses of intelligence tests. www.pearsoncustom. com/mi/msu_mylabs

◇ INTELLIGENCE BENCHMARKS: DIFFERENTIATING THE INTELLIGENT FROM THE UNINTELLIGENT

The Paris school system was faced with a problem at the turn of the twentieth century: A significant number of children were not benefiting from regular instruction. Unfortunately, these children—many of whom we would now say had mental retardation—were generally not identified early enough to shift them to special classes. The French minister of instruction approached psychologist Alfred Binet with the problem of devising a technique for the early identification of students who might benefit from instruction outside the regular classroom.

Binet tackled his task in a thoroughly practical manner. His years of observing school-aged children suggested to him that previous efforts to distinguish intelligent from unintelligent students—some of which were based on reaction time or keenness of sight—were off the mark. Instead, he launched a trial-and-error process in which items and tasks were administered to students who had been previously identified by teachers as being either "bright" or "dull." Tasks that the bright students completed correctly and the dull students failed to complete correctly were retained for the test. Tasks that did not discriminate between the two groups were discarded. The end result of this process was a test that reliably distinguished students who had previously been identified as fast or slow learners.

Binet's pioneering efforts in intelligence testing left three important legacies. The first was his pragmatic approach to the construction of intelligence tests. Binet did not have theoretical preconceptions about what intelligence was. Instead, he used a trial-and-error approach to psychological measurement that continues to serve as the predominant approach to test construction today. His definition of intelligence as that which his test measured has been adopted by many modern researchers, and it is especially popular among test developers who respect the widespread utility of intelligence tests but wish to avoid arguments about the underlying nature of intelligence.

Our second inheritance from Binet stems from his focus on linking intelligence and school success. Binet's reliance on teachers as the backbone for his procedure of constructing an intelligence test ensured that intelligence—defined as performance on the test—and school success—predicted by teachers—would be virtually one and the same. Binet's intelligence test and its current successors, then, have become reasonable indicators of the degree to which students possess attributes that contribute to successful school performance. Unfortunately, they do not provide particularly useful information regarding a vast number of other attributes that are largely unrelated to academic proficiency.

Finally, Binet developed a procedure of assigning each intelligence test score to a mental age, the age of the children taking the test who, on average, achieved that score. For example, if a six-year-old girl received a score of 30 on the test, and this was the average score received by ten-year-olds, her mental age would be considered 10 years. Similarly, a fifteen-year-old boy who scored a 90 on the test—thereby matching the mean score for fifteen-year-olds—would be assigned a mental age of 15 years.

Although assigning a mental age to students indicates whether or not they are performing at the same level as their peers, it does not permit adequate comparisons between students of different chronological (or physical) ages. By using mental age

The Wechsler Intelligence Scale for Children-Fourth Edition (WISC-IV) is widely used as an intelligence test that measures verbal and performance (nonverbal) skills.
(Wechsler Intelligence Scale for Children, Fourth Edition (WISC-IV).NCS Pearson, Inc. Reproduced with permission)

alone, for instance, one might assume that a fifteen-year-old responding with a mental age of 17 years would be as bright as a six-year-old responding with a mental age of eight years, when actually the six-year-old would be showing a much greater relative degree of brightness.

intelligence quotient, or IQ a score that takes into account a student's mental and chronological age

A solution to this problem comes in the form of the **intelligence quotient, or IQ**, a score that takes into account a student's mental and chronological age. The traditional method of calculating an IQ score uses the following formula, in which MA stands for mental age and CA for chronological age:

As a bit of trial-and-error with this formula demonstrates, people whose mental age (MA) is

$$IQ\ Score = \frac{MA \times 100}{CA}$$

equal to their chronological age (CA) will always have an IQ of 100. Furthermore, if the chronological age exceeds the mental age—implying below-average intelligence—the score will be below 100; and if the chronological age is lower than the mental age—suggesting above-average intelligence—the score will be above 100.

Using this formula, we can return to our earlier example of a fifteen-year-old who scores at a seventeen-year-old mental age. This student's IQ is 17/15 × 100, or 113. In comparison, the IQ of a six-year-old scoring at a mental age of eight is 8/6 × 100, or 133—a higher IQ score than the fifteen-year-old's.

Although the basic principles behind the calculation of an IQ score still hold, scores today are calculated in a more mathematically sophisticated manner and are known as deviation IQ scores. Rather than comparing performance to children who are younger and older, deviation IQ scores are computed by comparing other children of the same age. The average deviation IQ score remains set at 100, and tests are now statistically constructed so that approximately two-thirds of children of a given age fall within 15 points of the average score of 100, achieving scores between 85 and 115. As scores rise or fall beyond this range, the percentage of children in the same score category drops significantly (see Figure 7).

◆ MEASURING IQ: PRESENT-DAY APPROACHES TO INTELLIGENCE

Since the time of Binet, tests of intelligence have become increasingly accurate measures of IQ. Most of them can still trace their roots to his original work in one way or another. For example, one of the most widely used tests—the **Stanford-Binet Intelligence Scale, Fifth Edition (SB5)**—began as an American revision of Binet's original test. The test consists of a series of items that vary according to the age of the person being tested. For instance, young children are asked to answer questions about everyday activities or to copy complex figures. Older people are asked to explain proverbs, solve analogies, and describe similarities between groups of words. The test is administered orally, and test-takers are given progressively more difficult problems until they are unable to proceed.

The **Wechsler Intelligence Scale for Children-IV (WISC-IV)** and its adult version, the **Wechsler Adult Intelligence Scale-IV (WAIS-IV)**, are two other widely used intelligence tests. The tests provide separate measures of verbal and performance (or nonverbal) skills, as well as a total score. As you can see from the items similar to those actually on the test in Figure 8, the verbal tasks are traditional word problems testing skills such as understanding a passage, while typical nonverbal tasks are copying a complex design, arranging pictures in a logical order, and assembling objects. The separate portions of the test allow for easier identification of any specific problems a test-taker may have. For example, significantly higher scores on the performance part of the test than on the verbal part may indicate difficulties in linguistic development.

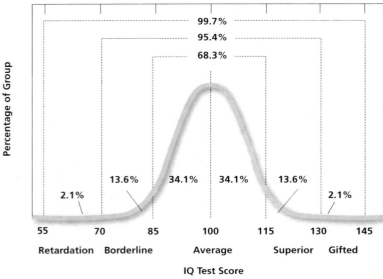

FIGURE 7 IQ Scores

The most common and average IQ score is 100, with 68.3 percent of all people falling within 15 points of 100. About 95 percent of the population has scores that are within 30 points above or below 100; fewer than 3 percent score below 55 or above 145.

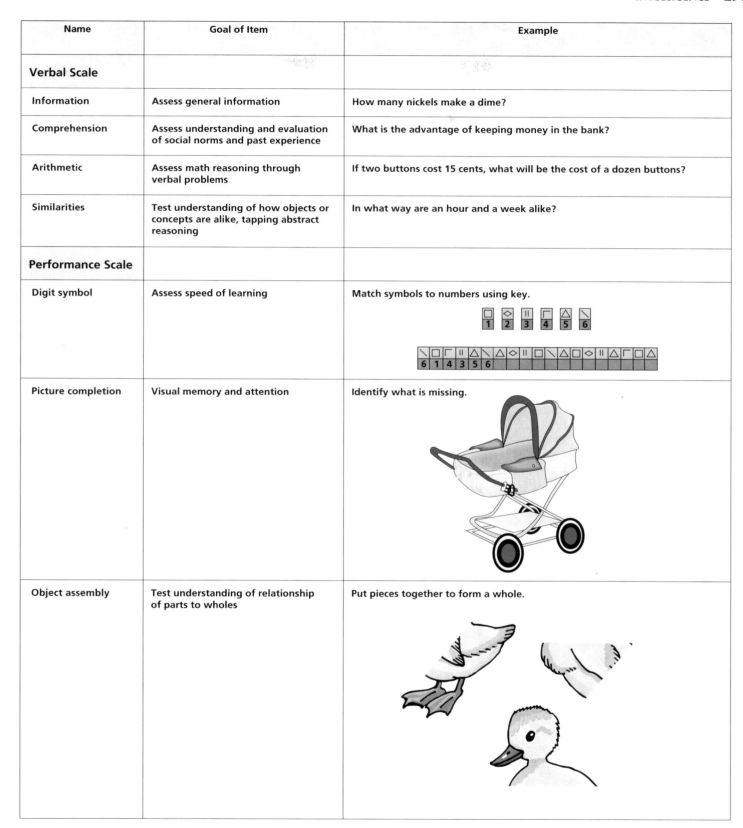

Name	Goal of Item	Example
Verbal Scale		
Information	Assess general information	How many nickels make a dime?
Comprehension	Assess understanding and evaluation of social norms and past experience	What is the advantage of keeping money in the bank?
Arithmetic	Assess math reasoning through verbal problems	If two buttons cost 15 cents, what will be the cost of a dozen buttons?
Similarities	Test understanding of how objects or concepts are alike, tapping abstract reasoning	In what way are an hour and a week alike?
Performance Scale		
Digit symbol	Assess speed of learning	Match symbols to numbers using key.
Picture completion	Visual memory and attention	Identify what is missing.
Object assembly	Test understanding of relationship of parts to wholes	Put pieces together to form a whole.

FIGURE 8   Measuring Intelligence

The Wechsler Intelligence Scale for Children-IV (WISC-IV) include s items such as these. What do such items cover? What do they miss?

Stanford-Binet Intelligence Scale, Fifth Edition (SB5)
A test that consists of a series of items that vary according to the age of the person being tested

Wechsler Intelligence Scale for Children-IV (WISC-IV)
A test for children that provides separate measures of verbal and performance (nonverbal) skills, as well as a total score

Wechsler Adult Intelligence Scale-IV (WAIS-IV)
A test for adults that provides separate measures of verbal and performance (nonverbal) skills, as well as a total score

Kaufman Assessment Battery for Children (KABC-II)
A children's intelligence test permitting unusual flexibility in its administration

The **Kaufman Assessment Battery for Children (KABC-II)** takes a different approach than the Stanford-Binet, WISC-IV, and WAIS-IV. In the KABC-II, children are tested on their ability to integrate different kinds of stimuli simultaneously and to use step-by-step thinking. A special virtue of the KABC-II is its flexibility. It allows the person giving the test to use alternative wording or gestures, or even to pose questions in a different language, in order to maximize a test-taker's performance. This makes testing more valid and equitable for children to whom English is a second language (Kaufman et al., 2005).

In addition to individualized IQ tests, there are also several tests designed to be administered to groups of children. Such group IQ tests require written answers to a series of written questions. Their great advantage over other types of IQ tests is the ease with which they can be administered.

Group IQ tests have several disadvantages, however. For one thing, the questions asked on group tests tend to be more restricted than those administered individually. In addition, children are often more motivated when they are asked questions individually by a test administrator than when they are responding in a group. Finally, outside factors, such as being distracted by other students, having their pencils break, or not paying attention to instructions, may interfere with children's performance. Ultimately, group-administered IQ tests may provide a far less accurate assessment of IQ than individually administered tests.

Some IQ tests have been specifically designed to overcome the potential for cultural bias. As we'll discuss later in the module, IQ tests have been criticized for discriminating against members of minority racial, ethnic, and cultural groups. In order to overcome this bias, *culture-fair IQ tests* are designed to be independent of the cultural background of test-takers. For example, the *Raven Progressive Matrices Test* asks test-takers to examine abstract designs that have a missing piece and choose the missing piece from several possibilities (see Figure 9).

The assumption behind culture-fair IQ tests is that no particular cultural group will be more or less acquainted with the test content, and consequently the test results will be free from cultural bias. Unfortunately, the culture-fair tests have not been very successful, and the disparities based on minority group membership still occur. A true culture-fair IQ test has yet to be developed (Sattler, 1992; Anastasi, 1997; Ostrosky-Solis & Oberg, 2006).

Reliability and Validity

Every time we measure our weight on a bathroom scale, we assume that any changes we find are due to fluctuations in our actual weight, and not produced by inaccuracies in the scale. In the same fashion, testing experts who produce IQ tests construct them to have reliability. **Reliability** exists when a test measures consistently what it is trying to measure. If we assume that IQ is a stable characteristic, then a test that has reliability will produce the same score each time it is administered to a particular person. If a test produced a score of 105 at one time, but the next time it produced a score of 130, then it is not reliable. On the other hand, if each time the test is administered to the same individual it yielded a score of 105, then the test is reliable.

Even if a test is reliable, it is not necessarily valid. A test has **validity** when it actually measures what it is supposed to measure. For instance, just as a valid bathroom scale should measure a person's weight correctly and unambiguously, a valid IQ test should measure an individual's underlying intelligence correctly and unambiguously.

Tests can be reliable without being valid. For example, we could devise a completely reliable test for intelligence if we made the assumption that skull circumference was related to intelligence. Because measuring skull size precisely is fairly easy, we would then have a very reliable measure. But would such a test of intelligence be valid? Hardly, because it seems far-fetched that skull size would have much to do with anyone's intelligence. Well, not far-fetched to everyone: There have been serious efforts in the past to match skull configuration to psychological attributes such as intelligence, although such attempts have, not surprisingly, proved unsuccessful (Gould, 1996; Deary et al., 2007).

To assess intelligence accurately, IQ tests must be both reliable *and* valid. Although there is wide agreement that well-established IQ tests meet the formal requirements of reliability, their validity, as we will see, is far more controversial.

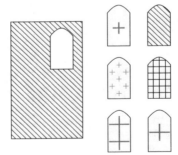

FIGURE 9 The Raven Progressive Matrices Test In the Raven Progressive Matrices Test, examinees are shown an abstract figure with a missing piece. They are asked to choose from several possibilities which piece would complete the figure. The Raven is designed to be free of cultural bias because it is assumed that no group is more or less familiar with the task.

IQ and School Achievement

What do IQ scores mean? For most children, they are reasonable predictors of school performance. That's not surprising, given that intelligence tests were developed to identify students who were having difficulties (Sternberg & Grigorenko, 2002).

But the story differs for performance outside of school. Although people with higher scores tend to finish more years of schooling, once this is statistically controlled for, IQ scores do not closely relate to income and later success in life. Two people with different scores may both earn bachelor's degrees at the same college, but the person with a lower IQ might have a higher income and a more successful career. These difficulties with traditional IQ scores have led researchers to consider alternative approaches (McClelland, 1993; Zagorsky, 2007).

Recall what the scores derived from IQ tests mean. For most children, IQ scores are reasonably good predictors of school performance. That's not surprising, given that the initial impetus for the development of intelligence tests was to identify children who were having difficulties in school.

But even within the academic sphere, IQ scores aren't always accurate predictors of school performance. For instance, 2.6 million school-age children in the United States are officially labeled as having learning disabilities. **Learning disabilities** are defined as difficulties in the acquisition and use of listening, speaking, reading, writing, reasoning, or mathematical abilities. A somewhat ill-defined, grab-bag category, learning disabilities are diagnosed when a discrepancy exists between children's actual academic performance and their apparent potential to learn as based on IQ scores and other ability measures (Lyon, 1996; Wong, 1996; Kozey & Siegel, 2008).

Several types of learning disabilities have been identified. The most common is *attention-deficit/hyperactivity disorder (ADHD)*. Children with ADHD are inattentive and impulsive, with a low tolerance for frustration and generally a great deal of inappropriate activity. Yet their IQ scores are either normal or above. Other children with learning disabilities suffer from *dyslexia*, a reading disability that can result in the misperception of letters during reading and writing, unusual difficulty in sounding out letters, confusion between left and right, and difficulties in spelling. Thus, normal IQ scores can fail to detect abnormal learning (Barkely, 1997; Byrne, Shankweiler, & Hine, 2008; Nicolson & Fawcett, 2008).

The utility of IQ scores becomes even less clear when we consider performance outside academic spheres. For instance, although people with higher IQ scores are apt to finish more years of schooling, once this is statistically controlled for, IQ scores are only moderately related to income and later success in life. Furthermore, IQ scores are frequently inaccurate when it comes to predicting a particular individual's future success. For instance, some minimal level of intelligence obviously is needed based on the demands of a specific profession. However, once a person enters a profession, IQ plays only a modest role in determining how successful a particular individual will be. Factors such as motivation, luck, and social skills account for a large part of occupational success (Sternberg, 1997; Wagner, 1997; Zagorsky, 2008).

In short, despite the frequent measurement and use of IQ scores, their relevance to nonscholastic domains is not clear. Because of these difficulties with traditional IQ scores, researchers have turned to alternative approaches to intelligence (McClelland, 1993; Pascual-Leone & Johnson, 2005).

What IQ Tests Don't Tell: Alternative Conceptions of Intelligence.

The intelligence tests schools use most today regard intelligence as a single factor, a unitary mental ability. This attribute is commonly called *g* (Spearman, 1927; Lubinski, 2004). Assumed to underlie performance on every aspect of intelligence, the *g* factor is what IQ tests presumably measure.

However, many theorists disagree that intelligence is unidimensional. As we will see in the next module, some developmentalists suggest that two kinds of intelligence exist: fluid and crystallized (Cattell, 1987, 2004). **Fluid intelligence** reflects information processing capabilities, reasoning, and memory; for example, a student asked to group a series of letters according to some criterion or to remember a set of numbers would be using fluid intelligence (Ziegler et al., 2012). In contrast, **crystallized intelligence** is the cumulative information, skills, and strategies people have learned and can apply in solving problems. A student would likely use crystallized

reliability
a quality of tests that measure consistently what they are trying to measure

validity
a quality of tests that actually measure what they are supposed to measure

learning disabilities
difficulties in the acquisition and use of listening, speaking, reading, writing, reasoning, or mathematical abilities

Bodily kinesthetic intelligence, as displayed by dancers, ballplayers, and gymnasts, is one of Gardner's eight intelligences. What are some examples of other Gardner intelligences?
(Jennie Woodcock/Bubbles PhotolibrarY/Alamy)

fluid intelligence
is intelligence that reflects information processing capabilities, reasoning, and memory

crystallized intelligence
the store of information, skills, and strategies that people have acquired through education and prior experiences and through their previous use of fluid intelligence

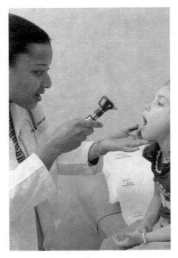

According to Robert Sternberg's triarchic theory of intelligence, practical intelligence is as important as traditional academic intelligence in determining success. (Robin Nelson/PhotoEdit, Inc.)

triarchic theory of intelligence
the belief that intelligence consists of three aspects of information processing: the componential element, the experiential element, and the contextual element

intelligence to solve a puzzle or find the solution to a mystery (Alfonso, Flanagan, & Radwan, 2005; McGrew, 2005).

Other theorists divide intelligence into even more parts. Psychologist Howard Gardner suggests that we have at least eight distinct intelligences, each of them relatively independent of the other (see Figure 10 on page 255). Gardner suggests that, for example, some people may be particularly skilled in linguistic intelligence, while others may be particularly skilled in musical intelligence. Others, in contrast, may show the opposite pattern (Chen & Gardner, 2005; Gardner & Moran, 2006; Roberts & Lipnevich, 2012; also see the *Neuroscience and Development* box on page 256).

The Russian psychologist Lev Vygotsky, whose cognitive development approach we discussed earlier, took a very different approach to intelligence. He suggested that we should assess intelligence by looking not only at fully developed cognitive processes, but at processes in development as well. To do this, he contended that assessment tasks should involve cooperative interaction between the assessed individual and the assessor—a process called *dynamic assessment*. In short, intelligence is reflected both in how children perform on their own and how they perform when helped by adults (Vygotsky, 1927/1976; Brown & Ferrara, 1999; Lohman, 2005).

Psychologist Robert Sternberg (2003a), taking another approach, suggests that intelligence is best viewed as information processing. In this view, how people store material in memory and later use it to solve intellectual tasks provides the most precise concept of intelligence. Rather than focusing on the subcomponents that make up the *structure* of intelligence, information processing approaches examine the *processes* underlying intelligent behavior.

Studies of the nature and speed of problem-solving processes show that people with higher intelligence levels differ from others in the number of problems they solve and the methods they use. People with high IQ scores spend more time on the initial stages of problem solving, retrieving relevant information from memory. In contrast, those who score lower tend to skip ahead and make less informed guesses. The processes used in solving problems may reflect important differences in intelligence (Sternberg, 1982, 1990; Sternberg, Kaufman, & Grigorenko, 2008).

Sternberg's work on information processing approaches led him to develop the triarchic theory of intelligence, which we will look at next.

◇ SMART THINKING: THE TRIARCHIC THEORY OF INTELLIGENCE

Your year on the job has been generally favorable. Performance ratings for your department are at least as good as they were before you took over, and perhaps even a little better. You have two assistants. One is quite capable. The other just seems to go through the motions and is of little real help. Even though you are well liked, you believe that there is little that would distinguish you in the eyes of your superiors from the nine other managers at a comparable level in the company. Your goal is rapid promotion to an executive position.

How do you meet your goal? (Based on Wagner & Sternberg, 1985, p. 447)

The way adults answer this question may affect their future success. The question is one of a series that psychologist Robert Sternberg designed to assess a particular type of intelligence that may have more of an impact on future success than the IQ measured by traditional tests.

In his **triarchic theory of intelligence**, Sternberg suggests that intelligence is made up of three major components: componential, experiential, and contextual. The *componential aspect* involves the mental components used to solve problems (e.g., selecting and using formulas, choosing problem-solving strategies, and in general making use of what has been learned in the past). The *experiential component* refers to the relationship between intelligence, prior experience, and the ability to cope with new situations. This is the insightful aspect of intelligence, which allows people to relate what they already know to a new situation and facts never before encountered. Finally, the *contextual component* of intelligence takes account of the demands of everyday, real-world environments. For instance, the contextual component is involved in adapting to on-the-job professional demands (Sternberg, 2005).

Traditional IQ tests tend to focus on the componential aspect. Yet increasing evidence suggests that a more useful measure, particularly when comparing and predicting adult success, is the contextual component—the aspect of intelligence that has come to be called practical intelligence.

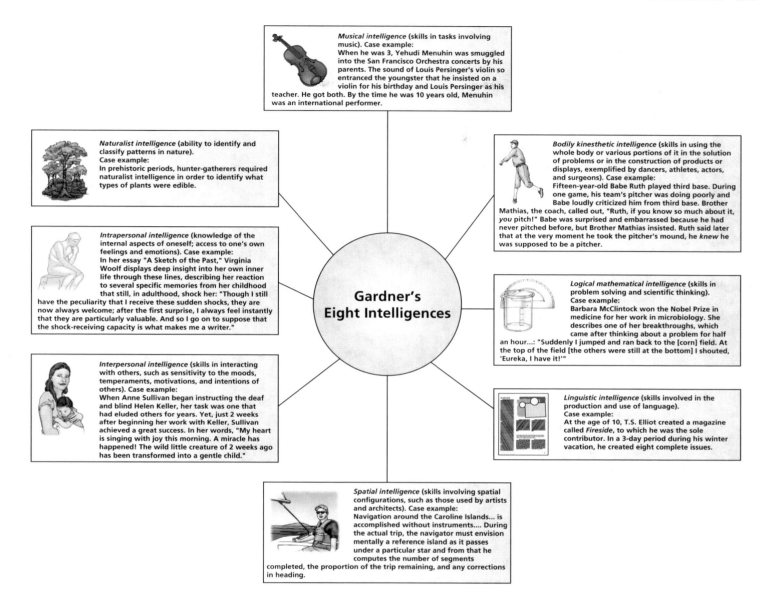

FIGURE 10 Gardner's Eight Intelligences

Howard Gardner has theorized that there are eight distinct intelligences, each relatively independent of one another. How do you fit into this categorization?

(*Source:* Based on Walters & Gardner, 1986.)

Practical and Emotional Intelligence

According to Sternberg, traditional IQ scores relate quite well to academic success but not to other types of achievement, such as career success. Although it is clear that success in business requires some level of the IQ sort of intelligence, the rate of career advancement and the ultimate success of business executives is only marginally related to IQ scores (Ree & Carretta, 2002; Cianciolo et al., 2006; Sternberg, 2006).

Sternberg contends that success in a career necessitates practical intelligence (Sternberg et al., 1997). While academic success is based on knowledge obtained largely from reading and listening, **practical intelligence** is learned primarily by observing others and modeling their behavior. People with practical intelligence have good "social radar." They understand and handle even new situations effectively, reading people and circumstances insightfully based on their previous experiences.

NEUROSCIENCE AND DEVELOPMENT

WHEN SONG IS SILENT: WHY AMUSIA SUFFERERS CAN'T HEAR A TUNE

As a preschooler, Alexa put her hands over her ears when her caregiver sang or played music. In third grade her teacher reported that Alexa was disruptive in music class—oftentimes singing the same note louder rather than following the melody of a song. It was not until she participated in a college psychology experiment that Alexa was diagnosed as one of five percent of the population with amusia, or tone deafness.

Some people cannot carry a tune, but they still process musical tones normally. In contrast, people with *amusia*, like Alexa, are unable to differentiate pitch and often are unaware when they are singing out of tune. They also may have difficulty recognizing familiar melodies without the assistance of lyrics (Peretz et al., 2009).

New brain imaging research provides insight into the brain's role in amusia. In a recent study, researchers investigated tone deafness and its association with one of the brain's neural highways and major fiber bundles called the arcuate fasciculus (AF). The AF is a white-matter, neural fiber tract that connects the right temporal lobe (where basic sound processing occurs) and frontal brain regions (where higher thinking occurs). It plays a major role in linking music and language perception with vocal production.

In the study, brain scans showed that people with amusia had less neural connectivity in the AF compared to 10 musically normal-functioning people. White matter of the people with amusia was smaller in size and possessed fewer fibers, suggesting a weaker connection. In addition, abnormal AF branching occurred, indicating that dendrites bringing information to the AF cells and axons taking information away from AF cells were less effective in processing music-related information (Loui, Alsop, & Schlaug, 2009).

This study represents the first investigation into the structural and neural correlates of tone deafness. So the next time you hear terrible singing in a karaoke bar, forgive the singer: He or she may be suffering from amusia.

- Based on these findings, do you think amusia can be corrected? Why or why not?
- What suggestions might you give to teachers working with children who are required to take music classes as part of their curriculum?

There is another related type of intelligence. **Emotional intelligence** is the set of skills that underlies the accurate assessment, evaluation, expression, and regulation of emotions. Emotional intelligence is what enables people to get along well with others, to understand what they are feeling and experiencing, and to respond appropriately to their needs. Emotional intelligence is of obvious value to career and personal success as a young adult (Mayer, Salovey, & Caruso, 2008; Kross & Grossmann, 2012).

Creativity: Novel Thought

The hundreds of musical compositions of Wolfgang Amadeus Mozart, who died at the age of 35, were largely written during early adulthood. This pattern—major works produced during early adulthood—is true of many other creative individuals (Dennis, 1966a; see Figure 11).

One reason for the productivity of early adulthood may be that after this period creativity can be stifled by a phenomenon that psychologist Sarnoff Mednick (1963) called "familiarity breeds rigidity." By this he meant that the more people know about a subject, the less likely they are to be creative. Early adulthood may be the peak of creativity because many problems encountered professionally are novel.

On the other hand, many people do not reach their pinnacle of creativity until much later in life. For instance, Buckminster Fuller did not devise the geodesic dome until he was in his 50s. Frank Lloyd Wright designed the Guggenheim Museum in New York at age 70. Charles Darwin and Jean Piaget were still writing influential works well into their 70s, and Picasso was painting in his 90s. Furthermore, overall productivity, as opposed to the period of a person's most important output, remains fairly steady throughout adulthood, particularly in the humanities (Simonton, 1989; Feist & Barron, 2003).

Overall, the study of creativity reveals few consistent developmental patterns. One reason is the difficulty of determining just what constitutes creativity, which is defined as combining responses or ideas in novel ways. Because definitions of what is "novel" may vary from one person to the next, it is hard to identify a particular behavior unambiguously as creative (Sasser-Coen, 1993; Kaufman & Sternberg, 2006).

This hasn't stopped psychologists from trying. One suggested component of creativity is a person's willingness to take risks that may yield high payoffs. Creative people are like successful stock market investors who follow the "buy low, sell high" rule. Creative people develop and endorse ideas that are

practical intelligence
according to Sternberg, intelligence that is learned primarily by observing others and modeling their behavior

emotional intelligence
the set of skills that underlies the accurate assessment, evaluation, expression, and regulation of emotions

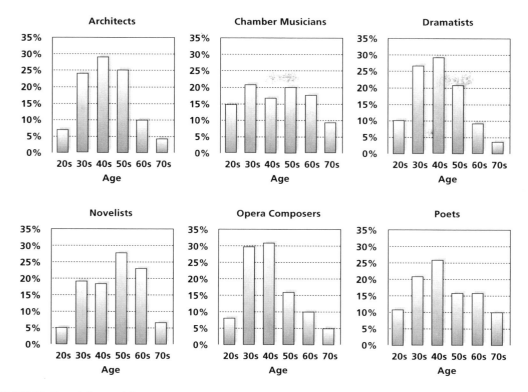

FIGURE 11 Creativity and Age

The period of maximum creativity differs depending on the particular field. The percentages refer to the percent of total lifetime major works produced during the particular age period. Why do poets peak earlier than novelists?

(*Source: Journal of Gerontology* by W. Dennis. Copyright 1966 by The Gerontological Society of America. Reproduced with the permission of The Gerontological Society of America in the format Textbook via Copyright Clearance Center.)

unfashionable or regarded as wrong ("buying low"), assuming that eventually others will see their value and embrace them ("selling high"). According to this theory, creative adults take a fresh look at ideas that were initially discarded, particularly if the problem is a familiar one. They are flexible enough to move away from tried and true ways of doing things and to consider new approaches (Sternberg & Lubart, 1992; Sternberg, Kaufman, & Peretz, 2002; Sawyer, 2012).

REVIEW AND APPLY

REVIEW

- Pinning down the meaning of intelligence and measuring it accurately have proven to be challenging tasks that have occupied psychologists for many years.

- The measurement of intelligence began in the twentieth century with the work of Alfred Binet, who took a trial-and-error approach to the question. His work is reflected in the most widely used IQ tests of today.

- To Binet we owe three legacies: his pragmatic, nontheoretical approach to intelligence testing; his linkage of intelligence to school success; and his derivation of a mathematical means of classifying children as more or less intelligent according to IQ scores.

- Measurements must have both reliability (defined as consistency across persons and over time) and validity (defined as measuring what they claim to measure).

- Learning disabilities are defined as difficulties in the acquisition and use of listening, speaking, reading, writing, reasoning, or mathematical abilities.

- While they are reasonably predictive of school success, IQ scores fall short in other realms. As a result, a number of alternative conceptions of intelligence have emerged that differentiate different kinds of intelligence.

REVIEW AND APPLY CONTINUED

- One of the most successful alternative conceptions is Robert Sternberg's *triarchic theory of intelligence*, which breaks the factor down into componential, experiential, and contextual components.

- Creativity is often, though not exclusively, a characteristic of young adults. This appears to be so because young adults' minds are flexible enough to explore novel approaches to problem solving.

APPLY

- If a perfectly valid and reliable measure of intelligence were developed, how would it best be used? What uses would be inappropriate?

- Do you think that practical and emotional intelligence are distributed equally along gender lines, or do women have more or less of one type than men do? What would be the consequences if the opposite of your answer were true?

LOOKING BACK

LO 1 What is intelligence, and how has it been measured over the years?

- It is difficult for developmental psychologists to define and measure intelligence. Alfred Binet is responsible for most twentieth-century approaches to the study of intelligence.

- Binet left three major contributions to the field of intelligence measurement: using a practical, nontheoretical approach; linking intelligence to academic success; and using IQ scores to quantify intelligence.

- Measurements must be consistent (i.e., have reliability) and measure what they are expected to measure (i.e., have validity).

LO 2 What are newer conceptions of intelligence?

- Alternative conceptions of intelligence have sprung up to explain different kinds of intelligence, including Robert Sternberg's triarchic theory of intelligence, which claims that intelligence is composed of componential, experiential, and contextual components.

- Creativity is often a young adult trait because young adults' minds are not set in habitual ways of solving problems.

◇ KEY TERMS AND CONCEPTS

intelligence (p. 249)
intelligence quotient, or IQ (p. 250)
Stanford-Binet Intelligence Scale, Fifth Edition (SB5) (p. 251)
Wechsler Intelligence Scale for Children-IV (WISC-IV) (p. 251)

Wechsler Adult Intelligence Scale-IV (WAIS-IV) (p. 251)
Kaufman Assessment Battery for Children (KABC-II) (p. 252)
reliability (p. 253)
validity (p. 253)

learning disabilities (p. 253)
fluid intelligence (p. 253)
crystallized intelligence (p. 253)
triarchic theory of intelligence (p. 254)
practical intelligence (p. 255)
emotional intelligence (p. 256)

◇ EPILOGUE

We opened the module with the question of what intelligence consists of and how it can be defined. We saw some of the ways in which intelligence has been measured, and we considered controversial topics such as group performance differences on IQ tests and the nature of cognitive decline that accompanies aging. Our discussion of intelligence concluded with a look at two groups with intellectual exceptionalities at opposite ends of the intelligence scale: people with intellectual disability and people who are gifted or talented.

Return to the prologue of this module, in which we met college student Paul Galesko. In light of what you now know about intelligence, answer the following questions.

1. How might Paul's parents have influenced his academic achievements in high school?
2. Paul was academically talented, but in what ways may he have been lacking in practical and emotional intelligence?

3. Is there a fair way to measure Paul's intelligence? Would Howard Gardner's theory work?

4. As Paul ages, should he expect his intellectual ability to increase, decrease, or remain stable?

◇ REFERENCES

Alfonso, V. C., Flanagan, D. P., & Radwan, S. (2005). The impact of the Cattell-Horn-Carroll theory on test development and interpretation of cognitive and academic abilities. In D. P. Flanagan & P. L. Harrison (Eds.), *Contemporary intellectual assessment: Theories, tests, and issues*. New York: Guilford Press.

Barkley, R. A. (1997a). *ADHD and the nature of self-control.* New York: Guilford Press.

Barkley, R. A. (1997b). Behavioral inhibition, sustained attention, and executive functions: Constructing a unifying theory of ADHD. *Psychological Bulletin, 121,* 65–94.

Brown, A. L., & Ferrara, R. A. (1999). Diagnosing zones of proximal development. In P. Llyod & C. Fernyhough (Eds.), *Lev Vygotsky: Critical assessments: The zone of proximal development Vol. III.* New York: Routledge.

Byrne, B., Shankweiler, D., & Hine, D. (2008). Reading development in children at risk for dyslexia. In *Brain, behavior, and learning in language and reading disorders*. New York: Guilford Press.

Cattell, R. (2004). The theory of fluid and crystallized intelligence; its relationship with "culture-free" tests and its verification with children aged 9–12 years. *European Review of Applied Psychology, 54,* 47–56.

Chen, J., & Gardner, H. (2005). Assessment based on multiple-intelligences theory. In D. P. Flanagan & P. L. Harrison (Eds.), *Contemporary intellectual assessment: Theories, tests, and issues*. New York: Guilford Press.

Cianciolo, A. T., Matthew, C., & Sternberg, R. J. (2006). Tacit knowledge, practical intelligence, and expertise. In K. A. Ericsson, N. Charness, P. J. Feltovich, & R. R. Hoffman (Eds.), *The Cambridge handbook of expertise and expert performance*. New York: Cambridge University Press.

Deary, I., Ferguson, K., Bastin, M., Barrow, G., Reid, L., Seckl, J., et al. (2007). Skull size and intelligence, and King Robert Bruce's IQ. *Intelligence, 35,* 519–528.

Dennis, W. (1966). Age and creative productivity. *Journal of Gerontology, 21,* 1–8.

Feist, G., & Barron, F. (2003). Predicting creativity from early to late adulthood: Intellect, potential, and personality. *Journal of Research in Personality, 37,* 62–88.

Gardner, H., & Moran, S. (2006). The science of multiple intelligences theory: A response to Lynn Waterhouse. *Educational Psychologist, 41,* 227–232.

Kaufman, J. C., & Sternberg, R. (2006). *The international handbook of creativity.* New York: Cambridge University Press.

Kaufman, J. C., Kaufman, A. S., Kaufman-Singer, J., & Kaufman, N. L. (2005). The Kaufman Assessment Battery for Children—Second Edition and the Kaufman Adolescent and Adult Intelligence Test. In D. P. Flanagan & P. L. Harrison (Eds.), *Contemporary intellectual assessment: Theories, tests, and issues*. New York: Guilford Press.

Kozey, M., & Siegel, L. (2008). Definitions of learning disabilities in Canadian provinces and territories. *Canadian Psychology/Psychologie canadienne, 49,* 162–171.

Kross, E., & Grossmann, I. (2012). Boosting wisdom: Distance from the self enhances wise reasoning, attitudes, and behavior. *Journal of Experimental Psychology: General, 141,* 43–48.

Lohman, D. (2005). Reasoning abilities. In *Cognition and intelligence: Identifying the mechanisms of the mind*. New York: Cambridge University Press.

Lubinski, D. (2004). Introduction to the special section on cognitive abilities: 100 years after Spearman's (1904) " 'General Intelligence,' objectively determined and measured." *Journal of Personality and Social Psychology, 86,* 96–111.

Lyon, G. R. (1996). Learning disabilities. *The Future of children, 6,* 54–76.

Mayer, J., Salovey, P., & Caruso, D. (2008). Emotional intelligence: New ability or eclectic traits? *American Psychologist, 63,* 503–517.

McClelland, D. C. (1993). Intelligence is not the best predictor of job performance. *Current Directions in Psychological Research, 2,* 5–8.

McGrew, K. S. (2005). The Cattell-Horn-Carroll theory of cognitive abilities: Past, present, and future. In D. P. Flanagan & P. L. Harrison (Eds.), *Contemporary intellectual assessment: Theories, tests, and issues*. New York, Guilford Press.

Mednick, S. A. (1963). Research creativity in psychology graduate students. *Journal of Consulting Psychology, 27*, 265–266.

Nicolson, R., & Fawcett, A. (2008). *Dyslexia, learning, and the brain.* Cambridge, MA: MIT Press.

Ostrosky-Solís, F., & Oberg, G. (2006). Neuropsychological functions across the world—common and different features: From digit span to moral judgment. *International Journal of Psychology, 41*, 321–323.

Pascual-Leone, J., & Johnson, J. (2005). A dialectical constructivist view of developmental intelligence. In *Handbook of understanding and measuring intelligence.* Thousand Oaks, CA: Sage Publications, Inc.

Ree, M., and Carretta, T. (2002). g2K. *Human Performance, 15,* 3–24.

Roberts, R. D., & Lipnevich, A. A. (2012). From general intelligence to multiple intelligences: Meanings, models, and measures. In K. R. Harris, S. Graham, T. Urdan, S. Graham, J. M. Royer, & M. Zeidner (Eds.), *APA educational psychology handbook, Vol 2: Individual differences and cultural and contextual factors.* Washington, DC: American Psychological Association.

Sasser-Coen, J. R. (1993). Qualitative changes in creativity in the second half of life: A life-span developmental perspective. *Journal of Creative Behavior, 27,* 18–27.

Sattler, J. M. (1992). *Assessment of children: WISC—III and WPPSI—R supplement.* San Diego, CA: Jerome M. Sattler.

Sawyer, R. (2012). *Explaining creativity: The science of human innovation (2nd ed.).* New York: Oxford University Press.

Simonton, D. K. (1989). The swan-song phenomenon: Last-works effects for 172 classical composers. *Psychology and Aging, 4,* 42–47.

Spearman, C. (1927). *The abilities of man.* London: Macmillan.Spen

Sternberg, J. (2005). The triarchic theory of successful intelligence. In D. P. Flanagan & P. L. Harrison (Eds.), *Contemporary Intellectual Assessment: Theories, Tests, and Issues.* New York: Guilford Press.

Sternberg, R. J. (1997). *Educating intelligence: Infusing the Triarchic Theory into school instruction.* New York: Cambridge University Press.

Sternberg, R. J. (1982). Reasoning, problems solving, and intelligence. In R. J. Sternberg (Ed.), *Handbook of human intelligence* (pp. 225–307). Cambridge, England: Cambridge University Press.

Sternberg, R. J. (1990). *Metaphors of mind: Conceptions of the nature of intelligence.* Cambridge, England: Cambridge University Press.

Sternberg, R. J. (2006). Intelligence. In K. Pawlik & G. d'Ydewalle (Eds.), *Psychological concepts: An international historical perspective.* Hove, England: Psychology Press/Taylor & Francis.

Sternberg, R. J., & Grigorenko, E. L. (Eds.). (2002). *The general factor of intelligence: How general is it?* Mahwah, NJ: Lawrence Erlbaum.

Sternberg, R. J., & Lubart, T. I. (1992). Buy low and sell high: An investment approach to creativity. *Current Directions in Psychological Science, 1,* 1–5.

Sternberg, R. J., Wagner, R. K., Williams, W. M., & Horvath, J. A. (1997). Testing common sense. In D. Russ-Eft, H. Preskill, & C. Sleezer (Eds.), *Human resource development review: Research and implications.* Thousand Oaks, CA: Sage Publications.

Sternberg, R. J., Kaufman, J. C., & Grigorenko, E. (2008). *Applied intelligence.* New York: Cambridge University Press.

Sternberg, R. J., Kaufman, J. C., & Pretz, J. E. (2002). *The creativity conundrum: A propulsion model of creative contributions.* Philadelphia, PA: Psychology Press.

Sternberg, R. J., Conway, B. E., Ketron, J. L., & Bernstein, M. (1981). Peoples' conceptions of intelligence. *Journal of Personality and Social Psychology, 41,* 37–55.

Wagner, R. K., & Sternberg, R. J. (1985). Alternate conceptions of intelligence and their implications for education. *Review of Educational Research, 54,* 179–223.

Walters, E., & Gardner, H. (1986). The theory of multiple intelligences: Some issues and answers. In R. J. Sternberg & R. K. Wagner (Eds.), *Practical intelligence.* New York: Cambridge University Press.

Weinberg, R. A. (1989). Intelligence and IQ: Landmark issues and great debates. *American Psychologist, 44(2),* 98–104.

Wong, B. Y. L. (1996). *The ABCs of learning disabilities.* San Diego, CA: Academic Press.

Zagorsky, J. (2007). Do you have to be smart to be rich? The impact of IQ on wealth, income and financial distress. *Intelligence, 35,* 489–501.

Ziegler, M., Danay, E., Heene, M., Asendorpf, J., & Bühner, M. (2012). Openness, fluid intelligence, and crystallized intelligence: Toward an integrative model. *Journal of Research in Personality, 46,* 173–183.

Name: _____   Date: _____

MODULE 7-C

ACTIVITY

◇ MAGICAL THINKING

Sometimes members of more traditional cultures are described as using forms of magical thinking that defy rules of logic and reason. Paul Rozin and Carol Nemeroff (2002) suggest that such thinking is not limited to traditional cultures, but exists in some aspects of daily life in highly industrialized cultures as well. Their research on college students in the United States indicates the two forms of magical thinking below, described a century ago by Sir James Frazer (1890/1959).

The law of contagion states that when two things (or beings) are in contact with each other the properties of one can permanently transfer to the other. For example,

Frazer describes an ancient Chinese practice in which burial clothes were sewn by young women with the reasoning that their longevity would somehow pass into the clactivityothes and ensure that the clothes themselves would live long (that is, not be used for many years).

The law of similarity holds that an image of an object or person takes on the characteristics of the actual object or person. For example, Frazer notes that in many cultures it was believed that by injuring footprints it is possible to injure the feet that made them.

The purpose of this activity is to explore the use of magical thinking among college students and consider the meaning of such thinking for understanding the link between culture and cognition.

Directions: Identify two college students to act as participants in this activity. Then, using the interview forms below, ask each participant the two questions about magical thinking based on the study by Rozin, Millman, and Nemeroff (1986). Please interview the two participants separately and do not tell them that you are studying magical thinking. The first item addresses the law of contagion and the second item addresses the law of similarity.

Taken from *Cross-Cultural Explorations: Activities in Culture and Psychology*, Second Edition, by Susan Goldstein.

Participant A

1. Would you rather wear a laundered shirt that had been previously worn by someone you like, someone you dislike, or someone you don't know? Please explain.

2. Would it be more difficult for you to throw darts at a dartboard depicting a picture of someone you like or someone you don't like? Please explain.

Participant B

1. Would you rather wear a laundered shirt that had been previously worn by someone you like, someone you dislike, or someone you don't know? Please explain.

2. Would it be more difficult for you to throw darts at a dartboard depicting a picture of someone you like or someone you don't like? Please explain.

Reactions:

1. To what extent did your participants manifest magical thinking (on item 1, choosing the shirt worn by the liked person, and on item 2, having more difficulty throwing darts at the liked person, indicates magical thinking).

2. Can you think of any alternative explanations for the "magical thinking" in the two questions asked of the participants?

3. Have you engaged in any other forms of magical thinking? Please explain.

4. To what extent does magical thinking interfere with rational thinking in everyday life in your culture?

◇ SOURCE

Based on Rozin, P., Millman, L., & Nemeroff, C. (1986). Operation of the laws of sympathetic magic in disgust and other domains. *Journal of Personality and Social Psychology*, 50, 703-712.

◇ REFERENCES

Frazer, J. G. (1959). *The new golden bough: A study in magic and religion*. New York: MacMillan (Edited by T. H. Gaster, 1922; Original work published 1890).

Rozin, P., & Nemeroff, C. (2002). Sympathetic magical thinking: The contagion and similarity "heuristics." In T. Gilovich, D. Griffin, & D. Kahneman (Eds.), *Heuristics and biases: The psychology of intuitive judgment* (pp. 201-215). New York: Cambridge University Press.

SECTION 8

SELF

MODULE 8-A

CULTURE, SELF, AND PERSONALITY

Sergej was happy, agreeable, and easy to care for as a child. He grew up on a kolkhozy *(collective farm) in the Ukraine, one of the fifteen republics in the former Soviet Union. Sergej was quiet, and even his adolescent years were not characterized by the confusion and psychological turmoil experienced by so many young people. Sergej did well in school, completed an apprenticeship, and, following the breakup of the Soviet Union, now works on his family's small farm. He has been married for several years, and his wife, Tamara, describes him as a "good husband" who works hard, stays at home, and cares for his family.*

Yuen, born in Guizhou province in south central China, was what her mother considered a difficult child. Her moods were unpredictable, and when upset she took a long time to calm down. Yuen never developed a regular sleeping and feeding schedule, making it difficult for her mother to coordinate her work and child care. Her adolescent years were equally challenging. Yuen had few friends and struggled with discipline problems at school. Now in her mid-thirties, she has assumed a leadership position in her work. Occasionally, she has to be reprimanded for her creative and sometimes radical ideas.

Sergej and Yuen clearly are very different people and showed very distinct character traits as children and as adults. Were they born with different personalities? Are these differences due to innate cultural patterns of personality? How much do cultural expectations about the course of one's life influence adult personality? We address these and other questions in this module by examining issues of personality, self, and individual differences and their embeddedness in a cultural context.

◇ ECOLOGICAL CONTEXT: TEMPERAMENT, PERSONALITY, AND SELF

Temperament and Heritability of Traits

Many of the childhood behaviors exhibited by Sergej and Yuen can be explained according to differences in **temperament,** or *a person's innate characteristic behavioral style or typical pattern of responding to events in the environment.* Individual differences in temperament can be observed in the earliest hours following birth. For example, while some newborns and infants are irritable and cry frequently, others appear to be good-natured and calm. During the first few months of life, some infants are extremely expressive and react to people and events by making sounds and waving their

Taken from *Lives Across Cultures: Cross-Cultural Development*, Fifth Edition, by Harry W. Gardiner and Corinne Kosmitzki.

arms; others are less active, may hardly respond to their environment, and appear withdrawn and uninvolved. Frequently, the differences we see in temperament among infants tend to be characteristically consistent throughout individual lives. In fact, some researchers maintain that infant temperament reliably predicts adult personality.

Personality can be described as a *unique system of identifiable, characteristic behavioral patterns that distinguish a person from others.* The infant who is shy and anxious around strangers is more likely to be a shy adult than is an infant who curiously approaches strangers. The potentially powerful relationship between infant temperament and adult personality has led many researchers to the conclusion that traits of temperament are, to a significant extent, inherited. They argue that environment and socialization can influence temperament only within the limits initially defined by heredity.

The concept of heritability of temperament has received support from careful studies of twins (identical and fraternal) reared together and apart (DiLalla & Jones, 2000). These studies are based on the hypothesis that identical twins share 100 percent of their genes and, therefore, should be identical in their temperamental dispositions at birth. In contrast, fraternal twins, like other siblings, share only 50 percent of their genetic makeup and, therefore, should be less similar in their temperament. Yet, like identical twins, they share a very similar environment. Studies such as these should be able to provide answers to such questions as the following: (1) Are identical twins more similar in their temperament than fraternal twins? (2) Are identical twins raised in different environments more similar in temperament than are fraternal twins reared together? (3) Are fraternal twins (who share half of their genes) more similar to each other than are adopted siblings (who do not share any genes)?

If the answer to all of these questions is "yes," we can conclude that genetic disposition, rather than environment, is responsible for the differences in temperament observed among people. However, to accurately assess the results of twin studies, it is important to understand the way heritability is measured. In general, the degree of heritability is expressed by the **heritability quotient,** which is *an estimate of the percentage of the variability in a given trait that can be attributed to genetic differences.* For example, a heritability quotient of 50 percent, for trait X means that approximately half of the variation, or individual difference, found in a sample is due to genetic differences among those subjects in the sample. The remaining half of the variation is assumed to be the result of complex environmental factors or, possibly, unexplained errors in measurement. With this in mind, let us consider some twin research and what it tells us about the inheritability of temperament.

In general, twin studies have produced moderately high heritability quotients. For example, a study of 250 Canadian twins showed broad genetic influence on the five dimensions of neuroticism, extraversion, openness, agreeableness, and conscientiousness. The genetic contribution to trait variation was estimated at 41 percent, 53 percent, 61 percent, 41 percent, and 44 percent, respectively (Jang, Livesly, & Vernon, 1996). Similarly, a study of 350 twins in Minnesota revealed that approximately 40 percent of variability among subjects in such traits as stress reaction (related to neuroticism and general anxiousness) and aggression could be attributed to genetics (Bouchard, Lykken, McGue, Segal, & Tellegen, 1990).

While results like these suggest that certain temperamental traits are genetically transmitted, they also suggest that in specific instances other traits are heavily influenced by socialization within the family environment. After all, a heritability quotient of 40 to 50 percent also means that 50 to 60 percent of variation is due to environmental rather than genetic factors. The debate around environmental and genetic influences on temperament continues, and researchers are not yet able to provide a definitive answer as to which plays the more significant role in determining differences in temperament and personality.

The Self: Some Cultural Perspectives

Our unique system of behavioral patterns, or personality, develops over time, shaped by the interaction between temperament (heritable traits) and the ecological system. As personality develops, it helps lay the foundation for development of the **self-concept**—*the perception of oneself as a person with identifiable behavioral patterns and characteristics, directed by desires, preferences, attributes, and abilities.* The unique structure and content of the self-concept, as well as some of the psychological dynamics related to it, are largely influenced by one's developmental niche and ecological systems (microsystem, meso-system, exosystem, or macrosystem) in which one finds oneself at a particular time in the lifespan.

Those who write most frequently about the topic of self-concept tend to discuss cultural variations in relation to the dimension of individualism-collectivism. Triandis (1989), who has written extensively about individualism-collectivism, suggests that culture-specific views of the self result from early exposure to differing values and beliefs. For example, childrearing patterns in collectivist cultures tend to introduce and reinforce the welfare of the collective over the welfare of the individual. In contrast, parents in individualistic cultures teach their children that the individual's primary goal is independence and the establishment of a unique self. Based on these fundamentally different approaches, it seems logical that individuals in collectivist and individualistic cultures should vary in how they view themselves. Some authors make a distinction between interdependent and independent selves (Gardiner & Mutter, 1994; Markus & Kitayama, 1991). Figure 1 depicts various conceptions of self as they may exist within a given culture and across many cultures. The individualistic/independent self-concept (a)-remains relatively stable and consistent because interrelations with others are not defining elements of one's identity. This is represented in the figure as a heavier circle that does not contact other individuals that surround the person.

The interdependent/collectivistic conception of self (b) is defined by the individual's relationship with individuals who are significant in that person's life. The heavier circle of self touches each individual illustrating the situational flexibility of the self-concept: The self must change if relationships change. These models of self are based on older work by Markus and Kitayama (1991) and Gardiner and Mutter (1994). The more recent findings we described above led Mascolo, Misra, and Rapisardi (2004) to propose two additional conceptions of self that could account for the coexistence of independent and interdependent elements within a person's self. In the relational understanding of self (c), self and other are neither entirely independent nor interdependent. Rather, aspects of the distinct self are defined in mutual relations with others. For example, self-characteristics such as hostile, friendly, or gregarious can only be derived from relationships with others. How would one be gregarious by oneself? Finally, with the "encompassing" sense of self (d), Mascolo and colleagues account for a self that derives from relationships that are unequal in social status. Such relationships define one person as responsible, protective, and caring for the other person. In turn, the "subordinate" person sees himself as obedient, respectful, and appreciative. This type of self-experience may occur in parent–child relationships, and, in many cultures, between husband and wife or siblings. One would also find it in very hierarchically structured groups, such as the military or in organized religion.

While the concepts of individualism and collectivism may be useful in describing general differences among cultures, critics point out that they disregard within-culture differences and neglect the fact that any culture includes both individualistic and collectivistic beliefs, values, and motives (Turiel, 2004). Applied to the concept of self, this means that a person's self can contain individualistic and collectivistic elements at the same time. In fact, one of the students who read an earlier edition of this book was concerned that she should be relegated to an "individualistic" concept of self just because she grew up in an individualistic culture. For example, she argued convincingly that some aspects of her self-concept and the belief that she is a "good" person are tied to her charity

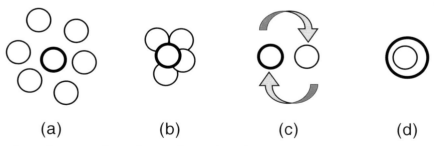

(a)   (b)   (c)   (d)

FIGURE 1   Independent, Interdependent, Relational, and Encompassing Concepts of the Self

Source: Adapted from M. F. Mascolo, G. Misra, and C. Rapisardi, "Individual and Relational Conceptions of Self-Experience in India and the U.S." in M. F. Mascolo and J. Li (Eds.), *Cultural and Developing Selves: Beyond Dichotomization*, 2004, pp. 9–26. New Directions in Child and Adolescent Development Series. W. Damon (Series Ed.). San Francisco: Jossey-Bass.

work and helping others. Research confirms this more complex understanding of self. Raeff (2004) reports that late adolescents recognize themselves in relation to others. When asked to describe themselves, most adolescents in Raeff's European American sample did use autonomous terms (e.g., I am insightful, I am athletic, I like to read). However, when they were prompted to explain why these self-characteristics are important, the answers revealed a clear connection between self-characteristics and social relationships. For example, one woman pointed out that being insightful" . . . is very important because communication's obviously a very important thing. . . . You know, and sometimes it's nice to have insight into what somebody else is thinking and feeling" (Raeff, 2004, p. 73). Equally poignant are Li and Yue's (2004) findings that Chinese adolescents can show strong individual goals and ambitions in the realm of learning, despite the generally more collectivistic values present in Chinese culture. How do you view yourself—as an individualist, collectivist, or a mixture of the two? What about other members of your family and your friends?

The ecological model is a useful tool in interpreting these findings. Viewed from this perspective, individual and collective orientations of self can coexist at different levels of the ecological model. Box 1 highlights several cultures that have a body of research focused on the concept of the self in relation to cultural values and beliefs—Japan, China, and India.

BOX 1

THE SELF AND PERSONALITY:
SOME CULTURAL PERSPECTIVES

Japan

Japan is considered to be a collective culture, where the Japanese place the group above the individual and tend to be other-directed. The Japanese are extremely sensitive to and concerned about relationships and maintaining harmony (an influence from Confucianism) and stress such values as filial piety, shame (as a method of reinforcing expectations and proper behavior), self-control, emphasis on consensus, and fatalism.

The Japanese view the self as consisting of two parts—the inner self and the outer self, also known as the social self (what is typically shown to others). At the core of the inner self is the *kokoro*, a reservoir of truthfulness and purity that remains private and is not shared with outsiders. Interestingly, the Japanese describe the self in concrete terms that are more contextual and relational than individuals in the United States. For example, while an American may say, "I am shy" (an abstract definition), a Japanese is more likely to say, "I am shy at work" (a contextual definition) or "I am shy with strangers" (a relational definition).

In addition, Japanese behavior often avoids direct communication and careful control over emotions and actions, allowing for the masking of feelings and the appearance of extreme modesty or shyness. The downplaying of one's performance may result in a nonthreatening atmosphere in which no one feels threatened, but the modesty displayed does not mean the person is not confident or he or she is shy. The individual may be extremely confident but, according to cultural expectations, is not to behave in an outwardly confident manner. Finally, the Japanese tend to be less unrealistically optimistic than Americans. Unrealistic optimism is the tendency for people to believe that, compared to others, they are more likely to experience positive events and less likely to experience negative events. The Japanese are believed to be less unrealistically optimistic, because the attention to the individual that self-enhancement engenders is not valued in Japanese culture.

China

An interest in understanding personality and the self is not new for the Chinese. An ancient theory held that personality is a result of the interaction of two forces—*yin* (passive, weak, and destructive) and *yang* (active, strong, and constructive)—and the Five Agents or *Wu-using* (metal, wood, water, fire, and earth), each of which has corresponding physical and temperamental characteristics. All of this is mediated by the Confucian Doctrine of the Mean, which states that there should be a balance of these forces and an avoidance of one-sidedness or extremity to maintain the Mean (moderation). This balance results in all things being in their proper order and thriving. If there is a balance, then

BOX 1 CONTINUED

the person is active or passive *according to the situation.* If the Doctrine of the Mean is violated, then the person is either extremely passive or extremely active.

A more modern Chinese theory of personality centers on Chinese social orientation or a person's tendency and desire to maintain harmonious relationships with others. An example is dedication to the family that results in Chinese merging their sense of self with the family and not focusing on personal interests, desires, or goals.

Beliefs about personality and the self are also influenced by Confucianism. Confucian personality is viewed as "the becoming process" and not an attained state of being. There is no fixed personality; rather, it is constantly evolving. A person becomes a personality by embodying a life worth living. At the same time, there is a belief in a "boundless" self, and the Chinese see the self as part of a larger vision of the universe.

Finally, while the Chinese focus greater attention on the inner self than individuals in Western cultures, their self-presentation is similar to the Japanese. In other words, the Chinese downplay their successes, engage in self-effacement, are less likely to demonstrate self-serving bias, and mask their feelings in social interactions.

India

India is predominantly Hindu, with large minorities of Sikhs and Muslims. To understand India's views on the self, an awareness and understanding of Hinduism is extremely helpful. Hinduism is multifaceted and encompasses a body of beliefs, philosophies, worship practices, and a code of conduct. According to Hinduism, all individuals have four basic aims in life that form the basis of Indian values: (1) *kama,* pleasure or enjoyment; (2) *artha,* wealth or success; (3) *dharma,* righteousness, faithful duty or code of conduct; and (4) *moksha,* liberation or salvation. Of these, dharma is the most relevant for the concept of self, because it deals with righteousness, faithful duty, or the code of conduct. In India rights and duties are defined separately for various segments of the society divided by age and social category (i.e., caste). In fact, the primary term for personhood has been *purusa,* meaning *man,* and the term conveys the privileged status of men.

The Indian view of the self is also related to the "Law of Karma," the guiding principle that assumes lawfulness and order in the physical, biological, mental, and moral realms. According to the law, each person must face the appropriate consequences for his or her actions regardless of whether the actions are good, bad, or indifferent. Because India, like many other Asian cultures, is generally a collective society, individuals are not identified by individual traits, but instead are described in terms of social relationships. Responsiveness to the needs of others is viewed as a high moral obligation.

Source: Adapted from *Personality, the Self, and Culture* by Vicki Ritts, 2001, unpublished manuscript, St. Louis Community College. Reprinted by permission.

◇ INFANCY

As of today, researchers have not found a definite answer to the question "what influences a person's personality more, temperament or socio-cultural factors?" Consequently, most recognize the existence of an intricate relationship between individual temperament and the sociocultural environment. In this section, we will discuss some theoretical perspectives that attempt to explain that relationship and how it shapes personality development early in life.

Temperament, Ecological Systems, and the Developmental Niche

As we pointed out in Module 2-A, a child's developmental environment consists of four basic subsystems: (1) the microsystem, consisting of interactions between the child and her immediate environment (e.g., home or day care center); (2) the mesosystem, made up of individual microsystems (e.g., family and preschool); (3) the exosystem, consisting of influential social settings (e.g., parents' place of work); and (4) the macrosystem, consisting of customs, values, and laws important to the child's culture. Together, these subsystems provide the individual child with her developmental niche, or unique combination of socialization experiences. Each of these subsystems is influenced by, and in turn influences, a child's individual temperament. A child's behavior will initiate a specific response from a caretaker in a particular setting (home or preschool). However, these responses differ from one environmental setting to another. For example, a mother's reaction to a child who exhibits irregular sleep and eating patterns differs from North America to East Africa. A North American mother typically pays more attention to an infant who is unpredictable in eating and sleeping patterns, and she arranges her schedule to take care of the child's needs. In contrast, Super and Harkness (1994a) report that mothers in Kokwet, a small farming town in Kenya, interact more with children who operate on a regular daily schedule. Knowing when her baby will be awake and alert, the mother can more easily arrange her many other duties and activities. Kokwet infants who are less predictable in their daily patterns are more often left to the care of an older sister or another caretaker.

This example illustrates how a child's temperament influences the environment. At the same time, however, specific patterns of response exhibited by others in the child's environment may facilitate or inhibit particular behavioral styles on the part of the child, thus making the child–environment relationship a two-way interaction. A fussy child receives more attention from the primary caretaker in most Western cultures, thus potentially rewarding and facilitating the child's dependency on the caretaker. In non-Western cultures, dependency and emotional attachment to the mother are often less pronounced, because mothers may not be available to respond with immediate emotional attention to fussy children.

Temperament and "Goodness of Fit"

Another theoretical explanation that contributes considerably to the understanding of how temperament, development, and culture relate to one another is that of **goodness of fit**—*the quality of the adaptation, or "match," between a child's temperament and the demands of his immediate environment.* This concept was introduced by Thomas and Chess (1977) in an elaborate longitudinal study of children's temperament that eventually included a wide range of environmental factors. The researchers began by interviewing and observing middle-class families of European background living in New York. They were able to identify clusters of traits that characterized three different temperament types among infants: (1) the "easy" child, (2) the "difficult" child, and (3) the "slow-to-warm-up" child.

An **easy child** was *characterized by a good mood, regular sleeping and eating cycles, and general calmness.* Mothers considered these babies unproblematic and easy to raise. On the other hand, temperament traits of a **difficult child** included a *negative mood, slow adaptation to and withdrawal from new experiences and people, irregular sleep and feeding patterns, and high emotional intensity.* Moreover, these "difficult" infants were found in later childhood to be less well adjusted and prone to more behavioral problems. A **slow-to-warm-up child** generally *showed few intense reactions, positive or negative, and tended to be mild and low in activity level.* Thomas and Chess assert that it is not the individual child's temperament itself that is related to future maladjustment, but rather the match or mismatch of the child's temperament with the environment that predicts problematic behavior. If "difficult" temperament disrupts family routine and leads to negative parental reactions, negative developmental outcome is likely.

A follow-up study by Korn and Gannon (1983) with Puerto Rican families in New York provided additional support for the goodness-of-fit concept but sounded a note of caution as well. For example, early "difficult" temperament did not predict poor adjustment and behavioral difficulties in later childhood. The researchers point out that in these families, characteristics that were originally classified as "difficult" were not perceived as necessarily problematic and therefore did not disrupt family life or evoke negative parental reactions toward the child. These studies and others provide convincing evidence that culture is a critical determinant of the "goodness of fit" between an individual child (temperament) and her environment.

DeVries (1994) and DeVries and Sameroff (1984) further illustrate this concept by describing two individual cases encountered in the study of infants from different parts of Kenya. The case of Hamadi, a Digo boy, demonstrates how an "easy" temperament can lead to poor adjustment due to a mismatch between the boy's temperament and his environment. For example, as an infant, Hamadi was energetic and active and exhibited healthy approach tendencies. He was described as one of the most advanced infants in the entire study. However, after starting school, Hamadi began to withdraw, became shy, and showed clear signs of distress through acting-out behavior.

What caused this transition? The researchers interviewed Hamadi's parents and teachers and were told that Hamadi's temperament did not fit with the cultural expectations of how a Digo boy his age should behave. The efforts of teachers and parents to control his energetic temperament and discourage his curiosity, instead of rewarding his enthusiasm and challenging his intellect, led Hamadi to withdraw and become angry and fearful.

The second case reported by DeVries introduces Enkeri, a Masai boy born in the same year as Hamadi. According to traditional temperament measures, Enkeri scored as "difficult." He was the classic "fussy" child—very intense, persistent, overactive, irregular in his daily behavior patterns, and not easily distracted or consolable. In a Western culture, these temperament traits would place Enkeri at risk for future adjustment problems. However, the behaviors that Western mothers dislike and describe as undesirable and difficult are valued highly in Masai society.

The Masai are an agricultural society and often have to struggle for survival in an extremely hostile environment. In times of drought, when herds of cattle and goats are destroyed,

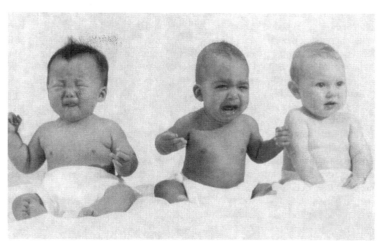

Differences in infant temperament can often be observed side-by-side within the same cultural context.
(© Gary Buss/Getty images)

infant mortality is high because families cannot rely on the usual supply of milk. Under these kinds of conditions, infants who show "difficult" behavior tend to survive at a higher rate than infants who are quiet and undemanding. Why? Because infants who cry are fed and attended to, whereas those who don't are assumed to be content. Consequently, infants who cry a lot are fed more and are in better physical condition, which contributes to their survival.

Finally, Meijer, Super, and Harkness (1997) attempted to further clarify the nature of "goodness of fit" and find a systematic relationship between maternal judgments of "difficult" and specific dimensions of child behavior. In a comparative study of mothers in Bloemenheim, Holland, and towns near Cambridge, Massachusetts, the researchers reported that parents in the two different cultural settings systematically interpreted the causes of difficult behavior differently. For example, while more American parents viewed difficulty as inherent in a child, more Dutch parents viewed it as a result of environmental factors. Clearly, the interaction of culture and individuality are different in these two ecological settings, and the resulting behavior and the interpretation of it are strongly influenced by the presence of different developmental niches.

Canadian researcher J. Phillipe Rushton (1998) pursues the "goodness of fit" hypothesis even further and in a very controversial direction. He argues that there are consistent "racial" differences in temperament that result from the unique survival challenges diverse groups of humans faced during evolutionary history. In particular, Rushton focuses on three categories of humans described as Mongoloid (Asian), Caucasoid (European), and Negroid (African). He argues that his research supports differences between these three groups in activity level, aggressiveness, cautiousness, dominance, impulsivity, and sociability. Rushton hypothesizes that the farther the populations migrated out of Africa, the more their temperament evolved over time to fit the survival challenges these populations faced. For example, the populations migrating north (Caucasoid and Mongoloid) spent long cold winters in closely knit social groups, requiring social cooperation and impulse control. Over time, these positive temperament traits (goodness of fit in these ecological settings) were passed on and became part of the "racial" temperament characteristics. While this perspective accounts for neither individual differences nor cultural influences and socialization, it does illustrate the principle of the "goodness-of-fit" idea and is, thus, worth mentioning.

◇ CHILDHOOD

The Emerging Self-Concept

If you were asked to draw a picture of yourself, what would your picture look like? Would it show a single figure in the middle of the page? Would you attempt to portray your most typical features (e.g., hairstyle, clothes, facial features)? Or, would you show yourself at work, at home, with friends, or with family? The way we think about ourselves, as individual entities or in a social context, is influenced by the cultural understanding of who a person is and what characterizes him or her.

In a cross-cultural study of self-concept in Japan and the United States, Cousins (1989) reported that subjects differed in the way they described themselves as individuals. Cousins used the Twenty Statements Test, which asks individuals to write twenty responses to the question "Who am I?" Results indicated that Americans used more psychological attributes, such as traits or dispositions, to describe themselves. In contrast, Japanese subjects frequently included the larger context when describing who they were. For example, Japanese subjects used more preferences and wishes, social categories, and activities in their self-descriptions.

Interestingly, the results from this study support several of the major themes we discussed in Module 1-B. For example, in terms of Bronfenbrenner's ecological model, Americans can be said to view the self as part of the microsystem. The individual selects characteristics derived from early interactions between the child and the immediate environment, most notably the family. This conception reflects the individualistic nature of the American culture. The Japanese, on the other hand, select characteristics that emerge from interactions in social settings or institutions—that is, in the exosystem or even the macrosystem—where they have come into contact with the customs, values, and laws of their culture. Such behavior reflects a collectivist society. This contrast can be seen in the examples of Sergej and Yuen in the opening vignettes of this module.

In another study using the same methodology (the Twenty Statement Test), Bochner (1994) reported similar results when comparing adults from Malaysia (a collectivist culture) with adults from Australia and Britain (individualist cultures). Interestingly, unlike Cousins's study cited earlier, Malaysians gave more responses referring to personal traits and dispositions than responses associated with social groups, and members of the two other cultures (Australia and Britain) gave more socially oriented responses. However, overall Bochner's cross-cultural comparison showed significantly fewer personal responses and significantly more group-related responses among Malaysians than in either the Australian or British samples.

Miller (1984) suggested that these differences are developmental in nature (another theme weaving through our topical discussions). He compared adults in North America and Hindus in India. The results seem to replicate other findings: Indians attributed their actions more to contextual factors, whereas Americans explained actions in terms of personal dispositions. On the other hand, self-descriptions among young American and Hindu children (eight to eleven years of age) did not differ in any significant way; both groups referred more to context than to personal characteristics. This suggests that Americans, with age, may learn to focus more on the person than on the context when perceiving and evaluating behavior. This also casts some doubt on the definition of the individualism-collectivism dichotomy and its effect on actual behavior (in this case, self description). After all, it would be naïve to assume that cultural effects on self-concept and behavior could be reduced to two distinct categories of cultural values. This might be an interesting area for future research.

Additional evidence for the early influence of culture comes from a study conducted in the Netherlands (Van den Heuvel, Tellegen, & Koomen, 1992). Moroccan, Turkish, and Dutch children in grades six through eight were asked to describe five things about themselves, about one classmate who is like them, and about one classmate who is different from them. As hypothesized by the researchers, children from the two more collectivist cultures (Morocco and Turkey) used more social statements indicating group memberships, social activities, or clearly interpersonal traits (e.g., friendly toward others) when describing themselves or a similar classmate. Dutch children used significantly more psychological attributes, such as traits and personal preferences, in their description of themselves or a similar classmate. The authors conclude that the significant psychological differences found between individuals with an individualistic cultural background and those with a collectivistic background emerge at an early age and continue to develop across the lifespan.

Development of self-concept is greatly aided by language development and the words we use to describe ourselves. Pronouns such as *me, mine, you, us,* and *them* distinguish between self and others. Through the use of such words, we learn to understand ourselves as unique and different from others. In an early study, Mead (1934) suggested that personal names were at the center of self-concept development. Personal names help identify the self and distinguish oneself from others who are not referred to by that name. In many cultures in which names are carefully selected for their meaning, the person is thought to adopt characteristics associated with that name. These attributes become part of their self-concept. How often have we met someone with the same name as someone else we know and compared the characteristics of the two individuals?

Self-Esteem and Self-Efficacy

A recurring question in the study of self-concept is whether we can and should separate how we *think* about ourselves from how we *feel* about ourselves. Some contend that the content of the self-concept and its evaluation, which results in self-esteem, are virtually inseparable. However, other self-concept research increasingly demonstrates that self-esteem may indeed be a distinct aspect of self-concept. From a developmental perspective, Harter (1982) has shown that a global sense of self-esteem (perceived self-worth), distinguishable from the descriptive aspects of self, emerges around the age of eight.

Watkins and Dhawan (1989) argue that the distinction or lack of distinction between self-esteem and self-concept may be a cultural phenomenon. In several studies, these investigators examined aspects of the self-concept and self-esteem of children and adults from diverse cultural groups. As before, they found distinct differences between members of Western and Asian cultures. For example, Dhawan and Roseman (1988) reported that 62 percent of responses of American young adults were classified as self-evaluations, compared with 35 percent of responses among Indians of the same age group. In addition, most of the self-evaluations made by Western subjects were positive rather than negative.

These results, along with others, suggest that the distinction between self-concept and self-evaluation is more pronounced in Asian cultures, whereas both aspects of self are intertwined in Western cultures. Once again, the explanation seems to lie in the individualistic or collectivistic orientation of the cultures involved. If an individual is independent and responsible for her success or failure, a focus on specific positive aspects of the self is an efficient protection against low self-esteem (Gardiner & Mutter, 1994). In contrast, in cultures in which individual success and enhancement are less important, personal attributes and accomplishments are not an immediate source of self-esteem and their value need not be emphasized.

As we noted previously, particularly in our discussion of the developmental niche and the ecological systems approach, childrearing practices and family environment are major contributors to cultural differences. These factors are also believed to be very influential in the development of personality and self-esteem, especially during the first years of life. Therefore, the fact that cultural differences in self-esteem are related to cultural differences in childrearing should not be surprising. Childrearing that emphasizes warmth and acceptance, together with consistent rules and achievement expectations, is clearly related to high self-esteem. For example, Olowu (1990) argues that many African children have higher self-esteem than children in Western countries because they enjoy the warmth and acceptance of an extended family. Such parental warmth can be provided by aunts and uncles as well as by grandparents. Western children, on the other hand, frequently rely on one or two caretakers for their self-esteem needs.

Akande (1999) comes to a similar conclusion after studying the self-esteem in post-apartheid black South African children. He points out that at the core of South African self-esteem is the social group (most notably, the family) that promotes personal achievement, good character ("iwa pele") influence, prestige, and hegemony.

Social psychologists recently have argued that we cannot understand a person's self by only considering the general sense of ourselves as a person distinct from another person (self-concept) and our general sense of self-worth (self-esteem). Bandura (1997) explores the construct of "self-efficacy" as an important factor in the development of self. **Self-efficacy** refers to *the general sense of one's ability to master tasks and to direct one's behavior toward a goal.* Although highly correlated with self-esteem (Judge, Erez, Bono, & Thoresen, 2002), self-efficacy adds important insights to our understanding of the developing self.

According to Bandura, self-efficacy, unlike self-esteem, influences personal goals and behavior. When children learn that they can influence their environment through their behavior, and they succeed in doing so, they develop a sense of efficacy. This sense of capabilities allows and motivates them to set goals and achieve them. As their world and their ecological systems expand, from family to peers to school, they develop self-efficacy in different domains. For example, Bandura's Children-Perceived Self-Efficacy

In Burkina Faso, a senior Lobi man shows warmth and affection toward a young friend.
(© Bertrand Rieger)

scales, or CPSE, (Bandura 1990) measure self-efficacy in three domains: academic self-efficacy (capable to manage one's learning and master academic subjects), social self-efficacy (capable to form and maintain social relationships and manage conflicts), and self-regulatory efficacy (capable to resist social pressure).

In a study involving ten- to fifteen-year-old Italian, Hungarian, and Polish children, Pastorelli and her colleagues (2001) showed that some national differences in academic and social efficacy exist. For example, Hungarian children were more confident in their ability to master academic subjects but had a lower sense of being able to take charge of their learning than Italians and Poles. The authors point to the differences in educational practices in the different countries. They suggest that students may develop high efficacy in subject mastery in an educational system that is highly structured and tightly controlled by teachers and parents. On the other hand, these students may perceive a lack of control in choosing and directing their own learning activities. Likewise, the explanation for the tendency of Italian children in this study to perceive themselves as more capable in the social domain than both Hungarian and Polish children may lie in the ecological system. The family exerts the earliest influence in a child's life and provides early opportunities to develop social efficacy. Italian culture is known for its emphasis on strong family relationships throughout life, so it might not be surprising to find that Italian children consider themselves socially competent. They may just have had more opportunities to develop social efficacy within their microsystem.

◇ ADOLESCENCE

Adolescence is a particularly interesting period of transition in the lifespan. It begins with biological maturation and ends with society's acceptance of the young person as an adult. Most Western societies have clear social markers that define when a young person is considered mature enough to assume adult responsibilities (e.g., voting in elections) and adult privileges (e.g., driving a car or consuming alcohol). In contrast to many nonindustrialized cultures, adolescence generally lasts several years in most modern Western cultures. Adolescents in non-Western societies assume adult responsibilities much earlier, because these societies cannot afford to let their young people be "nonproductive" and engage in idle "self-discovery" for an extended time.

Identity Formation

During the adolescent years, young people encounter one of the most important developmental tasks of their lives—the establishment of an individual identity. **Identity** is *a person's self-definition as a separate and distinct individual, including behaviors, beliefs, and attitudes.* Simply stated, the individual is trying to answer the question "Who am I?" Finding the answer isn't always easy and involves many of those within one's various ecological systems, including family and friends, members of peer groups, and teachers. Some adolescents find the journey particularly difficult and have to deal with serious issues, including antisocial or delinquent behavior. These topics receive attention in the section that follows.

Psychologist Erik Erikson is generally credited with the first complete analysis of identity development (Erikson's stage theory is discussed in detail in Module 2-A; see Table 3). Furthermore, he proposed the integration of identity, social roles, and the broader cultural context (Erikson, 1963). In his cross-cultural research, he collected evidence for the universal existence of identity development, yet the exact process by which individuals achieve an adult identity is influenced by specific contextual factors. The basic premise of identity development across cultures is that it is rooted in the physical and psychological developmental changes an individual experiences during the adolescent period.

It has long been assumed, particularly in Western societies, and most notably in the United States, that the transition to adulthood is a rather painful and psychologically challenging event (Hall, 1904). However, other research shows that the experience of stress during adolescence varies cross-culturally (Offer, Ostrov, Howard, & Atkinson, 1988). Some writers suggest that adolescence is more stressful when individuals are confronted with a large number of choices, as they frequently are in Western cultures. In non-Western societies, in which roles are frequently more clearly defined and choices are more limited, the transition to adulthood appears to be much smoother. For example, if the firstborn child is expected to take over the family business and assume care of the aging parents, it is not necessary for him to explore a variety of social roles in order to find a suitable adult identity. The important decisions have already been made for him. In contrast, those societies that value independence offer adolescents numerous opportunities to explore a variety of different social roles, thereby making the search for identity more difficult and of longer duration.

One study serves as an example of the influences of specific contextual factors on identity development. Tzuriel (1992) was interested in knowing whether adolescents exposed to multiple (and sometimes conflicting) sets of norms and expectations experience more identity conflict than adolescents with a less ambiguous environment. Israeli Arabs, who represent a relatively small minority in Israel, grow up experiencing elements of both their traditional culture and the Jewish majority culture. In contrast, Israeli Jews know a more homogeneous culture, in which their values and beliefs are reflected and reinforced. Would Israeli Arabs have a more negative view of themselves or express more confusion regarding their identity as a result of their different cultural experiences? Among the six factors of identity examined in this study, Arab youths expressed more self-confidence, a stronger sense of ideological and vocational commitment, and more genuineness. In contrast, Jewish adolescents reported more feelings of alienation and discontent with their appearance and behavior. However, they also recognized that others valued them and their abilities.

Personal identity is expressed in interesting ways throughout the world.
(© PhotoDisc/Getty images)

These findings suggest that Jewish adolescents experienced a somewhat different struggle in their identity formation than did Arabs. Tzuriel speculates that the ambiguous environment, especially among Israeli Arabs, may actually facilitate identity exploration and self-awareness in relation to identity issues. Thus, a seemingly ambiguous environment may have a more positive influence on identity formation than common sense would suggest. With the resolution of the identity conflict, most adolescents achieve an identity with which they are comfortable and adjust their behavior accordingly.

Social Identity Formation

We tend to think of identity as something that is very unique and represents the individual's personal history, experiences, and personality. However, our lives are inextricably connected with those around us—our family, our peers, our coworkers. Viewed from an ecological systems view, groups of people in a given context show a great degree of overlap. It is not surprising, therefore, that part of what we like to think of as our self results from what we share with others. Psychologists call these shared aspects of self "social identities." French psychologist H. Tajfel (1981) defines **social identity** as *"that part of an individual's self-concept which derives from his knowledge of his membership of a social group (or groups) together with the value and emotional significance attached to that membership"* (p. 255).

We tend to belong to multiple groups. Some are assigned to us (e.g., gender, nationality), while we choose others (e.g., political affiliation). Among these, ethnic or cultural identity has been singled out as particularly important to self-concept and the psychological functioning of ethnic group members. Phinney (1990) and others suggest that the formation of ethnic or cultural identity is similar to the formation of ego-identity as outlined by Erikson.

Ethnic or cultural identity formation appears to take place in three stages. The first stage, generally occurring in adolescence, is characterized by the lack of exploration of ethnic identity. The second stage involves becoming aware of one's ethnicity and actively exploring that ethnicity. At this stage, the person may engage in ethnic group activities, including reading and talking to people about the culture and participating in cultural events. The completion of this stage results in the final stage: ethnic identity achievement. This stage is characterized by a deeper understanding of one's ethnicity and the internalization of ethnic identity into the self. Because this understanding of ethnic identity varies from person to person, according to personal history and ecological systems, the implications for the self-concept and, ultimately, social behavior may also vary. For example, one person may become deeply involved in the activities of her ethnic group by maintaining the language, wearing traditional dress, and practicing ethnic rituals and customs. For another person, ethnic identity achievement may result in an intrinsic confidence in his ethnicity and not necessarily require strong ethnic involvement.

Cultural Influences on Social Identity

Just as the larger cultural context influences the specific content of adolescents' self-concepts and personal identity, culture also plays an important role in the progression of social identity formation. With regard to ethnic identity as an example of social identity, the position an ethnic group holds in the larger society (minority or majority status) and relationships among ethnic groups are the most influential of these cultural factors (Phinney, Lochner, & Murphy, 1990).

Research in the West Indies shows how general cultural conditions and beliefs (i.e., macrosystem) shape the basis from which young people begin their ethnic identity formation. Gopal-McNicol (1995) presented black and white preschool children with black and white dolls. The investigator asked the children questions such as "Which doll would you like to play with?" "Which doll do you want to be?" "Which doll is rich, ugly, pretty?" Similar to research in the United States, nearly five decades earlier (Clark & Clark, 1947), most of the children chose the white doll in response to the positive questions. The author concludes that colonialism, along with the representation of blacks and whites in the media, has made a marked impact on attitudes toward and perceptions of ethnic groups in the West Indies. It is not unreasonable to assume that these attitudes and perceptions play an important role in the eventual ethnic identity formation of those black and white children who participated in the study.

Contemporary adolescents are growing up in a world much more culturally diverse than that of their parents and grandparents. This increased globalization has implications for adolescents in many societies as they attempt to develop and establish their cultural identities. Jensen (2003) suggests that adolescents increasingly form multicultural identities as a result of their exposure to diverse cultural beliefs and behaviors either from first-hand contact with people from other cultures or through the media. She further argues that the process of developing a cultural identity during adolescence in a global society has become more complex and presents more challenges than it did just a generation or two ago.

As an example, Jensen (2003) discusses the changing view of marriage in India. The cultural tradition of arranged marriage in India is deeply rooted in values such as obligation to one's family and conforming to social roles rather than pursuing individual preferences. In today's more global Indian society, young Indian women and men are also exposed to values that emphasize freedom of choice and individual rights. Multiple traditional and nontraditional cultural values and practices influence adolescents' conceptions of who they are and how they fit into the world. The words of a young Indian woman exemplify this process of negotiating multiple cultural identities: "I've always insisted that I've got to have the right man and I won't just be able to adjust to anyone. . . . There have been pressures, if I can call them that, from family, but I've . . . not given in to it. I won't do that because I know the situation now. . . . From the very beginning things foreign and imported were very glamorous to me. From those days onward [when I became familiar with things foreign], I was against having an arranged marriage. Arranged marriages in India are becoming obsolete, I think" (Jensen, 2003, p. 4).

In addition to a general globalization that happens at the macrolevel of the ecological system, cultural influences that occur at the microlevel contribute to personal and social identity. Huntsinger and Jose (2006) discovered some systematic changes in self-reported personality characteristics among second-generation Chinese American and European American adolescents. First, all young people seemed to increase in extraversion and independence over the period of five years. This seems to be a result of normative developmental influences, such as becoming more independent from parents, building social relationship with peers, and defining one's independent identity.

Second, the two ethnic groups of adolescents became more similar in their self-reported personality characteristics over the span of five years. At the beginning of the study, the two groups differed significantly in eight of thirteen personality dimensions measured (i.e., emotional stability, excitability, dominance, cheerfulness, shrewdness, apprehension, sensitivity, and withdrawal). Five years later, the same two groups only differed in cheerfulness and boldness. The researchers attribute these changes in part to acculturative influences that may have affected particularly the Chinese American group in steering their development toward adopting qualities that are adaptive in the American cultural environment.

As researchers have begun to recognize increasing globalization of the adolescent world, they have come to adopt more complex models to interpret their research findings and understand adolescent identity development. In recent years, developmental researchers have pointed explicitly to ecological systems theory as a useful model to guide research and practice (Spencer et al., 2003; Swanson et al., 2003). In fact, globalization is a good example of a sociohistorical force that is captured by the "chronosystem" in the ecological model. As we saw in the preceding discussion of identity formation, the globalization of values, beliefs, and practices permeates all levels of the ecological system and greatly influences individuals' developmental paths.

◇ ADULTHOOD

A Time of Stability and Change

Given a secure identity by the early to mid-twenties, along with a set of relatively stable personality dispositions (traits), one might assume that personality would not change much after adolescence. However, distinct patterns of personality development, related to temperament traits, continue to occur. In particular, adults become more agreeable, more conscientious, more emotionally stable, but less extraverted and less open to experience. Numerous studies examining these "Big Five" personality traits have shown this pattern to be surprisingly consistent across many age groups and cultures, such as the United States, Germany, South Korea, Italy, Croatia, and Portugal (McCrae and Allik, 2002; McCrae et al., 1999; McCrae and Costa, 2003). See Table 1 for a description of these traits. (As a useful memory aid, you may want to note that the first letters of the five traits spell the word "OCEAN".)

The big five personality traits were "discovered" when researchers performed statistical analysis on adjectives that describe personality characteristics, as well as on existing personality tests (also based on language). They assumed that natural language, used to communicate differences and similarities between oneself and others, reflects the socially relevant dimensions of personality. Therefore, the analysis of natural language should reveal the characteristics that are important in describing oneself and others. Their analysis showed that all descriptors used in natural language, as well as test items designed to measure personality, can be represented by five common dimensions—the "Big Five" personality traits. Further research indicated that these five traits are also found in different languages and different cultures. For recent research on these traits, see Stankov and Lee (2009).

Robert McCrae (2004), one of the main proponents of the Five Factor Theory, even goes so far as to suggest that humans, as a species, have a genetic predisposition to develop in basically the same way, regardless of life experiences or cultural influences. McCrae cites the universal occurrence of the five traits and the seemingly universal pattern of personality change as evidence of a biological basis for personality and personality change.

Are we destined by biology to become more agreeable, conscientious, emotionally stable, and less sociable and open to experience, relative to when we were younger? Are we bound to change in much the same way as our parents and grandparents did?

TABLE 1 The Big Five Personality Traits

TRAIT	DESCRIPTION
Agreeableness	Tendency to be compassionate, cooperative, generous, trusting, sympathetic, and altruistic versus suspicious, critical, and antagonistic toward others
Conscientiousness	Tendency to be well-organized, reliable, hardworking, persistent, ambitious, reliable, and responsible versus disorganized, negligent, and irresponsible
Extroversion	Tendency to be energetic, active, outgoing, and sociable versus quiet, deliberate, reserved, and less involved in the social world
Openness to experience	Tendency to be curious, imaginative, creative, and artistic versus conventional, unimaginative, and uncreative
Neuroticism	Tendency to be emotional, anxious, unstable, temperamental, and worried versus unemotional, calm, stable, even-tempered, and not easily upset

Sources: Ahadi & Rothbart, 1994; McCrae & Costa, 1990; McCrae & Costa, 2003; McCrae & John, 1992.

While there seems to be a universal pattern of adult personality development and change, genetic influences offer one possible explanation. Roberts, Wood, and Smith (2005) adopt a different view. They suggest that it is not genetic "hardwiring" that predicts universal patterns of personality development. Rather, it is universally occurring tasks of social living that lead to a shared pattern of personality trait development.

Roberts and his colleagues argue that "the majority of people in a majority of different cultures go through similar life transitions at roughly the same age" (p. 173). All cultures have defined times at which certain life events are supposed to take place. For example, at some point in their lives, individuals in most cultures are expected to find a partner, start a family, produce offspring, work for a living, and contribute to one's community. These are normative tasks that, like Erikson's classic life stages, involve the conflict between acquiring new competencies and maintaining the status quo.

It has been suggested that these normative life tasks affect the adult personality in several ways. First, people adjust more easily to transitions that occur according to normative tasks than to transitions that are "not on time." The unexpected death of a child represents an "off-time" event, because parents are supposed to be survived by their children. However, the same event, while unexpected, is not considered "off-time" in societies with high infant mortality rates. Second, a new stage of life requires changes in behavior that frequently result in personality changes. Young adults who experience their first serious romantic relationship increase their emotional stability and conscientiousness (Neyer & Asendorpf, 2001). In turn, individuals who are more emotionally stable and conscientious tend to have relationships that last longer and are more satisfying (Roberts & Bogg, 2004).

Finally, certain personality traits appear to be associated with adherence or nonadherence to the normative tasks. Helson and her colleagues (1984) examined 141 women over a period of several decades and found that those whose lives followed the cultural expectations of women at that time (e.g., prescribed role of wife and mother) displayed an increase in tolerance, responsibility, nurturance, and self-control, but also a decrease in self-confidence and feelings of competence. Those women who chose a career path and departed from their prescribed roles as mothers adapted to this role by developing high levels of confidence, initiative, and intellectual independence. In conclusion, during adulthood personality develops within the ecological system in which a person finds herself, but the extent of this change is inhibited or promoted by genetic predisposition.

◇ LATE ADULTHOOD

Personality Changes in Senescence or Illness

Personality traits established throughout life continue to guide behavior into late adulthood. In fact, personality appears to "stabilize" in older age. Johnson and colleagues (2005) studied pairs of monozygotic and same-sex dizygotic twins between the ages of fifty and seventy. These adults completed the same personality questionnaires five years apart. Results revealed that personality traits were highly stable over time, strongly influenced by both genetics and nonshared environment. In their discussion, the authors point out that their study confirms the genetic influences on personality stability. On the other hand, they also observed that environmental influences appear to be more important in later life, perhaps because the environment in which people live tends to be more stable later in life. For example, people will have lived within the same community for many years, surrounded by long-time friends and family. Overall, there is much consensus that personality is very stable in older age and any changes that do occur are relatively minimal (Lautenschlager & Foerstl, 2007).

If that is the case, how does one explain the sometimes highly observable behavior changes in the elderly that are often reported by families or health care professionals? Such changes include increased anxiety, apathy, depression, and hostility. With increasing age, people tend to experience more chronic and severe illnesses. Both the organic changes associated with these illnesses (e.g., Alzheimer's disease) and the stressors related to coping with illnesses can lead to personality changes in older age. Lautenschlaeger and Foerstle conclude, "Conceptually, personality traits are considered to be stable.[. . .] More significant personality changes in old age need to be considered as warning signs for the potential presence of an underlying organic illness, most suspiciously due to different forms of dementia" (2007, p. 66).

The diagnosis of illness as well as the way individuals respond to illness and cope with it is largely influenced by the cultural and ecological system. For example, in two comparable samples of elderly individuals suffering from dementia, personality and behavioral disorders were more frequently observed in African Americans in Indianapolis than their African counterparts in Nigeria (Hendries, Gao, & Baiewu, 2000). In this case, increased stubbornness, irritability, and anger were more prevalent in American dementia patients than in Nigerian patients. Does this mean dementia affects the personality of individuals in one cultural group more than those in another? Most likely, this difference is a result of cultural expectations about aging, personality, and concepts of deviant behavior.

Just as personality change can be a result of illness, personality is also a predictor of health, illness, and mortality. For example, a longitudinal study of Japanese elderly revealed that conscientiousness, extraversion, and openness were associated with lower mortality rate (Iwasia et al., 2008). The authors speculate that more conscientious people take greater care of their health, more extraverted people are more socially active and have better support systems, and more open people adapt more easily to the changes and challenges of older age.

The "Aging" Self

As we have repeatedly pointed out throughout this book, adults face a number of unique developmental conditions in their later years of life. Aside from the challenges of physical aging, they frequently experience negative stereotypes and ageism. Yet, consistently, researchers find that the majority of adults maintain a positive self-concept, a sense of well-being, and continue to be productive members of society (Gething et al., 2003). This phenomenon seems to be rooted in the developing self, allowing it to remain stable and continuous, and, at the same time, flexible enough to assimilate to changing ecological conditions. Sneed and Whitbourne (2005) synthesize various motivation and self-theories and propose that "age-related changes in adulthood are negotiated through processes of identity assimilation, identity accommodation, and identity balance" (p. 382). In their theory, the successfully aging self is a combination of these three processes.

When faced with information that challenges the existing positive self-concept, a person will initially assimilate the environment in a way that is consistent with the self. For example, an adult suffering from hearing loss may explain his failure to have conversations on the telephone with "a bad connection" and, as a consequence, avoid the telephone. This strategy, identity assimilation, maintains a positive sense of self, but also limits a person's ability to seek out experiences and may restrict his behavior. After some time, assimilation may no longer be functional. Then, a person's well-being comes to depend on the self's ability to adapt to a changing environment. Identity accommodation involves changing the self-concept in response to challenging experiences. However, the accommodating self is less stable, and an inconsistent self is associated with low self-esteem. Thus, neither identity assimilation nor identity accommodation alone is conducive to prolonged well-being. Instead, Whitbourne and her associates conclude that identity balance is the most adaptive response to aging. Identity balance allows people to make favorable changes to their self-concept when challenged, but at the same time to maintain a consistent sense of solid identity. This model is echoed in work by Denise Tanner, a professor of social work in Britain, who interviewed several older British adults (aged 70–94) over a period of three years. Qualitative analysis of these interviews revealed that these aging adults indeed employed both assimilation and accommodation strategies to cope with threats to the self. In Figure 2, we show how the strategies that "sustain the self" through change and stability are embedded in the ecological system, which represents both resources and threats to self and well-being.

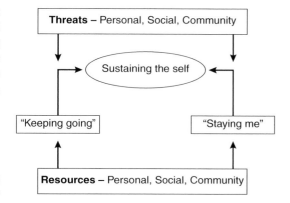

FIGURE 2   Sustaining the Self in Older Age

Source: Tanner, D. (2007). Reprinted by Permission of SAGE.

◇ SUMMARY

This chapter discusses the development of individual, self, and personality across cultures and in specific cultural contexts. Some aspects of personality and behavior are clearly influenced by innate temperamental dispositions. The ways in which individual temperament is expressed and what is considered acceptable are shown to be largely dependent on cultural values and practices. Discussion also focuses on cultural variations in the concept of person and self and their relationship to the early development of self-concept. While adolescents in most cultures experience the need to establish an identity, the manner in which they accomplish this and the specific issues and behaviors related to it show great cultural variation. Finally, we raise the question whether seemingly universal patterns of personality development in adulthood are the result of "hardwired" developmental processes or the result of universal socially prescribed "normative life tasks." We also establish that personality and self continue to develop and change throughout life, and in old age help the individual adapt to the unique challenges in later life.

◇ STUDY QUESTIONS

Use the examples of Hamadi and Enkeri to describe how children and their environment shape each other and create a "goodness of fit."

Using the ecological model, explain why the concept "individualism/collectivism" is limited in explaining cultural differences in self-concept.

Proponents of the Big Five personality theory claim that our personality changes in a distinctly universal pattern as we get older. What is this pattern?

◇ FURTHER READINGS

A. T. Church & M. S. Katigbak. (2002). Studying personality traits across cultures: Philippine examples. *Online Readings in Psychology and Culture* (Unit 6, Chapter 2). (http://orpc.iaccp.org) International Association for Cross-Cultural Psychology.

> This online chapter reviews the questions addressed by researchers who study personality traits across cultures, including whether traits are used in all cultures to understand persons and their behavior, the universality versus culture-specific traits, the validity of imported and indigenous measures of personality traits, and the meaningfulness of trait comparisons across cultures. Evidence relevant to these questions is summarized for one collectivistic culture—the Philippines.

Sigmund Freud. (1961). *Civilization and Its Discontents* (Vol. 21). London: Hogarth.

> One of the most important writings on the interaction between personality and culture by one of the most creative and influential contributors to the field of psychology.

R. R. McCrae. (2009). Cross-cultural research on the five-factor model of personality. *Online Readings in Psychology and Culture* (Unit 6, Chapter 1, Version 2). (http://orpc.iaccp.org) International Association for Cross-Cultural Psychology.

> An online chapter discussing the Five-Factor model, its use across cultures, and some recent research findings.

The Big Five Personality Test.

> If you are interested in learning more about the big five personality traits mentioned in this chapter, you can take a free, anonymous, online test that will help you understand the traits as they relate to your personality by going to http://www.outofservice.com/bigfive/.

◇ DEVELOPMENTAL ANALYSIS

CULTURE, SELF, AND PERSONALITY

As you read in this chapter, temperament, ecological systems, and the developmental niche all seem to be intertwined. This was certainly the case with me. At times, my mother said I was an "easy child" because I was usually happy, outgoing, and slept fairly well. I certainly enjoyed my meals, especially desserts, even as an infant in a high chair. However, occasionally I could be a "difficult child," as when I would insist on climbing trees and jumping to the ground! My younger sister was more difficult than I was—maybe because she was the middle child, and my brother, the youngest, was more "slow-to-warm-up." It is not unusual for a family to have all these types of children. Just when my husband and I (like most parents) thought we had learned all we needed to know about

◇ **DEVELOPMENTAL ANALYSIS** CONTINUED

successfully raising children, along came the next one who was so different, in many ways, from the previous child. Maybe this is true in your family, too.

Apparently, as a child, I was determined to establish my own personality. I didn't always conform to the norms in terms of clothes, play activities, and school interests. I felt confident in most of my emerging abilities (such as doing math and playing sports) and had a good self-concept—often to the point of being stubborn, especially during my adolescent years. I guess you might say I had high self-efficacy. Although our town didn't have the cultural diversity that many places have today, I found a large part of my cultural and ethnic identity in my Irish background (reflected in my red hair, freckles, and sense of humor).

In terms of personality, I have always tended to be extroverted and outgoing, agreeable and trusting, well-organized, hardworking, and ambitious (as reflected in my career accomplishments), curious, creative, and open to new experiences (demonstrated in my travels and efforts at cooking new foods). I see some of these same personality characteristics in our children and grandchildren.

As I approach the seventh decade of my life, I'm generally happy with the person I have become, and as I look back on my early life, I see the many influences that my family, culture, developmental niche, and unique ecological system had on the development of my self-concept and personality. Maybe I would have changed some things—but not many. It's been a good life so far.

Name: _____   Date: _____

MODULE 8-B

ACTIVITY

◇ THE INTERDEPENDENT AND INDEPENDENT SELVES

This activity focuses on a key distinction between cultures, whether the self is viewed as interdependent or independent (Markus & Kitayama, 1991). Collectivist cultures have been associated with a self-system that is inseparable from the social context. In other words, the self is defined in terms of relationships. The independent self, more typical of individualistic cultures, focuses on individual traits, abilities, goals, and preferences. The degree to which we hold an interdependent versus independent self-construal may impact how we process thoughts, how we experience and express our emotions, and how and when we are motivated.

Directions: Read each of the items in the two columns below and place a check next to the item in each pair that best describes you.

____ Success depends on help from others.   ____ Success depends on my abilities.

____ I know more about others than   ____ I know more about myself than
     I do about myself.   I do about others.

____ Being excluded from my group   ____ Being dependent on others would
     would be very hard on me.   be very hard on me.

____ Silence is comfortable.   ____ Silence is embarrassing.

____ It is important that my behavior   ____ It is important that my behavior and
     is appropriate for the situation.   attitudes correspond.

____ I sometimes feel ashamed.   ____ I sometimes feel guilty.

____ Friendships are difficult to establish,   ____ Friendships are fairly easy to establish,
     but are generally very intimate.   but often not very intimate.

____ I generally socialize in groups.   ____ I generally socialize in pairs.

____ **Total number of checks**   ____ **Total number of checks**

Taken from *Cross-Cultural Explorations: Activities in Culture and Psychology*, Second Edition, by Susan Goldstein.

Reactions:

1. The items in the column on the left indicate characteristics of the interdependent self whereas items in the column on the right indicate characteristics of the independent self. According to the total number of checks for each column, is your self-construal more interdependent or independent? To what extent does your cultural background explain this result?

2. Harry Triandis (1994) suggests that we may have both interdependent and independent aspects of self. Which one we draw from at any given moment may depend on our cultural experiences and the situation. Describe below an instance in which you acted from an interdependent self-construal and one in which you acted from an independent self-construal.

3. Research by Serge Guimond and colleagues (2006) and by Andreja Avsec (2003) suggests that women may maintain a more interdependent self-construal whereas men maintain a more independent self-construal. To what extent do you think your gender affected your responses to the checklists?

4. Shinobu Kitayama, Hazel Markus, and colleagues (1997) report that independent self-construal appears to be associated with more self-enhancement (that is, creating an overly positive view of oneself), whereas interdependent self-construal seems to be associated with more self-criticism. How might you explain this finding?

5. Ben C. H. Kuo and Laurie Gingrich (2004) suggest that counselors need to know their clients' type of self-construal. Why do you think this might be important?

◆ REFERENCES

Avsec, A. (2003). Masculinity and femininity personality traits and self-construal. *Studia Psychologica, 45,* 151-159.

Guimond, S., Chatard, A., Martinot, D., Crisp, R., & Redersdorff, S. (2006). Social comparison, self-stereotyping, and gender differences in self-construals. *Journal of Personality and Social Psychology, 90,* 221-242.

Kitayama, S., Markus, H. R., Matsumoto, H., & Norasakkunkit, V. (1997). Individual and collective processes in the construction of the self: Self enhancement in the United States and self-criticism in Japan. *Journal of Personality and social Psychology, 72,* 1245-1267.

Kuo, B. C. H., & Gingrich, L. (2004). Correlates of self-construals among Asian and Caucasian undergraduates in Canada.: Cultural patterns and implications for counseling. *Guidance and Counseling 20,* 78-88.

Markus, H., & Kitayama, S. (1991). Culture and self: Implications for cognition, emotion and motivation. *Psychological Review, 98,* 224-253.

Triandis, H. C. (1994). *Culture and social psychology*. New York: McGraw-Hill.

SECTION 9
GENDER AND SEXUALITY

GENDER IDENTITY, GENDER ROLES, AND GENDER DIFFERENCES

Rubberball/Mike Kemp/Getty Images

Preview

Prenatal Sexual Differentiation

- Describe the processes of prenatal sexual differentiation
- Discuss sex chromosomal abnormalities that may affect sexual differentiation

Gender Identity

- Define gender identity and the roles of nature and nurture in gender identity
- Discuss transgenderism

Gender Roles and Stereotypes

- Discuss gender roles and stereotypes
- Explain the relationship between gender roles and sexual behavior

Gender Differences

- Discuss gender differences in cognitive abilities
- Discuss gender differences in personality
- Discuss gender differences in social behavior

On Becoming a Man or a Woman: Gender Typing

- Discuss biological and psychological perspectives on gender typing

(*continued*)

Taken from *Human Sexuality in a World of Diversity*, Ninth Edition, by Spencer A. Rathus, Jeffrey S. Nevid, and Lois Fichner-Rathus.

Truth or Fiction?

Which of the following statements are the truth, and which are fiction? Look for the Truth-or-Fiction icons on the pages that follow to find the answers.

1. If male sex hormones were not present during critical stages of prenatal development, we would all develop external female sexual organs.   T   **F**?
2. A woman with Turner syndrome cannot become pregnant, but she can carry and deliver a baby.   T   **F**?
3. Seventeen of 18 boys who appeared to have female external sex organs suddenly developed male sex organs at puberty, when male sex hormones went to work.   T   **F**?
4. The gender of a baby crocodile is determined by the temperature at which the egg develops.   T   **F**?
5. Thousands of people have changed their anatomic sexes through gender-reassignment surgery.   T   **F**?
6. Men act more aggressively than women do.   T   **F**?
7. A 2½-year-old child may know that he is a boy but might think that he can grow up to be a mommy.   T   **F**?

Preview (Continued)

Psychological Androgyny and the Reconstruction of Masculinity–Femininity: The More Traits, the Merrier?

• Define psychological androgyny and discuss its possible advantages

My life, My Sexuality: Do You Fit the Masculine or Feminine Gender-Role Stereotype? (Do You Want to Fit One of Them?)

Jayne Thomas, Ph.D.—In Her Own Words

The 'Glass Ceiling,' male bashing, domestic violence, nagging, PMS, Viagra—these are but a few of the important issues examined in the Human Sexuality classes I instruct. As a participant-observer in my field, I see many of these topics aligning themselves as masculine/ feminine or male/female. Ironically, I can both see and not see such distinctions. Certainly women have bumped up against, smudged (and in some cases even polished) this metaphorical limitation of women's advancement in the workplace (i.e., that 'Glass Ceiling'). And most assuredly men have often found themselves 'bashed' by angry women intent upon extracting a pound of flesh for centuries of felt unjust treatment. As previously mentioned, these distinctions between masculine and feminine, for me often become blurred; I must add that, having lived my life in both the roles of man and woman, I offer a rather unique perspective on masculinity and femininity.

"All of my life, I harbored the strongest conviction that I was in appropriately assigned to the wrong gender—that of a man—when inside I knew myself to be a woman. Even so I continued a life-long struggle with this deeply felt mistake; I was successful in school, became a national swimming champion, received my college degrees, married twice (fathering children in both marriages) and was respected as a competent and good man in the workplace. However, the persistently unrelenting wrongfulness of my life continued. Not until my fourth decade was I truly able to address my gender issue.

"Jay Thomas, Ph.D., underwent gender reassignment and officially became Jayne Thomas, Ph.D., in November of 1985, and what has transpired in the ensuing years has been the most enlightening of glimpses into the plight of humankind. As teachers we are constantly being taught by those we purport to instruct. My students, knowing my background (I share who I am when it is appropriate to do so), find me accessible in ways that many professors are not. Granted, I am continually asked the titillating questions that one watching Geraldo might ask and we do have fun with the answers (several years ago I even appeared on a few of the Geraldo shows). My students, however, are able to take our discussions beyond the sensational and superficial, and we enter into meaningful dialogue regarding sex differences in society and the workplace, sexual harassment, power and control issues in relationships, and what it really means to be a man or a woman.

Challenging both the Masculine and the Feminine

"Iconoclastically, I try to challenge both the masculine and feminine. 'I know something none of you women know or will ever know in your lifetime,' I can provocatively address the females in my audiences as Jayne. 'I once lived as a man and have been treated as an equal. You never have nor will you experience such equality.' Or, when a male student once came to my assistance in a classroom, fixing an errant video playback device and then strutting peacock like back to his seat as only a satisfied male can, I teasingly commented to a nearby female student,' I used to be able to do that.'

"Having once lived as a man and now as a woman, I can honestly state that I see profound differences in our social/psychological/biological being as man and woman. I have now experienced many of the ways in which women are treated as less than men. Jay worked as a consultant to a large banking firm in Los Angeles and continued in that capacity as a woman following her gender shift. Amazingly the world pre-

sented itself in a different perspective. As Jay, technical presentations to management had generally been received in a positive manner and credit for my work fully acknowledged. Jayne now found management less accessible, credit for her efforts less forthcoming and, in general, found herself working harder to be well prepared for each meeting than she ever had as a male. As a man, her forceful and impassioned presentations were an asset; as a woman they definitely seemed a liability. On one occasion, as Jayne, when I passionately asserted my position regarding what I felt to be an important issue, my emotion and disappointment in not getting my point across (my voice showed my frustration) was met with a nearby colleague (a man) reaching to touch my arm with words of reassurance,' There, there, take it easy, it will be all right.' Believe me; that never happened to Jay. There was also an occasion when I had worked most diligently on a presentation to management only to find the company vice president more interested in the fragrance of my cologne than my technical agenda.

(Tom Grill/Spirit/Corbis)

"Certainly there are significant differences in the treatment of men and women, and yet I continue to be impressed with how similar we two genders really are. Although I have made this seemingly enormous change in lifestyle (and it is immense in so many ways), I continue as the same human being, perceiving the same world through these same sensory neurons. The difference—I now find myself a more comfortable and serene being, than the paradoxical woman in a man's body, with anatomy and gender that have attained congruence."

This module addresses the biological, psychological, and sociological aspects of gender. First we define **gender** as the psychological sense of being female or being male and the roles society ascribes to gender. Anatomic sex is based on, well, anatomy. But gender is a complex concept that is based partly on anatomy, partly on the psychology of the individual, and partly on culture and tradition.

Next we focus on **sexual differentiation**—the process by which males and females develop distinct reproductive anatomy. We then turn to gender roles—the clusters of behavior that are deemed "masculine" or "feminine" in a particular culture. The module examines research findings on gender differences. We next consider gender typing—the processes by which boys come to behave in line with what is expected of men (most of the time) and girls behave in accordance with what is expected of women (most of the time). We will also explore the concept of psychological androgyny, which applies to people who display characteristics associated with both gender roles in our culture.

Gender
The psychological state of being female or being male, as influenced by cultural concepts of gender-appropriate behavior. Compare and contrast the concept of gender with *anatomic sex*, which is based on the physical differences between females and males.

Sexual differentiation
The process by which males and females develop distinct reproductive anatomy.

◇ PRENATAL SEXUAL DIFFERENTIATION

Over the years, many ideas have been proposed to account for sexual differentiation. Aristotle believed that the anatomic difference between males and females was due to the heat of semen during sexual relations. Hot semen generated males, whereas cold semen made females (National Center for Biotechnology Information, 2006). Aristotle may have given in to stereotyping—the stereotypes of "hot-blooded male" and the "frigid female." Others believed that sperm from the right testicle made females, and sperm from the left testicle made males.

When a sperm cell fertilizes an ovum, 23 **chromosomes** from the male parent normally combine with 23 chromosomes from the female parent. The *zygote*, the beginning of a new human being, is only 1/175 of an inch long. Yet, on this tiny stage, one's stamp as a unique individual has already been ensured—whether one will have black or blond hair, grow bald or develop a widow's peak, or become female or male.

The chromosomes from each parent combine to form 23 pairs. The 23rd pair makes up the sex chromosomes. An ovum carries an X sex chromosome, but a sperm cell can carry either an X or a Y sex chromosome. The denotation of *X* and *Y* refers to the shapes of the chromosomes. If a sperm cell with an X sex chromosome fertilizes the ovum, the newly conceived individual will have an XX sex chromosomal structure and normally develop as a female. If the sperm cell carries a Y sex chromosome, the child will normally develop as a male (XY).

Chromosome
One of the rodlike structures found in the nucleus of every living cell that carries the genetic code in the form of genes.

After fertilization, the zygote divides repeatedly. After a few short weeks, one cell has become billions of cells. At about three weeks a primitive heart begins to drive blood through the embryonic bloodstream. At about five to six weeks, when the **embryo** is only ¼- to ½-inch long, primitive gonads, ducts, and external genitals whose anatomic sex cannot be distinguished visually have formed (see Figures 1 and 2). Each embryo possesses primitive external genitals, a pair of sexually undifferentiated gonads, and two sets of primitive duct structures, the Müllerian (female) ducts and the Wolffian (male) ducts.

During the first six weeks or so of prenatal development, embryonic structures of females and males develop along similar lines and resemble primitive female structures. At about the seventh week after conception, the genetic code (XX or XY) begins to assert itself, causing changes in the gonads, genital ducts, and external genitals. Genetic activity on the Y sex chromosome causes the testes to begin to differentiate (National Center for Biotechnology Information, 2006). Ovaries begin to differentiate if the Y chromosome is absent. The reproductive organs of some rare individuals who have only one X sex chromosome instead of the typical XY or XX arrangement also become female in appearance, because they too lack the Y sex chromosome. One could thus say that the basic blueprint of the human embryo is female (De Vries et al., 2002; Steinemann & Steinemann, 2005). The genetic instructions in the Y sex chromosome cause the embryo to deviate from the female developmental course.

By about the seventh week of prenatal development, strands of tissue begin to organize into seminiferous tubules. Female gonads begin to develop somewhat later than male gonads. The forerunners of follicles that will bear ova are not found until the fetal stage of development, about ten weeks after conception. Ovaries begin to form at 11 or 12 weeks.

Genetic Factors in Sexual Differentiation

What roles do genes play in sexual differentiation? Some of the answers to this question are fascinating. Animal studies suggest a role for genes in the determination of mating and other behavior patterns in humans. For example, the interaction of a number of genes has led to the development of three different types of males in a crustacean as well as to a quite complex mating strategy (Benvenuto & Weeks, 2012). One anatomic-sex-determining gene called *transformer (tra)* is needed in the development of female fruit flies. Chromosomal (XX) females with inactive tra attempt to mate with other females but they are attractive to males because they still emit female pheromones (Dauwalder, 2011). Researchers conclude that among fruit flies, sexual differentiation, sexual orientation, and sexual behavior are all determined by the interactions of genes (Meissner et al., 2011).

The SRY gene—which stands for *sex-determining region Y* gene—is also connected with sexual differentiation. In an article that could have been entitled "The Mouse That Roared," researcher

Embryo
The stage of prenatal development that begins with implantation of a fertilized ovum in the uterus and concludes with development of the major organ systems at about two months after conception.

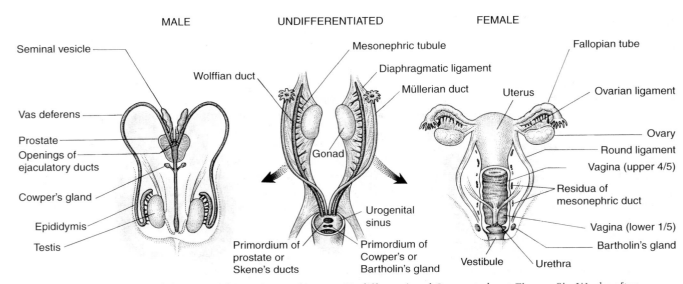

FIGURE 1 Development of the Internal Sex Organs from an Undifferentiated Stage at about Five or Six Weeks after Conception

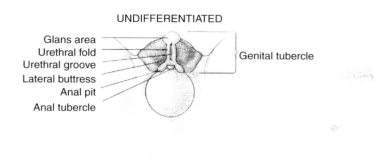

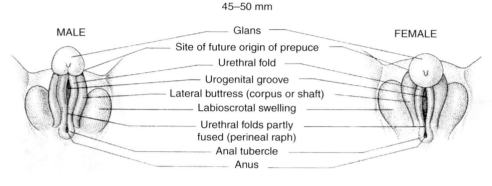

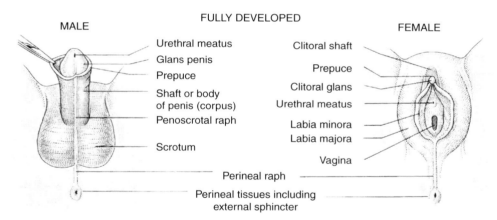

FIGURE 2   Development of the External Sex Organs from an Undifferentiated Stage at about Five or Six Weeks after Conception

Stephen Maxson (1998) reported that a number of genes that are involved in determining maleness in mice, including SRY, are connected with aggressiveness. SRY is also involved in anatomic sex determination in humans (Savic et al., 2010), leading to formation of the testes. Another gene involved in anatomic sex determination has also been researched in mice: *Sox 9*. Sox 9 appears to regulate the expression of SRY (Czech et al., 2012). Females with XX sex chromosomal structure normally suppress the action of their own Sox 9, which in turn prevents the expression of SRY. However, when these XX mice are chemically prevented from turning off Sox 9, they develop as males—albeit sterile males.

The Role of Sex Hormones in Sexual Differentiation

Once genes have done their work and testes develop in the embryo, they begin to produce male sex hormones, or androgens. Without androgens, we would all develop female external reproductive organs. The most important androgen, testosterone, spurs differentiation of the male (Wolffian)

duct system (see Figure 1). Each Wolffian duct develops into an epididymis, vas deferens, and seminal vesicle. The external genitals, including the penis, begin to take shape at about the eighth week of development under the influence of another androgen, dihydrotestosterone (DHT). **TRUTH OR FICTION** REVISITED: It is true that without male sex hormones, or androgens, we would all develop female external reproductive organs. However, *Müllerian inhibiting substance (MIS)*, a testicular hormone that is secreted during the fetal stage, prevents the Müllerian ducts from developing into the female duct system.

Small amounts of androgens are produced in female fetuses, but they are not normally sufficient to cause male sexual differentiation. In female fetuses, the relative absence of androgens causes degeneration of the Wolffian ducts and prompts development of female sexual organs. The Müllerian ducts evolve into fallopian tubes, the uterus, and the upper two-thirds of the vagina. Although female sex hormones are crucial in puberty, they are not involved in fetal sexual differentiation. If a fetus with an XY sex chromosomal structure failed to produce testosterone, it would develop external female sexual organs, but be infertile.

Inguinal canal
A fetal canal that connects the scrotum and the testes, allowing their descent.

Cryptorchidism
The condition defined by undescended testes.

Descent of the Testes and the Ovaries

The testes and ovaries develop from slender structures high in the abdominal cavity. By about ten weeks after conception, they have descended so that they are almost even with the upper edge of the pelvis. The ovaries remain there for the rest of the prenatal period. Later they rotate and descend farther to their adult position in the pelvis. About four months after conception, the testes normally descend into the scrotal sac via the **inguinal canal**. Then the passageway closes.

In a small percentage of males, one or both testes do not descend and remain in the abdomen at birth. The condition is termed **cryptorchidism.** In most cases of cryptorchidism, the testes migrate to the scrotum during infancy. In still other cases, the testes descend by puberty. Men with undescended testes are usually treated through surgery or hormonal therapy, because they are at higher risk for cancer of the testes. Sperm production is also impaired because the undescended testes are subjected to a higher-than-optimal body temperature, causing sterility.

Klinefelter syndrome
A sex-chromosomal disorder caused by an extra X sex chromosome.

Turner syndrome
A genetically determined condition associated with the presence of only one complete X chromosome and with characteristics including usually infertile ovaries, absence of menstruation, and short stature.

Sex Chromosomal Abnormalities

Abnormalities of the sex chromosomes can have profound effects on sexual characteristics, physical health, and psychological development. **Klinefelter syndrome**, a condition that affects about 1 in 500 males, is caused by an extra X sex chromosome, so the man has an XXY rather than an XY pattern. Men with this pattern fail to develop appropriate secondary sex characteristics. They have enlarged breasts, poor muscular development, and, because they fail to produce sperm, they are infertile. They may be mildly retarded.

Turner syndrome occurs in about 1 of every 2,500 females and is a consequence of having one rather than two X sex chromosomes. Individuals with this abnormality are at risk of developing heart disease, short arms and legs, kidney problems, hypothyroidism (producing too little thyroid hormone), and diabetes. Turner syndrome does not cause general cognitive impairment, but women may have specific problems in spatial relationships and math. Females with the syndrome may not naturally undergo puberty, so hormone treatments are usually begun when pubertal changes would start to spur growth of secondary sex characteristics. Nevertheless, nearly all women with the syndrome are infertile.

TRUTH OR **FICTION** REVISITED: Interestingly, however, if another woman donates an ovum (egg cell), and it is fertilized in a laboratory dish, it can usually be implanted in a woman with Turner syndrome and the embryo can develop normally to term.

The brain, like the genital organs, undergoes prenatal sexual differentiation. Testosterone causes cells in the hypothalamus of male fetuses to become insensitive to the female sex hormone estrogen. In female fetuses the hypothalamus develops sensitivity to estrogen.

Sensitivity to estrogen is important in the regulation of the menstrual cycle after puberty. The hypothalamus detects low levels of estrogen in the blood at the end of each cycle and initiates a new cycle by stimulating the pituitary gland to secrete follicle-stimulating hormone (FSH). FSH, in turn, stimulates estrogen production by the ovaries and the ripening of an immature follicle in an ovary.

◇ GENDER IDENTITY

Our **gender identity** is our psychological awareness or sense of being male or being female, and it's one of the most obvious and important aspects of our self-concepts. **Sex assignment** (also called *gender assignment*) reflects the child's anatomic sex and usually occurs at birth. A child's anatomic sex is so important to parents that they usually want to know "Is it a boy or a girl?" before they count fingers and toes.

Most children first become aware of their anatomic sex by about the age of 18 months. By 36 months, most children have acquired a firm sense of gender identity (Rathus, 2014).

Nature and Nurture in Gender Identity

What determines gender identity? Are our brains biologically programmed along masculine or feminine lines by prenatal sex hormones? Does the environment, in the form of postnatal learning experiences, shape our self-concepts as males or females? Or does gender identity reflect an intermingling of biological and environmental influences?

Gender identity is almost always consistent with chromosomal sex, but such consistency does not certify that gender identity is biologically determined. Caregivers also rear us as males or females, according to our anatomic sex. How, then, might we sort out the roles of nature and nurture, of biology and the environment?

Investigators have found clues in the experiences of rare individuals, **intersexuals**, who possess the gonads of one anatomic sex but external genitalia that are ambiguous or typical of the other anatomic sex. Intersexuals are sometimes reared as members of the other sex (the sex other than their chromosomal sex). Researchers have wondered whether the gender identity of these children reflects their chromosomal and gonadal sex or the gender to which they were assigned at birth, and according to which they were reared. Before going further, let us distinguish between true hermaphrodites and intersexuals.

Hermaphrodites and Intersexuals

Hormonal factors during prenatal development produce various congenital outcomes. Some individuals are born with both ovarian and testicular tissue. They are called **hermaphrodites**, after the Greek myth of the son of Hermes and Aphrodite, whose body became united with that of a nymph while he was bathing. True hermaphrodites may have one gonad of each anatomic sex (a testicle and an ovary), or gonads that combine testicular and ovarian tissue.

Regardless of their genetic sex, hermaphrodites often assume the gender identity and gender role of the gender assigned at birth. Figure 3 shows a genetic female (XX) with a right testicle and left ovary. This person married and became a stepfather with a firm male identity. The roles of biology and environment remain tangled, however, because true hermaphrodites have gonadal tissue of females and males.

Intersexualism

True hermaphroditism is quite rare. Less rare is intersexualism, which occurs in perhaps 1 infant in 5,000 or so (Intersex Society of North America [www.isna.org], 2012). Intersexuals have testes or ovaries, but not both. Unlike hermaphrodites, their gonads (testes or ovaries) match their chromosomal sex. Because of prenatal hormonal factors, however, their external genitals and sometimes their internal reproductive anatomy are ambiguous or resemble those of the other anatomic sex. Intersexualism has given scientists an opportunity to examine the roles of nature (biology) and nurture (environmental influences) in the shaping of gender identity. ◉

The most common form of female intersexualism is **congenital adrenal hyperplasia (CAH)**, in which a genetic (XX) female has female internal sexual structures (ovaries), but masculinized external genitals (www.congenitaladrenalhyperplasia.org, 2012; see Figure 4). The clitoris is enlarged and may resemble a small penis. CAH is caused by high levels of androgens, which are usually produced by the fetus's own adrenal glands. In other cases, mothers may have received synthetic androgens during their pregnancies. In the 1950s and 1960s, before these side effects were known, synthetic androgens were sometimes prescribed to help prevent miscarriages in women with histories of miscarriage.

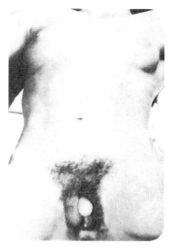

FIGURE 3
A Hermaphrodite

This genetic (XX) female has one testicle and one ovary and the gender identity of a male.

(reprinted courtesy of the John Money Collections at the Kinsey Institute for Research in Sex, Gender, and Reproduction, Inc.)

Gender identity
One's belief that one is male or female.

Sex assignment
The labeling of a newborn as a male or female. Also termed *gender assignment*.

Intersexual
A person who possesses the gonads of one anatomic sex but external genitalia that are ambiguous or typical of the other anatomic sex. Also termed *pseudohermaphrodite*.

Hermaphrodite
A person who possesses both ovarian and testicular tissue.

◉—⎤ **Watch the Video**
Intersexuals on www.
pearsoncustom.com/mi/
msu_mylabs

Congenital adrenal hyperplasia
A form of intersexualism in which a genetic female has internal female sexual structures but masculinized external genitals.

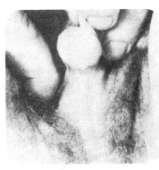

FIGURE 4

Intersexualism

In congenital adrenal hyperplasia, a genetic (XX) female has female internal sexual structures (ovaries) but masculinized external genitals.

Androgen-insensitivity syndrome

A form of intersexualism in which a genetic male is prenatally insensitive to androgens such that his genitals are not normally masculinized.

Dominican Republic syndrome

A form of intersexualism in which a genetic enzyme disorder prevents testosterone from masculinizing the external genitalia.

3

CRITICAL THINKING

How do intersexuals provide researchers with a special opportunity to explore the origins of gender identity?

Swedish investigator Anna Servin and her colleagues (2003) studied gender-typed behaviors and interests in 26 girls aged 2 to 10 who had CAH and in 26 girls without CAH who were matched for age. Girls with CAH showed more interest in masculine-typed toys, such as transportation toys, and less interest in feminine-typed toys, such as dolls. The girls with CAH were also more likely to have boys as playmates and to desire masculine-typed careers. Parents rated the behavior of daughters with CAH as being more "boy-like" in choice of toys and aggressiveness. Servin and her colleagues interpret the results as supporting a hormonal contribution to styles of play between girls with and without CAH, although other researchers also find a role for socialization (Wong et al., 2012).

There are several varieties of **androgen-insensitivity syndrome**, which is another type of intersexualism. One involves genetic (XY) males who, due to a mutated gene, have lower-than-normal prenatal sensitivity to androgens. As a result, their genitals do not become normally masculinized. At birth their external genitals are feminized, including a small vagina, and their testes are undescended. Because of insensitivity to androgens, the male duct system (epididymis, vas deferens, seminal vesicles, and ejaculatory ducts) fails to develop. Nevertheless, the fetal testes produce Müllerian inhibiting substance (MIS), preventing the development of a uterus or fallopian tubes. Genetic males with androgen-insensitivity syndrome usually have no or sparse pubic and axillary (underarm) hair, because the development of hair in these locations is dependent on androgens.

Girls with *partial androgen-insensitivity syndrome (PAIS)* or *complete androgen-insensitivity syndrome (CAIS)* are also intersexuals. PAIS and CAIS occur in 1 in 2,000 to 5,000 girls with a single X sex chromosome and in girls with XX chromosomal structure who lose some X sex chromosomal material. Girls with CAIS develop typical external genital organs, but their internal reproductive organs do not develop or function normally. By contrast, girls with PAIS develop masculinized external genitals and are sometimes raised as boys, sometimes as girls. A study by Melissa Hines and her colleagues (2003) compared 22 women with CAIS and single X sex chromosomal structure with 22 women who had the normal XX sex chromosomal structure. They found no differences between the women with CAIS and controls in self-esteem, general psychological well-being, gender identity, sexual orientation, gender-typed behavior patterns, marital status, personality traits, or hand preferences. The researchers conclude that two X sex chromosomes and ovaries are not essential to the development of feminine-typed behavior patterns in humans.

Dominican Republic syndrome is a form of intersexualism that was first documented in a group of 18 boys in two villages in the Dominican Republic (Lang & Kuhnle, 2008; Newman, 2012). Dominican Republic syndrome is a genetic enzyme disorder that prevents testosterone from masculinizing the external genitalia. The boys were born with normal testes and internal male reproductive organs, but their external genitals were malformed. Their penises were stunted and resembled clitorises. Their scrotums were incompletely formed and resembled female labia. They also had partially formed vaginas. Because the boys resembled girls at birth, they were reared as females. At puberty, however, their testes swung into normal testosterone production, causing startling changes: Their testes descended, their voices deepened, their musculature filled out, and their "clitorises" expanded into penises.

TRUTH OR **FICTION** REVISITED: Of the 18 Dominican Republic boys who were reared as girls, 17 shifted to a male gender identity. Sixteen of the 18 assumed a stereotypical masculine gender role. Of the remaining 2, 1 identified himself as a male but continued to maintain a feminine gender role, including wearing dresses. The 18th continued to see herself/himself as female and later sought gender-reassignment surgery to counter the pubertal masculinization. Despite being reared as girls, 16 of the 18 made the transition to the male role without problems, suggesting the importance of biology in gender identity (Bailey, 2003b).

Many scientists conclude that gender identity is influenced by complex interactions of biological and psychosocial factors. But could the "complex-interaction" approach be a way of avoiding the hot-potato issue as to whether nature (biological factors) or nurture (psychosocial factors) is more important? To place the emphasis on nature is to lessen the role of personal choice and thus has major political consequences. Although some place relatively greater emphasis on psychosocial factors (Bradley et al., 1998; Money, 1994), others emphasize the role of biological factors (Diamond, 2011; Savic et al., 2010). However, as noted in the nearby "A Closer Look" titled "Boys Who Are Reared as Girls," the theory that newborns are psychosexually neutral and that gender identity depends mainly on environmental factors has had rough sledding in recent years.

In case you have had enough discussion of the complex issues surrounding the origins of anatomic sex and gender identity in human beings, consider the crocodile. Crocodile eggs do not carry sex chromosomes. **TRUTH** OR **FICTION** REVISED: The crocodile offspring's anatomic sex is determined by the temperature at which the eggs develop (Ackerman, 1991). Some (males) like it hot (at least in the mid-90s F), and some (females) like it cooler, under the mid-80s F.

Transgenderism

In 1953, an ex-GI who journeyed to Denmark for a "sex-change operation" made headlines. She became known as Christine (formerly George) Jorgensen. Since then, thousands of transgendered individuals have undergone gender-reassignment surgery.

In **transgenderism**, the individual wishes to possess the anatomic features of people of the other sex and to live as a person of the other gender. The term *transsexualism* was earlier used for transgenderism.

Many transgendered individuals undergo hormone treatments and surgery to create the appearance of the external genitals typical of the other anatomic sex. This can be done more precisely with male-to-female than female-to-male transgendered individuals. After surgery, people can participate in sexual activity and even attain orgasm. One survey found that 85% of transgendered women attained orgasm during sexual activity (Lawrence, 2005). They cannot, however, conceive or bear children.

Is It a Boy or a Girl? *We haven't checked, but the answer has to do with the temperature at which the egg was incubated. Clue: Some like it hot.* (Roger de la Harpe/Gallo Images/Getty Images)

Transgenderism
A condition in which people strongly desire to be of the other anatomic sex and live the gender roles of the other anatomic sex.

TRUTH OR **FICTION** REVISITED: Gender-reassignment surgery cannot implant the internal reproductive organs of the other anatomic sex. Therefore, it is not accurate to say that people have actually changed their sexes through gender-reassignment surgery. Instead, surgery creates the appearance of the external genitals typical of the other anatomic sex.

What motivates transgendered people to wish to live as people of the other anatomic sex? It appears that they experience incongruity between their genital anatomy and their gender identity. Although they have the anatomic sex of a male or a female, they *feel* that they are members of the other anatomic sex. The discrepancy motivates them to wish to be rid of their own primary sex characteristics (their external genitals and internal sex organs) and to live as members of the other anatomic sex. A male-to-female transgendered individual perceives himself to be a female who, through some quirk of fate, was born with the wrong genital equipment. A female-to-male transgendered individual perceives herself as a man trapped in a woman's body.

But some researchers contend that many men who seek to become women tend to fall into other categories: either men who are extremely feminine or men who are sexually aroused by the idea of becoming a woman. The first category includes **homosexual transgendered men**—men who are extremely feminine gays and not fully satisfied by sexual activity with other males (Blanchard, 1989; Cantor, 2011). The second category refers to males who are **autogynephilic,** or sexually stimulated by fantasies of their own bodies as being female (Moser, 2010; Nuttbrock et al., 2011).

 5

Homosexual transgendered men
Extremely feminine gay males who seek gender reassignment.

Autogynephilic
Descriptive of transgendered men who are sexually stimulated by fantasies that their own bodies are female.

REAL STUDENTS, REAL QUESTIONS

Q *Can a man who has sex reassignment surgery get pregnant, or is that option futuristic?*

A No, he can't. Getting pregnant in the future is also unlikely. However—there's often a however in these matters—she could provide sperm prior to the change, use it to fertilize an egg from a donor, and the donor or another woman might carry the embryo to term.

Stockbroker/ SuperStock

A CLOSER LOOK

BOYS WHO ARE REARED AS GIRLS

Are children "psychosexually neutral" at birth? Can you surgically reassign a boy as a female, rear him as a girl, and have him feel that he is truly a girl as the years go on? Will cosmetic surgery, female sex hormone treatments, and laces and ribbons do it? Or will he be maladjusted and his male gender identity sort of "break through"? No one has sought to answer these questions by randomly selecting male babies and reassigning their genders. Evidence on the matter derives from studies of children who have lost their penises or failed to develop them through accidents or unusual medical conditions.

David Reimer
(REUTERS/Str Old)

Getting Down to Cases

For example, one of a pair of male twins, David Reimer, lost much of his penis as a result of a circumcision accident. As this case study is related by Colapinto (2000), the parents wondered what to do. Johns Hopkins sexologist John Money believed that gender identity was sufficiently malleable that the boy could undergo sex-reassignment surgery (have his testes removed and an artificial vagina constructed) and female hormone treatments and be successfully reared as a girl.

For a number of years, the case seemed to supply evidence for the view that children may be psychosexually neutral at birth. The sex-reassigned twin, unlike his brother, seemed to develop like a "real girl," albeit with a number of "tomboyish" traits. But at the age of 14, when "she" was informed about the circumcision accident and the process of sex reassignment, David immediately decided to pursue life as a male. As an adult, he recalled that he had never felt quite comfortable as a girl—a view confirmed by the recollections of his mother. At the age of 25, he married a woman and adopted her children. He reported being sexually attracted to women only. According to researchers such as Milton Diamond (1996), this outcome would appear to support the view that gender identity may be determined to a considerable extent in the uterus, as the fetal brain is being exposed to androgens.

Reimer committed suicide with a sawed-off shotgun in 2004, at the age of 38. When Colapinto received the news from David's father, he wrote, "I was shocked, but I cannot say I was surprised. Anyone familiar with David's life—as a baby, after a botched circumcision, [after] an operation to change him from boy to girl—would have understood that the real mystery was how he managed to stay alive for 38 years, given the physical and mental torments he suffered in childhood and that haunted him the rest of his life" (2004).

Another Case Study

Susan Bradley and her colleagues (1998) report on the development of another boy who suffered a circumcision accident in infancy. Again, John Money recommended sex reassignment, and the surgery was carried out at the age of 21 months. In this case, as Money found out in a follow-up at the age of 9, the individual was also tomboyish in behavior and personality traits but considered herself to be a girl.

She was interviewed subsequently at the ages of 16 and 26, and her situation had grown more complex. She considered herself to be bisexual and had sexual relationships with both men and women. However, when last interviewed, she had begun living with a woman in what the authors label a "lesbian" relationship. Of course, if one remembers that the individual has XY sex chromosomal structure, the relationship with the woman is not with a person of the same sex at all. On the other hand, the individual did retain the self-concept of being female.

A Larger Study

These celebrated cases are far from the only ones. On May 12, 2000, researchers from the Johns Hopkins Hospital, including William G. Reiner, a psychiatrist and urologist, presented a paper on the subject to the Lawson Wilkins Pediatric Endocrine Society Meeting in Boston. They recounted the development of 27 children who had been born without penises due to a rare condition called cloacal exstrophy. However, the children had normal testicles, male sex chromosomal structure, and male sex hormones.

Nevertheless, the sex of 25 of the 27 children was reassigned shortly after birth. They were surgically castrated and reared as girls by their parents. As the years went on, all 25—now 5 to 16 years old—showed the rough-and-tumble play considered stereotypical of males. Of the 25, 14 declared themselves to be males. Reiner (2000) suggests that "with time and age, children may well know what their gender is, regardless of any and all information and child-rearing to the contrary," he said. "They seem to be quite capable of telling

A CLOSER LOOK CONTINUED

us who they are." Reiner also noted that 2 of the 27 children who were not sex-reassigned fit in with male peers and appeared to be better adjusted than the children who were reassigned.

Swedish neuroscientists Ivanka Savic and her colleagues (2010) report evidence that gender identity and sexual orientation (heterosexual or homosexual) can develop during the intrauterine period. However, sexual differentiation of the sex organs occurs during the first two months of pregnancy, whereas sexual differentiation of the brain begins later, during the second half of pregnancy. Sexual differentiation of the genitals and the brain both depend on surges of testosterone, but because they happen at different times, they occur independently. Therefore, it is possible that an individual's sex organs can develop in one direction while his or her brain develops in the other direction. And, as in the case of David Reimer, it is possible that sexual differentiation can be ambiguous although sexual differentiation of the brain occurs more precisely later on.

As Marianne J. Legato (2000), a professor of medicine at Columbia University, describes it, "When the brain has been masculinized by exposure to testosterone, it is kind of useless to say to this individual, 'You're a girl.' It is this impact of testosterone that gives males the feelings that they are men." The view that newborns are psychosexually neutral and that gender identity depends mainly on nurture has become increasingly criticized in recent years.

Although the prevalence of transgenderism remains unknown, it is thought to be relatively rare. The number of transgendered people in the United States is estimated to be below 50,000. Of these, only a minority have undergone gender-reassignment surgery (Jones & Hill, 2002).

Homosexual transgendered males usually show cross-gender preferences in play and dress in early childhood. Some report that they felt they belonged to the other anatomic sex as long as they can remember (Zucker, 2005a, 2005b). Some male-to-female transgendered men recall that, as children, they preferred playing with dolls, enjoyed wearing frilly dresses, and disliked rough-and-tumble play. They were often perceived by their peers as "sissy boys." Some female-to-male transgendered people report that as children they disliked dresses and acted like "tomboys." They preferred playing "boys' games" and playing them with boys. Female-to-male transgendered individuals appear to have an easier time adjusting than male-to-female transgendered individuals. Even in adulthood, it may be easier for a female transsexual to don men's clothes and pass as a slightly built man than it is for a brawny man to pass for a tall woman.

Gender Reassignment

Surgery is one element of gender reassignment. Because the surgery is irreversible, health professionals conduct careful evaluations to determine that people seeking reassignment are competent to make such decisions and that they have thought through the consequences (Bockting & Fung, 2006). They usually require that the transsexual live openly as a member of the other sex for an extended trial period before surgery.

After the decision is reached, a lifetime of hormone treatments is begun. Male-to-female transsexuals receive estrogen, which fosters the development of female secondary sex characteristics. It causes fatty deposits to develop in the breasts and hips, softens the skin, and inhibits growth of the beard. Female-to-male transsexuals receive androgens, which promote male secondary sex characteristics. The voice deepens, hair becomes distributed according to the male pattern, muscles enlarge, and the fatty deposits in the breasts and hips are lost. The clitoris may also grow more prominent. In the case of male-to-female transsexuals, "phonosurgery" can raise the pitch of the voice (Bockting & Fung, 2006).

Despite its complexity and intimacy, sex-reassignment surgery is largely cosmetic. Medical science cannot construct internal genital organs or gonads. Male-to-female surgery is generally more successful. The penis and testicles are first removed. Tissue from the penis is placed in an artificial vagina so that sensitive nerve endings will provide sexual sensations. A penis-shaped form of plastic or balsa wood is used to keep the vagina distended during healing.

In female-to-male transsexuals, the internal sex organs (ovaries, fallopian tubes, uterus) are removed, along with the fatty tissue in the breasts. Some female-to-male transsexuals engage in a series of operations, termed **phalloplasty,** to construct an artificial penis, but the penises don't work

Phalloplasty
The surgical creation of an artificial penis.

Chaz Bono's Transition. *Chastity ("Chaz") Bono, 40, daughter of singers Cher (seen here on the left) and the late Sony Bono, announced in 2009 that she was undergoing the initial stages of gender reassignment surgery from female to male. Chaz expressed through a spokesperson the hope that this transition would open the "hearts and minds" of people toward transgendered individuals. (Mirek Towski/Contributor/Time & Life Pictures/ Getty Images)*

very well, and the procedures are costly. Therefore, most female-to-male transsexuals are content to have hysterectomies, mastectomies, and testosterone treatments (Bailey, 2003b).

Some transsexuals hesitate to undertake surgery because they are repulsed by the prospect of extreme medical intervention. Others forgo surgery so as not to jeopardize high-status careers or family relationships. Such people continue to think of themselves as members of the other sex, even without surgery.

REAL STUDENTS, REAL QUESTIONS

Q *Does an artificial penis get an erection? Can it ejaculate?*

A Yes and no. Female-to-male transsexuals who undergo phalloplasty (construction of an artificial penis) can have a pump installed that enables them to get erections, but medical science cannot create the glands that make ejaculation of seminal fluid possible.

RubberBall/ SuperStock

Outcomes of Sex-Reassignment Surgery

Most reports of the postoperative adjustment of transsexuals are positive (Smith et al., 2005). A Canadian follow-up study of 116 transsexuals at least one year after surgery found that most were content with the results and were reasonably well adjusted (Blanchard et al., 1985). Positive results for surgery were also reported in a study of 141 Dutch transsexuals (Kuiper & Cohen-Kettenis, 1988).

A study of 326 Dutch candidates for sex-reassignment surgery found that about two-thirds (222) began hormone treatment, whereas 103 did not (Smith et al., 2005). Of the 222, about 15% dropped out before surgery. Generally speaking, after surgery the group was no longer gender dysphoric and most individuals functioned well sexually, psychologically, and socially. Only two male-to-female transsexuals regretted their decision. Male-to-female transsexuals outnumbered female-to-males, but postoperative adjustment was more favorable for female-to-males. One reason may be that society is more accepting of women who desire to become men (Smith et al., 2005). Female-to-male transsexuals tend to be better adjusted socially before surgery as well so their superior postoperative adjustment may be nothing more than a selection factor.

CRITICAL THINKING
Why would a researcher bother to study whether traditional gender-role stereotypes are found around the world?

Stereotype
A fixed, conventional idea about a group of people.

Gender roles
Complex clusters of behavioral expectations for males and females.

◇ GENDER ROLES AND STEREOTYPES

"Why can't a woman be more like a man?" This is the title of a song in the musical *My Fair Lady*. In the song, Professor Henry Higgins laments that women are emotional and fickle, whereas men are logical and dependable. The "emotional woman" is a stereotype. The "logical man" is also a stereotype—albeit more generous. Even emotions are stereotyped. People assume that women are more likely to experience feelings of fear, sadness, and sympathy, whereas men are more likely to experience anger and pride (Plant et al., 2000). A **stereotype** is a fixed, conventional—and often distorted—idea about a group of people. Sex assignment—our identification of ourselves as female or male—does not determine the roles or behaviors that are deemed masculine or feminine in our culture. Cultures have broad expectations for the personalities and behaviors of men and women, and these are termed **gender roles**. A survey of 30 countries confirmed that these gender-role stereotypes are widespread (Williams & Best, 1994; see Table 1).

One of the effects of stereotyping is sexism, as we see in the following section.

TABLE 1   Gender-Role Stereotypes in 30 Nations

STEREOTYPES OF MALES		STEREOTYPES OF FEMALES	
Active	Opinionated	Affectionate	Nervous
Adventurous	Pleasure seeking	Appreciative	Patient
Aggressive	Precise	Cautious	Pleasant
Arrogant	Quick	Changeable	Prudish
Autocratic	Rational	Charming	Self-pitying
Capable	Realistic	Complaining	Sensitive
Coarse	Reckless	Complicated	Sentimental
Conceited	Resourceful	Confused	Sexy
Confident	Rigid	Dependent	Shy
Courageous	Robust	Dreamy	Softhearted
Cruel	Sharp witted	Emotional	Sophisticated
Determined	Show-off	Excitable	Submissive
Disorderly	Steady	Fault finding	Suggestible
Enterprising	Stern	Fearful	Superstitious
Hardheaded	Stingy	Fickle	Talkative
Individualistic	Stolid	Foolish	Timid
Inventive	Tough	Forgiving	Touchy
Loud	Unscrupulous	Frivolous	Unambitious
Obnoxious		Fussy	Understanding
		Gentle	Unstable
		Imaginative	Warm
		Kind	Weak
		Mild	Worrying
		Modest	

Note: Psychologists John Williams and Deborah Best (1994) found that people in 30 countries largely agreed on what constituted masculine and feminine gender-role stereotypes.

Source: Data from Williams and Best (1994, p. 193, Table 1).

Sexism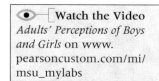

We have all encountered the effects of **sexism**—the prejudgment that because of her or his sex, a person will possess certain negative traits. These negative traits are assumed to disqualify the person for certain vocations or prevent him or her from performing adequately in these jobs or in some social situations.

Sexism may lead us to interpret the same behavior in prejudicial ways when performed by women or by men. A "sensitive" woman is simply sensitive, but a sensitive man may be seen as a "sissy." We may see a man as "self-assertive," but a woman who behaves in the same way is often seen as "pushy."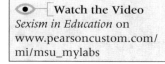

Children develop stereotypes about the differences between "man's work" and "woman's work" (Rathus, 2014). Women have been historically excluded from "male occupations," and stereotypical expectations concerning "men's work" and "women's work" filter down to the primary grades.

Watch the Video
Adults' Perceptions of Boys and Girls on www. pearsoncustom.com/mi/ msu_mylabs

Sexism
The prejudgment that, because of her or his sex, a person will possess negative traits.

Watch the Video
Sexism in Education on www.pearsoncustom.com/ mi/msu_mylabs

A WORLD OF DIVERSITY

THIRD GENDER/THIRD SEX

The terms *third gender* and *third sex* describe people who are considered to be neither women nor men, along with the social category in societies that recognize three or more sexes. Being neither male nor female has ramifications not only in terms of the person's sex but also in terms of the person's gender role, gender identity, and sexual orientation. In some cultures or to some individuals, a third sex or gender may represent an intermediate state between men and women, or it may represent a state of being both, as in the case of "the spirit of a man in the body of a woman." It may also represent the state of being neither (neuter), the ability to cross or swap sexes and gender roles, or another category that is independent of being male or being female. This last definition is favored by those who argue for a strict interpretation of the "third gender" concept.

The term *third gender* has been used to describe the Hijras of India and Pakistan, the Fa'afafine of Polynesia, and the Sworn virgins of the Balkans. In the Western world, lesbian, gay, transgender, and intersex people have also been described as belonging to a third sex or gender, although many object to being so categorized.

Third Sex in Biology

A small number of individuals within a population will not differentiate sexually into typical male or female bodies. They are sometimes called *hermaphrodites* or (especially among humans) *intersexuals*. Biologist and gender theorist Anne Fausto-Sterling (1993) proposed that five sexes may be more adequate than just two for describing human bodies. In addition to the physical morphology of sex, transgender biologist Joan Roughgarden argues that in some nonhuman animal species, there may be more than two *genders* (understood in terms of behavior and identity). She argues that there might be multiple behavior patterns available to individuals with a given biological sex.

Feminists distinguish between (biological) sex and (social/psychological) gender. Contemporary gender theorists usually argue that that a two-gender system is neither inborn nor universal. A sex/gender system that recognizes only the following two social norms has been labeled "heteronormativity," but feminists and queer theorists consider it to be too limited to describe the variety of sexual interests and behaviors we find in the real world:

- Female genitalia, female gender identity, feminine behavior, desire male partner
- Male genitalia, male gender identity, masculine behavior, desire female partner

Let's have a look at some *non*-heteronormative patterns around the world.

South-Central Asia

The Hijra of India, Pakistan, and Bangladesh are probably the most well known and populous third sex type in the modern world. The Mumbai-based community health organization called The Humsafar Trust estimates there are between 5 and 6 million hijras in India. In different areas they are known as Aravani/Aruvani or Jogappa. British photographer Dayanita Singh writes about her friendship with a Hijra, Mona Ahmed, and their two different society's beliefs about gender: "When I once asked her if she would like to go to Singapore for a sex change operation, she told me, 'You really do not understand. I am the third sex, not a man trying to be a woman. It is your society's problem that you only recognize two sexes'" (Singh et al., 1999). Hijra social movements have campaigned for recognition as a third sex, and in 2005, Indian passport application forms were updated with three gender options: M, F, and E.

The "Ladyboys" of Thailand

Also commonly referred to as a third sex are the *kathoeys* (or "*ladyboys*") of Thailand. However, although a significant number of Thais perceive kathoeys as belonging to a third gender, including many kathoeys themselves, others see them as either a kind of man or a kind of woman. Researcher Sam Winter (2003) writes:

> We asked our 190 [kathoeys] to say whether they thought of themselves as men, women, sao praphet song ["a second kind of woman"] or kathoey. None thought of themselves as male, and only 11% saw themselves as kathoey (i.e., "non-male"). By contrast 45% thought of themselves as women, with another 36% as sao praphet song.... Unfortunately we did not include the category phet tee sam (third sex/ gender); conceivably if we had done so there may have been many respondents who would have chosen that term.... Around 50% [of non-transgender Thais] see them as males with the mistaken minds, but the other half see them as either women born into the wrong body (around 15%) or as a third sex/gender (35%).

In 2004, the Chiang Mai Technology School allocated a separate restroom for kathoeys, with an intertwined male and female symbol on the door. The 15 kathoey students are required to wear male clothing at school but are allowed to sport feminine hairdos. The restroom features four stalls, but no urinals.

A WORLD OF DIVERSITY   CONTINUED

The Western World

Some writers suggest that a third gender emerged around 1700 in England: the male sodomite. According to these writers, this was marked by the emergence of a subculture of effeminate males and meeting places (molly houses), as well as a marked increase in hostility toward effeminate and/or homosexual males. People described themselves as members of a third sex in Europe from at least the 1860s with the writings of Karl Heinrich Ulrichs and continuing in the late nineteenth century with Magnus Hirschfeld, John Addington Symonds, Edward Carpenter, Aimée Duc, and others. These writers described themselves and those like them as being of an "inverted" or "intermediate" sex and experiencing homosexual desire, and their writing argued for social acceptance of such sexual intermediates.

Throughout much of the twentieth century, the term *third sex* was a popular descriptor for homosexuals and gender nonconformists, but after the gay liberation movement of the 1970s and a growing separation of the concepts of sexual orientation and gender identity, the term fell out of favor among LGBT (lesbian-gay-bisexual-transgender) communities and the wider public. With the renewed exploration of gender that feminism, the modern transgender movement, and queer theory has fostered, some in the contemporary West have begun again to describe themselves as a third sex. One well-known social movement of male-bodied people that identify as neither men nor women is the *Radical Faeries*. Other modern identities that cover similar ground include *pangender, bigender, genderqueer, androgyne, other gender,* and *differently gendered.*

The term *transgender,* which often refers to those who change their gender, is increasingly being used to signify a gendered subjectivity that is neither male nor female. One recent example is on a form for the Harvard Business School, which has three gender options: male, female, and transgender.

Indigenous Cultures of North America: "Two Spirits"

Native American cultures are also very much associated with multiple genders. They often contain social gender categories that are collectively known as "berdache" or Two-Spirit. Individual examples include the Winkte of Lakota culture, the ninauposkitzipxpe ("manly-hearted woman") of the North Piegan (Blackfoot) community, and the Zapotec Muxe. Various scholars have debated the nature of such categories, as well as the definition of the term *third gender.* Different researchers may characterize the berdache as a gender-crosser, a mixed gender, an intermediate gender, or distinct third and fourth genders that are not dependent on male and female as primary categories. Those (such as Will Roscoe) who have argued for the latter interpretation also argue that mixed-, intermediate-, cross-, or non-gendered social roles should not be understood as truly representing a third gender. According to Jean-Guy Goulet (2006):

"Berdache" may signify a category of male human beings who fill an established social status other than that of man or woman; a category of male and female human beings who behave and dress "like a member of the opposite sex"; or categories of male and female human beings who occupy well established third or fourth genders. Scheffler, however, sees Native American cases of "berdache" and "amazon" as "situations in which some men (less often women) are permitted to act, in some degree, as though they were women (or men), and may be spoken of as though they were women (or men), or as anomalous 'he-she' or 'she-he.'" In Scheffler's view, "Ethnographic data … provide definitive evidence that such persons were not regarded as having somehow moved from one sex category to the other, but were only metaphorically 'women' (or 'men')." In other words, according to Scheffler, we need not imagine a multiple gender system. Individuals who appeared in the dress and/or occupation of the opposite sex were only metaphorically spoken of as members of that sex or gender.

Sources: This feature is adapted from the Wikipedia entry on Third Gender and obtains information from Agrawal (1997), Fausto-Sterling (1993), Goulet (2006), Hester (2005), Murray and Roscoe (1997), Roscoe (2000), Roughgarden (2004), Stockett (2005), Totman (2004), and Winter (2003).

Thai "Ladyboys"
(Peter Treanor/Alamy)

A Nurse and a Patient. *If you think there is something wrong with this picture, could it be because you have fallen prey to traditional gender-role stereotypes? Tradition has prevented many women from seeking jobs in "male" preserves such as construction work and the military. Tradition has also prevented many men from obtaining work in "female" domains such as secretarial work, nursing, and teaching at the elementary level.*
(Taxi/Getty Images)

For example, according to traditional stereotypes, women are not expected to excel in math. Exposure to such negative expectations may discourage women from careers in science and technology. Even when they choose a career in science or technology, women are often subject to discrimination in hiring, promotions, allocation of facilities for research, and funds to conduct research (Loder, 2000). Similarly, only recently have men begun to enter occupational domains previously restricted largely to women, such as secretarial work, nursing, and teaching in the primary grades.

Sexism is psychologically damaging. One experiment found that women who were led to believe that sexism was pervasive reported lower self-esteem than women who were led to think that sexism was rare (Schmitt et al., 2003). In another experiment, men and women were led to believe that they were rejected from taking a course either due to sexism or personal reasons (Major et al., 2003). Attributing the rejection to prejudice rather than to personal deservingness had the effect of protecting their self-esteem ("It's not me; it's society").

Fortunately, it appears that education can modify sexist attitudes. One study reported on the degree to which women's studies courses can help individuals become more aware of sexism and develop more egalitarian attitudes (Stake & Hoffman, 2001). In the study, 548 women's studies students completed questionnaires prior to and following the courses in areas such as openness to women's studies, egalitarian attitudes toward females and gender issues, and awareness of sexism and discrimination against females. As compared with students who did not take women's studies, the students in the courses reported increased awareness of sexism and other kinds of prejudice, more egalitarian attitudes toward women and other stigmatized groups, and more interest in engaging in activism for social causes.

Gender Roles and Sexual Behavior

Gender roles affect relationships and sexual behavior. Children learn at an early age that men usually approach women and initiate sexual interactions, whereas women usually serve as the "gatekeepers" in romantic relationships. In their traditional role as gatekeepers, women are expected to wait to be approached and to screen suitors. Men are expected to make the first (sexual) move, and women are to determine how far they will go.

The cultural expectation that men are initiators and women are gatekeepers is embedded within the larger stereotype that men are sexually aggressive and women are sexually passive. Men are expected to have a higher number of sexual partners than women do (Fisher et al., 2012; Schmitt et al., 2012). Men not only initiate sexual encounters; they are also expected to dictate all the "moves" thereafter, just as they are expected to take the lead on the dance floor. People who adhere to the masculine gender-role stereotype, whether male or female, are more likely to engage in risky (unprotected) sexual behavior (Belgrave et al., 2000). According to the stereotype, women are supposed to let male partners determine the choice, timing, and sequence of sexual positions and techniques. Unfortunately, the stereotype favors men's sexual preferences, denying women the opportunity to give and receive their preferred kinds of stimulation.

According to another stereotype, men become sexually aroused at puberty and remain at the ready throughout adulthood. Women, however, do not share men's natural interests in sex, and a woman discovers her own sexuality only when a man ignites her sexual flame. Despite the stereotype, it is not clear that women are biologically less arousable than men; however, they are more likely to desire to limit sexual activity to intimate, committed relationships (Schmitt et al., 2012). On the other hand, researchers (Fisher et al., 2012) find consistent empirical support for the view that men generally have more sexual desire than women.

Questions remain as to the extent to which the gender differences associated with gender-role stereotypes reflect nature or the influences of culture and tradition. Gender differences are also vastly more pervasive than those involving sexual behavior, as we see next.

◇ GENDER DIFFERENCES

If females and males were not anatomically different, this book would never have been written. But how do females and males differ in cognitive abilities, personality, and social behavior, if at all?

Differences in Cognitive Abilities

Although females and males do not differ noticeably in overall intelligence (Halpern & LaMay, 2000), beginning in childhood, gender differences appear in certain cognitive abilities. Females are somewhat superior to males in verbal ability. Males seem somewhat superior in visual–spatial skills. The picture for mathematics appears to be much more complex, with females excelling in some areas and males in others.

Verbal Ability

Verbal abilities include reading, spelling, grammar, oral comprehension, and word fluency. As a group, females surpass males in verbal ability throughout their lives (Andreano & Cahill, 2009; Lohman & Lakin, 2009). These differences show up early. Girls seem to acquire language faster than boys. They make more prelinguistic vocalizations, utter their first word sooner, and develop larger vocabularies. Boys in the United States are more likely than girls to have reading problems, ranging from reading below grade level to learning disorders (Brun et al., 2009).

Why do females excel in verbal abilities? Biological factors such as the organization of the brain may play a role, but do not discount cultural factors—whether a culture stamps a skill as gender-neutral, masculine, or feminine (Goldstein, 2005). In Nigeria and England, reading is looked on as a masculine activity, and boys traditionally surpass girls in reading ability. But in the United States and Canada, reading tends to be stereotyped as feminine, and girls tend to excel.

Visual–Spatial Abilities

Visual–spatial ability refers to the ability to visualize objects or shapes and to mentally manipulate and rotate them. This ability is important in such fields as art, architecture, and engineering. Boys begin to outperform girls on many types of visual–spatial tasks starting at age 8 or 9, and the difference persists into adulthood (Andreano & Cahill, 2009; Yazzie, 2010). The gender difference is particularly notable on tasks that require imagining how objects will look if they are rotated in space (see Figure 5).

Some researchers link visual–spatial performance to evolutionary theory and sex hormones. It may be related to a genetic tendency to create and defend a territory (Ecuyer-Dab & Robert, 2004). An environmental theory is that gender stereotypes influence the spatial experiences of children. Gender-stereotyped "boys' toys," such as blocks, Legos, and Erector sets, provide more practice with spatial skills than gender-stereotyped "girls' toys." Boys are also more likely to engage in sports, which involve moving balls and other objects through space (Leaper & Bigler, 2011).

Mathematical Abilities

For half a century or more, it has been believed that male adolescents generally outperform females in mathematics, and research has tended to support that belief (Collaer & Hill, 2006; Halpern et al., 2007). But a study by Janet Hyde and her colleagues (2008) of some 7 million children in

CRITICAL THINKING
Why do you think some writers suggest that it is "politically correct" to minimize gender differences in cognitive abilities?

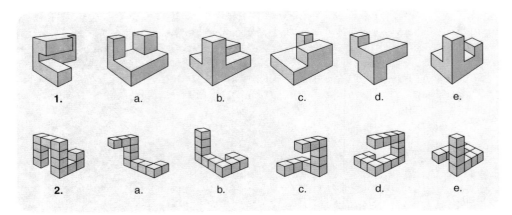

FIGURE 5 Rotating Geometric Figures in Space

Visual–spatial skills—for example, the ability to rotate geometric figures in space—are considered part of the male gender-role stereotype. But such gender differences are small and can be modified by training.

second through eleventh grade found no overall gender difference for performance in mathematics on standardized tests.

Regarding differences in verbal abilities and spatial-relations skills, note that the reported gender differences are group differences. There is greater variation in these skills among individuals within the groups than between males and females (Halpern, 2003). Millions of females outdistance the "average" male in math and spatial abilities. Men have produced their verbally adept Shakespeares. Moreover, in most cases, differences in cognitive skills are small in societies in which women are empowered, including most parts of the United States, Canada, Europe, Japan, and South Korea (Else-Quest et al., 2010; Else-Quest & Grabe, 2012).

Differences in Personality

There are also many gender differences in personality. According to a meta-analysis of the research literature, females exceed males in extraversion, anxiety, trust, and nurturance (Feingold, 1994). Overall, however, differences in personality tend to be small (Bailey, 2003b). Males do tend to exceed females in assertiveness, tough-mindedness, and self-esteem. Two factors may largely account for the relatively lower self-esteem of females:

Are There Gender Differences in Cognitive Abilities? *The physical differences between females and males are well established—and well celebrated! But are there cognitive differences between females and males? If so, what are they? How large are they? Are they the result of nature (heredity) or nurture (environmental influences such as educational experiences and cultural expectations)?*
(Adam Gault/Alamy)

- Parents, on average, prefer to have boys.
- Society has created an unlevel playing field in which females have to perform better than males to be seen as doing equally well.

Differences in Social Behavior

There are important gender differences in social behavior, particularly in matters concerning sex and aggression. Consider communication styles. Research shows that males tend to dominate classroom discussions unless teachers take steps to encourage gender equity in the classroom (McHugh & Hambaugh, 2010). As girls mature, it appears that they often learn to "take a backseat" to boys and let the boys do most of the talking when they are in mixed-gender groups, especially if they are reared in "traditional" communities or regions of the nation. Women are more willing than men to disclose their feelings and personal experiences, however

A WORLD OF DIVERSITY

WOMEN IN STEM FIELDS

Despite research findings that there is no overall gender difference in performance on standardized mathematics achievement tests, most Americans continue to have different expectations for boys and girls, and these expectations may still dissuade some math-proficient girls from entering so-called STEM (science, technology, engineering, and mathematics) fields (Hyde & Mertz, 2009).

Thus, there is reason to believe that women have the capacity to be entering STEM fields in greater numbers. So why, in the twenty-first century in the United States, do women remain underrepresented in STEM fields? According to psychologists Stephen Ceci, Wendy Williams, and Susan Barnett (2009), the reasons are likely as follows:

- Women who are proficient in math are more likely than math-proficient men to prefer careers that do not require skills in math.
- More males than females obtain extremely high scores on the SAT mathematics test and the quantitative reasons sections of the Graduate Record Exam.
- Women who are proficient in math are more likely than men with this proficiency to have high verbal competence as well, which encourages many such women to choose careers other than those in STEM fields.
- In some STEM fields, women with children find themselves penalized in terms of promotions.

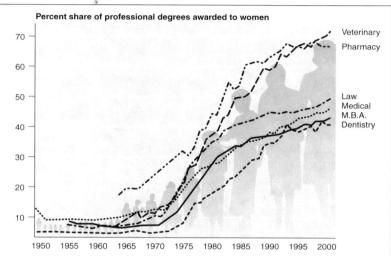

FIGURE 6 Women Flood Professions Once Populated Almost Exclusively by Men

Source: As appeared in "Scientists Are Made, Not Born" by W. Michael Cox and Richard Alm, *The New York Times*, February 28, 2005. Reprinted by permission of Management Design.

Women's preferences may well be a key reason that there are more men entering and remaining in STEM fields today. However, we need to note two caveats: First, women are in fact entering STEM fields in increasing numbers (see Table 2 and Figure 6). Second, women's preferences cannot be fully divorced from society's expectations. As long as gender stereotypes about who belongs in STEM fields remain, at least some women will be discouraged from entering them.

TABLE 2 Percentage of Bachelor's and Doctoral Degrees Earned by Women, According to Field of Study: Academic Years 1990–1991, 1995–1996, 2005–2006

BACHELOR'S DEGREES	1990–1991	1995–1996	2005–2006
Health professions & related clinical sciences	83.9	81.5	86.0
Biological & biomedical sciences	50.8	52.6	61.5
Physical sciences & science technologies	31.6	36.0	41.8
Mathematics & statistics	47.3	46.1	45.1
Engineering & engineering technologies	14.1	16.2	17.9
DOCTORAL DEGREES			
Health professions & related clinical sciences	57.7	60.3	72.5
Biological & biomedical sciences	36.9	41.8	49.2
Physical sciences & science technologies	19.6	22.9	30.0
Mathematics & statistics	19.2	20.6	29.5
Engineering & engineering technologies	9.3	12.6	20.2

Source: U.S. Department of Education, National Center for Education Statistics (NCES). Digest of Education Statistics, 2007 (NCES 2008-022), tables 258, 286, 288, 290–301, 303, 305, and 307, data from U.S. Department of Education, NCES, 1990–91, 1995–96, and 2005–06. Integrated Postsecondary Education Data System, "Completions Survey" (IPEDS-C91-96), and IPEDS, Fall 2006. Table 27.I.

(Valkenburg et al., 2011). The stereotype of the "strong and silent" male may not discourage men from hogging the conversation, but it may inhibit them from expressing their personal feelings.

Differences in Sexuality

According to almost any measure that is used, men show more interest in sex than women do, although the gender difference may not be as large as is generally believed and may also be influenced by sex-role expectations (Fisher et al., 2012). Women are more likely to want to combine sex with a romantic relationship (Thompson & O'Sullivan, 2011). Men also report being more interested than women in casual sex and in multiple sex partners (Schmitt et al., 2012).

Differences in Aggressiveness

6 **TRUTH** OR **FICTION** REVISITED: It is true that males tend to behave more aggressively than females, and that this gender difference emerges early (Hay et al., 2011). In almost all cultures, it is the males who march off to war and who battle for fame and glory (and shaving-cream-commercial contracts in stadiums and arenas). As we will see, the key question is: Why?

Differences in Willingness to Seek Health Care

Men's life expectancies are seven years shorter, on average, than women's. Female and male anatomy and physiology predispose them to different health issues, but part of the difference, according to surveys of physicians and of the general population, is women's greater willingness to seek health care (Glaesmer et al., 2012). Men often let symptoms go until a problem that could have been prevented or readily treated becomes serious or life-threatening. Women, for example, are much more likely to check themselves for breast cancer than men are to even recognize the symptoms of prostate cancer. Many men have a "bullet-proof mentality." They are too strong to see the doctor in their 20s, too busy in their 30s, and too frightened later on.

◇ ON BECOMING A MAN OR A WOMAN: GENDER TYPING

We have chronicled the biological processes of sexual differentiation, and we have explored gender differences in cognitive abilities, personality, and social behavior. In this section we consider various explanations of gender typing, the process by which males and females come to develop personality traits and behavior patterns that society considers to be consistent with their gender, male or female—at least most of the time. Researchers who investigate people's perceptions of gender differences in personality traits tend to find groups of "masculine" and "feminine" traits such as those shown in Table 1.

One study using the "Big Five Inventory" investigated gender differences in personality in 55 nations, with a sample size of 17,637 (Schmitt et al., 2008). Responses revealed that women reported higher levels of anxiety, extraversion (outgoingness), agreeableness, and conscientiousness than men did in most nations.

Biological Perspectives: It's Only Natural

Biological views on gender typing tend to focus on the roles of hormones, genetics, and brain structures in predisposing men and women to gender-linked behavior patterns. It is largely assumed that a major mechanism by which heredity expresses itself in this realm is through prenatal sex hormones.

Hormones

Researchers suggest that the development of gender differences in personality, along with the development of anatomic gender differences, may be related to prenatal levels of sex hormones. Although results of many studies attempting to correlate prenatal sex hormone levels with subsequent gender-typed play have been mixed, a study of 212 pregnant women conducted by Bonnie Auyeung and her colleagues (2009) found that fetal testosterone was related to masculine or feminine-typed play at the age of 8½ years. Other studies show that children display gender-typed preferences—with boys preferring transportation toys and girls preferring dolls—as early as the age of 13 months (Knickmeyer et al., 2005). Another study investigated the gender-typed visual preferences of 30 human infants at the early ages of 3 to 8 months (Alexander et al., 2009). The researchers assessed interest in a toy truck and a doll by using eye-tracking technology to indicate the direction of visual attention. Girls showed a visual preference for the doll over the truck (that is, they made a greater number of visual fixations on the doll), and boys showed a visual preference for the truck.

The Evolutionary Perspective

From the evolutionary perspective, the story of the survival of our ancient ancestors is etched in our genes. Genes that bestow attributes that increase an organism's chances of surviving to produce viable offspring are most likely to be transmitted to future generations. We thus possess the genetic remnants of traits that helped our ancestors survive and reproduce (Buss, 2009). This heritage influences our social and sexual behavior as well as our anatomic features.

According to the evolutionary perspective, men's traditional roles as hunters and warriors and women's roles as caregivers and gatherers of fruits and vegetables are bequeathed to us in our genes. Men are better suited to war and the hunt because of physical attributes passed along since ancestral times. Upper-body strength, for example, would have enabled them to throw spears and overpower adversaries. Men also possess perceptual–cognitive advantages, such as superior visual–motor skills that favor aggression. Visual–motor skills would have enabled men to aim spears or bows and arrows.

Women, it is argued, are genetically predisposed to be empathic and nurturant because these traits enabled ancestral women to respond to children's needs and to enhance the likelihood that their children would flourish and eventually reproduce, thereby transmitting their own genetic legacy to future generations. Prehistoric women thus tended to stay close to home, care for the children, and gather edible plants, whereas men ventured from home to hunt and raid their neighbors' storehouses.

The evolutionary perspective is steeped in controversy. Although scientists do not dispute the importance of evolution in determining physical attributes, many are reluctant to attribute complex social behaviors, such as aggression and gender roles, to heredity. The evolutionary perspective implies that stereotypical gender roles—men as breadwinners and women as homemakers, for example—reflect the natural order of things. Critics contend that, among humans, biology is not destiny, and behavior is not dictated by genes.

Prenatal Brain Organization

Researchers have sought the origins of gender-typed behavior in the organization of the brain. Is it possible that the cornerstone of gender-typed behavior is laid in the brain before the first breath is taken?

The hemispheres of the brain are specialized to carry out certain functions (Shaywitz et al., 1995). In most people, the right hemisphere ("right brain") appears to be specialized to perform visual–spatial tasks. The "left brain" appears to be more essential to verbal functions, such as speech, in most people.

We know that sex hormones are responsible for prenatal sexual differentiation of the genitals and for the gender-related structural differences in the hypothalamus of the developing prenatal brain. Sexual differentiation of the brain may also partly explain men's superiority at spatial-relations tasks, such as interpreting road maps and visualizing objects in space. Testosterone in the brains of male fetuses spurs greater growth of the right hemisphere and slows the rate of growth of the left hemisphere (Cohen-Bendahan et al., 2005; Siegel-Hinson & McKeever, 2002). This difference may be connected with the ability to accomplish spatial-relations tasks, and with preferences for childhood toys.

Might boys' inclinations toward aggression and rough-and-tumble play also be prenatally imprinted in the brain? Some theorists argue that prenatal sex hormones may masculinize or feminize the brain by creating predispositions that are consistent with gender-role stereotypes, such as rough-and-tumble play and aggressive behavior in males (Cohen-Bendahan et al., 2005).

The gender differences in activity preferences of children are also found in rhesus monkeys. For example, male rhesus juveniles and boys are more likely than female rhesus juveniles and girls to engage in rough-and-tumble play (Wallen & Hassett, 2009). Researchers also introduced wheeled toys and plush toys into a 135-member rhesus monkey troop and found that male monkeys, like boys, showed consistent,

CRITICAL THINKING
Why do you think many feminists and queer theorists argue that evolutionary theory is little more than a sophisticated excuse for maintaining the status quo in the centers of power in society?

A WORLD OF DIVERSITY

THE EYE THAT ROVES AROUND THE WORLD?

One of the more controversial gender differences is the suggestion that males are naturally polygamous and females are naturally monogamous (Schmitt, 2008). If this were so, it would place a greater burden on societies in which men are expected to remain loyal to their mates. If the man strayed, after all, he could have the attitude, "Don't blame me. It's in my genes." Women, moreover, might wonder how realistic it is to expect that their partners will remain faithful.

Evolutionary psychologists have hypothesized *sexual strategies theory*, which holds that men and women differ in their long-term and short-term mating strategies, with men more interested in sexual variety in the short term (Cohen & Belsky, 2008; Njus & Bane, 2009). In the long term, both males and females may seek a heavy investment in a relationship, and feelings of love, companionship, and a sharing of resources. Even so, men are hypothesized to place more value on signals of fertility and reproductive value, as found in a woman's youth and physical appearance. But women are hypothesized to place relatively more value on a man's social status, maturity, and resources—cues that are relevant to his ability to provide over the long term. The qualities that men and women seek are believed to help solve adaptive problems that humans have faced over their evolutionary history.

But in the short term, men are more interested in one-night stands and relatively brief affairs. Women, evolutionarily speaking, would have little to gain from such encounters. Impregnation requires a long-term commitment to childrearing, and evolutionary forces would favor the survival of the children of women who created a long-term nurturing environment. But men would have a greater chance of contributing their genes to future generations by impregnating as many women as possible.

Do Men around the World Have Roving Eyes? *A study of ten different areas of the world found that in every culture surveyed, men were more likely than women to desire multiple sex partners. According to the sexual strategies theory, this gender difference reflects human adaptation to environmental forces. Here's a question for critical thinking: Does this research finding mean that it is "unnatural" to expect men to remain faithful to their partners?*
(Buena Vista Images/The Image Bank/Getty Images)

Because a "universal" form of behavior is more likely to be embedded in people's genes, the evolutionary theory of different sexual strategies would find support if males and females from various cultures showed similar gender differences in short-term mating strategies. In seeking just such evidence, David Schmitt (2003) supervised a survey of 16,288 people across ten major regions of the world, including North America, South America, Western Europe, Eastern Europe, Southern Europe, Middle East, Africa, Oceania, South/Southeast Asia, and East Asia. He found that, indeed, gender differences in the desire for sexual variety were culturally universal.

Table 3 and Figure 7 reveal Schmitt's findings concerning desire for variety in short-term and long-term relationships. When asked whether they would like to have more than one sex partner in the next month, men from all ten areas of the world were significantly more likely than women to say that they would. For example, 23.1% of North American men would like more than one partner, as compared with just 2.9% of North American women (see Table 3). When asked about the mean (average) number of sex partners they would like to have over the next 30 years, men from every area said they would like to have significantly more sex partners than did the women (see Figure 7).

We cannot conclude that these research findings, intriguing as they are, "prove" the validity of the evolutionary approach to understanding gender differences in "sexual strategies." For example, we could point to details in Figure 7, such as the fact that Oceanic women reported that they wanted more sex partners in the long term than did African men. We can also accept the universality of the finding but consider rival explanations for the data. For example, in a world with common global communication, it might not be surprising that there is worldwide overlap in gender roles. This overlap might affect the ways in which parents and cultural institutions influence children around the world.

CRITICAL THINKING
According to evolutionary theory, men have inherited a tendency to be interested in having multiple sex partners. Does this mean that it is "unnatural" for society to promote monogamous relationships?

strong preferences for the wheeled toys, whereas female monkeys, like girls, showed greater flexibility in preferences, sometimes playing with the plush toys and sometimes playing with the wheeled toys (Hassett et al., 2008). Do these cross-species findings suggest that such preferences in humans can develop without human gender-typed socialization experiences?

Another study investigated the gender-typed visual preferences of human infants at the early ages of 3 to 8 months (Alexander et al., 2009). The researchers hypothesized that preferences for gender-typed toys might be at least in part inborn and would therefore emerge in children before they were self-aware of their gender identity. The researchers assessed interest in a toy truck and doll in 30 infants by using eye-tracking technology to indicate the direction of visual attention. They did find the hypothesized gender differences in visual interest: Girls showed a visual preference for the doll over the truck, and boys showed a higher number of visual fixations on the truck than on the doll. As noted, these gender differences emerge much earlier than self-awareness of one's sex, and there has been relatively little time for social influences to take effect.

Psychological Perspectives

Developmentally speaking, children acquire awareness of gender-role stereotypes by the tender ages of 2½ to 3½ (Rathus, 2014). When asked to describe gender differences, boys and girls generally agree that boys build things, play with transportation toys such as cars and fire trucks, enjoy helping their fathers, and hit other children. Both boys and girls also agree that girls enjoy playing with dolls, help their mothers cook and clean, and are talkative, dependent on others for help, and nonviolent. They perceive the label "cruel" to be a masculine trait, whereas "cries a lot" is perceived as feminine. By the time they are age 3, most children have become aware of the stereotypical ways in which men and women dress and the types of occupations that are considered appropriate for each (Rathus, 2014).

Many psychologists have attempted to explain how children acquire such knowledge and adopt stereotypical behavior patterns in terms of psychoanalytic, social–cognitive, or cognitive–developmental theories.

TABLE 3 Gender Differences in the Percentage of Men and Women Who Desire More Than One Sex Partner "in the Next Month" across 10 World Regions

WORLD REGION	PERCENTAGE OF MEN WANTING MORE THAN ONE SEXUAL PARTNER	PERCENTAGE OF WOMEN WANTING MORE THAN ONE SEXUAL PARTNER
North America	23.1	2.9
South America	35.0	6.1
Western Europe	22.6	5.5
Eastern Europe	31.7	7.1
Southern Europe	31.0	6.0
Middle East	33.1	5.9
Africa	18.2	4.2
Oceania	25.3	5.8
South/Southeast Asia	32.4	6.4
East Asia	17.9	2.6

Note: The chances that any gender differences within a given region are the result of chance is less than 1 in 1,000 (p < 0.001).

Source: David P. Schmitt (2003). Universal sex differences in the desire for sexual variety: Tests from 52 nations, 6 continents, and 13 islands. *Journal of Personality and Social Psychology,* 85(1), 85–104, Table 5. Copyright © 2003 by the American Psychological Association. Reprinted with permission.

REAL STUDENTS, REAL QUESTIONS

Q *Aren't there cultures in which women do the hunting/gathering and men take care of the children?*

A There certainly have been some. In her 1935 book *Sex and Temperament in Three Primitive Societies,* anthropologist Margaret Mead described the Tchambuli of New Guinea as follows: "The men 'primped' and spent their time decorating themselves while the women worked and were the practical ones—the opposite of how it seemed in early 20th century America." But, frankly, what makes this finding notable is its rarity.

(RubberBall/SuperStock)

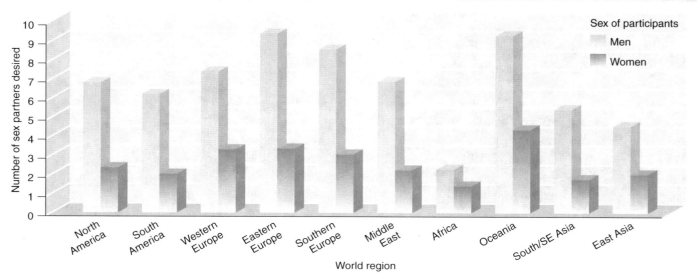

FIGURE 7 Mean Number of Sexual Partners Desired by Men and Women in the Next 30 Years, across 10 World Regions

Source: David P. Schmitt (2003). Universal sex differences in the desire for sexual variety: Tests from 52 nations, 6 continents, and 13 islands. *Journal of Personality and Social Psychology,* 85(1), 85–104. Copyright © 2003 by the American Psychological Association. Reprinted with permission.

Identification
In psychoanalytic theory, the process of incorporating within ourselves our perceptions of the behaviors, thoughts, and feelings of others.

Oedipus complex
According to psychoanalytic theory, a conflict of the phallic stage in which the boy wishes to possess his mother sexually and perceives his father as a rival in love.

Socialization
The process of guiding people into socially acceptable behavior patterns by means of information, rewards, and punishments.

Psychoanalytic Theory

Sigmund Freud explained gender typing in terms of identification. Appropriate gender typing, in Freud's view, requires that boys come to identify with their fathers and girls with their mothers. **Identification** is completed, in Freud's view, as children resolve the **Oedipus complex** (sometimes called the *Electra complex* in girls).

According to Freud, the Oedipus complex occurs during the phallic period of psychosexual development, from the ages of 3 to 5. During this period the child develops incestuous wishes for the parent of the other sex and comes to perceive the parent of the same sex as a rival. The complex is resolved by the child's forsaking incestuous wishes for the parent of the other sex and identifying with the parent of the same sex. Through identification with the same-sex parent, the child comes to develop preferences and behavior patterns that are typically associated with that sex. But children display stereotypical gender-typed behaviors earlier than Freud would have predicted. Babies show visual preferences for sex-typed toys at 3 to 8 months (Alexander et al., 2009). During the first year, boys are more independent than girls. Girls are more quiet and restrained. Because of their lack of empirical support, many researchers believe that Freud's views are now of historic interest only.

Social–Cognitive Theory

Social–cognitive theorists explain the development of gender-typed behavior in terms of processes such as observational learning, identification, and socialization (Golombok et al., 2008; Zosuls et al., 2009). In social–cognitive theory, identification is seen as a continuous learning process in which rewards and punishments influence children to imitate adult models of the same sex. In identification, the child not only imitates the behavior of the model but tries to become broadly like the model.

Socialization is thought to play a role in gender typing (Golombok et al., 2008; Zosuls et al., 2009). Almost from the moment a baby comes into the world, she or he is treated in ways that are consistent with gender stereotypes. Parents tend to talk more to baby girls, and fathers especially engage in more roughhousing with boys. When children are old enough to speak, caregivers and even other children begin to tell them how they are expected to behave. Parents may reward children for behavior they consider gender appropriate and punish (or fail to reinforce) them for behavior they consider inappropriate for their gender. Girls are encouraged to practice caregiving behaviors, which are intended to prepare them for traditional feminine adult roles. Boys are handed Legos or doctor sets to help prepare them for traditional masculine adult roles.

Fathers generally encourage their sons to develop assertive, instrumental behavior (that is, behavior that gets things done or accomplishes something) and their daughters to develop nurturant, cooperative behavior. Fathers are likely to cuddle their daughters gently. They are likely to carry their sons like footballs or toss them into the air. Fathers also tend to use heartier and harsher language with their sons, such as "How're yuh doin', Tiger?" and "Hey you, get your keester over here." Being a nontraditionalist, your first author made sure to toss his young daughters into the air, which raised immediate objections from the relatives, who chastised him for being too rough. This, of course, led him to modify his behavior. He learned to toss his daughters into the air when the relatives were not around.

In traditional households, boys are more likely to receive toy cars and guns and athletic equipment and to be encouraged to compete aggressively from an early age. Girls are spoken to more often, whereas boys are handled more frequently and more roughly.

Parental roles in gender typing are apparently changing. With more mothers working outside the home in our society, daughters are exposed to more women who represent career-minded role models than was the case in earlier generations. More parents today are encouraging their daughters to become career minded and to engage in strenuous physical activities, such as organized sports. Many boys today are exposed to fathers who take a larger role than men used to in child care and household responsibilities.

Social–cognitive theorists believe that aggression is largely influenced by learning. Boys are permitted, even encouraged, to engage in more aggressive behavior than girls.

Gender Typing through Observational Learning. *According to social–cognitive theory, people learn about the gender roles that are available to them—and expected of them—at an early age. Gender schema theory adds that once children have learned the expected gender roles (i.e., the gender schema of their culture), they blend these roles with their self-concepts. Their self-esteem comes to be dependent on their adherence to the expected gender roles.* (Tony Freeman/PhotoEdit, Inc.)

Cognitive theorists address ways in which children integrate gender-role expectations within their self-concepts. Let us consider two cognitive approaches to gender typing: cognitive–developmental theory and gender schema theory.

Cognitive–Developmental Theory

Psychologist Lawrence Kohlberg (1966) proposed a cognitive–developmental view of gender typing. Children form concepts, or **schemas**, about gender and then conform their behavior to their gender concepts. These developments occur in stages and are entwined with general cognitive development.

According to Kohlberg, gender typing entails the emergence of three concepts: *gender identity, gender stability,* and *gender constancy.* Gender identity is usually acquired by the age of 3. By the age of 4 or 5, most children develop a concept of **gender stability**—the recognition that people retain their genders for a lifetime.

TRUTH OR **FICTION** REVISITED: Prior to the age of 4 or 5 or so, children may have not developed the concept of gender stability. As a result, boys may think that they will become mommies when they grow up, and girls may believe that they can become daddies.

The more sophisticated concept of **gender constancy** develops in most children by the age of 7 or 8. They recognize that gender does not change, even if people alter their dress or behavior. So gender remains constant even when appearances change. A woman who wears her hair short (or shaves it off) remains a woman. A man who dons an apron and cooks dinner remains a man.

According to cognitive–developmental theory, children are motivated to behave in gender-appropriate ways once they have established the concepts of gender stability and gender constancy. Boys and girls who come to recognize that their genders will remain a fixed part of their identity will show preferences for "masculine" and "feminine" activities, respectively. Researchers find, for instance, that boys who had achieved gender constancy played with an uninteresting gender-typed toy for a longer period of time than did boys who hadn't yet achieved gender constancy (Frey & Ruble, 1992). Both groups of boys played with an interesting gender-typed toy for about an equal length of time.

Cross-cultural studies of the United States, Samoa, Nepal, Belize, and Kenya find that the concepts of gender identity, gender stability, and gender constancy emerge in the order predicted by Kohlberg. However, gender-typed play often emerges at an earlier age than would be predicted by the cognitive–developmental theory. Many infants show visual preferences for gender-typed toys by 3 to 8 months (Alexander et al., 2009).

Gender Schema Theory

Gender schema theory proposes that children develop a **gender schema** as a means of organizing their perceptions of the world (Bem, 1993). A gender schema is a cluster of mental representations about masculine and feminine physical qualities, behaviors, and personality traits. Gender gains prominence as a schema for organizing experience because of society's emphasis on it.

Children's gender schemas determine how important gender-typed traits are to them. Consider the dimension of *strength–weakness*. Children may learn that strength is connected with maleness and weakness with femaleness. (Other dimensions, such as *light–dark*, are not gender-typed and thus may fall outside children's gender schemas.) Children also gather that some dimensions, such as *strong–weak*, are more important to one sex (in this case, the male) than the other.

Once children acquire a gender schema, they begin to judge themselves according to traits considered appropriate to their sex (Fagot et al., 2000; Grace et al., 2008). In doing so, they blend their developing self-concepts with the prominent gender schema of their culture. Children with self-concepts that are consistent with the prominent gender schema of their culture are likely to develop higher self-esteem than children whose self-concepts are inconsistent. Jack learns that muscle strength is a characteristic associated with "manliness." He is likely to think more highly of himself if he perceives himself as embodying this attribute than if he does not. Jill is likely to discover that the dimension of kindness–cruelty is more crucial than strength–weakness to the way in which women are perceived in society.

According to gender schema theory, gender identity itself is sufficient to inspire gender-appropriate behavior. Once children develop a concept of gender identity, they begin to seek information concerning gender-typed traits and try to live up to them. Jack will retaliate when provoked, because boys are expected to do so. Jill will be "sugary and sweet" if such is expected of little girls. Thus, gender-typed behavior would emerge earlier than would be proposed by cognitive–developmental

Schema
Concept; way of interpreting experience or processing information.

Gender stability
The concept that people retain their genders for a lifetime.

 7

Gender constancy
The concept that people's genders do not change, even if they alter their dress or behavior.

Gender schema
A cluster of mental representations about male and female physical qualities, behaviors, and personality traits.

theory. But even gender-schema theory cannot explain why boys and girls tend to show visual preferences for gender-typed toys before they are 1 year old.

In the following section, we see that some people have traits that are stereotypical of both males and females and that they promote psychological adjustment to a complex society.

◇ PSYCHOLOGICAL ANDROGYNY AND THE RECONSTRUCTION OF MASCULINITY–FEMININITY: THE MORE TRAITS, THE MERRIER?

Most people think of masculinity and femininity as opposite ends of one continuum. People tend to assume that the more masculine a person is, the less feminine he or she must be, and vice versa. So a man who exhibits stereotypical feminine traits of nurturance, tenderness, and emotionality is often considered less masculine than other men. Women who compete with men in business are perceived not only as more masculine but also as less feminine than other women.

Some investigators, such as Sandra Bem, argue that masculinity and femininity comprise separate personality dimensions (DiDonato & Berenbaum, 2011). A person who is highly masculine, whether male or female, may also possess feminine traits—and vice versa. People who exhibit "masculine" assertiveness and instrumental skills (skills in the sciences and business, for example) along with "feminine" nurturance and cooperation fit both the masculine and feminine gender-role stereotypes. They are said to show **psychological androgyny.** Assertiveness and instrumental skills are consistent with the masculine stereotype. Nurturance and cooperation are consistent with the feminine stereotype. People low in the stereotypical masculine and feminine traits are "undifferentiated," according to gender-role stereotypes.

Psychological androgyny
A state characterized by possession of both stereotypical masculine traits and stereotypical feminine traits.

People who are psychologically androgynous may be capable of summoning a wider range of masculine and feminine traits to meet the demands of various situations and to express their desires and talents (Cooper et al., 2011; Prakash et al., 2010). Researchers, for example, have found psychologically androgynous persons of both genders to show "masculine" independence under group pressures to conform and "feminine" nurturance in interactions with children (DiDonato & Berenbaum, 2011). Psychologically androgynous adolescents are less likely to stereotype occupations as masculine or feminine (Kulik, 2000).

Many people who oppose the constraints of traditional gender roles may perceive psychological androgyny as a desirable goal. Some feminist writers, however, have criticized psychological androgyny on grounds that the concept is defined in terms of, and thereby perpetuates, belief in the existence of masculine and feminine gender roles (Denmark et al., 2008).

CRITICAL THINKING
Explain why feminists have criticized the concept of psychological androgyny.

Other critics suggest that some benefits of psychological androgyny are actually confounded with masculinity. For example, psychologically androgynous people tend to have higher self-esteem and to be generally better adjusted psychologically than people who are feminine or undifferentiated (DiDonato & Berenbaum, 2011; Parent et al., 2011). Does this mean that masculine traits such as assertiveness and independence may be related to psychological well-being, whether or not they are combined with feminine traits such as warmth, nurturance, and cooperation?

In any event, not all males are extremely "masculine," and not all females are overwhelmingly "feminine." Perhaps it is fortunate that few of us are completely masculine or feminine, despite our anatomic sex.

In this module we have explored what it means to be female, male, or another sex within a cultural setting such as ours. In the following module we consider how feelings of attraction and love develop in females, males, and others.

REAL STUDENTS, REAL QUESTIONS

Q *Are there more similarities or differences between men and women?*

A Here's a shocking answer: It depends on how you look at it. We are used to focusing on the differences, but we'll take a flyer and say there are more similarities. For example, men and women share well over 99% of their genetic material. They both walk upright, use language, think, perform in the sciences and the arts, play tennis and golf, have iPods and cell phones attached to their ears, and on and on. And, sadly, they both pay taxes and carry mortgages.

◆ MODULE REVIEW

LO1   Describe the processes of prenatal sexual differentiation

During the first six weeks or so of prenatal development, embryonic structures of both sexes resemble female structures. At about the seventh week, the genetic code (XX or XY) begins to cause changes in the gonads, genital ducts, and external genitals. Testosterone spurs differentiation of the male (Wolffian) duct system. In the absence of testosterone, the Wolffian ducts degenerate, and female sex organs develop. The testes and ovaries develop in the abdominal cavity. A few months after conception, the ovaries descend to the pelvic region, and the testes descend into the scrotal sac.

LO2   Discuss sex chromosomal abnormalities that may affect sexual differentiation

These abnormalities include Klinefelter syndrome (in which a male has an XXY sex chromosomal structure) and Turner syndrome (in which a woman has just one X sex chromosome).

LO3   Define gender identity and the roles of nature and nurture in gender identity

Gender identity is almost always consistent with anatomic sex. However, research with intersexuals suggests that prenatal exposure to androgens may masculinize the brain as well as the sex organs.

LO4   Discuss transgenderism

Transgenderism is the desire to have the genital organs of, and to live as, a member of the other sex. The third gender area addresses matters that have to do with people whose anatomy and/or patterns of sexual behavior or sexual desire do not fit "heteronormativity."

LO5   Discuss gender roles and stereotypes

Cultures have broad expectations of men and women that are termed *gender roles*. In our culture the stereotypical female is seen as nurturant, gentle, dependent, kind, helpful, patient, and submissive. The stereotypical male is self-assertive, tough, competitive, gentlemanly, and protective. Sexism is the prejudgment that because of gender, a person will possess negative traits.

LO6   Explain the relationship between gender roles and sexual behavior

Gender roles encourage many males to take the initiative in matters of sex.

LO7   Discuss gender differences in cognitive abilities

Females excel somewhat in verbal skills, and males somewhat in spatial-relations skills. Recent research challenges the view that males perform better in math, showing no overall differences on math achievement tests.

LO8   Discuss gender differences in personality

Females are usually more extraverted and nurturing. Males are usually more aggressive and tough minded.

LO9   Discuss gender differences in social behavior

Males often dominate classroom discussions, and females are usually more likely to share their feelings. Men are relatively more interested in sex with multiple partners, and women are usually more interested in combining sex with romance.

LO10   Discuss biological and psychological perspectives on gender typing

Evolutionary theory explains gender differences in terms of adaptation to environmental forces. Testosterone in the brains of male fetuses spurs greater growth of the right hemisphere, which may be connected with spatial-relations tasks. Freud explained gender typing in terms of identification with the parent of the same sex. Social–cognitive theorists explain the development of gender-typed behavior in terms of processes such as observational learning, identification, and socialization. According to Kohlberg, gender typing entails the emergence of gender identity, gender stability, and gender constancy. Gender schema theory proposes that children blend their developing self-concepts with the prominent gender schema of their culture.

LO11   Define psychological androgyny and discuss its possible advantages

There is a question as to whether masculinity and femininity comprise two independent personality dimensions or a single bipolar dimension. People who combine stereotypical masculine and feminine behavior patterns are termed *psychologically androgynous*.

◇ TEST YOUR LEARNING

1. Müllerian inhibiting substance prevents the Müllerian ducts from developing into
   a. the female duct system.
   b. the male duct system.
   c interstitial cells.
   d. external genital organs.

2. Congenital adrenal hyperplasia is caused by excessive levels of
   a. androgens.
   b. estradiol.
   c. pheromones.
   d. Müllerian inhibiting substance.

3. Transgendered people are most likely to have
   a. an extra X chromosome.
   b. androgen insensitivity syndrome.
   c. aggressive tendencies.
   d. gender dysphoria.

4. The masculine gender-role stereotype is seen as all of the following *except*
   a. sensitive.
   b. tough.
   c. protective.
   d. gentlemanly.

5. Which gender difference is supported by evidence?
   a. Males are better writers.
   b. Females are better in math and science.
   c. Females are more aggressive.
   d. Males have more reading problems.

6. According to sexual strategies theory,
   a. women choose the best-looking men.
   b. only humans have long-term mates.
   c. men are more interested in short-term sexual variety.
   d. women seek sex without commitment.

7. According to Kohlberg, gender _____ develops last.
   a. stability
   b. identity
   c. exclusivity
   d. constancy

8. The concept of the third gender challenges
   a. feminist theory.
   b. queer theory.
   c. heteronormativity.
   d. transgender activism.

9. Research shows that following sex reassignment, most male-to-female transsexuals
   a. are orgasmic during sexual intercourse.
   b. regret their decision to have the operation.
   c. develop psychological disorders they did not show evidence of previously.
   d. eventually discontinue hormone treatments.

10. The most common form of female intersexualism is
    a. Dominican Republic syndrome.
    b. congenital adrenal hyperplasia.
    c. transgenderism.
    d. gender instability.

Answers: 1. a; 2. a; 3. d; 4. a; 5. d; 6. c; 7. d; 8. c; 9. a; 10. b

◇ REFERENCES

Ackerman, D. (1991). *The moon by whale light.* New York: Random House.

Agrawal, A. (1997). Gendered bodies: The case of the "third gender" in India. *Contributions to Indian Sociology, 31,* 273–97.

Alexander, G. M., Wilcox, T., & Woods, R. (2009). Sex differences in infants' visual interest in toys. *Archives of Sexual Behavior, 38*(3), 427–433.

Andreano, J. M., & Cahill, L. (2009). Sex influences on the neurobiology of learning and memory. *Learning and Memory, 16,* 248–266.

Auyeung, B., et al. (2009). Fetal testosterone predicts behavior in girls and in boys. *Psychological Science, 20*(2), 144–148.

Bailey, J. M. (2003b). *The man who would be queen: The science of gender-bending and transsexualism.* Washington, DC: Joseph Henry Press.

Belgrave, F. Z., van Oss Marian, B., & Chambers, D. B. (2000). Cultural, contextual, and intrapersonal predictors of risky sexual attitudes among urban African American girls in early adolescence. *Cultural Diversity and Ethnic Minority Psychology, 6*(3), 309–322.

Bem, S. L. (1993). *The lenses of gender.* New Haven: Yale University Press.

Benvenuto, C., & Weeks, S. C. (2012). Coflict during mate guarding in an androdioecious crustacean. *Ecology, 23*(1), 218-224.

Blanchard, R. (1989). The concept of autogynephilia and the typology of male gender dysphoria. *Journal of Nervous & Mental Disease, 177*(10), 616–623.

Blanchard, R., Steiner, B. W., & Clemmensen, L. H. (1985). Gender dysphoria, gender reorientation, and the clinical management of transsexualism. *Journal of Consulting and Clinical Psychology, 53,* 295–304.

Bockting, W. O., & Fung, L. C. T. (2006). Genital reconstruction and gender identity disorders. In D. B. Sarwer (Ed.), *Psychological aspects of reconstructive and cosmetic plastic surgery: Clinical, empirical, and ethical perspectives* (pp. 207–229). New York: Lippincott Williams & Wilkins.

Bradley, S. J., Oliver, G. D., Chernick, A. B., & Zucker, K. J. (1998). Experiment of nurture: Ablatio penis at 2 months, sex reassignment at 7 months, and a psychosexual follow-up in young adulthood. *Pediatrics, 102*(1), e9.

Brun, C. C., et al. (2009). Sex differences in brain structure in auditory and cingulate regions. *NeuroReport: For Rapid Communication of Neuroscience Research, 20*(10), 930.

Buss, D. M. (2009). An evolutionary formulation of person–situation interactions. *Journal of Research in Personality, 43*(2), 241–242.

Cantor, J. M. (2011). New MRI studies support the Blanchard typology of male-to-female transsexualism. *Archives of Sexual Behavior, 40*(5), 863–864.

Ceci, S. J., Williams, W. M., & Barnett, S. R. (2009). Women's underrepresentation in science. *Psychological Bulletin, 135*(2), 218–261.

Cohen, D. L., & Belsky, J. (2008). Individual differences in female mate preferences as a function of attachment and hypothetical ecological conditions. *Journal of Evolutionary Psychology, 6*(1), 25–42.

Cohen-Bendahan, C. C. C., van de Beek, C., & Berenbaum, S. A. (2005). Prenatal sex hormone effects on child and adult sex-typed behavior: Methods and findings. *Neuroscience & Biobehavioral Reviews, 29*(2), 353–384.

Colapinto, J. (2000). *As nature made him: The boy who was raised as a girl.* New York: HarperCollins.

Collaer, M. L., & Hill, E. M. (2006). Large sex difference in adolescents on a timed line judgment task: Attentional contributors and task relationship to mathematics. *Perception, 35*(4), 561–572.

Cooper, S. M., Guthrie, B. J., Brown, C., & Metzger, I. (2011). Daily hassles and African American adolescent females' psychological functioning: Direct and interactive associations with gender role orientation. *Sex Roles, 65*(5–6), 397–409.

Cox, W. M., & Alm, R. (2005, February 25). Scientists are made, not born. *The New York Times* (Online).

Czech, D. P., et al. (2012). The human testis-determining factor SRY localizes in midbrain dopamine neurons and regulates multiple components of catecholamine synthesis and metabolism. *Journal of Neurochemistry, 122*(2), 260–271.

Dauwalder, B. (2011). The roles of *fruitless* and *doublesex* in the control of male courtship. In N. Atkinson (Ed.). *International Review of Neurobiology: Recent advances in the use of Drosophila in neurobiology and neurodegeneration, 99* (pp. 87–107). London: Academic Press.

De Vries, G. J., et al. (2002). A model system for study of sex chromosome effects on sexually dimorphic neural and behavioral traits. *Journal of Neuroscience, 22*(20), 9005–9014.

Denmark, F., Paludi, M. A., & Lott, B. (2008). *Psychology of women: A handbook of issues and theories.* Santa Barbara, CA: Greenwood Press.

Diamond, M. (1996). Prenatal predisposition and the clinical management of some pediatric conditions. *Journal of Sex & Marital Therapy, 22*(3), 139–147.

Diamond, M. (2011). Developmental, sexual and reproductive neuroendocrinology: Historical, clinical and ethical considerations. *Frontiers in Neuroendocrinology, 32*(2), 255–263.

DiDonato, M. D., & Berenbaum, S. A. (2011). The benefits and drawbacks of gender typing: How different dimensions are related to psychological adjustment. *Archives of Sexual Behavior, 40*(2), 457–463.

Ecuyer-Dab, I., & Robert, M. (2004). Have sex differences in spatial ability evolved from male competition for mating and female concern for survival? *Cognition, 91*(3), 221–257.

Else-Quest, N. M., & Grabe, S. (2012). The political is personal: Measurement and application of nation-level indicators of gender equity in psychological research. *Psychology of Women Quarterly*, 36(2), 131–144.

Else-Quest, N. M., Hyde, J. S., & Linn, M. C. (2010). Cross-national patterns of gender differences in mathematics: A meta-analysis. *Psychological Bulletin, 136*(1), 103–127.

Fagot, B. I., Rodgers, C. S., & Leinbach, M. D. (2000). Theories of gender socialization. In T. Eckes & H. M. Trautner (Eds.), *The developmental social psychology of gender* (pp. 65–89). Mahwah, NJ: Erlbaum.

Fausto-Sterling, A. (May/April 1993). The five sexes: Why male and female are not enough. *The Sciences*, 20–25.

Feingold, A. (1994). Gender differences in personality: A meta-analysis. *Psychological Bulletin, 116*, 429–456.

Fisher, A. D., Bandini, E., Casale, H., & Maggi, M. (2012). Paraphilic disorders: Diagnosis and treatment. In M. Maggi (Ed.). *Hormonal therapy for male sexual dysfunction* (pp. 94–110). Hoboken, NJ: Wiley.

Frey, K. S., & Ruble, D. N. (1992). Gender constancy and the "cost" of sex-typed behavior: A test of the conflict hypothesis. *Developmental Psychology, 28,* 714–721.

Glaesmer, H., et al. (2012). Gender differences in healthcare utilization. *Journal of Applied Social Psychology,* DOI:10.1111/j.1559-1816.2011.00888.x

Golombok, S., et al. (2008). Developmental trajectories of sex-typed behavior in boys and girls: A longitudinal general population study of children aged 2.5–8 Years. *Child Development, 79*(5), 1583–1593.

Goulet, J. (2006). The "berdache"/"two-spirit": A comparison of anthropological and native constructions of gendered identities among the Northern Athapaskans. *Journal of the Royal Anthropological Institute, 683*(19).

Grace, D. M., David, B. J., & Ryan, M. K. (2008). Investigating preschoolers' categorical thinking about gender through imitation, attention, and the use of self-categories. *Child Development, 79*(6), 1928–1941.

Halpern, D. F. (2003). Sex differences in cognitive abilities. *Applied Cognitive Psychology, 17*(3), 375–376.

Halpern, D. F., & LaMay, M. L. (2000). The smarter sex: A critical review of sex differences in intelligence. *Educational Psychology Review, 12*(2), 229–246.

Halpern, D. F., et al. (2007). The science of sex differences in science and mathematics. *Psychological Science in the Public Interest, 8*(1), 1–51.

Hassett, J. M., Siebert, E. R., & Wallen, K. (2008). Sex differences in rhesus monkey toy preferences parallel those of children. *Hormones and Behavior, 54*(3), 359–364.

Hay, D. F. et al. (2011). The emergence of gender differences in physical aggression in the context of conflict between young peers. *British Journal of Developmental Psychology, 29*(2), 158–175.

Hester, J. D. (2005). Eunuchs and the postgender Jesus: Matthew 19:12 and transgressive sexualities. *Journal for the Study of the New Testament, 28*(1), 13–40.

Hines, M., Ahmed, S. F., & Hughes, I. A. (2003). Psychological outcomes and gender-related development in complete androgen insensitivity syndrome. *Archives of Sexual Behavior, 32*(2), 93–101.

Hyde, J. S., & Mertz, J. E. (2009). Gender, culture, and mathematics performance. *Proceedings of the National Academy of Sciences, 106*, 8801–8807.

Hyde, J. S., Lindberg, S. M., Linn, M. C., Ellis, A. B., & Williams, C. C. (2008). Gender similarities characterize math perfromance. *Science, 321*, 494–495.

Jones, B. E., & Hill, M. J. (2002). *Mental health issues in lesbian, gay, bisexual, and transgender communities: Review of Psychiatry* (vol. 21). Washington, DC: American Psychiatric Publishing.

Knickmeyer, R., et al. (2005). Gender-typed play and amniotic testosterone. *Developmental Psychology, 41*, 517–528.

Kohlberg, L. (1966). A cognitive-developmental analysis of children's sex-role concepts and attitudes. In E. E. Maccoby (Ed.), *The development of sex differences.* Stanford, CA: Stanford University Press.

Kuiper, B., & Cohen–Kettenis, P. (1988). Sex reassignment surgery: A study of 141 Dutch transsexuals. *Archives of Sexual Behavior, 17,* 439–457.

Kulik, L. (2000). Gender identity, sex typing of occupations, and gender role ideology among adolescents: Are they related? *International Journal for the Advancement of Counselling, 22*(1), 43–56.

Lang, C., & Kuhnle, U. (2008). Intersexuality and alternative gender categories in non-Western cultures. *Hormone Research in Paediatrics, 69*(4), 240–250.

Lawrence, A. A. (2005). Sexuality before and after male-to-female sex reassignment surgery. *Archives of Sexual Behavior, 34*(2), 147–166.

Leaper, C., & Bigler, R. S. (2011). In M. K. Underwood & L. H. Rosen (Eds.). *Social development* (pp. 289–315). New York: Guilford.

Legato, M. J. (2000, May 12). Cited in "Study of children born without penises finds nature determines gender." The Associated Press online.

Loder, N. (2000). US science shocked by revelations of sexual discrimination. *Nature, 405,* 713–714.

Lohman, D. F., & Lakin, J. M. (2009). Consistencies in sex differences on the Cognitive Abilities Test across countries, grades, test forms, and cohorts. *British Journal of Educational Psychology, 79*(2), 389–407.

Major, B., Kaiser, C. R., & McCoy, S. K. (2003). It's not my fault: When and why attributions to prejudice protect self-esteem. *Personality & Social Psychology Bulletin, 29*(6), 772–781.

Maxson, S. C. (1998). Homologous genes, aggression, and animal models. *Developmental Neuropsychology, 14*(1), 143–156.

McHugh, M. C., & Hambaugh, J. (2010). She said, he said: Gender, language, and power. *Handbook of Gender Research in Psychology, 5,* 379–410.

Meissner, G. W., et al. (2011). Functional dissection of the neural substrates for sexual behaviors in *Drosophila melanogaster*. *Genetics, 189*(1), 195–211.

Money, J. (1994). The concept of gender identity disorder in childhood and adolescence after 39 years. *Journal of Sex and Marital Therapy, 20*(3), 163–177.

Moser, C. (2010). Blanchard's autogynephilia theory: A critique. *Journal of Homosexuality, 57*(6), 790–809.

Murray, S. O., & Roscoe, W. (1997). *Islamic homosexualities: Culture, history, and literature.* New York: New York University Press.

National Center for Biotechnology Information (NCBI). (2006, February 1). National Institute of Health. [Online]. www.ncbi.nlm.nih.gov/entrez/query.fcgi?=CMD=Search&db= homologene&term=SRY.

Newman, L. (2012). Questions about gender: Children with atypical gender development. *Disorders of Sex Development,* 31–39. DOI:10.1007/978-3-642-22964-0_4.

Njus, D. M., & Bane, C. M. H. (2009). Religious identification as a moderator of evolved sexual strategies of men and women. *Journal of Sex Research,* DOI: 10.1080/00224490902867855.

Nuttbrock, L., et al. (2011). A further assessment of Blanchard's typology of homosexual versus non-homosexual or autogynephilic gender dysphoria. *Archives of Sexual Behavior, 40*(2), 247–257.

Parent, M. C., Moradi, B., Rummell, C. M., & Tokar, D. M. (2011). Evidence of construct distinctiveness for conformity to masculine norms. *Psychology of Men and Masculinity, 12*(4), 354–367.

Plant, E. A., Hyde, J. S., Keltner, D., & Devine, P. G. (2000). The gender stereotyping of emotions. *Psychology of Women Quarterly, 24*(1), 81–92.

Prakash, J., et al. (2010). Does androgyny have psychoprotective attributes? A cross-sectional community-based study. *Industrial Psychiatry Journal, 19*(2), 119–124.

Rathus, S. A. (2014). *Childhood and adolescence: Voyages in development* (5th ed.). Belmont, CA: Cengage.

Reiner, W. G. (2000). Cited in Study of children born without penises finds nature determines gender. Associated Press. (Online).

Roscoe, W. (2000). *Changing ones: Third and fourth genders in native North America.* Palgrave: Macmillan.

Roughgarden, J. (2004). *Evolution's rainbow: Diversity, gender, and sexuality in nature and people.* University of California Press.

Savic, I., Garcia-Falgueras, A., & Swaab, D. F. (2010). Sexual differentiation of the human brain in relation to gender identity and sexual orientation. In I. Savic (Ed.), *Sex differences in the human brain, Their underpinnings and implications. Progress in Brain Research, 186* (pp. 41–64). New York: Elsevier.

Schmitt, D. (2008). An evolutionary perspective on mate choice and relationship initiation. In S. Sprecher, A. Wenzel, & J. Harvey (Eds.), *Handbook of relationship initiation* (pp. 55–74). New York: CRC Press.

Schmitt, D. P. (2003). Universal sex differences in the desire for sexual variety: Tests from 52 nations, 6 continents, and 13 islands. *Journal of Personality and Social Psychology, 85*(1), 85–104.

Schmitt, D. P., et al. (2012). A reexamination of sex differences in sexuality: New studies reveal old truths. *Current Directions in Psychological Science, 21*(2), 135–139.

Schmitt, D., Jonason, P. K., Byerley, G. J., Flores, S. D., Illbeck, B. E., O'Leary, K. N., & Qudrat, A. (2012). A reexamination of sex differences in sexuality: New studies reveal old truths. *Current Directions in Psychological Science, 21*(2), 135–139.

Schmitt, M. T., Branscombe, N. R., & Postmes, T. (2003). Women's emotional responses to the pervasiveness of gender discrimination. *European Journal of Social Psychology, 33*(3), 297–312.

Servin, A., Nordenström, A., Larsson, A., & Bohlin, G. (2003). Prenatal androgens and gender-typed behavior: A study of girls with mild and severe forms of congenital adrenal hyperplasia. *Developmental Psychology, 39*(3), 440–450.

Shaywitz, B. A., et al. (1995). Sex differences in the functional organization of the brain for language. *Nature, 373*, 607–609.

Siegel-Hinson, R. I., & McKeever, W. F. (2002). Hemispheric specialisation, spatial activity experience, and sex differences on tests of mental rotation ability. *Laterality: Asymmetries of Body, Brain and Cognition, 7*(1), 59–74.

Singh, D., Vidaurri, M., Zambrano, R. J., & Dabbs, J. M., Jr. (1999). Lesbian erotic role identification: Behavioral, morphological, and hormonal correlates. *Journal of Personality & Social Psychology, 76*(6), 1035–1039.

Smith, Y. L. S., Van Goozen, S. H. M., Kuiper, A. J., & Cohen-Kettenis, P. T. (2005). Sex reassignment: Outcomes and predictors of treatment for adolescent and adult transsexuals. *Psychological Medicine, 35*(1), 89–99.

Stake, J. E., & Hoffman, F. L. (2001). Changes in student social attitudes, activism, and personal confidence in higher education: The role of women's studies. *American Educational Research Journal, 38*(2), 411–436.

Steinemann, S., & Steinemann, M. (2005). Retroelements: Tools for sex chromosome evolution. *Cytogenetic and Genome Research, 110*, 134–143.

Stockett, M. K. (2005). On the importance of difference: Re-envisioning sex and gender in ancient Mesoamerica, *World Archaeology, 37*(4), 566–578.

Thompson, A. E., & O'Sullivan, L. F. (2011). Gender differences in associations of sexual and romantic stimuli. *Archives of Sexual Behavior, 41*(4), 949–957.

Totman, R. (2004). *The third sex: Kathoey: Thailand's ladyboys.* London: Souvenir Press.

Valkenburg, P. M., Sumter, S. R., & Peter, J. (2011). Gender differences in online and offline self-disclosure in pre-adolescence and adolescence. *British Journal of Developmental Psychology, 29*(2), 253–269.

Wallen, K., & Hassett, J. M. (2009). Sexual differentiation of behaviour in monkeys: Role of prenatal hormones. *Journal of Neuroendocrinology, 21*(4), 421–426.

Williams, J. E., & Best, D. L. (1994). Cross-cultural views of women and men. In W. J. Lonner & R. Malpass (Eds.), *Psychology and culture*. Boston: Allyn & Bacon.

Winter, S. (2003). *Research and discussion paper: Language and identity in transgender: Gender wars and the case of the Thai kathoey.* Paper presented at the Hawaii conference on Social Sciences. Waikiki, HI.

Wong, W. I., Pasterski, V., Hindmarsh, P. C., Geffner, M. E., & Hines, M. (2012). Are there parental socialization effects on the sex-typed behavior of individuals with congenital adrenal hyperplasia? *Archives of Sexual Behavior.* DOI:10.1007/s10508-012-9997-4.

Yazzie, A. (2010). Visual-spatial thinking and academic achievement: A concurrent and predictive validity study. *Dissertation Abstracts International: Section A, Humanities and Social Sciences, 70*(8-A), 2897.

Zosuls, K. M., et al. (2009). The acquisition of gender labels in infancy: Implications for gender-typed play. *Developmental Psychology, 45*(3), 688–701

Zucker, K. J. (2005a). Gender identity disorder in children and adolescents. *Annual Review of Clinical Psychology, 1*(1), 467–492.

Zucker, K. J. (2005b). Gender identity disorder in girls. In D. J. Bell, S. L. Foster, & E. J. Mash (Eds.), *Handbook of behavioral and emotional problems in girls. Issues in clinical child psychology* (pp. 285–319). Kluwer Academic/Plenum Publishers.

MODULE 9-B

ACTIVITY

◇ CULTURE AND GENDER ROLE EXPECTATIONS

An important aspect of culture is expectations about gender-based behaviors and attributes. Researchers have investigated advertisements in many different countries, to determine the messages conveyed about gender roles. These studies consistently find gender stereotyping across cultures (Milner & Collins, 2000). This activity uses a content analysis of magazine advertisements in order to explore culture and gender role expectations.

Directions: Select two recent magazines, one targeted to men and one targeted to women (avoid purely fashion magazines). Carefully read the descriptions of coding categories and then, using the coding sheet provided, tally the number of advertisements that fall under each category. Note any additional findings of interest that may not be reflected by the number of advertisements. For example, you may find the same number of car advertisements in both men=s and women=s magazines, but may find more sports cars in the men=s magazines and more minivans in the women=s magazines. Once you have coded your data, respond to the questions that follow.

Coding Categories:
Alcohol – Such as beer, wine, liquor, or any alcoholic beverage or beverage mix.
Apparel – Such as clothes, shoes (except sports shoes), glasses, watches, jewelry, handbags, wallets, and other accessories.
Automotive – Such as cars, trucks, car repair services.
Beauty and Personal Care – Such as cosmetics, hair products, skin lotions or cleansers, deodorants, toothpastes, feminine hygiene products, cologne/perfume, and breath fresheners.
Child and Baby Care – Such as diapers, baby food, children=s toys, books, or music.
Cleaning – Household cleaning products such as laundry detergent, furniture polish, dishwashing liquid, floor cleaner, glass cleaner, or disinfectants.
Crafts and Collectibles – Including hobby-related products, and collectible dolls, dishes, or figurines.
Electronic Products – Such as computers and software, fax machines, pagers, phones, televisions, video or stereo equipment.
Entertainment – Such as products relating to movies, music, television, and events.
Financial Services – Such as banking or brokerage services, tax preparation services, or financial consulting services.

Taken from *Cross-Cultural Explorations: Activities in Culture and Psychology*, Second Edition, by Susan Goldstein.

Food and (Nonalcoholic) Beverages – Any food or (nonalcoholic) drink in a prepared or natural state including mixes, canned, or frozen products, bottled water, candy, or gum.

Home Products – Such as furniture, appliances, house paint, flooring, or fixtures.

Medications and Vitamins – Such as pain relievers, antacids, laxatives, contraceptives, antidepressants, vitamins, weight control products, or nutritional supplements.

Pets – Including pet food, pet care items, and accessories.

Sports and Outdoor Equipment – Such as exercise equipment, bicycles, roller blades, gym bags, or sports shoes.

Tobacco Products – Such as cigarettes, cigars, or chewing tobacco.

Travel – Including information on travel destinations, tours, or travel products.

Weight Loss and Fitness – Including fitness equipment, health clubs, and diet medications, plans, or products.

Magazine Coding Sheet

PRODUCT	WOMEN'S MAGAZINE	MEN'S MAGAZINE
Alcohol		
Apparel		
Automotive		
Beauty & Personal Care		
Child & Baby Care		
Cleaning		
Crafts & Collectibles		
Electronic Products		
Entertainment		
Financial Services		
Food and (Nonalcoholic) Beverages		
Home Products		
Medications & Vitamins (Not for Weight Loss)		
Pets		
Sports & Outdoor		
Tobacco		
Travel		
Weight Loss and Fitness		

Reactions:

1. Based on the data you collected, describe below the cultural expectations of women and of men as depicted in the magazine advertisements.

2. To what extent do you believe these messages shape gender-typed behavior? Are these messages primarily reinforced or contradicted elsewhere in the culture? Please explain.

3. John Williams and Deborah Best (1990) found a great deal of consensus across cultures in the attributes associated with males and females. In a study of sex role stereotypes involving 30 different countries, being female in these countries was associated with, for example, being attractive, dependent, emotional, sensitive, and weak whereas being male was associated with being adventurous, dominant, independent, and strong. Did you find any indications of these attributes in the magazine ads you examined? If so, please give an example.

◇ REFERENCES

Milner, L. M., & Collins, J. M. (2000). Sex-role portrayals and the gender of nations. *Journal of Advertising,* *29*, 67–79.

Williams, J., & Best, D. (1990). *Measuring sex stereotypes: A thirty-nation study* (rev. ed.). Newbury Park, CA: Sage.

SECTION 10

HEALTH

MODULE 10-A

BIRTH AND THE NEWBORN CHILD

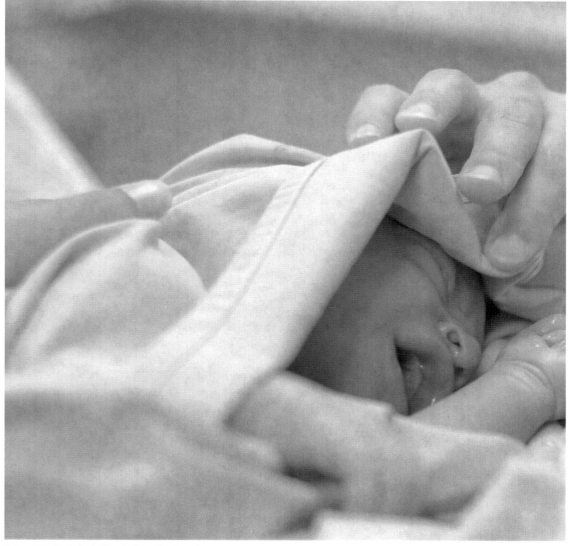

(Hagai Nativ/PhotoStock-Israel/Alamy)

Taken from *Human Development: A Cultural Approach*, by Jeffrey Jensen Arnett.

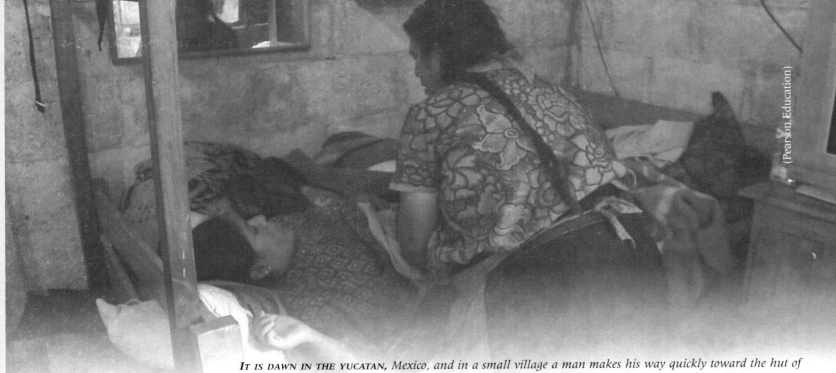

(Pearson Education)

Across cultures, the birth of a new human being is usually regarded as a joyful event

IT IS DAWN IN THE YUCATAN, *Mexico, and in a small village a man makes his way quickly toward the hut of Dona Juana, the village midwife. The man's wife has been pregnant for nearly nine months, and now it seems her time has come. He awakens Dona Juana, who gathers her birth equipment and follows him to his hut.*

When they arrive they greet the mother-to-be, lying comfortably on a hammock, and the women who will help during the birth process: her own mother, her aunt, and her sister. Dona Juana inquires and learns that for several hours the contractions have been weak and far apart but persistent, and now they seem to be growing stronger and closer together. Nevertheless, it appears that the birth is still some hours off, and Dona Juana and the other women settle in and begin to share tales of their own birth experiences and other births they have witnessed. Dona Juana explains the birth process to the expectant mother, demonstrating different birthing positions as she speaks. The other women—all mothers themselves—join in, demonstrating their own favorite birth positions.

The Yucatan Maya, like people in many cultures, believe that the time surrounding birth is a time of great vulnerability to evil spirits. As the birth approaches, the midwife directs the helpers to keep all doors and windows shut and stuff all cracks in the hut with rags, to keep the evil spirits out.

Some births are easy and some are difficult, and this one is going to be on the difficult side. Labor now continues for several hours, with the contractions growing steadily more frequent and intense. With each contraction, the expectant mother throws her arms back around the neck of her own mother and lifts herself up on the hammock almost to a sitting position, making use of gravity to position the baby for exiting through the birth canal. When the contraction subsides, the woman reclines again to rest as the midwife and the other birth helpers massage her abdomen, back, and legs.

By now it is nearly midday, and the midwife is becoming concerned. She fears that at this rate the woman will be too exhausted to push adequately once the time comes. Cracking a raw egg into a cup, she gives it to the woman to swallow. Immediately the woman vomits, and this brings on an especially strong contraction.

Now the contractions are reaching a new level of intensity, and the midwife instructs the woman to push as hard as she can with each one. During the contractions the other women urge the mother-to-be on with a rhythmic chorus of words: "Come on, bring it down, let's go!" In between contractions the expectant mother complains of the pain, and the other women scold her gently. "Don't be lazy! Just push like you're supposed to, and everything will be fine."

On the third contraction that follows the baby at last emerges, to exclamations of joy and relief. It's a girl! Dona Juana quickly suctions the mucus from her nose and mouth so she can breathe, then lays her on the mother's abdomen. The mother smiles wearily and looks down at her new daughter. A few minutes later the placenta is delivered, and the midwife hands it carefully to a helper who will bury it later in a special ritual. Now the midwife cuts the umbilical cord and cauterizes the stump with the flame of a candle. While the helpers clean up, the mother breast-feeds her baby for the first time. (Adapted from Jordan, 1993.)

Across cultures, the birth of a new human being is usually regarded as a joyful event, worthy of celebration (DeLoache & Gottlieb, 2000). At the same time, it is often a physically challenging and potentially perilous process, for both mother and child, especially when modern medical assistance is not available. In this module we will look at the birth process, followed by cultural variations in birth beliefs, then at the history of birth in the West and birth variations today around the world. We will then move on to care of the newborn, before ending with the characteristics of the newborn child.

PART 1   BIRTH AND ITS CULTURAL CONTEXT

LEARNING OBJECTIVE

1. Describe the three stages of the birth process and methods for easing its discomfort.
2. Name two common types of birth complications and explain how they can be overcome by cesarean delivery.
3. Compare and contrast cultural variations in birth beliefs.
4. Explain the role of the midwife and compare and contrast cultural practices and medical methods for easing the birth process.
5. Summarize the history of birth in the West from the 15th century to today.
6. Describe the differences in maternal and neonatal mortality both within and between developed countries and developing countries.

◇ THE BIRTH PROCESS

Toward the end of pregnancy, hormonal changes take place that trigger the beginning of the birth process. Most importantly, the hormone **oxytocin** is released from the woman's pituitary gland. When the amount of oxytocin in the expectant mother's blood reaches a certain threshold level, her uterus begins to contract on a frequent and regular basis, and the birth process begins.

oxytocin
hormone released by pituitary gland that causes labor to begin

Stages of the Birth Process

Describe the three stages of the birth process and methods for easing its discomfort.

LEARNING OBJECTIVE 1

The birth process is generally divided into three stages: labor, delivery of the baby, and delivery of the placenta and umbilical cord, as shown in **Figure 1** (Mayo Clinic Staff, 2011). There is immense variability among women in the length and difficulty of this process, depending mostly on the size of the woman and the size of the baby, but in general it is longer and more difficult for women giving birth to their first child.

Stage 1: Labor

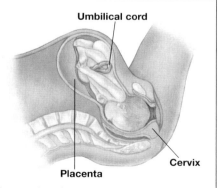

Contractions increase in duration, frequency, and intensity, causing the cervix to dilate.

Stage 2: Delivery

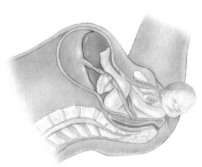

The mother pushes, and the baby crowns and then exits the birth canal and enters the world.

Stage 3: Expelling of Placenta & Umbilical Cord

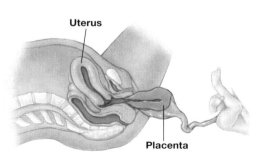

Contractions continue as the placenta and umbilical cord are expelled.

FIGURE 1 The Three Stages of the Birth Process Which stage is longest and most difficult? (Angela Hampton Picture Library/Alamy)

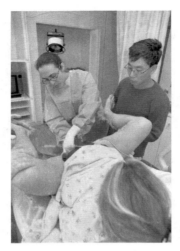

In developed countries, the husband or other family members often assist with strategies to ease the birth process. Here, an American man assists as his wife gives birth.

(Rich Legg/Getty Images)

The First Stage: Labor

The first stage of the birth process, **labor**, is the longest and most taxing stage, averaging about 12 hours for first births and 6 hours for subsequent births (Lyons, 2007). During labor, contractions of the muscles in the uterus cause the woman's cervix to dilate (open) in preparation for the baby's exit. By the end of labor, the cervix has opened to about 10 centimeters (4½ inches). Labor is painful because the contractions of the muscles of the uterus must occur with increasing intensity, frequency, and duration in order to dilate the cervix and move the fetus down the neck of the uterus and through the vagina. The contractions of the uterus are painful in the same way (and for the same reasons) a cramp is painful—pain results when muscles contract intensely for an extended period.

In the early part of labor, as the cervix opens, there may be a thick, stringy, bloody discharge from the vagina known as *bloody show*. Women often experience severe back pain as labor continues. Nausea and trembling of the legs are also common. Here are some strategies recommended by health professionals to ease the woman's discomfort (Mayo Clinic Staff, 2011):

- Rock in a rocking chair.
- Roll on a birthing ball.
- Breathe in a steady rhythm, fast or slow, depending on what is most comfortable.
- Take a warm shower or bath.
- Place a cool, damp cloth on the forehead.
- Take a walk, stopping to breathe through contractions.
- Have a massage between contractions.

Emotional support is also crucial to the woman's experience during labor (daMotta et al., 2006). In developed countries she may have her husband present, whereas he would usually be excluded from the birth in developing countries (DeLoache & Gottlieb, 2000). She may have her mother present, or her mother-in-law, and one or more sisters. There may also be a midwife, especially in developing countries, and health personnel, especially in developed countries. These caregivers may assist the woman with the comfort strategies just listed.

The Second and Third Stages: Delivery and Expelling the Placenta and Umbilical Cord

labor
first stage of the birth process, in which the cervix dilates and the muscles of the uterus contract to push the fetus into the vagina toward the cervix

delivery
second stage of the birth process, during which the fetus is pushed out of the cervix and through the birth canal

episiotomy
incision to make the vaginal opening larger during birth process

The second stage of the birth process, **delivery**, usually takes a half hour to an hour, but again there is wide variation (Murkoff & Mazel, 2008). So far in the birth process there has been not much the expectant mother could do to influence it, other than bear the pain and discomfort as well as possible. Now, however, her efforts to push will help move the fetus through the cervix and out of the uterus. Contractions continue to help, too, but for most women the contractions are now less frequent, although they remain 60–90 seconds long. Usually the woman feels a tremendous urge to push during her contractions.

At last *crowning* occurs, meaning that the baby's head appears at the outer opening of the vagina. The woman often experiences a tingling or burning sensation at her vaginal opening as the baby crowns. At this point, if she is giving birth in a hospital she may be given an **episiotomy**, which is an incision to make the vaginal opening larger. The purpose of the episiotomy is to make the mother's vagina less likely to tear as the fetus's head comes out, and to shorten this part of the birth process by 15 to 30 minutes. However, critics of episiotomies say they are often unnecessary, and in response to such criticism the rate of episiotomies in the United States declined from about 90% in 1970 to just 20% in 2000 (Cassidy, 2006).

Now the baby has arrived, but the birth process is not yet over. In this third and final stage, contractions continue as the placenta and umbilical cord are expelled from the uterus (Lyons, 2007). This process usually happens within a few minutes, at most a half hour. The contractions are mild and last about a minute each. Although the expulsion of the placenta and umbilical cord is usually brief, care must be taken that the entire placenta comes out. If it does not, the uterus will be unable to contract properly and the mother will continue to bleed, perhaps even to the point of threatening her life. Beginning to breast-feed the newborn triggers contractions that help expel the placenta, and when advanced medical care is available the mother may be given an injection of synthetic oxytocin for the same purpose.

If the mother has had an episiotomy or her vagina has torn during delivery, she will be stitched up at this time. At this point, too, the umbilical cord must be cut and tied. There are many interesting cultural beliefs surrounding the cutting of the umbilical cord and the disposal of the placenta, as we will see later in the module.

Birth Complications

> Name two common types of birth complications and explain how they can be overcome by cesarean delivery.

LEARNING OBJECTIVE 2

We have just examined the birth process as it occurs if all goes well, but of course there are many times when all does not go well. Two of the most common birth complications are *failure to progress* and the *breech presentation* of the fetus.

Failure to Progress and Breech Presentation

"Failure to progress" means that the woman has begun the birth process but it is taking longer than normal. The woman may stimulate progress by walking around, taking a nap, or having an enema. She may also be given herbal medicines or synthetic oxytocin to stimulate her contractions.

Breech presentation is when the fetus is turned around so that the feet or buttocks are positioned to come first out of the birth canal, rather than the head. About 4% of fetuses present in the breech position (Martin et al., 2005). Breech births are dangerous to the baby because coming out feet- or buttocks-first can cause the umbilical cord to be constricted during delivery, potentially leading to insufficient oxygen and brain damage within minutes. Consequently, attempts are usually made to avoid a breech presentation. Midwives have long used their skills to massage the expectant mother's abdomen and turn the fetus from breech presentation to headfirst, but it must be done with extreme care to avoid tearing the placenta from the uterine wall. Today physicians in hospitals also seek to turn breech fetuses at about the 37th week of pregnancy. Doctors often use drugs to relax the muscles of the uterus as they attempt to turn the fetus with the massage (Hofmeyr, 2002).

Cesarean Delivery

If failure to progress takes place during delivery, or if a fetus in breech position cannot be turned successfully, or if other problems arise in the birth process, the woman may be given a **cesarean delivery,** or **c-section**. The c-section involves cutting open the mother's abdomen and retrieving the baby directly from the uterus. The c-section has been around for a long time—according to legend it is named for the Roman emperor Julius Caesar, who supposedly was born by this method about 2,000 years ago—but until recent decades mothers nearly always died from it, even as the baby was saved. Today, with the standardization of sterile procedures and the use of antibiotics, it is very safe, although it takes women longer to heal from a cesarean than from a vaginal birth (Connolly & Sullivan, 2004). C-sections are generally safe for infants as well, and if the mother has a sexually transmitted infection, such as HIV or genital herpes, it is safer than a vaginal birth because it protects the infant from the risk of contracting the disease during the birth process. As **Map 1** on page 334 shows, rates of c-sections vary widely among countries and do not seem to be related to world region or level of economic development (Organisation for Economic Co-operation and Development [OECD], 2009; World Health Organization [WHO], 2010).

Critics of high c-section rates claim that they are performed far more than is necessary, and that they are often performed not so much to protect the mother and baby as to fatten the wallets

Applying Your Knowledge . . . as a Nurse

One of your patients is a pregnant woman who is HIV positive and is nervous about having a C-section delivery. What might you say to reassure her of its benefits?

breech presentation
positioning of the fetus so that feet or buttocks, rather than the head, are positioned to come first out of the birth canal

cesarean delivery, or **c-section**
type of birth in which mother's abdomen is cut open and fetus is retrieved directly from the uterus

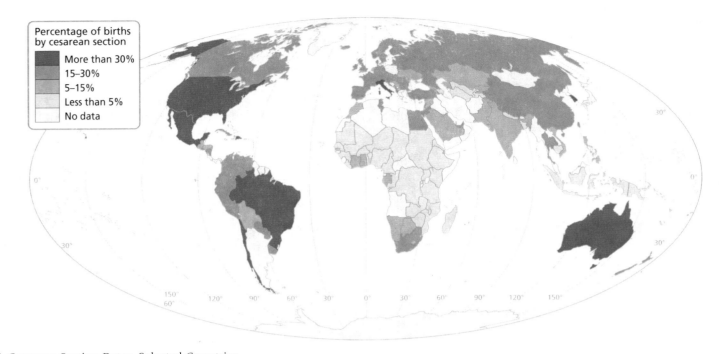

MAP 1 Cesarean Section Rates, Selected Countries

Which countries have the highest rates of cesarean sections? What determines whether a country has high or low rates?

of doctors (c-sections are a type of surgery and thus cost far more than a vaginal birth). However, c-section rates are not substantially higher in countries that rely mostly on private medical insurance and where doctors get paid more for doing more c-sections (like the United States), than in countries like China, Italy and Canada that have a national health care system that does not pay doctors per c-section (WHO, 2010). More likely, high rates of c-sections result from extreme caution by doctors seeking to avoid disaster during births.

Some of the countries that have the lowest rates of c-sections also have very low rates of birth complications, which seems to indicate that many c-sections performed in other countries are unnecessary (WHO, 2010). Specifically, the countries that have the lowest rates of birth problems as well as the lowest rates of c-sections are the countries of northern Europe, where doctors and mothers alike share a cultural belief that birth should be natural and that technical intervention should take place only when absolutely necessary (Ravn, 2005). However, rates of c-sections are also low in countries like India and in most of Africa, where many people lack access to hospital facilities that could provide c-sections when necessary (WHO, 2010).

For women who have had a c-section, there is a possibility of having a vaginal birth with the next baby, a procedure known as a VBAC (*vaginal birth after cesarean section*; Shorten, 2010). As part of a more general movement in developed countries toward natural, less technological birth experiences, rates of VBAC rose in the 1980s and 1990s, and by the late 1990s about one-fourth of American women who had their first baby by c-section had a VBAC with their next baby (Roberts et al., 2007). However, evidence began to indicate that having a VBAC raised birth risks in several ways in comparison to repeat c-sections, most notably the risk of uterine rupture. This occurred rarely, in only about 1% of VBACs, but when it did it sometimes resulted in death of both mother and fetus from the mother's loss of blood (WebMD, 2011). Consequently, the American College of Obstetricians and Gynecologists issued guidelines advocating that an emergency c-section be available for every woman attempting VBAC, and rates of VBACs among American women plummeted, to just 10% a decade later (Shorten, 2010). After an National Institutes of Health (NIH) panel reviewed the evidence in 2010 and declared that a VBAC is safe for nearly all women, the American College of Obstetricians and Gynecologists revised their guidelines in July 2010 to state that "Attempting a vaginal birth after cesarean (VBAC) is a safe and appropriate choice for most women who have had a prior cesarean delivery" (WebMD, 2011, p. 2). In other developed countries as well, VBAC guidelines are in flux as professional groups and policy makers respond to new evidence and shifting views (Foureur et al., 2010).

WHAT HAVE YOU LEARNED?

1. What role does oxytocin play in the birth process?
2. What is an episiotomy and how often is it performed in the United States today?
3. Why is it important that the entire placenta be expelled?
4. Which countries have the highest c-section rates and which the lowest? What explains the differences?

◇ CULTURAL AND HISTORICAL VARIATIONS IN BIRTH BELIEFS AND PRACTICES

Around nine months after conception, if survival has been sustained through the amazing, dramatic, and sometimes hazardous events of the germinal, embryonic, and fetal periods, a child is born. Even for the child who has made it this far, the hazards are far from over. Birth inspires especially intense beliefs in every culture because it is often difficult and sometimes fatal, to mother or child or both. The difficulties and dangers of birth are unique to the human species (Cassidy, 2006). Polar bear mothers, who weigh an average of 500 pounds, give birth to cubs whose heads are smaller than the heads of newborn humans. Even gorillas, one of our closest primate relatives, have babies who average only 2% of their mother's weight at birth, compared to 6% for humans.

Over the course of human evolutionary history, the size of the brain more than tripled. Yet the rest of the female body did not grow three times larger, nor did the female pelvis triple in size. Consequently, birth became more problematic among humans than among any other animal, as it became increasingly difficult for the large-brained, big-headed fetus to make it through the birth canal out into the world.

Humans responded to this danger by developing cultural beliefs and practices intended to explain why labor is difficult and to alleviate the pain and enhance the safety of mother and child. Some of these beliefs and practices were surely helpful; others were indisputably harmful. Some of the most harmful beliefs and practices were developed not in traditional cultures but in the West, through the interventions of the medical profession from the 18th to the mid-20th century. It is only in the past 50 years that scientifically-based medical knowledge has led to methods that are genuinely helpful to mothers and babies in the birthing process.

Cultural Variations in Birth Beliefs

Compare and contrast cultural variations in birth beliefs	LEARNING OBJECTIVE 3

Cultural beliefs about birth are sometimes designed to protect mother and baby, and sometimes designed to isolate them and protect others. The placenta is one aspect of the birth process that is often the focus of distinct beliefs.

Beliefs and Rituals Surrounding Birth

As noted at the outset of the module, across cultures a successful birth is marked with a joyful celebration (Newton & Newton, 2003). For example, among the Ila people of Zimbabwe, women attending the birth will shower praise upon the woman having the baby. After the birth, her husband comes in to congratulate her, and other male relations also enter the hut to clasp her hand and provide her with gifts.

However, there are also cultural practices that frame birth and its aftermath with some degree of fear and wariness. Perhaps because birth is often dangerous, many traditional cultures have developed beliefs that it puts a woman in a state of being spiritually unclean (Newton & Newton, 2003). In some cultures, birth must take place away from where most people reside, so that others will not be contaminated by it. For example, among the Arapesh of New Guinea, birth is allowed to take place only at the outskirts of the village, in a place reserved for other contaminating activities such as excretion and menstruation.

Many cultures have beliefs that the mother remains unclean long after the birth and must be kept away from others, for her own sake as well as theirs (Newton & Newton, 2003). In traditional Vietnam (but not today), the mother was to avoid going out for at least 30 days after birth, in order not to contaminate the rest of the village or endanger herself or her infant; even her husband could not enter her room but could only speak to her from outside the door. Some cultures have rituals for women to purify themselves after birth, and not just non-Western cultures. In the Bible, the twelfth chapter of the book of Leviticus is devoted to ritual purification of women after childbirth, and until recent decades the Catholic church had a special ritual for new mothers to purify themselves.

Why would such beliefs develop? A frequent motivation for the development of cultural beliefs appears to be the desire for control. As the great early 20th century anthropologist Bronislaw Malinowski observed, "the function of [magical beliefs] is to ritualize optimism, to enhance [our] victory in the faith of hope over fear . . . [people] resort to magic only where chance and circumstances are not fully controlled" (Jones & Kay, 2003, p. 103). Birth is often fraught with pain and peril. Humans, faced with this unpleasant prospect, develop beliefs they hope will enable them to avoid, or at least minimize, the pain and peril. It is a comfort to believe that if certain rituals are performed, the mother, the baby, and everyone else will make it through the process unscathed.

Thinking Culturally

In your own culture, in what ways (if any) is birth viewed as potentially contaminating? In what ways is it celebrated?

Meanings of the Placenta

The placenta is a component of the birth process that has often carried its own special cultural beliefs. Perhaps because delivery of the placenta is potentially dangerous, many cultures have developed beliefs that the placenta itself is potentially dangerous and must be disposed of properly so that no unpleasant consequences will result (Jones & Kay, 2003). Failure to do so is believed to carry consequences as minor as pimples on the baby or as major as the baby's death.

In some cultures the methods for disposing of the placenta are clear and simple: burial, burning, or throwing it in a river, or keeping it in a special place reserved for placentas. For example, among the Navajo, a Native American culture, the custom was to bury the placenta in a sacred place to underscore the baby's bonds to the ancestral land (Selander, 2011). In other cultures, the traditions surrounding the placenta are more elaborate and involve beliefs that the placenta has a spirit or soul of its own. In these cultures, the placenta is not simply thrown away but given a proper burial similar to that given to a person. For example, in several parts of the world, including Ghana, Malaysia, and Indonesia, the placenta is treated as the baby's semihuman sibling (Cassidy, 2006). Following delivery, the midwife washes the placenta and buries it as she would a stillborn infant. In some cultures the burial includes prayers to the placenta requesting it to not to harm the newborn child or the mother.

In developed countries the placenta is recognized as having special value as a source of hormones and nutrients. Hospitals give their placentas to researchers, or to cosmetic manufacturers who use them to make products such as hair conditioner (Jones & Kay, 2003). Some people in Western countries even advocate consuming part of the placenta, on top of "placenta pizza" or blended into a "placenta cocktail" (Weekley, 2007)! Maybe this explains why the word "placenta" is derived from the Latin word for "cake"?

Well, probably not. More likely, this (rare) practice is inspired by the fact that many other mammalian mothers, from mice to monkeys, eat the placenta. The placenta is full of nutrients that can provide a boost to an exhausted new mother about to begin nursing. It also contains the hormone oxytocin, which helps prevent postpartum hemorrhage. Few human cultures have been found to have a custom of eating the placenta, although in some parts of the Philippines midwives add placental blood to a porridge intended to strengthen the new mother (Cassidy, 2006). Also, in

Applying Your Knowledge . . . as a Nurse

Suppose you were attending a birth, and afterward the new mother told you she would like to take the placenta with her in order to bury it at home, in accordance with the customs of her culture. How would you respond?

traditional Chinese medicine dried placenta is sometimes used to stimulate maternal milk production (Tierra & Tierra, 1998).

Cultural Variations in Birth Practices

Explain the role of the midwife and compare and contrast cultural practices and medical methods for easing the birth process.

LEARNING OBJECTIVE 4

Although there is great cultural variation in beliefs about birth, there is relatively little variation among traditional cultures in who assists with the birth. Almost always, the main assistants are older women (Bel & Bel, 2007). In one early study of birth practices in 60 traditional cultures, elderly women assisted in 58 of them (Ford, 1945). Rarely, men have been found to be the main birth attendants, such as in some parts of Mexico and the Philippines. More typically, not only are men not the main attendants at birth but they are forbidden from being present (Newton & Newton, 2003). However, sometimes fathers assist by holding up the mother as she leans, stands or squats to deliver the baby (Jordan, 1993).

Who Helps?

Although a variety of women are typically present with the mother at birth, especially her relatives, the women who are charged with managing the birth process usually have a special status as midwives. Midwives tend to be older women who have had children themselves but are now beyond childbearing age. They have direct experience with childbirth but no longer have young children to care for, so that they are available and able when called to duty.

There are a variety of ways a woman may become a midwife (Cosminsky, 2003). In some cultures, such as in Guatemala and the Ojibwa tribe of Native Americans, she receives what she believes to be a supernatural calling in a dream or vision. In other cultures, the position of midwife is inherited from mother to daughter. Still other cultures allow women to volunteer to be midwives. Regardless of how she comes to the position, typically the woman who is to be a midwife spends several years in apprenticeship to a more experienced midwife before taking the lead in assisting with a birth. Through apprenticeship she learns basic principles of hygiene, methods to ease the birth, and practices for prenatal and postnatal care.

Cultures have varied widely in how they regard midwives. Most often, the midwife has a highly respected status in her culture, and is held in high regard for her knowledge and skills. However, in some cultures midwives have been regarded with contempt or fear. In India, for example, midwives come from the *castes* that have the lowest status (Cosminsky, 2003). Birth is believed to be unclean and polluting, so only the lowest castes are deemed fit to be involved in it. In Western cultures, from the 15th through the 17th centuries midwives were frequently accused of being witches and many of them were executed (Cassidy, 2006). However, in recent decades midwifery has become more prevalent and accepted in Western countries, as we will see in more detail later in the module.

Midwives are usually the main birth assistants in rural areas of developing countries. Here, a midwife attends to a pregnant woman in her Cambodian village home.
(Borderlands/Alamy)

Easing the Birth

Cultures have devised many ways of attempting to ease the birth process. These strategies begin long before birth. Often the role of midwife includes prenatal visits, every few weeks beginning in about the fourth month of pregnancy. When visiting the prospective mother, the midwife typically gives her an abdominal massage. This is believed to make the birth easier, and it also allows the midwife to determine the position of the fetus. If the fetus is in the breech position, she turns it.

Applying Your Knowledge . . . as a Nurse

You have a patient who wants to include a midwife in the birthing room. The hospital where you work allows this. Why might a midwife be helpful to the mother?

In addition to massaging the pregnant woman's abdomen, the midwife often gives the mother herbal tea, intended to prevent miscarriage and promote healthy development of the fetus. She also gives the mother advice on diet and exercise. In many cultures in Asia and South America, foods are classified as "hot" or "cold" (a cultural definition, not on the basis of whether they are actually hot or cold), and the mother is forbidden from eating "hot" foods (Cosminsky, 2003). These food classifications have no scientific basis, but they may help to reassure the expectant mother and enhance her confidence going into the birth process.

When the woman begins to go into labor, the midwife is called, and the expectant mother's female relatives gather around her. Sometimes the midwife gives the mother-to-be medicine intended to ease the pain of labor and birth. Many cultures have used herbal medicines, but in the Ukraine, traditionally the first act of the midwife upon arriving at the home of a woman in labor was to give her a generous glass of whiskey (Newton & Newton, 2003). Expectant mothers may be fed special foods to strengthen them for the labor to come. In some cultures women are urged to lie quietly between contractions, in others they are encouraged to walk around or even to exercise.

During the early part of labor, the midwife may use the intervals between contractions to explain to the expectant mother what is to come—how the contractions will come more and more frequently, how the woman will eventually have to push the baby out, and what the woman's position should be during the birth (Bel & Bel, 2007). Sometimes the other women present add to the midwife's advice, describing or even demonstrating their own positioning when giving birth. As labor continues, often the midwife and other women present with the mother will urge her on during contractions with "birth talk," calling out encouragement and instructions, and sometimes even scolding her if she screams too loud or complains too much (Bergstrom et al., 2009, 2010).

The longer the labor, the more exhausted the mother and the greater the potential danger to mother and child. Consequently, cultures have created a wide variety of practices intended to speed it up, as we'll see in the **Cultural Focus: Easing Birth Among the Cuna Indians** feature. The most widespread approach, appearing in cultures in all parts of the world, is to use some kind of imagery or metaphor associated with opening up or expulsion (Bates & Turner, 2003). For example, in the Philippines a key (for "opening" the cervix) and a comb (for "untangling" the umbilical cord) are placed under the laboring woman's pillow. In parts of Southeast Asia, people assisting the laboring woman unlock all doors, windows, and cupboards, and forbid others from uttering words such as "stuck" or "fastened." In other cultures, ropes are unknotted, bottles are uncorked, or animals are let out of their pens. Several cultures use the imagery of the flower, placing flowers in the room with the woman in the hope that as the buds of the flower open, so will her cervix. These methods have no direct effect on the birth, of course, but they may give the birth mother emotional and social support.

Emotional and social support help ease the birth for women in developed countries as well (daMott et al., 2006). As we have seen earlier in the module, methods of easing the birth may include practices such as rhythmic breathing or taking a warm bath. Medical interventions are also common in developed countries. Women in labor often receive an **epidural**, which involves the injection of an anesthetic drug into the spinal fluid to help them manage the pain while remaining alert (Vallejo et al., 2007). If administered in the correct dosage, an epidural allows enough feeling to remain so that the woman can push when the time comes, but sometimes synthetic oxytocin has to be administered because the epidural causes contractions to become sluggish. Rates of receiving epidurals for women having a vaginal birth vary widely in developed countries, for example 76% in the United States, 52% in Sweden, 45% in Canada, and 24% in New Zealand (Lane, 2009). The reasons for these variations are not clear.

An important part of the strategy for easing the birth in many cultures is the physical position of the mother. In nearly all cultures some kind of upright position is used, most commonly kneeling or sitting, followed in prevalence by squatting or standing (Newton & Newton, 2003). Often a woman will lean back on a hammock or bed between contractions, but take a more upright position as birth becomes imminent. Lying flat was the most prevalent delivery position in developed countries during the 20th century, but it is rarely used in traditional cultures, as it makes delivery more difficult by failing to make use of gravity. Today

epidural
during birth process, injection of an anesthetic drug into the spinal fluid to help the mother manage the pain while also remaining alert

CULTURAL FOCUS

EASING BIRTH AMONG THE CUNA INDIANS

In many parts of the world today, birth is a social and religious event. Women give birth in their own homes, in the company of their closest female relatives and friends; the birth is assisted by a midwife whom the woman knows well. In many places the woman is believed to be especially vulnerable during birth, not just physically but spiritually. Consequently, many cultures have developed religious beliefs and methods in an attempt to ensure the safety of mother and child.

One example was described by the French anthropologist Claude Levi-Strauss, who did ethnographic research on the Cuna Indians of Panama (Levi-Strauss, 1967). Normally, Cuna women are attended during birth by a midwife and female relatives. However, if labor becomes difficult, the midwife often calls on spiritual assistance from a shaman, a religious leader believed to have special powers and knowledge of the spirit world. Shamans are common in traditional cultures around the world.

Among the Cuna Indians, difficult births are believed to be caused by the spirit of the womb, Muu, who may, for no apparent reason, decide to hold on to the fetus and prevent it from coming out. The shaman's job is to invoke magic that will release the fetus from Muu's grip. He sits down next to the woman giving birth and begins by singing a long and detailed song describing why he has been summoned to help her and how he and his fellow spirits plan to launch an attack on Muu. Then, as the song continues, he calls upon the spirits of other animals for assistance, such as wood-boring insects to cut through Muu's fingers and burrowing insects to help push the fetus along the birth canal. The shaman's own spirit joins the animal spirits inside the womb to wage combat against Muu.

(Paul Gapper/Alamy)

Does any of this do any good to the woman suffering a difficult labor? Medically, obviously not, but be careful before you dismiss the effects of the shaman's song too easily. There is abundant evidence of the **placebo effect**, which means that sometimes if people believe something affects them, it does, just by virtue of the power of their belief. In the classic example, if people are given a sugar pill containing no medicine and told it is a pain reliever, many of them will report experiencing reduced pain (Balodis et al., 2011). It was not the sugar pill that reduced their pain but their belief that the pill would reduce their pain.placebo effect psychological phenomenon in which people believe something affects them and it does, just by virtue of the power of their belief

The shaman's song may have a placebo effect on the Cuna woman giving birth, if not to promote her labor than at least to ease her pain. Furthermore, according to Levi-Strauss, the shaman's song and the spiritual world it invokes allow the woman to make sense of her pain. By connecting her labor pain to the symbolic worldview of her culture, she gives it meaning and order. For a woman who believes in the spiritual world the shaman describes, "The impact of the symbolic environment is to concentrate the whole of the woman's being, psychologically and physiologically, upon the task at hand" (Bates & Turner, 2003, pp. 93–94).

in developed countries many hospitals use a semisitting, half-reclining position (Eisenberg et al., 2011).

After birth, typically the baby is laid on the mother's abdomen until the placenta and umbilical cord are expelled from her uterus. Although there is often great joy and relief at the birth of the baby, the attention of the birth attendants and the mother is immediately directed toward delivering the placenta. A variety of strategies are used to promote the process, such as massage, medication, rituals involving opening or expelling, or attempts to make the woman sneeze or vomit (Cosminsky, 2003). Most common across cultures is the use of herbal medicines, administered as a tea or a douche (a liquid substance placed into the vagina). In developed countries, synthetic oxytocin may be used to promote contractions that will expel the placenta.

After the placenta is expelled, the umbilical cord is cut. Usually the cord is tied with thread, string, or plant fiber. In traditional cultures, some of the customs involved in cutting or treating the cord are unwittingly hazardous to the baby (Cosminsky, 2003). Tools used to cut the cord include bamboo, shell, broken glass, sickles, and razors, and they may not be clean, resulting in transmission of disease to the baby. Methods for treating the cut cord include, in one part of northern India, ash from burned cow dung mixed with dirt, which is now known to increase sharply the baby's risk of tetanus.

placebo effect
psychological phenomenon in which people believe something affects them and it does, just by virtue of the power of their belief

The Peculiar History of Birth in the West

| LEARNING OBJECTIVE 5 | Summarize the history of birth in the West from the 15th century to today. |

Given the perils of birth throughout human history one might assume that once modern scientific medicine developed, mothers and babies were safer than in the superstitious past. However, this is not quite how the story goes. On the contrary, making birth "medical" made the dangers for mothers and babies worse, not better, for *over a century*. Here we'll look first at the struggle between midwives and doctors for priority in assisting the birth. Then we'll look at the problems involved in medical approaches to birth in the 20th century, and the more favorable trends of recent decades.

Midwives Versus Doctors

forceps
pair of tongs used to extract the baby's head from the womb during delivery

obstetrics
field of medicine that focuses on prenatal care and birth

In the West as in other cultures, most births throughout most of history were administered by midwives (Ehrenreich, 2010). The role of midwife was widely valued and respected. Most did their work for little or no pay, although families would often present them with a gift after the birth.

This began to change in the 15th century, as a witch-hunting fervor swept over Europe. In 1486 an influential witch-hunting manual was published by two monks, declaring that "No one does more harm to the Catholic faith than midwives" (Cassidy, 2006, p. 33). Midwives became widely suspected of being witches, and many of them were put to death. After the witch-hunting fervor passed, midwifery revived, but to keep out any remaining witches midwives were required to have licenses, issued by the Catholic church.

HISTORICAL FOCUS

THE TRAGIC HISTORY OF DOCTOR-ASSISTED BIRTHS IN THE 19TH CENTURY

In the course of the 19th century it became increasingly common for doctors in the West to be called upon to assist in births. The medical profession was gaining in prestige, and the care and assistance of expectant mothers became a distinct field within medicine called **obstetrics**. Increasingly, mothers felt they would be safer if attended by a physician. Unfortunately, medical training at the time often included virtually nothing about assisting a birth. All the doctors-to-be were men, and in many medical schools it was considered improper for a man to see a woman's genitals under any circumstances. Consequently, medical students learned about assisting a birth only from reading books and attending lectures, which sometimes included a demonstration with a mannequin playing the role of Mom and a rag doll to play the baby (Cassidy, 2006).

This may sound humorously idiotic, but the consequences of doctors' ignorance were anything but amusing for mothers and babies. For many physicians, the first birth they assisted after medical school was also the first birth they ever witnessed; for years they learned by trial and error, at the mothers' and babies' expense. Many of the doctors used forceps, a set of "iron hands" intended to help ease the baby's head out of the vagina. Forceps were first invented in the 16th century, but came into widespread use in the 18th and 19th centuries. By the end of the 19th century, half of all American births involved the use of forceps (Ehrenreich, 2010). Forceps were sometimes useful in the hands of an experienced, well-trained doctor—and still are, in rare cases—but doctors of the time were rarely experienced or well trained. Consequently, the use of forceps frequently resulted in damage to the baby or the mother. In the course of the 20th century, as the damage done by forceps was increasingly recognized, their use diminished. By the early 21st century they were used in only 4% of American births (Cassidy, 2006).

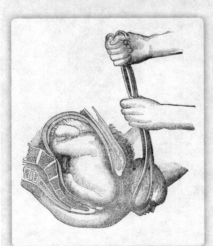

19th-century illustration of use of forceps
(Emilio Ereza/Alamy)

Even worse than the pervasive and unnecessary use of forceps in doctor-assisted births in the 19th century was the spread of disease. At the time, it was not known that disease is transmitted by bacteria and viruses, so no one understood that it was necessary for doctors to wash their hands before examining a patient to avoid spreading infection. Consequently, hospitals became disease factories, and as more and more mothers gave birth in hospitals—hoping they would be safer there than at home—more and more of them became afflicted with diseases spread by doctors. And as medical schools in the United States and Europe began providing students with more direct involvement in births, the students, too, became carriers of disease.

Doctors and medical students would go from doing an autopsy on a cadaver to examining the vagina of a woman in labor, unwittingly spreading disease along the way. Vast numbers of women died following childbirth from what was called *childbed fever* or *puerperal sepsis*. Records show that in many European and American hospitals in the 19th century about 1 in 20 mothers died from childbed fever, and during occasional epidemics the rates were much higher (Nuland, 2003). Records from one Boston hospital in 1883 showed that 75% of mothers giving birth suffered from childbed fever, and 20% died from it (Cassidy, 2006). Few people realized that doctors were contaminating the mothers, and doctors were reluctant to accept the evidence once it began to emerge (Nuland, 2003). For centuries childbed fever had been attributed to causes such as bad air, self-poisoning by the mother's vaginal fluids, or the mother's milk gone astray in her body; doctors, who saw themselves as bringing enlightened science to the birth process, were not eager to accept that they were actually making it worse.

In the early 18th century a new challenge arose to the status of midwives. Medical schools were established throughout Europe, and many of the new doctors considered delivering babies to be the domain of physicians. Doctors developed new methods of assisting births, such as using **forceps**, a pair of tongs used to extract the baby's head from the womb, often damaging the brain in the process. Gradually in the course of the 18th and 19th centuries, as doctors became more numerous they took over a steadily higher proportion of births, at first with unfortunate results for mothers as we'll see in the **Historical Focus: The Tragic History of Doctor-Assisted Births in the 19th Century** feature. Even in the early 20th century midwives still assisted at about 50% of births, but by 1930 this proportion had dwindled to 15%, and by 1973 to just 1% (Cassidy, 2006).

In recent decades midwifery has seen a revival, and currently about 10% of births in the United States are assisted by midwives (MacDorman et al., 2010). Many now receive formal training and are certified and licensed as nurse-midwives, rather than simply learning their skills from an older midwife as in the past. In Europe, midwives are much more common than in the United States, especially in northern Europe. In Norway, for example, 96% of births are assisted by midwives (Cosminsky, 2003).

The 20th Century: Slow Progress

In obstetrics as in other branches of medicine, a more scientific basis of knowledge, care, and treatment developed during the 20th century. However, progress was slow. In the early decades of the 20th century medical training remained inadequate. A 1912 survey of 120 medical schools found that the majority of professors of obstetrics admitted that they were inadequately trained to teach their subject (Cassidy, 2006). And these were the *professors*, so you can imagine how little their students knew. Childbed fever remained a persistent problem. Although hand washing became standard among doctors by the early 20th century, inadequate washing still caused many deaths. It was not until the 1940s that childbed fever was finally vanquished in the United States and Europe as it became standard for obstetricians to wash their hands and also wear rubber gloves in examining women. The development of antibiotics at this time cured the cases of childbed fever that did occur (Carter & Carter, 2005).

In some ways, obstetrical care of women grew still worse in the early 20th century. Episiotomies became more prevalent, when some medical authorities claimed (without evidence) that the procedure made birth safer for mothers and babies. Doctors increasingly used drugs to relieve mothers' pain during birth. As discussed earlier in this module, methods to ease the pain of childbirth have a long history in human cultures and have long been part of the midwife's repertoire. In the 19th century physicians developed stronger drugs to relieve pain during birth, first using ether and later, chloroform. However, these drugs could be used only just before the birth, because if used earlier they might interfere with the woman's contractions. In addition, these drugs had dangerous side effects that could cause maternal hemorrhage and breathing difficulties in babies.

In the early 20th century a new drug method was developed that resulted in a condition that became known as *Twilight Sleep* (Cassidy, 2008). After being injected with narcotics (mainly morphine), a woman giving birth in Twilight Sleep became less inhibited, which helped her relax during her contractions and promoted dilation of her cervix, making the use of forceps less likely. Women still felt pain—in fact, screaming and thrashing were so common in Twilight Sleep that women were often strapped in helmets and handcuffed to the birth bed—but afterward they remembered none of it, so as far as they were concerned, the birth had been painless and problem free. From the 1930s through the

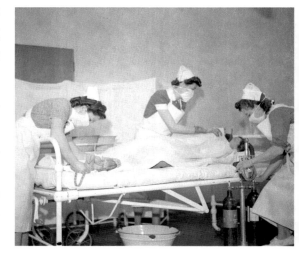

In the mid-20th century birth in developed countries often took place in a condition of "Twilight Sleep," in which the mother was heavily medicated. Shown here is a 1946 photo of a new mother under sedation after giving birth in a London hospital.
(Bush/Express/Getty Images)

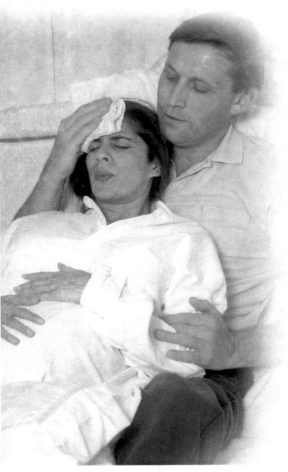

In natural childbirth, husbands or partners often assist with breathing techniques designed to manage the pain.
(Angela Hampton Picture Library/Alamy)

natural childbirth
approach to childbirth that avoids medical technologies and interventions

electronic fetal monitoring (EFM)
method that tracks the fetus's heartbeat, either externally through the mother's abdomen or directly by running a wire through the cervix and placing a sensor on the fetus's scalp

Applying Your Knowledge . . . as a Nurse

If you were pregnant or the partner of a pregnant woman, how "natural" would you want the childbirth to be, and why?

1960s use of Twilight Sleep and other drug methods was standard practice in hospitals in Western countries, and women nearly always gave birth while heavily medicated (Cassidy, 2006). If you live in a Western country, ask your grandmother about it.

During the late 1960s a backlash began to develop against the medicalization of birth (Lyon, 2009). Critics claimed that medical procedures such as forceps, episiotomies, and drugs were unnecessary and had been created by the medical profession mainly to make childbirth more profitable. These critics advocated **natural childbirth** as an alternative. Although this term was first proposed in the 1930s, it was only in the 1960s and the decades that followed that a variety of drug-and-technology-free approaches to birth became popular, as part of more general trends toward greater rights for women, a greater push for consumer rights, and a growing interest in natural health practices (Thompson, 2005). Natural childbirth methods vary in their details, but all reject medical technologies and interventions as unhelpful to the birth process or even harmful. The premise is that a substantial amount of the pain women experience in childbirth is based on the anxiety created by fear of the medical setting and lack of understanding of the birth process. Consequently, natural childbirth entails a nonmedical setting for birth, and includes classes in which the parents-to-be learn about the birth process. The remainder of the pain experienced in childbirth can be managed by learning relaxation and breathing techniques. Another important component of natural childbirth approaches is for the expectant mother to have the physical and emotional support of her husband or partner or others who could assist with the relaxation and breathing techniques.

No differences have been found in maternal and neonatal health outcomes between natural childbirth and medical methods (Bergstrom et al., 2009). However, most participants in natural childbirth methods report that it lowered their anxiety about the birth and made them feel that they were more knowledgeable about and more in control of the birth process (Westfall & Benoit, 2004). Natural childbirth methods remain popular today, especially in northern Europe. In most countries where women have the option of medical methods to lower the pain of birth most of them choose these methods, but in northern Europe the majority of women choose to make the birth experience as natural as possible, in a home rather than a hospital (Ravn, 2005).

Birth Today in Developed Countries

In developed countries today, the birth process is better than it has ever been before, for both mothers and babies. The natural childbirth movement has had many positive effects on how birth is assisted in mainstream medicine. Although most births in developed countries still take place in a hospital, birth has become less like an operation performed by a physician and more of a collaboration between doctors, nurses (often including nurse-midwives), and mothers.

Fathers are now involved, too. Prior to the 1960s they were totally excluded from the birth, but by the late 1970s the majority of fathers were present when their wives gave birth (Simkin, 2007). In general, the father's presence seems to benefit the mother during birth (Kainz et al., 2010). When fathers are present, mothers experience slightly shorter labor and express greater satisfaction with the birth experience (Hodnett et al., 2007). For fathers, being present at the birth evokes intense feelings of wonder and love for the mother and child (Erlandsson & Lindgren, 2009). However, some fathers also experience intense fears for their health and well-being (Eriksson et al., 2007).

Several technological developments have made the birth process less painful and safer for both mother and baby. Epidurals are a great improvement over being knocked out by Twilight Sleep and similar drug methods. The "vacuum," a cup attached to the head of the fetus and linked to an extracting machine that uses vacuum power to pull firmly but steadily, serves the same function as forceps but with less likelihood of damage to either mother or baby (WHO, 2011). **Electronic fetal monitoring (EFM)** is another common technology used in births in developed countries. EFM tracks the fetus's heartbeat, either externally through the mother's abdomen or directly by running a wire through the cervix and placing a sensor on the fetus's scalp. In the United States, about 85% of births include EFM (Martin et al., 2005). Changes in the fetal heart rate may indicate distress and call for intervention (Sachs et al., 1999). However, heart rate changes are not easy to interpret and do not necessarily indicate distress, so use of EFM may increase the rate of unnecessary c-sections (Thaker & Stroup, 2003). EFM is probably most useful in preterm or other high-risk deliveries, when fetal distress is most likely to occur.

Cultural Variations in Neonatal and Maternal Mortality

> Describe the differences in maternal and neonatal mortality both within and between developed countries and developing countries.

LEARNING OBJECTIVE 6

Outside developed countries, few pregnant women have access to any modern medical technologies. As you can see from **Map 2,** rates of infant and maternal mortality are vastly higher in developing countries than in developed countries. In the over 80% of the world's population that lives outside developed countries, birth remains fraught with pain and peril. However, there are some hopeful signs. Maternal mortality has decreased substantially in developing countries over the past 30 years, due to improvements in nutrition and access to health care (Hogan et al., 2010; Rajaratnam et al., 2010).

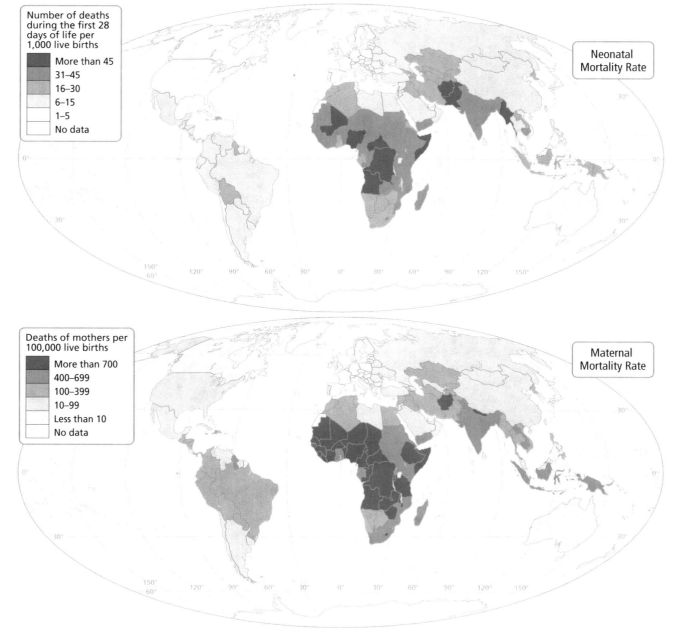

MAP 2 Neonatal and Maternal Mortality Worldwide
How do neonatal and maternal mortality rates compare? What factors might explain why mortality rates are higher in developing countries than in developed countries?

There is also substantial variation in neonatal and maternal mortality within developed countries, especially within the United States (UNDP, 2011). Neonatal mortality is over twice as high for African Americans as for Whites, due primarily to greater poverty and lower access to high-quality medical care among African Americans (CDC, 2010). However, neonatal mortality has dropped steeply in the United States since 1980, by over half among Whites and by nearly half among African Americans (U.S. Bureau of the Census, 2010). Current rates among Latinos and Asian Americans are similar to those for Whites (CDC, 2010). For maternal mortality, the trends are in the opposite direction. Maternal mortality is over 3 times as high among African Americans as among Whites and has been rising steadily in both groups since 1980, for reasons that are not clear (U.S. Bureau of the Census, 2010).

WHAT HAVE YOU LEARNED?

1. Provide two examples of cultural beliefs regarding birth, one that reflects a negative view and one that reflects a positive view.
2. What are some cultural beliefs and practices concerning the disposal of the placenta?
3. Who is typically present at birth, across cultures, and who is not?
4. What position do mothers typically take when giving birth, and why?
5. What was Twilight Sleep, and what birthing methods developed as a counterreaction to the medicalized approach to birth?
6. What are the factors influencing maternal and neonatal mortality today within both developed countries and developing countries?

PART 1 VIDEO GUIDE

LABOR (LENGTH: 10:35)

This video gives an overview of labor and delivery. It contains a video simulation of the process as well as actual footage of labor and delivery from a real birth.

1. While the video narrator tells us that the actual trigger for labor is still a mystery, he provides a few possibilities. Explain those possibilities.
2. List at least three of the signals a woman may experience to let her know she is about to begin labor.
3. Describe in detail the three stages of labor.

> ● | **Watch the Video** Labor at www.pearsoncustom.com/mi/msu_mylabs

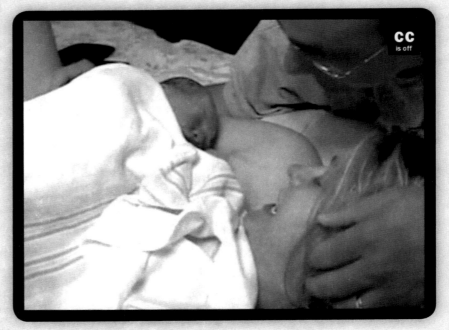

PART 2   THE NEONATE

LEARNING OBJECTIVE

7. Identify the features of the two major scales most often used to assess neonatal health.

8. Identify the neonatal classifications for low birth weight and describe the consequences and major treatments.

9. Describe neonates' patterns of waking and sleeping, including how and why these patterns differ across cultures.

10. Describe the neonatal reflexes, including those that have a functional purpose and those that do not.

11. Describe the neonate's sensory abilities with respect to touch, taste and smell, hearing, and sight.

◇ THE NEONATE'S HEALTH

And so out comes baby at last, after nine months or so inside the womb. If you were expecting cuddly and cute from the beginning, you may be in for a surprise. The baby may be covered with fine, fuzzy, hair called lanugo, a vestige of our hairy primate ancestors. This hair will be shed after a few days, fortunately. The skin may also be coated all over with an oily, cheesy substance called vernix, which protected the skin from chapping while in the womb. When my twins were born I was amazed to see that they were covered with this white substance, which I had never known about until that moment.

The head may be a bit misshapen as a consequence of being squeezed through the birth canal. One evolutionary solution to the problem of getting large-brained human fetuses out of the womb is that the skull of the infant's head is not yet fused into one bone. Instead, it is composed of several loosely joined pieces that can move around as necessary during the birth process. In between the pieces are two soft spots called **fontanels**, one on top and one toward the back of the head. It will take about 18 months before the pieces of the skull are firmly joined and the fontanels have disappeared.

It was only 9 months ago that sperm and ovum united to make a single cell, but by birth the newborn baby has 10 trillion cells! The typical newborn child, or **neonate**, is about 50 centimeters (20 in.) long and weighs about 3.4 kilograms (7.5 lb). Neonates tend to lose about 10% of their weight in their first few days, because they lose fluids and do not eat much (Verma et al., 2009). By the 5th day they start to regain this weight, and by the end of the second week most are back up to their birth weight.

About half of all neonates have a yellowish look to their skin and eyeballs in the first few days of life. This condition, known as **neonatal jaundice**, is due to the immaturity of the liver (Madlon-Kay, 2002). In most cases, neonatal jaundice disappears after a few days as the liver begins to function normally, but if it lasts more than a few days it should be treated, or it can result in brain damage (American Academy of Pediatrics [AAP] Committee on Quality Improvement, 2002). The most effective treatment is a simple one, *phototherapy*, which involves exposing the neonate to colored light; blue works best (American Academy of Pediatrics [AAP], 2009).

fontanels
soft spots on the skull between loosely joined pieces of the skull that shift during birth process to assist passage through the birth canal

neonate
newborn baby, up to 4 weeks old

neonatal jaundice
yellowish pallor common in the first few days of life due to immaturity of the liver

At birth, babies are covered with vernix, which protects their skin. (Buddy Mays/Alamy)

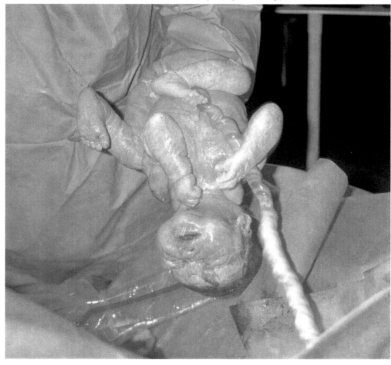

Measuring Neonatal Health

Identify the features of the two major scales most often used to assess neonatal health.

anoxia
deprivation of oxygen during birth process and soon after that can result in serious neurological damage within minutes

In the transition from the fetal environment to the outside world, the first few minutes are crucial. Especially important is for neonates to begin to breathe on their own, after months of obtaining their oxygen through their mothers' umbilical cord. Most neonates begin to breathe as soon as they are exposed to air, even before the umbilical cord is cut. However, if they do not, the consequences can become severe very quickly. Deprivation of oxygen, a condition known as **anoxia**, results in swift and massive death of brain cells. If a neonate suffers anoxia for even a few minutes, the result can be permanent cognitive deficits, including mental retardation (Hopkins-Golightly et al., 2003).

Because the transition from the fetal environment is crucial and occasionally problematic, methods have been developed for assessing neonatal health. In Western countries, two of the most widely used methods are the Apgar scale and the Brazelton Neonatal Behavioral Assessment Scale (NBAS).

The Apgar Scale

The **Apgar scale** is named after its creator, the pediatrician Virginia Apgar (1953). The letters *APGAR* also correspond to the five subtests that comprise the scale: **A**ppearance (color), **P**ulse (heart rate), **G**rimace (reflex irritability), **A**ctivity (muscle tone), and **R**espiration (breathing). The neonate is rated on each of these five subscales, receiving a score of 0, 1, or 2 (see **Table 1**), with the overall score ranging from 0–10. Neonates are rated twice, first about a minute after birth and then after 5 minutes, because sometimes a neonate's condition can change quickly during this time, for better or worse.

Apgar scale
neonatal assessment scale with five subtests: Appearance (color), Pulse (heart rate), Grimace (reflex irritability), Activity (muscle tone), and Respiration (breathing)

A score of 7 to 10 means the neonate is in good to excellent condition. Scores in this range are received by over 98% of American babies (Martin et al., 2003). If the score is from 4 to 6, anoxia is likely and the neonate is in need of assistance to begin breathing. If the score is 3 or below, the neonate is in life-threatening danger and immediate medical assistance is required. In addition to their usefulness immediately after birth, Apgar scores indicate the neonate's risk of death in the first month of life, which can alert physicians that careful monitoring is necessary (Casey et al., 2003).

TABLE 1 The Apgar Scale

Total Score: 7–10 = Good to excellent condition; 4–6 = Requires assistance to breathe; 3 or below = Life-threatening danger

SCORE	0	1	2
Appearance (Body color)	Blue and pale	Body pink, but extremities blue	Entire body pink
Pulse (Heart rate)	Absent	Slow—less than 100 beats per minute	Fast—100–140 beats per minute
Grimace (Reflex irritability)	No response	Grimace	Coughing, sneezing, and crying
Activity (Muscle tone)	Limp and flaccid	Weak, inactive, but some flexion of extremities	Strong, active motion
Respiration (Breathing)	No breathing for more than 1 minute	Irregular and slow	Good breathing with normal crying

Sources: Based on Apgar, 1953

The Brazelton Scale

Another widely used scale of neonatal functioning is the **Brazelton Neonatal Behavioral Assessment Scale (NBAS)**. The NBAS rates neonates on 27 items assessing *reflexes* (such as blinking); *physical states* (such as irritability and excitability), *responses to social stimulation*, and *central nervous system instability* (indicated by symptoms such as tremors). Based on these 27 items, the neonate receives an overall rating of "worrisome," "normal," or "superior" (Nugent & Brazelton, 2000; Nugent et al., 2009).

In contrast to the Apgar scale, which is administered immediately after birth, the NBAS is usually performed about a day after birth but can be given any time in the first 2 months. The NBAS most effectively predicts future development if it is given a day after birth and then about a week later. Neonates who are rated normal or superior at both points or who show a "recovery curve" from worrisome to normal or superior have good prospects for development over the next several years, whereas neonates who are worrisome at both points or go down from normal or superior to worrisome are at risk for early developmental problems (Ohgi et al., 2003).

For at-risk neonates as well as others, the NBAS can help inform parents about the abilities and characteristics of their infants. In one study of Brazilian mothers, those who took part in an NBAS-guided discussion of their infants a few days after birth were more likely to smile, vocalize, and establish eye contact with their infants a month later, compared to mothers in a control group who received only general health care information (Wendland-Carro et al., 1999). In an American study of full-term and preterm neonates, parents in both groups who participated in an NBAS program interacted more confidently with their babies than parents who did not take part in the program (Eiden & Reifman, 1996).

The NBAS has also been used in research to examine differences among neonates across cultures and how those differences interact with parenting practices (Nugent et al., 2009). For example, studies comparing Asian and White American neonates on the NBAS have found the Asian neonates tend to be calmer and less irritable (Muret-Wagstaff & Moore, 1989). This difference may be partly biological, but it also appears to be related to parenting differences. Asian mothers tended to respond quickly to neonates' distress and attempt to soothe them, whereas White mothers were more likely to let the neonates fuss for awhile before tending to them. In another study, in Zambia, many of the infants were born with low birth weights and were rated worrisome on the NBAS a day after birth (Brazelton et al., 1976). However, a week later most of the worrisome neonates had become normal or superior on the NBAS. The researchers attributed this change to the Zambian mothers' custom of carrying the infant close to their bodies during most of the day, providing soothing comfort as well as sensory stimulation.

Brazelton Neonatal Behavioral Assessment Scale (NBAS) 27-item scale of neonatal functioning with overall ratings "worrisome," "normal," and "superior"

Low Birth Weight

Identify the neonatal classifications for low birth weight and describe the consequences and major treatments.

LEARNING OBJECTIVE 8

The weight of a baby at birth is one of the most important indicators of its prospects for survival and healthy development. Neonates are considered to have **low birth weight** if they are born weighing less than 2,500 grams (about 5.5 pounds). Some neonates with low birth weights are **preterm**, meaning that they were born 3 or more weeks earlier than the optimal 40 weeks after conception. Other low-birth-weight neonates are **small for date**, meaning that they weigh less than 90% of other neonates who were born at the same *gestational age* (number of weeks since conception). Small-for-date neonates are especially at risk, with an infant death rate 4 times higher than that of preterm infants (Regev et al., 2003).

Rates of low-birth-weight neonates vary widely among world regions (UNICEF, 2004). As Map 3 shows, the overall rate worldwide is 14%. Asia and Africa have the highest rates, and Europe the lowest. The current rates in the United States (8%) and Canada (6%) are lower than in developing regions of the world but higher than in Europe. Within the United States, rates of low birth weight are about twice as high among African Americans as among other ethnic groups, for reasons that may include lower likelihood of good prenatal care and higher levels of stress (Casey Foundation, 2010; Giscombe & Lovel, 2005).

low birth weight term for neonates weighing less than 2,500 grams (5.5 lb)

preterm babies born at 37 weeks gestation or less

small for date term applied to neonates who weigh less than 90% of other neonates who were born at the same gestational age

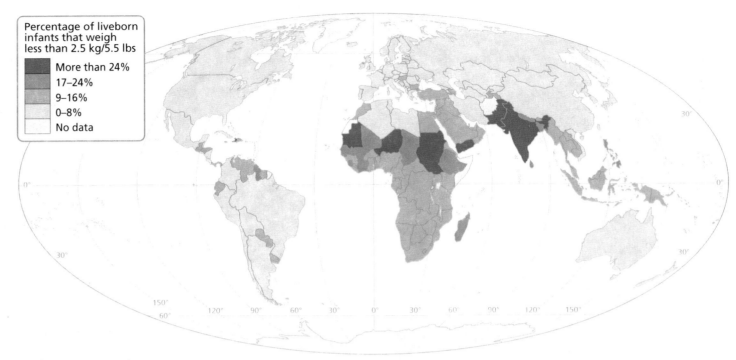

Percentage of liveborn infants that weigh less than 2.5 kg/5.5 lbs

- More than 24%
- 17–24%
- 9–16%
- 0–8%
- No data

MAP 3 Rates of Low Birth Weight Around the World
Why are rates so high in developing countries?

The causes of low birth weight also vary widely among world regions. In developing countries, the main cause is that mothers are frequently malnourished, in poor health, and receive little or no prenatal care. In developed countries, the primary cause of low birth weight is the mother's cigarette smoking (Rückinger et al., 2010). Other contributors to low birth weight are multiple births (the more babies in the womb at once, the lower the birth weights), use of alcohol or other drugs during pregnancy, and young or old maternal age (under 17 or over 40) (Gavin et al., 2011).

Consequences of Low Birth Weight

very low birth weight
term for neonates who weigh less than 1,500 grams (3.3 lb) at birth

extremely low birth weight
term for neonates who weigh less than 1,000 grams (about 2.2 lb) at birth

surfactant
substance in lungs that promotes breathing and keeps the air sacs in the lungs from collapsing

kangaroo care
recommended care for preterm and low-birth-weight neonates, in which mothers or fathers are advised to place the baby skin-to-skin on their chests for 2–3 hours a day for the early weeks of life.

Low-birth-weight babies are at high risk of death in their first year of life. Even in developed countries with advanced medical care, low birth weight is the second most common cause of death in infancy, next to genetic birth defects (Martin et al., 2005). **Very low-birth-weight** neonates, who weigh less than 1,500 grams (about 3.3 lb) at birth, and **extremely low-birth-weight** neonates, who weigh less than 1,000 grams (about 2.2 lb) at birth, are at especially high risk for early death (Tamaru et al., 2011). Usually these neonates are born many weeks before full term. Even in the United States, which has the most advanced medical technology in the world, the chance of surviving through the first year is only 50% for a baby born before 25 weeks gestation (National Institute of Child Health and Human Development [NICHD], 2004). In developing countries, where low birth weight is most common, deaths due to low birth weight contribute to higher overall rates of infant mortality, which we will discuss in more detail later in the module.

Why are low-birth-weight neonates at such high risk for death? If they were small for date at birth, it was likely due to factors that interfered with their prenatal development, such as poor maternal nutrition, maternal illness or disease, or exposure to teratogens such as nicotine or alcohol. Consequently, they were already less healthy than other neonates when they were born, compounding their risk.

For preterm neonates, their physical systems are inadequately developed at birth. Their immune systems are immature, leaving them vulnerable to infection (Stoll et al., 2004). Their central nervous systems are immature, making it difficult for them to perform basic functions such as sucking to obtain nourishment. Their little bodies do not have enough fat to insulate them, so they are at risk of dying from insufficient body heat. Most importantly, their lungs are immature, so they are in danger of dying from being unable to breathe properly. The lungs of a mature neonate are coated with a substance called **surfactant** that helps them breathe and keeps the air sacs in the lungs from collapsing, but preterm infants often have not yet developed surfactant, a deficiency with potentially fatal consequences (Porath et al., 2011). Where advanced medical care is available, mainly in developed countries, preterm neonates are often given surfactant at birth (via a breathing tube), making their survival much more likely (Mugford, 2006).

Treatment for Low-Birth-Weight Babies

What else can be done for low-birth-weight babies? In developing countries, where few of them receive medical treatment, traditional methods of infant care are helpful. In many traditional cultures, young infants are strapped close to their mother's body for most of the time as she goes about her daily life (Small, 1998). In the West, this has been studied as a method called **kangaroo care**, in which mothers or fathers are advised to place their preterm newborns skin-to-skin on their chests for 2–3 hours a day during the early weeks of life (Warnock et al., 2010).

Research has shown that kangaroo care has highly beneficial effects on neonatal functioning. It helps newborns stabilize and regulate bodily functions such as heart rate, breathing, body temperature, and sleep–wake cycles (Ferber & Makhoul, 2004; Reid, 2004). Preterm infants treated with kangaroo care are more likely to survive their first year, and they have longer periods of sleep, cry less, and gain weight faster than other preterm infants (Charpak et al., 2005; Kostandy et al., 2008). Mothers benefit as well. Kangaroo care gives them more confidence in caring for their tiny, vulnerable infant, which leads to more success in breast feeding (Feldman et al., 2003; Ferber & Makhoul, 2004). The effects of kangaroo care on low-birth-weight babies are so well established that now it is used in over three-fourths of neonatal intensive care units in the United States (Engler et al., 2002). An Italian study found that kangaroo care was practiced in two-thirds of the neonatal intensive care units (de Vonderweid & Leonessa, 2009).

The other traditional method of infant care that is helpful for low-birth-weight babies is *infant massage*. This is a widespread custom in Asia, India, and Africa, not just for vulnerable babies but for all of them (McClure, 2000). In the West, infant massage developed because low-birth-weight babies are often placed in an *isolette*, a covered, sterile chamber that provides oxygen and a controlled temperature. The isolette protects neonates from infection but also cuts them off from sensory and social stimulation. Infant massage, pioneered in the West by Tiffany Field and her colleagues (Field, 1998; Field et al., 2010), was intended to relieve the neonate's isolation.

Research has now established the effectiveness of massage in promoting the healthy development of low-birth-weight babies. Preterm neonates who receive three 15-minute massages a day in their first days of life gain weight faster than other preterm babies, and they are more active and alert (Field, 2001; Field et al., 2010). The massages work by triggering the release of hormones that promote weight gain, muscle development, and neurological development (Dieter et al., 2003; Ferber et al., 2002; Field et al., 201). In the United States, currently 38% of hospitals practice massage in their neonatal intensive care units (Field et al., 2010).

Although kangaroo care and massage can be helpful, low-birth-weight babies are at risk for a variety of problems throughout childhood, adolescence, and adulthood. In childhood, low birth weight predicts physical problems such as asthma and cognitive problems that include language delays and poor school performance (Davis, 2003; Marlow et al., 2005). In adolescence, low birth weight predicts relatively low intelligence-test scores and greater likelihood of repeating a grade (Martin et al., 2008). In adulthood, low birth weight predicts brain abnormalities, attention

Babies born with low birth weights are at risk for multiple problems. Unlike this neonate in Uganda, most low-birth-weight neonates in developing countries do not have access to advanced medical care.

(Jake Lyell/Alamy)

Kangaroo care has many benefits for low-birth-weight babies.
(Hypermania/Alamy)

deficits, and low educational attainment (Fearon et al., 2004; Hofman et al., 2004; Strang-Karlsson et al., 2008).

The lower the birth weight, the worse the problems. Most neonates who weigh 1,500 to 2,500 grams at birth (3.3 to 5.5 lb) are likely to show no major impairments after a few years as long as they receive adequate nutrition and medical care, but neonates weighing less than 1,500 grams, the very low-birth-weight and extremely low-birth-weight babies, are likely to have enduring problems in multiple respects (Davis, 2003; Saigal et al., 2003; Taylor et al., 2000). With an unusually healthy and enriched environment, some of the negative consequences of low birth weight can be avoided, even for very low-birth-weight babies (Doyle et al., 2004; Martin et al., 2008). However, in developed countries as well as in developing countries, low-birth-weight babies are most likely to be born to parents who have the fewest resources (UNICEF, 2004; WHO, 2011).

WHAT HAVE YOU LEARNED?

1. Why do neonates have fontanels?
2. What does APGAR stand for, and what constitutes a "good" or "excellent" score on the scale?
3. How has the NBAS been used to inform parents and in neonatal research?
4. What distinguishes a small-for-date infant from a preterm infant?
5. What physical systems of preterm babies are inadequately developed at birth? What are some health implications of this?
6. What are the long-term consequences for low birth weight?

◇ PHYSICAL FUNCTIONING OF THE NEONATE

Physical functioning in the first few weeks of life is different in some important ways when compared to the rest of life. Neonates sleep more and have a wider range of reflexes than the rest of us do. Their senses are mostly well developed at birth, although hearing and especially sight take some weeks to mature.

Neonatal Sleeping Patterns

LEARNING OBJECTIVE 9

Describe neonates' patterns of waking and sleeping, including how and why these patterns differ across cultures.

Even in the womb there are cycles of waking and sleeping, beginning at about 28 weeks gestation. Once born, most neonates spend more time asleep than awake. The average for neonates is 16 to 17 hours of sleep a day, although there is great variation, from about 10 hours to about 21 (Peirano et al., 2003).

Neonates not only sleep much of the time, the pattern and quality of their sleep is different than it will be later in infancy and beyond. Rather than sleeping 16–17 hours straight, they sleep for a few hours, wake up for awhile, sleep a few more hours, and wake up again. Their sleep–wake patterns are governed by when they get hungry, not whether it is light or dark outside (Davis et al., 2004). Of course, neonates' sleep–wake patterns do not fit very well with how most adults prefer to sleep, so parents are often sleep-deprived in the early weeks of their children's lives (Burnham et al., 2002). By about 4 months of age most infants have begun to sleep for longer periods, usually about 6 hours in a row at night, and their total sleep has declined to about 14 hours a day.

rapid eye movement (REM) sleep
phase of the sleep cycle in which a person's eyes move back and forth rapidly under the eyelids; persons in REM sleep experience other physiological changes as well

Another way that neonates' sleep is distinctive is that they spend an especially high proportion of their sleep in **rapid eye movement (REM) sleep**, so called because during this kind of sleep a person's eyes move back and forth rapidly under the eyelids. A person in REM sleep experiences other physiological changes as well, such as irregular heart rate and breathing and (in males) an erection. Adults spend about 20% of their sleep time in REM sleep, but neonates are in REM sleep about one-half the time they are sleeping (Burnham et al., 2002). Furthermore, adults do not enter REM until about an hour after falling asleep, but neonates enter it almost immediately. By about

3 months of age, time spent in REM sleep has fallen to 40%, and infants no longer begin their sleep cycle with it.

In adults, REM sleep is the time when dreams take place. Are neonates dreaming during their extensive REM sleep periods? It is difficult to say, of course—they're not telling—but researchers in this area have generally concluded that the answer is no. Neonate's brain-wave patterns during REM sleep are different from the patterns of adults. For adults, REM brain waves look similar to waking brain waves, but for infants the REM brain waves are different than during either waking or non-REM sleep (Arditi-Babchuck et al., 2009). Researchers believe that for neonates, REM sleep stimulates brain development (McNamara & Sullivan, 2000). This seems to be supported by research showing that the percentage of REM sleep is even greater in fetuses than in neonates, and greater in preterm than in full-term neonates (Arditi-Babchuck et al., 2009; de Weerd & van den Bossche, 2003).

In addition to neonates' distinctive sleep patterns, they have a variety of other states of arousal that change frequently. When they are not sleeping, they may be alert but they may also be drowsy, dazed, fussing, or in a sleep–wake transition.

So far this description of neonates' sleep–wake patterns has been based on research in Western countries, but infant care is an area for which there is wide cultural variation that may influence sleep–wake patterns. In many traditional cultures, neonates and young infants are in physical contact with their mothers almost constantly, and this has important effects on the babies' states of arousal and sleep–wake patterns. For example, among the Kipsigis of Kenya, mothers strap their babies to their backs in the early months of life as they go about their daily work and social activities (Anders & Taylor, 1994; Super & Harkness, 2009). Swaddled cozily on Mom's back, the babies spend more time napping and dozing during the day than a baby in a developed country would. At night, Kipsigis babies are not placed in a separate room but sleep right alongside their mothers, so they are able to feed whenever they wish. Consequently, for the first year of life they rarely sleep more than 3 hours straight, day or night. In contrast, by 8 months of age American babies typically sleep about 8 hours at night without waking.

Most neonates sleep 16–17 hours a day.
(Rohit Seth/Shutterstock)

Neonatal Reflexes

Describe the neonatal reflexes, including those that have a functional purpose and those that do not.

LEARNING OBJECTIVE 10

Looking at a newborn baby, you might think that it will be many months before it can do much other than just lie there. Actually, though, neonates have a remarkable range of **reflexes**, which are automatic responses to certain kinds of stimulation. A total of 27 reflexes are present at birth or shortly after (Futagi et al., 2009). Some examples are shown in Table 2. 👁

Some reflexes have clear survival value. Sucking and swallowing reflexes allow the neonate to obtain nourishment from the mother's breast. The **rooting reflex** helps neonates find the breast, because it causes them to turn their heads and open their mouths when touched on the cheek or the side of the mouth. The grasping reflex helps neonates hang on when something is placed in their palms. The **Moro reflex** serves a similar function, causing neonates to arch their backs, fling out their arms, and then bring their arms quickly together in an embrace, in response to a sensation of falling backward or a loud sound. Reflexes for coughing, gagging, sneezing, blinking, and shivering regulate neonates' sensory systems and help them avoid things in the environment that may be unhealthy. 👁

Some reflexes are precursors of voluntary movements that will develop later. The stepping reflex can be observed

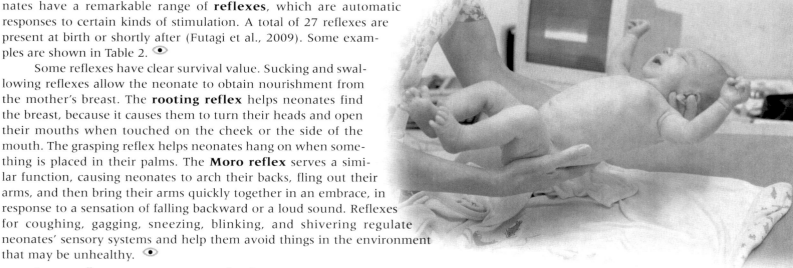

The Moro reflex is present at birth, but disappears by 3 months of age.
(Picture Partners/Alamy)

reflex
automatic response to certain kinds of stimulation

▶ Watch the Video
Reflexes at www.pearson custom.com/mi/msu_mylabs.com

▶ Watch the Video
Development of the Grasp Reflex at www.pearson custom.com/mi/msu_mylabs.com

rooting reflex
reflex that causes the neonate to turn its head and open its mouth when it is touched on the cheek or the side of the mouth; helps the neonate find the breast

Moro reflex
reflex in response to a sensation of falling backward or to a loud sound, in which the neonate arches its back, flings out its arms, and then brings its arms quickly together in an embrace

about a month after birth, by holding an infant under the arms at a height that allows its feet to just touch the floor. Stepping disappears after about two months, but will reappear as voluntary movement later in the first year when the infant starts walking. The swimming reflex is one of the most surprising and remarkable. At about 1 month old, an infant placed face down in water will automatically hold its breath and begin making coordinated swimming movements. After 4 months this reflex has disappeared, and will become voluntary swimming movements only many years later.

Other reflexes appear to have no apparent purpose, other than their obvious entertainment value. With the *Babkin reflex*, a neonate whose palms are firmly stroked will open its mouth, close its eyes, and tilt its head forward. With the *Babinski reflex*, when the sole of the neonate's foot is stroked, it will respond by twisting its foot inward as it fans out its toes (Singerman & Lee, 2008).

TABLE 2 Neonatal Reflexes

REFLEX	STIMULATION	RESPONSE	DISAPPEARS BY . . .
Stepping	Hold baby under arms with feet touching floor	Makes stepping motions	2 months
Moro	Dip downward suddenly, or loud sound	Arch back, extend arms and legs outward, bring arms together swiftly	3 months
Babkin	Press and stroke both palms	Mouth opens, eyes close, head tilts forward	3 months
Sucking	Object or substance in mouth	Sucking	4 months
Rooting	Touch on cheek or mouth	Turn toward touch	4 months
Grasping	Object placed in palm	Hold tightly	4 months
Swimming	Baby is immersed in water	Holds breath, swims with arms and legs	4 months
Tonic neck	Baby laid on back	Head turns to side, legs and arms take "fencing position" with arms and legs extended on side head is turned, flexed on the other side	5 months
Babinski	Stroke sole of foot	Foot twists in, toes fan out	8 months

Most neonatal reflexes fade away after a few months, as they are replaced by voluntary behavior. However, in the early weeks of life, reflexes serve as important indicators of normal development and healthy functioning (Schott & Rossor, 2003). Both the Apgar and the NBAS include items on reflex responses as an indirect measure of the neonate's neurological development.

Neonatal Senses

LEARNING OBJECTIVE 11   **Describe the neonate's sensory abilities with respect to touch, taste and smell, hearing, and sight.**

The neonate's senses vary widely in how well developed they are at birth. Touch and taste are well developed, even in the womb, but sight does not mature until several months after birth. Let's look at each of the neonate's senses, from the most to the least developed.

Touch

Touch is the earliest sense to develop. Even as early as 2 months gestation, the rooting reflex is present. By 7 months gestation, 2 months before a full-term birth, all the fetus's body parts respond to touch (Tyano et al., 2010). Most neonatal reflexes involve responses to touch.

Given that touch develops so early and is so advanced at birth, it is surprising that until recent decades, most physicians believed that neonates could not experience pain (Noia et al., 2008). In fact, surgery on neonates was usually performed without anesthetics. Physicians believed that even if neonates felt pain, they felt it only briefly, and they believed that the pain was less important than the danger of giving anesthetic medication to such a young child. This belief may have developed because neonates who experience pain (for example, boys who are circumcised) often either recover quickly and behave normally shortly afterward, or fall into a deep sleep immediately afterward, as a protective mechanism. Also, in response to some types of pain, such a being pricked on the heel, neonates take longer to respond (by several seconds) than they will a few months later (Tyano et al., 2010).

In recent years, research has established clearly that neonates feel pain. Their physiological reactions to pain are much like the reactions of people at other ages: their heart rates and blood pressure increase, their palms sweat, their muscles tense, and their pupils dilate (Warnock & Sandrin, 2004; Williams et al., 2009). They even have a specific kind of high-pitched, intense cry that indicates pain (Simons et al., 2003). Evidence also indicates that neonates who experience intense pain release stress hormones that interfere with sleep and feeding and heighten their sensitivity to later pain (Mitchell & Boss, 2002). For these reasons, physicians' organizations now recommend pain relief for neonates undergoing painful medical procedures (Noia et al., 2008). To minimize the dangers of anesthetics, nonmedical methods such as drinking sugar water can be used, or local rather than general anesthesia (Holsti & Grunau, 2010).

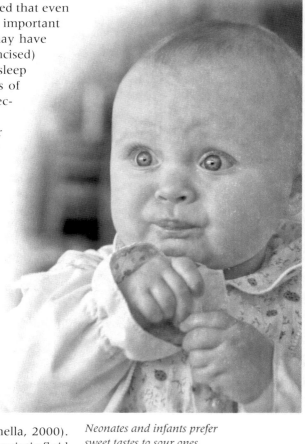

Neonates and infants prefer sweet tastes to sour ones.
(Kathleen Nelson/Alamy)

Taste and Smell

Like touch, taste is well developed even in the womb. The amniotic fluid that the fetus floats in has the flavor of whatever the mother has recently eaten, and neonates show a preference for the smells that were distinctive in the mother's diet in the days before birth (Schaal et al., 2000). In one study, when women drank carrot juice during pregnancy, their neonates were more likely to prefer the smell of carrots (Menella, 2000). Neonates exposed to the smell of their mother's amniotic fluid and another woman's amniotic fluid orient their attention to their mother's fluid (Marlier et al., 1998). In fact, neonates find the smell of their mother's amniotic fluid soothing, and cry less when it is present (Varendi et al., 1998).

In addition to showing an early preference for whatever is familiar from the womb, neonates have a variety of innate responses to tastes and smells. Like most children and adults, neonates prefer sweet tastes and smells over bitter or sour ones (Booth et al., 2010). If they smell or taste something bitter or sour, their noses crinkle up, their foreheads wrinkle, and their mouths show a displeased expression (Bartoshuk & Beauchamp, 1994).

Preference for sweet tastes is present before birth. When an artificial sweetener is added to amniotic fluid, fetuses' swallowing becomes more frequent (Booth et al., 2010). After birth, preference for sweet tastes is demonstrated with a facial expression that looks like pleasure, and with a desire to consume more. As just noted, tasting something sweet can have a calming effect on neonates who are in pain. Preference for sweet tastes may be adaptive, because breast milk is slightly sweet (Porges et al., 1993). Enjoying the sweet taste of breast milk may make neonates more likely to nurse successfully.

In addition to their innate preferences, neonates quickly begin to discriminate smells after birth. At 2 days after birth, breast-feeding neonates show no difference in response between their mother's breast smell and the breast smell of another lactating mother, but by 4 days they orient more toward their mother's smell (Porter & Reiser, 2005).

Hearing

Hearing is another sense that is quite well developed before birth. Fetuses become familiar with their mother's voice and other sounds. After birth, they recognize distinctive sounds they heard in the womb.

Neonates have an innate sensitivity to human speech that is apparent from birth (Vouloumanos & Werker, 2004). Studies on this topic typically assess neonates' preferences by how vigorously they suck on a plastic nipple; the more frequently they suck, the stronger their

Applying Your Knowledge . . . as a Researcher

Why is it adaptive for neonates to be able to distinguish sounds such as "*ba*" and "*ga*" and stress patterns such as ma-*ma* and *ma*-ma?

preference for or attention to the sound. Using this method, studies have found that neonates prefer their mother's voice to other women's voices, and their mother's language to foreign languages (Vouloumanos et al., 2010). However, they show no preference for their father's voice over other male voices (Kisilevsky et al., 2003). This may be partly because they heard his voice less while in the womb, and partly because neonates generally prefer high-pitched voices over low-pitched voices.

Neonates can distinguish small changes in speech sounds. In one study, neonates were given a special nipple that would produce a sound of a person saying "ba" every time they sucked on it (Aldridge et al., 2001). They sucked with enthusiasm for a minute so, then their sucking pace slowed as they got used to the sound and perhaps bored with it. But when the sound changed to "ga," their sucking pace picked up, showing that they recognized the subtle change in the sound and responded to the novelty of it. Changes in neonate's sucking patterns show they also recognize the difference between two-syllable and three-syllable words, and between changes in emphasis such as when ma-*ma* changes to *ma*-ma (Sansavini et al., 1997).

In addition to their language sensitivity, neonates show a very early sensitivity to music (Levitin, 2007). At only a few days old, they respond when a series of musical notes changes from ascending to descending order (Trehub, 2001). After a few months, infants respond to a change in one note of a six-note melody, and to changes in musical keys (Trehub et al., 1985). One study even found that neonates preferred classical music over rock music (Spence & DeCasper, 1987).

Like language awareness, musical awareness begins prenatally. Neonates prefer songs their mother's sang to them during pregnancy to songs their mother sang to them for the first time after birth (Kisilevsky et al., 2003). Neonate's musical responses may simply reflect their familiarity with sounds they heard before birth, but it could also indicate an innate human responsiveness to music (Levitin, 2007). Music is frequently a part of human cultural rituals, and innate responsiveness to music may have served to enhance cohesiveness within human cultural groups.

Although neonates hear quite well in many respects, there are also some limitations to their hearing abilities that will improve over the first 2 years of life (Tharpe & Ashmead, 2001). One reason for these limitations is that it takes awhile after birth for the amniotic fluid to drain out of their ears. Another reason is that their hearing system is not physiologically mature until they are about two years old.

Neonates are unable to hear some very soft sounds that adults can hear (Watkin, 2011). Overall, their hearing is better for high-pitched sounds than for midrange or low-pitched sounds (Aslin et al., 1998; Werner & Marean, 1996). They also have difficulty with **sound localization**, that is, with telling where a sound is coming from (Litovsky & Ashmead, 1997). In fact, their abilities for sound localization actually become worse for the first 2 months of life, but then improve rapidly and reach adult levels by 1 year old (Watkin, 2011).

Sight

Sight is the least developed of the neonate's senses (Atkinson, 2000; Dobson, 2000). Several key structures of the eye are still immature at birth, specifically, (1) the muscles of the *lens*, which adjust the eyes' focus depending on the distance from the object; (2) the cells of the *retina*, the membrane in the back of the eye that collects visual information and converts it into a form that can be sent to the brain; (3) *cones*, which identify colors and (4) the *optic nerve*, which transmits visual information from the retina to the brain.

At birth, neonates' vision is estimated to range from 20/200 to 20/600, which means that the clarity and accuracy of their perception of an object 20 feet away is comparable to a person with normal 20/20 vision looking at the same object from 200 to 600 feet away (Cavallini et al., 2002). Their visual acuity is best at a distance of 8–14 inches. Vision improves steadily as their eyes mature, and reaches 20/20 some time in the second half of the first year. Their capacity for *binocular vision,* combining information from both eyes for perceiving depth and motion, is also limited at birth but matures quickly, by about 3–4 months old (Atkinson, 2000). Color vision matures at about the same pace. Neonates can distinguish between red and white but not between

---

Applying Your Knowledge . . . as a Parent

Given what you have learned here about neonate's sight preferences, how would you design a mobile for your newborn's room?

sound localization
perceptual ability for telling where a sound is coming from

white and other colors, probably because the cones are immature (Kellman & Arterberry, 2006). By 4 months old, infants are similar to adults in their perception of colors (Alexander & Hines, 2002; Dobson, 2000).

Just as with taste and hearing, neonates show innate visual preferences (Columbo & Mitchell, 2009). ("Preference" is measured by how long they look at one visual stimulus compared to another. The longer they look, the more they are presumed to prefer the stimulus.) Even shortly after birth they prefer patterns to random designs, curved over straight lines, three-dimensional rather than two-dimensional objects, and colored over gray patterns. Above all, they prefer human faces over any other pattern (Pascalis & Kelly, 2009). This indicates that they are born with cells that are specialized to detect and prefer certain kinds of visual patterns (Csibra et al., 2000).

WHAT HAVE YOU LEARNED?

1. How are neonates' sleep patterns distinct from those of adults?
2. What function does the rooting reflex serve?
3. When do neonatal reflexes disappear?
4. Which senses are most developed at birth? Which least?
5. What does research indicate concerning neonates' experience of pain?
6. Which visual pattern do neonates prefer the most?

PART 2 VIDEO GUIDE

PREMATURE BIRTHS AND THE NICU (LENGTH: 5:11)

This video contains an overview of information about premature births and the Neonatal Intensive Care Unit.

1. What are some of the advances in care that technology has provided to the NICU?
2. In this video, the speaker discusses several reasons why babies might end up in the NICU. List some of the causes that were mentioned and highlight those that can be controlled by the mother as well as those that cannot be controlled by the mother.
3. What are some of the complications (both long and short term) that premature babies might encounter?

PART 3 CARING FOR THE NEONATE

LEARNING OBJECTIVES

12. Describe the cultural customs surrounding breast feeding across cultures and history.
13. Identify the advantages of breast feeding and where those advantages are largest.
14. Describe neonates' types of crying and how crying patterns and soothing methods vary across cultures.
15. Describe the extent to which human mothers "bond" with their neonates and the extent to which this claim has been exaggerated.
16. Describe the reasons for postpartum depression and its consequences for children.

◇ NUTRITION: IS BREAST BEST?

One of the most heavily researched topics regarding neonates is the question of how they should be fed. Specifically, attention has focused on whether breast feeding should be recommended for all children, and if so, for how long. Here we examine the evolutionary and historical basis of breast feeding, the evidence for its benefits, and the efforts to promote breast feeding in developing countries.

Evolutionary and Historical Perspectives on Breast Feeding

LEARNING OBJECTIVE 12 | Describe the cultural customs surrounding breast feeding across cultures and history

mammary glands
in females, the glands that produce milk to nourish babies

let-down reflex
in females, a reflex that causes milk to be released to the tip of the nipples in response to the sound of her infant's cry, seeing its open mouth, or even thinking about breast feeding

wet nursing
cultural practice, common in human history, of hiring a lactating woman other than the mother to feed the infant

Both mother and baby are biologically prepared for breast feeding. In the mother, the preparation begins well before birth. Early in pregnancy the **mammary glands** in her breasts expand greatly in size as milk-producing cells multiply and mature. By 4 months gestation the breasts are ready to produce milk. At birth, the mother's **let-down reflex** in her breasts causes milk to be released to the tip of her nipples whenever she hears the sound of her infant's cry, sees its open mouth, or even thinks about breast feeding (Walshaw, 2010).

Infants are ready for breast feeding as soon as they are born. The sucking and rooting reflexes are at their strongest 30 minutes after birth (Bryder, 2009). As noted earlier in this module, within a few days neonates recognize their mother's smell and the sound of her voice, which helps orient them for feeding.

Our closest primate relatives, chimpanzees, breast-feed for about 4 years. In the human past, archeological and historical evidence indicate that in most cultures infants were fed breast milk as their primary or sole food for 2-3 years, followed by 2–3 more years of occasional nursing. There are also indications that breast feeding in the human past took place at frequent intervals. Among the !Kung San of Central Africa, a modern hunter-gatherer culture, infants feed about every 13 minutes, on average, during their first year of life (Sellen, 2001). In traditional, nonindustrial cultures it is typical for infants to be bound to or close to their mothers almost constantly, day and night, allowing for frequent feeding. This has led anthropologists to conclude that this was probably the pattern for 99% of human history (Small, 1998).

Such frequent feeding is, of course, very demanding on the mother, and many cultures have developed ways of easing this responsibility. One common way has been substituting mothers' milk with milk from other species, especially cows or goats, two species that are domesticated in many cultures and so readily available. Another way is **wet nursing**, which means hiring a lactating woman other than the mother to feed the infant. Wet nursing is a widespread custom as old as recorded human history. European records indicate that by the 1700s in some countries a majority of women employed a wet nurse to breast-feed their babies. (Fildes, 1995)

In the late 1800s, manufactured substitutes such as condensed milk and evaporated milk began to be developed and marketed in the West by large corporations such as Borden and Nestlé (Bryder, 2009). The corporations claimed that these milk substitutes were not only more convenient than breast milk but also cleaner and safer. Doctors were persuaded—thanks in part to generous payments from the corporations—and they in turn persuaded new mothers to use the milk substitutes. By the 1940s only 20–30 percent of babies in the United States were breast-fed, and the percentage stayed in this range until the 1970s (Small, 1998). By then, scientific evidence was accumulating that breast milk was far better than any substitute, and health organizations such as UNICEF and the World Health Organization (WHO) began to wage worldwide campaigns to promote breast feeding.

In recent years, rates of breast feeding have risen to over 70% in the United States and Canada due to government-sponsored campaigns touting the health benefits, and breast feeding has become nearly universal in northern Europe (Greve, 2003; Ryan et al., 2006). In developed countries, the higher the mother's age, educational level, and socioeconomic status, the more likely she is to breast-feed her infant (Schulze & Carlisle, 2010). Within the United States, rates of breast feeding are higher among Latinos (80%) and Whites (79%) than among African Americans (65%), but rates have risen across all ethnic groups in recent years (CDC, 2008). It should be noted that these rates are for *any duration* of breast feeding; across ethnic groups, less than half the neonates who breast-feed initially are still breast-feeding at age 6 months. Worldwide only about half of all infants are breast-fed even for a short time (UNICEF, 2011).

Wet nursing has a long history in Europe. Here, a wet nurse and baby in France in 1895.
(Henri Roger/Roger-Viollet/The Image Works)

Benefits of Breast Feeding

Identify the advantages of breast feeding and where those advantages are largest.   **LEARNING OBJECTIVE 13**

What benefits of breast feeding have been demonstrated by scientific research in recent decades? The list is a long one, and includes:

Disease protection. Breast milk contains antibodies and other substances that strengthen the baby's immune system, and breast feeding has been found to reduce the risk of a wide range of illnesses and diseases, such as diphtheria, pneumonia, ear infections, asthma, and diarrhea, among many others (American Academy of Pediatrics [AAP] Section on Breastfeeding, 2005; Godfrey et al., 2009).

Cognitive development. Breast-fed infants tend to score higher than bottle-fed infants on measures of cognitive functioning, perhaps because the nutrients in breast milk promote early brain development (Kramer et al., 2008). This finding holds up even after controlling for many other factors such as parents' intelligence and education (Feldman & Eidelman, 2003). The benefits are mainly for infants who are preterm or low birth weight and consequently are at risk for cognitive difficulties (Ip et al., 2007; Schulze & Carlisle, 2010).

Reduced obesity. Breast feeding for at least 6 months reduces the likelihood of obesity in childhood (AAP Section on Breastfeeding, 2005; Shields et al., 2010). This is especially important in developed countries, where rates of obesity have risen dramatically in recent decades.

Better health in childhood and adulthood. In addition to protection from illnesses and disease early in life, breast feeding promotes long-term health in a variety of ways, such as promoting bone density, enhancing vision, and improving cardiovascular functioning (Gibson et al., 2000; Owen et al., 2002).

Mothers also benefit from breast feeding (Godfrey & Meyers, 2009). In the days following birth, breast feeding triggers the release of the hormone oxytocin, which reduces bleeding in the uterus and causes the uterus to return to its original size. Nursing the neonate also helps mothers

The benefits of breast feeding are especially important in developing countries, where risks to early development are higher. Here, a mother nurses her baby in the Southeast Asian country of Laos.

(Alain Evrard/PhotoLibrary)

◉ Watch the Video
Breastfeeding at www.
pearsoncustom.com/mi/
msu_mylabs

Applying Your Knowledge

Given that the benefits of breast feeding in developed countries are genuine but small, should public policies encourage or discourage more women to breast-feed for longer? Consider the arguments that breast feeding makes returning to the workplace difficult for women and makes it hard for mothers and fathers to share the infant care equally.

---

return to their pre-pregnancy weight, because it burns 500–1000 calories per day. Nursing has long-term effects as well on mothers' health, strengthening their bones, and reducing their risk of ovarian and breast cancer even many years later (Ip et al., 2007). Furthermore, breast feeding acts as a natural form of birth control because it suppresses ovulation, making it less likely that a woman will conceive another child quickly once she resumes sexual contact with her husband (Bellamy, 2005). However, breast feeding has no influence on the emotional development of the infant or the social relationship between infant and mother (Schulze & Carlisle, 2010).

How long should mothers breast-feed their infants? The World Health Organization (WHO) recommends breast feeding for 2 years, with solid foods introduced to supplement breast milk at 6 months of age. As just noted, few women today breast-feed for the recommended time. However, even breast-feeding for only a few days after birth provides important benefits for infants. The first milk the mother produces is **colostrum**, a thick, yellowish liquid that is extremely rich in protein and antibodies that strengthen the neonate's immune system (Napier & Meister, 2000). Colostrum is especially important for neonates to receive, but it lasts only a few days. Perhaps because of its odd appearance, colostrum is erroneously believed in many cultures to be bad for babies. For example, in India many mothers avoid giving colostrum to their babies, substituting it with a mix of butter and honey they believe is healthier (Small, 1998).

Even in developed countries, where good health care is widely available, breast feeding provides advantages for infants and mothers. However, in developed countries the advantages of breast feeding are relatively small, as we will see in the **Research Focus: How Much Does Breast Feeding Matter?** feature on page 359. In contrast, breast feeding is crucial in developing countries, where risks of many diseases are higher and infants may not receive the vaccinations that are routine in developed countries. In developed countries, breast feeding helps infants avoid illnesses such as gastrointestinal infections, but in developing countries breast feeding can be literally a matter of life and death. UNICEF estimates that 1.5 million babies die each year in developing countries because they are bottle-fed rather than breast-fed (UNICEF, 2011). This is not only due to losing the advantages of breast feeding but to making infant formula with unsafe water, as we will soon see in more detail. ◉

If breast feeding is so important to infants' health, why don't more mothers nurse in the early months of their children's lives? Some women have difficulty with breast feeding, either because their infant cannot latch on properly (often a problem with low-birth-weight babies) or because they produce insufficient breast milk (Bryder, 2009). However, there are a number of practical obstacles as well. In developed countries, many mothers are employed outside the home, which makes breast feeding more difficult (but not impossible; some use a breast pump to make milk available in their absence). Breast feeding also makes it more difficult for fathers to take part in feeding (except via the pumped breast milk) and more challenging for fathers and mothers to share the care of the baby more or less equally, as many couples in developed countries would prefer (Gennesoni & Tallandini, 2009; Wolf, 2007). One of my most cherished memories of early fatherhood is of the nights in their first few months of life when I would get up to do the 3 A.M. feeding and it would be just me and the twins, the whole world silent and sleeping around us. When fathers are able to feed the neonate it also helps mothers recover from the physical strain of giving birth (Simkin, 2007).

In developing countries, sometimes mothers have infectious diseases such as HIV/AIDS, tuberculosis, or West Nile virus that could be transmitted through breast milk, so they are advised not to breast-feed (Centers for Disease Control & Prevention, 2002). However, only a small percentage of women have such diseases. A much larger contributor to low rates of breast feeding is that many mothers in developing countries have been deceived, by the marketing campaigns of corporations selling infant formula, into believing the formula is actually better for infants than breast milk is.

This is false. Infant formula today is better than the condensed or evaporated milk of a century ago, because it is fortified with many of the components that make breast milk healthy, but even the best infant formula today is not as good for infants as breast milk is. Worse yet, infant formula is typically mixed with water, and in many developing countries the available water is not purified and may contain disease. Consequently, not only do infants fed with formula miss out on the health benefits of breast milk, but they are imperiled by the diseases that may be contained in the water mixed with the powdered formula.

In response to this situation, the WHO and UNICEF initiated a worldwide effort beginning in the early 1990s to promote breast feeding (UNICEF, 2011; WHO, 2000). These organizations have attempted to educate women about the advantages of breast feeding for them and their infants. They have also worked with hospitals to implement programs to get breast feeding off to a good start in the first days of the neonate's life. In this "Baby-Friendly Hospital Initiative," hospital personnel educate mothers about breast feeding prior to the birth, help them with the first feeding shortly after birth, show them how to maintain lactation (milk flow), and organize them into breast-feeding support groups (Merewood et al., 2005; Merten et al., 2005).

The WHO/UNICEF initiative has been successful, with rates of breast feeding increasing wherever it has been implemented (UNICEF, 2011). However, because most births in developing countries today take place in homes, most mothers are unlikely to come into contact with the Baby-Friendly Hospital Initiative. With only half of infants worldwide breast-fed for even a short time, clearly there remains much room for improvement.

colostrum
thick, yellowish, milky liquid produced by mammalian mothers during the first days following birth, extremely rich in protein and antibodies that strengthen the baby's immune system

meta-analysis
statistical technique that combines the results from many studies into one summary statistic to evaluate the overall outcome of research in an area

confounded
problem in statistical analyses when variables are entwined in people's lives in a way that is not easy to disentangle

RESEARCH FOCUS

HOW MUCH DOES BREAST FEEDING MATTER?

Numerous studies have found benefits of breast feeding for children and mothers alike across a wide range of areas. In developing countries, breast feeding is crucial to infant health, because these populations receive little in the way of vaccines and other medical care to protect them from widespread diseases. But what about in developed countries? How much difference does breast feeding make to the long-term development of children?

There are so many studies of breast feeding in developed countries that it is sometimes difficult to make sense of them all and come to a general conclusion about their results and implications. One way of boiling down a large number of studies into a comprehensible summary is a statistical method called a **meta-analysis**, which combines the results from many studies to estimate the overall conclusion to be drawn from the research.

In the most comprehensive meta-analysis of breast-feeding studies yet conducted, Stanley Ip and colleagues (2007) screened

(Pavel Filatov/Alamy)

over 9,000 studies and selected nearly 500 that met their criteria for valid research methods and design. The conclusions of their meta-analysis generally support the conclusions stated in this module, that breast feeding is associated with a wide variety of benefits for infants and mothers.

However, the authors of the meta-analysis also warned that readers "should not infer causality based on these findings" (Ip et al., 2007, p. v). Why not? Because most studies of breast-feeding benefits find a correlation between breast feeding and benefits, correlation does not mean causation. One reason to be skeptical of causation claims in studies of breast feeding is that breast-feeding status is based on *self-selection*, meaning that women choose to breast-feed (or not), and those who choose to breast-feed tend to be different in many ways than women who do not. Most notably, the authors observed, women who breast-feed generally have more education and higher IQs. Consequently, the differences between the two groups that are attributed to breast-feeding may actually be due to their differences in education and IQ.

To get around this problem, studies sometimes *control* for education when comparing breast-feeding and non-breast-feeding groups. This means that the educational differences between the two groups are taken into account statistically. Although controlling for education is helpful in assessing more accurately the consequences of breast feeding, it does not entirely resolve the issue. The problem is that breast feeding and education are **confounded**, which means that they are entwined in people's lives in a way that is

RESEARCH FOCUS CONTINUED

not easy to disentangle through statistical strategies. Education tends to be connected to a lot of other aspects of mothers' lives, such as attention to prenatal care, access to health care resources, likelihood of having a stable partner, likelihood of smoking, and household income, among others. Controlling for education in statistical analyses does not make all those other differences disappear.

So what can be done to find out accurately how much difference breast feeding makes in babies' and mothers' outcomes? Ethical standards probably would prohibit assigning new mothers into breast-feeding and non-breast-feeding groups, given what appear to be the benefits of breast feeding. However, one study that approximated this design was conducted by Canadian researcher Michael Kramer and his colleagues in Belarus in Eastern Europe. The researchers gained the cooperation of 31 maternity hospitals and clinics and the study involved over 17,000 women who—note carefully—stated their intention to breast-feed. Kramer and colleagues randomly assigned the women into two groups, with one group receiving an intervention designed to promote and support breast feeding by providing women with advice, information, and instruction, whereas the women in the control group received no intervention.

The women and their babies were then followed up by Kramer and colleagues for the next 7 years (so far). Over the course of the first year, women in the intervention group were more likely to exclusively breast-feed when their babies were 3 months old (46% to 11%) and more likely to be breast-feeding at any level at 12 months (19% to 11%), although by then breast-feeding rates were low in both groups (Kramer et al., 2001). Babies in the intervention group were less likely to have gastrointestinal infections during their first year (Kramer et al., 2001). However, at age 6, there were no differences between children in the two groups in asthma or allergy problems (Kramer et al., 2007), nor in the likelihood of obesity (Kramer et al., 2009). Perhaps the most striking finding was that, at age 6, the children in the intervention group were significantly higher in IQ, by 6 points (Kramer et al., 2008). This is especially notable because most studies on the cognitive effects of breast feeding find that no effects remain after controlling for education and other confounding variables, unless the children were born preterm or low birth weight (Schulze & Carlisle, 2010). The result found by Kramer and colleagues seems to indicate a small but clear positive effect of breast feeding on children's cognitive development.

However, this study, impressive as it is, is hardly the last word on this complex topic. Remember, all the mothers in the study had indicated their intention to breast-feed; all were self-selected, in other words. So, the results do not apply to mothers who do not intend to breast-feed, or to their children. Also, how important is it that the study was conducted in Belarus? Belarus is not easily classified as either a developed country or a developing country. It is part of Europe, but it is a relatively poor European country (United Nations Development Programme [UNDP, 2011]), and its median levels of income, education, and health care access are nowhere near that of Western European countries. Would the same benefits from a breast-feeding intervention be found in a more developed country than Belarus? Like most studies, the research by Kramer and colleagues opens up new questions to be investigated.

Thinking Culturally

Given that marketing infant formula in developing countries persuades many women to bottle-feed rather than breast-feed, in the mistaken belief that drinking formula will be better for their babies, should developing countries make it illegal to sell infant formula?

WHAT HAVE YOU LEARNED?

1. What cultural pattern of breast feeding do anthropologists believe has prevailed for most of human history?
2. In what parts of the world is breast feeding most and least prevalent today?
3. Where in the world are the advantages of breast feeding most important, and why?
4. What is colostrum and what role does it have in breast feeding?
5. Is infant formula an adequate substitute for breast milk? Why or why not? Where and where not?

◇ SOCIAL AND EMOTIONAL ASPECTS OF NEONATAL CARE

There are few events that change the life of an adult more than having a baby! My wife and I had our twins relatively late—I was 42 and she was 33—and by then we had been together as a couple for over ten years. We were used to late and long dinners, and to lazy weekends waking up late, reading for hours, and taking long walks. All that went out the window when the twins were born. In the early weeks it seemed like all we did all day long—and half the night—was feed them, change them, dress them, walk them, and adore them.

Neonates not only need protection and nutrition, they need social and emotional care as well. Here we look at neonates' crying patterns and the soothing methods that cultures have developed, and at the first social contacts between neonates and others, sometimes called "bonding." In closing the module we examine the postpartum depression sometimes experienced by new mothers.

Crying and Soothing

Describe neonates' types of crying and how crying patterns and soothing methods vary across cultures.

Because human newborns are so immature and dependent in the early months of life, they need some way of signaling their needs to those who care for them, and their most frequent and effective signal is crying. Adults tend to find the crying of an infant hard to bear, so they have developed many creative ways of soothing them.

Crying

Three distinct kinds of crying signals have been identified (Wood & Gustafson, 2001):

Fussing: This is a kind of warm-up cry, when babies are mildly distressed. If no response comes soon, it develops into full-blown crying. It is fairly soft in volume, an unsteady whimper punctuated by pauses and long intakes of breath.

Anger cry: A cry that expels a large volume of air through the vocal cords.

Pain cry: Sudden onset, with no fussing to herald it. Baby takes a large intake of breath and holds it, then lets loose.

Most parents can tell the difference between an anger cry and a pain cry by the time the infant is about a month old (Zeskind et al., 1992). However, there are lots of other reasons an infant may cry, without a distinctive cry to go with them: hungry, lonely, wet or soiled diaper, tired, uncomfortable, too warm, too cold, or any other kind of frustration. Crying that falls into this general category is usually referred to as a *basic cry* or *frustration cry* (Wood & Gustafson, 2001).

Across a variety of cultures with different infant-care practices, crying frequency follows what is known as the "crying curve" (Barr, 2009): stable for the first 3 weeks of life, rising steadily and reaching a peak by the end of the second month, then declining. **Figure 2** shows the pattern for American infants. Sometimes crying has a clear source, but there is a lot of crying in the early months for no particular reason. This is important for parents to remember, because distress in neonates often triggers distress in those around them (Out et al., 2010). **Table 3** presents a way to remember the normal features of crying in the first 3 months of life.

Soothing and Responding to Cries

Although daily crying duration is consistent across cultures, there is wide variation in the *duration* and *intensity* of crying in infancy. Crying episodes are longer and more intense in cultures where infants are left on their own a lot and have relatively little time when they are being carried around. Four out of 5 American infants have daily crying episodes in the early months of life of at least 15 minutes that do not have any apparent cause (Eisenberg et al., 2011). In contrast, infants in cultures where babies are held or carried around much of the day rarely have prolonged episodes of crying. For example, in a study comparing infants in South Korea and the United States, the

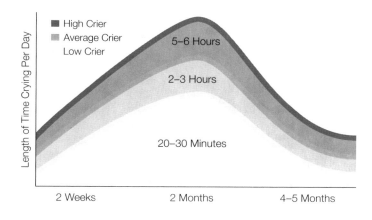

FIGURE 2 Daily Crying Duration in the Early Months

In their first months of life, infants often cry for no apparent reason.

Source: Barr, 2009.

Thinking Culturally

How does the framework of individualism and collectivism help to explain the Korean practice of carrying their infants much of the time and responding immediately to their cries and the American practice of leaving infants on their own much of the time and sometimes letting them "cry it out"?

Applying Your Knowledge . . . as a Day Care Provider

You have children of different ages in your day care. Would it be all right for the 5-year-olds to help you care for the newborns?

swaddling
practice of infant care that involves wrapping an infant tightly in cloths or blankets

Crying spells are longer and more intense in cultures where neonates are left alone for a substantial part of the day. (BananaStock/Thinkstock)

TABLE 3 Period of PURPLE Crying in the Early Months

A crying baby is difficult for others to bear, especially when the crying is frequent and does not appear to take place for an evident reason. Here is a way to remind parents and others of the normal features of crying in the early months of life. /

P	Peak pattern	Crying peaks around age 2 months and then declines
U	Unpredictable	Crying in the early months often comes and goes unpredictably, for no apparent reason
R	Resistant to soothing	Crying may continue despite parents' best soothing efforts
P	Pain-like face	Crying babies may look like they are in pain even though they are not
L	Long lasting	Babies cry for longer in the early months, sometimes 30–40 minutes or more
E	Evening crying	Babies usually cry most in the afternoon and evening

The word *Period* means that the crying has a beginning and an end.

Sources: Barr, 2009 [see http://www.purplecrying.info/sections/index.php?sct=1&]

American infants cried for much longer periods, and this appeared to be explained by differences in parenting (Small, 1998). Korean infants spent much less of their time alone than American infants did, Korean mothers carried their infants twice as long per day as the American mothers did, and Korean mothers responded immediately to their infants' cries whereas American mothers often let the infant cry it out.

The relation between parenting and infant crying has also been demonstrated experimentally. In one study, researchers divided American mothers and their newborns into two equal groups (Hunziker & Barr, 1986). The mothers in Group A were asked to carry their babies for at least 3 hours a day, and mothers in Group B were not given any special instructions. Infants' mothers in both groups kept diaries of when and how long their babies cried. When the infants were 8 weeks old, the frequency of crying was the same in both groups, but the duration of crying was only about half as long in Group A, the babies who were held more often, as it was in Group B.

In traditional cultures babies are typically held for most of the day, either by their mothers or by another adult woman or an older sister. When neonates in traditional cultures cry, two common responses are breast-feeding and swaddling (DeLoache & Gottlieb, 2000). Crying often signals hunger, so offering the breast soothes the baby, but even if babies are not hungry they can find consolation in suckling, in the same way that babies in developed countries are soothed by a pacifier.

In **swaddling**, babies are wrapped tightly in cloths so that their arms and legs cannot move. Often the baby is laid on a cradle board and the cloths are wrapped around the board as well as around the baby. Swaddling is an ancient practice, with evidence of it going back 6,000 years (DeMeo, 2006). Swaddling has long been widely used in many cultures, from China to Turkey to South America, in the belief that neonates find it soothing and that it helps them sleep and ensures that their limbs grow properly (van Sleuwen et al., 2007). It fell out of favor in Western cultures in the 17th century, when it became regarded as cruel and unnatural. However, swaddling has recently become more common in the West as studies have indicated that it reduces crying and does not inhibit motor development (Thach, 2009).

What else can parents and other caregivers do to soothe a crying neonate? First, of course, any apparent needs should be addressed, in case the baby is hungry, cold, tired, uncomfortable, injured, or needs a diaper change. For crying that has no apparent source, parents have devised a wide range of methods, such as (Eisenberg et al., 2011):

- Lifting baby up and holding to the shoulder
- Soothing repetitive movements such as rocking gently back and forth or riding in a car or carriage
- Soothing sounds such as singing, a fan or vacuum cleaner, or recordings of nature sounds like waves breaking on a beach
- A warm-water bath
- A pacifier or a finger to suck on
- Distraction, with some new sight or sound

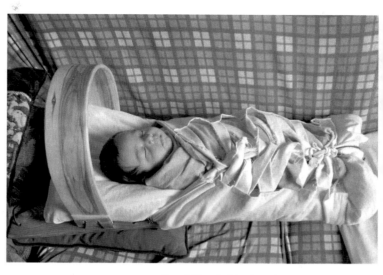

The common theme of these methods appears to be offering a new source of sensory stimulation, especially something gently repetitive. When my twins were neonates we usually tried to soothe them by holding them to the shoulder or singing to them, but if those methods did not work their crying was almost always soothed by the gentle movements of the battery-operated infant seat we called their "wiggly chair." Parents with a crying neonate will often go to great lengths to make the crying stop, so there are many such items on the market today that promise to help parents achieve this goal.

There is also the option of not responding to crying, until the infant stops. For decades, developmental psychologists have debated whether ignoring crying is a good or bad idea. Some argue that ignoring it is a good idea (unless of course the infant has a clear need for food or other care), because parents who respond will reinforce the infant's crying and thus make crying more likely the next time the infant wants attention (Crncek et al., 2010; Gewirtz, 1977; van Ijzendoorn & Hubbard, 2000). Others argue that ignoring it is a bad idea, because infants whose cries are ignored will cry even more in order to get the attention they need (Bell & Ainsworth, 1972; Lohaus et al., 2004). Different studies have reported different findings, so all that can be concluded at this point is that responses to crying do not appear to be strongly related to infants' development (Alvarez, 2004; Hiscock & Jordan, 2004; Lewis & Ramsay, 1999).

About 1 in 10 Western babies have crying patterns of extreme duration, a condition known as **colic**. Babies are considered to be colicky if they fit the "rule of threes" (Barr, 2009): the crying goes on for more than 3 hours a day over more than 3 days at a time for more than 3 weeks. Colic usually begins in the second or third week of life and reaches its peak at 6 weeks, thereafter declining until it disappears at about 3 months of age (Barr & Gunnar, 2000; St. James-Roberts et al., 2003).

The causes of colic are unknown, but it exists primarily in Western cultures, where infants receive relatively little carrying time (Richman et al., 2010). Remedies for colic are also unknown. Babies with colic are inconsolable. None of the soothing methods described above work with them. Fortunately, there appear to be no long-term effects of colic, in babies' physical, emotional, or social development (Barr, 2009; Eisenberg et al., 1996). However, this may be of little comfort to parents who must endure the persistent crying of an inconsolable infant for many weeks. Colic is a risk factor for parents' maltreatment of their babies (Zeskind & Lester, 2001), so it is important for parents to seek help and support if they feel themselves reaching the breaking point.

Swaddling babies to reduce crying spells is a long tradition in many cultures. Here, a Navajo baby in Arizona is swaddled to a traditional backboard.
(Aurora Photos/Alamy)

Applying Your Knowledge . . . as a Researcher

Considering that colic places neonates at risk for parental maltreatment, how would you design a program to prevent such maltreatment?

colic
infant crying pattern in which the crying goes on for more than 3 hours a day over more than 3 days at a time for more than 3 weeks

Bonding: Myth and Truth

Describe the extent to which human mothers "bond" with their neonates and the extent to which this claim has been exaggerated.

LEARNING OBJECTIVE 15

In some species, especially among birds such as geese, the first minutes after birth are a critical period for relations between mother and offspring. Geese form an instant and enduring bond to the first moving object they see, a phenomenon known as **imprinting**. Usually this first object is their mother, of course, and imprinting quickly to her promotes their survival because they

imprinting
instant and enduring bond to
the first moving object seen
after birth; common in birds

bonding
concept that in humans the
first few minutes and hours
after birth are critical to
mother–infant relationships

Goslings will imprint to the first moving object they see, which is usually—but not always—the mother goose. Here, the biologist Konrad Lorenz leads three goslings on a swim.
(Nina Leen//Time Life Pictures/Getty Images)

will follow her everywhere she goes when they begin waddling around soon after birth. Konrad Lorenz (1957), who first identified the imprinting process, showed that geese would imprint to any moving object they saw soon after birth (including him—see the photo on this page).

Some physicians, learning of this research, applied it to humans and asserted that in humans, too, the first few minutes and hours after birth are critical to mother–infant **bonding** (Klaus & Kennell, 1976). Without contact with the mother shortly after birth, these physicians claimed, the baby's future development is jeopardized. However, when systematic research was done to test this hypothesis, it turned out not to be true (Lamb, 1994; Redshaw, 1997; Weinberg, 2004). Humans are not birds, and they are not at risk for later emotional and social problems if they do not bond with a caregiver in the first minutes, hours, or days after birth.

Nevertheless, this is a rare example of a false idea having good effects. As described earlier in the module, in developing countries the birth process had become overly medical by the 1950s and 1960s. Although bonding claims were false, the possibility that they were true led hospitals all over the world to reexamine their policies of sedating the mother and separating mother and child immediately after birth (Lamb, 1994). Subsequently, during the 1970s and after, hospital policies changed so that mother, child, and even father could all be in close contact after the birth. This may not be necessary for the baby's successful later development, but there is no reason not to allow it, and it does alleviate parents' anxieties and promotes feelings of warmth and confidence in caring for their newborn child (Bergstrom et al., 2009).

Postpartum Depression

LEARNING OBJECTIVE 16   Describe the reasons for postpartum depression and its consequences for children.

postpartum depression
in parents with a new baby,
feelings of sadness and
anxiety so intense as to
interfere with the ability to
carry out simple daily tasks

Although the birth of a child is generally greeted with joy, some parents experience a difficult time emotionally in the early months of their baby's life. In one study of new mothers in 11 countries, **postpartum depression** was found at similar rates in all of them, about 10% (Oates et al., 2004). In Western countries this condition was often seen as an illness requiring possible intervention of health professionals, whereas in non-Western countries social support from family members was relied upon for making it through. Studies in the United States and the United Kingdom report that about 4% of fathers also experience postpartum depression in the months following the birth of their child (Dennis, 2004; Ramchandani et al., 2005).

Low emotional states in mothers following birth may be due to rapid hormonal changes, as the high concentrations of estrogen and progesterone in the mother's body return to normal levels. However, postpartum depression is deeper and more enduring. Feelings of sadness and anxiety become so intense that they interfere with the ability to carry out simple daily tasks. Other symptoms include extreme changes in appetite and difficulty sleeping. Postpartum depression often peaks about four weeks after childbirth—long after the mother's hormones would have returned to normal levels—and in 25–50% of mothers who experience postpartum depression it lasts 6 months or longer (Beck, 2002; Clay & Seehusen, 2004).

Why do some women and not others develop postpartum depression? Women are more at risk for postpartum depression if they have had previous episodes of major depression or if they have close family members who have experienced major depression (Bloch et al., 2006). This suggests that for postpartum depression, as for other forms of depression, some people may have a genetic vulnerability to becoming depressed when they experience intense life stresses. Women are also more likely to experience postpartum depression if they lack social support from a husband or partner (Iles et al., 2011). Thus even if a mother has a genetic vulnerability to depression, it is unlikely to be expressed unless she also experiences a social and cultural context in which social support is lacking. For fathers, postpartum depression may result from the challenges of reconciling their personal and work-related needs with the demands of being a father (Genesoni & Tallandini, 2009; Ramchanandi et al., 2005).

Across countries, about 10% of new mothers experience postpartum depression. (VOISIN/PHANIE/Photo Researchers, Inc.)

Mothers' and fathers' postpartum depression is related to children's developmental problems in infancy and beyond. Numerous studies of mothers with postpartum depression have found that their infants are more likely than other infants to be irritable, to have problems eating and sleeping, and to have difficulty forming attachments (Herrera et al., 2004; Martins & Griffin, 2000). In later development, the children are at risk for being withdrawn or displaying antisocial behavior (Nylen et al., 2006). Children of fathers with postpartum depression have been found to have similar risks for their development (Kane & Garber, 2004; Ramchanandi et al., 2005).

Of course, all of these studies are subject to the research design problem of passive and evocative genotype → environment effects. That is, the children in these studies received not only their environment from their parents but also their genes, and it is difficult to tell whether the relation between their problems and their parents' depression is due to genetics or environment (the problem of passive genotype → environment effects). Also, the studies usually assume that the mother's depression affected the child, but it could also be that the mothers became depressed in part because their infant was especially irritable and difficult (evocative genotype → environment effects). However, observational studies of mothers with postpartum depression have found that they talk to and look at their infant less than other mothers, and that they also touch them less and smile less often at them (Righetti-Veltema et al., 2002). This suggests that the behavior of depressed mothers is different in ways that may affect infants, even if passive and evocative genotype → environment effects are also involved.

WHAT HAVE YOU LEARNED?

1. Describe the "crying curve." When does crying reach its peak in neonates?
2. What is the relation, if any, between parenting practices and infant crying?
3. How have claims that humans bond with their neonates influenced hospital policies in the United States?
4. What are the consequences of postpartum depression for children? Why do genotype → environment effects make it difficult to tell?

PART 3 VIDEO GUIDE

BREASTFEEDING PRACTICES ACROSS CULTURES (LENGTH: 6:19)

In this video mothers, and expectant mothers, from various countries are interviewed about their views on breastfeeding.

1. Were you surprised to see that many of the women interviewed have similar reasons for breastfeeding (regardless of their culture)? What are some of the benefits of breastfeeding that they mentioned?

2. Although she was not asked the question about how she would comfort her child, how do you think the expectant mother from the U.S. would answer? Do you think that she would answer in a way similar to the mothers from the other countries? Would the American mother have additional options that the other mothers may not?

3. What are your thoughts on the lengths of time that the mothers planned to breastfeed and the reasons that they had for the lengths?

Watch the Video Breastfeeding Practices Across Cultures at www.pearsoncustom.com/mi/msu_mylabs

SUMMING UP

PART 1   BIRTH AND ITS CULTURAL CONTEXT

1. **Describe the three stages of the birth process and methods for easing its discomfort.**

   The three stages of the birth process are labor, delivery, and expelling of the placenta and umbilical cord. During labor, the contractions of the muscles in the uterus cause the mother's cervix to dilate in preparation for the baby's exit. By the end of labor, the cervix has opened to about 10 centimeters. During delivery, the woman pushes the fetus through the cervix and out of the uterus. In the final stage of the birth process, contractions continue as the placenta and umbilical cord are expelled. Both emotional support and physical methods such as breathing techniques and massage may help ease the discomfort of labor.

2. **Name two common types of birth complications and explain how they can be overcome by cesarean delivery.**

Two common birth complications are failure to progress, which occurs when the birth process is taking longer than normal, and the breech presentation of the fetus, which means the fetus is turned around so that the feet or buttocks are positioned to come first out of the birth canal. Both complications can be overcome through the use of a c-section, which today is generally safe for mothers and infants.

3. **Compare and contrast cultural variations in birth beliefs.**

Because birth is often dangerous, many traditional cultures–such as the Arapesh of New Guinea and the traditional Vietnamese—have developed beliefs that childbirth puts a woman in a state of being spiritually unclean. The placenta is often disposed of with care in traditional cultures because of beliefs that it is potentially dangerous or even semihuman.

4. **Explain the role of the midwife and compare and contrast cultural practices and medical methods for easing the birth process.**

In most cultures, women giving birth are attended by female relatives and an older woman ("midwife" or similar title) who has experience assisting in the birth process. The midwife eases birth pain through massage techniques, reassurance, and herbal medicines. In developed countries, an anesthetic drug called an epidural is often injected into a woman's spinal fluid to help manage the pain.

5. **Summarize the history of birth in the West from the 15th century to today.**

There have been attempts over the past several centuries to make birth safer for baby and mother alike. Some of those attempts were disastrous, such as the deadly infections spread to mothers unwittingly by 19th-century doctors. In the early 20th century the attempts were overzealous and overly medical, as birth was taken over by doctors and hospitals, with the maternal experience disregarded. In the past 50 years most of the West has moved toward a more reasonable middle ground, seeking to minimize medical intervention but making it available when necessary.

6. **Describe the differences in maternal and neonatal mortality both within and between developed countries and developing countries.**

In recent decades birth has become routinely safe and humane in developed countries, although there is considerable variation based on SES and ethnicity. Childbirth remains highly dangerous in developing countries where little medical intervention is available, although mortality rates are decreasing due to recent improvements in nutrition and access to health care.

◇ KEY TERMS

oxytocin *p. 331*
labor *p. 332*
delivery *p. 332*

episiotomy *p. 332*
breech presentation *p. 333*
cesarean delivery (c-section) *p. 333*

epidural *p. 338*
placebo effect *p. 339*
forceps *p. 340*

obstetrics *p. 340*
natural childbirth *p. 342*
electronic fetal monitoring (EFM) *p. 342*

PART 2 THE NEONATE

7. **Identify the features of the two major scales most often used to assess neonatal health.**

Two of the most widely used methods of assessing neonatal health are the Apgar scale and the Brazelton Neonatal Behavioral Assessment Scale (NBAS). The Apgar scale, which is administered immediately after birth, assesses infants on 5 subtests with a total rating of 1–10. The NBAS, which is administered any time from 1 day to 2 months after birth, relies on a 27-item scale and assigns infants an overall rating of "worrisome," "normal," or "superior."

8. **Identify the neonatal classifications for low birth weight and describe the consequences and major treatments.**

Low-birth-weight neonates weigh less than 5.5 pounds and very low-birth-weight neonates weigh less than 3.3 pounds; extremely low-birth-weight babies weight less than 2.2 pounds. Low birth weight is related to a variety of physical, cognitive, and behavioral problems, not just in infancy but throughout life. Close physical contact and infant massage can help ameliorate the problems.

9. **Describe neonates' patterns of waking and sleeping, including how and why these patterns differ across cultures.**

Neonates sleep an average of 16 to 17 hours a day (in segments of a few hours each), about 50% of it in REM sleep. By 4 months old the typical infant sleeps for 14 of every 24 hours, including about 6 hours straight at night, and the proportion of REM sleep declines to 40%. These patterns may vary across cultures due to differences in parenting practices such as how much time mothers spend holding their babies.

10. Describe the neonatal reflexes, including those that have a functional purpose and those that do not.

There are 27 reflexes present at birth or shortly after, including some related to early survival (such as sucking and rooting) and others that have no apparent function (such as the *Babkin* and *Babinski* reflexes).

11. Describe the neonate's sensory abilities with respect to touch, taste and smell, hearing, and sight.

Touch and taste develop prenatally to a large extent, and neonate's abilities are similar to adults'. Neonates also quickly begin to discriminate smells after birth, showing a preference for the smell of their mother's breast. Hearing is also quite mature at birth, although neonates hear high-pitched sounds better than other sounds and their ability to localize sound does not mature until about one year old. Sight is the least developed of the senses at birth, due to the physiological immaturity of the visual system at birth, but it reaches maturity by the end of the first year.

◇ KEY TERMS

fontanels *p. 345*

neonate *p. 345*

neonatal jaundice *p. 345*

anoxia *p. 346*

Apgar scale *p. 346*

Brazelton Neonatal Behavioral Assessment Scale (NBAS) *p. 347*

low birth weight *p. 347*

preterm *p. 347*

small for date *p. 347*

very low birth weight *p. 348*

extremely low birth weight *p. 348*

surfactant *p. 348*

kangaroo care *p. 348*

rapid eye movement (REM) sleep *p. 350*

reflex *p. 352*

rooting reflex *p. 352*

Moro reflex *p. 352*

sound localization *p. 354*

PART 3   CARING FOR THE NEONATE

12. Describe the cultural customs surrounding breast feeding across cultures and history.

n the human past, evidence indicates that in most cultures children were fed breast milk as their primary or sole food for 2 to 3 years. To ease the burden of frequent feedings, the custom of wet nursing (hiring a lactating woman other than the mother to feed the infant) is a widespread custom as old as recorded human history.

13. Identify the advantages conferred by breast feeding and where those advantages are largest.

Breast feeding is beneficial to infants in many ways, including offering protection from disease in infancy and better health in childhood and adulthood, healthy cognitive development, and reduced obesity. For mothers, breast-feeding helps their bodies return to normal after pregnancy and serves as a natural contraceptive. The advantages are especially pronounced in developing countries. Nevertheless, worldwide only about half of all infants are breast-fed even for a short time.

14. Describe neonates' types of crying and how crying patterns and soothing methods vary across cultures.

Three distinct kinds of crying signals have been identified: fussing, anger, and pain. Crying frequency rises steadily beginning at 3 weeks of age and reaches a peak by the end of the second month, then declines. This pattern is similar across cultures, but duration and intensity of crying are lower in cultures where babies are held or carried throughout much of the day and night.

15. Describe the extent to which human mothers "bond" with their neonates and the extent to which this claim has been exaggerated.

Some physicians have claimed on the basis of animal studies that the first few minutes and hours after birth are critical to mother–infant "bonding." This has now been shown to be false, but the claims had the beneficial effect of changing hospital policies to allow more contact between mothers, fathers, and neonates.

16. Describe the reasons for postpartum depression and its consequences for children.

Many mothers experience mood fluctuations in the days following birth as their hormones return to normal levels, but some mothers experience an extended period of postpartum depression, as do some fathers. The basis of postpartum depression appears to be a combination of genetic vulnerability to depression and a social and cultural context that does not provide enough social support.

◇ KEY TERMS

mammary glands *p. 356*

let-down reflex *p. 356*

wet nursing *p. 356*

colostrum *p. 359*

meta-analysis *p. 359*

confounded *p. 359*

swaddling *p. 362*

colic *p. 363*

imprinting *p. 364*

bonding *p. 364*

postpartum depression *p. 364*

◇ PRACTICE TEST

1. Juanita's cervix is 10 centimeters dilated so she
   a. is just beginning the labor stage.
   b. requires an episiotomy.
   c. has completed labor and is ready to deliver the baby.
   d. requires a c-section.

2. C-sections
   a. are performed when the baby is in the breech position and attempts to turn the baby into a head first position have not been successful.
   b. require the same recovery time as a vaginal birth if they are performed correctly.
   c. have only been proven safe in the case where there is a failure to progress.
   d. are performed at equally small rates around the world because they are seen as a last resort.

3. In traditional cultures, birth is only allowed to take place in certain settings. The LEAST LIKELY explanation is
   a. so others will not be contaminated.
   b. to feel a sense of control over an often perilous situation.
   c. to find a place where medical help is available if complications arise.
   d. so that the mother or her infant will not be endangered.

4. Surita is a midwife in a traditional culture. She is most likely to
   a. have spent time as an apprentice to a more experienced midwife.
   b. be childless so she is able to devote more time to this work.
   c. be a young woman because she will be able to practice midwifery for longer than her older counterparts.
   d. exclude other relatives from being present to reduce possible contamination.

5. Which of the following is true about birthing practices?
   a. Recently, midwifery has seen a revival, and about 50% of births in the United States are assisted by midwives.
   b. In the early 1900s, the intervention of doctors often made the birth process less dangerous because they now had better expertise and medical equipment.
   c. In the 1960s, doctors began administering drugs such as ether and chloroform, which offered pain relief without any side effects.
   d. Twilight Sleep was a drug used in the early 20th century that promoted dilation of the cervix and resulted in mothers forgetting the events of birth.

6. In developing countries
   a. most pregnant women now have access to modern medical technologies.
   b. giving birth is relatively free of risks because of modernization and globalization.
   c. maternal mortality has decreased over the past 30 years.
   d. rates of infant mortality are lower than in developed countries because of more holistic and natural approaches to childbirth.

7. The five characteristics that are evaluated in the Apgar scale are
   a. the Babinski, Moro, stepping, swimming, and grasping reflexes.
   b. color, heart rate, reflex irritability, muscle tone, and breathing.
   c. reaction to cuddling, startling, intelligence, vocal response, and visual response.
   d. sucking reflex, responses to social stimulation, and disease symptoms.

8. Preterm babies are considered at risk because
   a. their immune systems are immature.
   b. they have too much surfactant in their lungs.
   c. their bodies generate too much heat.
   d. their gestational age is 40 weeks and that is still too early to perform basic functions such as sucking.

9. Compared to adults, neonates
   a. spend a lower proportion of their sleep in REM.
   b. enter REM sooner after falling asleep.
   c. spend less time sleeping.
   d. do not experience eye movements under the eyelids or brain-wave changes during REM sleep.

10. Which of the following reflexes has no apparent survival value?
    a. the rooting reflex
    b. the Moro reflex
    c. the Babinski reflex
    d. the grasping reflex

11. The earliest sense to develop is
    a. taste.
    b. touch.
    c. vision.
    d. hearing.

12. Breast feeding

    a. is more common among women from low socioeconomic status groups.

    b. increased in popularity as formulas came on to the market because the formulas were very expensive and women worried about product safety.

    c. is something both mother and baby are biologically prepared to do.

    d. rates have stayed about the same in the United States since the 1940s.

13. Which of the following statements about breastfeeding is most accurate?

    a. Babies in developing countries are more at risk for health problems if their mothers do not breast-feed them than are babies in developed countries.

    b. Breast feeding promotes better health in childhood, but does not have any influence on long-term health.

    c. Breast-fed babies are more likely than bottle-fed babies to become obese in childhood because they are used to eating on demand.

    d. The colostrum that mothers produce in the first weeks after birth can be dangerous to babies so doctors advise using formula until the mother begins producing milk.

14. American infants

    a. are less likely to experience colic than are babies in non-Western cultures.

    b. typically experience colic until they are about a year of age.

    c. show the same frequency, intensity, and duration of crying as babies from all over the world.

    d. have been found to cry more than babies from cultures where they are held or carried for much of the day.

15. Which of the following statements about bonding is most accurate?

    a. There is a critical period for mother–child relations in all species.

    b. Imprinting is another name for the stepping reflex.

    c. In humans, if there is no contact with the mother shortly after birth, the baby's future development is at risk.

    d. Konrad Lorenz showed that following the first moving object after birth has survival value.

16. Postpartum depression

    a. is less common among women who have had previous episodes of major depression because they tend to seek preventive treatment.

    b. is experienced by men as well as by women.

    c. has a genetic component and, therefore, has not been correlated with levels of social support.

    d. has been linked with developmental outcomes for babies, but only among male babies.

Answers: 1. C (L.O. 1); 2. A (L.O. 2);3. C (L.O. 3); 4. A (L.O. 4); 5. D (L.O. 5); 6. C (L.O. 6); 7. B (L.O. 7); 8. A (L.O. 8); 9. B (L.O. 9); 10. C (L.O. 10); 11. B (L.O. 11); 12. C (L.O. 12); 13. A (L.O. 13); 14. D (L.O. 14); 15. D (L.O. 15); 16. B (L.O. 16).

◆ REFERENCES

Aldridge, M. A., Stillman, R. D., & Bower, T. G. R. (2001). Newborn categorization of vowel-like sounds. *Developmental Science, 4,* 220–232.

Alexander, G. M., & Hines, M. (2002). Sex differences in response to children's toys in nonhuman primates. *Evolution and Human Behavior, 23,* 467–479.

Alvarez, M. (2004). Caregiving and early infant crying in a Danish community. *Journal of Developmental and Behavioral Pediatrics, 25,* 91–98.

American Academy of Pediatrics. (2005). Breastfeeding and the use of human milk: Policy statement. *Pediatrics, 115,* 496–506.

Anders, T. F., & Taylor, T. (1994). Babies and their sleep environment. *Children's Environments, 11,* 123–134.

Arditi-Babchuk, H., Eidelman, A. I., & Feldman, R. (2009). Rapid eye movement (REM) in premature neonates and developmental outcome at 6 months. *Infant Behavior & Development, 32,* 27–32.

Aslin, R. N., Jusczyk, P. W., & Pisoni, D. B. (1998). Speech and auditory processing during infancy: Constraints on and precursors to language. In W. Damon (Ed.), *Handbook of child psychology* (5th ed., Vol. 2). New York, NY: Wiley.

Atkinson, J. (2000). *The developing visual brain.* Oxford, UK: Oxford University Press.

Balodis, I.M., Wynne-Edwards, K.E., & Olmstead, M.C. (2011). The stress-response-dampening effects of placebo. *Hormones and behavior, 59,* 465-472.

Barr, R. G. (2009). The phenomena of early infant crying and colic. Paper presented at the Centre for Community and Child Health, Melbourne, Australia, March 2.

Barr, R. G., & Gunnar, M. (2000). Colic: The 'transient responsivity' hypothesis. In R. G. Barr, B. Hopkins, & J. A. Green (Eds.), *Crying as a sign, a symptom, and a signal* (pp. 41–66). Cambridge, UK: Cambridge University Press.

Bartoshuk, L. M., & Beauchamp, G. K. (1994). Chemical senses. *Annual Review of Psychology, 45,* 419–449.

Bates, B., & Turner, A. N. (2003). Imagery and symbolism in the birth practices of traditional cultures. In L. Dundes (Ed.), *The manner born: Birth rites in cross-cultural perspective* (pp. 85–97). Walnut Creek, CA: Altamira Press.

Beck, C. T. (2002). Theoretical perspectives on postpartum depression and their treatment implications. *American Journal of Maternal/Child Nursing, 27*, 282–287.

Bel, A., & Bel, B. (2007). Birth attendants: Between the devil and the deep blue sea. In B. Bel, J. Brouwer, B. T. Das, V. Parthasarathi, & G. Poitevin (Eds.), *Communication processes 2: The social and the symbolic* (pp. 353–385). Thousand Oaks, CA: Sage.

Bell, S. M., & Ainsworth, M. D. S. (1972). Infant crying and maternal responsiveness. *Child Development, 43*, 1171–1190.

Bellamy, C. (2005). *The state of the world's children: 2005.* New York, NY: UNICEF.

Bergström, L., Richards, L., Morse, J. M., & Roberts, J. (2010). How caregivers manage pain and distress in second-stage labor. *Journal of Midwifery & Women's Health, 55*, 38–45.

Bergström, M., Kieler, H., & Waldenström, U. (2009). Effects of natural childbirth preparation versus standard antenatal education on epidural rates, experience of childbirth and parental stress in mothers and fathers: A randomised controlled multicentre trial. *BJOG: An International Journal of Obstetrics & Gynaecology 116*, 1167–1176.

Bloch, M., Klein, E., Koren, D., & Rotenberg, N. (2006). Risk factors for early postpartum depressive symptoms. *General Hospital Psychiatry, 28*, 3–8.

Booth, D. A., Higgs, S., Schneider, J., & Klinkenberg, I. (2010). Learned liking versus inborn delight: Can sweetness give sensual pleasure or is it just motivating? *Psychological Science, 21*, 1656–1663.

Brazelton, T. B., Koslowski, B., & Tronick, E. (1976). Neonatal behavior among urban Zambians and Americans. *Journal of the American Academy of Child Psychiatry, 15*, 97–107.

Bryder, L. (2009). From breast to bottle: a history of modern infant feeding. *Endeavour 33*, 54–59.

Burnham, M., Goodlin-Jones, B., & Gaylor, E. (2002). Nighttime sleep–wake patterns and self–soothing from birth to one year of age: A longitudinal intervention study. *Journal of Child Psychology & Psychiatry & Allied Disciplines, 43*, 713–725.

Carter, K. C., & Carter, B. R. (2005). *Childbed fever. A scientific biography of Ignaz Semmelweis.* Edison, NJ: Transaction.

Casey Foundation (2010). *2010 Kids Count data book.* Baltimore, MD: Annie E. Casey Foundation.

Cassidy, T. (2006). *Birth: The surprising history of how we are born.* New York, NY: Atlantic Monthly Press.

Cassidy, T. (2008). *Taking Great Pains: An Abridged History of Pain Relief in Childbirth.* Retrieved from http://wondertime.go.com/learning/article/childbirth-pain-relief.html

Cavallini, A., Fazzi, E., & Viviani, V. (2002). Visual acuity in the first two years of life in healthy term newborns: An experience with the Teller Acuity Cards. *Functional Neurology: New Trends in Adaptive & Behavioral Disorders, 17*, 87–92.

Centers for Disease Control (CDC). (2010). *U.S. Obesity Trends: Trends by State 1985–2009.* Atlanta, Georgia: AuthorAARP (2002). *The Grandparent Study 2002 report.* Washington, DC: Author.

Centers for Disease Control and Prevention (CDC) (2002). Infant mortality and low birth weight among Black and White infants: United States, 1980–2000. *Morbidity & Mortality Weekly Report, 51*, 589–592.

Charpak, N., Ruiz-Pelaez, J. G., & Figueroa, Z. (2005). Influence of feeding patterns and other factors on early somatic growth of healthy, preterm infants in home-based kangaroo mother care: A cohort study. *Journal of Pediatric Gastroenterology and Nutrition, 41*, 430–437.

Clay, E. C. & Seehusen, D. A. (2004). A review of postpartum depression for the primary care physician. *Southern Medical Journal, 97*, 157–162.

Connolly, M., & Sullivan, D. (2004). *The essential c-section guide: Pain control, healing at home, getting your body back, and everything else you need to know about a cesarean birth.* New York: Broadway Books.

Cosminsky, S. (2003). Cross-cultural perspectives on midwifery. In L. Dundes (Ed.), *The manner born: Birth rites in cross-cultural perspective* (pp. 69–84). Walnut Creek, CA: Altamira Press.

Csibra, G., Davis, g., Spratling, M. W., & Johnson, M. H. (2000). Gamma oscillations and object processing in the infant brain. *Science, 290*, 1582–1585.

da Motta, C. C. L., Naziri, D., & Rinne, C. (2006). The Influence of emotional support during childbirth: A clinical study. *Journal of Prenatal & Perinatal Psychology & Health, 20*, 325–341.

Davis, D. W. (2003). Cognitive outcomes in school-age children born prematurely. *Neonatal Network, 22*, 27–38.

Davis, K. F., Parker, K. P., & Montgomery, G. L. (2004). Sleep in infants and young children. Part I: Normal sleep. *Journal of Pediatric Health Care, 18*, 65–71.

de Vonderweid, U., & Leonessa, M. (2009). Family centered neonatal care. *Early Human Development, 85,* S37–S38.

De Weerd, A. W., & van den Bossche, A. S. (2003). The development of sleep during the first months of life. *Sleep Medicine Reviews, 7,* 179–191.

DeLoache, J., & Gottlieb, A. (2000). *A world of babies: Imagined childcare guides for seven societies.* New York, NY: Cambridge University Press.

DeMeo, J. (2006). *Saharasia: The 4000* bce *origins of child abuse, sex-repression, warfare and social violence, in the deserts of the old world* (Revised 2nd ed.). El Cerrito, CA: Natural Energy Works.

Dennis, C. L. (2004). Can we identify mothers at risk for postpartum depression in the immediate postpartum period using the Edinburgh Postnatal Depression Scale? *Journal of Affective Disorders, 78,* 163–169.

Doyle, L. W., Faber, B., Callanan, C., Ford, G. W., & Davis, N. M. (2004). Extremely low birth weight and body size in early adulthood. *Archives of Disorders in Childhood, 89,* 347–350.

Ehrenreich, B. (2010). *Witches, midwives, and nurses: A history of women healers.* New York, NY: Feminist Press.

Eiden, R. D., & Reifman, A. (1996). Effects of Brazelton demonstrations on later parenting: A meta-analysis. *Journal of Pediatric Psychology, 21,* 857–868.

Engler, A. J., Ludington-Hoe, S. M., Cusson, R. M., Adams, R., Bahnsen, M., Brumbaugh, E.,…Williams, D. (2002). Kangaroo care: National survey of practice, knowledge, barriers, and perceptions. *American Journal of Maternal/Child Nursing, 27,* 146–153.

Eriksson, C., Hamberg, K., & Salander, P. (2007). Men's experiences of intense fear related to childbirth investigated in a Swedish qualitative study. *Journal of Men's Health & Gender, 4,* 409–418.

Erlandsson, K., & Lindgren, H. (2009). From belonging to belonging through a blessed moment of love for a child—The birth of a child from the fathers' perspective. *Journal of Men's Health,* 338–344.

Fearon, P., O'Connell, P., Frangou, S., Aquino, P., Nosarti, C., Allin, M.,…Murray, R. (2004). Brain volumes in adult survivors of very low birth weight: A sibling–controlled study. Q *Pediatrics, 114,* 367–371.

Feldman, R., & Eidelman, A. I. (2003). Skin-to-skin contact (kangaroo care) accelerates autonomic and neurobehavioral maturation in preterm infants. *Developmental Medicine and Child Neurology, 45,* 274–281.

Feldman, R., Weller, A., Sirota, L., & Eidelman, A. I. (2003). Testing a family intervention hypothesis: The contribution of mother–infant skin-to-skin (kangaroo care) to family interaction, proximity, and touch. *Journal of Family Psychology, 17,* 94–107.

Ferber, S. G., & Makhoul, I. R. (2004). The effect of skin-to-skin contact (kangaroo care) shortly after birth on the neurobehavioral responses of the term newborn: A randomized, controlled trial. *Pediatrics, 113,* 858–865.

Ferber, S. G., Kuint, J., Weller, A., Feldman, S. D., Arbel, E., & Kohelet, D. (2002). Massage therapy by mothers and trained professionals enhances weight gain in preterm infants. *Early Human Development, 67,* 37–45.

Field, T. M. (1998). Massage therapy effects. *American Psychologist, 53,* 1270–1281.

Field, T. M. (2001). Massage therapy facilitates weight gain in preterm infants. *Current Directions in Psychological Science, 10,* 51–55.

Field, T., Diego, M., & Hernandez-Reif, M. (2010). Preterm infant massage therapy: A review. *Infant Behavior and Development, 33,* 115–124.

Fildes, V. (1995). The culture and biology of breastfeeding: An historical review of Western Europe. In P. Stuart-Macadam & K.A. Dettwyler (Eds.), *Breastfeeding: Biocultural perspectives* (pp. 101-131). Hawthorne, NY: Aldein de Gruyter.

Ford, C. S. (1945). *A comparative study of human reproduction.* New Haven, CT: Yale University Press.

Foureur, M., Ryan, C. L., Nicholl, M., & Homer, C. (2010). Inconsistent evidence: Analysis of six national guidelines for vaginal birth after cesarean section. *Birth: Issues in Perinatal Care, 37,* 3–10.

Futagi, Y., Toribe, Y., & Suzuki, Y. (2009). Neurological assessment of early infants. *Current Pediatric Reviews, 5,* 65–70.

Gavin, A. R., Hill, K. G., Hawkins, J. D., & Maas, C. (2011). The role of maternal early-life and later-life risk factors on offspring low birth weight: Findings from a three-generational study. *Journal of Adolescent Health, 49,* 166–171.

Genesoni, L., & Tallandini, M. A. (2009). Men's psychological transition to fatherhood: An analysis of the literature, 1989–2008. *Birth: Issues in Perinatal Care, 36,* 305–318.

Gewirtz, J. (1977). Maternal responding and the conditioning of infant crying: Directions of influence within the attachment–acquisition process. In B. C. Etzel, J. M. LeBlanc, & D. M. Baer (Eds.), *New developments in behavioral research* (pp. 31–57). Hillsdale, NJ: Lawrence Erlbaum.

Gibson, J. H., Harries, M., Mitchell, A., Godfrey, R., Lunt, M., & Reeve, J. (2000). Determinants of bone density and prevalence of osteopenia among female runners in their second to seventh decades of age. *Bone, 26,* 591–598.

Giscombé, C. L., & Lobel, M. (2005). Explaining disproportionately high rates of adverse birth outcomes among African Americans: The impact of stress, racism, and related factors in pregnancy. *Psychological Bulletin, 131,* 662–683.

Godfrey, J. R., & Meyers, D. (2009). Toward optimal health: Maternal benefits on breastfeeding. *Journal of Women's Health, 18,* 1307–1310.

Greve, T. (2003). Norway: The breastfeeding top of the world. *Midwifery Today International, 67,* 57–59.

Herrera, E., Reissland, N., & Shepherd, J. (2004). Maternal touch and maternal child-directed speech: Effects of depressed mood in the postnatal period. *Journal of Affective Disorders, 81,* 29–39.

Hiscock, H., & Jordan, B. (2004). Problem crying in infancy. *Medical Journal of Australia, 181,* 507–512.

Hodnett, E. D., Gates, S., Hofneyr, G. J., & Sakala, C. (2007). Continuous support for women during childbirth. *Cochrane Database of Systematic Reviews, 3.*

Hofman, P. L., Regan, F., Jackson, W. E., Jefferies, C., Knight, D. B., Robinson, E. M., & Cutfield, W. S. (2004). Premature birth and later insulin resistance. *New England Journal of Medicine, 351,* 2179–2186.

Hofmeyr, G. J. (2002). Interventions to help external cephalic version for breech presentation at term. *Cochrane Database of Systematic Reviews, 2,* CD000184.

Hogan, M. C., Foreman, K. J., Naghavi, M., Ahn, S. Y., Wang, M., Makela, S. M.,…Murray, C. J. L. (2010). Maternal mortality for 181 countries, 1980–2008: A systematic analysis of progress toward Millennium Development Goal 5. *The Lancet, 375,* 1–15.

Holsti, L., & Grunau, R. E. (2010). Considerations for using sucrose to reduce procedural pain in preterm infants. *Pediatrics, 125,* 1042–1049.

Hopkins-Golightly, T., Raz, S., & Sander, C. (2003). Influence of slight to moderate risk for birth hypoxia on acquisition of cognitive and language function in the preterm infant: A cross–sectional comparison with preterm–birth controls. *Neuropsychology, 17,* 3–13.

Hunziker, U. A., & Barr, R. G. (1986). Increased carrying reduces infant crying: A randomized controlled trial. *Pediatrics, 77,* 641–648.

Iles, J., Slade, P., & Spiby, H. (2011). Posttraumatic stress symptoms and postpartum depression in couples after childbirth: The role of partner support and attachment. *Journal of Anxiety Disorders, 25,* 520–530.

Ip, S., Chung, M., Raman, G., Chew, P., Magula, N., DeVine, D.,…Lau, J. (2007). *Breastfeeding and maternal and infant health outcomes in developed countries. Evidence Report/Technology Assessment No. 153.* Rockville, MD. Agency for Healthcare Research and Quality.

Jones, E., & Kay, M. A. (2003). The cultural anthropology of the placenta. In L. Dundes (Ed.), *The manner born: Birth rites in cross-cultural perspective* (pp. 101–116). Walnut Creek, CA: Altamira Press.

Jordan, B. (1993). *Birth in four cultures: A cross-cultural investigation of childbirth in Yucatan, Holland, Sweden, and the United States.* Long Grove, Illinois: Waveland.

Kainz, G., Eliasson, M., & von Post, I. (2010). The child's father, an important person for the mother's well–being during the childbirth: A hermeneutic study. *Health Care for Women International, 31,* 621–635.

Kane, P., & Garber, J. (2004). The relations among depression in fathers, children's psychopathology, and father–child conflict: A meta-analysis. *Child Psychology Review, 24,* 339–360.

Kellman, P. J., & Arterberry, M. E. (2006). Infant visual perception. In W. Damon & R. Lerner (Eds.), & D. Kuhn & R. Siegler (Vol. Eds.), *Handbook of child psychology: Vol. 2. Cognition, perception, and language* (6th ed., pp. 109–160). New York, NY: Wiley.

Kisilevsky, B. S., Hains, S. M., Lee, K., Xic, X., Huang, H., Ye, H. H., Zhang, K. & Wang, Z. (2003). Effects of experience on fetal voice recognition. *Psychological Science, 14,* 220–224.

Klaus, M. H., & Kennell, J. H. (1976). *Maternal–infant bonding: The impact of early separation or loss on family development.* St. Louis, MO: Mosby.

Kostandy, R. R., Ludington-Hoe, S. M., Cong, X., Abouelfettoh, A., Bronson, C., Stankus, A., & Jarrell, J. R. (2008). Kangaroo care (skin contact) reduces crying response to pain in preterm neonates: Pilot results. *Pain Management Nursing, 9,* 55–65.

Kramer, M. S., Aboud, F., Mironova, E., Vanilovich, I., Platt, R. W., Matush, L.,…Promotion of Breastfeeding Intervention Trial (PROBIT) Study Group (2008). Breastfeeding and child cognitive development: New evidence from a large randomized trial. *Archives of General Psychiatry, 65,* 578–584.

Kramer, M. S., Lidia, M., Vanilovich, I., Platt, R. W., & Bogdanovich, N. (2009). A randomized breast–feeding promotion intervention did not reduce child obesity in Belarus. *Journal of Nutrition, 139,* 417S–421S.

Lamb, M. E. (1994). Infant care practices and the application of knowledge. In C. B. Fisher & R. M. Lerner (Eds.), *Applied developmental psychology* (pp. 23–45). New York, NY: McGraw-Hill.

Lane, B. (2009). *Epidural rates in the U.S. and around the world: How many mothers choose to use an epidural to provide pain relief?* Retrieved from http://www.suite101.com/content/epidural-for-labor-a168170

Levitin, D. (2007). *This is your brain on music.* New York, NY: Plume.

Lewis, M., & Ramsay, D. S. (1999). Effect of maternal soothing and infant stress response. *Child Development, 70,* 11–20.

Litovsky, R. Y., & Ashmead, D. H. (1997). Development of binatural and spatial hearing in infants and children. In R. H. Gilkey & T. R. Anderson (Eds.), *Binaural and spatial hearing in real and virtual environments* (pp. 571–592). Mahwah, NJ: Erlbaum.

Lohaus, A., Keller, H., Ball, J., Voelker, S., & Elben, C. (2004). Maternal sensitivity in interactions with three– and 12–month–old infants: Stability, structural composition, and developmental consequences. *Infant and Child Development, 13,* 235–252.

Lorenz, K. (1957). Companionship in bird life. In C. Scholler (Ed.), *Instinctive behavior: The development of a modern concept* (pp. 83–128). New York, NY: International Universities Press.

Lyon, E. (2007). *The big book of birth.* New York, NY: Plume.

MacDorman, M. F., Menacker, F., & Declercq, E. (2010). Trends and characteristics of home and other out–of–hospital births in the United States, 1990–2006. *National Vital Statistics Reports, 58,* 1–14, 16.

Madlon-Kay, D. J. (2002). Maternal assessment of neonatal jaundice after hospital discharge. *The Journal of Family Practice, 51,* 445–448.

Marlier, L, Schaal, B., & Soussignan, R. (1998). Neonatal responsiveness to the odor of amniotic and lacteal fluids: A test of perinatal chemosensory continuity. *Child Development, 69,* 611–623.

Marlow, N., Wolke, D., Bracewell, M. A., & Samara, M. (2005). Neurologic and developmental disability at six years of age after extremely preterm births. *New England Journal of Medicine, 352,* 9–19.

Martin, A., Brooks-Gunn, J., Klebanov, P., Buka, S., & McCormick, M. (2008). Long-term maternal effects of early childhood intervention: Findings from the Infant Health and Development Program (IHDP). *Journal of Applied Developmental Psychology, 29,* 101–117.

Martin, J. A., Hamilton, B. E., Sutton, P. D., Ventura, S. J., Menacker, F., & Munson, M. L (2005). Births: Final data for 2003. *National vital statistics Reports, 54,* 1–116.

Martins, C., & Gaffan, E. A. (2000). Effects of maternal depression on patterns of infant–mother attachment: A meta-analytic investigation. *Journal of Child Psychology and Psychiatry, 41,* 737–746.

Mayo Clinic Staff (2011). *Stages of Labor: Baby, it's time!* Retrieved from http://www.mayoclinic.com/health/stages-of-labor/PR00106/NSECTIONGROUP=2

McClure, V. S. (2000). *Infant massage—Revised Edition: A handbook for loving parents.* New York, NY: Bantam.

McNamara, F., & Sullivan, C. E. (2000). Obstructive sleep apnea in infants. *Journal of Pediatrics, 136,* 318–323.

Menella, J. (2000, June). The psychology of eating. Paper presented at the annual meeting of the American Psychological Society, Miami, FL.

Merewood, A., Mehta, S. D., Chamberlain, L. B., Phillipp, B. L., & Bauchner, H. (2005). Breastfeeding rates in U.S. baby-friendly hospitals: Results of a national survey. *Pediatrics, 116,* 628–634.

Merten, S., Dratva, J., & Achermann-Liebrich, U. (2005). Do baby-friendly hospitals influence breastfeeding duration on a national level? *Pediatrics, 116,* c702–c708.

Mitchell, A., & Boss, B. J. (2002). Adverse effects of pain on the nervous systems of newborns and young children: A review of the literature. *Journal of Neuroscience and Nursing, 34,* 228–235.

Mugford, M. (2006). Cost effectiveness of prevention and treatment of neonatal respiratory distress (RDS) with exogenous surfactant: What has changed in the last three decades? *Early Human Development, 82,* 105–115.

Muret-Wagstaff, S., & Moore, S. G. (1989). The Hmong in America: Infant behavior and rearing practices. In J. K. Nugent, B. M. Lester, & T. B. Brazelton (Eds.), *Biology, culture, and development* (Vol. 1, pp. 319–339). Norwood, NJ: Ablex.

Murkoff, H., & Mazel, S. (2008). *What to expect when you're expecting.* New York, NY: Workman.

Napier, K., & Meister, K. (2000). *Growing healthy kids: A parents' guide to infant and child nutrition.* New York, NY: American Council on Science and Heath.

National Institute of Child Health and Development (NICHD) (2004). Follow-up care of high-risk infants. *Pediatrics, 114,* 1377–1397.

Newton, N., & Newton, M. (2003). Childbirth in cross–cultural perspective. In L. Dundes (Ed.), *The manner born: Birth rites in cross–cultural perspective* (pp. 9–32). Walnut Creek, CA: AltaMira.

Noia, G., Cesari, E., Ligato, M. S., Visconti, D., Tintoni, M., Mappa, I.,…Caruso, A. (2008). Pain in the fetus. *Neonatal Pain, 2,* 45–55.

Nugent, K. J., Petrauskas, B. J., & Brazelton, T. B. (Eds.). (2009). *The newborn as a person: Enabling healthy infant development worldwide.* Hoboken, NJ: John Wiley & Sons.

Nugent, K., & Brazelton, T. B. (2000). Preventive infant mental health: Uses of the Brazelton scale. In J. D. Osofsky & H. E. Fitzgerald (Eds.), *WAIMH Handbook of infant mental health* (Vol. 2). New York, NY: Wiley.

Nuland, S. B. (2003). *The doctor's plague: Germs, childbed fever, and the strange story of Ignac Semmelweis.* New York, NY: Norton.

Nylen, K., Moran, T., Franklin, C., & O'Hara, M. (2006). Maternal depression: A review of relevant treatment approaches for mothers and infants. *Infant Mental Health Journal, 27,* 327–343.

Oates, M. R., Cox, J. L., Neema, S., Asten, P., Glangeaud-Freudenthal, N., Figueiredo, B.,…TCS–PND Group. (2004). Postnatal depression across countries and cultures: A qualitative study. *British Journal of Psychiatry, 184,* s10–s16.

OECD (2009). *Health at a glance 2009: OECD indicators.* Author.

Ohgi, S., Arisawa, K., Takahashi, T., Kusomoto, T., Goto, Y. & Saito, A .T. (2003). Neonatal behavioral assessment scale as a predictor of later developmental disabilities of low birth-weight and/or premature infants. *Brain Development, 25,* 313–321.

Out, D., Pieper, S., Bakermans-Kranenburg, M. J., Zeskind, P. S., & van IJzendoorn, M. H. (2010). Intended sensitive and harsh caregiving responses to infant crying: The role of cry pitch and perceived urgency in an adult twin sample. *Child Abuse & Neglect, 34,* 863–873.

Owen, C. G., Whincup, P. H., Odoki, K., Gilg, J. A. & Cook, D. G. (2002). Infant feeding and blood cholesterol: A study in adolescents and a systematic review. *Pediatrics, 110,* 597–608.

Pascalis, O., & Kelly, D. J. (2009). The origins of face processing in humans: Phylogeny and ontogeny. *Perspectives on Psychological Science, 4,* 200–209.

Peirano, P., Algarin, C., & Uauy, R. (2003). Sleep–wake states and their regulatory mechanism throughout early human development. *Journal of Pediatrics, 143*(Suppl.), S70–S79.

Porath, M., Korp, L., Wendrich, D., Dlugay, V., Roth, B., & Kribs, A. (2011). Surfactant in spontaneous breathing with nCPAP: Neurodevelopmental outcome at early school age of infants = 27 weeks. *Acta Paediatrica, 100,* 352–359.

Porges, S. W., & Lispitt, L. P. (1993). Neonatal responsitivity to gustatory stimulation: The gustatory–vagal hypothesis. *Infant Behavior & Development, 16,* 487–494.

Porter, R. H., & Rieser, J. J. (2005). Retention of olfactory memories by newborn infants. In R. T. Mason, P. M. LeMaster, & D. Müller-Schwarze (Eds.), *Chemical Signals in Vertebrates* (pp. 300–307). New York, NY: Springer.

Ramchandani, P., Stein, A., Evans, J., O'Connor, T. G., & the ALSPAC Study Team. (2005). Paternal depression in the postnatal period and child development: A prospective population study. *Lancet, 365,* 2201–2205.

Ravn, M. N. (2005). A matter of free choice? Some structural and cultural influences on the decision to have or not to have children in Norway. In C. B. Douglas (Ed.), *Barren states: The population "implosion" in Europe* (pp. 29–47). New York, NY: Berg.

Redshaw, M. E. (1997). Mothers of babies requiring special care: Attitudes and experiences. *Journal of Reproductive & Infant Psychology, 15,* 109–120.

Reid, C. (2004). Kangaroo care. *Neonatal Network, 23,* 53.

Richman, A. L., Miller, P. M., & LeVine, R. A. (2010). Cultural and educational variations in maternal responsiveness. In R. A. LeVine (Ed.), *Psychological anthropology: A reader on self in culture* (pp. 181–192). Malden, MA: Wiley-Blackwell.

Righetti-Veltema, M., Conne-Perreard, E., Bousquest, A., & Manzano, J. (2002). Postpartum depression and mother–infant relationship at 3 months old. *Journal of Affective Disorders, 70,* 291–306.

Roberts, R. G., Deutchman, M., King, V. J., Fryer, G. E., & Miyoshi, T. J. (2007). Changing policies on vaginal birth after cesarean: Impact on access. *Birth: Issues in Perinatal Care, 34,* 316–322.

Rückinger, S., Beyerlein, A., Jacobsen, G., von Kries, R., & Vik, T. (2010). Growth in utero and body mass index at age 5 years in children of smoking and non-smoking mothers. *Early Human Development, 86,* 773–777.

Rückinger, S., Rzehak, P., Chen, C-M., Sausenthaler, S., Koletzko, S.…?? (2010). Prenatal and postnatal tobacco exposure and behavioral problems in 10–year–old children: Results from the GINI-plus Prospective Birth Cohort Study. *Environmental Health Perspectives, 118,* 150–154.

Ryan, A.S., Zhou, W., & Arensberg, M.B. (2006). The effects of employment status on breastfeeding in the United States. *Women's Health Issues, 16,* 243-251.

Sachs, B. P., Kobelin, C., Castro, M. A., & Frigoletto, F. (1999). The risks of lowering the cesarean–delivery rate. *New England Journal of Medicine, 340,* 54–57.

Saigal, S., den Ouden, L., Wolke, D., Hoult, L., Paneth, N., Streiner, D. L., Whitaker, A., & Pinto-Martin, J. (2003). School–age outcomes in children who were extremely low birth weight from four international population–based cohorts. *Pediatrics, 112,* 943–950.

Sansavani, A., Bertoncini, J., & Giovanelli, G. (1997). Newborns discriminate the rhythm of multisyllabic stressed words. *Developmental Psychology, 33,* 3–11.

Schaal, B., Marlier, L., & Soussignan, R. (2000). Human fetuses learn odours from their pregnant mother's diet. *Chemical Senses, 25,* 729–737.

Schott, J. M., & Rossor, M. N. (2003). The grasp and other primitive reflexes. *Journal of Neurological and Neurosurgical Psychiatry, 74,* 558–560.

Schulze, P. A., & Carlisle, S. A. (2010). What research does and doesn't say about breastfeeding: A critical review. *Early Child Development and Care, 180,* 703–718.

Selander, J. (2011). *Cultural beliefs honor placenta.* Retrieved from http://placentabenefits.info/culture.asp

Sellen, D. W. (2001). Comparison of infant feeding patterns reported for nonindustrial populations with current recommendations. *Journal of Nutrition, 131,* 2707–2715.

Shields, L., Mamun, A. A., O'Callaghan, M., Williams, G. M., & Najman, J. M. (2010). Breastfeeding and obesity at 21 years: A cohort study. *Journal of Clinical Nursing, 19,* 1612–1617.

Shorten, A. (2010). Bridging the gap between mothers and medicine: "New insights" from the NIH Consensus Conference on VBAC. *Birth: Issues in Perinatal Care, Vol 3,* 181–183.

Simkin, P. (2007). *The birth partner, Third edition: A complete guide to childbirth for dads, doulas, and all other labor companions.* Boston, MA: Harvard Common Press.

Simons, S. H. P., van Dijk, M., Anand, K. S., Roofhooft, D., van Lingen, R., & Tibboel, D. (2003). Do we still hurt newborn babies: A prospective study of procedural pain and analgesia in neonates. *Archives of Pediatrics & Adolescent Medicine, 157,* 1058–1064.

Singerman, J., & Lee, L. (2008). Consistency of the Babinski reflex and its variants. *European Journal of Neurology, 15,* 960–964.

Small, M. F. (1998). *Our babies, ourselves: How biology and culture shape the way we parent.* New York, NY: Anchor.

Spence, M. J., & DeCasper, A. J. (1987). Prenatal experience with low-frequency maternal voice sounds influences neonatal perception of maternal voice samples. *Infant Behavior and Development, 10,* 133–142.

St. James-Roberts, I., Bargn, J. G., Peter, B., Adams, D., & Hunt, S. (2003). Individual differences in responsivity to a neurobehavioural examination predict crying patterns of 1–week–old infants at home. *Developmental Medicine & Child Neurology, 45,* 400–407.

Stoll, B., Hansen, N. I., Adams-Chapman, I., Fanaroff, A. A., Hintz, S. R., Vohr, B.,...Human Development Neonatal Research Network (2004). Neurodevelopmental and growth impairment among extremely low–birth–weight infants with neonatal infection. *JAMA: Journal of the American Medical Association, 292,* 2357–2365.

Strang-Karlsson, S., Räikkönen, K., Pesonen, A-K., Kajantie, E., Paavonen, J., Lahti, J.,...Andersson, S. (2008). Very low birth weight and behavioral symptoms of Attention Deficit Hyperactivity Disorder in young adulthood: The Helsinki Study of very–low–birth–weight adults. *American Journal of Psychiatry, 165,* 1345–1353.

Super, C. M., & Harkness, S. (2009). The developmental niche of the newborn in rural Kenya. In K. J. Nugent, B. J. Petrauskas, & T. B. Brazelton (Eds.), *The newborn as a person: Enabling healthy infant development worldwide* (pp. 85–97). Hoboken, NJ: John Wiley & Sons.

Tamaru, S., Kikuchi, A., Takagi, K., Wakamatsu, M., Ono, K., Horikoshi, T., Kihara, H., & Nakamura, T. (2011). Neurodevelopmental outcomes of very low birth weight and extremely low birth weight infants at 18 months of corrected age associated with prenatal risk factors. *Early Human Development, 87,* 55–59.

Taylor, H. G., Klein, N., Minich, N. M., & Hack, M. (2000). Middle-school-age outcomes with very low birth weight. *Child Development, 71,* 1495–1511.

Thach, B. T. (2009). Does swaddling decrease or increase the risk for Sudden Infant Death syndrome? *Journal of Pediatrics, 155,* 461–462.

Thacker, S. B., & Stroup, D. E. (2003). Revisiting the use of the electronic fetal monitor. *Lancet, 361,* 445–446.

Tharpe, A. M., & Ashmead, D. H. (2001). A longitudinal investigation of infant auditory sensitivity. *AJA: American Journal of Audiology, 10,* 104–112.

Thompson, C. J. (2005). Consumer risk perceptions in a community of reflexive doubt. *The Journal of Consumer Research, 32,* 235–248.

Tierra, L., & Tierra, M. (1998). *Chinese traditional herbal medicine.* Twin Lakes, WI: Lotus Light.

Trehub, S. E. (2001). Musical predispositions in infancy. *Annals of the New York Academy of Sciences, 930,* 1–16.

Trehub, S. E., Thorpe, L. A., & Morrongiello, B. A. (1985). Infants' perception of melodies: Changes in a single tone. *Infant Behavior and Development, 8,* 213–223.

Tyano, S., Keren, M., Herrman, H., & Cox, J. (2010). *The competent fetus.* New York, NY: Wiley.

U.S. Bureau of the Census (2010). *Statistical abstract of the United States.* Washington, DC: Author.

U.S. Bureau of the Census (2010). *Statistical abstracts of the United States.* Washington, DC: U.S. Government Printing Office.

UNICEF (2004). *Low birth weight: Country, regional, and global estimates.* New York, NY:Author.

UNICEF (2004). *The state of the world's children 2002.* Geneva, Switzerland: Author.

UNICEF (2011). *Breastfeeding Initiatives Exchange.* Retrieved from http://www.unicef.org/programme/breastfeeding/

United Nations Development Programme (UNDP) (2011). *Human development report.* New York, NY: Author.

Vallejo, M. C., Ramesh, V., Phelps, A. L., & Sah, N. (2007). Epidural labor analgesia: Continuous infusion versus patient–controlled epidural analgesia with background infusion versus without a background infusion. *The Journal of Pain, 8,* 970–975.

van IJzendoorn, M. H., & Hubbard, F. O. A. (2000). Are infant crying and maternal responsiveness during the first year related to infant–mother attachment at 15 months? *Attachment and Human Development, 2,* 371–391.

van Sleuwen, B. E., Engelberts, A. C., Boere-Boonekamp, M. M., Kuis, W., Schulpen, T. W. J., & L'Hoir, M. P. (2007). Swaddling: A systematic review. *Pediatrics, 120,* e1097–e1106.

Varendi, H., Christensson, K., Porter, R. H., & Wineberg, J. (1998). Soothing effect of amniotic fluid smell in newborn infants. *Early Human Development, 51,* 47–55.

Verma, R. P., Shibli, S., Fang, H., & Komaroff, E. (2009). Clinical determinants and the utility of early postnatal maximum weight loss in fluid management of extremely low birth weight infants. *Early Human Development, 85,* 59–64.

Vouloumanos, A., & Werker, J. F. (2004). Tuned to the signal: The privileged status of speech for young infants. *Developmental Science, 7,* 270–276.

Vouloumanos, A., Hauser, M. D., Werker, J. F., & Martin, A. (2010). The tuning of human neonates' preference for speech. *Child Development, 81,* 517–527.

Warnock, F. F., Castral, T. C., Brant, R., Sekilian, M., Leite, A. M., De La Presa Owens, S., & Schochi, C. G. S. (2010). Brief report: Maternal Kangaroo Care for neonatal pain relief: A systematic narrative review. *Journal of Pediatric Psychology, 35,* 975–984.

Warnock, F., & Sandrin, D. (2004). Comprehensive description of newborn distress behavior in response to acute pain (newborn male circumcision). *Pain, 107,* 242–255.

Watkin, P. M. (2011). The value of the neonatal hearing screen. *Paediatrics and Child Health, 21,* 37–41.

WebMD (2011). *Vaginal birth after cesarean (VBAC)—Risks of VBAC and cesarean deliveries.* Retrieved from http://www.webmd.com/baby/tc/vaginal-birth-after-cesarean-vbac-risks-of-vbac-and-cesarean-deliveries

Weekley, A. (2007). *Placentophagia: Benefits of eating the placenta.* Retrieved from http://www.associated-content.com/article/289824/placentophagia_benefits_of_eating_the.html?cat=51

Weinberg, R. A. (2004). The infant and the family in the twenty-first century. *Jouranl of the American Academy of Child & Adolescent Psychiatry, 43,* 115–116.

Wendland-Carro, J., Piccinini, C. A., & Millar, W. S. (1999). The role of an early intervention on enhancing the quality of mother–infant interaction. *Child Development, 70,* 713–731.

Werner, L. A., & Marean, G. C. (1996). *Human auditory development.* Boulder, CO: Westview Press.

Werner, L. A., & Marean, G. C. (1996). *Human auditory development.* Madison, WI: Brown & Benchmark.

Westfall, R. E., & Benoit, C. (2004). The rhetoric of "natural" in natural childbirth: Childbearing women's perspectives on prolonged pregnancy and induction of labour. *Social Science & Medicine, 59,* 1397–1408.

Williams, A. L., Khattak, A. Z., Garza, C. N., & Lasky, R. E. (2009). The behavioral pain response to heelstick in preterm neonates studied longitudinally: Description, development, determinants, and components. *Early Human Development, 85,* 369–374.

Wolf, J. B. (2007). Is breast really best? Risk and total motherhood in the national breastfeeding awareness campaign. *Journal of Health Politics, Policy and Law, 32,* 595–63.

Wood, R. M., & Gustafson, G. E. (2001). Infant crying and adults' anticipated caregiving responses: Acoustic and contextual influences. *Child Development, 72,* 1287–1300.

World Health Organization (WHO) (2000). WHO Global Data Bank on Breastfeeding. Available: http://www.who.int/nut/db_bfd.htm.

World Health Organization (WHO) (2010). Method of delivery and pregnancy outcomes in Asia: The WHO global survey on maternal and perinatal health, 2007–2008. *The Lancet, 375,* 490–499.

World Health Organization (WHO) (2010). *Towards universal access: Scaling up priority HIV/AIDS interventions in the health sector.* Geneva, Switzerland: Author.

World Health Organization (WHO) (2010). WHO vaccine-preventable diseases: Monitoring system—2010 global summary. Geneva, Switzerland: Author.

World Health Organization (WHO) (2011). Cigarette consumption. Retrieved February 21, 2011, from http://www.who.int/tobacco/en/atlas8.pdf

World Health Organization (WHO) (2011). *Vacuum extraction versus forceps for assisted vaginal delivery.* Retrieved from http://apps.who.int/rhl/pregnancy_childbirth/childbirth/2nd_stage/facom/en/

World Health Organization [WHO] (2010). *World Health Statistics 2010.* Geneva, Switzerland: Author.

Zeskind, P. S., & Lester, B. M. (2001). Analysis of infant crying. In L. T. Singer & P. S. Zeskind (Eds.), *Biobehavioral assessment of the infant* (pp. 149–166). New York, NY: Guilford.

Zeskind, P. S., Klein, L., & Marshall, T. R. (1992). Adults' perceptions of experimental modifications of durations and expiratory sounds in infant crying. *Developmental Psychology, 28,* 1153–1162.

HEALTH IN THE 21ST CENTURY: NEW CHALLENGES, NEW CHOICES

- The current life expectancy at birth in the United States is 78.7 years.

- Just four bad habits—eating poorly, being physically inactive, smoking, and drinking too much—can prematurely age you by up to 12 years.

(Shannon Fagan/The Image Bank/Getty Images)

Taken from *Health: Making Choices for Life*, by April Lynch, Berry Elmore, and Jerome Kotecki.

HEALTH MATTERS

LEARNING OBJECTIVES

Identify and describe the multiple dimensions of health.
Compare health challenges across America and around the world.
Identify four lifestyle choices that profoundly influence health.
Provide examples of the six categories of determinants of health.
Describe three models of behavior change.
List seven steps for creating an effective behavior-change contract.

Have you ever noticed that, when you're ill, stressed, or sleep deprived, you're more likely to doubt yourself, argue with your roommate, and feel overwhelmed by even simple tasks? But when you're bursting with strength and stamina, you feel calm and confident. Even daunting challenges—like hiking a grueling trail or solving a complex calculus proof—can seem like fun.

Intuitively, you know health matters. But do your choices each day—what to eat, how much to sleep, whether to exercise, smoke, or abuse alcohol—really make health a priority? A theme of this textbook is that these so-called *lifestyle choices* can have a profound influence on your health. That's because, over many years, the cumulative effects of lifestyle choices can greatly increase or decrease your risk for disease, injury, disability, and early death. If health matters, then your choices matter, too.

This textbook provides the facts you need to begin evaluating your current lifestyle choices. But information is just a first step. Each module concludes by identifying a variety of practical strategies to improve your own health, as well as ways to get involved in promoting a more healthful environment on campus. With this support, you can start making healthy changes for yourself and your world.

Let's begin by exploring the concept of health: its definitions, dimensions, and unique terminology.

◇ WHAT IS HEALTH?

A century ago, the term **health** was used to mean merely the absence of illness or injury. Then in 1948, the newly formed World Health Organization (WHO)—the global health unit of the United Nations—published a radical new definition of health as "a state of complete physical, mental, and social well-being, and not merely the absence of disease or infirmity."[1]

This holistic view of health acknowledges that, in a healthy person, many different dimensions of life are working harmoniously.

Although the WHO's definition of health has been broadly accepted for decades, some researchers have objected to the concept of "complete" well-being, or asserted that the definition lacks practical value. In 1986, in the Ottawa Charter for Health Promotion, the WHO offered the following context for its definition of health:[2]

> To reach a state of complete physical, mental, and social well-being, an individual or group must be able to identify and to realize aspirations, to satisfy needs, and to change or cope with the environment. Health is, therefore, seen as a resource for everyday life . . .

This emphasis on health as a resource we use to reach our goals and satisfy our needs helps us view health less as a stable state and more as an active process. This is true as well for the closely related concept of **wellness**. Some public health authorities view wellness as a state in which we realize our fullest potential as individuals and as members of our community. But others see wellness as a process in which we actively make choices to achieve optimal health.[3] People who have a high level of wellness continually make decisions that promote health in multiple areas of their

---

Health Online
icons are found throughout the module, directing you to web links, videos, podcasts, and other useful online resources.

health
More than merely the absence of illness or injury, a state of well-being that encompasses physical, social, psychological, and other dimensions and is a resource for everyday life.

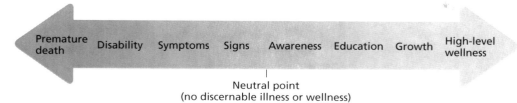

Neutral point
(no discernable illness or wellness)

FIGURE 3 The Illness-Wellness Continuum

Your general direction on the continuum matters more than your specific point on it at any given time.

Source: Adapted with permission, from *Wellness Workbook*, 3rd edition, © 2004 by John W. Travis, MD, and Regina Sara Ryan, Celestial Arts. www.thewellspring.com.

lives. On the other hand, a low level of wellness is characterized by poor decisions that increase the risk of illness, injury, disability, and premature death.

The Illness-Wellness Continuum

In 1975, wellness pioneer John W. Travis, M.D., published a book on the *illness-wellness continuum*. He envisioned a continuum with two extremes: premature death at one end and high-level wellness on the other **(Figure 3)**. Most of us fall somewhere in between, shifting between states of feeling sick, "neutral," and vibrantly healthy. Your general direction on the continuum (either toward optimal wellness or toward premature death) matters more than your place on it at any given time. You may have a cold, for instance, and not feel particularly well—but if you are taking care of yourself and have a positive attitude, your general direction will be toward greater wellness. Likewise, you may consider yourself healthy—but if you are under a great deal of stress, eating poorly, and drinking excessively, your general direction on the continuum will be toward reduced wellness.

Dimensions of Health and Wellness

Recall that the WHO definition of health identifies three dimensions—physical, mental, and social—all of which are working harmoniously. Though some researchers accept these three dimensions as adequate, others have identified more or different dimensions appropriate for the populations they serve. We acknowledge the following seven dimensions of health: physical, intellectual, psychological, spiritual, social, environmental, and occupational **(Figure 4)**. (Note that because wellness is the process of achieving optimal health, wellness, too, is multidimensional.) Let's take a closer look at each of these dimensions.

Physical Health

Physical health focuses on the body: how well it functions, and how well you care for it. Optimal physical health includes being physically active, eating nutritiously, getting enough sleep, making responsible decisions about sex, drinking, and drugs, and taking steps to avoid injuries and infectious diseases.

wellness
The process of actively making choices to achieve optimal health.

FIGURE 4 Dimensions of Health.

Health is more than just the absence of injury or illness; it encompasses multiple dimensions.
(Daniel Hurst Stock Connection Worldwide/Newscom)

Intellectual Health

Intellectual health is marked by a willingness to take on new intellectual challenges, an openness to new ideas and skills, a capacity to think critically, and a sense of humor and curiosity. People who have a high level of intellectual health not only recognize problems quickly, but also seek and create solutions. These characteristics are important not only during your years of formal education, but throughout your lifetime.

Psychological Health

Psychological health is a broad category encompassing autonomy, self-acceptance, and the ability to respond appropriately to our environment. It also includes the ability to maintain nurturing relationships with others and to pursue meaningful goals. Finally, people who are psychologically healthy sense that they are continually growing and developing as individuals.

Spiritual Health

Closely related to psychological health is spiritual health, which is influenced by the beliefs and values we hold and the ways in which we express them—for instance, in humanitarian activities, religious practices, or efforts to preserve nature and the environment. Spiritual health contributes to a sense of place and purpose in life, and can be a source of support when we face challenges.

Social Health

Social health describes the quality of our interactions and relationships with others. How satisfying are your relationships with your family, your friends, your professors, and others in your life? How do you feel about your ability to fulfill social roles, whether as a friend, roommate, or community volunteer? Good social health is also characterized by an ability to provide support to others and receive it in return.

Environmental Health

Environmental health describes the quality of our home, work, school, and social environments—as well as the health of our planet. Air quality, availability of clean water and nutritious food, crime rates, weather, pollution, and exposure to chemicals are just a few of the variables that factor into environmental health.

◇ PROUD OF MY SCARS

STUDENT STORY

"Hi, I'm Corey. I'm 19 and I'm a sophomore park and rec management major. I was born with a skeletal condition where the left side of my body is bigger than the right side. The doctors had to even out my legs so that I could walk flat-footed and wouldn't have back problems later in life. I've had a total of three surgeries, which left me with some scars. I also have a scar from my belly button all the way to the side of my rib cage. Growing up, I was always self-conscious, especially during the summer when everybody was out at the beach in swimsuits, and all these guys had six-pack abs. I knew I'd never be able to have abs like that because I have this scar running straight through my abdominal muscle.

Now, though, I've realized that my scars are a great conversation starter. People will see me and ask 'Oh, cool scar, how'd you get it?' I've learned over the years that everybody has a fail point and mine just happens to be physical. I've just learned to live with it. Those scars are what make me 'me.' I also have friends who don't really care what I look like or whether I'm the strongest or best-looking guy in the world. My friends are there whether I'm having surgeries or I'm on top of the world."

1. Where do you think Corey falls on the wellness continuum?
2. Assess how Corey is doing in at least three different dimensions of wellness.

(John Dawson, Pearson Education)

Occupational Health

Occupational health describes the quality of your relationship to your work. Rather than a paying job, your "work" may consist of your studies, an athletic endeavor, or an artistic pursuit—whatever it is that you consider your primary occupation. Does this work feel fulfilling? Do you have opportunities to advance and learn? Do you feel respected by your colleagues or peers? Challenges to occupational health include stress, lack of fulfillment in the work, poor relationships with colleagues, poor performance, inadequate compensation, and sudden unemployment.

Terminology of Health

As you can see, health and wellness are as broad as life itself. So it's not surprising that health-care providers and researchers in public health have developed an extensive vocabulary with which to communicate health-related concepts and statistics. The following are some of the most important of these terms, which you'll encounter not only throughout this textbook, but also in media reports on health-related topics:

- **Acute versus chronic illness.** An acute illness is one that comes on suddenly and intensely, like a headache or a bout of food poisoning. It typically resolves quickly, too, sometimes in a matter of hours, sometimes in a week or two. Medical treatment may or may not be required. Significant acute illnesses—like heat stroke or an infection involving the brain—can be fatal. In contrast, chronic illnesses become noticeable only gradually, often over months or years. They are initially very mild, and may continue that way, or may progress in severity. Examples are arthritis, heart disease, and age-related dementia.

- **Morbidity and mortality.** Morbidity is a clinical term meaning illness, especially the prevalence of a disease within a population. Mortality, of course, means death, but public health researchers use the term when referring to the number of deaths in a certain population or from a certain cause. For instance, a country's infant mortality rate—the percentage of babies who die before their first birthday—is often used as a general indicator of a nation's overall health status.

- **Signs and symptoms.** In the language of health care, a sign is an objective indication of a person's health status. For example, body weight, pulse, blood pressure, lab test results, and X-rays and scans are measures that can suggest the presence or absence of disease. Signs also include things we can't measure, but simply hear or see, such as wheezing, slurred speech, or a rash. In contrast, a symptom is a subjective experience reported by a patient—such as pain, shortness of breath, dizziness, or fatigue.

- **Health promotion and disease prevention.** At its simplest, health promotion is the process of helping people improve their health.[4] For instance, a campus campaign to get students to increase their hours of sleep each night qualifies as health promotion. So does reading this textbook. In contrast, disease prevention refers more specifically to actions taken to reduce the incidence of diseases. For instance, your campus health center might offer free latex condoms to reduce the incidence of sexually transmitted infections.

- **Causes and risk factors.** A cause is a factor that is directly responsible for a certain result. For example, a particular genetic defect is known to result in a disease called cystic fibrosis. And consuming food contaminated with a type of bacteria called *Salmonella* causes the infection salmonellosis. In contrast, a risk factor is a characteristic that increases the likelihood that an individual will develop a particular disease or experience an injury. For example, obesity is a risk factor for heart disease, and alcohol abuse is a risk factor for involvement in a motor vehicle accident. Notice that risk factors don't directly *cause* disease or injury; that is, not everyone who is obese develops heart disease, and many people who have heart disease are not obese. Instead, risk factors tell us about relationships; for example, 40% of deaths in motor vehicle accidents involve alcohol.[5]

The U.S. Centers for Disease Control and Prevention publishes the *Morbidity and Mortality Weekly Report (MMWR)*. Listen to short podcasts from the MMWR on a variety of health topics, from salt intake to sleep, at www.cdc.gov/mmwr/mmwrpodcasts.html.

Notice that, although you can reduce your risk for many health problems, few are entirely preventable. For example, for decades, a series of reports from the U.S. Surgeon General have stated unequivocally that smoking and exposure to secondhand smoke cause cancer; in fact, more than 440,000 Americans die each year as a direct result of their own or others' smoking.[6] But every day, people who have never smoked and have never lived with smokers learn that they have lung cancer. That's because many diseases, including cancer, are *multifactorial;* that is, they develop as a result of multiple factors, including some—such as your genetic inheritance and your age—that are not within your control. Still, the lifestyle choices you make—such as to avoid smoking and to eat a nutritious diet—can dramatically reduce your risk, or reduce the severity of your signs and symptoms should the disease develop.

◇ CURRENT HEALTH CHALLENGES

In the past century, dramatic technological advances have enabled people worldwide to enjoy longer, healthier lives. Advances in public health, such as municipal water purification, sanitation, and food service inspection, have decreased the prevalence of disease. At the same time, new diagnostic techniques such as MRI scans and DNA testing, as well as advances in vaccines, medications, radiation, and surgery, have helped us to treat disease earlier and more successfully when it does occur. Despite such progress, many health challenges remain.

Health Across America

life expectancy
The average number of years a person may expect to live.

By one very basic measure of health—how long the average person born in the United States can expect to live—we are in far better shape than our predecessors. The current **life expectancy** at birth in the United States is a record 78.7 years—more than 15 years longer than it was in 1940.[7] The causes of death have also changed dramatically over the years. In 1900, the leading causes of death were infectious diseases such as pneumonia, influenza, and tuberculosis.[8] Today, the leading causes of death in the United States are chronic diseases (see **Table 4**).[9]

America's Health Challenges

Want to know your life expectancy? Try an online longevity calculator like the ones at www. northwesternmutual.com/ learning-center/ the-longevity-game.aspx and www.livingto100.com.

In 2010, just two chronic diseases—heart disease and cancer—were responsible for almost half of all deaths (47.4%) in the United States.[9] Almost 1 out of every 2 adults has at least one chronic disease.[10] These statistics are all the more shocking when you realize that chronic diseases are among the most preventable of all health problems in the United States.[10] That's why one of the world's oldest and largest public health agencies—the U.S. Centers for Disease Control and Prevention (CDC)—is sponsoring a national initiative to reduce our rate of chronic disease. As part of this initiative, the CDC has identified four common behaviors that are responsible for most of the illness, suffering, and early death related to chronic diseases (**Figure 5**). They are:[10]

TABLE 4   Top Five Causes of Death in the United States

CAUSE OF DEATH	
All ages	1. Heart disease
	2. Cancer
	3. Chronic lower respiratory disease
	4. Stroke
	5. Accidents/unintentional injuries
15–24 years old	1. Accidents/unintentional injuries
	2. Assault/homicide
	3. Suicide
	4. Cancer
	5. Heart disease

Data from Deaths: *Preliminary Data for 2010* by S. L. Murphy, J. Xu, and K. D. Kochanek, 2012, *National Vital Statistics Reports*, 60 (4), pp. 1–69.

Motor vehicle accidents *are the leading cause of death among people aged 15 to 24 in the United States.*
(Lane Erickson/Dreamstime)

- Lack of physical activity
- Poor nutrition
- Tobacco use
- Excessive alcohol consumption

Are Americans paying attention, and if so, are we changing our behaviors? Recent national health surveys reveal the following trends among U.S. adults:

- More than 65% do not engage in regular leisure-time physical activity.[11]
- More than 34% are overweight and another 33.9% are obese.[12]
- Almost 20% smoke.[11]
- Almost 23% admitted to binge drinking within the last year.[11]

As these statistics suggest, it's time for Americans to make healthful lifestyle choices a priority.

FIGURE 5 Four Keys to Good Health
These four behaviors can significantly reduce your risk of chronic disease and early death.

Organizations That Promote America's Health

The U.S. Department of Health and Human Services (HHS) is the U.S. government's principal agency for protecting the health of all Americans and providing essential human services, especially for those who are least able to help themselves.[13] Its primary division is the U.S. Public Health Service (PHS), which is directed by the Office of the Surgeon General. The PHS includes a dozen operating divisions that work together to promote and protect the health of Americans. Among these is the CDC, as well as the following:[13]

- The *Food and Drug Administration (FDA)* is responsible for protecting the public health by assuring the safety, efficacy, and security of medications, medical devices, the food supply, cosmetics, and products that emit radiation.
- The *National Institutes of Health (NIH)* is the primary center for medical research in the United States. It comprises many institutes, such as the National Cancer Institute and the National Center for Complementary and Alternative Medicine.
- The *Substance Abuse and Mental Health Services Administration* is an agency whose mission is to reduce the impact of substance abuse and mental illness on America's communities.

Healthy People initiative
A federal initiative to facilitate broad, positive health changes in large segments of the U.S. population every 10 years.

health disparities
Gaps in the rate and burden of disease and the access to and quality of health care among various population groups.

The Healthy People Initiative

In 1979, HHS launched the **Healthy People initiative** with a report of the Surgeon General on health promotion and disease prevention efforts in the United States. This laid the groundwork for the publication in 1980 of *Healthy People 1990,* a set of 10-year objectives for improving the health of all Americans. Every decade since, HHS has updated *Healthy People* to include both new objectives and a report of the progress made over the previous decade. Called both a "road map and a compass for better health," the most recent effort, *Healthy People 2020,* was released in December 2010.[14]

Healthy People 2020 poses two main questions:[14]

- What makes some people healthy and others unhealthy?
- How can we create a society in which everyone has a chance to live long, healthy lives?

In exploring these questions, *Healthy People 2020* emphasizes an *ecological approach* to health, one that considers the relationship between an individual's health and the many factors that influence it—from biology and lifestyle choices to level of education, access to health-care services, and even the foods available in the individual's neighborhood. Later in this module, we'll discuss these influences in more detail.

One of the primary goals of the Healthy People initiative is to achieve *health equity*—the attainment of the highest level of health for all people.[14] This requires the elimination of **health**

disparities—differences in the rate and burden of disease and the access to and quality of health care among various population groups. Health disparities adversely affect groups of people who have systematically experienced greater obstacles to health based on their racial or ethnic group; religion; socioeconomic status; sex; age; mental health; cognitive, sensory, or physical disability; sexual orientation or gender identity; geographic location; or other characteristics historically linked to discrimination or exclusion.[14] For example, gays and lesbians experience certain health disparities—including a lower quality of health care—associated with the discrimination they experience. The nearby **Diversity & Health** box examines health disparities specific to race and ethnicity, and we'll examine the role of poverty and other disparities as we continue in this module.

For more information on *Healthy People 2020*, visit www.healthypeople.gov.

The behaviors that increase the risk of developing chronic diseases—including unhealthy eating habits and a lack of physical activity—are common among college students."

Health on America's Campuses

Centers of higher learning, as microcosms of our larger society, have come to recognize that promoting students' health helps the institution meet its goal of providing the best education possible. Stress, sleep deprivation, poor nutrition, depression, anxiety, alcohol and tobacco use, and sexually transmitted infections are just a few of the health issues that can affect academic performance and achievement.

DIVERSITY & HEALTH

HEALTH DISPARITIES AMONG DIFFERENT RACIAL AND ETHNIC GROUPS

Whether the causes are socioeconomic, biological, cultural, or still not well understood, health disparities exist among different racial and ethnic populations. For example:

- As a group, Hispanics are more likely to be overweight or obese than are Caucasians, more likely to die from complications of stroke or diabetes, less likely to receive all recommended childhood vaccinations, and less likely to receive prenatal care early in pregnancy.[1]
- African Americans experience the same leading causes of death as the general population, but tend to experience these illnesses and injuries more often and die of them at younger ages and higher rates than other groups. These differences start in infancy, when African American babies experience a higher infant mortality rate. Later in life, issues such as injury, violence, being overweight and obese, and chronic illnesses become especially pressing concerns. When it comes to cancer care, for example, African Americans are less likely to be diagnosed with many types of cancer early, when the disease is easier to treat, and less likely to survive 5 years after diagnosis.[2]
- Asians and Asian Americans, overall, tend to have a life expectancy longer than that of the general population. But as a highly diverse group with ancestries encompassing dozens of countries and regions throughout Asia and the Indian subcontinent, there are also significant differences in health concerns among subgroups of Asians. For example, people from parts of northeast Asia with high levels of hepatitis B tend to experience higher rates of this infectious illness (and the liver damage and liver cancer that can follow it) than other Asian subgroups.[3]

(Tetra Images/SuperStock)

- Native Americans experience lower than average rates of some of the more common health concerns in the United States, such as heart disease or cancer.[4] But they also tend to have a shorter life expectancy than the general population, due to factors including unintentional injuries, substance abuse, and suicide.[4] Diabetes and its complications are an especially important concern—Native Americans as a group have the highest rate of diabetes in the world.[4]
- Caucasians are more susceptible to cystic fibrosis (a genetic disease) than are other populations.[5] In addition, Caucasian women have a higher incidence of breast cancer than other racial or ethnic populations.[6] One recent study found that middle-aged white men and women had the fastest growing rates of suicide compared with other ethnic groups, whose rates were holding steady or declining.[7]

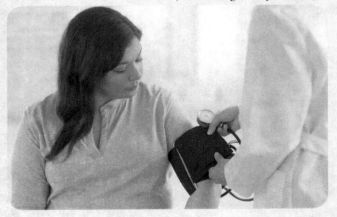

DIVERSITY & HEALTH   CONTINUED

References: **1.** "Health Disparities Experienced by Hispanics—United States," by Centers for Disease Control and Prevention, 2005, *Morbidity and Mortality Weekly Report, 53* (4), pp. 935–937. **2.** "Health Disparities Experienced by Black or African Americans—United States," by Centers for Disease Control, 2005, *Morbidity and Mortality Weekly Report, 54* (1), pp. 1–3. **3.** "Hepatitis B" by S. Chavez, 2009, *Travelers' Health – Yellow Book,* retrieved from the Centers for Disease Control, http://www.nc.cdc.gov/travel/yellowbook/2010/chapter-2/hepatitis-b.aspx. **4.** "Health Disparities Experienced by American Indians and Alaska Natives," by Centers for Disease Control and Prevention, 2003, *Morbidity and Mortality Weekly Report, 52* (30), p. 697. **5.** "Cystic Fibrosis," by the U.S. National Library of Medicine, 2008, retrieved from http://ghr.nlm.nih.gov/condition/cystic-fibrosis. **6.** "Breast Cancer Rates by Race and Ethnicity," by the Centers for Disease Control and Prevention, 2009, retrieved from http://www.cdc.gov/cancer/breast/statistics/race.htm. **7.** "Mid-life Suicide: An Increasing Problem in U.S. Whites, 1999–2005" by G. Hu, H. Wilcox, L. Wisslow, and S. Baker, 2008, *American Journal of Preventive Medicine, 35* (6), pp. 589–593.

Campus Health Challenges

The **Student Stats** box lists common health issues reported by college students in a recent nation-wide study.[15] The same study reported that nearly 60% of students describe their health as either "very good" or "excellent."

Among Americans aged 15 to 24, the leading causes of death are unintentional injuries, homicide, and suicide.[9] These sudden, traumatic deaths lead mortality in this age group because younger people do not experience the same high rates of chronic illnesses (such as heart disease and cancer) that increase mortality among the adult population as a whole. However, the behaviors that increase the risk of developing chronic diseases—including unhealthy eating habits and a lack of physical activity—are common among college students. Although 62.7% of students report being at a healthy weight, 21.4% are overweight and 11% are obese.[15] Furthermore, although 48.3% of college students meet national recommendations for physical activity (moderate exercise for at least 30 minutes at least 5 days per week or vigorous exercise for at least 20 minutes at least 3 days per week), more than half do not.[15]

Interestingly, research has shown that students tend to vastly overestimate how many of their peers are regularly using alcohol, tobacco, or other drugs.[15] For example:

- Students believe that 93.8% of their peers consumed alcohol during a given 30-day period. The actual percentage was 65.9%.

- Students believe that 81.8% of their peers had smoked cigarettes during a given 30-day period. The actual percentage was 15.2%.

- Students believe that 80.3% of their peers had smoked marijuana during a given 30-day period. The actual percentage was 15.9%.

- Students believe that 75.5% of their peers used illicit drugs (excluding marijuana) during a given 30-day period. The actual percentage was 12.9%.

The lesson here: When it comes to drugs and alcohol, it's simply not true that "everyone is doing it."

The Healthy Campus Initiative

In conjunction with the Healthy People initiative, the American College Health Association publishes an initiative called **Healthy Campus** for use in student settings. Colleges and universities participating in this program can choose to focus on improving health topics most relevant to them, such as:

- Reducing stress and depression
- Decreasing student abuse of alcohol and drugs
- Improving opportunities for daily physical activity on campus
- Improving sexual health among students

Specific objectives for *Healthy Campus 2020* are currently under development.

STUDENT  STATS

Common Health Problems Reported by College Students

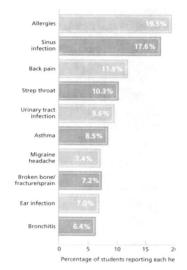

Allergies	19.5%
Sinus infection	17.6%
Back pain	11.9%
Strep throat	10.3%
Urinary tract infection	9.6%
Asthma	8.5%
Migraine headache	7.4%
Broken bone/fracture/sprain	7.2%
Ear infection	7.0%
Bronchitis	6.4%

Percentage of students reporting each he

Data from *American College Health Association National College Health Assessment (ACHA-NCHA II) Reference Group Executive Summary, Spring 2011,* by the American College Health Association, 2011, retrieved from http://www.acha-ncha.org/docs/ACHA-NCHA_Reference_Group_ExecutiveSummary_Spring2011.pdf. (Imagestate Media Partners Limited - Impact Photos/Alamy)

Healthy Campus
An offshoot of the Healthy People initiative, specifically geared toward college students.

The Healthy Campus initiative aims to improve the health of college students nationwide.

For more information on infectious diseases around the world, visit the World Health Organization website at www.who.int/topics/infectious_diseases/en.

determinants of health
The range of personal, social, economic, and environmental factors that influence health status.

Health Around the World

In our increasingly mobile and connected world, where a country experiencing a dangerous infectious disease is just a plane ride away, global health has become a top concern.

Some countries with lower levels of economic development and less stable political systems continue to experience high rates of infectious diseases that have largely been eradicated in other parts of the world. For example, parts of Africa, Asia, and South America continue to grapple with cholera, an infectious disease transmitted via unclean water supplies, and malaria, which is transmitted by mosquitoes. Although infections from the human immunodeficiency virus (HIV) have dropped in number in more-developed countries, HIV/AIDS continues to be a serious concern worldwide. More than 33 million people around the world are living with HIV infection; more than 67% of them live in sub-Saharan Africa. China, India, and Russia have seen a substantial increase in HIV infections in recent years.[16]

Some infections are now resisting conventional treatment with antimicrobial drugs. A wide range of disease-causing microorganisms—including the bacteria that cause tuberculosis and staph infections, the viruses that cause influenza, the parasites that cause malaria, and the fungi that cause yeast infections—are becoming resistant to the antimicrobial agents used for treatment.[17] People infected with resistant strains of microorganisms are more likely to have longer hospital stays and to die as a result of the infection.[17] This is a concern around the globe.

Nutritional diseases are also still a concern in developing nations: More than 1 billion people in the world go hungry, and nearly 99% of these live in the developing world.[18] Deficiency of certain vitamins and minerals causes a variety of diseases rarely seen in the United States and Europe, such as night blindness, which develops when vitamin A is deficient, and a form of mental retardation called cretinism, which is due to iodine deficiency. Malnutrition also increases an individual's susceptibility to infection, as well as the risk that infection will result in death.

To address these global disparities, a number of privately funded international health organizations have joined with public efforts in recent years. Groups founded by prominent business leaders such as Microsoft founder Bill Gates and former U.S. presidents Jimmy Carter and Bill Clinton now provide funds for public health initiatives such as immunizations, mosquito nets, water filters, vitamin drops, and the addition of iodine to salt. In the next decade, it will become clear how well these initiatives are improving global health, and how well they complement the public health efforts carried out by international agencies such as the WHO.

Whereas global rates of HIV and certain other infectious diseases have begun to stabilize or decline, rates of chronic diseases such as heart disease and type 2 diabetes are rising worldwide, including in developing nations. That's because obesity—a risk factor for chronic diseases—is increasing. Two trends contribute to the rising prevalence of "globesity": A greater percentage of the world's population now has access to high-fat, high-sugar processed foods. At the same time, more people have access to motorized transportation, labor-saving devices, and sedentary forms of entertainment. These trends have contributed to an alarming statistic: The WHO estimates that in developing nations 115 million people now suffer from obesity-related disease.[19]

HIV/AIDS continues to be a serious concern worldwide, especially in sub-Saharan Africa.
(Friedrich Stark Alamy)

To watch a video explaining and providing examples of how determinants influence an individual's health, go to www.healthypeople.gov/2020/about/DOHAbout.aspx.

◇ DETERMINANTS OF HEALTH

Earlier we noted that *Healthy People 2020* takes an ecological approach to health—one that considers the relationship of individual human beings to their environment. In this view, individuals bear some, but not all, responsibility for the state of their health. A wide range of social, economic, and environmental factors are also recognized to influence heath. The WHO, as well as the CDC and other agencies of the HHS, refer to these factors as **determinants of health.** Any steps taken to improve health—both for individuals and for populations—are likely to be more successful when they target multiple determinants of health.[20]

Determinants of health fall into six broad categories, all of which overlap to a greater or lesser extent (Figure 6). Let's take a closer look.

determinants of health
The range of personal, social, economic, and environmental factors that influence health status.

Biology and Genetics

Biologic and genetic determinants influence your health but are beyond your control. The following are the most significant determinants in this category:

- **Age.** Think back to childhood and your visits to the pediatrician. The kinds of health issues your doctor likely focused on then—ear infections, tooth eruption, and tracking your growth and development—are not relevant for young and middle adults. At the other end of the age spectrum, the physical and cognitive effects of aging increase an older adult's vulnerability to poor health.[20] Chronic illnesses like heart disease, for example, are much more common among older adults, and infectious diseases like influenza can have far more serious consequences.

- **Sex.** The genes you inherited at conception determined your sex—that is, the anatomical and physiological features that differentiate males from females. Sex has a powerful role on health, with biological differences between men and women resulting in many different health outcomes. Women tend to live about 4 years longer than men, for example, but have higher rates of some disabling health problems, such as arthritis and osteoporosis. Men are more likely to experience other serious chronic conditions, such as high blood pressure and cancer.[21]

- **Genetics.** Not only your sex, but many other aspects of your genetic inheritance influence your health. Most obviously, these include the presence or absence of any of a variety of genetic conditions such as color-blindness or hemophilia (a failure of blood clotting). You may also have inherited from one or both parents a particular gene or genes that increases your susceptibility to a disease. For instance, women who carry the BRCA1 or BRCA2 gene have an increased risk for breast and ovarian cancer.

- **Race/Ethnicity.** Although some researchers argue that race and ethnicity are social rather than biological concepts, certain population groups do have an increased or decreased risk for certain diseases when compared with the general population. (See the **Diversity & Health** box on page 386.) Awareness of these differences can prompt you to make better lifestyle choices, and can prompt your physician to provide more targeted care. For example, because African American men tend to develop aggressive prostate cancer at a higher rate than the general population, informed doctors may start screening these men for the condition earlier than others. Because Caucasians are more likely to carry genetic mutations for cystic fibrosis, doctors may consider making genetic screening before or during pregnancy a priority. Groups such as the National Coalition for Health Professional Education in Genetics are working to make medical professionals more aware of these diverse needs.

- **Health history.** Some conditions that you experienced in the past may still be influencing your health today. For instance, have you ever had chickenpox? If so, you're at increased risk for a disorder called shingles, which is characterized by a painful, itchy rash that forms blisters. After a person recovers from chickenpox, the virus remains in the body, and can become active at a later time as shingles. Similarly, many sexually transmitted infections can reduce your fertility and cause other persistent health problems. Past injuries—from a minor fracture to head trauma or a spinal cord injury—can also permanently affect health.

Create and print out your own family health history tree using the interactive tool *My Family Health Portrait* from the U.S. Surgeon General at https://familyhistory.hhs.gov/fhh-web/home.action.

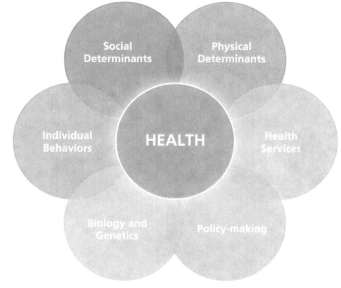

FIGURE 6 Determinants of health.

An ecological approach to health acknowledges the influence of six categories of determinants on an individual's or population's health status. Notice that the categories overlap.

- **Family history.** You—and your children—are at increased risk for developing some of the same diseases that members of your family have experienced. This is true not only for recognized genetic diseases such as sickle-cell anemia and cystic fibrosis, but also for many chronic diseases such as high blood pressure, type 2 diabetes, and osteoporosis (low bone density), and even for some psychological disorders such as depression. It's important to know your family health history so that you and your health-care provider can monitor your risk. Moreover, if you know you're at risk for a particular condition, you may be able to change your lifestyle behaviors to reduce that risk.

Individual Behaviors

Although you can't turn back the clock on aging or select different genes, other health determinants—such as your individual lifestyle choices—are very much within your ability to control.

We noted earlier that the CDC has identified four behavioral decisions with a profound ability to influence your health. These are: (1) the level of physical activity you engage in, (2) the type of diet you eat, (3) your choice about whether or not to smoke, and (4) how much alcohol you consume. Making healthful choices in these four key areas can greatly decrease your risk of developing serious illnesses later in life. On the other hand, poor choices in these areas can prematurely age you by up to 12 years![22]

Other lifestyle choices that play a significant role in promoting health include: managing your stress level, getting enough sleep, refraining from illicit drug use, developing supportive relationships with others, making responsible sexual health decisions, and taking basic steps to ensure your personal safety, such as wearing a seat belt. These behaviors are discussed later in this text.

Social Determinants

Individual behaviors are undeniably important in determining health, and are the emphasis of most personal health courses. But the ecological approach also recognizes the influence of a variety of social conditions that you can work to improve, but can't fully control. Social determinants are the economic and societal conditions in which people live—and which can impair their health or help them to thrive. They include, for example:[20]

*Regular **physical activity** is a key component of staying healthy.*
(Fancy/Alamy)

- Availability of resources to meet daily needs, such as educational and job opportunities, living wages, or healthful foods
- Social attitudes, such as discrimination
- Public safety versus exposure to crime
- Social support and social interactions
- Exposure to mass media and emerging technologies, such as the Internet or cell phones
- Socioeconomic conditions, such as concentrated poverty
- Availability of quality schools
- Transportation options

Research over the past two decades has increasingly acknowledged the significant role that social determinants play in influencing health. For example, a family may understand the value of regular physical activity, but live in a high-crime area where they're afraid to go out walking or running, and can't afford the cost of membership in a fitness club. These social determinants limit their options for physical activity. In 2012, the American Academy of Pediatrics released a policy statement associating poverty, domestic violence, and other forms of "childhood adversity" with a wide range of physical and mental health problems across the lifespan.[23]

If you're getting the sense that poverty is a fundamental social determinant of health, you're right: Rates of both disease and premature death are dramatically higher among the poor than among the rich.[24] Called the **status syndrome,** this disparity in health and mortality has been observed not only in developing nations, but also in Europe and the United States. The status syndrome has traditionally been attributed to a poor person's reduced access to quality health care, health information, nutritious foods, safe, adequate shelter, and opportunities for physical activity. However, some researchers believe that it occurs because, in people who are poor, two fundamental human needs go unmet: These are the needs for autonomy and for full social participation. Deprived of a clean, safe neighborhood, meaningful work, opportunities for quality children's education, and freedom from violence and aggression, it is harder to have control over one's life or be a full social participant.[24] These factors—lack of control and low social participation—are known to dramatically increase stress, causing physiologic changes that can lead to a variety of diseases.[24]

*These boys live in a poor area of South Bronx, NY. Living in a neighborhood that **lacks access to resources** increases their risk for a variety of health problems.*
(Visions of America/SuperStock)

Physical Determinants

Physical determinants are physical conditions in the environment. Examples include:[20]

- Aspects of the natural environment, such as plants, weather, or climate change
- Aspects of the so-called *built environment*, which includes all buildings, spaces, and products that are made or modified by people, such as homes, schools, factories, roads, subway systems, parks, and the tools, equipment, and objects within them
- Presence or absence of toxic substances and other physical hazards

For example, heat waves, floods, earthquakes, blizzards, and other natural hazards are aspects of the physical environment that influence health. Pollutants in the air, soil, and water are largely invisible, but can significantly increase disease rates. For instance, people living in regions with high levels of air pollution, such as Detroit, Michigan, or California's Central Valley, experience higher rates of asthma and other respiratory ailments.[25]

Health Services

Health services include availability of quality preventive and medical care as well as access to that care. Health literacy is also included in health services.

Access to Health Services

In countries with a national health service, health insurance status does not usually affect access to quality care. In the United States, health insurance status directly affects access to health services. People who lack adequate health insurance are less likely to have a regular doctor or place of care. They are also less likely to receive a wide range of health services, including preventive care, and more likely to delay medical treatment. Many uninsured wait until a condition has advanced to a crisis stage before visiting a local hospital emergency room—a habit that greatly increases the level of care required as well as the cost and outcome of that care. In one national survey, about 15% of respondents said they had no regular place where they sought or received health care.[11] And in 2011, the CDC reported that over 48 million Americans had no health insurance.[26] Not only people from lower socioeconomic brackets, but also members of ethnic minorities are generally less likely to have health coverage than the population overall.

Supporting the understanding that access to quality care is a key determinant of health, studies have found that while higher-income Caucasians have enjoyed a wide range of health gains, these improvements have not been shared by lower-income Caucasians and ethnic minorities.[27] In part to address this disparity, in 2010 the U.S. Congress passed into law a set of comprehensive new health-care reforms. Called the Affordable Care Act, the legislation aims to substantially reduce the number of Americans who do not have health insurance.[28]

Regardless of your income, the region you call home also influences your access to quality care. For example, Americans living in rural areas (that is, places with fewer than 2,500 residents)

status syndrome
The disparity in health status and rates of premature mortality between the impoverished and the affluent within any given society.

For updates on the Affordable Care Act, visit www.healthcare.gov.

*Can you trust **medical information** from doctors (real or fictional) on TV?*
(FOX Broadcasting Company/Album/Newscom)

have less access to specialized medical care or emergency services, and are more likely to die from heart attacks, serious injuries, and other medical emergencies.

Moreover, cultural and language barriers can limit access to quality care. All people deserve care provided by staff who understand relevant cultural concerns and can communicate with them effectively if they speak limited English. Medical translation services, available with a quick phone call, now help many care providers care for patients who otherwise might not be able to communicate with doctors or staff effectively.

Health Literacy

In the 21st century, quality health care increasingly depends upon **health literacy,** the ability to evaluate and understand health information and to make informed choices for your own care. It includes the ability to read, understand, and follow instructions in medical brochures and prescription drug labels; the ability to listen to health-care providers, ask good questions, and analyze the information you receive; and the ability to navigate an often-confusing and complex health-care system.[29] Increasingly, health literacy also requires a degree of computer literacy and media awareness. New health programs aimed at specific communities help build health literacy. In communities with sizeable Asian American populations, for example, targeted public awareness campaigns are emphasizing the need for screening and treatment for hepatitis B, which is more prevalent in several Southeast Asian countries and is often acquired in infancy or early childhood.[30]

health literacy
The ability to evaluate and understand health information and to make informed choices for your health care.

Another goal of this text is to increase your health literacy by providing you with strategies to critically evaluate all the health information that you are exposed to—whether from books, magazines, newspapers, television, advertisements, or the Internet. Online search engines like Google are increasingly the first place many people turn when seeking health information, but search results don't distinguish between sites that provide unbiased, up-to-date, scientifically sound information and sites that contain inaccurate or misleading content. The accompanying **Spotlight** will help you evaluate health information in the media.

Policy-Making

Policies at the local, state, and federal levels also affect health. Increasing taxes on cigarettes, for example, improves health by reducing the number of people who smoke. Similarly, regulations to increase motor vehicle safety—for example, establishing speed limits, mandating seat belt use, and outlawing texting while driving—reduce traumatic injuries and deaths in motor vehicle accidents. Other examples of public policy-making include changes in city zoning ordinances to promote small gardens, state programs to provide free health screenings such as mammograms to low-income families, HHS provision of health insurance for older Americans (Medicare) and Americans in need (Medicaid), efforts by the FDA to improve food safety, and the establishment of standards for air, water, and soil quality set by the U.S. Environmental Protection Agency (EPA).

Policy-making also includes corporate initiatives. For example, in 2011, Walmart—the nation's largest grocer and the world's largest retailer—collaborated with First Lady Michelle Obama's efforts to reduce childhood obesity by announcing new policies to make fresh, local foods more affordable, and to increase support for nutrition programs.

◇ ACHIEVING SUCCESSFUL BEHAVIOR CHANGE

We can't change our biology or genetics, but we can modify and change individual behaviors. Every day, we encounter opportunities to make choices that will benefit our health. Making the right choices, however, can be a challenge. We often have a good idea of what choices we *ought* to be making—for instance, eating more fruits and vegetables, setting aside time each day to exercise, or getting more sleep—but actually doing these things and achieving true **behavior change** is the hard part.

behavior change
A sustained change in a habit or pattern of behavior that affects health.

SPOTLIGHT

EVALUATING HEALTH INFORMATION IN THE MEDIA

Is the health information you just researched on the Internet accurate? Can you trust your favorite actor's television advertisement for a weight-loss product? Was last week's episode of *The Dr. Oz Show* based on any kind of medical reality? How can you make sense of the endless stream of media headlines trumpeting health studies that sometimes contradict one another?

The term *media* can mean a variety of things. We use it here to include books, newspapers, magazines, television, and Internet/web programming, as well as advertisements. To get a sense of how frequently you're inundated with health information from the media, consider the following:

- How often do you encounter an advertisement for prepackaged snack foods or meals? In contrast, how often have you encountered an advertisement for fresh fruits and vegetables?
- How often have you seen an advertisement promoting prescription drugs—for everything from weight loss to social anxiety?

(alvarez/iStockphoto)

- How regularly are you exposed to images of seemingly perfect celebrities? How does this affect your feelings about your own body and your self-esteem?

Whenever you encounter information from the media, critically assess it. Is someone trying to sell you something? Are there other ways to solve problems like being overweight without resorting to pills? Do you realize that many of the images of celebrities you see in magazines have been digitally altered to make them look more attractive than they really are?

When you come across an article about the results of the latest health-related study, consider: Was the study conducted by an unbiased source, or was it carried out by an individual or organization with a vested interest in the outcome? Have the results been replicated by other researchers? Was the sample size of the study large or small? Was the study conducted over a short or long period of time? Is the study only showing what may be a coincidental *correlation* between two things, or is it truly showing that one variable is the direct result of another variable?

The Internet deserves special attention in discussions of health in the media, as it is increasingly where people turn for information. In one survey of more than 70,000 college students, students listed the Internet as their second most often used source of health information.[1] The only source they turned to more often was their parents. When you're evaluating health information online, ask yourself the following questions to determine whether or not the information is credible:

- Is the sponsor of the site identified? Is it a commercial, nonprofit, academic, or government site? In general, sites with URLs ending in ".gov" (signifying a U.S. government site) or ".edu" (signifying an educational institution) are more likely to provide credible information than those that end in ".com." Note that the domain ".org" is used by many credible, nonprofit, noncommercial sites, but it is sometimes used by commercial entities as well.
- What is the purpose of the site? Is it to inform and educate, or is it to sell you something? If it is to sell you something, be aware that the information presented is more likely to be biased.
- Does the site tell you where the information it presents is coming from? If so, is the content based on scientific evidence, or was it written by someone hired by the site to produce marketing information? Sites that are able to provide citations and links to scientific studies and journals are more likely to be credible than sites lacking these references.
- Does the site specify when its content was last updated? Health information can sometimes change quickly, so you want to seek out information that is as current as possible.
- Does the site list a reputable professional accreditation? Many reputable health sites, for example, are accredited by the Health on the Net Foundation, and bear an insignia reading "HON."

Throughout this text, the **Get Connected** feature lists health-related websites where you can obtain reliable health information. Still, keep in mind that information on the Internet is never a substitute for consulting a health-care professional. Do not rely solely on online information to make important decisions about your health! Make an appointment with your doctor and don't be afraid to ask questions to be certain that you are receiving the most accurate information about any health issue you may be facing

Reference: **1.** *American College Health Association—National College Health Assessment Spring 2007 Reference Group Data Report (abridged),* by the American College Health Association, 2008, *Journal of American College Health, 56* (5), pp. 469–479.

predisposing factor
A physical, mental, emotional, or surrounding influence that shapes current behavior.

Factors That Influence Behavior Change

Let's begin our discussion of behavior change by taking a look at some factors that influence our success in making and maintaining change: *predisposing factors, enabling factors,* and *reinforcing factors.* Notice that these factors can help you make positive change, or can hinder your attempts to change.

Predisposing Factors

Predisposing factors are the physical, mental, emotional, and environmental factors that shape current behavior. They include your knowledge of health issues, your beliefs about how susceptible you are to illness or injury, and your attitude toward how behavior change can benefit your health. For instance, someone whose best friend died in a car crash while driving intoxicated might be predisposed to avoid drunk driving.

The values you hold are predisposing factors that can and do shape behaviors—but what if you hold conflicting values? For instance, most people value a long life free of disease and disability. But what if you're a woman who so highly values a slender appearance that you deprive yourself of adequate, nourishing food—putting yourself at risk for anemia, low bone density, and even death?

Your age, sex, race, income, and family background can also be predisposing factors in your health behavior. If you have a family history of cancer, for instance, and you believe in the wisdom of regular screenings to allow for early detection, you may be predisposed to schedule and obtain these screenings yourself. On the other hand, if you grew up in a family of smokers, you may be more likely to take up smoking yourself.

Enabling Factors

Enabling factors are the skills, assets, capacities, and resources you have at your disposal to help you make lasting changes. Examples of individual enabling factors include strong motivation and willpower, as well as the understanding and physical health necessary to embark on a program of change, such as regular exercise.

Social factors can also enable change: The education you'll get in your personal health course is likely to help you make and maintain positive health behaviors. Your peers are key enablers: If you smoke, but start hanging out with nonsmokers, you're likely to quit. Of course, peer pressure often works the other way, prompting college students to adopt behaviors—like drinking too much or experimenting with drugs—that can initiate a pattern of increasingly negative behavior change.

Aspects of your physical environment can also enable change. If you wanted to eat more nutritiously, access to a neighborhood grocery store stocked with fresh, affordable produce would be an enabling factor.

Of course, access to health information and preventive care is a critical enabling factor. Access to a registered dietitian can enable you to design a healthful diet and stick to it, and access to a smoking cessation program can enable you to quit. Policy-making that supports such resources can be a powerful enabler within a population. If you smoked marijuana throughout high school, but now want to quit, enrolling in a college with a chemical-free campus would strongly enable that change.

Support groups *for quitting smoking or drinking can play a key role in lasting behavior change.*
(Cultura Creative/Alamy)

Reinforcing Factors

Reinforcing factors include encouragements and rewards that promote positive behavior change. They include support and praise from others around you. A support group for anger management, encouragement from family members if you are trying to lose weight, or the companionship (and positive peer pressure) of a workout partner are all examples of reinforcing factors. Reinforcing factors also include barriers that can oppose, impede, or entirely derail your efforts to change. Perhaps you've begun a strength-training program to increase your level of fitness. All goes well for the first 3 weeks—but then you prematurely increase the weights and throw out your lower back. You'll need persistence and determination to overcome this negative reinforcer.

Think about a health behavior you'd like to change in your own life, and then consider the predisposing, enabling, and reinforcing factors that may affect your attitude and/or ability to implement that change.

Models of Behavior Change

A *model* is a description that helps you understand something you can't directly observe. If you've ever attended a 5-year sobriety celebration or discovered that a formerly obese friend from high school has lost a lot of weight, you might have wondered how—exactly—they did it. And would the method they used work for you?

Over many decades, public health researchers have proposed at least a dozen different models identifying a method by which they believe lasting behavior change happens. They've based their models on their work with different populations facing different health challenges at different times. So as you might expect, no single model dominates.[31] Two of the oldest and most established models are the transtheoretical model and the health belief model. More recently, researchers have developed a variety of ecological models of behavior change. Let's take a look.

The Transtheoretical Model

The **transtheoretical model of behavior change,** also called the *stages of change* model, was developed by psychologist James Prochaska and his colleagues. Its basic premise is that behavior change is a process and not an event, and that individuals are at varying levels of motivation, or readiness, to change.[31] The model identifies six stages of change that a person progresses through before achieving sustained behavior change (see **Figure 7**).[32]

- **Precontemplation,** during which a person may or may not recognize a health challenge, and in either case has no intention of making changes to address it in the near future (that is, within the next 6 months).

- **Contemplation,** during which a person acknowledges the health challenge and thinks about making a change within the next 6 months. At this stage, the person is still not ready to take action but is thinking about it.

- **Preparation,** during which a person intends to change the behavior within the next month and has a plan of action in mind (such as enrolling in a class or joining a support group).

- **Action,** during which a person modifies the behavior in an observable way—for example, quits smoking, begins jogging each week, etc. In this stage, the change is initiated, but is not yet consistent over time.

- **Maintenance,** in which a person has maintained the new behavior for 6 months or more, and continues to actively work to prevent relapse (reverting to old habits). Maintenance can last months or even years, and relapse is not unusual.

- **Termination,** during which a person has successfully achieved behavior change to the point where he or she is completely confident that relapse will not occur.

The transtheoretical model has its share of critics. The research is inconclusive, for instance, on whether application of the model truly results in lasting changes in behavior. However, the model is widely used as a framework for research studies in public health, and can be useful to consider when you think about embarking on a behavior-change plan in your own life.

enabling factor
A skill, asset, or capacity that influences an individual's ability to make and sustain behavior change.

reinforcing factor
An encouragement or a reward that promotes positive behavior change, or a barrier that opposes change.

transtheoretical model of behavior change
A model of behavior change that focuses on decision-making steps and abilities. Also called the *stages of change* model.

FIGURE 7 The Transtheoretical Model of Behavior Change
Developed by James Prochaska, this model outlines six stages of behavior change.

The Health Belief Model

health belief model
A model of behavior change emphasizing the influence of personal beliefs on the process of creating effective change.

In the 1950s, researchers at the U.S. Public Health Service developed a model of behavior change called the **health belief model**.[31] This model identifies four factors as instrumental in predicting behavior change:[31]

- **Perceived threat.** The person perceives that he or she is at risk of a threat (such as illness or injury) and perceives that this threat is real.

- **Perceived severity.** The person understands that the threat could have serious consequences in terms of pain, lost work time, financial loss, or other consequences.

- **Perceived benefit.** The person believes that the benefits of making the behavior change will outweigh the costs, inconveniences, and other challenges, and that the change is possible for him or her to make and maintain.

- **Cues to action.** The person witnesses or experiences a precipitating force that causes him or her to commit to making the change. For example, a young person at risk for diabetes witnesses a parent attempting to cope following a foot amputation as a result of the disease.

Like the transtheoretical model, the health belief model has been widely studied and used in different research designs. One survey looked at how useful this model is in weight management, and found that the greatest motivation came from the perceived threat of obesity, while the greatest resource for change came from a person's belief in his or her ability to lose weight or to maintain a healthy weight.[33] Critics, meanwhile, say the model does not adequately gauge the effect that a person's family or friends, or other aspects of the environment, have on his or her ability to make successful changes. In any case, it may help to consider the health belief model when you are assessing your own readiness for changing a health behavior: Do you perceive a serious threat to your health? If so, can you identify real benefits to making changes—benefits that outweigh the time and other costs involved in change?

◆ SLEEP DEPRIVED

STUDENT STORY

"Hi, I'm Jasmine. I'm a freshman and I'm a child development major. Each night, I'm very lucky if I get 4 hours of sleep. I'm just a night owl. I like staying up at night. My father's the exact same way. It's like 3 o'clock in the morning and we'll still be up watching the food channel. Around exam time, I find myself awake at 7:30 in the morning, still up—knowing that I have a test at 9:30. Why, I don't know.

I don't think I'm doing my best right now because when I drag myself to class, I'm half asleep. I do need to change and get better rest so that I can do better in school. I don't think I've gotten 8 hours of sleep since I was 13. I'm 19, so that's 6 years of not getting a full night's sleep. That takes a toll on your body and your mind."

(John Dawson, Pearson Education)

1: What stage of the transtheoretical model of behavior change would you guess that Jasmine is in?

2: Apply the health belief model to Jasmine's situation. What is the perceived threat? What is the perceived benefit to changing her behavior? What are the perceived barriers she may face?

3: Look at Jasmine's situation through an ecological model approach. What factors in her environment are reinforcing her late-night behavior? What factors are going against it?

Ecological Models

A criticism of most models of behavior change is that they emphasize individual actions and disregard the influence of social and physical determinants, health services, and policy-making on the initiation and maintenance of behavior change. This has led to the development of a variety of **ecological models** of behavior change, in which the creation of a supportive environment is acknowledged to be as important to achieving change as an individual's acquisition of health information and development of personal skills.[34]

Ecological models emphasize the following principles:[34]

- Multiple levels of factors—from individual behavior to family values, community support, and public policy—influence health behaviors (**Figure 8**).

- Influences at different levels interact in a positive way.

- For successful behavior change, interventions at multiple levels are most effective.

For example, an individual's motivation to lose weight might interact positively with a physician's advice to exercise, an employer's financial incentive for logging time at the company gym, and a city's construction of a new bike path. On the other hand, personal motivation is less effective when environments and policies make it difficult to choose healthful behaviors.

This means that, if you want to make lasting change, you shouldn't try to go it alone. You're more likely to succeed if you reach out for support from your health-care provider, your campus health services, and other resources in your community. In the next section, we talk more about recruiting support for your change. And if the resources you need don't currently exist—advocate for them! Every module of this text concludes with ideas on campus advocacy for health-related change.

Even with support, making healthful behavior change is still tough, so it helps to follow a systematic plan. The plan provided ahead uses an ecological framework to help you make effective and lasting behavior change.

◇ CHANGE YOURSELF, CHANGE YOUR WORLD

By enrolling in a personal health course and reading this textbook, you've already taken the initial step toward achieving better health and wellness. Throughout this book you'll find **Self-Assessments** that will help you assess your current health status, as well as **Choosing to Change Worksheets** that guide you on how to set appropriate goals and implement plans for behavior change. Each Choosing to Change Worksheet will prompt you to list your level of readiness for change—also known as your stage of behavior change—based on the transtheoretical model you read about earlier in this module. The Worksheets will then walk you through behavior-change techniques appropriate for your stage of change, promoting a greater chance of success. You can also find online versions of all of these worksheets at **www.pearsonhighered.com/lynchelmore**.

This module's **Self-Assessment: How Healthy Is Your Current Lifestyle?** is a general self-survey evaluating your current health behaviors. Complete the survey, then read the instructions for interpreting your score. Now, is there a particular area of health you'd like to turn around? Once you've identified the health behavior you most want to change . . . how do you begin? Let's look at the personal choices that help people succeed in making behavior change.

ecological model
Any of a variety of behavior-change models that acknowledge the creation of a supportive environment as equally important to achieving change as an individual's acquisition of health information and development of personal skills.

FIGURE 8 An Ecological Model of Behavior Change
Like ecological approaches to health itself, ecological models of behavior change acknowledge the influence of many factors at different levels, from individual to societal. They also emphasize the effectiveness of interventions at multiple levels. (Lissandra/Shutterstock; Tom Mareschal/Alamy; Monkey Business Images/Shutterstock; Katrina Brown/Shutterstock)

Personal Choices

Changing your targeted behavior will require more than a quick decision to "just do it." Effective change is a process and starts with information, a SMART goal, and a practical plan. You also need to identify and tackle your barriers, work your environment, promise yourself some rewards—and commit. Let's consider these seven steps one at a time.

Step 1. Get Informed

You've identified a goal—"Quit smoking" or "Get fit"—but how much do you really know about the behavior you want to change? For instance, what are the components of fitness, what are the benefits, how is it achieved, and how is it measured? If you're going to set a fitness goal and create a plan for reaching it, you need to be able to answer these questions. So your first step is to do some homework. The information in this text, together with the **Get Connected** link at the end of the module, are good resources for researching your health concerns. You can also find information at your campus health services center, from your health-care provider, and from reputable professional journals. Jot down the facts that seem most important for changing your targeted behavior. What rate of weight loss is reasonable per week, for instance? Or what's your target heart rate during aerobic exercise? Is it more effective to quit smoking "cold turkey" or gradually? Answering these questions will, among other things, help you identify a more effective behavior-change goal; that is, a SMART goal.

Step 2. Set a SMART Goal

If you don't know precisely where you're going, how will you know when you've arrived? Experts in business, education, health care, and personal development agree that goals are more likely to be achieved when they're SMART. The acronym SMART, which was first used in project management in the early 1980s, stands for the five qualities of an effective goal:[35]

- **Specific.** Your goal for change should be well-defined and entirely clear to you. For example, "I'm going to try to lose weight" is not a SMART goal. How much weight do you want to lose? Or if precise numbers don't motivate you, decide specifically how you want to look or feel: "When I'm wearing my new jeans, I want to be able to slide my finger comfortably between me and the waistband."
- **Measurable.** Include in your goal statement objective criteria for evaluating your success. What data would make it clear to anyone that you have succeeded? For instance, "By the end of this semester . . . I'll have lost 10 pounds . . . I'll be meditating for at least 20 minutes a day . . . I'll have paid off my credit card debt . . ."
- **Attainable.** Does the research you did earlier convince you that you can achieve your goal? If not, you probably won't. So make sure your goal isn't unreasonable. For instance, for most people who are overweight, it's sensible to aim to lose about ½–1 pound of body weight per week; however, 3 pounds a week is not attainable without putting your health at risk.
- **Relevant.** Don't borrow somebody else's health goal! Make sure that the goal you're working toward feels right for you. For instance, let's say you're overweight, and can't even climb a flight of stairs without feeling winded. You've been looking for some inspiration to get moving when a friend invites you to join him in training for a local marathon. Your friend has been involved in track since middle school. The goal is relevant for him, but it's not SMART for you.
- **Time based.** A SMART goal has a time frame. For instance: "For the next 6 months, each time I weigh myself—on the 15th and the 30th of each month—I'll have lost at least 1 pound. In 5 months' time, by December 30th, I'll have lost 10 pounds."

The National Institutes of Health also advises that your goal be *forgiving*.[36] That is, it should allow for the occasional intervention of unforeseen events. A goal of walking for 30 minutes a day, 5 days a week, is forgiving. A goal of walking for 30 minutes a day, every day, is not.

Step 3. Make a Plan

A SMART goal is like a guiding vision: "In 6 months, I'm going to get on that scale and see that I've lost 20 pounds!" But to make it happen, you need an action plan, and that means you need to break down your goal into specific, achievable, day-to-day actions that will enable you to accomplish it. In doing this, it helps to use a technique called **shaping;** that is, breaking a big goal into a series of smaller, measurable steps. If you'd like to eventually run a 10K, for instance, set yourself a goal of a shorter distance at first, and then gradually increase your distance a little each week.

Many people who want to lose weight think that a good action plan would be: "I'll eat right and exercise every day." But what does it mean to "eat right"? And what kind of exercise? For how long? Where and when? When shaping, it can be helpful to ask yourself questions like: who, what, when, where, why, how, and how long? Here is an example:

*Keep in mind your current situation when setting goals. Set a goal that is **relevant** and **attainable** and you're more likely to reach it.*
(Supri Suharjoto/Shutterstock)

- On Sunday morning, I'll weigh myself and write down my weight.

- Monday to Friday, on my morning break between classes, I'll skip the mocha and have a plain coffee with skim milk. At lunch, instead of a regular soda, I'll get a diet soda or water. And I'll skip the fries with my sandwich.

- Also, after my last class on M/W/F, I'll walk to the fitness center. I'll do at least 10 minutes on the treadmill, 10 minutes on the stationary bike, and 10 minutes on the stair-climber. On Saturday morning, I'll take the drop-in yoga class.

- On Sunday morning, I'll weigh myself again. If I've lost 1 pound or more, I'll continue with my plan for another week. And I'll call my best friend to celebrate! If I haven't, I'll increase my exercise next week to 15 minutes per machine.

Step 4. Identify Barriers and How You'll Overcome Them

Barriers are factors that stand in the way of successful change. You can think of them as the "disabling" factors and "negative reinforcers" we discussed earlier. In an ecological model of behavior change, barriers can emerge from any of the multiple levels of influence on human behavior. For instance, emotional factors like fear and anxiety are common barriers, as is a factor called low self-efficacy.[37] One of the most important psychological factors influencing our ability to change, **self-efficacy** is both the conviction that you can make successful changes and the ability to take appropriate action to do so. If you believe in your own ability to get in better shape, for example, you'll keep exercising, even if a few workouts leave you tired or frustrated. If you have low self-efficacy, you may give up, or never attempt an exercise program in the first place.

Your sense of self-efficacy, and the actions that stem from it, are closely tied to your **locus of control.** If you have an *internal* locus of control, you are more likely to believe that you are the master of your own destiny. When a barrier presents itself, you'll look for ways to overcome it. If you have an *external* locus of control, you are more likely to believe that events are out of your hands—that there's little you can do to overcome barriers.

What barriers might exist in your social environment? Let's say you want to lose weight, but your roommate is a culinary arts major who's constantly cooking and baking the most delectable treats—and asking you to try them. You might overcome this barrier by telling your roommate about your weight-loss plan, and asking him or her to create some low-calorie meals and snacks. Self-advocacy is an essential—though sometimes uncomfortable—skill to practice in demonstrating self-efficacy.

Aspects of your physical environment can act as barriers, too. But with some ingenuity, you can often find ways to overcome them. If you're trying

shaping
A behavior-change technique based on breaking broad goals into more manageable steps

self-efficacy
The conviction that you can make successful changes and the ability to take appropriate action to do so.

locus of control
A person's belief about where the center of power lies in his or her life; it can be external or internal.

*Factors in your **environment** can be barriers to behavior change. If you'd like to adopt a more healthy diet, you may want to limit your trips to the bakery!*

(Helen King/Lithium/AGE Fotostock)

to stop smoking, but there's an enticing smoke shop in your neighborhood with a variety of tobacco products from around the world, that's a barrier—especially if you tend to walk past it several times a day. A simple way to overcome this barrier would be to choose a different route. If you're trying to lose weight and struggle with binge eating, make sure you go through your apartment or dorm room and get rid of any junk foods.

We discussed earlier the significant disparity in access to health services in the United States. Lack of access to consistent, high-quality care is a barrier to change for millions of Americans. As a college student, you may have access to low-cost health services, from preventive and clinical care to counseling and support groups, as well as classes and programs in stress management, smoking cessation, and other health topics.

People with a high level of self-efficacy and an internal locus of control may be able to overcome most barriers to behavior change. You can increase your self-efficacy and shift your locus of control by turning to clearly defined techniques that help change behavior in positive ways specific to your health concerns. Throughout this book, we offer **Practical Strategies** boxes to help you do just that.

Step 5. Recruit Some Support

According to the ecological models of behavior change, your plan for change will be more likely to succeed if you have different levels of support. Start with your family members and friends. With whom do you feel comfortable sharing your plans for change? Give your support group specific instructions about how they can help; for instance, if you want to lose weight, you might ask your mom to stop sending you care packages loaded with cookies and other sweets. When your motivation wanes, call on your support group to cheer you on. If family members and friends can't provide the consistent support you need, consider joining a campus or community self-help group. Many such programs pair you up with a coach, mentor, or buddy you can call on for advice and caring.

modeling
A behavior-change technique based on watching and learning from others.

A subtle form of social support comes through **modeling**, learning behaviors by watching others. This strategy enables you to learn from the experiences of others who have already made successful change. If you'd like to eat less junk food, for example, observe the habits of a health-conscious friend who has already scoped out the options for healthy eating on campus. A rarely acknowledged benefit of modeling is that it lets you imagine yourself engaging in the same healthful behavior—in a sense, it allows you to *rehearse* it. Frequent rehearsal through modeling helps you become more and more familiar and comfortable with the actions required for the behavior change. You don't have to be personally acquainted with your model, either: Reading a biography of someone who has successfully overcome alcohol addiction, for example, can help you understand how to change aspects of your personal life and your environment to achieve a similar change.

Don't ignore campus resources as a source of support for your plan for change. Remember all that campus-services information you got at the start of your freshman year? Take a look back through it, and you may be surprised to find a department or organization ideally suited to support your targeted change.

Step 6. Promise Yourself Rewards

reinforcement
A motivational behavior-change technique that rewards steps toward positive change.

Rewards keep you motivated to sustain change. For example, you might promise yourself new clothing after you've reached a target weight goal. However, **reinforcement** doesn't have to be a material object. For instance, the natural "high" people often feel after physical exercise can be its own positive reinforcement. Many people who are trying to quit smoking set aside the money they would have spent on cigarettes daily, with the promise of travel or another significant reward when they've reached a time goal—say, 6 months or a year—smoke free.

End-goal rewards are important, but it's also important to reward yourself for small steps along the way. For instance, if you enroll in an aerobics class held on T/TH throughout the current semester, you might promise yourself that, when you attend both sessions, you'll reward yourself with an act of "self-kindness," such as a long-distance call to a loved one that weekend.[36]

> "End-goal rewards are important, but it's also important to reward yourself for small steps along the way."

Step 7. Commit in Writing

Many people find it helps to write out and sign their name at the bottom of a behavior-change contract—indicating that they've made a pact with themselves that they intend to keep. So if you're ready to take the plunge, turn to the **Choosing to Change Worksheet** on page 405 for a form you can use. Notice that the steps in this contract follow those just discussed.

Make copies of your behavior-change contract, and place them anywhere you want support: on the refrigerator, your full-length mirror . . . or scan your contract and use it as your screensaver image on your laptop so you see it several times throughout the day!

Believe It!

Once you have your contract, it's time to make it happen. When barriers arise—and they will—don't give in to discouragement. Try to fill your mind with positive **self-talk**—thoughts that affirm your ability to change and acknowledge the help available to you from your environment. At all costs, avoid negative self-talk—the inner chatter that says you can't do this, or you don't have the

self-talk
A person's internal dialogue.

PRACTICAL STRATEGIES FOR CHANGE

CHANGING YOUR SELF-TALK

Psychotherapists and personal development coaches know that a first step for changing your behavior is to change your thoughts about that behavior. Here are some proven strategies for becoming your own best behavior-change coach:

- **Bust the myth of "I can't."** You wrote a SMART—and forgiving—goal, right? That means it's *Attainable*, which in turn means, "You can." To bust the myth of "I can't," try expanding the statement with an action within your control. For instance, "I can, because I'm going to walk on the indoor track at the fitness center today, and whenever it snows." Or, "I can, because not even this friendship is worth more than my staying sober."

- **Affirm yourself, and then affirm yourself again.** Positive affirmations are often the subject of spoofs, but they can be highly effective in supporting change, because they force you to envision yourself as you plan to be. For instance: "I am fully able to handle anything that comes along today," or "My body is fit and strong," or, "Alcohol has no power over me." Experts suggest that you repeat your affirmation three or four times as soon as you wake up, and then several more times throughout the day. Tape your affirmation to your bathroom mirror, the glove compartment of your car, the back of your cell phone . . . anywhere you'll see it and say it.

- **Dump the disaster script.** Let's say you want to cut down on your drinking, but at a party after your last final exam, you

(Maridav/Shutterstock)

blow it. Sick and discouraged the next day, you might be tempted to think of yourself as "a loser." Instead, recognize that what happened is not a disaster. You didn't drive while drunk and get in a car crash. Okay, you're sick, but not dangerously so. Switch your disaster script for a learning script: "I guess last night shows me that, when I'm letting down from stress, I'm more vulnerable than usual to binge drinking. I'm not a loser. I can control my drinking. From now on, I'm going to make sure I drink something non-alcoholic before going to a party, so I'm not thirsty when I get there, and I'll bring along a couple of bottles of non-alcoholic beer to have in between alcoholic drinks while I'm there."

In short, rather than dwelling on roadblocks, look for solutions. The result will help you feel better about yourself and solve your problems more effectively.

self-monitoring
A behavior-change technique in which the individual observes and records aspects of his or her behavior-change process.

time or money, or it's not important anyway. The nearby **Practical Strategies for Change** can help you turn negative chatter into positive self-talk.

Another tip for maintaining your belief in yourself is to engage in **self-monitoring;** that is, to observe and record aspects of your behavior-change process, such as how many servings of fruits and vegetables you eat each day, or how many hours of sleep you get each night. Such self-monitoring can provide solid evidence of improvement at times when you're not sure how you're doing, and can boost your confidence when it starts to slip. Your record can also show you when it's time to shift your change plan into higher gear. In all these ways, self-monitoring of a behavior can move you closer to your goal; for example, when the record shows that your level of physical activity is increasing, you'll be encouraged to keep it up.[36]

Cope With Relapse

relapse
A return to the previous state or pattern of behavior.

When people attempt to change a long-term behavior, a lapse—a temporary "slip" back to the previous behavior—is highly likely.[38] For instance, a person trying to quit smoking who takes a drag on a friend's cigarette is experiencing a lapse. In contrast, a **relapse** is a return to the previous state or pattern of behavior: The person completely gives up the attempt to quit. Relapse is common; for example, according to the American Cancer Society, a majority of the people who successfully quit smoking have tried to quit—and relapsed—several times before.[39]

Certain conditions influence the likelihood that a lapse will devolve into a full-blown relapse. For instance, if the person views the lapse as due to external circumstances within the individual's control—"My roommate left an open pack of cigarettes out in full view, but from now on, has agreed to keep them out of sight."—then relapse is unlikely. By viewing a lapse as a learning experience, the person can then experiment with different strategies for changing or coping with the stimulus that provoked the lapse. In contrast, if a person views a lapse as due to factors that are internal, global, and/or uncontrollable—"My parents are alcoholics, so it's in my genes. I can't change."—then true relapse is more likely to occur.[38] See the **Practical Strategies for Change** for information on changing your self-talk to "dump the disaster script" and learn from your lapses.

Preventing a relapse is easy if you can prevent a lapse in the first place! To do it, take an inventory of the full ecological spectrum of factors that might trigger a lapse, and then identify strategies for coping. Two strategies for preventing lapses include the following:

cue control
A behavior-change technique in which the individual learns to change the stimuli that provoked the lapse.

- **Control cues.** With **cue control,** you learn to change the stimuli that provoke your unwanted behavior. For example, you may learn from your self-monitoring records that you're more likely to overeat while you're watching television, or whenever your mom leaves her latest batch of homemade cookies on the kitchen counter, or when you're around a certain friend. You might then try to change the behavior by:[36]

  - Separating the behavior from the cue (don't eat while watching television)
  - Taking action to avoid or eliminate the cue (ask your mom to put her cookies in a closed container out of sight)
  - Changing the environment or other circumstances surrounding the cue (plan to meet your friend in a nonfood setting)

counter-conditioning
A behavior-change technique in which the individual learns to substitute a healthful or neutral behavior for an unwanted behavior triggered by a cue beyond his or her control.

- **Find a substitute.** For cue control to work, you have to have the capacity to change the stimulus. But in our complex lives, this isn't always possible. Fortunately, there's a technique called **counter-conditioning,** in which you learn to substitute a healthful or neutral behavior for the unwanted behavior when it's triggered by a cue beyond your control. One of the simplest examples is the urge to have something in their mouths that strikes most smokers repeatedly in the first few weeks after they quit. With counter-conditioning, the person replaces cigarette smoking with chewing on something, whether gum, licorice, or even a toothpick. Peer pressure commonly triggers lapses, but countering can be surprisingly effective in overcoming it. Write out and memorize one or more short, assertive statements such as, "No thanks, I've had enough." Then, in situations in which you'd usually give in, substitute your assertion.

Campus Advocacy

When a barrier to change exists in your social or physical environment, or results from poor health services or policy-making, your best chance for change might just be in **advocacy**; that is, working independently or with others to directly improve services in or other aspects of your environment, or to change related policies or legislation. You may think of advocacy as lobbying to legislators, and while that's one form, there are many others available to you in your role as a college student. These include the following:

- Get better informed about the issue, especially what's happening on campus and within your community.
- Use your social networking pages to heighten awareness of the issue among your contacts.
- Meet directly with campus faculty or staff members to share your experiences, feelings, and suggestions on the issue.
- Write about the issue for campus news services.
- Speak about the issue at campus gatherings.
- Organize a letter-writing campaign to your dean of students or other decision-makers.
- Organize a petition drive or student demonstration related to the issue.
- Join a campus organization already working on the issue.
- Found an organization of your own.

Concluding every module of this book, you'll find suggestions for campus advocacy specific to the topics addressed in that module, from fitness to discrimination to climate change. These suggestions may or may not be appropriate for your campus. Still, we hope they'll provide you with practical examples of strategies that have worked for others, and some inspiration for advocacy of your own. The bottom line is, even in the face of health disparities that may seem beyond your personal control—poverty, pollution, lack of access to health services, restrictive policies—one voice can start a chain reaction that leads to change. Make it yours.

advocacy
Working independently or with others to directly improve services in or other aspects of the environment, or to change related policies or legislation.

Watch videos of real students discussing their health at: www. pearsonhighered.com/ lynchelmore.

SELF-ASSESSMENT

HOW HEALTHY IS YOUR CURRENT LIFESTYLE?

Complete one section at a time by circling the number under the answer that best describes your behavior. Then add the numbers you circled to get your score for that section. Write the score on the line provided at the end of each section.

CIGARETTE SMOKING	ALMOST ALWAYS	SOMETIMES	ALMOST NEVER
If you are currently a nonsmoker, enter a score of 10 for this section and go to the next section on Alcohol and Drugs.			
1. I avoid smoking cigarettes.	2	1	0
2. I smoke only low-tar and -nicotine cigarettes or I smoke a pipe.	2	1	0
		SMOKING SCORE ————	
ALCOHOL AND DRUGS			
1. I avoid drinking alcoholic beverages or I drink no more than 1 (for women) or 2 (for men) drinks a day.	4	1	0
2. I avoid using alcohol or other drugs (especially illegal drugs) as a way of handling situations or problems.	2	1	0

ALCOHOL AND DRUGS

3. I am careful not to drink alcohol when taking certain medicines (for example, medicine for sleeping, pain, colds, and allergies) or when pregnant.	2	1	0
4. I read and follow the label directions when using prescribed and over-the-counter drugs	2	1	0

ALCOHOL AND DRUGS SCORE ————

EATING HABITS

1. I eat a variety of foods each day, such as fruits and vegetables; whole-grain breads and cereals; lean meats; low-fat dairy products; beans and legumes; nuts and seeds.	4	1	0
2. I limit the amount of fat, saturated fat, *trans* fat, and cholesterol I eat (including fat on meats, eggs, butter, cream, shortenings, and organ meats such as liver).	2	1	0
3. I limit the amount of salt I eat by cooking with only small amounts, not adding salt at the table, and avoiding salty snacks.	2	1	0
4. I avoid eating too much sugar (especially frequent snacks of sticky candy or soft drinks).	2	1	0

EATING HABITS SCORE ————

EXERCISE/FITNESS

	ALMOST ALWAYS	SOMETIMES	ALMOST NEVER
1. I do vigorous exercises for 30 minutes a day at least 5 times a week (examples include jogging, swimming, brisk walking, or bicycling).	4	2	0
2. I do exercises that enhance my muscle tone for 15–30 minutes at least 3 times a week (examples include using weight machines or free weights, yoga, calisthenics).	3	1	0
3. I use part of my leisure time participating in individual, family, or team activities that increase my level of fitness (such as gardening, dancing, bowling, golf, baseball).	3	1	0

EXERCISE/FITNESS SCORE ————

STRESS CONTROL

1. I have a job, go to school, or do other work that I enjoy.	2	1	0
2. I find it easy to relax and express my feelings freely.	2	1	0
3. I recognize early, and prepare for, events or situations likely to be stressful for me.	2	1	0
4. I have close friends, relatives, or others with whom I can talk about personal matters and call on for help when needed.	2	1	0
5. I participate in group activities (such as religious worship and community organizations) and/or have hobbies that I enjoy.	2	1	0

STRESS CONTROL SCORE ————

SAFETY/HEALTH

1. I wear a seat belt while riding in a car.	2	1	0
2. I avoid driving while under the influence of alcohol and other drugs, or riding with someone else who is under the influence.	2	1	0
3. I obey traffic rules and avoid distractions like texting and talking on the phone when driving.	2	1	0
4. I am careful when using potentially harmful products or substances (such as household cleaners, poisons, and electrical devices).	2	1	0
5. I get at least 7 hours of sleep a night.	2	1	0

SAFETY/HEALTH SCORE ————

HOW TO INTERPRET YOUR SCORE

Examine your score for each section and refer to the key below for a general assessment of how you are doing in that particular area of health.

Scores of 9 and 10

Excellent. Your answers show that you are aware of the importance of this area to your health. More important, you are putting your knowledge to work for you by practicing good health habits. As long as you continue to do so, this area should not pose a serious health risk. It's likely that you are setting an example for the rest of your family and friends to follow. Because you got a very high test score on this part of the test, you may want to consider other areas where your scores indicate room for improvement.

Scores of 6 to 8

Good. Your health practices in this area are good, but there is room for improvement. Look again at the items you answered with a "Sometimes" or "Almost Never." What changes can you make to improve your score? Even a small change can help you achieve better health.

Scores of 3 to 5

At Risk. Your health risks are showing. Would you like more information about the risks you are facing? Do you want to know why it is important for you to change these behaviors? Perhaps you need help in deciding how to make the changes you desire. In either case, help is available. You can start by contacting your health-care provider or a registered dietitian.

Scores of 0 to 2

Seriously at Risk. Obviously, you were concerned enough about your health to take this test. But your answers show that you may be taking serious risks with your health. Perhaps you were not aware of the risks and what to do about them. You can easily get the information and help you need to reduce your health risks and have a healthier lifestyle if you wish. Are you ready to take the next step?

CHOOSING TO CHANGE WORKSHEET

The Choosing to Change Worksheets guide you on how to implement your behavior-change plans based on the stages of change identified by the transtheoretical model.

Stages of Behavior Change:

Precontemplation: I do not intend to make a change in the next 6 months.

Contemplation: I might make a change in the next 6 months.

Preparation: I am prepared to make a change in the next month.

Action: I have been making a change for less than 6 months.

Maintenance: I have been maintaining a change for more than 6 months.

After you have completed the Self-Assessment on the previous page, consider what stage of change you are in for each of the behaviors listed. Then, select one behavior—in which you are at either the contemplation or preparation stage—that you would like to target for change over the next few months. Next, fill out the Behavior Change Contract below. Make sure you sign it, and either display it where you'll see it often, or consider discussing it with your health instructor as part of your work toward your long-term goal.

BEHAVIOR CHANGE CONTRACT

My behavior change: _____

1. Three important benefits of changing my behavior are:

  1._____

  2._____

  3._____

2. My SMART goal for this behavior change is:

_____

_____

_____

3. Keeping my current stage of behavior change in mind, these short-term goals and rewards will make my SMART goal more attainable:

Short-term goal	Target date	Reward
Short-term goal	Target date	Reward
Short-term goal	Target date	Reward

4. Barriers I anticipate to making this behavior change are:

  1._____

  2._____

  3._____

The strategies I will use to overcome these barriers are:

  1._____

  2._____

  3._____

5. Resources I will use to help me change this behavior include:

  • a friend, partner, or relative: _____

  • a school-based resource: _____

  • a health-care resource: _____

  • a community-based resource:_____

  • a book or reputable website: _____

6. When I achieve the long-term behavior change described above, my reward will be:

_____   _____
                                              Target date

7. I intend to make the behavior change described above. I will use the strategies and rewards above to achieve the goals that will contribute to a healthy behavior change.

Signed: _____

◇ MODULE SUMMARY

- *Health* is more than merely the absence of disease or injury. In a healthy person, many different dimensions of life are working harmoniously.

- *Wellness* is the process of actively making choices to achieve optimal health.

- Although you can reduce your risk for many health problems, many are multifactorial, and some of the contributing factors are not within individual control.

- Although life expectancy in the United States is a record 78.7 years, many health challenges remain. For example, just two chronic diseases—heart disease and cancer—are responsible for almost half of all deaths in the United States.

- The four common behaviors responsible for most of the illness, suffering, and early death related to chronic disease in the United States are lack of physical activity, poor nutrition, tobacco use, and excessive alcohol consumption.

- The U.S. Department of Health and Human Services (HHS) is the U.S. government's principal agency for protecting the health of all Americans. Its primary division is the U.S. Public Health Service, and one of its leading agencies is the Centers for Disease Control and Prevention (CDC).

- The HHS initiative known as Healthy People takes an ecological approach to health that seeks to achieve health equity and the elimination of health disparities.

- Among Americans aged 15 to 24, the leading causes of death are unintentional injuries, homicide, and suicide. Stress, depression, anxiety, alcohol and tobacco use, and sexual health compromises are all common health concerns faced by college students.

- Global health problems include infection, malnutrition, and obesity-related diseases.

- The six broad categories of determinants of health include: biology and genetics, individual behaviors, social determi-nants, physical determinants, health services—including access to quality health care and health literacy—and policy-making.

- *Predisposing, enabling,* and *reinforcing factors* can all influence our success in making and maintaining health-related behavior change.

- The *transtheoretical model of behavior change* proposes six stages that a person progresses through before achieving sustained behavior change.

- The *health belief model* identifies four factors as instrumental in predicting health-related behavior change, including perceptions of threat, severity, benefit, and cues to action.

- Ecological models of behavior change acknowledge that the creation of a supportive environment is as important to achieving change as an individual's acquisition of health information and development of personal skills.

- After identifying a health-related behavior you want to change, seven steps for implementing that change include: becoming informed; setting a SMART goal; breaking down your goal into a sequential action plan; identifying barriers to change and how you'll overcome them; recruiting support; promising yourself rewards; and committing in writing.

- As you put your plan into action, identify thoughts constituting negative self-talk and replace them with affirmations and other examples of positive self-talk. Use self-monitoring to see your real progress and move closer to your goal.

- Prevent relapse by taking inventory of the full ecological spectrum of factors that might trigger a lapse, and then identifying strategies for coping, including cue control and counter-conditioning.

- Advocacy can be effective when a barrier to change exists in your social or physical environment, or results from poor health services or policy-making.

◇ TEST YOUR KNOWLEDGE

1. Which dimension of health is characterized by the quality of your interactions and relationships with other people?
   - **a.** physical health
   - **b.** intellectual health
   - **c.** social health
   - **d.** occupational health

2. The process of actively making choices to achieve optimal health is called
   - **a.** psychological health.
   - **b.** wellness.
   - **c.** self-efficacy.
   - **d.** precontemplation.

3. Which of the following behaviors can have profound health benefits?
   - **a.** eating nutritiously
   - **b.** being physically active
   - **c.** not smoking and not drinking excessively
   - **d.** all of the above

4. The ability to read, understand, and follow instructions in medical brochures and prescription drug labels is an example of
   - **a.** health literacy.
   - **b.** wellness.
   - **c.** behavior change.
   - **d.** occupational health.

5. You've decided to get fit. The fact that you live in a warm, sunny climate is an example of
   - **a.** a predisposing factor for behavior change.
   - **b.** an enabling factor for behavior change.
   - **c.** a reinforcing factor for behavior change.
   - **d.** none of the above.

6. In the transtheoretical model of behavior change, which stage indicates the period during which a person has modified the behavior in an observable way?

   a. precontemplation

   b. contemplation

   c. preparation

   d. action

7. Which of the following is a principle of the ecological models of behavior change?

   a. The individual's belief that making a change will reduce a threat to his or her health is the primary factor in behavior change.

   b. Interventions at multiple levels—from individual to society—are most effective in making health-related behavior change.

   c. Influences at multiple levels interact in a negative way.

   d. The individual must be able to admit the potential environmental consequences of changing a behavior.

8. The belief that events are out of your control is characteristic of

   a. self-efficacy.

   b. a strong internal locus of control.

   c. a strong external locus of control.

   d. the termination stage of behavior change.

9. Adopting a behavior by watching and learning from others is characteristic of

   a. modeling.

   b. shaping.

   c. reinforcement.

   d. changing self-talk.

10. Relapse is

   a. a temporary "slip" back to the previous behavior.

   b. uncommon.

   c. almost always due to circumstances beyond the person's individual control.

   d. less likely when the person views the lapse as due to external circumstances.

Answers: 1. C; 2. B; 3. D; 4. A; 5. B; 6. D; 7. B; 8. C; 9. A; 10. D

GET CRITICAL

WHAT HAPPENED

In the fall of 2009, British celebrity chef Jamie Oliver arrived in Huntington, West Virginia, and declared a "food revolution." With its soaring obesity rates, Huntington had recently been named the unhealthiest city in the United States by the Centers for Disease Control. Oliver's goal was to educate the residents of Huntington on the basics of good nutrition and to encourage behavior change at both the individual level and the community level (for example, making school lunches more nutritious), and to film his efforts for a nationally broadcast reality television show. Although the project had many supporters, critics charged that Oliver was a celebrity opportunist with a condescending attitude toward the citizens of Huntington.

WHAT DO YOU THINK?

1: What's your opinion of Jamie Oliver's "food revolution"? Are you in favor of his efforts or do you find them offensive?

2: Recall the ecological models of behavior change. With what principle(s) are Oliver's efforts aligned?

3: Does a celebrity-driven health campaign make you more motivated to change a health behavior? Why or why not?

(Press Association via AP Images)

GET CONNECTED

Health Online Visit the following websites for further information about the topics in this module:

- Centers for Disease Control and Prevention
  www.cdc.gov

- Go Ask Alice (answers to health questions, sponsored by Columbia University)
  www.goaskalice.columbia.edu

- U.S. Department of Health and Human Services' healthfinder.gov
  http://healthfinder.gov

- U.S. Department of Health and Human Services' *Healthy People 2020*
  www.healthypeople.gov

- Medline Plus
  www.nlm.nih.gov/medlineplus

- Mayo Clinic
  www.mayoclinic.com

- World Health Organization
  www.who.int/en

- New Mexico Media Literacy Project
  http://medialiteracyproject.org

Mobile Tips!

Scan this QR code with your mobile device to access additional health tips. Or, via your mobile device, go to *http://mobiletips. pearsoncmg.com* and navigate to Chapter 1.

◆ REFERENCES

i.   Murphy, S. L., Xu, J., & Kochanek, K. D. (2012, January 11). Deaths: preliminary data for 2010. *National Vital Statistics Reports*, 60 (04). Available at www.cdc.gov/nchs/data/nvsr/nvsr60/nvsr60_4.pdf.

ii. Kvaavik, E., Batty, G., Ursin, G., Huxley, R., & Gale, C. (2010). Influence of individual and combined health behaviors on total and cause-specific mortality in men and women. *Archives of Internal Medicine*, 170 (8), 711–718.

1.   World Health Organization. (1948). Preamble to the Constitution of the World Health Organization as adopted by the International Health Conference, New York, 19–22 June, 1946; signed on 22 July 1946 by the representatives of 61 States (Official Records of the World Health Organization, no. 2, p. 100) and entered into force on 7 April 1948. Available at http://www.who.int/about/definition/en/print.html.

2.   World Health Organization. (1986). Ottawa Charter for Health Promotion. First International Conference on Health Promotion. (21 November, 1986). WHO/HPR/HEP/95.1. Available at http://www.who.int/hpr/NPH/docs/ottawa_charter_hp.pdf.

3.   National Wellness Institute. (2010). *Defining wellness*. Retrieved from http://www.nationalwellness.org/index.php?id_tier=2&id_c=26.

4.   O'Donnell, M. P. (2009). Definition of health promotion. *American Journal of Health Promotion*, 24 (1), iv. Available at http://www.healthpromotionjournal.com/index.html.

5.   National Institute on Alcohol Abuse and Alcoholism. (2010). *Rethinking drinking: Alcohol and your health*. Retrieved from http://rethinkingdrinking.niaaa.nih.gov/WhatsTheHarm/WhatAreTheRisks.asp.

6.   U.S. Department of Health and Human Services. (2010). *How tobacco smoke causes disease: The biology and behavioral basis for smoking-attributable disease. A report of the Surgeon General*. Retrieved from http://www.surgeongeneral.gov/library/tobaccosmoke/report/index.html.

7.   World Bank. (2011, April 1). Life expectancy at birth: Total years. *World Development Indicators*. Retrieved from http://data.worldbank.org/indicator/SP.DYN.LE00 .IN?cid=GPD_10.

8.   Centers for Disease Control. (2000). *Leading causes of death*, 1900–1998. Retrieved from http://www.cdc.gov/nchs/data/dvs/lead1900_98.pdf.

9.   Murphy, S. L., Xu, J., & Kochanek, K. D. (2012, January 11). Deaths: preliminary data for 2010. *National Vital Statistics Reports*, 60 (04). Available at www.cdc.gov/nchs/data/nvsr/nvsr60/nvsr60_4.pdf.

10. U.S. Centers for Disease Control. (2010, July 7). Chronic diseases and health promotion. Available at http://www.cdc.gov/chronicdisease/overview/index.htm.

11. U.S. Department of Health and Human Services. (2011). *Vital and health statistics: Early release of selected estimates based on data from the January–September 2010 National Health Interview Survey*. Available at http://www.cdc.gov/nchs/nhis/released201103.htm#9.

12. Ogden, C. L., & Carroll, M. D. (2010, June). Prevalence of overweight, obesity, and extreme obesity among adults: United States, trends 1976–1980 through 2007–2008. National Center for Health Statistics. Available at http://www.cdc.gov/NCHS/data/hestat/obesity_adult_07_08/obesity_adult_07_08.pdf.

13. U.S. Department of Health and Human Services. (2011). About HHS. Available at http://www.hhs.gov/about.

14. U.S. Department of Health and Human Services. (2010, December 2). What's new for 2020. Available at http://www.healthypeople.gov/2020/about/new2020.aspx.

15. American College Health Association. (2011). *ACHA-NCHA II: Reference group executive summary, Spring 2011*. Retrieved from http://www.achancha.org/docs/ACHA-NCHA-II_ReferenceGroup_ExecutiveSummary_Spring2011.pdf.

16. Joint United Nations Program on HIV/AIDS. (2009). *09 AIDS epidemic update*. Retrieved from http://data.unaids.org/pub/Report/2009/JC1700_Epi_Update_2009_en.pdf.

17. U.S. Centers for Disease Control. (2010, July 19). Antibiotic/Antimicrobial resistance. Available at http://www.cdc.gov/drugresistance/DiseasesConnectedAR.html.

18. Food and Agriculture Organization (FAO). (2009, October 14). The state of food insecurity in the world, 2009. FAO Media Centre. Available at http://www.fao.org/news/story/en/item/36207/icode/.

19. World Health Organization. (2011). Nutrition: Controlling the global obesity epidemic. Available at http://www.who.int/nutrition/topics/obesity/en/index.html.

20. U.S. Department of Health and Human Services. (2010, December 2). Determinants of health. Available at http://www.healthypeople.gov/2020/about/DOHAbout.aspx.

21. Williams, D. R. (2008). The health of men: Structured inequalities and opportunities. *American Journal of Public Health*, 93,150–157.

22. Kvaavik, E., Batty, G., Ursin, G., Huxley, R., & Gale, C. (2010). Influence of individual and combined health behaviors on total and cause-specific mortality in men and women. *Archives of Internal Medicine*, 170 (8), 711–718.

23. American Academy of Pediatrics. (2012, January). Early childhood adversity, toxic stress, and the role of the pediatrician: Translating developmental science into lifelong health. *PEDIATRICS, 129* (1), e224–e231. Retrieved from http://aappolicy.aappublications.org/cgi/reprint/pediatrics;129/1/e224.pdf.

24. Marmot, M. G. (2006, March 15). Status syndrome: A challenge to medicine. *JAMA, 295* (11). Available at http://www.psr.org/assets/pdfs/status-syndrome.pdf.

25. American Lung Association. (2010). *State of the air 2010*. Retrieved from http://www.stateoftheair.org/2010/assets/SOTA2010.pdf.

26. U.S. Centers for Disease Control and Prevention/National Center for Health Statistics. (2011). Health Insurance Coverage: Early Release of Estimates from the 2010 National Health Interview Survey, 2011. Available at http://www.cdc.gov/nchs/nhis/released201106.htm.

27. Krieger, N., Rehkopf, D., Chen, J., Waterman, P., Marcelli, E., & Kennedy, M. (2008). The fall and rise of U.S. inequities in premature mortality: 1960–2002. *Public Library of Science Medicine*, 5 (2), e46.

28. The Henry J. Kaiser Family Foundation. (2010). *Focus on health reform: Summary of patient coverage provisions in the Patient Protection and Affordable Care Act*. Retrieved from http://www.kff.org/healthreform/upload/8023-R.pdf.

29. National Network of Libraries of Medicine. (2010). *Health literacy*. Retrieved from http://nnlm.gov/outreach/consumer/hlthlit.html.

30. American Liver Foundation. (n.d.). *Hepatitis B and Asian Americans*. Retrieved from http://www.thinkb.org/professionals/asianamericans.

31. Breslow, L., ed. (2002). Health-related behavior. In *Encyclopedia of public health*. Farmington Hills, MI: Gale Cengage Learning.

32. Prochaska, J., & Velicer, W. (1997). The transtheoretical model of health behavior change. *American Journal of Health Promotion*, 12 (1), 38–48.

33. Daddario, D. (2007). A review of the use of the health belief model for weight management. *Medsurg Nursing*, 16 (6), 363–366.

34. Sallis, J. F., Owen, N., & Fisher, E. B. (2008). Ecological models of health behavior. In Glanz, K., Rimer, B. K., & Viswanath, K. *Health behavior and health education*. San Francisco: John Wiley & Sons.

35. Doran, G. T. (1981). There's a S.M.A.R.T. way to write management's goals and objectives. *Management Review*, 70 (11) (AMA FORUM), 35–36.

36. National Institutes of Health. (2011, April 15). Guide to behavior change. Available at http://www.nhlbi.nih.gov/health/public/heart/obesity/lose_wt/behavior.htm.

37. Olson, J. M. (1992, February). Psychological barriers to behavior change. *Can Fam Physician*, 38, 309–319.

38. Marlatt, A., & Witkiewitz, K. (2005). Relapse prevention for alcohol and drug problems. In Marlatt, A., & Donovan, D. M., eds. *Relapse prevention: Maintenance strategies in the treatment of addictive behaviors*, 2nd ed. NY: The Guilford Press.

39. American Cancer Society. (2010, November 3). Helping a smoker quit: Do's and don'ts. Available at http://www.cancer.org/healthy/stayawayfromtobacco/helping-a-smoker-quit.

Name: _____   Date: _____

MODULE 10-C

ACTIVITY

◇ CULTURE AND HEALTH: THE NI HON SAN ACTIVITY

Several studies of culture and health have taken advantage of what one might consider a natural experiment; that is, changes in health as a specific ethnic group migrates to another culture. By comparing the health measures of members of an ethnic group who do not migrate with those who do, it is possible to separate genetic from behavioral influences on health. An example of this type of research is the landmark Ni Hon San study described below. The purpose of this activity is to encourage you to think about how culturally imbedded behaviors may influence health. In addition, this activity will familiarize you with a form of research that provides significant insights into issues of culture and health.

Directions: Read the description of the Ni Hon San study below (based on Benfante, 1992) and then answer the questions that follow.

◇ THE NI HON SAN STUDY

The Ni Hon San study began in 1964 as part of the ongoing Honolulu Heart Study. This research compared health data from three groups of men: Japanese men living in Hiroshima and Nagasaki, Japan; descendants of Japanese migrants to Hawaii; and descendants of Japanese migrants to San Francisco, California. One of the most striking findings of this study is that the rate of cardiovascular disease (heart disease) was lowest in the Japan group, highest in the California group, and intermediate in the Hawaii group.

1. What conclusions can you draw from the findings of the Ni Hon San study about the role of genetics and behavior in the development of cardiovascular disease?

Taken from *Cross-Cultural Explorations: Activities in Culture and Psychology*, Second Edition, by Susan Goldstein.

2. What assumptions can you make about the distinction between individuals of Japanese ancestry living in Hawaii as opposed to California?

3. List some behavioral factors (things people do in daily life) that may have affected the findings of the Ni Hon San study.

4. List some environmental factors (aspects of the setting in which people live) that may have affected the findings of the Ni Hon San study.

5. The participants of the Ni Hon San study were all male. Would you have any concerns about extrapolating from this study to draw conclusions about the health practices of women? Please explain.

6. Since the conclusion of the Ni Hon San study, investigations of a number of other immigrant groups have found a disturbing pattern -- the longer the amount of time spent in the United States, the higher the risk of cardiovascular disease (Mooteri, Petersen, Dagubati, & Pai, 2004). What measures might be taken to prevent this problem among people who immigrate?

◇ REFERENCES

Benfante, R. (1992). Studies of cardiovascular disease and cause-specific mortality trends in Japanese-American men living in Hawaii and risk factor comparisons with other Japanese populations in the Pacific region: A review. *Human Biology*, 64, 791-805.

Mooteri, S. N., Petersen, F., Dagubati, R., & Pai, R. G. (2004). Duration of residence in the United States as a new risk factor for coronary artery disease (The Konkani Heart Study). *American Journal of Cardiology*, 93, 359-361.

SECTION 11

DEATH AND DYING

MODULE 11-A

DEATH AND AFTERLIFE BELIEFS

(MERVYN REES/Alamy)

Taken from *Human Development: A Cultural Approach*, by Jeffrey Jensen Arnett.

PART 1 SOCIOCULTURAL AND EMOTIONAL RESPONSES TO DEATH

LEARNING OBJECTIVES

1. Compare and contrast the benefits and drawbacks of dying at home versus in a hospital.
2. Summarize the options and controversies that exist regarding end-of-life care and death.
3. Describe how the emotional responses associated with grief change over time.
4. Describe variations in the grieving process, and identify factors that influence these variations.
5. Summarize Kübler-Ross's theory of death and dying, and identify some limitations of this theory.

◇ THE SOCIOCULTURAL CONTEXTS OF DEATH

We have examined many differences in the course of this book between developed countries and developing countries, and death is one of the areas where the difference is largest. Most people in developing countries today die as people have always done through human history—at home among family, or through accidents or wars. In contrast, death in developed countries today is usually a highly technological event, because it typically takes place in the context of the advanced medical technologies used to try to keep the dying person alive. We first examine homes and hospitals as sociocultural contexts for death, then look at the hospice approach as an alternative that is rising in acceptance. Then we look at the difficult questions raised by the use of medical methods not to keep people alive but to ease them into death. Finally we consider the increasing use of written plans to direct others in what steps to take if the dying person is incapacitated.

Where We Die: Homes and Hospitals

LEARNING OBJECTIVE 1   Compare and contrast the benefits and drawbacks of dying at home versus in a hospital.

For most of human history, death has most commonly occurred at home. Most people died of infectious diseases, and they experienced a relatively short period of illness before their death, ranging from a few days to a few weeks. Today, most people in developing countries die at home because they rarely have access to medical care in a hospital or clinic setting. Even in developed countries, surveys indicate that 80–90% of people would prefer to die at home (National Hospice and Palliative Care Organization [NHPCO], 2008). Actually, however, only about 20% die at home. Most people in developed countries die in hospitals, about 60%, and another 20% die in nursing homes (Gruneir et al., 2007).

The prospect of dying at home appeals to many people because they imagine facing the uncertainty and pain of death in the context of the security and comfort of home, cared for by the familiar people they know and love (Germino, 2003; NHPCO, 2008). However, the reality of dying at home is considerably more challenging and difficult, especially for the caregivers. Because the major causes of death in developed countries are not infectious diseases but heart disease and cancer, and because modern medications and technology make it possible to keep people alive long past when they would have died in previous eras, dying often takes place slowly and gradually over a period of many months or even years. During this time, as the dying person's health declines, the home caregivers are often required to help them with daily activities of eating, using the toilet, bathing, and taking medications (Singer et al., 2005).

This is often a tremendous physical and psychological strain on the caregivers, and even nearly a year after a home death, family caregivers report higher levels of stress than persons whose family member died in a hospital (Addington-Hall, 2000). The strain is reduced if caregivers have support from health care professionals, but even then most homes are not suited to providing well for the physical and medical needs of a dying person (Perrault et al., 2004). Most older adults anticipate the difficulty of home care, and even though they would prefer to die at home, they realize the burden this would place on their family members (Gott et al., 2004).

Hospitals can provide the necessary medical care when a person is dying, but hospitals also have their drawbacks as a setting for death (O'Connor, 2003). Dying people and their families often complain that hospital care is impersonal and dehumanizing, because the focus of medical personnel is on the technology and medications intended to keep the person alive rather than on emotional and social needs (Open Society Institute, 2003). A large American study of seriously ill and dying hospital patients found that most physicians and their patients did not discuss the prospect of the patient's death or make plans for end-of-life care (Christopher, 2003). Dying in a hospital often means experiencing loneliness, fear, and untreated pain (Gruneir et al., 2007; Weitzen et al., 2003).

Options and Decisions Regarding the End of Life

> Summarize the options and controversies that exist regarding end-of-life care and death.

Now that people in developed countries live so much longer than in the past, societies have had to develop ways of addressing the issues that arise when older adults are near the end of their lives and in declining health. Hospice care provides a humane setting that allows terminally ill people to live the final module of their lives with dignity. Euthanasia is sometimes considered when death is near and there is no possibility of recovery, although it is highly controversial. Many older adults in developed countries now record instructions for their end-of-life care long before they become ill, so that their loved ones will not be faced with making difficult choices on their behalf.

The Hospice Approach to Care of the Dying

In response to widespread dissatisfaction with end-of-life hospital care, the **hospice** approach has become increasingly popular in developed countries. Hospice care aims to address not just medical issues but the physical, emotional, social, and spiritual needs of dying persons and their families (NHPCO, 2008). The hospice approach only begins when medical interventions to extend life have ceased and the person is considered to have 6 months or less to live. The focus of medical efforts is on **palliative care**, that is, on relieving the patient's pain and suffering and providing care in a way that allows the person to die with dignity.

Sometimes the hospice approach is implemented at a separate institution devoted to hospice care, but more often the hospice approach is applied in the home or hospital setting or at an assisted living or nursing home facility. Hospice care takes place at home more commonly than in any other setting, making it possible for people to die among family members as they prefer (Centers for Medicare and Medicaid Services, 2009; Muramatsu et al., 2008). In contrast to the usual pattern of home care for dying persons described earlier, family members who care for the dying person with hospice support have better psychological functioning two years later, compared to family members without hospice support (Ragow-O'Brien et al., 2000). ⊙

In addition to palliative care, the hospice approach has the following features (NHPCO, 2008):

- Interdisciplinary care team including medical personnel, counselors, and volunteers;

- Psychological and spiritual counseling available for patients and family members;

- For family members providing home hospice care, housekeeping support and periodic relief from care for a few hours;

- Psychological support and comfort for the dying person, sometimes including music therapy and celebrations of special events such as birthdays and holidays;

- Bereavement care for family and friends after the patient dies.

Hospice care has expanded greatly in recent years in developed countries, in part because research has shown that dying persons and their

hospice
alternative to hospital care at the end of life that emphasizes the physical, emotional, social, and spiritual needs of dying persons and their families

palliative care
for terminally ill persons, a type of care that focuses on relieving the patient's pain and suffering and allows the person to die with dignity

⊙ **Watch the Video**
Hospice Care at www.pearsoncustom.com/mi/msu_mylabs

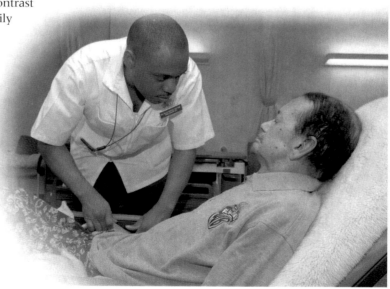

Hospice care attends not only to medical issues of a terminally ill person, but to emotional, social, and spiritual issues.
(Robin Nelson/PhotoEdit)

families respond much more favorably to it than to standard hospital care (Muramatsu et al., 2008; Tang et al., 2004). Another key reason for the expansion of hospice care is that it is much less expensive than standard hospital care (Morrison et al., 2008). With medical costs escalating and nearly every developed country facing the prospect of a rapidly aging population over the decades to come, hospice care is likely to grow further.

Despite the evidence of the advantages of the hospice approach, currently only about 40% of deaths in the United States involve a hospice program (NHPCO, 2008). Furthermore, hospice care tends to be applied only at the very end of life, with a median length of just 20 days. There are also sharp ethnic differences within the United States in hospice care, with the majority of Whites receiving such care at the end of life but just 10% of African Americans (Cohen, 2008).

There are a variety of reasons why the prevalence of hospice care is limited so far. Physicians are trained to heal people and keep them alive, and some tend to be optimistic about recovery prospects and reluctant to cease medical interventions even when the patient has an illness that is typically terminal (Hooyman & Kiyak, 2011). Many patients and their families are reluctant to accept hospice care because it means giving up the hope of a cure and acknowledging that death is imminent (Waldrop, 2006). African American families tend to be more likely to prefer aggressive medical treatments rather than accepting end-of-life palliative care, in part because they often believe that the more aggressive approach shows respect and love for elders and leaves the decision of the timing of death in God's hands (Dula et al., 2005). In response to such concerns, some hospice service providers are instituting "open access" policies that combine the hospice approach with continued cure efforts such as chemotherapy and dialysis (Wright & Katz, 2007).

Euthanasia

There are few objections to the hospice approach, as it seems to offer a humane, compassionate, dignified way of reaching the end of life. However, some related approaches are regarded with far more ambivalence and ethical objections. **Euthanasia**, which means "good death," is the term for the practice of ending the life of a person who is suffering from an incurable disease or severe disability. There are two types of euthanasia.

euthanasia
practice of ending the life of a person who is suffering from an incurable disease or severe disability

- *Passive euthanasia* involves ceasing medical interventions that would prolong a persons' life. For example, this would include ending chemotherapy for a person who had been receiving this treatment for cancer, or removing the respirator from a person whose brain activity had ceased but whose lungs were continuing to function with medical assistance. Passive euthanasia allows death to take place but does not cause it.

- *Active euthanasia* involves not just ceasing treatment but taking steps to hasten death. It may take place when medical personnel provide a dying person with the medical means to die without pain, for example when a physician prescribes a terminally ill person with a prescription for a drug that will end life, at the person's request. This is also known as *assisted suicide*. Or, medical personnel or persons close to the dying person may take deliberate steps to end life, for example by administering a lethal injection.

These seem to be two quite different types of euthanasia. However, in practice the distinctions between them may be harder to draw. Take this hypothetical example. A 92-year-old woman is in the last stages of colon cancer. She was diagnosed when the cancer was far advanced, and her doctor told her she probably had only 3 months to live. For 2 months, at her request the doctor tries chemotherapy and radiation, but the treatments make her feel miserable and do little to reverse the progress of the cancer, so she requests an end to them. She leaves the hospital and returns home, where her son, taking a leave from work, moves in with her and cares for her with the help of visits by health workers and others providing assistance. In the weeks to come her condition deteriorates further, and early one morning she wakes up crying in pain and begging her son to relieve her pain, telling him she is ready to die. He calls her doctor, who sends over a nurse with a bottle of morphine and prescribes a heavy dosage. The nurse administers the morphine and tells the son how to administer another dosage if the pain continues. The patient falls deeply asleep in response to the morphine, but wakes up later in the day, groggy and disoriented but still complaining desperately of the pain. Her son administers another dosage of the morphine, and that night she dies.

So, what happened? Was this passive euthanasia, because the treatment for the terminal condition was ended and the patient subsequently died in about the expected interval? Or was it active euthanasia, because the physician provided a prescription for a dose of morphine strong enough to end her life and because the administration of morphine probably ended the patient's life more quickly than if she had not received it?

Perhaps because the types of euthanasia are difficult to distinguish in real-life cases, surveys of people in developed countries indicate broad public support for both passive and active euthanasia. A survey on attitudes toward active euthanasia in five developed countries showed strong support (at least 70%) across all five (World Federation of Right to Die Societies, 2006). However, when "assisted suicide" is surveyed it receives lower support, slightly less than 50% (DiCamillo & Field, 2006; Pew Research Center, 2006). This may be due to the visceral response to the word *suicide*. When the survey question asks if physicians should be allowed to provide life-ending prescriptions at the request of terminally-ill persons but does not use the term *assisted suicide*, support rises to three-fourths of respondents (Journal of Pain and Palliative Care Pharmacotherapy, 2006).

In the legal arena as in the real world, the distinction between the different types of euthanasia appears at first to be clear but then turns out not to be. In virtually all countries, passive euthanasia is legal but active euthanasia is illegal (World Federation of Right to Die Societies, 2006). Major medical societies such as the American and Canadian Medical Associations support passive euthanasia but oppose active euthanasia. However, courts generally accept the judgment of physicians in providing medications to relieve the pain of dying persons, even to the point of "terminal sedation" (Hooyman & Kiyak, 2011). Providing drugs to ease pain is legally acceptable and providing drugs with the intent to cause death is not, but in practice it is nearly impossible to tell where the easing of pain ends and the hastening of death occurs. Consequently, end-of-life decisions made between physicians and patients and patients' families are rarely questioned by the courts.

Only one developed country explicitly allows assisted suicide, the Netherlands, where these procedures have been legal for several decades. There are several conditions that must be followed under the law: the patient has clearly indicated a desire to die; the patient's physical and/or mental suffering is severe and unlikely to improve; all other options for care have been attempted or refused by the patient; and a second doctor has been consulted to ensure that these conditions have been met (Dees et al., 2010).

How well is the law succeeding, in practice? Over half of Dutch doctors report performing active euthanasia, usually with terminally ill cancer patients (Rurup et al., 2005). However, in an anonymous survey many physicians admitted that the conditions specified by the law are frequently ignored, especially the requirement of consulting a second doctor (Onwuteaka-Philipsen et al., 2005). Some physicians also admit to providing assisted suicide to elderly persons who are not terminally ill but simply "weary of life" (Rurup et al., 2005). This finding has provided fuel to critics who fear that laws allowing active euthanasia send society down a slippery slope that may lead to elderly ill persons feeling an obligation to die sooner rather than later (Jost, 2005).

Another place where active euthanasia is legal is the state of Oregon, where it has been allowed since 1997 for persons who are terminally ill and are diagnosed as having less than 6 months to live. Despite their legality, these procedures remain rare in Oregon, accounting for only one-tenth of one percent of deaths (Niemeyer, 2006). Notably, 10 times as many people initiate the process of approval for assisted suicide as carry it through to the end. The law is not controversial in Oregon, where residents generally approve of the law and appreciate having the option of active euthanasia even if they do not intend to make use of it (Hedberg et al., 2003).

Easing the Exit: Advance Directives

Perhaps the most controversial part of euthanasia involves cases where the dying person is incapacitated and therefore unable to make the decision about which medical treatments should—or should not—be provided. In such cases it is often left to medical personnel and family members to decide, and they may have conflicting views as to what the person would have wanted.

One increasingly prevalent method for avoiding this dilemma is the used of an **advance directive**, a person's written and oral instructions concerning end-of-life care (Mitty et al., 2008). Advance directives may include a *living will*, which is a document specifying the treatments the person does or does not want in case of terminal illness, coma, or brain death. Living wills may include a **Do Not Resuscitate (DNR)** provision, indicating that medical personnel are not to attempt to prolong life if the heart stops or the person stops breathing (Hanson et al., 2009). Advanced directives also may specify a *health care proxy*, which is a person (usually a family member) designated to make treatment decisions on behalf of the dying person in the event of incapacitation.

Thinking Culturally

What cultural reasons might there be for the fact that the Netherlands is the only developed country that allows assisted suicide?

Applying Your Knowledge . . . as an Emergency Responder

You rush to a nursing home where 88-year-old Roberto is not breathing. The nurse on call tells you that Roberto has a DNR provision. What do you do?

advance directive
person's written and oral instructions concerning end-of-life care

Do Not Resuscitate (DNR)
provision in a living will indicating that medical personnel are not to attempt to prolong life if the heart stops or the person stops breathing

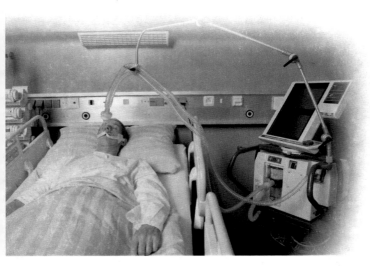

Many older adults prepare an advance directive in case they become incapacitated, but physicians often ignore them.
(Zefa RF/Alamy)

Although advance directives have been legally approved in most developed countries and are recommended by medical authorities, they do not solve all end-of-life dilemmas. One study found that even when patients had an advance directive, fewer than half the physicians overseeing their care were aware it existed (Kass-Bartelmes & Hughes, 2003). Other research has found that even when physicians have been informed of the patient's advance directive, they are often reluctant to follow it, partly from fear of legal vulnerability and partly because they have been trained to do all they can to save patients, not to let them die (Gorman et al., 2005; McArdle, 2002).

WHAT HAVE YOU LEARNED?

1. What challenges do caregivers face when someone dies at home?
2. What could hospitals do to make end-of-life care less impersonal and more humane for patients?
3. What are the main features of hospice care, and why is hospice care limited in the United States?
4. How is passive euthanasia different from active euthanasia, and why is it sometimes difficult to distinguish between them?
5. Why is it important for a terminally ill patient to have an advance directive?

◇ BEREAVEMENT AND GRIEF

bereavement
experience of losing a loved one

grief
intense psychological response that often accompanies bereavement

In addition to facing the prospect of our own death, nearly all of us also experience the death of people we love and value. **Bereavement** is the experience of losing a loved one, and **grief** is the intense psychological response that often accompanies bereavement. Grief is perhaps the most intense and complex psychological process we experience throughout the course of a human lifetime, and there is no simple or easy way to characterize it. With this in mind, first let us look at the general pattern of the grief process, then at some of the major sources of variability.

The Emotional Arc of Grief

LEARNING OBJECTIVE 3

Describe how the emotional responses associated with grief change over time.

In the initial hours, days, and perhaps weeks following bereavement, grief often involves shock, numbness, and disbelief. At first we find it hard to believe that the person we loved could really be gone forever. This is often accompanied by an intense yearning to see and hear the person again.

As the initial shock fades, it is frequently succeeded by a cascade of powerful, unsettling, and shifting emotions, possibly including sadness, anger, anxiety, loneliness, guilt, and helplessness (Scannell-Desch, 2003). These intense emotional states may alternate with states that resemble the symptoms of depression: lethargy, aimlessness, confusion, and disorganization (Hensley, 2006). Simply getting out of bed in the morning and going through the tasks of the day may seem overwhelming. There may be difficulty sleeping and a loss of interest in eating.

Applying Your Knowledge . . . as a Counselor

One of your clients, who recently lost his mother to cancer, is concerned about how his 87-year-old father is dealing with the death. He refuses to eat more than a few crackers each day, and sleeps a lot. What can you tell him about how the grieving process might be affecting his father?

After some time has passed—perhaps weeks later, perhaps months—the intense emotions of grief begin to subside, and the bereaved person is able to resume previous daily activities and social relationships (Bonanno, 2004). New activities may be taken up, as part of the reorganization of life now that the loved person is gone. New relationships may be formed, to provide support and companionship that had been missed as a consequence of the loved one's death. The survivor's identity may change, too, to incorporate the recognition of the death. For example, a woman who has lost her spouse may now think of herself as a widow rather than as a wife. After my mom died, my dad continued to wear his wedding ring for several years afterward. When he finally took it off, it symbolized his acceptance that his identity had changed and he was now a widower.

Grief subsides for most people over time, but when there was a close attachment to the person who died, the feelings of loss and yearning may never entirely fade (Worden, 2009). Survivors may not so much recover from their loss as learn to live with it (Levin, 2004). They may also maintain a persistent sense of the dead person's psychological presence.

Variations in Grieving

Describe variations in the grieving process, and identify factors that influence these variations.

LEARNING OBJECTIVE 4

Within the general pattern of grieving just described, there is a substantial amount of variability. The variations in forms and patterns of grieving depend on *who* has died and *how* the death occurred.

Regarding the question of who, the more intense the attachment had been, the more intense the grief is likely to be (Bonanno, 2004). In general, the deaths that provoke the most grief are of parents, children, and spouses. Children who experience the death of a parent tend to be deeply affected, even years later (Dowdney, 2000). Their grief depends in part on how old they are when the parent dies and how much support they receive from others, but in general the death of a parent places them at risk for emotional difficulties, especially depression, in both the near term and the long term (Shear, 2009). Similarly, parents who experience the death of a child tend to have a severe and enduring reaction (Dent & Stewart, 2004). They tend to report high levels of distress even years later, and the death also places them at high risk for divorce (Kreicbergs et al., 2004).

Death of a spouse has profound effects on the widowed, but these effects are complex and vary by gender. Among older adults, a wide variety of psychological problems are nearly 10 times higher among the newly bereaved as among their married peers, including depression, anxiety, substance use, and cognitive difficulties with memory and concentration (Hooyman & Kiyak, 2011). In the first year following the death of a spouse, the risk of mortality for the bereaved person is 7 times as high as among married peers (Subramanian et al., 2008).

Because men tend to be older than the women they marry and women tend to live longer than men do, over 80% of wives outlive their husbands (Hooyman & Kiyak, 2011). This pattern is consistent across cultures, nations, and historical periods. Widows often struggle financially after their husbands die, and if widowed in late adulthood they are unlikely to remarry (Angel et al., 2003; Schulz et al., 2006). However, they often show considerable resilience as they strengthen their relations with children and friends and build new lives for themselves (Cheng, 2006; Rossi et al., 2007). In contrast, men are more likely to experience physical and mental health problems following their bereavement, and they recover their emotional equilibrium more slowly (Berg et al., 2009). Widowers are 7 times more likely than widows to remarry late in life, in part because there are so many more women available than men but also because men feel less able than women to face the challenges of life on their own, without a spouse (Ajrouch et al., 2005).

The *how* of death also affects the course of grief, specifically how expected or unexpected the death is. Sudden death tends to evoke grief that is especially intense. In one study, the experience adults ages 18–45 rated as most stressful was the sudden death of a loved one (Breslau et al., 1998). A sudden death often shatters the survivors' assumptions that the world is benevolent, just, and predictable, and the psychological effects are evident for years afterward (Burton et al., 2006). Suicide is

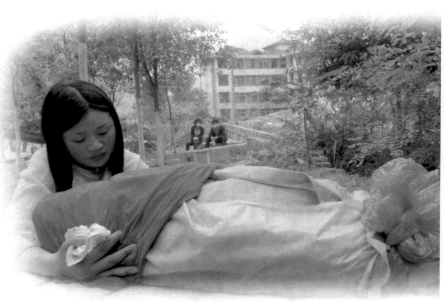

The sudden death of a loved one is often highly stressful and evokes grief that is especially intense. Here, a Chinese mother mourns the death of her son, who perished in an earthquake.

(Imaginechina via AP Images)

especially devastating, as it frequently arouses feelings not only of sorrow but of guilt and shame (Dunne & Dunne-Maxim, 2004).

In contrast, when death is expected because it takes place after a long illness or when the person is very old, the survivors are able to prepare themselves through *anticipatory grief*, as they accept that death is inevitable and begin to adapt to it emotionally. Especially for family members who have attended to a dying loved one through a long illness, grief may be combined with relief at being able to return to their own lives (Keene & Prokos, 2008).

Grief is complicated and various, and there is no one "best way" to grieve (Wortman, 2008). Because grief is so emotionally challenging, cultures around the world have developed mourning rituals to structure it and make it comprehensible and bearable, as we will see later in the module.

Confronting Death

LEARNING OBJECTIVE 5 Summarize Kübler-Ross's theory of death and dying, and identify some limitations of this theory.

People have to adapt not only to the deaths of those they love but also to the prospect of their own death. One person who has been influential in describing people's psychological responses to awareness of a fatal illness is Elizabeth Kübler-Ross (1969, 1982). Based on her interviews with 200 terminally ill patients, she proposed that people go through a series of five stages in their responses to imminent death.

1. **Denial.** Many people with a diagnosis of terminal illness initially refuse to believe it. *No, it can't be true,* they might think. *There must be some mistake. Perhaps my test results got mixed up with someone else's.* Kübler-Ross advised family members and health professionals not to encourage denial, because doing so would prevent the person from going ahead with making arrangements to prepare for death. However, other therapists have framed denial more positively, as a way of protecting the ego while the person adjusts to the psychological blow of a terminal diagnosis (Schacter, 2009).

2. **Anger.** After denial fades, anger is next. *It's not fair,* the person may reason. *I'm a good person. Look at all the people who are much worse than me and yet they're still healthy.* The anger may be felt toward family members, medical personnel, God, or healthy people generally.

In Chinese culture, the grieving process often focuses on how death will change relationships with others.
(REUTERS/NIR ELIAS)

3. **Bargaining.** Anger, too, eventually fades, and now the terminally ill person tries to bargain for extra time. Usually the bargaining is directed toward God or the fates or some vague spiritual entity. *Just let me live, and I promise I'll dedicate my life to healing others. Just give me one more year, so I can see my child get married. Please, let me live to celebrate one more holiday with my family.*

4. **Depression.** After bargaining, depression often sets in. Despite the attempts to bargain, the terminally ill person's condition steadily worsens. Invasive medical procedures are painful and result in a loss of dignity. The person realizes that death is growing nearer and there is little that can be done.

5. **Acceptance.** Finally, the person comes to accept death. There may be a feeling of peace as resistance to death is abandoned, or there may be little feeling at all, but rather a sense of disengagement and a desire to be with only the few people most valued.

Kübler-Ross's theory had an enormous impact on the care of terminally ill patients. Many health care professionals found it to be useful in understanding and caring for their patients. However, it has not held up well in subsequent research. Few people go through the five stages in a sequence as Kübler-Ross claimed, and many people experience few or none of the stages. The theory also oddly overlooks fear as a response to a diagnosis of terminal illness, which research shows is very common (Langner, 2002). And of course, it overlooks cultural context entirely, whereas other studies show that people often interpret impending death through a framework of cultural beliefs (Hooyman & Kiyak, 2011).

Despite its lack of validity, Kübler-Ross's theory has been influential not only in the care of terminally ill patients but in American cultural views of death. According to Ruth Konigsberg (2011), the theory is invoked to explain everything from how we will recover from the death of a loved one to a sudden environmental catastrophe or to the trading away of a basketball star, even though abundant research contradicts it. As Konigsberg describes, responses to a terminal illness are highly variable, and there is no common series of stages and no one healthy way to respond. Konigsberg also presents examples of how people in other cultures respond to terminal illness and grief, noting, for example, how in Chinese culture the focus is on the ways the prospect of death will change relationships with others, rather than being focused on the individual's emotions.

WHAT HAVE YOU LEARNED?

1. How is bereavement different from grief?
2. What emotions typically come after the initial shock of the death of a loved one?
3. How do men and women differ in the way they experience the death of a spouse?
4. What is anticipatory grief, and how is it different from the grief that accompanies a sudden death?
5. What are the five stages of grief in Kübler-Ross's theory, and how well is the theory supported by research?

PART 1 VIDEO GUIDE

GRIEVING: PART 2 (LENGTH: 6:49)

A series of interviews are conducted in this video. Each of the persons interviewed discusses the impact and emotional feeling that they experienced with the death of their spouse or mother.

1. The son in this video mentions that his mother's death has left a "big void", while the husband mentions that he feels that nothing was taken from what he had. Compare and contrast these differing views.
2. The husband in the video states that he did not even acknowledge that his kids had lost their mother until several months after her death. As a family member, how can you use this information to better understand grieving within others?
3. We learned that children in early childhood acquire the ability to see things from another person's point of view. How would you apply that "perspective taking" ability to the emotions discussed in this video?

PART 2 BELIEFS ABOUT DEATH AND THE AFTERLIFE

LEARNING OBJECTIVES

6. Describe how children's understanding of death changes from childhood to adolescence.
7. Describe how beliefs and fears about death change throughout adulthood.
8. Explain how individual beliefs about the afterlife vary across countries and within the United States.
9. Compare and contrast the mourning rituals of Hinduism, Buddhism, Judaism, Christianity, and Islam.
10. Describe the rituals and traditions used by various religions to remember and honor the dead.

◇ BELIEFS ABOUT DEATH THROUGHOUT THE LIFE SPAN

We are, so far as we know, the only animal who anticipates death. That unusually large cerebral cortex of ours, which is built so well for anticipating future events, allows us to realize that among those future events will be our own death. But how do thoughts and beliefs about death change in the course of human development? Let us examine changes in *awareness* of death and *anxiety* about death with age. As we will see, awareness and anxiety about death do not always go hand in hand.

Beliefs About Death in Childhood and Adolescence

LEARNING OBJECTIVE 6 | Describe how children's understanding of death changes from childhood to adolescence.

Even in early childhood most children have some experience with death, but do they really understand what death is?

(imagebroker/Alamy)

By the age of 3 or 4, most children have some experience with death. They may know of a family member or neighbor or family friend who died. They have almost certainly seen dead animals, perhaps a family pet, or a dead bird, or at least a dead bug. But do they really understand what it means to be dead?

In some ways they do, and in some ways they do not (Kenyon, 2001). Even in early childhood, most children understand that death is *permanent*. They realize the dead bug is not going to get up and walk away. However, for most children it is not until middle childhood that they realize that death is *inevitable*. It is not just bugs and bad people who die, but every living thing, including "me."

One reason for children's limited understanding of death is that most cultures have customs of using euphemisms to refer to death and withholding the full truth about death from children, in an effort to protect them from the pain of losing a loved one and the fear of the death of loved ones and themselves (Cicirelli, 2006; Wass, 2004). Thus adults might tell children "Grandma has passed on" or the family pet has "gone to sleep," rather than being told bluntly of their death. Furthermore, as we will see later in the module, nearly all cultures have beliefs about life after death. Nearly always, these beliefs make death seem neither permanent nor inevitable, and children learn the afterlife beliefs of their culture early (Wass, 2004).

In adolescence, beliefs about death become more abstract and more complex, reflecting adolescents' more general gains in cognitive development. When describing their thoughts about death, adolescents often use abstractions such as "eternal light" and "nothingness," whereas children usually do not (Brent et al., 1996; Wenestam & Wass, 1987). Adolescents are also more likely than children to discuss religious concepts of death, such as reincarnation, heaven and hell, and the existence of a soul that endures after death (Mearns, 2000; Noppe & Noppe, 1997; Yang & Chen, 2002).

Adolescents understand death better than children in some ways, but do they really understand the reality of their own death? This question is more difficult to answer. Adolescence is the life stage of the *personal fable,* the belief that they are unique and special and that bad things will not happen to them. Some scholars on adolescence believe that adolescents' participation in risk behavior such as cigarette smoking and high-speed driving is due partly to the way the personal fable dulls their awareness that the risks they take could lead to an early death (Alberts et al., 2007; Arnett, 2000). Some adolescents who are diagnosed with a terminal illness have a personal fable so resilient that they refuse to believe they really will die soon (Blumberg et al., 1984).

Beliefs About Death in Adulthood

Describe how beliefs and fears about death change throughout adulthood.

LEARNING OBJECTIVE 7

You might think that the older people are, the closer they are to death, and so the more they fear dying. However, research shows that the pattern in adulthood is just the opposite. Death anxiety is highest in emerging adulthood, then declines with age and is lowest in late adulthood (Russac et al., 2007). Greater fear of death at the younger life stages appears to be due mainly to having plans and goals that remain to be accomplished. By late adulthood, especially among persons beyond age 80, most people feel they are nearing the end of their life span and they no longer feel they need to stay alive in order to reach the goals they had set out for themselves (Cicirelli, 2006). For many people late adulthood is a time of what psychologist Robert Butler calls **life review**, thinking about the life they have lived and coming to an acceptance of it, both the lows and the highs (Butler, 2002). Erikson (1950) proposed that the main crisis of late adulthood is *ego integrity versus despair,* and research indicates that most people end up with a state of ego integrity, accepting what their life has been for better and worse. Although they may not fear death itself, older adults often do have some fears associated with death, such as suffering and pain, loss of self-control, and the effects of their death on loved ones (Cicirelli, 2006; Kwak et al., 2008).

life review
according to Robert Butler, the process in late adulthood when people reflect on the life they have lived and come to an acceptance of it

Within each life stage, death anxiety is lowest in people who have the strongest religious faith, because they are more likely than others to be confident that there is a pleasant life after death awaiting them (Cicirelli, 2002). Death anxiety is highest not in atheists and agnostics but in people who are unsure believers and inconsistent participants in religious activities (Cicirelli, 2006). Apparently their involvement in religion is enough to make them contemplate death but not enough to provide consolation. Death anxiety is also consistently higher among women than among men, across cultures, but why this is so is not clear (Russac et al., 2007; Tomer et al., 2000).

In addition to changes in death anxiety, thoughts about death change in other ways in the course of adulthood (Cicirelli, 2006). In young adulthood, fears of death tend to be focused on fear for one's children, both the fear of the children dying and the fear that the children would be vulnerable if their parents died. In middle adulthood, people often become aware that they have passed the half-way point and have fewer years remaining than they have lived so far. For some, this sharpens their awareness of death and makes them reexamine their lives to see if they need to make changes in order to make the most of the years they have left.

In late adulthood, people become more familiar with death because this is where death is concentrated, especially in developed countries. In the course of late adulthood, the longer they live the more likely they are to witness the deaths of parents, friends, and siblings. This experience, combined with their own closer proximity to death, leads them to think and talk more about death than younger people do (Hayslip & Hansson, 2003). Talking about death helps them cope effectively with it, using mutual consolation and sometimes humor (Lamberg, 2002; Tomer & Ellison, 2000). It also enables them to address practical concerns such as making a will and arranging for the distribution of their personal possessions (Kastenbaum, 2007).

WHAT HAVE YOU LEARNED?

1. In what ways is children's understanding of death limited?
2. How are adolescents' beliefs about death more abstract and complex than children's?
3. What is a life review and how does it help people in late adulthood prepare for death?
4. What impact does religiosity have on death anxiety?

◇ AFTERLIFE BELIEFS AND MOURNING RITUALS

This book has been devoted to explaining what happens in the course of human development, from beginning to end, from womb to tomb, from lust to dust. But one remarkable feature of the human species, at least since the Neolithic revolution 40,000 years ago, is that we are the only creature that believes that death is not the end, that part of us—the soul, the spirit, some indefinable essence of ourselves—goes on. Here we examine what people in a variety of countries believe about life after death. Then we look at how the mourning rituals and remembrance practices of the major religions reflect afterlife beliefs and assist the mourners in carrying on with life.

What Do Individuals Believe About Life After Death?

LEARNING OBJECTIVE 8 Explain how individual beliefs about the afterlife vary across countries and within the United States

Over the past several thousand years, vast changes have taken place in how people live; yet over that same time, how people explain death has been surprisingly enduring and stable. The early Egyptian and Greek beliefs about life after death, developed thousands of years ago, are still evident in several major religions, as we'll see in the **Historical Focus: Afterlife Beliefs in Ancient Egypt and Greece** feature on page 429. Many of the beliefs of the major religions today date from around 3,500 to 2,000 years ago; even the most recent major religion, Islam, is about 1,500 years old. Afterlife beliefs are part of all the major religious traditions, including Hinduism, Buddhism, Judaism, Christianity, and Islam.

There are some striking similarities across these beliefs. First, in every religion death is not the end. In some religions the body continues on in some way after death and in some it does not, but in all religions there is a belief in a soul that remains in existence. Second, in every religion the determination of the soul's destiny in the afterlife depends on the kind of moral life the person has lived. Good people are rewarded after death, either with a higher reincarnation status (Hinduism and Buddhism) or with entry to heaven (Christianity and Islam). Bad people are punished, either with a lower reincarnation status (Hinduism and Buddhism) or the torments of hell (Judaism, Christianity, and Islam). Judaism and Christianity may seem to be exceptions to this rule, because they assert that believing in the faith is ultimately the most important criterion for an afterlife reward, but even in these religions faith and works are supposed to go together. That is, an essential part of following the faith in these religious traditions is leading a good moral life.

But what do individual people actually believe about the afterlife? After all, each of these religions (except Judaism) has hundreds of millions of adherents, so it seems likely there must be some variability of afterlife beliefs with each faith. Next, we take a closer look at what people around the world have reported about their afterlife beliefs.

Afterlife Beliefs Around the World

Several times over the past 20 years, the International Social Survey Program (http://www.issp.org/) has surveyed people in 32 countries around the world about a wide range of topics, including their afterlife beliefs. According to this survey, people in different countries vary widely in how they view the prospect of life after death. As shown in **Figure 1**, for the question "Do you believe in life after death?" there were only 3 of the 32 countries where a majority of adults responded "definitely yes": the Philippines, the United States, and Chile. Adding "probably yes" and "definitely yes" together, in about half of the countries a majority of adults answered with one of the "yes" responses, whereas in the other half a majority answered "no" ("probably no" or "definitely no").

Some other patterns can be seen in the responses across countries. "Yes" responses were highest in the two least economically developed countries in the survey, the Philippines and Chile, as well as in the United States, which has long been found to be more religious than most other developed countries and which has a large population of Latinos (13%), who tend to be more religious than the general population (Pew Forum on Religion and Public Life, 2008). "No" responses were highest in the countries of eastern Europe such as Russia, Czech Republic, and Slovenia, all countries in which religious observances were suppressed when atheism was the official state policy during their decades under Communist rule in the 20th century. "No" responses were also high in

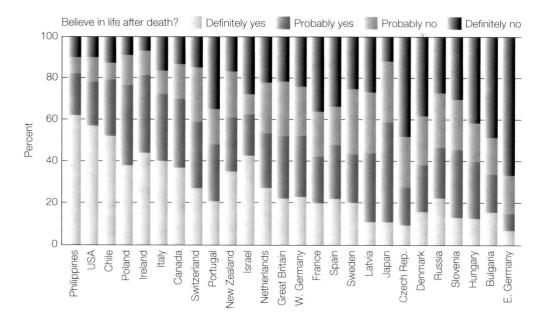

Believe in life after death? ■ Definitely yes ■ Probably yes ■ Probably no ■ Definitely no

FIGURE 1 ISSP Survey on Belief in Life After Death.
Source: ISSP (1998)

Japan and in the prosperous northern European countries of Denmark and Sweden. In these countries, participation in organized religion has faded substantially in the course of the past century and few people participate actively in religious institutions today.

HISTORICAL FOCUS

AFTERLIFE BELIEFS IN ANCIENT EGYPT AND GREECE

Beginning about 5,000 years ago, with the origins of civilizations, evidence of afterlife beliefs becomes more abundant because, unlike previous human cultures, civilizations kept written records. Two of the belief systems of early civilizations that influenced the beliefs later found in major religions are from Egypt and Greece (Segal, 2004).

The ancient Egyptians believed that after death, the body enters the afterlife along with the soul (Meskel, 2001). Consequently, Egyptians developed an elaborate process of preserving the corpse through mummification. Eventually the soul, ka, would form a spiritual body, but the physical body was a temporary necessity in the afterlife until the spiritual body was ready. At first only pharaohs were mummified, but eventually the practice became typical at all levels of Egyptian society.

Belief in the necessity of mummification remained distinctly Egyptian, but another Egyptian innovation became popular all throughout the world: the belief that the dead would be judged and their fate in the afterlife would depend on their

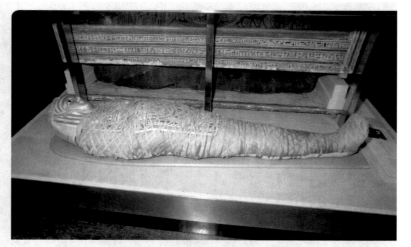

Ancient Egyptians took care to preserve the body of deceased persons, as with this mummy, because they believed the body entered the afterlife.
(Ancient Art & Architecture Collection Ltd/Alamy)

moral behavior on earth. Upon death, a person's ka appeared before Osiris, king of the underworld, and their good and bad deeds, represented in the form of a heart, were weighed against a feather. Those who failed the test experienced a "second death" in which they were devoured by the crocodile-headed god Attim, resulting in total annihilation. However, those who passed the test rose from the earth to join the sun god Ra in his daily passage across the sky. In another version of this belief, the blessed were allowed entry to a heavenly realm called the *Field of Rushes*, where they continued to enjoy the best of earthly pleasures.

The Egyptians believed that many problems among the living were caused by the unhappy dead, from bad moods to deadly illnesses. Reasons for the disgruntlement of the dead were that they had not been buried properly, or they died too young, or they had been murdered. Magicians arose who claimed to be able to contact the dead and discover the reason for their dissatisfaction with the living. This is another practice first recorded in Egypt that became widespread around the world.

HISTORICAL FOCUS CONTINUED

In contrast to the Egyptians, who left little in the way of written records, the ancient Greeks left abundant records that allow us to understand their afterlife beliefs. The main sources are the epic poems the *Iliad* and the *Odyssey*, believed to have been passed down orally through many generations before being written down about 3,000 years ago by the fabled poet Homer.

The Greeks believed that the soul, or *psyche*, survived after death, but in a grim and somber underworld, "the joyless region" (Segal, 2004). This land of the dead, called *Tartarus*, was ruled by the god of the underworld, Hades, and was also referred to as the *House of Hades* or simply as *Hades*. In Tartarus the dead were mere shadows of their earthly selves, without feeling or desire, except that they envied the living. In this passage from the *Odyssey*, Achilles observes wistfully

> Better, I say, to break sod as a farm hand
> For some poor country man, on iron rations,
> Than to be lord among the exhausted dead.

Nearly all the dead shared this dismal eternity, except for a few who were singled out for special rewards or punishments. Special heroes of Greek mythology were granted entry into the *Isles of the Blessed*, a paradise where they lived like gods. In contrast, notable villains were singled out for eternal torture. For example, Ixion, a mortal, was invited to dine with the gods but made the mistake of attempting to have sexual relations with Hera, wife of Zeus, the most powerful god. He was punished by being banished to Tartarus and strapped to an eternal wheel of flames representing his burning lust.

Over the centuries the bleak afterlife described by Homer gave way to a more hopeful vision among the Greeks. By the time of Socrates and Plato about 2,500 years ago, there was a widespread belief in reincarnation, which Plato described. In this view, souls are judged in the underworld after death. As in Homer's conception, those who have been exceptionally good ascend to the heavenly Isle of the Blessed, and those who have been exceptionally evil (usually by defying the gods) are tortured eternally in Tartarus. However, for the rest, the fate of their souls was not the shadowy and empty eternity Homer had described but a brief period of purgatory where their souls were prepared to be reborn on earth. According to Plato, after successive rebirths the ultimate goal was to reach a high state of philosophical understanding that would end the cycle of rebirth and allow the individual soul to be reunited with the One, the great soul from which all the individual souls originally came. Nevertheless, the soul retains something of an individual identity and consciousness even after uniting with the One.

In the afterlife beliefs of the ancient Egyptians and Greeks, we can see the outlines of what eventually became the afterlife beliefs of the major religions described in this module. Most notable is the belief that death is a moral event. Both ancient civilizations came to believe that upon death we are judged for our moral conduct, and our destination in the afterlife depends on the outcome of that judgment. The afterlife beliefs of the major religions are quite diverse, but all of them have this belief in common, and it is a belief that first developed in the ancient civilizations.

Afterlife Beliefs in the United States

More detailed information about afterlife beliefs is available for the United States in the surveys of the Pew Forum on Religion and Public Life (2008). Because the United States has immigrants from many countries, the Pew survey provides information about afterlife beliefs among adherents of many different religions.

As Table 1 shows, about three-quarters of Americans in the Pew survey said they believe in life after death, with one-half stating that they are "absolutely certain" there is an afterlife and another one-fourth stating that they are "fairly certain." Afterlife beliefs were highest among those in two branches of Christianity, Protestants (the average of Evangelical and Mainline Protestant churches was 82%) and Catholics (77%), but were also high among Muslims (77%), Hindus (65%) and Buddhists (68%). Only 39% of Jews expressed a belief in an afterlife, consistent with Judaism's focus on life in this world rather than on the afterlife. It is also worth noting that even 18% of atheists and 35% of agnostics said they believe in an afterlife.

Beliefs in heaven are prevalent among Protestants and Catholics, as well as among Muslims (Pew Forum on Religion, 2008, p. 33). Jews, Buddhists, and Hindus are relatively unlikely to believe in heaven. Across religious groups, people are somewhat less likely to believe in hell than to believe in heaven. The survey also found that 61% of Hindus believe in **reincarnation** (being born again into the world after death) and 62% of Buddhists believe in *nirvana* (release from the cycle of death and rebirth).

Perhaps because there so many different religious groups living together in the United States, people are generally tolerant of different views about religion and the afterlife. The Pew survey found that in all faiths a majority of respondents agreed that "many religions can lead to eternal life" (p. 58). This view is in direct contradiction to the traditional doctrine of both Christianity and Islam, which emphasize belief in their faith as a requirement for being rewarded in the afterlife.

reincarnation
belief that after death the soul returns again to earth in another bodily form

Thinking Culturally

How might one's cultural or religious beliefs about the afterlife affect the way that person views the death of a loved one?

TABLE 1 Americans' Belief in an Afterlife Responses to the Question: "Do you believe in life after death?"

	YES, BELIEVE IN LIFE AFTER DEATH	NO, DO NOT BELIEVE IN LIFE AFTER DEATH	OTHER (VOL.)	DON'T KNOW/ REFUSED
Total	74	18	2	7
Evangelical Churches	86	10	1	3
Mainline Churches	78	14	1	7
Historically Black Churches	79	14	1	6
Catholic	77	15	1	7
Mormon	98	1	0	1
Orthodox	74	19	1	6
Jehovah's Witness	42	45	9	4
Other Christian	82	10	3	5
Jewish	39	45	2	14
Muslim	77	18	2	3
Buddhist	68	24	2	6
Hindu	65	26	1	7
Other Faiths	68	19	3	10
Unaffiliated	48	39	2	11

Sources: U.S. Religious Landscape Survey, Pew Center's Forum on Religion & Public Life, © 2008, Pew Research Center. http://religions.pewforum.org/

Mourning Rituals of the Major Religions

Compare and contrast the mourning rituals of Hindusim, Buddhism, Judaism, Christianity and Islam

LEARNING OBJECTIVE 9

Each of the major religions has mourning rituals that help survivors adjust to the death of a loved one. As you read about the mourning rituals, keep in mind that in each religion there are local and regional variations and the rituals described here may not match precisely how they are performed in each specific place.

Reincarnation is a key part of Hindu beliefs. (Eye Ubiquitous/Photo- Library)

Hinduism

In Hinduism, reincarnation is the central afterlife belief. When a person dies, the body no longer functions but the soul returns to the earth in a new form, perhaps again as a human, perhaps in animal form, depending on the overall moral balance of good and evil that has accumulated in the person's life. However, before the soul returns to earth there is a period when its bodily destination in the next life is still to be determined. It is here that Hindu mourning rituals are crucial, because the devotion of the survivors to performing these rituals is a key influence on what the soul's status will be in the next life (Hockey & Katz, 2001). The rituals are highly elaborate, so only a brief version is described here.

Most Hindus die at home, as most people in India live in rural villages far from any hospital, but even in urban areas persons who are in hospitals on the verge of death are usually transported home to die among family members. When death is imminent, family members keep

a vigil all day and night, singing hymns, praying, and reading Hindu scriptures. Holy ashes are applied to the forehead, and a few drops of milk or holy water may be trickled into the mouth.

Upon death, a lamp is lit and incense is burned continually. The thumbs are tied together, as are the big toes. Religious pictures are turned to the wall, and mirrors may be covered to signify that mourners should not be thinking of themselves during this time. Extended kin are called together to bid farewell to the deceased and sing sacred songs beside the body.

The mourning rituals that follow are led by the "chief mourner," who is usually the eldest son; if there is no son, the nearest male relative serves this role. The body of the deceased is carried to a private area where, with only same-gender family members present, the clothes of the deceased are removed and the body is bathed with holy water, then draped with a white cloth and placed in a coffin or on a burial slab. Led by the chief mourner, men carry the body to a special shelter built for the occasion, where a sacred fire is burning. Young children, holding lighted sticks, circle the body singing hymns. The women then walk around the body, sprinkling puffed rice on the mouth of the deceased to symbolize nourishment for the journey ahead into death. If the dead person was a married man, his wife places her *tali* (wedding pendant) on his chest to signify their enduring bond.

Next the body is taken to be **cremated**, that is, burned to ashes. Sometimes this is done on an open fire, but increasingly it occurs at a place designated for the purpose, called a *crematorium*. Only men go the site of the cremation, regardless of the gender of the deceased. Led by the chief mourner, the men carry the body three times counterclockwise around the funeral pyre, then place it upon the pyre. Men offer puffed rice to the mouth of the deceased as the women did earlier, and place wood and incense upon the body. The chief mourner now circles the body with a clay pot on his shoulder, containing holy water. At each turn, one of the other men knocks a hole in the pot, to symbolize life leaving its vessel. At the end of the third turn, the chief mourner drops the pot to the ground. Then the chief mourner starts the fire, and as cremation begins he leaves the site, followed by the others. All of them bathe upon returning to the home, to wash themselves of the spiritual impurity associated with death.

About 12 hours after cremation, the family men return to collect the ashes. The ashes are then scattered in a holy body of water, ideally the holy Ganges river, along with flowers. In the days that follow, family members are not to visit each others' homes, attend festivals or temple, or make wedding arrangements. Pictures remained turned to the wall, and all religious icons are covered with white cloths. About a week after the death, family members gather to share a meal of the deceased's favorite foods. A portion is offered before a photo of the deceased.

A memorial service is held 31 days after the death. Afterward, all join in cleaning the house and the period of spiritual impurity is considered to be over. Although some families observe the prohibitions just described for up to a year, Hindu tradition generally discourages prolonged mourning and encourages the survivors to move on with life after the 31st day.

> **Watch the Video**
> *Buddhist and Christian Funeral Rituals* at www.pearsoncustom.com/mi/msu_mylabs

In Buddhist mourning rituals, an important role is played by monks, such as the Cambodian monks shown here.
(Kruppa/Caro/Alamy)

Buddhism

Like Hinduism, Buddhism includes belief in reincarnation, and as in Hinduism, cremation is the prescribed practice upon death. Furthermore, in both religions it is believed that the period immediately following death is of special importance, and mourning rituals must be followed scrupulously to lessen the soul's suffering during the interim period between death and rebirth and to ensure the soul as favorable a reincarnation as possible. In Buddhism as in Hinduism, there are differences in mourning rituals by region and sect, so the information that follows describes the general pattern (Wilson, 2009).

In Buddhist mourning rituals, monks play a prominent role. They arrive at the home when death is near to comfort the dying person and the family. At this time the monks begin chanting verses about the brevity of life and the inevitability of death. It is believed that if the person's thoughts are on Buddhist beliefs at death, afterlife prospects will be enhanced. If the person is unconscious, the beliefs may be written on paper and placed in the mouth.

After death, there is a bathing ceremony in which relatives and friends pour water over one hand of the deceased. The body is then placed in a coffin and flowers, candles, and incense are placed alongside it, perhaps along with a picture of the deceased. Monks continue chanting throughout the ceremony in order to ease the passage of the soul from the body.

Cremation usually takes place within 3 days. Each day monks come to the house to chant prayers for the soul of the deceased. Food is offered to the monks by the family. Both the prayers and the food offered to the monks are believed to enhance the soul's store of merit and its afterlife prospects. Neighbors and family also arrive each day to feast, share fellowship, and observe the prayers offered by the monks.

On the day of cremation, the monks lead a prayer service at the home and then lead the procession of mourners to the temple, where the cremation takes place. The coffin is carried to the temple by mourners and placed on a stand of brick built for this purpose. More prayers are chanted, and then mourners approach the coffin with lighted torches of wood, incense, and candles and toss them beneath to begin the cremation process. Later the ashes will be collected and kept in an urn.

In Judaism, when a family member dies the surviving family members recite the Kaddish prayer every day for 11 months.
(Bill Aron/PhotoEdit)

On the evening of the cremation ritual one last feast is held. Now instead of prayers there is music, and the feast is intended to banish sorrow and fear of the spirits of the dead through fellowship among the survivors. In some Buddhist traditions prayers for the deceased continue to be chanted every 7 days for 49 days; in others, every 10 days for 100 days. As long as the rituals continue they are believed to benefit the soul of the deceased.

Judaism

In Judaism, upon death the eyes are closed, the body is covered and laid on the floor, and candles are lit nearby (Wahlhaus, 2005). The body is not to be left alone, so various family members remain beside it at all times. Eating and drinking are forbidden in the same room as the body, as this would mock the deceased who is no longer able to enjoy these pleasures. For the same reason flowers are not present at the funeral, nor are they sent to the family. ◉

Jewish communities usually have a special group of volunteers, the "holy society," who are endowed with the responsibility of caring for the dead. They wash the body and then purify it spiritually by pouring 24 containers of water over it in a continuous flow. Then the body is dried and wrapped in a simple burial shroud of white linen, the same for rich and poor so that they will be equally honored.

The body may or may not be buried in a coffin. When the body is placed in the grave, a handful of dirt from Israel is thrown on top of it, reflecting the belief that the dead will rise and be gathered in Israel upon the coming of the Messiah. Following the burial there is usually a "meal of condolence" consisting of eggs and bread (symbolizing life), for family members only. Visitors may come to offer condolences following the meal.

Although Judaism emphasizes life after death less than any other major religion, its mourning rituals after death are among the most highly ritualized. Upon hearing of the death of a family member or close friend the tradition is to express grief by tearing one's clothing (although today often a black ribbon is worn instead). After the burial, family members enter an intense 7-day period called sitting *shiva* (meaning "seven"). During this time they sit only on low stools or on the floor, and they do not work, bathe, shave, cut their hair, wear cosmetics, have sexual relations, or change their clothes (they still wear the clothes torn upon hearing the news). Mirrors in the house are covered. Prayer services are held that include family and friends.

Following shiva, another period of restrictions lasts until 30 days after burial, called *schloshim* (meaning "thirty"). Mourners may not shave or cut their hair, attend parties, or listen to music. A further period, lasting until a year after death, is observed for parents' death only. Children of the deceased parent are not to attend parties, theatre performances, or concerts during this time. Furthermore, they must recite a prayer called the *Kaddish* every day for 11 months.

Christianity

Christianity has more adherents worldwide (about 2 billion) than any other religion, and the mourning rituals of Christianity often take local forms. However, there are two main general types of mourning rituals in Christianity: Catholic and Protestant (Hunter, 2007). Both are considerably simpler than any of the rituals previously described.

◉──Watch the Video
Jewish and Islamic Funeral Rituals at www.pearson custom.com/mi/msu_ mylabs.com

In the Catholic church, when a person is ill and near death there is a traditional ritual called *Anointing of the Sick*. The purpose of this ritual is to bring comfort to the sick person and family members who may be anguished over the impending death, to forgive any sins the sick person may not have repented, and to prepare the person's soul for passing over to eternal life. It can take place in a home, hospital, or church. The rite is administered by a priest, who begins by reading a Bible verse, then places his hands on the dying person's head, then blesses the oil and applies it to the forehead of the dying person.

After the person dies, a *vigil* (also called a *wake*) is held in the home or the church. Family members and friends gather to share food and drink, pray for the deceased person, remember the person's life, and comfort one another. The deceased is in a coffin, which is usually open, and often there are candles, flowers, and a crucifix. In some cultures, mirrors are covered or turned to the wall if the vigil takes place at home. The vigil can last from a few hours to 2 days.

The day following the end of the vigil, a *Requiem Mass* is held. After the Mass is over, the coffin is immediately taken to the cemetery to be buried. At the gravesite the priest sprinkles holy water on the coffin and on the grave. Special prayers are said, asking that the soul rest in peace and receive God's mercy. After the burial it is customary to gather again at the home of the deceased for food, drink, remembrance, and consolation.

The Protestant funeral service resembles the Catholic service in some ways, but is much less standardized and ritualized, and much more variable. There is no standard custom for the period before death, although it is common for a dying person's minister to visit during the time when death is near. After death, there is a period of visitation for 1 or 2 days resembling the Catholic vigil, taking place in the home of the deceased or a funeral home.

The funeral service varies widely because there is no standard form, but typical elements include prayers, music, and reading of scripture, led by a minister. One common element of Protestant funeral services that is unique is that there is often a *eulogy*, which is a special sermon on the life of the deceased, usually performed by the minister. Following the funeral service the mourners proceed to the grave if the body is to be buried, where there may be a short prayer and scripture reading as the coffin is lowered into the grave. If the body has been cremated, this part of the service may involve the scattering of the ashes.

Islam

When a Muslim is near death, loved ones gather near the deathbed and recite verses from the Koran (Gatrad, 1994). They try to make the dying person comfortable, and encourage the person to recite words of remembrance and prayer.

After death occurs, the body is bathed and wrapped in a simple plain cloth. Family, friends, and others close to the deceased may come by to offer their respect and condolences. Burial takes place within a short time after death, because Islam does not allow embalming or otherwise disturbing the body after death. Cremation is forbidden, because Muslims believe that there will be a Day of Judgment in which their bodies will be raised from the dead.

The body is taken to the cemetery, where funeral prayers are recited. Then the body is laid in the grave with only the cloth shroud, no coffin (unless required by local law). It is placed on its right side, facing Mecca, the holiest site in Islam. More prayers are recited, asking for Allah's forgiveness of the deceased. Only a simple grave marker is planted, because lavish displays are discouraged in Islam.

Loved ones observe a 3-day mourning period, during which they are to pray, receive visitors and condolences, and avoid decorative clothing and jewelry. Widows are committed to a mourning period of 4 months and 10 days. During this period they are not to marry, move from their homes, or wear jewelry.

Thinking Culturally

Since periods of mourning vary between religions, do you think labor policies should accommodate people's religious beliefs and allow people to take extended periods off from work to grieve?

Remembering and Honoring the Dead

LEARNING OBJECTIVE 10   Describe the rituals and traditions used by various religions to remember and honor the dead.

When someone we love dies, we grieve and we mourn their passing, and we miss them. After the mourning rituals and the prescribed periods of mourning are over we resume our daily lives, but we never forget those who have died. In all human cultures, there are customs for remembering and honoring the dead.

Ritual honoring of the dead is an important part of life for Hindus (Knipe, 2008). Each year, on the anniversary of a family member's death, a meal is prepared of dishes the deceased person enjoyed in life, and the food is served as an offering in a ritual ceremony led by a male, usually the oldest son. A special dish called *pinda* (rice balls) is prepared for the occasion and set out for the spirit of the ancestor on the roof of the family home. If a crow comes and devours the rice balls the offering is believed to be accepted, as crows are believed to be messengers of Yama, the god of the dead. In addition, every year there is a 16-day period called *Fortnight of the Ancestors* devoted to honoring the dead.

Buddhist rituals honoring the dead are blended with traditions of ancestor worship that have existed for millennia. The Chinese tradition of ancestor worship is described in the **Cultural Focus: Ancestor Worship and Hungry Ghosts in China** feature.

In the Jewish tradition, the death of parents, siblings, spouses, or children is commemorated each year on the anniversary of death, a custom called the *Yahrzeit* (Marcus, 2004). A special Yahrzeit candle is lit and burns for 24 hours. The Kaddish prayer recited at funerals is now recited three times (evening of the previous day, morning, and afternoon), and many attend synagogue on this day. Some people observe a custom of fasting on the day of the Yahrzeit, or at least refraining from meat and wine. Many synagogues will have lights on a special memorial plaque on one of the synagogue's walls, with names of synagogue members who have died. Each of these lights will be lit for individuals on their Yahrzeit.

On the Day of the Dead in Mexico, families sometimes have a picnic at the gravesite of the loved one.
(PEROUSSE Bruno/Hemis/Alamy)

In Christian tradition, the dead are especially remembered and honored during a 3-day period beginning on the last night in October. This tradition began many centuries ago in Ireland, where it was believed that this is a time when the boundary between the spirit world and the earthly world is at its thinnest and when spirits are most likely to be roaming the earth. Fires and pumpkin lanterns were lit to frighten away witches and ghosts. Eventually this night became known as *All Hallows' Eve* (*hallows* means "spirits"), or Halloween. November 1, the day after Halloween, is All Saints' Day, when the lives of saints and martyrs are remembered and praised. The next day, November 2, is All Souls' Day, when people pray for all their loved ones who have died.

A distinctive form of the Christian observance of All Souls' Day takes place in Mexico, where it is known as *Día de los Muertos,* the Day of the Dead (Beatty & Brandes, 2009). Friends and family gather to pray for and remember the dead, but the Day of the Dead is a time of celebration when eating and parties are common. Families may build small shrines or altars in their homes on this occasion. Sometimes families go to the cemetery to be with the soul of the deceased. There, they clean and decorate the grave, and perhaps present the favorite food and drink of the dead as an offering. Celebrants may recall humorous events and stories from the life of the deceased. In some parts of Mexico the family picnics at the gravesite, and in others the family may stay beside the grave all night long. A common symbol of the holiday is the skull, a tradition believed to have originated in the pre-Christian past, when it was common to display skulls to symbolize death and rebirth. Today the skulls are often made of sugar or chocolate and inscribed with the name of the loved one who has passed away.

Muslims are encouraged to visit the graves of their loved ones, to show their respect and to remind them of the afterlife to come. Prayers should be offered at home before going to the cemetery. Shoes are to be taken off before entering the graveyard, and prayers are recited at the grave. The death anniversaries of saints are observed as religious days, when believers are obliged to gather, recite the Koran, and do charitable works.

In sum, the major religions have different ways of remembering and honoring the dead, but across religions these customs allow the survivors to maintain a sense of psychological contact with the dead. The death of someone we love is among the most difficult human experiences, and ritual ways of remembering those we have lost provide consolation and a mode of expression for the feelings that still exist even though the person who was the object of those feelings is with us no longer.

CULTURAL FOCUS

ANCESTOR WORSHIP AND HUNGRY GHOSTS IN CHINA

Most cultures have customs and rituals for honoring the dead, but China is a place where those practices are especially elaborate. In other cultures it is common for the dead to be remembered on a special day each year, but in China ceremonies worshipping the ancestors are held several times a year, including on Chinese New Year, a Chinese All Soul's Day, and seasonal festivals in autumn, winter, and spring (Chung & Wegars, 2009). On these occasions, offerings of food and other gifts are made to the ancestors, gratitude is expressed for past favors granted, and appeals are made for the protection of the family from misfortunes and disasters, as well as for good fortune and prosperity in the future. These practices honoring deceased ancestors are one reflection of the Chinese value of filial piety. Parents and other elders are to be obeyed and honored not only during their lifetimes but for generations after their deaths.

In addition to the many occasions each year when the living pay their respects to the dead, there is a period each year during which the souls of the dead are believed to visit the living. This period is called the Ghost Month, and during this month the gates of the underworld are said to be opened up and ghosts are free to roam the earth where they seek food and entertainment (Zhang, 2009). Families pray to their ancestors and prepare elaborate meals as an offering to them. They also burn, as an offering to the ancestors, paper fashioned into valued items such as money, cars, houses, and televisions. Historians believe that this is an echo of a previous custom in which valuable objects were actually buried with the dead.

The high point of the month is the Hungry Ghost Festival, in which families gather and prepare a large meal and place the dishes on an offering table to please the ghosts and ward off bad luck. Why are the ghosts hungry? Because they may not have been given proper food offerings by their families during the year, and by the time of Ghost Month they are emaciated and have long thin necks. At the end of the festival families take lanterns in the shape of lotus flowers and place them on boats and set them in water, to direct the ghosts back to the underworld. Thus the Hungry Ghost Festival is held not just to honor the dead but to pacify them so that they will not be angry at the living and cause them harm.

WHAT HAVE YOU LEARNED?

1. Do most Americans believe in life after death? How do the beliefs vary based on one's religion?
2. What is involved in the Jewish tradition of sitting shiva?
3. What is the proper way to deal with a body after death, according to the Muslim religion?
4. What is the Day of the Dead?

PART 2 VIDEO GUIDE

REMEMBERING AND HONORING THE DEAD ACROSS CULTURES (LENGTH: 8:36)

A variety of people from various countries are interviewed in this video about how they honor their ancestors.

1. What is one common tribute that all of the individuals interviewed in this video do to honor their ancestors?
2. Compare and contrast at least two of the practices discussed in this video.
3. Discuss the concept of "feeding the dead" and list your thoughts about this concept.

> ◉— **Watch the Video**   *Remembering and Honoring the Dead Across Cultures* at
> www.pearsoncustom.com/mi/msu_mylabs

SUMMING UP

PART 1   SOCIOCULTURAL AND EMOTIONAL RESPONSES TO DEATH

1. **Compare and contrast the benefits and drawbacks of dying at home versus in a hospital.**

    Most people would prefer to die at home, yet few do in developed countries. Dying at home often takes place slowly and gradually, leaving caregivers under the strain of helping the dying person with daily activities of eating, using the toilet, bathing, and taking medications. Hospitals offer medical care and support but are often seen as impersonal and dehumanizing.

2. **Summarize the options and controversies that exist regarding end-of-life care and death.**

    Hospice care provides a humane setting that allows terminally ill people to live the final module of their lives with dignity. Euthanasia, which involves either ceasing medical interventions or taking steps to bring about death, is sometimes considered when death is near and there is no possibility of recovery, although it is highly controversial. Many older adults in developed countries now create advance directives before they become ill so that their loved ones will not be faced with making difficult choices on their behalf.

3. **Describe how the emotional responses associated with grief change over time.**

    The early stages of grief often involve shock, numbness, and disbelief followed by a period of intense emotions alternating with states that resemble the symptoms of depression. Grief gradually subsides and the bereaved person is able to resume previous daily activities and social relationships although feelings of loss and yearning may never entirely fade.

4. **Describe variations in the grieving process, and identify factors that influence these variations.**

    There are variations in grieving depending on *who* has died and *how* the death occurred, with most intense grief for deaths of a parent, child, or spouse, and for deaths that occurred suddenly. Men and women generally deal with the death of a spouse differently, with men more likely to experience physical and mental health problems.

5. **Summarize Kübler-Ross's theory of death and dying, and identify some limitations of this theory.**

    Kübler-Ross proposed that people go through a series of five stages in their responses to imminent death: denial, anger, bargaining, depression, and acceptance. Her theory has been influential but has not held up well in subsequent research. Few people go through the five stages in this sequence, and many people experience few or none of the stages.

◇ KEY TERMS

hospice *p. 419*	euthanasia *p. 420*	Do Not Resuscitate	bereavement *p. 422*
palliative care *p. 419*	advance directive *p. 421*	(DNR) *p. 421*	grief *p. 422*

PART 2   BELIEFS ABOUT DEATH AND THE AFTERLIFE

6. **Describe how children's understanding of death changes from childhood to adolescence.**

    Children have a limited understanding of death: They realize that death is permanent, but not until middle childhood do they realize that death is inevitable. In adolescence, beliefs about death become more abstract and more complex, reflecting adolescents' more general gains in cognitive development

7. **Describe how beliefs and fears about death change throughout adulthood.**

    Death anxiety is highest in emerging adulthood, then declines with age and is lowest in late adulthood, as many adults undergo a life review and come to accept the life they have lived. Death is also more familiar to those in late adulthood, so they spend more time talking about it and planning for it than younger adults do.

8. **Explain how individual beliefs about the afterlife vary across countries and within the United States.**

    Belief in life after death varies by country, but the majority of people in most countries believe in some kind of afterlife. Americans are more likely than people in other developed countries to believe in life after death, although fewer than half of American Jews hold this belief.

9. **Compare and contrast the mourning rituals of Hinduism, Buddhism, Judaism, Christianity, and Islam.**

   Mourning rituals are important to Hindus and Buddhists, as they believe that these rituals will help influence what a soul's status will be in the next life. Both religions practice cremation. Jewish mourning rituals after death are among the most highly ritualized, and include sitting shiva with the deceased. Christian rituals may include the anointing of the sick, vigils, and a mass. Muslim burial takes place within a short time after death, because Islam does not allow embalming or otherwise disturbing the body after death. Prayers are recited outdoors and the body is laid to rest in a grave.

10. **Describe the rituals and traditions used by various religions to remember and honor the dead.**

    Rituals and traditions for remembering and honoring the dead exist in all traditions. They vary greatly, but many include leaving an offering such as food for the deceased, lighting candles in remembrance, saying prayers, and visiting the grave.

◇ KEY TERMS

life review *p. 427*   reincarnation *p. 430*   cremation *p. 432*

◇ PRACTICE TEST

1. In developed countries today, most people die
   a. at home.   b. in hospitals.
   c. in nursing homes.   d. in private homelike hospice facilities.

2. Research on hospice has found that
   a. it is more expensive than standard hospital care.
   b. it is more common among African Americans who tend to be higher than other groups in spirituality.
   c. those who are dying respond to it more favorably than to standard hospital care, but their families find it to be more stressful.
   d. family members who provide for the dying person with hospice support have better psychological functioning two years later, compared to family members without hospice support.

3. Research on grief has shown that
   a. after a loved one dies, people have difficulty sleeping or eating, but this tends to occur only in the first week after the loss.
   b. the survivor's identity may change.
   c. talking to the deceased spouse was found only among those who had psychological disorders before the loss.
   d. after the initial shock fades, people who were not depressed before the loss will not be depressed after it because of their innate resiliency.

4. Following the death of a spouse
   a. women are more likely than men to experience mental health problems because they are less likely to get remarried.
   b. the risk of mortality is about the same as among married peers because older adults are often given a lot of social support.
   c. older adults are more at risk for psychological problems and cognitive difficulties with memory and concentration than their married counterparts.
   d. older adults tend to grieve similarly regardless of how their spouse died because of deeply engrained beliefs of what is "appropriate."

5. Which of the following is considered a critique of the research on Kübler-Ross's theory?
   a. It doesn't have enough stages.
   b. It has not been influential in the care of terminally ill patients in this country.
   c. The brief questionnaire reports provided very limited information on the experiences of terminally ill patients.
   d. It overlooks the cultural context.

6. Lia discussed the existence of her friend's soul that will endure after death. It is most likely that Lia is a
   a. 4-year-old.   b. 6-year-old.
   c. 9-year-old.   d. 13-year-old.

7. Research on death anxiety has shown that
   a. death anxiety is higher among women than men.
   b. strength of religious faith is unrelated to level of death anxiety.
   c. younger people talk more about death than older people do because they see it as further away.
   d. older adults are the most afraid of death since they've witnessed the death of friends and family members.

8. Which of the following statements best reflects the results of the Pew survey on afterlife beliefs within the United States?
   a. Only a small percentage of Americans believe in life after death.
   b. Americans who adhere to a religion believe in life after death, but atheists and agnostics do not.
   c. Most Americans are tolerant of different views about religion and the afterlife, believing that many religions can lead to eternal life.
   d. Christians and Jews believe in life after death, but no research has been done yet on the beliefs of Americans who are Muslim, Hindu, or Buddhist.

9. In which religion is cremation forbidden?
   a. Islam   b. Protestant
   c. Hinduism   d. Buddhism

10. Shulamit, who is Jewish, would be most likely to do which of the following on the anniversary of her son's death?

a. have a party and celebrate by sharing humorous stories about her son's life

b. prepare an elaborate meal and set aside a special dish for the spirit of the ancestor

c. light a candle

d. erect a shrine or alter in her home

Answers: 1. B (L.O. 1); 2. D (L.O. 2); 3. B (L.O. 3); 4. C (L.O. 4); 5. D (L.O. 5); 6. D (L.O. 6); 7. A (L.O. 7); 8. C (L.O. 8); 9. A (L.O. 9); 10. C (L.O. 10)

◆ REFERENCES

Addington-Hall, J. (2000). Do home deaths increase distress in bereavement? *Palliative Medicine, 14,* 161–162.

Ajrouch, K., Blandon, A., & Antonucci, T. (2005). Social networks among men and women: The effects of age and socioeconomic status. *Journal of Gerontology: Social Sciences, 60B,* S311–S317.

Alberts, A., Elkind, D., & Ginsberg, S. (2007). The personal fable and risk-taking in early adolescence. *Journal of Youth and Adolescence, 36,* 71–76.

Angel, J. L., Douglas, N., & Angel, R. J. (2003). Gender, widowhood, and long-term care in the older Mexican population. *Journal of Women and Aging, 15,* 89–105.

Arnett, J. J. (2000). Emerging adulthood: A theory of development from the late teens through the twenties. *American Psychologist, 55,* 469–480.

Beatty, A., & Brandes, S. (2009). Skulls to the living, bread to the dead: The Day of the Dead in Mexico and beyond. *Journal of the Royal Anthropological Institute, 15,* 209–211.

Berg, A. I., Hoffman, L., Hassing, L. B., McClearn, G. E., & Johansson, B. (2009). What matters, and what matters most, for change in life satisfaction in the oldest-old? A study of over 6 years among individuals 80+, *Aging & Mental Health, 13,* 191–201.

Blumberg, B. D., Lewis, M. J., & Susman, E. J. (1984). Adolescence: A time of transition. In M. G. Eisenberg, L. C. Sutkin, & M. A. Jansen (Eds.), *Chronic illness and disability through the life span: Effects on self and family* (pp. 133–149). New York, NY: Springer.

Bonanno, G. A. (2004). Loss, trauma, and human resilience: Have we underestimated the human capacity to thrive after extremely aversive events? *American Psychologist, 59,* 20–28.

Brent, S. B., Speece, M. W., Lin, C., Dong, Q., & Yang, C. (1996). The development of the concept of death among Chinese and U.S. children 3–17 years of age: From binary to "fuzzy" concepts? *Omega, 33,* 67–83.

Breslau, N., Kessler, R. C., Chilcoat, H. D., Schultz, L. R., Davis, G. C., & Andreski, P. (1998). Trauma and posttraumatic stress disorder in the community: The 1996 Detroit Area Survey of Trauma. *Archives of General Psychiatry, 55,* 626–632.

Burton, A., Hayley, W., & Small, B. (2006). Bereavement after caregiving or unexpected death: Effects on elderly spouses. *Aging & Mental Health, 10,* 319–326.

Butler, R. N. (2002). The life review. *Journal of Geriatric Psychiatry, 35,* 7–10.

Carnelly, K. B., Wortman, C. B., Bolger, N., & Burke, C. T. (2006). The time course of grief reactions to spousal loss: Evidence from a national probability sample. *Journal of Personality and Social Psychology, 91,* 476–492.

Centers for Medicare and Medicaid Services. (2009). Hospice payment system. Retrieved from http://www.cms.hhs.gov/mlnproducts/downloads/hospice_pay_sys_fs.pdf

Cheng, C. (2006). Living alone: The choice and health of older women. *Journal of Gerontological Nursing, 32,* 24–25.

Christopher, M. J. (2003). The new place of end-of-life issues on the policy agenda. *Public Policy and Aging Report, 13,* 23–26.

Chung, S. F., & Wegars, P. (Eds.). (2009). *Chinese American death rituals: Respecting the ancestors.* New York, NY: AltaMira Press.

Cicirelli, V. G. (2002). *Older adults' views on death.* New York, NY: Springer.

Cicirelli, V. G. (2006). Fear of death in mid-old age. *Journal of Gerontology: Psychological Sciences, 61B,* P75–P81.

Cohen, L. L. (2008). Racial/ethnic disparities in hospice care: A systematic review. *Journal of Palliative Medicine, 11,* 763–768.

Dees, M., Dekkers, W., van Weel, C., & Vernooij–Dassen, M. (2010). Review unbearable suffering of patients with a request for euthanasia or physician–assisted suicide: An integrative review. *Psycho-Oncology, 19,* 339–352.

Dent, A., & Stewart, A. (2004). *Sudden death in childhood: Support for the bereaved family.* London, UK: Butterworth-Heinemann.

DiCamillo, M., & Field, M. (2006). *Continued support for doctor-assisted suicide. Most would want their physician to assist them if they were incurably ill and wanted to die.* San Francisco, CA: Field Research Corporation.

Dowdney, L. (2000). Annotation: Childhood bereavement following parental death. *Journal of Child Psychology and Psychiatry and Allied Disciplines, 41,* 819–830.

Dula, A., & Williams, S. (2005). When race matters. *Clinical Geriatric Medicine, 21,* 239–253.

Dunne, E. J., & Dunne-Maxim, K. (2004). Working with families in the aftermath of suicide. In F. Walsh & M. McGoldrick (Eds.), *Living beyond loss: Death in the family* (2nd ed., pp. 272–284). New York, NY: Norton.

Erikson, E. H. (1950). *Childhood and society.* New York, NY: Norton.

Gatrad, A. R. (1994). Muslim customs surrounding death, bereavement, postmortem examinations, and organ transplants. *BMJ, 309,* 521.

Germino, B. B. (2003). Dying at home. In I. Corless, B. B. Germino, & M. A. Pittman (Eds.), *Dying, death, and bereavement: A challenge for the living* (pp. 105–116). New York, NY: Springer.

Gorman, T. E., Ahern, S. P., Wiseman, J., & Skrobik, Y. (2005). Residents' end-of-life decision making with adult hospitalized patients: A review of the literature. *Academic Medicine, 80,* 622–633.

Gott, M., Seymour, J., Bellamy, G., Clark, D., & Ahmedzai, S. (2004). Older people's views about home as a place of care at the end of life. *Palliative Medicine, 18,* 460–467.

Grunier, A., Vincent, M., Weitzen, S., Truchil, R., Teno, J., & Roy, J. (2007). Where people die: A multi-level approach to understanding influence on site of death in America. *Medical Care Research & Review, 64,* 351–378.

Hayslip, B., & Hansson, R. (2003). Death awareness and adjustment across the life span. In C. D. Bryant (Ed.), *Handbook of death and dying* (pp. 437–447. Thousand Oaks, CA: Sage.

Hedberg, K., Hopkins, D., & Kohn, M. (2003). Five years of legal physician-assisted suicide in Oregon. *New England Journal of Medicine, 348,* 961–964.

Hensley, P. (2006). Treatment of bereavement-related depression and traumatic grief. *Journal of Affective Disorders, 92,* 117–124.

Hockey, J. L., & Katz, J. (2001). *Grief, mourning and death rituals.* London, UK: McGraw Hill.

Hooyman, N. R., & Kiyak, H. A. (2011). *Social gerontology: A multidisciplinary perspective* (9th ed.). Boston, MA: Pearson.

Hunter, J. (2007). Bereavement: An incomplete rite of passage. *OMEGA—Journal of Death and Dying, 56,* 153–173.

Jost, K. (2005). Right to die. *The CQ Researcher,* 423–438.

Journal of Pain and Palliative Care Pharmacotherapy. (2006). News and innovations: Physicians and general public support for physician-assisted suicide. *Journal of Pain and Palliative Care, 20,* 100.

Kass-Bartelemes, B. L., Hughes, R., & Rutherford, M. K. (2003). *Advance care planning: Preferences for care at the end of life.* Rockville, MD: Agency for Healthcare Research and Quality.

Kastenbaum, R. (2007). *Death, society, and human experience* (9th ed.). Boston, MA: Allyn & Bacon.

Keene, J. R., & Prokos, A. H. (2008). Widowhood and the end of spousal care-giving: Relief or wear and tear? *Aging & Society, 28,* 551–570.

Kenyon, B. L. (2001). Current research in children's conceptions of death: A critical review. *Omega, 43,* 63–91.

Knipe, D. M. (2008). Make that sesame on rice, please! Appetites of the dead in Hinduism. *Indian Folklore Research Journal, 5,* 27–45.

Konigsberg, R. D. (2011). *The truth about grief: The myth of its five stages and the new science of loss.* New York, NY: Simon & Schuster.

Kreicbergs, U., Valdimarsdottir, U., Onelov, E., Henter, J.-I., & Steineck, G. (2004). Anxiety and depression in parents 4–9 years after the loss of a child owing to a malignancy: A population-based follow-up. *Psychological Medicine, 34,* 1431–1441.

Kübler-Ross, E. (1969). *On death and dying.* New York, NY: Macmillan.

Kübler-Ross, E. (1982). *Working it through.* New York, NY: Macmillan.

Kwak, J., Haley, W. E., & Chiraboga, D. A. (2008). Racial differences in hospice use and in-hospital death among Medicare and Medicaid dual-eligible nursing home residents. *The Gerontologist, 48,* 32–41.

Lamberg, L. (2002). "Palliative care" means "active care:" It aims to improve quality of life. *JAMA: Journal of the American Medical Association, 288,* 943–944.

Langner, T. S. (2002). *Choices for living: Coping with fear of dying.* New York, NY: Kluwer Academic.

Levin, B. G. (2004). Coping with traumatic loss. *International Journal of Emergency Mental Health, 6,* 25–31.

Marcus, I. G. (2004). *The Jewish life cycle: Rites of passage from biblical to modern times.* Seattle, WA: University of Washington Press.

McArdle, E. F. (2002). New York's Do-Not-Resuscitate law: Groundbreaking protection of patient autonomy or a physician's right to make medical futility determinations? *DePaul Journal of Health Care Law, 8,* 55–82.

Mearns, S. (2000). The impact of loss on adolescents: Developing appropriate support. *International Journal of Palliative Nursing, 6,* 12–17.

Meskel, L. (2001). The Egyptian ways of death. *Archeological Papers of the American Anthropological Association, 10,* 27–40.

Mitty, E. L., & Ramsey, G. (2008). Advance directives. In E. Capezuti, D. Zwicker, & T. Fulmer (Eds.), *Evidence-based geriatric nursing protocols for best practice* (3rd ed., pp. 539–563). New York, NY: Springer.

Morrison, R. S., Penrod, J. D., Cassel, J. B., Caust-Ellenbogen, M., Litke, A., Spragens, L.,…Meier, D. E. (2008). Cost savings associated with U.S. hospital palliative care consultation programs. *Archives of Internal Medicine, 168,* 1784–1790.

Muramatsu, N., Hoyem, R. L., Yin, H., & Campbell, R. T. (2008). Place of death among older Americans: Does state spending on home and community-based services promote home death? *Medical Care, 46,* 829–838.

National Hospice and Palliative Care Organization and Research Department. (2008). *Hospice facts and figures.* Retrieved from http://www.nhpco.org/files/public/Statistics_Research/NHPCO_facts-and-figures_2008.pdf

Niemeyer, D. (2006). *Eighth annual report on Oregon's Death with Dignity Act.* Portland, OR: Oregon Department of Human Services.

Noppe, I. C., & Noppe, L. D. (1997). Evolving meanings of death during early, middle, and later adolescence. *Death Studies, 21,* 253–275.

O'Connor, P. (2003). Dying in the hospital. In I. Corless, B. B. Germino, & M. A. Pitman (Eds.), *Dying, death, and bereavement: A challenge for the living* (2nd ed., pp. 87–103). New York, NY: Springer.

Onwuteaka-Philipsen, B. D., van der Heide, A., Muller, M. T., Rurup, M., Rietjens, J. A. C., & Georges, J.-J. (2005). Dutch experience of monitoring euthanasia. *British Medical Journal, 331,* 691–693.

Open Society Institute. (2003). *Project on death in America.* New York, NY: Author.

Perrault, A., Fothergill-Bourbonnais, F., & Fiset, V. (2004). The experience of family members caring for a dying loved one. *International Journal of Palliative Nursing, 10,* 133–143.

Pew Forum on Religion & Public Life (2008). *U.S. religious landscape survey.* Washington, DC: Author.

Pew Research Center. (2006). *Strong public support for right to die.* Retrieved from http://people-press.org/reports.

Ragow-O'Brien, D., Hayslip, B., Jr., & Guarnaccia, C. A. (2000). The impact of hospice on attitudes toward funerals and subsequent bereavement adjustment. *Omega, 41,* 291–305.

Rossi, N. E., Bisconti, T. L., & Bergeman, C. S. (2007). The role of dispositional resilience in regaining life satisfaction after the loss of a spouse. *Death Studies, 31,* 863–883.

Rurup, M. L., Muller, M. T., Onwuteaka-Philipsen, B. D., van der Heide, A., van der Wal, G., & van der Maas, P. J. (2005). Requests for euthanasia or physician-assisted suicide from older persons who do not have a severe disease: An interview study. *Psychological Medicine, 35,* 665–671.

Russac, R. J., Gatliff, C., Reece, M., & Spottswood, D. (2007). Death anxiety across the adult years: An examination of age and gender effects. *Death Studies, 31,* 549–561.

Scannell-Desch, E. (2003). Women's adjustment to widowhood: Theory, research, and methods. *Journal of Psychosocial Nursing and Mental Health Services, 41,* 28–36.

Schulz, R., Boerner, K., Shear, K., Zhang, S., & Gitlin, L. N. (2006). Predictors of complicated grief among dementia caregivers: A prospective study of bereavement. *American Journal of Geriatric Psychiatry, 14,* 650.

Schachter, S. R. (2009). Cancer patients facing death: Is the patient who focuses on living in denial of his/her death? In M. K. Bartalos (Ed.), *Speaking of death: America's new sense of mortality* (pp. 42–77). Westport, CT: Praeger.

Segal, A. F. (2004). *Life after death: A history of the afterlife in Western religion.* New York, NY: Doubleday.

Shear, M. K. (2009). Grief and depression: Treatment decisions for bereaved children and adults. *American Journal of Psychiatry, 166,* 746–748.

Singer, Y., Bachner, Y. G., Shvartzman, P., & Carmel, S. (2005). Home death—the caregivers' experiences. *Journal of Pain and Symptom Management, 30,* 70–74.

Subramanian, S. V., Elwert, F., & Christakis, N. (2008). Widowhood and mortality among the elderly: The modifying role of neighborhood concentration of widowed individuals. *Social Science & Medicine, 66,* 873–884.

Tang, W. R., Aaronson, L. S., & Forbes, S. A. (2004). Quality of life in hospice patients with terminal illnesses. *Western Journal of Nursing Research, 26,* 113–128.

Tomer, A., & Eliason, G. (2000). Attitudes about life and death: Toward a comprehensive model of death anxiety. In A. Tomer (Ed.), *Death attitudes and the older adult: Theories, concepts and applications* (pp. 3-22). Philadelphia, PA: Taylor and Francis.

Wahlhaus, E. (2005). The psychological benefits of the traditional Jewish mourning rituals: Have the changes instituted by the Progressive movement enhanced or diminished them? *European Judaism, 38,* 95–109.

Waldrop, D. P. (2006). At the eleventh hour: Psychosocial dynamics in short hospice stays. *The Gerontologist, 46,* 106–114.

Wass, H. (2004). A perspective on the current state of death education. *Death Studies, 28,* 289–308.

Weitzen, S., Teno, J., Fennell, M., & Mor, V. (2003). Factors associated with site of death: A national study of where people die. *Medical Care, 41,* 323–335.

Wenestam, C. G., & Wass, H. (1987). Swedish and U.S. children's thinking about death: A qualitative study and cross-cultural comparison. *Death Studies, 11,* 99–121.

Wilson, J. (2009). *Mourning the unborn dead: A Buddhist ritual comes to America.* New York: Oxford University Press.

Worden, W. J. (2009). *Grief counseling and grief therapy: A handbook for the mental health practitioner* (4th ed). New York, NY: Springer.

World Federation of Right to Die Societies. (2006). Public opinion. Retrieved from www.worldrtd.net

Wright, A. A., & Katz, I. T. (2007). Letting go of the rope: Aggressive treatment, hospice care, and open access. *New England Journal of Medicine, 357,* 324–327.

Yang, S. C., & Chen, S.-F. (2002). A phenomenographic approach to the meaning of death: A Chinese perspective. *Death Studies, 26,* 143–175.

Zhang, W. (2009). How do we think about death?—A cultural glance of superstitious ideas from Chinese and Western ghost festivals. *International Education Studies, 2,* 68–71.

MODULE 11-B

ACTIVITY

◇ THE RESILIENCE OF CHILD SOLDIERS

Sadly, millions of children and adolescents throughout the world face the challenge of surviving natural and human-made disasters. These catastrophic events include tsunamis and hurricanes, war and terrorist attacks, gang violence and school shootings. For example, although the Geneva Conventions forbid the use of children under age 15 as soldiers, current estimates are that 300,000 children in over 50 countries have been recruited or forced into armed forces (Singer, 2006). Increasingly, mental health professionals have focused their efforts on understanding the psychological impacts of catastrophic events. In fact, the World Psychiatric Association (2006) now recognizes *Disaster Psychiatry* as a new specialty. Research indicates that children and adolescents in these circumstances are susceptible to developmental delays, family conflict, depression and other symptoms of post-traumatic stress (Joshi, O'Donnell, Cullins, & Lewin, 2006; Williams, 2006). Yet, some studies point to the remarkable resilience of these children and adolescents in that many continue to thrive despite these conditions (Unger, Lee, Callaghan, & Boothroyd, 2005). This activity will encourage you to think about the qualities of resilience.

Directions: Read the descriptions of resilient youth below and then answer the questions that follow about children and adolescents who become soldiers.

Michael Ungar and colleagues' (2006) International Resilience Project has conducted research with at-risk children on five continents in order to identify the conditions that enable young people to cope with disaster. They have identified seven tensions that young people must negotiate in order to thrive in spite of their environments (Unger, 2006, p.57):

1. **Access to material resources:** Availability of financial, educational, medical and employment assistance and/or opportunities, as well as access to food, clothing, and shelter.
2. **Relationships:** Relationships with significant others, peers, and adults within one's family and community.
3. **Identity:** Personal and collective sense of purpose, self-appraisal of strengths and weaknesses, aspirations, beliefs and values, including spiritual and religious identification.
4. **Power and control:** Experiences of caring for oneself and others; the ability to affect change in one's social and physical environment in order to access health resources.
5. **Cultural adherence:** Adherence to ones local and/or global cultural practices, values, and beliefs.

Taken from *Cross-Cultural Explorations: Activities in Culture and Psychology*, Second Edition, by Susan Goldstein.

6. **Social justice:** Experiences related to finding a meaningful role in community and social equality.

7. **Cohesion:** Balancing one's personal interests with a sense of responsibility to the greater good; feeling a part of something larger than oneself socially and spiritually.

Grigorenko and O'Keefe (2004) discuss child soldiers as an extraordinary example of resilience in that they often develop skills that enable them to cope with an extremely hostile environment. These authors describe the behaviors and attributes required of child soldiers as follows:

- running errands

- acting as spies and informants

- handling and caring for weapons

- handling wounds and personal needs

- understanding the hierarchy of the army

- reading and interpreting maps

- identifying with the army and seeking revenge on the enemy

- having self-pride, unit pride, and patriotism

1. Based on the seven tensions attained by resilient children, discuss why child soldiers might develop resilience.

2. In what type of disaster might you expect children to be the most resilient?

3. In what type of disaster might you expect children to be the least resilient?

4. How might cultural differences impact the ability to develop resilience?

◇ REFERENCES

Grigorenko, E. L., & O'Keefe, P. A. (2004). What do children do when they cannot go to school? In R. J. Sternberg, & E. L. Grigorenko (Eds.), *Culture and competence: Contexts of life success* (pp. 23-53), Washington, DC: American Psychological Society.

Joshi, P. T., O'Donnell, D. A., Cullins, L. M., & Lewin, S. M. (2006). Children exposed to war and terrorism. In M. M. Feerick & G. B. Silverman (Eds.). *Children exposed to violence (pp53-84)*. Baltimore, MD: Paul H. Brookes Publishing.

Singer, P. W. (2006). *Children at war*. Berkeley, CA: University of California Press.

Ungar, M. (2006). Nurturing hidden resilience in at-risk youth in different cultures. *Journal of the Canadian Academy of Child and Adolescent Psychiatry*, 15, 53–58.

Unger, M., Lee, A. W., Callaghan, T., & Boothroyd, R. A. (2005). An international collaboration to study resilience in adolescents across cultures. *Journal of Social Work Research and Evaluation*, 6, 5–23.

Williams, R. (2006). The psychosocial consequences for children and young people who are exposed to terrorism, war, conflict, and natural disasters. *Current Opinion in Psychiatry*, 19, 337–349.

World Psychiatric Association (2006). *World Psychiatry*, 5, 1–4.

SECTION 12

ETHICAL ISSUES AND
A LOOK TO THE FUTURE

MODULE 12-A

FUTURE TRENDS AND APPLICATIONS

Phyllidia Ramirez is eleven and lives with her mother, Nina, in a village high in the mountains in the middle of Nicaragua's Central Highlands. Like many Nicaraguan women, Nina has lived a large part of her life as a single mother. Her husband, Luis, was a migrant laborer who left home each year for several months to harvest cotton in the lowlands of the Pacific region. The long absences caused serious disruptions, and he abandoned the family when Phyllidia was five years old. Nina and Phyllidia both work part-time harvesting coffee. Although schools in the area are underfunded and inadequate, family and kinship are important, and through compadrazgo—a system of "coparenthood" that links parents, children, and godparents—Phyllidia is learning Spanish and weaving skills from her godmother, Maria.

Montreal, the largest city in the province of Quebec, differs greatly from the rest of Canada due to the prominence of its French culture and language, as well as the fact that most of its inhabitants belong to the Roman Catholic Church. Michel Lamoureux, thirteen years old, lives here with his mother Sylvie, father Jacques, brother Pierre, and sister Lise. His parents are well-to-do and are able to send their children to private Catholic schools and provide private lessons in foreign language, golf, and tennis. They set high standards for their children and, because their careers frequently keep them away from home, give Michel, the oldest child, a great deal of responsibility for the care of his younger brother and sister.

Our exploration of lives across cultures is nearly over. Before our journey comes to an end, we would like to briefly revisit our major themes, reconsider some of the theories we have discussed, and offer suggestions for modifying these to meet the needs of a rapidly changing world. A few simple revisions in specific theoretical positions might help make these theories more useful and appropriate for the study of lives across cultures. Finally, as we come to the end of our journey, we would like to gaze into our crystal ball and speculate as to where the young field of cross-cultural human development might be heading and make some recommendations for future research as we move toward the end of the first decade of the twenty-first century.

◇ LOOKING BACK: A REVIEW OF MAJOR THEMES AND THEORIES

We begin with a brief review of the major theories introduced in Module 2-A and addressed throughout subsequent modules. Our purpose in doing this is to take one last look at the ideas we have scattered throughout modules and pull them together into a final statement stressing the importance of viewing human development from a cross-cultural perspective and within a cultural context.

Taken from *Lives Across Cultures: Cross-Cultural Development*, Fifth Edition, by Harry W. Gardiner and Corinne Kosmitzki.

The module closes with a look at the future—the theories, topics, issues, and research that will determine the directions that the study of cross-cultural human development will take in the future and how this new knowledge will lead to a better understanding of the effects of culture on behavior as well as behavior on culture and how these might help improve lives across cultures.

Ecological Model

As you will recall, the ecological model of Bronfenbrenner focuses on the reciprocal relationships between and among children, their parents, and other family members and their connection with larger social and cultural traditions as well as the interaction among biological, sociocultural, and psychological factors in human development. Throughout the pages of this book, we have seen, through the use of opening vignettes, how the lives of individuals are deeply embedded in distinctly different ecocultural systems reflecting long-held and well-established patterns of thought and behavior governed by the interaction of micro-, meso-, exo-, and macrosystems.

In terms of the microsystem (the cultural setting in which adult–child interactions take place at home or at school), we can see that the young lives of Phyllidia in Nicaragua and Michel in Canada, at the opening of this module, have been influenced in a variety of ways by their cultural surroundings.

At the same time, parts of each of their microsystems have been in contact with a second, larger circle of influence, the mesosystem, consisting of a number of overlapping social settings that have also helped to shape the individual development of Phyllidia and Michel. For example, Michel's private tutorial sessions are a routine activity among the upper-middle-class families in the educational community in Montreal.

Beyond this is the exosystem, consisting of community institutions that individuals experience indirectly. In Michel's case, his private school curriculum reflects the content and skill areas believed to be important in attaining competency, even though he was not directly involved in setting the curricula.

The work of harvesting coffee is regularly performed by Nicaraguan women and girls.
(© Larry Luxner/D. Donne Bryant Stock)

Then, there is the macrosystem made up of the prominent cultural values and attitudes that influence a person's maturation. In Michel's case, religious beliefs provide the foundation for worship and daily living. In Phyllidia's single-parent household, her part-time job and close contact with extended family reflect the values of the macrosystem found in most Nicaraguan villages.

As we saw in earlier modules, sometimes several macrosystems operate within a single culture. In Malaysia and Singapore, for example, one macrosystem consists of a rapidly emerging group of young middle-class wage earners who are moving out of their parents' homes in an effort to achieve personal success and financial independence. Another represents the more traditional extended family system, in which parents and grandparents serve as principal caregivers for children, even those well into their adult years.

Since one of the major goals of cross-cultural research is to be aware of the varying influences of culture on behavior, by looking at how children interact within their culture's unique ecological system and gradually carve out a developmental niche, we hopefully have laid the foundation for a better understanding of how these forces shape and change development across the cultures we have considered, as well as those the reader may encounter in the future.

Developmental Niche

The concept of a developmental niche has contributed greatly to our understanding of the ways in which different components of a culture work together as a system and how parents and children behave within normal everyday settings.

Applying the developmental niche concept to the vignettes at the opening of this module, we can see how Nina's experience as a single mother affects her daughter Phyllidia's views of work and family relationships. Similarly, Michel's parents' expectations regarding his responsibilities toward caring for his younger brother and sister help shape Michel's values and attitudes. Each of these vignettes presents the child's unique developmental niche and how it operates within the larger ecological system (see Figure 2 in Module 2-A). Over the lifespan, Phyllidia and Michel will each continue to react and respond to thousands of cultural messages that will eventually become internalized and help them understand their world and themselves.

While relatively few cross-cultural studies have been specifically designed to compare cultures based on the developmental niche framework, a recent example is worth noting. Schwarz, Schafermeier, and Trommsdorff (2005) report results of two studies on the relationship among cultural values, parental beliefs, and parenting practices, with a focus on similarities and differences between German and South Korean mothers. Among the findings were those that showed Korean mothers to be less individualistic than German mothers, with a preference for group-oriented and achievement-oriented child-rearing goals. They were also more strict and controlling with their children. The authors emphasize that the results " . . . have shown that child-rearing goals are related to parenting behavior . . . [and] . . . this is in line with some of the assumptions of the developmental niche" (p. 224). We have seen these connections many times throughout this book.

Vygotsky's Sociocultural Theory

As we discussed in Module 2-A, Vygotsky offers a contextualist's approach to the study of cognitive development. While most mainstream Western developmental theories have traditionally viewed individuals as separate from their physical and social environments, Vygotsky believed that human development occurs over time *within* the context of culture. His influential mentor and friend, Alexandria Luria (1981), captured the essence of Vygotsky's theory best when he stated, "In order to explain the highly complex forms of human consciousness one must go beyond the human organism. One must seek the origins of conscious activity . . . in the external processes of social life, in the social and historical forms of human existence" (p. 25). Notice the contrast between the strong individualistic assumptions found in much of the psychological research conducted in Western societies and the historical and sociocultural contextualist approach employed by Vygotsky.

If we apply Vygotsky's zone of proximal development (the amount of assistance an individual needs from others in contrast to how much he can do without help) to this module's opening vignettes, we see that the guided instructions provided by Phyllidia's godmother in the teaching and learning of weaving reflects both the family's ecological surroundings, as well as her developmental niche. As Maria, the godmother, mentors Phyllidia's apprenticeship, she will move through the zone and increase her weaving skills. Her contributions to the family's collection of woven blankets and other objects strengthen her creativity, while promoting family cohesiveness, cultural identification, and interdependency.

In the case of Michel, he is being carefully trained by his golf coach to develop good putting skills. In the early stages, Michel needed lots of advice and practice drills to master the basics of good form. As Michel has improved and moved through the zone, demonstrating increased competency, his coach gradually removes the amount of assistance offered until Michel can proceed without further help. In both of these situations, it is likely that elements of the ecological context—such as climate, types of terrain, urban or rural setting, population density, health care, and other factors—will be intertwined within a variety of social contexts. In short, culture is, to a large extent, a group's response to its physical ecology, ancestral heritage, and developmental niche.

While Vgotskly's theory does have its problems (little attention to gender differences, lack of emphasis on individuals, and informal research methods), we believe it is certain to receive increased attention from cross-cultural developmental researchers in the decades ahead. This has surely been the case with the theorist we look at next—Jean Piaget.

Piaget's Cognitive Developmental Theory

Applying Piaget's theory to our opening vignettes, it is clear that eleven-year-old Phyllidia's ability to recreate her godmother's weaving skills requires that she has the ability to distinguish between types and amounts of materials used, to be able to use symbols creatively, and to infer cause-and-effect relationships—all characteristics of concrete operational thinking described in Module 2-A. On the other hand, Michel's ability to hold the golf club properly and to speculate what will happen if the ball is driven 300 yards or more requires that he be able to make use of hypotheses and form abstractions regarding golf skills. When he is able to do this, he displays some of the characteristics associated with formal operational thinking.

While each of these vignettes describes life in different cultures, the unique ecological settings, specific developmental niche, and distinctive social interactions experienced by Michel and Phyllidia strongly influence the nature and timing of the development of their cognitive abilities.

Kohlberg's Theory of Moral Development

According to Kohlberg, morality is based on a belief in general principles of justice and consists of six levels, ranging from an immature obedience and punishment orientation to an advanced application of universal ethical principles (see Module 2-A for a detailed description).

Gilligan (1982) severely criticized Kohlberg's approach and suggested that moral reasoning among women is more likely defined by a caring attitude and the maintenance of a network of relationships rather than by rules and abstract principles of justice. However, Gilligan did not take the next logical step and formulate an alternative developmental model that would integrate both orientations (caring and justice) into an understanding of moral development.

From a cross-cultural perspective, Kohlberg's model is clearly limited in its research application. Based on Gilligan's critique that the justice orientation is not the only way of viewing morality, we wonder how many other moral orientations may be present in other cultures. For example, in Japan, an individual frequently makes moral decisions based on a strict code of honor in which behavior is seen as right because it is the honorable thing to do. A common example involves the resignation of a company's president when someone in the organization behaves badly or commits an immoral act (e.g., overbilling), even though the president had no direct knowledge of, or connection to, the misbehavior. Moral reasoning such as this fits neither the justice nor the caring orientation and suggests that there are significant opportunities for more research in the area of moral development.

In this regard, a rarely cited model of moral development has been put forth by Haan, Aerts, and Cooper (1985). She and her colleagues propose that development of moral reasoning is not determined by general orientations, such as caring or justice, but is the result of understanding the interdependence of self and others that occurs in social interactions. In her model, morality is viewed as a form of social agreement that equalizes individuals' relations with each other, taking into account that when disagreements or disputes arise, all parties make their issues clearly known (Haan, 1991). Thus, moral solutions generally focus on a specific situation, involving a specific group of people, at a given time, and devote careful consideration to what each person needs and deserves, recognizing that these may vary at different times. In other words, the most mature moral reasoner attempts to make a moral decision that balances her needs, desires, strengths, and weaknesses with those of others affected by a particular moral issue. Situations involving conflicting needs frequently become severely emotional, because the fundamental form of moral action is dialogue or talk, which often provokes high levels of stress, which, in turn, also play a major role in moral decision making. In her research focusing on stressful moral situations, Haan found that individuals who were able to control their emotions, objectively consider a variety of possible solutions, be empathetic, and demonstrate the ability to "cope rather than defend" showed higher levels of moral action. In this view, moral reasoning would take on different forms in different cultures, simply because of wide variations in what is considered a need, desire, strength, or weakness and, unlike many other models of moral development, emphasizes the interactional nature of morality.

The potential usefulness of Haan's model (1991) for the study of moral development across cultures, as well as its relevance to the major themes expressed throughout this book, permit us to study moral reasoning within the context of culture-specific interactions and culture-specific moral issues, resulting in an emic approach to moral development. For example, in a highly individualistic culture such as the United States, most individuals accept as fair the notion that those of greater ability receive higher pay. However, in a collective setting, like the one found in a kibbutz, it may be equally fair that individuals get paid according to their needs, not what they actually earn by their own work. While both concepts of what is fair or right are valid in each culture, they can only be reasonably evaluated within the appropriate context.

Applying these concepts of moral development to our opening vignettes suggests that Michel's view of what is right or wrong is strongly influenced by the religious values taught as part of his Roman Catholic faith, a centerpiece of the Quebec culture in which he lives. Although the majority of Nicaraguans during the early 1990s were nominally Roman Catholic, the church influenced most Nicaraguans only sporadically at best. Like most living in rural villages far from an organized church, Phyllidia has likely been taught the basics of moral behavior as defined by her parents and community—for example, being nice to others, saying only good things, not stealing, and "having a strong belief in divine power over human affairs . . . reflected in the use of phrases such as 'God willing' or 'if it is God's desire.'

Erikson's Theory of Psychosocial Development

We can think of Erikson's theory as analogous to a book with eight modules. Like chapters in a "Book of Life," his developmental stages follow one another. Sometimes an issue introduced in one chapter is carried over into the next and may not be fully resolved until much later in the book. In order to understand the story completely and make sense of the plot, the reader must read the eight chapters in chronological order. As infants and children pass through the first four stages of Erikson's theory, they are confronted by a series of psychosocial crises (turning points with two possible resolutions, one positive and one negative) requiring successful resolution if healthy development is to take place at a later stage. These crises center on trust versus mistrust, autonomy versus shame and doubt, initiative versus guilt, and industry versus inferiority. The adolescent and young adult encounters the issue of identity versus role confusion, or identity diffusion. The mature adult first faces the challenge of intimacy versus isolation, followed by generativity versus stagnation or self-absorption. Finally, the older adult needs to resolve issues related to integrity versus despair. Erikson views these crises as a natural development common to everyone, regardless of their culture, through which we come to understand ourselves and our relationships with others. However, as with other stage theories, Erikson's approach is subject to the criticism that stages may vary from one culture to another in the time of occurrence, duration, and content.

Considering what we know about the subjects in our opening vignettes, we might hypothesize that Phyllidia and Michel have both been raised in warm and caring family environments, in which they developed the trust that allowed them to explore their surroundings and establish positive social relationships with family members. With supportive parents, they gradually developed control over their behavior, realizing that their intentions could be acted out through imitation of those around them. Michel, guided by his teachers in school, influenced by his golfing instructor in private lessons, and encouraged by his parents to take responsibility for his younger siblings, has developed a strong sense of industry and is on the verge of establishing a strong personal identity. Phyllidia, working part-time alongside her mother, harvesting coffee as well as learning her culture's weaving skills from her godmother, feels an equally strong sense of industry and, in the life of her village, is on the verge of womanhood and preparing to assume an adult identity.

While Erikson's theory works well as a general framework within which some specific lifespan changes can be described and interpreted, it is less useful as a model for cross-cultural experimentation. This is not to say, that with some modification and attention to cultural considerations, his ideas could not be usefully applied to human development within the cultural context. In fact, efforts directed at such endeavors might prove quite interesting as we have shown at various places throughout this book. On the other hand, an approach that may be more useful in accounting for the cultural context of lifespan development has been offered by Cantor and her associates (Cantor, Norem, Niedenthal, Langston, & Brower, 1987; Cantor et al., 1991).

Using the concept of "life-tasks" (the underlying goals that guide an individual's life or everyday behavior at a given time), Cantor and others (1987) studied a group of undergraduate students in the United States by having them keep records detailing their daily activities. While recording their activities, they also answered questions about the people they were with and their feelings about the activities. Findings revealed that students shared several "life-tasks," the two most important being "making friends" and "getting good grades." One advantage of using an approach like Cantor's in cross-cultural research is that it relies on self-generated "themes" based on people's culture-specific experience. This makes for a more emic approach than imposing a set of preformulated "themes" on individuals, as is the case with universalist theories such as Erikson's.

We are encouraged by the development of approaches like this and encourage others to consider using them in formulating their cross-cultural human development research efforts.

✛ WHERE DO WE GO FROM HERE?

No one can know for certain what the field of cross-cultural human development will look in the years ahead. Traditionally, the literature in mainstream developmental psychology has emphasized a Western European and North American orientation. For too long there has been what we might call a "psychological research ethnocentrism," that is, the assumption that research findings reported from studies conducted in one culture applied equally well to other cultures. The reader now knows that this is not always true. Yet, Harkness and Keefer (2000) caution that "in our search for cross-cultural validity in comparative research, we must make sure to avoid a new kind of ethnocentrism based on non-Western constructs or measures. Such an approach would be as unrealistic as the former mistake of imposing Western measures on other contexts . . . [and we must avoid the] . . . problem of oversimplification of cultural variability—complete relativism, in which cross-cultural comparisons become impossible" (p. 105).

Although Harkness and Keefer's point is well-taken, we do believe it is important to continue to conduct additional indigenous developmental studies. Recent research has demonstrated that concepts first identified indigenously (in one culture, often non-Western) frequently have a significant degree of validity when operationally defined and incorporated into multicultural studies and frequently broaden our understanding of important issues. For example, Yamuguchi's (2004) study of *amae* has shown that this concept is related to constructs (e.g., attachment) in the United States (and other cultures). Japanese researchers, as well as others, admit that the term **amae,** a Japanese word, is difficult to define. It is generally used to describe *behavior aimed at inducing another person, such as a parent, spouse, teacher, boss or other individual, to take care of oneself.* Takeo Doi (1973), the first to discuss the concept, defined it as *indulgent dependency.* In other words, the person who is carrying out *amae* may selfishly beg, plead, or act childishly, knowing that the caregiver will forgive and indulge the person. While once thought to be unique to Japan, similar behavior has been observed throughout Asia and may have its equivalent in some Western or African countries as well (Smith & Nomi, 2000). Here is an emic or culture-specific concept that, with further research, may be shown to be an etic or universal or culture-general concept. For these reasons, we welcome additional research conducted on this interesting cultural concept like the recent work of Niiya, Ellsworth, and Yamaguchi (2006) and Jordan (2005).

Other research worthy of recognition and further investigation includes the work of Cheung and Leung (1998) on indigenous measures of Chinese personality dimensions, and Kwan, Bond, and Singelis (1997) on measurement of relationship harmony. In addition, measures of **budi values** (*generosity, respect, sincerity, and righteousness*) in Malaysia have been shown to account for variances explained by Schwartz's value survey items (an approach receiving increasing attention among cross-cultural developmentalists). Finally, Boski (2005) has identified **humanism** (defined as *a concern for personal relationships combined with endorsement of personal responsibility and a rejection of materialism*) and **sarmatism** (*a mix of impulsive self-assertion and social hedonism*, deriving from values once espoused by the Polish nobility) as key Polish values.

Although we have seen a steady increase in developmental studies in recent years, much of this research still focuses on childhood and adolescence within a Western context. By comparison, relatively few studies have addressed cultural variations in adulthood and old age, and even fewer have examined the end of the lifespan in non-Western societies. With individuals living to increasingly older ages and with the percentage of elderly growing in most cultures, we would certainly benefit from more research on these life stages.

A welcome addition to the applied developmental literature is a recent volume that focuses on the contemporary culture of Japan, but demonstrates the universality of the research problems discussed (Shwalb, Nakazawa, & Shwalb, 2005). Included among the topics are the effects of video games, *manga*, comics, and television on children's development, literacy acquisition (Japan's rate is nearly 100 percent), innovative techniques for dealing with children's disabilities, and concern with bullying. One of the strengths of this book is the easy access for international researchers and readers to important findings by contemporary Japanese developmentalists. Another strength is the authors' choice of key issues and an emphasis on how culture guides research and theory and ways in which findings have been shown to have universal applications beyond the culture in which they were found if only we had more books like this one. We are hopeful that the authors' strong emphasis on originality of topics and research approaches, along with attempts at universal applications, will serve as a model for activities in other cultural contexts.

In the next several years, we predict, based on much of what has been discussed in the current book, an increasing interest in viewing human development within an ecological and cross-cultural developmental perspective. Several efforts are at the forefront of this movement. One example is an extensive study by Mishra, Sinha, and Berry (1996), examining the psychological adaptation of tribal groups in India. Three groups (the Asur, Oraon, and Birhar), differing in settlement and occupation patterns, were compared in terms of cultural lifestyles, patterns of child socialization, cognitive behavior, and acculturation attitudes and experiences. These authors also focus on the application of their findings, this time to problems of acculturative stress. In the decades ahead, we predict there will be more studies that focus on the practical application of findings to real-world problems such as immigration and psychological, social, and emotional adjustments to new cultures. We only wish there were more such examples at the present time.

In a review of cultural influences on child development, Super and Harkness (1997) have presented theoretical principles and research evidence in support of three specific approaches that, while varying in focus, emphasize "the structured, dynamic and integrative nature of the environment." These approaches include their developmental niche concept, which we have referred to extensively throughout this book, Worthman's proposed theory of developmental microniche (1994, 1995), and Weisner's work on the ecocultural niche (Weisner, 2002), all of which show promising potential.

In a review of cross-cultural human development research, Gardiner (2004) raised several critical and challenging questions that need to be answered in the near future: What types of cross-cultural developmental studies will be conducted in the future? How similar or different should these be to current research? In what ways will these studies contribute to our understanding of human development and the ever-changing and increasingly complex world in which people live? What implications will future research findings have for the construction of new developmental theories, and how will these new theories affect the design of even newer studies?

We are, in fact, beginning to see some possible answers to a few of these questions (Smith, 2004). Before we bring our discussions to a close, let us look at some of the topics to which we have given a great deal of attention, consider the implications of recent research and some of the proposals for future research, and comment on the benefits of understanding cross-cultural development and how this might help readers apply the ideas and findings to their own everyday lives. We shall do this, more or less, in the order in which topics were originally introduced, beginning with theories and methodology.

In Module 2-A, we pointed out that a single macrotheory (one designed to describe, explain, understand, and predict all aspects of an individual's development) is unlikely ever to appear, although some theories will explain more behavior than will others. Instead, recent trends toward the development of "minitheories" (efforts focused on limited and specific facets of development and behavior) are likely to continue in the future. In a summary of recent trends in human development theorizing, Thomas (2001) asserts that a conflict exists between traditional and more recent interpretations of development, and this is expected to continue "with traditional belief systems probably losing adherents as a result of the spread of literacy and the inevitable increase in international communication and intercultural exchange during the coming years" (p. 278).

Also in Module 2-A, we identified some of the problems in conducting cross-cultural research. A researcher who has dealt extensively with these issues, Fons van de Vijver, looks at the future in this way: "The major methodological task ahead of us is the change from an 'adjustment perspective,' by which we adopted and adjusted prevailing methodologies, to a truly cultural perspective that transcends the borders of a specific cultural context" (2001, p. 91). He proposes that future efforts will be directed at developing methodologies "tailor-made" for cross-cultural research and, in order to accomplish this, he suggests that the field draw on experiences from the various branches of psychology (e.g., developmental, experimental, social, abnormal). We would also encourage, as we have many times before, closer interdisciplinary cooperation and sharing of ideas with our colleagues in sociology and anthropology who, in many cases, are confronting similar problems and concerns.

Before these long-term goals of cross-cultural research can be accomplished, van de Vijver cites the need for two antecedent developments: (1) innovations in statistical approaches; for example, development of multilevel models allowing for the simultaneous study of individual and cultural differences to determine if a concept such as individualism is the same at the individual and cultural levels and (2) wider distribution and acceptance of guidelines for the appropriate design and carrying out of cross-cultural research; for example, awareness of bias in selection of subjects and populations, equivalence in meaning of concepts, instruments, methodology, interpretation of scores. See our earlier discussion in Module 2-A regarding some of these guidelines.

Finally, there are significant problems in interpreting findings across studies that lack consistency in definitions, approaches, and methodology. We are in need of studies that use culturally sensitive theoretical approaches that look at issues of education, immigration, and acculturation. Such studies will assist in understanding the relationships between ethnicity and culture as they affect mate selection, relationships among siblings, and the roles of grandparents.

In Module 3-A, we focused on what we believe to be one of the most important concepts in human development, namely socialization. In a review of parental socialization and children's values, Grusec (2002) points out that researchers have significantly altered their theoretical approaches to the study of socialization and introduced more refined and sophisticated methods for measuring its dimensions and outcomes. She states that, "At the moment, developmentalists are only beginning to understand how biology, context, and environment interact, and the amount of variance explained in studies is generally not large" (p. 162). However, she asserts that future studies that employ longitudinal designs, larger sample sizes, variables in interaction, "will help to untangle the specific contributions of parent and child to the socialization process . . . [and will] . . . allow the use of causal modeling techniques . . . to suggest the relative contributions of parent and child at given points in time to various outcomes having to do with socialization" (p. 162). Many of these ideas and suggestions for future research are discussed in *Handbook of Socialization* by Grusec and Hastings (2008). Also contributing to a better understanding of parenting and socialization, will be findings emerging from the field of molecular genetics and the associations beginning to be made between genes and behavioral traits and characteristics (Plomin & Rutter, 1998).

We looked at families in cultural context and learned that it is a complex topic, including mate selection, marriage and other long-term relationships, birth, transition to parenthood, parental belief systems, grandparenthood, and the need to care for elderly parents. While a great deal of progress has been made in describing diverse family systems and the variety of cultural contexts in which they develop and thrive much remains to be done. For example, we need to broaden our examination of different forms of families (e.g., extended or multigenerational, single-parent, stepfamilies, and families headed by gay and lesbian parents). Cross-culturally, we need to encourage indigenous researchers to take an emic (culture-specific) approach to the study of families, parenting, and development to refine and extend our understanding of family dynamics and processes in diverse ecological settings, setting the stage for more etic (universal or cultural general) studies and comparisons.

In their book, *Handbook of Parenting*, Hoghughi and Long (2004) assess the current status of parenting around the world and discuss possible trends affecting parents and children in the twenty-first century. These include onset of earlier sexual activity in children and parents' role in sex education, increasing influence of entertainment media and new technologies on children, the increasing exposure of children to dysfunctional parenting models in the media, the trend for children in their early twenties to continue living (or returning to live) with parents and the effects on all involved, advances in genetic engineering and the ability to create "designer babies," increased family mobility and erosion of neighborhood ties, and increase in frequency and severity of children's emotional and behavioral problems throughout the world. Each of these topics is worthy of further cross-cultural investigation.

Advances in reproductive technology (e.g., *in vitro* fertilization—IVF—or "test-tube" babies, donor insemination or egg donation, surrogate parenting) have dramatically changed the way in which some families are formed and the manner in which some individuals become parents. Much of this technology is still new enough that we are uncertain how it affects parents and the psychological, social, and emotional development of their children. Golombok (2002) sums it up this way: "Although existing knowledge about the impact of the contemporary reproductive technologies does not give undue cause for concern, there remain many unanswered questions about the consequences for parenting of creating families in this way" (p. 355).

As we pointed out earlier, the transition to parenthood represents a major change in most people's lives. To understand how this transition takes place, the manner in which parent–child relationships are formed, and the effects on children's development, Cowan, Powell, and Cowan (1998) have proposed that future research employ a family systems model of parenting that collects information on six critical aspects of family functioning, including the quality of relationships: (1) among parents, grandparents, and grandchildren; (2) between siblings; (3) between each parent and child; (4) between nuclear family members and individuals or institutions outside the family (e.g., friends, peers, school, child care, government); (5) between parents and their roles and communication patterns within the family; and (6) the biological and psychological characteristics of each family member.

What parents know and believe about parenting is, in large part, a result of the way their parents raised them. While the scientific study of parental beliefs is about fifty years old and has been characterized by a variety of perspectives, Sigel and McGillicuddy-De Lisi (2002) suggest a new approach to the topic that views cognition as the core component, especially the effects on children's cognitive and social development and academic achievement. At the same time, they admit that their approach is controversial with the strongest arguments against it being made by Wachs (2000a). However, they believe their dynamic belief systems model deserves further attention and provides evidence from cross-cultural studies of parental beliefs within specific cultures, across cultures, and between groups from different cultural backgrounds within a society to bolster their view of cultural perspectives.

We can think of many questions related to families and parents that might lead to interesting and beneficial research projects. For example, what do we know about the ecological contexts of new family structures such as gay and lesbian couples with children, transnational families living in one culture that communicates through e-mail, travel, and other means with members of their families living abroad? How do families like these deal with issues of identity—how do they define "family" and which values and customs do they decide to maintain, adapt, reject? How will the expanding global society of cultures influence future family research? Why are some people considered "good" parents and others "poor" parents? What does this mean? What role does age and gender play in parenting? What cultural factors determine the amount and quality of father involvement with their children in different cultures? How can we design more cross-cultural human development research that is experimental rather than correlational? Can we design more longitudinal studies of parenting that incorporate contextual factors that help to sort out the bidirectional and interactive variables involved in parent-child interactions? How does immigration influence parenting styles and practices?

We devoted attention to grandparenthood and the roles played by grandparents in several cultures, including those of Japan, China, and the United States. While information on this topic has grown rapidly over the past twenty years, there are limitations, including limited methodology (interviews or structured questionnaires), narrow range of cultures (primarily in the United States), and a lack of theoretical structuring. To improve and extend our knowledge of grandparenting, we need to use a wider range of methods (e.g., naturalistic home observations of grandparent–grandchild interactions, children's drawings of grandparents, and essays written about them), employing more cultures (e.g., those in Asia, Africa, and Latin America), and greater use of theoretical frameworks, like those mentioned previously, to interpret new and previously collected data.

In addition to these topics, even less is known about step-grandparenthood, the role of grandparents in lesbian and gay families, and the extended intergenerational role of great-grandparenthood. There are numerous opportunities to explore these topics in a wide variety of cultural and cross-cultural contexts.

We learned that individuals throughout the world tend to use the same or similar cognitive processes, but that cultural differences distinguish the way they are employed in specific cultural contexts. Our understanding of the relationship between culture and cognition requires a careful synthesis of what is currently known about these topics. Norbert Ross (2003), who knows both cognitive anthropology and cognitive psychology well, has provided such a synthesis in his book—*Culture and Cognition: Implications for Theory and Method*—and suggests a number of useful directions for future investigation that are not only interesting but could be quite productive.

Williams and Sternberg (2001), building on the ideas of Vygotsky and Rogoff, have set forth ten lessons parents can use to maximize children's cognitive abilities (e.g., recognizing what can and cannot be changed, aiming to *meaningfully challenge* them, and teaching them to take responsibility both for their successes and their failures).

Regarding the topic of children's temperament discussed in Module 8-A, individual differences can be observed in the earliest hours following birth, become more apparent during infancy, and remain an important although often modifiable influence (depending on age, gender, social and cultural factors, and parental characteristics) on later developments in behavioral, social, and cognitive areas.

As to future research, Rothbart and Bates (1998) point out that even the best contemporary measures of temperament are inadequate, and future research should be directed at the development of measures with better construct validity—the extent to which a test measures the construct it is designed to measure (e.g., temperamental characteristics of Indonesian infants). See also the work of Rothbart and Hwang (2005). Efforts should also be made to examine parental expectations before the birth of a child to determine how these may influence socialization strategies employed with a child's actual behavior after birth. For example, imagine you are expecting a child. You or your mate may be "hoping for" a boy or a girl. When the baby arrives, whether it is or isn't the gender you expected, you may already have preconceived ideas about how the child will behave and how you will react to those behaviors, which may or may not be appropriate. Knowing more about temperament, the characteristic styles of children and typical parental patterns of responding, will help you to be a more effective parent as you provide socialization experiences appropriate to the culture and world in which your newborn child will live. Recall the interesting ideas of Kara Smith on prenatal socialization and prebirth gender talk (2005) discussed in Module 3-A.

Carefully designed longitudinal studies, beginning at infancy, may help to explain observed gender and cultural differences in temperament. In addition, a number of researchers have drawn attention to the importance of replicating previous parent-temperament interaction findings to be certain they are accurate—an argument we have made several times with regard to other types of research findings as well.

Putnam, Sanson, and Rothbart (2002) recommend that future research on temperament can be greatly improved by moving away from global measures (e.g., "difficult," "easy," and "slow-to-warm-up"), which can vary significantly from one study to another, to more specific measures (e.g., irritability, fear, self-regulation, and shyness). This suggests another promising area—the testing of hypotheses that focus on specific combinations of parenting characteristics and temperament traits (e.g., how fear might lead to a lessening of aggressive responses). These authors also note that almost all temperament research has focused on mothers and, with changes in parental roles, more attention should be given to the caregiving role of fathers and others (e.g., grandparents, extended family members).

Finally, and perhaps of greatest importance to those interested in human development within cultural contexts, is the issue of the generalizability of findings. Almost all of the research on temperament, with the exception of a few anthropological studies (e.g., Margaret Mead's work in New

Guinea), has been conducted in individualistic Western cultures. As Kitayama and Markus (1994) have suggested, individuals raised in collectivist cultures (e.g., those in Asia, Africa, and among Indian tribes in the United States and Canada) are more frequently identified by their relationship to various groups, and, as a result, variations in temperament may, therefore, be less noticeable and relevant. We suggest that indigenous researchers should carefully examine the relationship between temperament and parenting within their cultures to expand our understanding of this crucial topic and provide parents with relevant information as they attempt to deal with their children's developing personalities. Putnam, Sanson, and Rothbart have expressed it well: "The task then for the parent and the practitioner is to foster 'respect for the individuality and integrity of each child, and flexibility in creating environments that may lead to positive outcomes for them and for us'" (2002, p. 272).

We discussed some aspects of culture and social behavior. What kinds of developments might we expect in the future, particularly from a cross-cultural perspective? Smith, Bond, and Kagitcibasi (2006) have suggested several possible areas of interest, including (1) expansion of our cultural theory base (e.g., consideration of cultural factors contributing to aggression and conflict resolution, as well as movement from Western, individualized theories of development to non-Western, collectivized theories of relatedness and interdependence), (2) universalization of social science measures (e.g., movement away from predominantly American instruments written in English to development of "cultural scripts" consisting of simple sentences that capture cultural norms from the point of view of "natives" and expresses these norms in terms of universal human concepts), and (3) diversification of input (e.g., greater interdisciplinary and cultural cooperation among social scientists in both the development of research projects and authorship of published writings). The authors speculate that attention to a number of dimensions of cultural variation is beginning to emerge. These include increasing contributions by Asian researchers from collectivist cultures interested in comparative studies, examination of relationships between cultural masculinity/femininity and measures of sexual norms and behaviors, as well as gender-related beliefs represented by the work of Hofstede (1996, 2001, 2004), and studies of values at the individual and cultural level (Knafo & Schwartz, 2003; Schwartz, 1995). In an expansion of his pioneering research on cultural values, Hofstede (2004) maintains that individuals carry around "mental programs," developed within the family during the years of early childhood, containing elements of national culture, reinforced in organizations and schools. The clearest expression of these "programs" can be found in the cluster of values that characterize and distinguish one cultural group from another. According to Smith and Bond (1999), these changes had to "await the diffusion of 'Western' psychology to different cultural milieux and the nurturing of local psychologists who are capable of challenging the biases of the discipline in its own terminology, using its established procedures" (p. 322). Now that cross-cultural social psychology has reached this stage, the authors believe there will be "an intellectual synergy that will enable us to transcend the limitations imposed by our different cultural origins. We may then be able to claim that we have a more truly universal understanding of humanity's social behaviour" (p. 323).

In the view of Waters and Cummings (2000), "Cross-cultural research on key issues in attachment theory is one of the most exciting prospects for the next generation of attachment research" (p. 169). Rothbaum and Morelli (2005) express a similar view by pointing out the necessity of understanding how "biological dispositions to develop attachments and real environments in which these attachments occur are co-mingled" (p. 119). They suggest a multimethod approach to look at cultural variations that will lead to better understanding of child security and caregiver behavior. For more information on recent attachment measures and a discussion of issues and difficulties in assessing the topic of attachment, visit this Web site: *http://www.psychology.sunysb.edu/ attachment/measures/measures_index.html*. For a comprehensive review of theory, research and clinical applications, see the second edition of the *Handbook of Attachment* by Cassidy and Shaver (2008).

Issues of gender and sexuality have been of increasing interest in cross-cultural psychology and anthropology. Best and Williams (2001) have provided one of the most comprehensive reviews of research on culture and gender. Based on their knowledge of these issues, Best and Williams pose a number of questions and challenges for the future of cross-cultural gender research. First, they express surprise that more of the cross-cultural research on gender is not "theory-driven," that is, based on hypotheses derived from current theories (e.g., social learning, cognitive developmental, and gender schema). They suggest conducting longitudinal studies in societies experiencing rapid changes in socioeconomic development to determine if gender concepts change in theoretically predicted directions. Second, Best and Williams note that the relationship between cultural practices (e.g., initiation rites or rites of passage), frequently studied by anthropologists, and individual development (more often the focus of psychologists), needs greater research attention. The authors argue, as we have before, that psychologists and anthropologists, with shared interests in understanding how culture affects human behavior, should work more closely together and, thereby, learn from each other. They express this well when they suggest that, "Perhaps the growing field of cultural psychology, together with cross-cultural psychology, will provide a bridge between disciplines, recognizing that culture serves as both an independent and an organizing variable" (p. 212).

We noted that when it comes to health and related issues, we often do not consider the many ways these might be affected by culture. In their *Handbook of Cultural Health Psychology*, two Canadian researchers, Kazarian and Evans (2001), have set forth a conceptual framework that considers the interface between health behavior and cultural psychology, a necessary step for the advancement of a more culturally competent and ethnically sound approach to health. Some of the topics discussed by contributors to this handbook are (1) approaches to multiculturalism, the relationship between culture and health, and the need to understand variations in health concepts and practices in multicultural societies, including the physical, popular, and folk sectors; (2) provider–patient relationships and the success or failure of treatments that are frequently embedded in cultural differences in individualism and collectivism and the illness models and cultural expectations for health care that result from these differences; (3) the need to more fully integrate the role of culture into the critical topics of health promotion and disease prevention, areas from which it has been conspicuously absent; (4) health concerns of Latinos (e.g., heart disease, HIV/AIDS, cancer, and diabetes); (5) clinical issues encountered by professionals working with native peoples, specific health-related issues they face, and a proposal for a "culturally congruent model" that integrates the values and beliefs of the target groups (e.g., present-time orientation, harmony with nature, sharing, respect for elders, and nonmaterialism); and (6) discussion of the principles of Confucianism and Taoism as they apply to beliefs about health and illness and some of the ways in which the cultural context shapes both collective and individual health behaviors in traditional and contemporary Chinese societies.

This collection provides a state-of-the-art understanding of what is known and not known about the rapidly emerging field of cultural health psychology, along with valuable detailed suggestions for designing much needed multicultural studies to expand the field and lead to important findings related to each of the health issues discussed.

In another timely effort, Tinsley et al. (2002) reviewed and attempted to integrate research findings concerned with specific ways parents try to promote children's health in a variety of cultural settings. They examine traditional approaches to child health care and more contemporary developmental models. They also discuss parents' socialization of children's sick role behavior as well as their wellness behavior. The authors conclude that health research is limited (e.g., focusing on mother's role in health promotion). They would like to see more attention given to the role of fathers, and the influence of entire families as they function in a cultural and ecological context.

In another effort to understand and explain the relationship between culture and health, Maclachlan (2006) introduces new techniques for assessment and treatment of disorders found in a variety of cultures. Making use of psychological, anthropological, sociological, and medical research, the author provides case studies and guidelines for good practice that show promise for future research.

An area of the world that has not received as much cross-cultural attention as it deserves, particularly in light of recent global events, is the Middle East/North Africa, sometimes referred to as MENA. In fact, until recently we have known relatively little about the people living in this important region of the world. A major contribution to our understanding of the societies and cultures that exist here, along with insights into their struggles with traditions and modernity, self and identity, stereotypes and misunderstandings and the universality as well as unique behaviors that characterize their citizens, are discussed in a book by Gary Gregg, *The Middle East: A Cultural Psychology* (2005). Most importantly, he provides a "social ecology" of psychological development and explores development across the same life stages as we have from infancy to adulthood. His contributions are theoretical, empirical, pragmatic, and add significantly to our cross-cultural understanding of societies we do not know very well but certainly should. In addition, the majority of the reported research has been conducted by Arab-Muslim scholars and has previously been unavailable to Westerners and others.

As stated in the Foreword to this book, "The theoretical perspectives on culture, personality, self, identity, and development; empirical contributions of the study of lives approach; and the carefully crafted writing make this volume one that is sure to make a strong and lasting contribution to the scholarly literature on culture, psychology, and the Middle East/North Africa" (p. vii).

Gregg closes with thoughtful suggestions for further research based on the writings of indigenous scholars with a focus on emic-etic influences on development. Among the priorities that researchers might consider are care practices among the growing urban poor, mastering of the "honor-modesty" system, the nature and consequences of patriarchal or authoritarian parenting styles, adolescent dealings with the contradictory world views associated with tradition and modern institutions, as well as their effect on identity formation. The book contains a wealth of ideas that can be applied not only to the study of MENA cultures but to other cultures as well.

In bringing the fourth edition of *Lives Across Cultures* to a close, we said that "Cross-cultural study of development frequently resembles a confused mosaic of often contradictory findings. Yet therein lies the promise and excitement of future endeavors. . . . Much more needs to be done, and as the cross-cultural perspective reveals, discovery of similarities and dissimilarities in human behavior will make our understanding both easier and more difficult" (2008, p. 310). This was true then, and it is even truer now.

Ahead of us lie tremendous challenges and opportunities. Speculating about where our cross-cultural journey will take us next is difficult. Wherever we go, it is certain to be an interesting and exciting adventure. Perhaps some of you will be the pioneer theorists and researchers who take us to the next point on this journey. We eagerly look forward to that day.

◇ SUMMARY

In this final module, we look back at the major theories introduced at the beginning of our journey into human development and comment on their usefulness for explaining cultural similarities and differences in behavior across the lifespan. These include the ecological systems approach and developmental niche as well as the work of Piaget, Vygotsky, Erikson, and Kohlberg. We conclude with our view of some of the current challenges we face and promising directions the field of cross-cultural human development will (or should) take as it attempts to expand our knowledge and understanding of a most fascinating topic—ourselves.

◇ STUDY QUESTIONS

Comment critically on the theories of Kohlberg and Erikson, and explain how these theories might be made more useful to cross-cultural researchers.

Explain why there is a need for conducting more comparative cross-cultural studies of human development.

Describe some of the examples of the type of research the authors outlined in "Thoughts and Challenges for the Future."

◇ FURTHER READINGS

Roy D'Andrade. (2000). The sad story of anthropology 1950–1999. *Cross-Cultural Research, 34,* 219–232.
> The author discusses how changing political attitudes over the past fifty years have affected the field of anthropology and its effectiveness as a discipline and what directions it might take in the future.

Wolfgang Friedlmeier, Pardeep Chakkarath, & Beate Schwarz. (2005). *Culture and Human Development.* New York: Psychology Press.
> This book provides an interdisciplinary approach to key developmental processes, with particular focus on theoretical and methodological issues in cross-cultural research. An invaluable source of information and very readable.

Gary S. Gregg. (2005). *The Middle East: A Cultural Psychology.* New York: Oxford University Press.
> A book that provides a long-overdue synthesis of psychological research on Middle Eastern and North African societies. Readers will become familiar with the lives of individuals in this critical region of the world who are attempting to resolve differences between adherence of traditional values and the attraction of Westernized lifestyles.

Heidi Keller & Patricia M. Greenfield. (2000). History and future of development in cross-cultural psychology. *Journal of Cross-Cultural Psychology, 31,* 52–62.

    It provides a view of the future of cross-cultural human development and how developmental issues and methods can be used to advance theory and research.

David Shwalb, Jun Nakazawa, & Barbara J. Shwalb (Eds.). (2005). *Applied Developmental Psychology: Theory, Practice, and Research from Japan.* Greenwich, CT: Information Age Publishing.

    This book consists of sixteen chapters in which the editors and authors provide valuable insights into theories, approaches, and applications of findings in a non-Western culture, which have important implications for other cultures. Not only are the presentations original, but easy to read and understand.

Name: _____ Date: _____

MODULE 12-B

 ACTIVITY

◇ **ACCULTURATION STRATEGIES**

Much cross-cultural research has focused on acculturation. That is, the process by which people adjust to contact with a culture other than their own. John Berry (1994; 2001) has developed a model for understanding the strategies that people use in acculturation. This activity involves applying Berry's model to your own acculturation experience in order to better understand this process.

Directions: Think about an experience you have had acculturating, or adjusting, to another culture. You may have traveled outside of your country or to an unfamiliar region of your own country. Perhaps you have spent time with an ethnic group or social class different from your own. For people entering an unfamiliar academic culture, adjusting to college may even involve acculturation. In the space provided below, describe your acculturation experience. Then answer the questions based on Berry's model in order to analyze your own acculturation experience.

Description of your acculturation experience:

Taken from *Cross-Cultural Explorations: Activities in Culture and Psychology*, Second Edition, by Susan Goldstein.

John Berry's (1994; 2001) model includes four types of acculturation strategies: Integration, Assimilation, Separation, and Marginalization. Read the descriptions of these strategies below and think about which best describes your own acculturation strategy.

- *Integration* – The individual maintains his or her own cultural identity while at the same time becomes a participant in the host culture.
- *Assimilation* – The individual gives up his or her own cultural identity and becomes absorbed into the host culture.
- *Separation* – The individual maintains his or her own cultural identity and rejects involvement with the host culture.
- *Marginalization* – The individual does not identify with or participate in either his or her own culture or the host culture.

1. Which of the four modes above best characterizes your acculturation strategy? Please explain.

Berry's (2001) model also includes four types of acculturation strategies adopted by the host culture: Multiculturalism, Melting Pot, Segregation, and Exclusion. Read the descriptions of these strategies below and think about which best describes the orientation of the society or group into which you acculturated.

- *Multiculturalism* – The society values and fosters diversity.
- *Melting Pot* – The society seeks assimilation.
- *Segregation* – The society forces separation.
- *Exclusion* – The society imposes marginalization.

2. Which of the four modes above best characterizes the acculturation orientation adopted by the host culture in your experience? Please explain.

3. Given the acculturation orientation of the host culture, do you believe that the acculturation strategy you adopted was effective? Please explain.

4. One criticism of Berry's model is that it treats acculturation as if it is static. A different model of acculturation, created by Teresa LaFramboise and colleagues (1993), addresses this concern. Their model, developed to address the acculturation experiences of ethnic minority groups within a dominant culture, includes the strategy of *Alternation*. Alternation refers to a strategy in which one moves back and forth between one's own culture and the host culture depending on the situation. Did you use alternation as a strategy in your acculturation experience? Please explain.

5. How would you apply the different acculturation strategies to attitudes about bilingualism and language use? Please consider both the perspective of the individual and the society at large.

◇ REFERENCES

Berry, J. W. (1994). Acculturative stress. In W. J. Lonner & R. S. Malpass (Eds.), *Psychology and culture* (pp. 211–215). Boston: Allyn & Bacon.

Berry, J. W. (2001). A psychology of immigration. *Journal of Social Issues, 57*, 615–631.

LaFramboise, T. D., Coleman, H. L. K., & Gerton, J. (1993). Psychological impact of biculturalism: Evidence and theory. *Psychological Bulletin, 114*, 395–412.

NAME INDEX

Aber, J. L., 116, 118, 120
Abu-Lughod, L., 15
Ackerman, D., 299
Adams, C., 234
Adamson, D., 108
Addington-Hall, J., 418
Aerts, E., 452
Agrawal, A., 305
Aguiar, A., 232
Ahadi, S. A., 279
Ahnert, L., 120
Ainsworth, M. D. S., 363
Ajrouch, K., 423
Akande, 275
Alberman, E., 103
Alberts, A., 427
Aldridge, M. A., 354
Alexander, G. M., 311, 312, 314, 315, 355
Alfonso, V. C., 254
Allen, M., 77
Allik, J., 279
Alm, R., 309
Alsop, D., 256
Alter, J., 115
Alvarez, M., 363
Ambady, N., 213
American Academy of Pediatrics (AAP), 345, 357, 390
American Cancer Society, 402
American College Health Association, 387, 393
Anastasi, 252
Anders, T. F., 351
Anderson, B., 11
Anderson, P. J., 99
Andreano, J. M., 307
Andrews, G., 233
Angel, J. L., 423
Anwo, J., 80
Apgar, V., 346
Arcus, D., 107
Arditi-Babchuk, H., 351
Arnett, J. J., 329, 417, 427
Arnold, R., 117, 118
Arterberry, M. E., 355
Asendorpf, J., 280

Ashmead, D. H., 354
Aslin, R. N., 354
Atkins, R., 116
Atkinson, J., 276, 354
Atkinson, P., 58
Auyeung, B., 310
Avsec, A., 286
Azuma, H., 29

Baiewu, O., 281
Bailey, J. M., 298, 302, 308
Baillargeon, R., 232
Baker, S., 387
Balakrishnan, V., 237
Baldwin, J. R., 39
Balodis, I. M., 339
Baltes, P. B., 125
Bandura, A., 275, 276
Bane, C. M. H., 312
Barkley, R. A., 253
Barnes, G. M., 118
Barnett, S., 309
Barr, R. G., 77, 361, 362, 363
Barron, F., 256
Barry, H., 80
Bartoshuk, L. M., 353
Basseches, M., 235
Basso, K., 14
Bates, B., 338, 339
Bates, J. E., 124, 458
Baumslag, N., 76
Bean, S., 206
Beatty, A., 435
Beauchamp, G. K., 353
Beck, C. T., 365
Becker, B. E., 114
Becker, G., 120
Becker, K., 129
Beidelman, 80
Bel, A., 337, 338
Bel, B., 337, 338
Belgrave, F. Z., 306
Bell, S. M., 363
Bellamy, C., 115, 358
Belsky, J., 312
Bem, S. L., 315, 316

Bemmels, H. R., 127
Benarroch, F., 101
Benedict, R., 48, 52, 58
Benfante, R., 411
Benoit, C., 342
Bentler, P. M., 122
Benvenuto, C., 294
Berenbaum, S. A., 316
Berg, A. I., 423
Bergelson, E., 239
Bergen, D., 53
Bergström, L., 338, 342, 364
Bergström, M., 338
Berk, L. E., 93
Berkowitz, R. L., 105
Berlin, B., 195, 196, 197
Berry, J. W., 28, 31, 50, 57, 59, 146, 455, 463, 464, 465
Best, D. L., 302, 303, 459, 460
Bhagavath, B., 97
Bharti, B., 75
Bigler, R. S., 307
Bimmel, N., 107
Binet, A., 52, 249, 250, 252, 257, 258
Bjorklund, D. F., 232
Blackman, M., 167
Blanchard, R., 299, 302
Blank, M., 238
Bledsoe, C., 175
Bloch, M., 365
Bloom, P., 201
Bloomfield, L., 195
Blumberg, B. D., 427
Boardman, J. D., 117
Boas, F., 161
Bochner, 274
Bockting, W. O., 301
Bogg, T., 280
Bohannan, L., 18, 19
Bonanno, G. A., 422, 423
Bond, M. H., 454, 459
Bones, J., 14
Bono, M. A., 275
Bonvillain, N., 3, 149, 158, 185, 207
Booth, D. A., 353
Borgatti, S., 60

SUBJECT INDEX